Making It Happen

From Interactive to
Participatory Language Teaching

Theory and Practice

Third Edition

Patricia A. Richard-Amato

Longman

In loving memory of my father,
Wallace Marvin Abbott

Making It Happen, Second Edition

Copyright © 2003 by Pearson Education, Inc.
All rights reserved.
No part of this publication may be reproduced,
stored in a retrieval system, or transmitted
in any form or by any means, electronic, mechanical,
photocopying, recording, or otherwise,
without the prior permission of the publisher.

Pearson Education, 10 Bank Street, White Plains, NY 10606

Acquisitions editior: Virginia L. Blanford
Vice president, director of design and production: Rhea Banker
Executive managing editor: Linda Moser
Production editor: Michael Mone
Production coordinator: Melissa Leyva
Director of manufacturing: Patrice Fraccio
Senior manufacturing buyer: Edie Pullman
Cover design: Joe dePinho
Text design adaptation: Curt Belshe
Text composition: Color Associates
Text art: Color Associates
Text credits: See pages xv–xvi.

Library of Congress Cataloging-in-Publication Data

Richard-Amato, Patricia A.
Making it happen: from interactive to participatory language teaching: a more critical
view of theory and practice/Patricia A. Richard-Amato.—3rd ed. p. cm.
Includes bibliographical references and index.
ISBN 0-13-060193-4
1. Language and languages—Study and teaching. 2. Second language acquisiton.
3. English language—Study and teaching—Foreign speakers. I. Title

P53.R49 2003
418'.007—dc21   2002031280

Printed in the United States of America
1 2 3 4 5 6 7 8 9 10–RRD–07 06 05 04 03

Contents

Preface

In recent years, we have witnessed a dramatic shift in language teaching from grammar-based approaches to interactive approaches. Although the latter generally acknowledge sociocultural and affective factors, we are just beginning to realize how very important these forces are to the process of language acquisition. Perhaps it is through an interaction of top-down and bottom-up processes that we have been able to arrive at a crossroads, and many are now ready to take the path requiring another look at critical pedagogy and all of its ramifications. And, in spite of a less-than-favorable political climate, two-way bilingual programs in particular have gained the respect and protection of parents, teachers, and communities in many parts of the country. At last, portions of society are beginning to acknowledge (however painfully) that students *do* indeed benefit from having more than one language and that effectively implemented bilingual education just might be a good way to achieve that goal, as well as other academic objectives.

At the same time, we are witnessing a movement toward longitudinal and ethnographic research and research components and toward various applications of teacher research. These will be instrumental to our knowledge of the structure of the larger society, how classrooms are organized socially, how languages are learned in them, and how well we are doing with our own students. Although our own experiences as learners and as teachers are important to our development, we must take full advantage of what others have to offer. We owe it to ourselves and to our students to keep abreast of what is happening in our own field and in closely related fields so that we do not stagnate.

This book is an attempt to present, for your critical consideration, some of the important theoretical concepts and research supporting *interaction* in the classroom and to examine where we might go from here. By "interaction" I am not referring to the mechanistic definition given to it in many scientific paradigms in which the entities that come together remain unchanged as a result of their contact. Rather, interaction as I define it incorporates elements of a *transactional* nature. In other words, *the entities doing the interacting are affected and often changed by the contact and by the total social situation surrounding it*. This definition of the interactional process has important implications for what goes on in classrooms and why interaction, as I have defined it, doesn't occur there as often as we might like it to. Without such interaction, students are likely to play only passive or superficial roles in the classroom.

But this book goes beyond a discussion of interactive teaching. It also includes a description of *participatory teaching* and how it might evolve. In order for transactional elements to be fully realized, a *classroom community* needs to develop within the context of the larger world. In a classroom community, teaching transcends organizing a curriculum, deciding upon an overall pedagogical strategy, and executing a program. It means facilitating learning and seeking learner input into the decision-making process. It means forming dialectical relationships with students in which they are considered important sources of knowledge and experience, in addition to the teacher. It means accommodating students linguistically and culturally, having high expectations of them, and believing that they are intelligent human beings who can achieve academically. And it means involving parents and others in the school environment and the outside community in the learning/teaching process.

The information presented here is not intended as the final word on second and foreign language teaching nor is it intended to be prescriptive. Every teacher needs to develop his or her own philosophical foundation and ways of doing things. This book is simply a resource from which to draw.

Patricia Abbott Richard-Amato
Professor Emeritus
California State University, Los Angeles

Acknowledgments

I must first thank the students and colleagues with whom I have worked over the years. Many of them have been very influential in my own development as a teacher, from my first teaching position at Pueblo High School in Tucson, Arizona, to my later experiences at the university level as a graduate student and professor. I am most grateful to all those who learned with me and challenged me to do better.

John Oller, Jr., was particularly influential as my graduate committee chair at the University of New Mexico, Albuquerque. Although we didn't always agree when co-authoring the first edition of *Methods that Work*, his seminal ideas about naturalness in language testing and about episodic structure made a huge impact on me and my later work.

Appreciation also goes to the many people with whom I exchanged ideas and developed friendships while teaching at several TESOL Institutes: at the Mediterranean Institute in Barcelona, Spain in 1994; and at two TESOL Academies. Many a fleeting notion became fleshed out through lengthy discussions in the classroom and out.

Although he probably doesn't remember me, I owe much to James Banks, who several years ago spoke to our faculty and whose book *Multicultural Education* became a text for a course I taught. His perspective helped me realize what it might be like for language minority students enrolled in institutions that do not value diversity.

But there are many other authors to whom I am indebted for their influence, particularly on this edition. Names that come to mind are Paulo Freire and Gordon Wells, and, more recently, Sonia Nieto and Leo van Lier. Freire's *Pedagogy of the Oppressed* and his discussion with me and other faculty members at Cal State, Los Angeles, made lasting impressions. Wells's *Learning Through*

Interaction also influenced my thinking early on. But his later book *Dialogic Inquiry* both surprised and delighted me. Many of his applications of Vygotsky were similar to my own, although he had described them much more eloquently than I. Nieto's book *The Light In Their Eyes* reinforced what Banks and Friere had taught me and presented a rich account of teachers' experiences from their own perspectives. Leo van Lier's *Interaction in the Language Curriculum* gave me greater insight into the language learning process and helped me clarify my own thinking. And, of course, I cannot forget Alastair Pennycook and Elsa Auerbach for their influence on my ideas about participatory teaching which changed the focus of this book.

I am grateful also to Kathy Weed and Leslie Jo Adams, who critiqued the second edition and contributed many thoughtful comments and suggestions for the third edition. Both are very experienced teacher educators in the field. Kathy Weed first made me aware of the Valley Center Two-Way Developmental Language Program (described on pages 446–454) and Leslie Jo Adams is among those who, over the years, have shared so willingly with me their thoughts and viewpoints.

I also owe appreciation to two of the best editors in publishing with whom I have had the pleasure of working: Ginny Blanford and Eleanor Barnes. Ginny's knowledge and experience, as an editor and as an author herself, have been invaluable to me in the revision process; Eleanor's devotion to task and insightful suggestions were immensely helpful at earlier stages. And to my production editor, Michael Mone, whose professional manner and expertise made working with him a pleasure, and to my copyeditors, Sharon Gold and Mike Isralewitz, whose careful readings of the manuscript saved me from embarrassment more than once. Thanks also to Louisa Hellegers, whose encouragement and advice over the years have meant a lot to me; and to Joanne Dresner, who first published my work and has been a great inspiration ever since.

And, of course, I cannot forget those people who contributed so much to the last edition: Allen Ascher, Jessica Miller, and Christine Cervoni (all at Pearson Education), Holbrook Mann, Linda Sasser, Kathleen Bailey, Mary Ann Christison, José Galván, Barbara Kroll, Diane Larsen-Freeman, Barbara Penman, Ann Snow, Fred Tarpley, Armando Baltra, Fred Carrillo, and Kathy Weed. Their expert advice was invaluable.

In addition, I am grateful to those who contributed to the first edition: John Oller, Jr. (who suggested that I write this book in the first place), Ruth Larimer, Mary McGroarty, Carolyn Madden, Leslie Jo Adams, Marty Furch, Alan Crawford, James Wiebe, Robert White, Rod Young, Steve Strauss, Bess Altwerger, Wendy Hansen, Jennifer Claire Johnson, Pamela Branch, Ramon Díaz, Sue Gould, and Rey Baca.

I want to express my appreciation also to the following publishing companies and individuals for permission to reprint or adapt materials for which they own copyrights:

Bonne, Rose. Excerpt from "There Was an Old Lady Who Swallowed a Fly," illustrated by Pam Adams. Copyright © 1973 Michael Twinn, Child's Play Ltd. Reprinted by permission of Michael Twinn, Child's Play (International) Ltd. An excerpt only—taken from last page in book.

Christison, Mary Ann. Illustration by Kathleen Peterson, *English Through Poetry*, p. 29, 1982. Reprinted by permission of Alemany Press/Janus Book Publishers, Inc., Haywood, California.

Evans, Joy and Moore, Jo Ellen. Adaptation of illustration, p. 57, from *Art Moves the Basics Along: Units About Children*; Copyright © 1982. Reprinted by permission of Evan-Moor, Carmel, California.

Krashen, Stephen. Figure 2, "The Relationship between Affective Factors and Language Acquisition," p. 110 in *Second Language Acquisition and Second Language Learning*; Copyright © 1981 by Stephen Krashen. Reprinted by permission of Oxford: Pergamon.

Krashen, Stephen. Figure from "Immersion: Why it Works and What it Taught Us," in *Language and Society* 12 (Winter 1984), p. 63. Copyright © 1981 by Stephen Krashen. Reprinted by permission of the Office of Official Language, Ontario, Canada and the Minister of Supply and Services, Canada.

Krashen, Stephen. Figure 2.1 from *Principles and Practice in Second Language Acquisition*. Copyright © 1982 by Stephen Krashen. Reprinted by permission of Oxford: Pergamon.

Krashen, Stephen and Terrell, T. From *The Natural Approach*, pp. 67–70. Copyright © 1983. Reprinted by permission of Alemany Press/Janus Book Publishers, Inc. Haywood, California.

Levelt, Willem. *Speaking: From Intention to Articulation*. Copyright © 1989. Reprinted by permission of The MIT Press, Cambridge, Massachusetts.

Nieto, Sonia. pp. 130–161 from *The Light in Their Eyes*. Copyright © 1999 by Teachers College, Columbia University. Reprinted by permission of Teachers College Press, New York. All rights reserved.

Palmer, Hap. "Put Your Hands Up in the Air," from *Songbook: Learning Basic Skills Through Music*. Copyright © 1971. Reprinted by permission of Educational Activities, Inc., Baldwin, New York.

Pennycook, Alastair. "The Social Politics and the Culture Politics of Language Classrooms," pp. 89–103 from *The Sociopolitics of English Language Teaching*. Copyright © 2000. Reprinted by permission of Multilingual Matters Ltd., New York.

Prelutsky, Jack. "The Creature in the Classroom," from *The Random House Book of Poetry for Children*, selected and introduced by Jack Prelutsky. Copyright © 1983 by Random House, Inc. Reprinted by permission of the publisher.

Shulman, Judith H., and Amalia Mesa-Bains, eds. "My Good Year Explodes: A Confrontation with Parents," pp. 85–86 in *Diversity in the Classroom: A Casebook for Teachers and Teacher Educators*. Copyright © 1993. Reprinted by permission of Lawrence Erlbaum Associates, Mahwah, New Jersey.

Shulman, Judith H., and Amalia Mesa-Bains, eds. "Please, Not Another ESL Student," pp. 37–39 in *Diversity in the Classroom: A Casebook for Teachers and Teacher Educators*. Copyright © 1993. Reprinted by permission of Lawrence Erlbaum Associates, Mahwah, New Jersey.

Silverstein, Shel. "Gooloo" from *A Light in the Attic*. Copyright © 1981 by Evil Eye Music, Inc. Reprinted by permission of Edite Kroll Literary Agency. Used by permission of HarperCollins Publishing

Whitecloud, Thomas. Adaptation of "Blue Winds Dancing." Reprinted with the permission of Scribner, an imprint of Simon and Schuster Adult Publishing Group from *Scribner's Magazine*. Copyright © 1938 by Charles Scribner's Sons; copyright renewed © 1966.

I thank also the following individuals for allowing me to summarize their programs:

Christine Schulze, Denise Phillippe, and Donna Clementi (Concordia Language Villages, Bemidji, Minnesota); Marguerite Straus and Good Jean Lau (Public School No. 1, New York); Lydia Vogt and Sarah Clayton (Valley Center School District, Valley Center, California); Sally Cummings and Carolyn Duffy (Saint Michael's College, Colchester, Vermont); Blanca Arazi (Instituto Cultural Argentina Norteamericano, Buenos Aires); Ann Snow and Janet Tricamo (California State University, Los Angeles); Linda Sasser (Alhambra School District, Alhambra, California); Pamela Branch and Christina Rivera (ABC Unified School District, Cerritos, California); Sandra Brown (North Hollywood Adult Learning Center, North Hollywood, California); Brandon Zaslow, Eva Wegrzecka-Monkiewicz and Beverly McNeilly (Los Angeles Unified School District; Los Angeles, California); and Ken Cressman (Lakehead Board of Education, Thunder Bay, Ontario, Canada).

And last to my husband, Jay. His patience, love, and good advice over the years remain a source of strength for me.

Introduction

CHANGE AND CHANGING[1]

Change is inevitable. We have come to expect it. It has brought new ways of looking at learning/teaching and at the teacher's role in these processes. Sometimes we resist new ways of looking—at least at first. If we discover some truth in them based on our own experience, we are more likely to give them serious consideration, to talk (perhaps argue) about them with colleagues and other associates and, eventually, to take action and incorporate from them what makes sense to us and disregard the rest. We have learned through our own experience that innovations in thought and action can make a big difference, not only for us personally, but for our students. The innovations we often find most acceptable and enduring are those that do not bluntly tear down what already exists. Advocates of change would be wise to find its roots, not only in the present, but also in history and to approach mainstream thought gingerly, realizing that others have also had their truths.

Unfortunately, those promoting change sometimes inadvertently fall into that great abyss—dichotomous thinking. To them every controversy involves an either/or situation—transformational education *or* transmission education; instructed grammar *or* no grammar focus at all; whole language strategies *or* phonics instruction; methods in teacher preparation *or* an absence of methods; and the list goes on. Try to imagine what these opposites might look like at the ends of a continuum rather than in a dichotomy. What if language teachers wanted to help students better their lives through critical thinking processes and, at the same time, help them master some of the disciplinary knowledge required to meet immediate needs through transmission? What if teachers used whole language strategies but become aware that the student would benefit from the ability to better distinguish /b/ and /v/? What if they taught a few grammar rules because research told them that these rules would benefit students, but at the same time believed (again because of research) that other rules would be best learned through actual *use* of language? And what if in teacher preparation programs, participants realized that they just might need to experiment, both as learners and teachers, with various methods, not because they slavishly planned to follow their tenets and practices, but because they could

---

[1] Some of the words you see here first appeared in a plenary I gave at the California TESOL State Conference, April 20, 2001, in Ontario and in *ESL Magazine*, January/February 2002, pp. 16–18. The article in *ESL Magazine* was adapted in part from the manuscript for this book.

1

be important sources from which to draw. When involved in real classrooms, teachers become pragmatic. They realize that the distinctions are not so clear-cut after all.

This new edition of *Making It Happen* is based on the premise that teachers are pragmatic beings. In their efforts to be effective in classrooms, they will pick and choose whatever strategies are needed at the moment, depending upon the situation and the participants involved—their histories, their preferred modes of learning, their personal, social, and political concerns, and their immediate as well as long-term goals.

Making It Happen draws from two major sources: psychology and sociology. Although each emphasizes a different aspect of the learning process, both are essential to understanding how humans learn language. From psychology, we take a close look at the *psycholinguistic* focus in *Second Language Acquisition Theory and Research*; and from sociology, we examine the renewed belief in the *sociocultural* focus in *Critical Pedagogy*.

SECOND LANGUAGE ACQUISITION THEORY AND RESEARCH

Modern psycholinguists view language acquisition as a developmental process. Second language learners move from little knowledge of the target language to fuller knowledge of it in somewhat nebulous stages. Modern psycholinguists have assumed that the goal is to communicate like a native speaker. This assumption alone raises the ire of the critical pedagogists. To them, the concept "native-speaker" brings with it certain baggage; i.e., a wish to divide up the world into a colonial "us and them" dichotomy (see Y. Kachru, 1994; Brutt-Griffler and Samimy, 1999; and Sridhar, 1994). Although I don't feel the motivation (at least not conscious) of most of these linguists has been to "colonize" others, some of the terminology they use, such as "interlanguage" and "fossilization," unfortunately does lend itself to that interpretation. Although I have used such terms in my own writing, I must admit that I never felt entirely comfortable with them, but didn't have a conscious realization of why. Fortunately, we now recognize that many Englishes are spoken by close to 600 million people around the world. The native-speaker standard is no longer the only model for English Language Learners (ELLs), nor should it be the only one.[2] Not that we should do away with having a goal, as some in the field seem to be suggesting. We still need a target language. However, it can and should be the *language*

---

[2] Widdowson (1996) argues that there is still just one "standard" model and that the other models of English are nonstandard dialects which co-exist with standard English and have their own appropriate smaller domains of use. He goes on to say that there are good reasons for teaching standard English to those who want membership in the wider community of English speakers.

of proficient second language users in whatever environment we find them. In this context, the terms "interlanguage" and "fossilization" are still useful and lose some of their negative overtones. Not only is the more loosely defined target language less condescending, but it presents a more realistic goal for language learners, although many of them do approximate native-like proficiency under the right conditions (see Klein, 1995; Marinova-Todd, Marshal, and Snow, 2000; and Flege and Liu, 2001). Moreover, this new definition recognizes that multilingual minds differ from monolingual minds (see Cook, 1999) and that both cannot be expected to come up with exactly the same end product. However, both can and should be considered proficient speakers of the language. As Cook reminds us, second language speakers should not be treated as failed native speakers.

Second Language Acquisition (SLA) has come under recent criticism for other reasons as well, particularly from the critical pedagogists. Some say that it downplays sociocultural factors too much in favor of psycholinguistic ones (see especially M. Gebhard, 1999). Others claim that SLA overemphasizes developmental stages and end points, rather than viewing language development as fluid and largely influenced by social circumstances (see Genishi, 1999). Still others argue that it maintains an unhealthy reliance on "experts" and divorces itself too readily from pedagogy, focusing instead on how languages are learned rather than how they are taught (see Thomas, 1998).

As a former ESL teacher myself, one additional failure of SLA, as I see it, is its failure to meaningfully address the relationship between student and teacher, student and student, and the importance of the learning environment. Are these relationships and environments mostly accepting, positive, and encouraging? Or do they tend to be judgmental, negative, and uncompromising? To language and cultural minorities, this issue is especially critical, for it can determine whether or not these students learn in our classrooms.

However, in spite of the apparent shortcomings of SLA, it has indeed presented us with valuable psycholinguistic knowledge to help us understand how languages are learned and taught in various settings and circumstances. Part I of *Making It Happen* brings to light some of this important psycholinguistic knowledge.

CRITICAL PEDAGOGY

One of the most interesting and, at the same time, controversial movements in second language teaching is the contemporary treatment of Paulo Freire's critical pedagogy. Freire believed that students should not be considered empty heads waiting to be filled with information through transmission. Rather, they should be considered valuable sources of knowledge, instrumental to their own learning and empowerment (see Chapters 3 and 4).

Perhaps the renewed interest in critical pedagogy has been given impetus by the fact that English is quickly becoming a global language. With that comes the awesome responsibility of making sure power and influence are shared as much as possible throughout the world. Not to do so would perpetuate and extend the "us and them" thinking which has followed humankind all the way into the twenty-first century.

Critical pedagogy considers itself postmodern. It goes beyond humanistic education, which assumes that individuals have the freedom to rise above their circumstances. Instead, critical pedagogy is based on the premise that such freedom may or may not exist and that powerful forces are determined to hold cultural minorities or persons with diminished influence in a state of oppression. For example, Pennycook (1999) points to the deterministic thinking often found in our classrooms and in the literature of our discipline, in which different cultures are given distinctive labels and treated as the "exotic other" so typical of colonial discourse (see also Kubota, 1999, 2001).

Unfortunately, teachers sometimes view their students' languages and cultures negatively. Some teachers feel that complete assimilation or acculturation is necessary in order to access the new societies in which students find themselves. Although the teachers' intentions may be good, the message students often receive is that their first languages and first cultures are inferior, perhaps even dysfunctional. All teachers need to show respect for their students' first languages and first cultures and realize that political empowerment in a global society comes from the ability to function in more than one cultural environment.

Critical pedagogists showcase Foucault (1980), who claimed early on that politics is the main factor influencing *all* social interaction, inside the classroom and out. They are convinced that teaching English as a Second Language is in itself a political act, and is not neutral (see Cox and Assis-Peterson, 1999). They believe that teaching English (or any second language, for that matter) is fraught with arbitrary implications about power and who has it and who does not, based on the values of the most influential in society.

Critical pedagogy aims to take students beyond a modernistic awareness about what oppresses them and keeps them marginalized. Its goal is and always has been to encourage critical engagement, problem solving, and the kind of action that leads to political/personal empowerment through participation and action. The issues critical to the students' own lives become focal points of learning and teaching. Students and teachers together identify and pursue the areas of knowledge relevant to them. Thus, students can gain perspective on those societal forces that help to shape their lives.

But critical pedagogy, too, has its critics. One bone of contention concerns power and how it is perceived. For example, Gore (1992) concludes that critical pedagogists consider power a *product* that teachers have, that can be "bestowed" upon their students. Even the very words "empowerment" and "transformation" carry a modicum of colonial baggage. Bill Johnston (1999), while emphasizing that power is not a commodity to be given away, argues that it is a *process* to be negotiated and that the teacher in the classroom will, in the end, always be the authority. He is convinced that teaching is neither about power nor politics; rather it is about a moral relationship between student and teacher.

A second criticism has to do with the claim made by the critical pedagogists that teaching English is a political act and is not neutral. Ghim-Lian Chew (1999) argues that learning English can indeed be neutral to many who use it around the world. She points to Nigeria, where English now has a pragmatic function in the society. And to Singapore, where the speakers have accepted the English language but not its cultural values. She is convinced that bilingualism does not have to be accompanied by biculturalism. Byram clarified this point in 1998 by distinguishing between "biculturalism" and "interculturalism." *Biculturalism*, according to him, implies that the learner identifies with the new culture and accepts it. *Interculturalism*, on the other hand, implies that the learner may know about the new culture, but does not accept it or internalize it. One can be bilingual without being bicultural. Sandra McKay (2000) takes the argument even further. She claims that in English as an International Language, the language belongs to its users and that interculturalism rather than biculturalism should be the goal. She suggests that, instead of choosing materials reflecting mainly American or British culture, we choose ones reflecting the *source culture*; in other words, the culture of the country in which English is being learned. Another alternative is to choose and/or create materials that incorporate the cultures of many countries around the world.

A third criticism of critical pedagogy concerns its stand on genre theory and its attitude toward "expertness" and authority opinion. It argues that a study of the conventional genres and how they are constructed perpetuates and reinforces structures of inequity (Luke, 1996). However, the fact that many students want (and even need) to know the literary conventions of a given society must be recognized. Such knowledge provides access to that society, making critical analysis and transformation possible (see especially Chapter 4). Because students understand and use the constructs of a given genre, doesn't mean that it has to control them. And just because they seek out the opinions of "experts," it doesn't mean they need to accept what these "experts" say. Students need to know that they have the same freedoms we do—to deconstruct what they read and hear, to accept what makes sense, and to reject the rest. This is, in part, what empowerment is all about.

We *can* share power in the classroom with our students and establish a more dialectical relationship with them. We *can* respect their first languages and cultures by learning about them and using them to inform our own teaching. We *can* realize that the language we are teaching is greatly influenced by social factors and study these influences. We *can* explore how discourse and language are influenced by power relationships and struggles for justice and equality. And we *can* encourage students to consider the viewpoints of others, reflect upon them, and be transformed by them, even if only in small ways.

TEACHER EDUCATION: WHAT ARE THE POSSIBILITIES?

Today, teacher education itself has been transformed. Once considered predominantly a training process, teacher education has taken on new dimensions through participants' experience, collaboration, and reflection.[3] Indoctrinating teachers in "how to" prescriptions represented by a dogmatic methods approach to teaching has given way to a constructivist focus on critical exploration, decision making, question posing, problem solving, and strategy modification.

But this doesn't mean that a disciplinary knowledge base from which to draw should be discarded. On the contrary, the contributions of applied linguists, socioculturalists, cognitive theorists, and researchers are still essential to teachers in developing their own principles of second language teaching. Most teachers do not want to be spoon-fed someone else's set of principles; nor do they want to simply be left to "discover" for themselves the theories and research that have taken decades to develop. From the interaction of teachers' values, what they are currently learning and experiencing, and their prior knowledge, a set of principles begins to take shape, which then evolves throughout lifetimes of teaching. The teachers, too, experience and benefit from transformational processes.

AN INTERACTIVE CONCEPTUALIZATION FOR SECOND LANGUAGE TEACHER EDUCATION

The rudimentary conceptualization I present below is still in the process of evolving since the last edition of *Making It Happen*. The conceptualization comprises three basic components: The *Affective Base*, the *Disciplinary Knowledge Base*, and the *Experience/Research Base* (see Figure I.1).

Each component consists of at least the items enumerated within the boxes below. Related factors include the personal qualities of the individual: openness to others, creativity, flexibility, intelligence, the ability to empathize with students and to make decisions (with their input). The conceptualization is *symbiotic* in that the components are interdependent, and *interactive* in that the influence that each has on any other is two-way (notice the arrows). Each component informs and validates the others. Another feature is that the conceptualization is independent of any specific method or methodology.

---

[3] See especially Richards, 1989, 1991, 1998; Prabhu, 1990; Richards and Nunan, 1990; Freeman, 1991, 1992, 1998; Fanselow, 1992; Freeman and Richards, 1996; Kumarvadivelu, 1994, 1999, 2001.

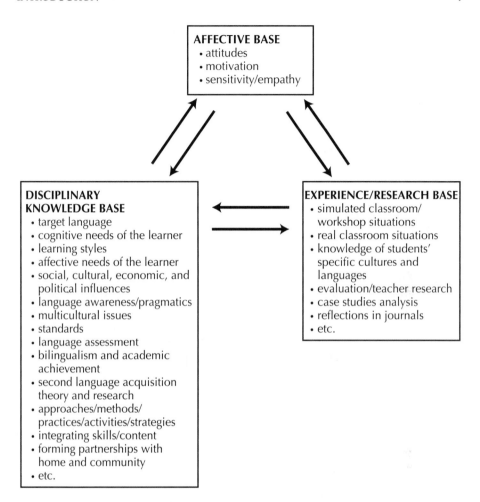

Figure I.1. An Interactive Conceptualization for Second-Language Teacher Education

Making It Happen provides a disciplinary knowledge and experience base which second and foreign language[4] teachers in-preparation can use to help them develop an informed critical perspective. Teachers are encouraged

---

[4] Second language teaching usually refers to a target language that is being taught in a country or domain where it is a dominant language. Foreign language teaching, on the other hand, usually refers to a target language that is being taught in a country or domain where it is not a dominant language. However, now that English has become global, the distinctions are not so clear. See pages 297–299 for a more adequate description and for the teaching implications related to each type of language teaching. Note that sometimes the terms are used when contrasting "first language acquisition" and "second language acquisition." In this case, "second" usually refers to any language that is not the first one learned.

throughout the book to examine what is here and to integrate what they accept with what they already know and believe about second language learning and teaching.

The text also encourages simulated experience in supportive environments. Teachers in preparation are encouraged to try out their own adaptations of various methods and activities, learn from them, critically analyze them with the help of peers, reflect upon their use, and take from them what they want. Simulated experience can be particularly valuable in such an investigation early on. Moreover, teachers, during simulated phases, are often exposed to a target language with which they are not familiar and are asked to reflect upon that experience. Thus, they become *learners* themselves and are asked to respond to each other from a *learner's point of view*. Too often, this component is missing from teacher education programs.

In the context of this book, methods are considered dynamic, sensitive to local factors, and fed by the teacher's own developing philosophy. At the same time, methods are likely to contribute to that philosophy. Participants' exposure to methods does not preclude their own generation of methods and strategies; indeed they may even stimulate such generation. If teacher education is to be transformative, participants must have access to current practice and they must be encouraged to explore together the information they consider valuable.

However, a teacher's knowledge of current practice, no matter how extensive, will not mean much if the school environment does not foster respect and mutual understanding. If the school and community atmosphere is one of hostility (even though subtle), if students are expected to do all the accommodation and have little power in the decision-making process, and if students are not made to feel capable of academic work, then nothing teachers do to teach the subject matter will be of consequence. Only when all students are valued for who they are will learning be successful.

PARTICIPATORY TEACHER EDUCATION

Just as language students are not empty heads waiting to be filled with information, neither are their teachers. Even before entering education programs, teachers know what they value, what their political and cultural concerns are, and what they already know. Teacher educators would be wise to tap into this resource and encourage participants in their programs to reflect on what they are learning and to deconstruct it on their own terms.

In addition, teachers in-preparation often need and want assistance deciding which directions to take and/or which questions about their teaching need to be addressed. They often want advice and "expert" input from a supervisor who is generally more experienced and may have critical information to share. At the same time, supervisors should avoid authoritarian approaches, no matter how practical or expedient they appear. Active collaboration between teachers and their supervisors, each showing respect for the other's viewpoint and expertise, usually brings about the best results.

NONNATIVE SPEAKERS IN TEACHER EDUCATION PROGRAMS

Nonnative-speaking teachers need to be welcomed with open arms into teacher education programs. They make excellent role models for students learning a second language. Most have already successfully overcome language and cultural shock (see Chapter 6), and most have attained or are close to attaining proficient L2 use. Because of their experience learning another language, they are generally more aware of helpful strategies, pitfalls to avoid, language learning difficulties, and the personal and social needs of their students.

Brutt-Griffler and Samimy (1999, p. 428) suggest that we take a close look at the concerns of nonnative-speaking students in these programs. Among their suggestions are the re-examination of nonnative speakers' experiences through self-representation, including goals and values; incorporation of discursive practices which downplay the native/nonnative dichotomy; and a broadening of program goals to reflect the diversity of experience from both second and foreign language contexts (see also Kamhi-Stein, 2000).

Participatory teacher education, where it is practiced, can provide the access nonnative speakers need to realize their full potential within teacher education programs. However, the educational institutions that do the hiring also need to become aware of the strengths that nonnative-speaking teachers can bring to their schools, especially to those programs designed for language-minority students.

OVERVIEW

In this edition of *Making It Happen,* as in the others, I have responded to the feedback and suggestions of many teacher educators and students who have used the book in the past or are currently using it. In addition to updating the supporting research, I have added the following:

- three new programs in action, including dual language programs and a village immersion program
- a separate chapter on participatory teaching
- separate and/or expanded sections on teacher research, connectionism, critical literacy, ESL and Foreign language standards, investigative inquiry, bilingual education, Vygotsky's and Freire's theories, the Levelt Model and its implications, and Internet applications for language teaching
- case studies from various levels for reflection and discussion

This edition concentrates on ways of providing opportunities for meaningful interaction in participatory second language classroom settings. **Part I** presents a theoretical orientation to the remaining chapters. It begins with an overview of the grammar-focused methods of the past and goes on to highlight some of the seminal ideas of Chomsky, Wilkins, Widdowson, Breen, Candlin, and others (Chapter 1). Then Part I presents evidence supporting the notion that acquisition can and does take place in the classroom under certain conditions (Chapter 2). Next, it describes the role of interaction in the acquisition process drawing from Vygotsky, Freire, Wells, Krashen, Bruner, van Lier, Levelt, Pienemann, and many others (Chapter 3). Part I then examines participatory language teaching and its ramifications, drawing from Freire, Pennycook, Auerbach, and other advocates (Chapter 4). Next, it explores literacy development and skills integration by looking at a natural language framework (Chapter 5). This section continues by examining the important role played by the affective domain in second language acquisition in the classroom (Chapter 6). Finally, it discusses language assessment, standards, and ways of making evaluation an integral part of the classroom environment (Chapter 7).

Part II examines several methods and activities that can be, for the most part, compatible with interactional/participatory teaching: physical involvement in the language learning process (Chapter 8); communicative language teaching focusing on Terrell's natural approach (Chapter 9); chants, music, and poetry (Chapter 10); storytelling, role play, and drama (Chapter 11); games (Chapter 12); ways to promote literacy development (Chapter 13); and affective activities (Chapter 14).

Several considerations to be taken into account when one is developing and implementing programs are discussed in **Part III**. They include devising a plan (Chapter 15); the selection of tools for teaching languages, including textbooks, computer programs, videos, and film (Chapter 16); and program designs and political implications (Chapter 17).

Part IV presents programs in action. Chapter 18 (ESL Programs) discusses a college English language program at Saint Michael's College in Colchester, Vermont; a university support program at California State University, Los Angeles; a life-skills adult basic education program at the North Hollywood Adult Learning Center in North Hollywood, California; a secondary sheltered English model at Artesia High School in Artesia, California; a high school ESL academic program at Thomas Jefferson High School in Los Angeles; an elementary district-wide program in the Alhambra School District in Alhambra, California; and a kindergarten ESL program within a Spanish bilingual school at Loma Vista Elementary in Maywood, California. Chapter 19 (Foreign Language Programs) describes a village immersion program for global understanding near Bemidji, Minnesota; a French immersion program for elementary students in Thunder Bay, Ontario, Canada; a bicultural institute for children, adolescents, and adults at the Instituto Cultural Argentine Norteamericano

(ICANA) in Buenos Aires, Argentina; a middle school Spanish language program at Millikan Junior High School in Los Angeles; and a high school Spanish program at Artesia High School in Artesia, California. Chapter 20 (Two-Way Bilingual Programs) presents a Spanish/English dual language program in Valley Center, California and a Cantonese/English dual language program in Lower Manhattan. All these programs were selected because of the quality of some of their more salient features. However, they are not meant to be representative of all the programs available.

Part V, Related Readings, presents edited readings from two professionals who have contributed, both directly and indirectly, to the development of second language pedagogy: Alastair Pennycook and Sonia Nieto. While the section is intended for anyone desiring supplemental materials, it will probably be especially useful to the teaching of graduate-level theory and/or methods courses, since it offers additional areas for thought, classroom discussion, and/or research.

Part VI presents four case studies for reflection and discussion. Each pertains to a different age group: elementary, middle school, high school, and college/university.

PART   I

Theoretical Considerations: Developing Your Own Language Teaching Principles

The selected theories and hypotheses presented here are intended to serve as a foundation for the methods, activities, and ideas presented in the remainder of the book—but the intent is not to divorce the theoretical from the practical. Rather, readers are encouraged to explore these ideas with a critical mind, and to create *praxis*—a blending of theory and practice—at every possible juncture. This section is intended to be representative, not all-inclusive. Research and scholarship in communicative language learning and teaching has expanded to the point where no single volume can reflect it all.

Because second language acquisition is so complex, no two learners will get there by exactly the same route. In spite of the variations, however, we can describe some of the processes that seem to be common to large numbers of people struggling with a new language and, in many cases, a new culture. Most people agree that simple exposure to the new language and/or culture is not enough. *By understanding more about the processes that language learners seem to share, we can be in a better position to develop our own language teaching principles and to make possible classroom experiences that are conducive to second language acquisition and to personal and collective empowerment.* Thus we can continue to develop means by which language, culture, and influence are made more accessible to second language learners, while at the same time preserving their first languages and cultures as much as possible.

Part I will contribute to the reservoir—which also includes your own interactions, experiences, and prior knowledge—from which you draw as your own principles as a language teacher evolve.

CHAPTER 1

From Grammatical to Communicative Approaches

Not to let a word get in the way
of its sentence
Nor to let a sentence get in the way
of its intention,
But to send your mind out to meet the
intention
as a guest;
That is understanding.

Chinese proverb,
Fourth Century B.C.
(in Wells, 1981)

QUESTIONS TO THINK ABOUT

1. How do humans learn language? Are we born with something that helps us learn language?

2. With what approaches to second or foreign language teaching are you already familiar? Are these primarily grammar-based? Do you know of any other approaches to second or foreign language teaching?

3. How would you envision an effective communicative approach? How would it differ from other approaches with which you are familiar?

Because grammar has traditionally been the focus of second and foreign language teaching over the years, the fact that many people still cling to the notion that grammar and the teacher (the grammar "expert") should take center stage in language programs isn't surprising. Even though Canale and Swain as far back as 1980 derogated grammar's role when they laid out the basic components of communicative competence,[1] grammar nevertheless has remained the approach of choice until the last decade or so.

GRAMMAR-BASED APPROACHES

Grammar-based approaches advocate language structure as the main content for study in language learning and expose students to isolated aspects of the grammar system consecutively—present tense before past, comparative before superlative, first-person singular before third-person singular, and so forth. These approaches include:

- grammar-translation
- audiolingualism
- the direct method
- cognitive-code

The characteristic features of each of these approaches are presented below, but many variations exist that are not included in this brief analysis.

Grammar-Translation

Grammar-translation, also known as the "Prussian Method," was popular in Europe and America from about the mid-nineteenth to the mid-twentieth century. Versions of it still exist today in many countries around the world. The goal of this approach was to produce students who could read and write in the target language by teaching them rules and applications.

A typical grammar-translation lesson began with a reading followed by the grammar rule it illustrated. Often several strings of unrelated sentences were given to demonstrate how the rule worked. New words were presented in a list, along with definitions in the first language. These new words were also included in the reading, which, more often than not, was syntactically and semantically far above the learner's level of proficiency. Students were asked to translate the readings into their first language. Lessons were grammatically

---

[1] In addition to linguistic competence (grammatical knowledge, mainly at the subconscious level), the components of communicative competence include discourse competence (how things get done with language, using logical sequence, etc.), sociolinguistic competence (using language appropriately), and strategic competence (compensation strategies such as requests for repetition or clarification, rephrasing, etc.).

sequenced, and learners were expected to produce errorless translations from the beginning. Little attempt was made to communicate orally in the target language. Directions and explanations were always given in the first language.

Audiolingualism

Audiolingualism (ALM), a new "scientific" oral method, was based on behaviorism (Skinner, 1957) and adhered to the theory that language is acquired through habit formation and stimulus/response association. Learning a second language was thought to be a matter of fighting off the habits of the first. First introduced as a component of the "Army Method" used by the United States government during World War II, audiolingualism was developed to replace or enhance grammar-translation. A version of it had been developed earlier by Bloomfield for linguists to use when studying languages. This approach was labeled the "audiolingual method" when it began to gain favor in teaching English as a Foreign Language and English as a Second Language in the 1950s. In the United States, the rise of audiolingual instruction was closely related to scholarship on structural linguistics and contrastive analysis[2] (see Fries, 1945; Lado, 1977).

In the audiolingual method, structures of the target language were carefully ordered and dialogues repeated in an attempt to develop correct habits of speaking. Sentences in substitution activities, mim-mem (mimic and memorize), and other drills were usually related only syntactically ("I go to the store," "You go to the store," "He goes to the store"), and they generally had nothing to do with actual events or narrative. Sometimes, however, these sentences did resemble real communication in that the situational scenarios to be memorized included greetings and idiomatic expressions. Rules were presented but often not formally explained, and activities such as minimal pairs (seat-sit, yellow-Jell-O, etc.) were commonly used in an effort to overcome the negative transfer (interference) of first language (L1) sounds. Listening and speaking skills took precedence over reading and writing skills. However, in most of the applications, there was very little use of creative language,[3] and a great deal of attention was paid to correct pronunciation. Often practice sessions took place in fully equipped language laboratories.

---

[2] *Structural linguistics* is a grammatical system whereby the elements and rules of a language are listed and described. Phonemes, morphemes and/or words, phrases, and sentences are ordered linearly and are learned orally as a set of habits. *Contrastive analysis*, emphasizing the differences between the student's first language and the target language, was relied upon in an effort to create exercises contrasting the two. The first language was thought of chiefly as an interference, hindering the successful mastery of the second.

[3] One exception was Fries's own language program at the University of Michigan. According to Morley, Robinett, Selinker, and Woods (1984), Fries utilized a two-part approach: one part focused on the structural points being drilled and the second part on automatic use through meaning. The "personalized" elements that were considered vital to the program somehow became lost in most of its adaptations.

The Direct Method

Also known today as "Berlitz," this approach was derived from an earlier version called the "Natural Method" developed by Sauveur in the mid-nineteenth century and later applied by de Sauzé. The direct method was natural in the sense that it made an effort to "immerse" students in the target language. Teacher monologues, formal questions and answers, and direct repetitions of the input were frequent. Although the discourse used today in Berlitz schools is often structured temporally, the topic for discussion is often the grammar itself. The students inductively discover the rules of the language. Books based on the direct method often move students so quickly through new syntactic structures that their internalization becomes difficult, if not impossible.

Cognitive-Code Approaches

Cognitive-code approaches, most evident since the 1960s, are described rather vaguely in the literature. According to Richards and Rodgers (1986, p. 60), the term *cognitive-code* refers to any attempt to rely consciously on a syllabus based on grammar, but at the same time to allow for the practice and use of language in meaningful ways. Subskills in listening, speaking, reading, and writing such as sound discrimination, pronunciation of specific elements, distinguishing between letters that are similar in appearance, and so on, need to be mastered before the student can participate in real communication activities. Phonemes need to be learned before words, words before phrases and sentences, simple sentences before more complicated ones, and so forth.

Lessons are highly structured through a deductive process, and the "rule of the day" is practiced. Although creative language is used at later levels during the practice, learners generally need to produce correctly from the start. A great deal of time is devoted to temporally related but often unmotivated (contextually unjustified) discourse (see Chapter 16).

Analysis

Although grammar-based methods varied, they all adhered to the same central principle: Grammar is the foundation upon which language should be taught. Even as early as 1904, Otto Jespersen saw the artificiality inherent in this principle. He criticized the French texts of his era by saying,

> The reader often gets the impression that Frenchmen must be strictly systematical beings who one day speak merely in futures, another day in *passé définis* and who say the most disconnected things only for the sake of being able to use all the persons in the tense which for the time being happens to be the subject for conversation while they carefully postpone the use of the subjunctive until next year (1904, p. 17; also in Oller and Obrecht, 1969, p. 119).

Advocates of cognitive-code approaches are particularly interesting with respect to their interpretation of Chomsky's *transformational grammar*, a complex description of the language system in which Chomsky claims that sentences are "transformed" within the brain to other sentences by the application of what he calls *phrase structure rules*. For example, a phrase structure rule known as *extraposition* applied to the sentence, "That summer follows spring is a known fact," transforms it into, "It is a known fact that summer follows spring." The first sentence is what is called the "deep structure" (also referred to as a *kernel sentence* by some cognitive-code advocates). The sentence into which it is transformed is called the "surface form."

Some applications of cognitive-code approaches began instruction with the translation of kernel sentences. Chomsky felt that kernel sentences of different languages would probably be very similar, and that positive transfer would then occur between languages.

Second language (L2) teachers who used cognitive-code approaches often taught sentences that were neither temporally sequenced nor logically motivated. Instead, their main reason for existence seemed to be to demonstrate the use of a particular grammatical structure to aid the development of linguistic competence. These teachers were disappointed to find that Chomsky himself did not advocate such a method—nor any specific method for that matter. In his address to the 1965 Northeast Conference on the Teaching of Foreign Languages, Chomsky stated that neither the linguist nor the psychologist had enough knowledge about the process of language acquisition to serve as a basis for methodology.

> I am, frankly, rather skeptical about the significance, for the teaching of languages, of such insights and understanding as have been attained in linguistics and psychology. . . . I should like to make it clear from the outset that I am participating in this conference not as an expert on any aspect of the teaching of languages, but rather as someone whose primary concern is with the structure of language and, more generally, the nature of cognitive processes (in Allen and Van Buren, 1971, p. 152).

Chomsky cautioned teachers against passively accepting theory on grounds of authority, real or presumed.

CHOMSKY'S CONTRIBUTIONS

Inferences drawn from Chomsky's innatist theory are perhaps more important to second language teaching than any of the applications of transformational grammar. He argued that language development is too complicated a phenomenon to be explained on the basis of behaviorism alone (Chomsky, 1959). That children seem to have mastered the structure of their first language by the age of five or earlier suggests that at least some aspects of language are innate or inborn.

Chomsky opposed the idea that the mind is simply a *tabula rasa*, or a blank slate on which to store impressions. He refused to believe that grammar is simply an "output" based on a record of data. However, he did not deny that the mind is capable of the abilities attributed to it by behaviorism. He reminded us that language is not "made" by us but rather develops as a result of the way we are constituted when we are placed in the "appropriate external environment" (1980, p. 11). For Chomsky, the jury is still out concerning how much of language is shaped by experience and how much is intrinsically determined.

Support for the idea that certain aspects of language are innate first came from early psycholinguistic research. Roger Brown (1973) discovered universal trends in language acquisition after studying the speech of several children in natural situations over a period of years. Slobin (1971) and others added to this body of research. They found that children across languages use similar linguistic structures in their language development, and that they make the same kinds of errors. In addition, they concluded that linguistic structures are learned in the same order.

These findings have led researchers to agree with Chomsky that the brain is not a blank slate, but rather contains highly complex structures that seem to come into operation through an interactional process. To house these complex structures of the brain, Chomsky proposed the notion of a "language organ" which he called the *Language Acquisition Device* (LAD). Critics over the years have ridiculed the possibility that such an "organ" could "magically" appear, but Pinker (1994) argues that such a device or networking might have evolved through natural selection.

The Language Acquisition Device

To Chomsky, the Language Acquisition Device is associated with all that is universal in human languages. Its structures (or networking of structures) are activated when we are exposed to natural language. To help clarify what happens during the process of activation, Chomsky compares the LAD to a computer (see Gliedman, 1983) that contains a series of preprogrammed subsystems responsible for meaning, syntax, relationships between various types of words, and their functions. Within each subsystem, the individual, through experience, makes subconscious choices from a linguistic menu.

For the purpose of much simplified illustration, let's say that the menu contains choices about word order when using an object. Perhaps the choices consist of something like this: Subject-Verb-Object (SVO), Verb-Subject-Object (VSO), Subject-Object-Verb (SOV), and Object-Subject-Verb (OSV). Children born into Spanish, Chinese, and English environments, for example, subconsciously select SVO; a child born into an Arabic environment subconsciously selects VSO; one born into a Korean environment SOV, and so forth. Other choices might be available for varying degrees of inflection, the dropping of pronouns under certain conditions, and so on. Depending on the language environment in which it finds itself, the brain selects items appropriate to the specific language to which it is exposed. All humanly possible options are included in this computer within the brain.

Universal Grammar

Another related perspective explored by Chomsky is Universal Grammar, the embodiment of the basic principles shared by all languages. Because all humans are born with this set of principles, they are able to acquire something as complex as the structure of their first language at a very early age.

The shared principles can vary along certain parameters which, in newborn children, are called *unmarked* (that setting which is most common and most restrictive to all languages). As the child is exposed to the language of the environment, the initial settings are reset to *marked* forms, reflecting the less common features of a particular language.

To return to our example, let's say that the parameter for using an object is first set to SVO (assuming that SVO is the unmarked setting). The brain of a child born into an Arabic environment would then quickly reset this parameter to VSO, since that is the order to which the child is exposed through the input from the community. Some rules of language are thought to be so marked that they can only be acquired by experience because they are not parameterized (Larsen-Freeman and Long, 1991, p. 231).

Implications for Second Language Acquisition

Some linguists believe that the brain *resets* parameters only when it is exposed to a language that deviates from the parameters set for the first language (see especially White, 1989, 1990). White maintains that Universal Grammar is indeed available to second language learners. If it were not, the learner would need to depend wholly upon input and the cognitive domain to acquire a second language. She argues that the learner would not be able to acquire the more abstract and complex knowledge necessary to learn a second language without having access to Universal Grammar (see also Flynn, 1987, 1990; and Hulk, 1991). But there remains considerable controversy concerning whether the brain can reset parameters as easily as it did originally, considering that second language learners are usually older when exposed to their second language. Perhaps, a *critical period* (an optimal time) exists for the resetting of parameters (see especially Schachter, 1990, and J. Johnson, 1992). Such speculation, however, does not negate the possibility that the brain may indeed be capable of resetting parameters for a second language (see also Felix, 1988; and Tomaselli and Schwartz, 1990).

Although some innatists feel that simple exposure is enough to trigger the appropriate settings, at least for children learning a first language, many others take an interactionist point of view and insist that, for normal development to occur, the individual must receive input tailored to his or her developing proficiency. In other words, the child must receive *motherese* or *caretaker* speech, if not from parents then from siblings or others in the environment willing to give it. Motherese consists of generally shorter utterances, the use of high frequency vocabulary, a slower rate, some exaggeration in expression, redundancy, frequent explanations, repetitions, and the like. Furthermore, the topics are usually about the *here and now* rather than about something removed in time and space from the immediate environment. Interestingly, the speech addressed to second language learners by fluent speakers of the target language often contains many of the same modifications in the input (see Chapter 3).

While the theories of Universal Grammar based on Chomskyan thought are highly abstract, they may well give us clues about what is actually happening in the brain when we acquire language—either first or second.

THE CONNECTIONISTS

Other theories abound in the more recent literature. Of particular interest is the *connectionist approach* to how language develops. Connectionism considers the brain a *neural network of networks* consisting of nodes that operate in nonlinear ways when stimulated. Connectionism, however, is not an anti-nativist concept (see especially Elman, et al, 1996). While knowledge of language itself is not considered innate in this view, the constraints that are imposed on that knowledge are. Connectionists believe that a structure of the networks in the brain controls and constrains the kinds of information that the brain can internalize, the tasks that it can perform, and the things that it can store. Elman and his colleagues are looking for a unified theory that will make connectionism compatible with some form of innateness theory. Their hope is that a connectionist model will provide a framework for examining more closely what may or may not be innate.

Deacon (1997) argues that the human brain is pre-equipped by evolutionary forces for dealing with the symbolic representation that distinguishes human languages. However, he is convinced that the language acquisition device does *not* contain a universal grammar, and that Chomsky's computer analogy is incorrect—that the brain does not innately contain that kind of knowledge. But neither does he believe that learning alone can account for the complex phenomenon of human language. Deacon argues that the fact that children master a great deal of the grammatical system at an early age is due to the *evolution of the language itself to fit the child's capacity for learning*. The capacity to learn language also goes through evolutionary changes, but very slowly. A language that does not evolve to fit the child's early learning biases, which are universal, will quickly disappear because it cannot be passed to the next generation of speakers through the process of socialization. To Deacon, this explains why languages independently resemble one another structurally. Children take many years to develop the vocabulary of a language, but they quickly master its grammatical system through trial and error by making "lucky" guesses due to their *innate biases*. Children who are isolated during their immature period—the so-called feral or wild children that we have read about—will not develop a full language system, for *it is that very immaturity that allows them to minimize cognitive interference and develop the fundamentals of language.*

> Being unable to remember the details of specific word associations, being slow to map words to objects that tend to co-occur in the same context, remembering only the most global structure-function relationships of utterances, and finding it difficult to hold more than a few words of an utterance in short-term memory at a time may all be advantages for language learning. . . . Precisely because of children's learning constraints, the relevant large-scale logic of language "pops out" of a background of other details too variable for them to follow, and paradoxically gives them a biased head start. Children cannot tell the trees apart at first, but they can see the forest and eventually the patterns of growth within it emerge (Deacon, 1997, p. 135).

Thus the same limitations that make it difficult for children to learn other things make it possible for them to access something as complex as their first language.

The connectionists' theories offer yet another way to look at first language acquisition. What implications these theories may have for second language development remains unclear at present.

WILKINS AND BEYOND

Chomsky also drew severe criticism (and perhaps deservedly) from those who pointed out early on that his basic linguistic model[4] failed to adequately address the social aspects of language (Hymes, 1970; Halliday, 1979; and many others). Most agreed with the competence/performance distinction drawn by Chomsky but felt that competence should include not only grammatical sectors, but also psycholinguistic, sociocultural, and *de facto* sectors (to use Hymes's terms). Halliday rejected the distinction between competence and performance altogether, calling it misleading or irrelevant. Halliday felt that the more we are able to relate the grammar system to meaning in social contexts and behavioral settings, the more insight we will have into the language system. It was this basic idea that Wilkins used in constructing his notional-functional syllabus as a structure for input in the classroom.

---

[4] Chomsky's basic linguistic model distinguished two aspects of language: competence (the underlying knowledge of the grammatical system) and performance (the use of that knowledge to communicate).

The Notional-Functional Syllabus

Wilkins was concerned with helping the learner meet specific communication needs through input. The notional-functional framework he proposed organized input into a set of notional categories for the purpose of syllabus design. For example, a category may have included various ways to express probability: I am *certain* this project will be finished by Friday. *Maybe* it will be finished by Friday. I *doubt* if it will be finished by Friday, and so forth. Syllabi based on a notional approach often included such topics as accepting/rejecting invitations, requesting information, and expressing needs or emotions of various kinds.

Although Wilkins felt that this kind of notional syllabus was superior to a grammatical one, he was not yet ready to replace grammatically focused systems with functionally focused ones. He did, however, see a notional approach as providing another dimension to existing systems. It "can provide a way of developing communicatively what is already known, while at the same time enabling the teacher to fill the gaps in the learners' knowledge of the language." (1979, p. 92).

Not everyone agreed with Wilkins. Henry Widdowson, for example, warned that although some linguists might boast of ensuring communicative competence through the use of a notional syllabus, this approach did not necessarily ensure such competence as its result. For one thing, a notional syllabus isolates the components of communication. Widdowson argued:

> There is one rather crucial fact that such an inventory [typically included in a notional syllabus] does not, and cannot of its nature, take into account, which is that communication does not take place through the linguistic exponence of concepts and functions as self-contained units of meaning. It takes place as discourse, whereby meanings are negotiated through interaction (1979, p. 253).

Because a notional approach uses an artificial breakdown of communication into discrete functions, most of its applications lose their potential as providers of effective input. Activities based on a notional approach do not always involve real communication situations any more than repetitive dialogues or "structures for the day" do.

Consider the following excerpt from an early textbook employing a notional approach (Jones and von Baeyer, 1983):

> Here are some useful ways of requesting. They are marked with stars [in this case asterisks] according to how polite they are.
>
>   * Hey, I need some change. I'm all out of change.
>   ** You don't have a quarter, do you? Have you got a quarter, by any chance? Could I borrow a quarter?
>   *** You couldn't lend me a dollar, could you? Do you think you could lend me a dollar? I wonder if you could lend me a dollar.

**** Would you mind lending me five dollars? If you could lend me five dollars, I'd be very grateful.
***** Could you possibly lend me your typewriter? Do you think you could possibly lend me your typewriter? I wonder if you could possibly lend me your typewriter.
****** I hope you don't mind my asking, but I wonder if it might be at all possible for you to lend me your car.

Decide with your teacher when you would use these request forms. Can you add any more forms to the list?

Not only would such an analysis be superficial, but the subtleties involved would be very difficult for English Language Learners (ELLs), even at an advanced level. Native speakers also might have trouble determining the differences. For example, is "Would you mind lending me five dollars?" more or less polite than "Do you think you could lend me a dollar?" In addition to the activity's syntactic problems, semantic and situational differences are not at all clear. Asking someone for a car is certainly different from asking someone for a quarter. Important variables are missing, such as the positions, ages, and other characteristics of the interlocutors and their relationships to one another. Thus the activity lacks not only meaning but comprehensibility.

What kinds of activities then would be meaningful and comprehensible? Although some organizing principles might lend themselves to effective communicative approaches more than others, the organizational principle is not what necessarily makes the difference. Nor does content. For some students and teachers, for example, even grammar is a stimulating topic (see especially Fotis and Ellis, 1991). A discussion of function, too, may both be of interest and raise pragmatic awareness in a given classroom. But any discussion of a specific item and its alternatives will probably be most effective if it grows out of whatever relevant communication is taking place at the time.

An Effective Communicative Approach

Breen and Candlin (1979) characterized an effective communicative approach as one in which a shared knowledge is explored and then modified. Such an approach implies a negotiation of "potential meanings in a new language," as well as a socialization process. Breen and Candlin rejected systems in which the learner is separated from that which is to be learned, as though the target language could be objectively broken down into isolated components. They argued further that:

In a communicative methodology, content ceases to become some external control over learning-teaching procedures. Choosing directions becomes a part of the curriculum itself, and involves negotiation between learners and learners, learners and teachers, and learners and text.

They felt that a *negotiation for meaning* in general was crucial to a successfully applied communicative methodology.[5] This idea seemed to suggest the need for greater interdependence and a greater flexibility on the parts of teachers and learners to allow the syllabus and its content to develop in ways that make acquisition of the target language most likely.

SUMMARY

Although methodologies have changed over the years, the content of language teaching has remained basically the same until the past decade or so. Meaningful interaction critical to acquisition itself has taken a back seat to an analysis of language until fairly recently.

Chomsky's transformational grammar had been mistakenly used to justify and perpetuate a focus on structure in language teaching while his real contributions to the field remained largely ignored until recent years. Although we are not sure where it will lead us, his concepts of a possible language acquisition device and Universal Grammar may have profound consequences for classroom practice once we have more understanding of the content, structure(s), and networking involved. In the meantime, we will want to keep a close eye on the evolving work of the connectionists to discover how neural networks in the brain might operate as language develops. Compatible theories are taking shape combining certain aspects of innateness with those of connectionism, and we will not want to miss examining their implications.

Hymes, Halliday, Wilkins, Widdowson, Breen and Candlin, and many others have added to our knowledge of sociocultural aspects in defining a language system. In addition, their ideas have been influential in the development of communicative approaches that involve students in meaningful experiences in their new language.

READINGS, REFLECTION, AND DISCUSSION

Suggested Readings and Reference Materials

Brumfit, C. J., and Johnson, K., eds. (1979). *The communicative approach to language teaching*. Oxford: Oxford University. This classic book presents an in-depth analysis of the fundamental arguments underlying communicative approaches. Included are key writings of Hymes, Halliday, Wilkins, Widdowson, and many others who have led the way to a new look at language teaching processes.

---

[5] That is not to say, however, that all attempts to negotiate meaning result in comprehensive language. It is the intention to understand and to be understood that is most important here.

Canale, M., and Swain, M. (1980). Theoretical bases of communicative approaches to second language teaching and testing. *Applied Linguistics*, 1 (1), 1–47. The authors define communicative competence and identify and describe its basic components.

Chomsky, N. (1995). *The minimalist program*. Cambridge, MA: MIT Press. Chomsky reiterates his basic assumption that there is a component of the human brain whose functions (both cognitive and performance) are devoted solely to language and that this component interacts with other systems in ways that still remain a mystery. He speculates that this language faculty relies on a single computational system which limits what is possible in language syntactically and allows for limited lexical variation—thus making the word "minimalist" appropriate to his analysis.

Deacon, T. (1997). *The symbolic species: The co-evolution of language and the brain*. New York: Norton. As fascinating as it is controversial, this book takes a close look at the kind of symbolic thinking that distinguishes humans from other living things and at the role evolution has had in the process. The author's disagreements with Chomsky are discussed at length.

Elman, J., Bates, E., Johnson, M., Karmiloff-Smith, A., Parisi, D., and Plunket, K. (1996). *Rethinking innateness: A connectionist perspective on development*. Cambridge, MA: MIT Press. A difficult but important book in the development of connectionist theory. It examines the origins of knowledge in the human brain and looks at the role played by the interaction of innateness, neurobiology, and learning in cognitive development.

Questions and Projects for Reflection and Discussion

1. Many have speculated about the existence of Chomsky's language acquisition device, what it might contain, and how it might work. Both the computer analogy and the notion of parameter setting have been posited as possibilities. Discuss the feasibility of Chomsky's theories. Consider what you know about the views of the connectionists in your discussion. Do you have any hypotheses of your own about how first languages may develop within the brain? What about second languages? What role might social interaction play in each?

2. Widdowson, as early as 1978, argued that "we do not progress very far in our pedagogy by simply replacing abstract isolates of a linguistic kind by those of a cognitive or behavioral kind." Explain what you think he meant. Can you think of abstract isolates, other than those mentioned in this chapter, on which programs might attempt to focus?

3. Begin a journal. In it include your questions and reflections concerning the issues about which you are reading. Relate your responses to the notions you already had about language learning, based on your prior knowledge and experience. What ideas or concepts will you want to apply to your own teaching? In addition, at the ends of Chapters 1–17 you will find at least one question or task description that will specifically suggest that you respond in your journal. You may wish to respond in your journal to other questions and issues as well.

If you are currently teaching in a classroom, reflect in your journal upon your own practice and how it relates to what you are learning. From time to time, include answers to questions such as these: What am I doing that is different from what I did in the past? How well is it working? What other alternatives might I try? What have I learned from these experiences? What evidence do I see of my growth over time?

You may want to share some of your journal entries with a peer to get his or her response. If so, leave room after these entries for the peer response.

CHAPTER 2

The Classroom as an Environment for Language Acquisition

This would not necessarily mean changing or disguising the classroom in the hope that it will momentarily serve as some kind of "communicative situation" resembling situations in the outside world. The classroom itself has a unique social environment with its own human activities and its own conventions governing these activities.

M. Breen and C. Candlin, 1979

QUESTIONS TO THINK ABOUT

1. Is it possible to become fluent in a second or foreign language in a classroom? How can this happen?

2. How is learning a second or foreign language like learning a first? How is it different? How will this knowledge help you plan classroom experiences?

3. Have you attempted to learn another language in a classroom setting? Did you eventually become fluent in the second language you studied? At what point did you feel fluent? What kinds of experiences seemed necessary to your fluency?

The positions taken in the remainder of this book are based on the following assumptions:

- Although important differences must be taken into account, a sufficient number of similarities between first and second language acquisition support a common theory, particularly when it comes to process.
- The classroom can indeed be an appropriate environment for language acquisition.

A COMPARISON BETWEEN FIRST AND SECOND LANGUAGE ACQUISITION

Similarities

As early as 1974, Ervin-Tripp directly challenged the idea that it is not logical to develop a similar theory for first and second language acquisition. She maintained that the notion that first language (L1) and second language (L2) acquisition have little in common theoretically has been based on two common misconceptions:

- The foundation for L2 is built largely from a transfer of the rules of L1.
- Only L2 is constructed from prior conceptual knowledge within the learner.

Concerning the first misconception, Newmark (1983) argued that students who have a need to perform before they are ready will revert to L1 syntactic rules—more as a result of ignorance than of interference. The dependence on L1 seems to occur predominantly at the beginning of the acquisition process when there is an intense desire to communicate. Sometimes the student at this level will use not only L1 structures with L2 words, but L1 words as well. While beginning learners may rely heavily on L1 during initial attempts at communication, students depend less and less on it in the L2 environment as they gain proficiency in the L2.

Regarding the second misconception, researchers now agree that L1, like L2, is constructed from prior conceptual knowledge. Bruner, referring to L1, observed that "language emerges as a procedural acquisition to deal with events that the child already understands conceptually and to achieve communicative objectives that the child, at least partially, can realize by other means" (1978b, p. 247).

Ervin-Tripp felt that if the human brain is equipped to handle language, then certainly this ability is not confined to L1 (see also O'Grady, 1999). To show that the brain uses many similar strategies for L2 acquisition, she pointed to her study of American children learning French in Geneva in which children used three sources for acquiring French:

- peers (interaction in and out of the classroom)
- school (content-area subject matter was taught in French)
- home (exposure to parents who often spoke French to servants and to the mass media)

Generally speaking, "the conclusion is tenable that first and second language learning is similar in natural situations . . . the first hypothesis we might have is that in all second language learning we will find the same processes: overgeneralizations, production simplification, loss of sentence medial items, and so on" (1974, p. 205).[1]

Others, too, found credible evidence that second language learners use many strategies similar to those used for learning a first language. For example, B. Taylor looked at the use of overgeneralization and transfer made by elementary and intermediate students of ESL. By examining errors, he found that "reliance on overgeneralization is directly proportional to proficiency in the target language, and reliance on transfer is inversely proportional" (1980, p. 146). In other words, learners may depend quite heavily on first language knowledge to communicate in the target language at first, but they will begin to work within the framework of the target language—without harming the framework for the first language—once they are able to form hypotheses about the new language. Students will then make errors mainly due to overgeneralization of the newly acquired structures. For example, a student of English who has just hypothesized that past tense verbs end with "ed" may put "ed" on everything that happens in the past. Thus, "sat" (the correct form already picked up from the input) may become "sitted" or maybe even "satted." Taylor points out that overgeneralization (and transfer, too, for that matter) is the result of a necessity to reduce language to the simplest possible system. He referred to Jain's (1969) observation that this phenomenon represents an effort to lessen the cognitive burden involved in trying to master something as complex as language. The second language learner, like the first, attempts to "regularize, analogize, and simplify" in an effort to communicate.

Both first and second languages appear to develop in predictable ways. In reference to the natural order hypothesis, Krashen (1982) points to some striking similarities between L1 and L2 acquisition orders. If valid, these similarities may add credence to the argument that there are many parallels in cognitive strategies. He based his early conclusions on the following morpheme studies:

- Dulay and Burt (1974), who found in their research done on Spanish and Chinese children learning English, what may be a universal order in L2 morpheme acquisition

---

[1] See Slobin (1973) for the "Operating Principles" associated with the acquisition of L1.

- Bailey, Madden, and Krashen (1974), who found that adults and children followed a similar order in learning a second language
- R. Brown (1973) and DeVilliers and DeVilliers (1973), who reached similar conclusions in their well-known findings on the L1 morpheme acquisition order

"In general," Krashen argues, "the bound morphemes have the same relative order for first and second language acquisition (*ing, plural, ir past, reg past, third person singular,* and *possessive*) while the auxiliary and copula (*to be*) tend to be acquired later in first language acquisition than in second language acquisition" (1982, p. 13). Larsen-Freeman (1978) found in her study that morpheme orders seem to reflect the frequency of certain morphemes in the input. She stressed the importance of carefully examining the input when investigating such orders.[2]

However, we should be cautious in interpreting the morpheme studies. Although the evidence appears impressive, equating accuracy order with acquisition order (as was done in the cross-sectional studies)[3] is a questionable assumption at best. Structures are known to fluctuate within given speakers. Because the student uses "sat" at one point in time does not mean that it has been acquired.

More convincing evidence supporting a common theory began with Cazden (1972) and others who based their conclusions on longitudinal studies.[4] To illustrate, Ellis (1986) pointed out that the L1 orders Cazden noted in the acquisition of the transitional forms of negatives and interrogatives are very similar to those of L2 acquisition. For example, negatives begin with the "no" attachment (no can walk here) followed by "no" moving to an internal position (Juan no can walk here). Finally, "no" is part of the verb (Juan can't walk here). Concerning question formation, rising intonation is used to mark questions before the incorporation of *wh-* structures, and word order inversion does not occur until later.

Similarity between speech addressed to children in their first language (motherese) and speech addressed to foreigners (foreigner talk) is evidence that others at least perceive the process of L1 and L2 acquisition to be similar in many ways. Shorter sentences, high-frequency vocabulary, "here and now" items (but to a lesser extent), indirect correction, frequent gesture, and lack of overt attention to form, are among the many similarities observed in situations in which the interlocutors were involved in real communication (Henzl, 1973; Freed, 1978; Hatch, Shapira, and Gough, 1978; Arthur, Weiner, Culver,

---

[2] Interestingly, frequency effect is currently being looked at as a possible component of an informed model of second language acquisition (see especially the N. Ellis, Gass and Mackey, Larsen-Freeman, and Tarone articles in the special issue of *Studies in Second Language Acquisition*, 24(2), June 2002.)

[3] Cross-sectional studies measure what students can do at a specified point in time.

[4] Longitudinal studies measure long-term effects and development over a period of time.

Young, and Thomas, 1980; Long, 1981; Wesche and Ready, 1985; Richard-Amato, 1984).

Additional support for a common theory comes from Asher: "[A] reasonable hypothesis is that the brain and nervous system are biologically programmed to acquire language, either the first or second, in a particular sequence and in a particular mode." He stressed that both require a *silent period*, i.e., time to simply comprehend language without having to orally produce it. "If you want to learn a second language gracefully and with a minimum of stress, then invent a learning strategy that is in harmony with the biological system" (1972, p. 134), he suggested.

We already know that children learning their first language require a fairly extensive silent period before they begin to produce utterances that are meaningful. Postovsky (1977) demonstrated the benefits of a silent period for second language learners in a study of adult American students of Russian at the Defense Language Institute in Monterey, California. The students in the experimental group were asked to *write* their responses to input rather than *speak*; in contrast, the control group had to produce orally right from the beginning. The first group did better than the second, not only in syntactic control of the language, but also in accuracy of pronunciation.

Gary's (1975) research also gives strength to arguments for a silent period. The study involved fifty American children learning Spanish. Half the students were allowed a silent period during which they could respond with nods, pointing, and other gestures. The other half had to respond orally using an audiolingual format. The experimental group outperformed the control group in both listening comprehension and speaking performance.

Differences

Because learners are usually older when acquiring a second language,[5] they are more developed cognitively than first language learners. (See especially Marinova-Todd, Barshall, and Snow, 2000, for an up-to-date review of the literature on older learners.) Older learners appear to have distinct advantages in several areas:

- they tend to learn more quickly
- they have a greater knowledge of the world in general
- they have more control over the input they receive (e.g., they are able to ask for repetitions, renegotiate meaning, change the topic, and so forth, more readily)
- they are able to learn and apply rules that can aid in facilitating the acquisition process (unless they are still very young children)

---

[5] An exception would be the compound bilingual, one who learns the second language at the same time as the first.

- they have a first language (and perhaps one or more second languages) from which they can transfer strategies and linguistic knowledge[6]
- they have one or more cultures that give them advanced information about expectations, discourse in general, and how to get things done with language (Of course, there will be many differences between the first language and culture and the second with which the learners will eventually become familiar.)

But being older may not always be advantageous in learning a second language. Although we don't yet know enough about this area to reach conclusions, it seems likely that older learners have some maturational constraints affecting the language acquisition process (see especially Long, 1990). Learners may lose some of their earlier abilities and gain others as they age. However, many areas of difficulty for older learners may be found mainly in the affective realm (see Chapter 6). Older learners may have increased inhibitions and anxiety (see MacIntyre and Charos, 1996), for example, and they may find themselves afraid to make errors. The latter may be the result of an undue emphasis on form in their earlier experiences with language learning and on the pressure they may have felt to perform in "nativelike" ways. In addition, they may have poor attitudes and lack motivation, depending upon their feelings about and the conditions under which they are learning the second language. Perhaps they are studying the language only because it is required in their program of study, or they find themselves in a country with a language and culture in which they have little interest. Although the influence of the first language is usually positive in learning the second, interference may occur later on, particularly for items that are similar in the two languages either structurally or semantically (Newmark, 1983). Moreover, students may avoid using certain structures altogether because they are not part of their first language repertoire (see Schachter, 1974 and Kleinmann, 1977). One thing we do know for certain is that older learners demonstrate much greater variation in their rate of acquisition and in their degree of ultimate proficiency than do younger learners. This indicates that biology may not be the major determining factor here.

The chart in Figure 2.1 summarizes some of the first and second language learner characteristics that we have mentioned so far.[7] You will probably want to add other characteristics as you read further.

Important differences between first and second language acquisition development appear to center on affective factors, cognitive functioning abilities and preferences, and certain kinds of knowledge. The similarities appear to

---

[6] However, usually one of the languages will take precedence over the other and will be considered the first language.

[7] The assumption is made here that second language learners are usually older than first language learners except in the case of compound bilinguals. Thus qualifiers such as "generally" and "in most cases" are used.

Characteristics	L1 Learner	L2 Learner
constructs language from prior conceptual knowledge	✓	✓
is an active learner who tests and revises hypotheses	✓	✓
requires an interactional process	✓	✓
uses cognitive strategies (oversimplification, etc.)	✓	✓
is aided by modified input	✓	✓
develops language in predictable stages	✓	✓
makes developmental errors	✓	✓
requires a silent period	✓	
benefits from a silent period		✓
is usually cognitively more highly developed		✓
generally has a greater knowledge of the world		✓
in most cases, can learn and apply rules more readily		✓
usually has more control over the input		✓
has an L1 as a resource		✓
may have other second languages from which to draw		✓
is familiar with one or more other cultures		✓
may have a problem with attitude and/or motivation		✓
is more likely to be inhibited, anxious, and/or afraid of making errors		✓

Figure 2.1 A Comparison Between First and Second Language Learners

lie mainly in the process itself, although there are some differences here to look for as well. Future research on the human brain and how it functions and changes over time may shed light on this critical, but little understood area.

THE PROCESS OF LEARNING A SECOND LANGUAGE

We need to examine the differences between *contrastive analysis* and *error analysis* (proposed by Corder in 1967) in order to get perspective on the process of learning a second language in general.

Contrastive Analysis

Contrastive analysis is based on behaviorism. It considers L1 to be mainly an interference to the mastery of L2. In order to become proficient in L2, the habits of L1 need to be "broken" before the habits of L2 can become firmly established. Thus audiolingualism, its most well-known manifestation (see Chapter 1), presented us with mim-mem drills and practice with minimal pairs such as *chew* and *shoe* (for Spanish speakers), *glass* and *grass* (for Japanese speakers), and dialogues to be memorized so that students could avoid errors in the new language and take on its proper forms.

One problem with this philosophy is that contrastive analysis is not a good predictor of errors in L2. The fact is that most of the errors students made in L2 cannot be traced to the differences between L1 and L2. In addition, regardless of the features of the students' first languages, they appear to go through similar variable stages in the second language anyway. For example, those students whose first languages use inversion to form questions (as does English) still go through the same process as other students for interrogatives. They usually will use intonation initially to mark a question (He is going?) before they use inversion (Is he going?) during the second language learning process.

Error Analysis

Error analysis, on the other hand, is based on *developmentalism* (learning develops in variable stages as learners interact with the environment). It looks at the errors made by learners while they are learning and asks questions about them.

- Why are these errors being made?
- What do they suggest about the hypotheses being tested (generally subconsciously) by learners?
- Do they mean that the learners are doing something wrong? Or do they mean that the learners have acquired a rule and are, in reality, progressing in the language?

Take, for example, the student who may change "sat" to "sitted" or "sat-ted" because the past tense "ed" has just been internalized. Error analysis looks at such errors positively and considers them necessary to the development of language, be it first or second. Used appropriately, then, error analysis should not pinpoint deficits in the student's use of the new language, but rather should help determine in what ways the student is progressing in the developmental process.

Overall, error analysis considers L1 to be mainly beneficial to the development of L2, as we learned earlier from Newmark (1983). At first, students rely heavily on L1 structures and sometimes even vocabulary to get meaning across. As the L2 becomes internalized and students move toward proficiency, L1 is relied upon less and less. Interestingly, the interim language that develops is neither L1 nor L2. It not only has some features of each, but also has features that are not found in either language. It is called *interlanguage* (Selinker, 1972).

Interlanguage Development

The term *interlanguage* refers to the variable progression through which each language learner constructs a system of abstract linguistic rules (Ellis, 1997). This process reflects the systematic development of the syntax, semantics, and pragmatics of the second language and is very similar to the process followed by first language learners. Throughout, hypothesis testing occurs usually at the subconscious level and predictable errors are made along the way, regardless of what first language the students speak (see Fuller and Gundel, 1987; Butterworth and Hatch, 1978; Ravem, 1978, and many others).

The progression toward proficient L2 use is not linear, and it does not have to be at the expense of the first language. Students move forward and back, and forward and back again, all the while stretching to increasingly more advanced levels. Thus the word "variable" is used throughout this book to describe stages and progression of development. Although students regress frequently, the general movement is forward, toward the goal: proficient L2 use. We need considerably more research to understand this progression fully. We do have evidence about how students progress, particularly in the formation of negatives and interrogatives, as well as the formation of relative clauses. For example, Schumann (1980) looked at the speech of five Spanish speakers learning English and found that clauses first are used to modify objects: "Roberto has a book is about electricity." Notice that the relative pronoun is missing. This will come later to form "Roberto has a book that is about electricity." Bardovi-Harlig (1992), too, looked at the acquisition of several morpheme and syntactic constructions and found, as did her predecessors, that these constructions emerge in variable stages throughout the acquisition process. One of her findings concerning past tense acquisition is that both tutored and untutored learners begin with no explicit time reference, slowly begin to incorporate adverbials (*last week*, *then*, *after*, etc.), and gradually add verb endings that indicate past tense. Both groups gradually increased systematic use of past tense verbs; however, in her study, the tutored learners demonstrated higher rates of appropriate use at upper levels (see discussion of instructed learning on pages 60–65).

Fossilization

Although the progression is generally forward, students will sometimes seem to reach a plateau. We say that at this point or for that particular structure (sometimes called a "pidginized form") the students' interlanguage has *fossilized*. When pidginized forms become obligatory in the students' production, we say that fossilization has occurred. Interestingly, fossilization is unique to second language learners and does not occur in first language learners (Ellis, 1997).

We know relatively little about what causes fossilization in second language learners and what can be done to reverse its effects. We do know that there are many related factors, some of which are:

- increased anxiety about the learning situation
- wanting to be "native-like" (which for many is an unrealistic and inappropriate goal)
- lack of competent linguistic models
- not enough flexibility within the learner
- insufficient motivation

In some cases, the learner may have reached specific communicative goals and no longer feels the need to become more competent. The language of many adults will tend to fossilize at some point in the interlanguage process, particularly in the area of pronunciation (see especially Mendes Figueiredo, 1991), but this should not be a great cause for concern unless it interferes with communication.

Defining and Reaching a Goal

Adults have been known to acquire *all* aspects of a second language under the right conditions. Sorenson (1967) studied the Tukano tribes of South America who must, according to their culture, marry someone outside of their first language group. He found that adults in this situation do indeed learn second languages and reach high levels of proficiency, even in pronunciation. (Incidentally, they are permitted a very long silent period.) Ioup, Boustagui, El Tigi, and Moselle (1994) found that their subject, Julie from the United Kingdom, gained native-like proficiency with Egyptian Arabic (she was married to an Egyptian). In both studies, continual access to the language was available, and the motivation to speak in native-like ways seemed very high.[8] While we obviously cannot provide students with access to a second language around-the-clock or heighten motivation to this level in our classrooms, we can do a great deal to prevent fossilization from occurring prematurely and maybe even keep it from happening at all. Klein (1995), who sees the phenomenon from a psychosocial perspective,[9] concludes that older learners who have sufficient access to input in the second language (see also Flege and Liu, 2001) and who have high motivation to speak it can, indeed, reach native-like levels. However, native-like proficiency should clearly *not* be the goal for all second language learners (see Cook, 1999; M. Gebhard, 1999; Liu, 1999). A more realistic and appropriate goal is to be understood by the group with which the second language learner needs to communicate. Now that English has become global, many "Englishes" have developed around the world, any one of which could become the target language for any given group of people (see also pages 2–3).

Bringing students into increased contact with competent speakers of the language, especially peers, may increase motivation to an optimal level for each person. Such contact might include:

- setting up peer-teacher situations (see Chapter 15)
- inviting fluent speakers of the target language to the classroom (including administrators, counselors, teachers, adults from the community, as well as peers and other L2 users)
- organizing pen-pal relationships with peers who are more advanced in the language
- arranging field trips and planning celebrations with more advanced speakers of the language

Situations such as these can provide enough motivation to prevent fossilization or, in some cases, get students moving again in the language development process.

Although error analysis is an important tool in studying interlanguage, we must move beyond that to include discourse and performance analyses as well as ethnography. We have much to learn about the total situations of L2 users, the details of the interactional events, the feelings, attitudes, political concerns, and motivational factors relevant to the process of learning another language in the classroom.

---

[8] The researchers noted, in the case of Julie, that she seemed to be an outstanding language learner and paid close attention to form. Of course, without strong motivation in the first place, she probably would not have been able to achieve what she did in spite of her abilities as a language learner.

[9] For neurobiological perspectives on the issue of age, see especially Lenneberg (1967) and Scovel (1988).

LANGUAGE ACQUISITION IN THE CLASSROOM

At the beginning of this chapter, we mentioned two assumptions: that first and second language acquisition processes share enough similarities that a single theory can address both; and that the classroom can be an appropriate environment for language acquisition. Two models have been advanced in the last couple of decades to support the second assumption: the Monitor Model (Krashen) and the Variable Competence Model (Ellis, 1986). The better known of these, the Monitor Model, is probably also the more controversial.

The Monitor Model

Krashen distinguished between two different linguistic systems: *acquisition* and *learning* (Krashen, 1981b, 1982). Acquisition, he suggested, is *subconscious*, and learning is *conscious*.

  Acquired items (Figure 2.2) are those that are able to pass through an "affective filter" of inhibitions, motivation, personality factors, and so on. The input then moves into the subconscious to become *intake*, a term proposed by Corder in 1967 to describe what is actually internalized. *Learned* items, on the other hand, become part of a monitor (see Figure 2.3) and are used in production only if they are relatively simple, if the speaker is focused on form, and if there is time to apply them.

  In the flow of normal discourse, the speaker does not have the opportunity to monitor the output to any great extent unless he or she is what Krashen called a "super monitor user"—in other words, one who is adept at applying rules and communicating simultaneously. Now and then a language learner appears not to monitor at all. Such learners make many errors in form; Krashen referred to them as "underusers." However, Krashen (1981b) also identified the "optimal user," one who applies the monitor appropriately. There are situations, he believed, in which the monitor can be maximally effective—for example, when the language learner is taking grammar tests, writing papers, or preparing planned speeches. Although items in the learning store do not directly become part of the acquisition store, according to Krashen, the rules of the target

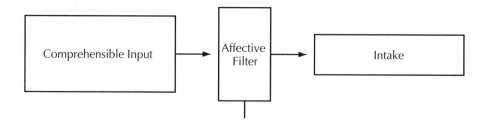

Figure 2.2. The Acquisition Process (Krashen, 1981b)

(Learned Rules)

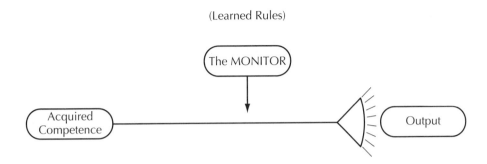

Figure 2.3. Performance Model (Krashen, 1982)

language do become acquired, but only by exposure to language that students can understand.[10]

Criticism of the Monitor Model

Krashen's learning/acquisition and subconscious/conscious distinctions within the Monitor Model were targets of considerable criticism. Many argued that it is possible for rules that have been consciously applied over and over in a variety of situations to become automatic and thus internalized (Ellis, 1986; Gregg, 1984; Sharwood-Smith, 1981; Stevick, 1980; McLaughlin, 1978; Bialystok and Fröhlich, 1977). Learners also seem continually to "monitor" subconsciously, and they become aware of doing so only when there has been a mismatch between their acquired hypotheses and what they would hear and/or produce (see Morrison and Low, 1983). Thus the issues involved here may be more complicated than many at first thought. Learning and acquisition may indeed be part of the same component (see the Ellis and Levelt models below).

McLaughlin, Rossman, and McLeod (1984) also criticized the distinctions Krashen draws. They preferred to speak of *controlled* and *automatic* information processing, as opposed to *learning* and *acquisition*. They suggested that either one can be the focus of attention (although this is usually true of controlled processes) or on the periphery of attention (usually true of automatic

---

[10] Krashen cited supportive evidence from the descriptive studies of Stafford and Covitt (1978) and Krashen and Pon (1975). Stafford and Covitt's subject V demonstrated a high level of proficiency with spoken English but, in an interview with him, they discovered that he showed no conscious knowledge of the rules. Conversely, Krashen and Pon's subject P proved to be an optimal monitor user when writing English but did not apply the well-learned, well-practiced rules to her speech production. Instead she made many errors. However, McLaughlin, Rossman, and McLeod (1984) pointed out that the brain often has difficulty in handling two competitive cognitive demands at once—carrying on a conversation and being accurate grammatically. It is possible that once the cognitive burden is lessened, the learner might be able to apply some of the rules.

processes). Unlike Krashen's divisions, controlled and automatic processes do not fall unequivocally into a conscious/subconscious dichotomy. These researchers saw both processes as falling somewhere on a continuum between conscious and subconscious functioning. They emphasized that individual learning styles must also be considered. They did concede that when input is comprehensible, implicit learning might be most successful, but they pointed out that some adults prefer working from the rules, whereas others prefer working from the input.

Krashen nevertheless has had an important impact on second language classrooms all across the United States and elsewhere. His model made sense to teachers, and through it he brought the point home that the classroom does not have to confine itself to formal instruction in the target language. Rather, it can provide input that better facilitates second language learning—input that is, according to him, comprehensible, interesting, and/or relevant, not grammatically sequenced, and is present in sufficient quantity.

The Variable Competence Model

Ellis (1984, 1986) called his conceptualization of second language acquisition the Variable Competence Model. While Krashen's Monitor Model emphasized the importance of *providing comprehensible input*, Ellis's model focused on *interaction*. Ellis suggested that appropriate input is not enough, but that a key factor in second language acquisition is "the opportunity afforded the learner to *negotiate* meaning with an interlocutor, preferably one who has more linguistic resources than the learner and who is adept at 'foreigner/teacher talk'" (1984, p. 184). (See Chapter 3 for the development of a similar idea.) Ellis recognized a *single* knowledge store containing variable transitional rules, some of which tend to be more automatic, others more analyzed.

The second language learner demonstrates variation in the production of interlanguage forms (see also Larsen-Freeman, 1991). Sometimes the learner will appear to have mastered a particular structure; other times he or she will regress to earlier forms. The variation, according to Ellis, is often the result of whether the process is a primary one (using automatic rules) in unplanned discourse or a secondary one (using analyzed rules) in planned discourse. (See Figure 2.4.)

According to this model, primary processes utilize and facilitate the *automatic system*, and secondary processes utilize and facilitate the *analytic system*. Both systems represent a continuum rather than a dichotomy. The rate of acquisition depends upon the quantity and quality of the interaction in which the learner is involved. Ellis argued that "rapid development along the 'natural' route occurs when the learner has the chance to negotiate meaning in unplanned discourse" (1984, p. 186). However, he reminded us that this process is influenced by such affective factors as motivation and personality (see Chapter 6).

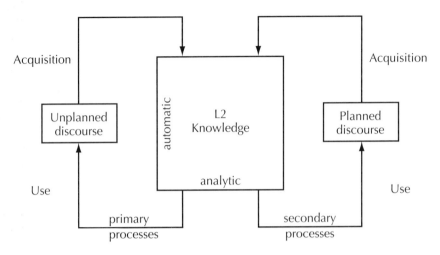

Figure 2.4. Variable Competence Model of SLA

Levelt's First Language Model and Its Implications

Levelt (1989) proposed an interesting model that, while it did not aim to explain second language comprehension and production as such, nevertheless illuminated the process, particularly concerning the monitor and how it works (see also Kormos, 1999). This model has also been applied to the study of vocabulary acquisition in second language learners (see de Bot, Paribakht, and Wesche, 1997) and to bilingual production (see de Bot, 1992). It may prove to have other applications in areas of second language acquisition as well. In his attempt to integrate theoretical approaches to understanding adults' abilities to produce their first languages. Levelt proposed a blueprint for the speaker (see Figure 2.5). Note that the boxes represent processing components and the circle and ellipse represent the stores of knowledge.

In the blueprint, you can see that the output of one component more often than not becomes the input for the next. At the risk of oversimplification, here are the functions of each component.

- The *Conceptualizer* produces preverbal messages reflecting the speaker's intentions. It is also responsible for monitoring.
- The *Formulator* consists of two subcomponents:
  1. The *Grammatical Encoder* retrieves lemmas (declarative information about the meaning and sense of lexical items) from the lexicon and comes up with grammatical relations to show how the concepts relate within the message (in other words, it produces the surface structure)
  2. The *Phonological Encoder* designs a phonetic plan (internal speech) based on the surface structure.

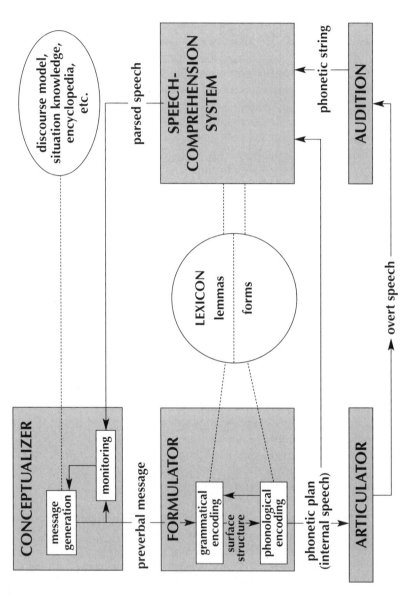

Figure 2.5. The Levelt Model: A Blueprint for the Speaker

- The *Articulator* lays out and implements the phonetic plan in the form of neuromuscular instructions.
- The *Speech-Comprehension System* makes *internal speech* and *overt speech* available to the conceptual system which gives the speaker a chance to monitor his or her own utterances.

All of the components operate autonomously in transforming input into output without further help or hindrance from any other component.

According to this model, generating messages and monitoring are *controlled* processes, which require the speaker's continuing attention. Grammatical encoding, form encoding, and articulation, on the other hand, are highly *automatic* processes that require little attention or intention on the part of the speaker.

Notice that there is no separate monitor. The monitoring of self and others is accomplished by the Conceptualizer because it alone has the abilities and knowledge necessary to do the job. Meaning and form are blended. In the case of self-monitoring, the Conceptualizer can monitor both internal speech and overt speech. Both are fed first to the Speech Comprehension System where they are parsed (broken down into their various components) and then looped back to the Conceptualizer where they are monitored. The first is accomplished *internally* at the phonetic planning stage; the second is accomplished *externally*, once the utterance is actually produced. This whole process is referred to as the *perceptual loop theory of monitoring*. It is important to remember, however, that not all self-monitoring goes through the loops. Monitoring is also done before the message even leaves the Conceptualizer.

Levelt's model holds much promise for second language process research, especially in the areas of self-correction (including consciousness raising, noticing, and attention to form—see also pages 60–65 in Chapter 3) and vocabulary development. However, this model's purpose is not to address how second language is acquired, nor to consider the impact of affective and sociocultural factors on language comprehension and production. Perhaps future models that draw from this one and the others will relate their components specifically to second language processes, as well as include the important affective and sociocultural influences. Unfortunately, we don't yet know what such a model might look like or if the process is even possible to codify. But ongoing brain research makes the possibility of developing an integrated model seem tantalizingly close.

EARLY RESEARCH ON ACQUISITION IN SECOND LANGUAGE CLASSROOMS

Although scant research (particularly longitudinal) has been done on the second language acquisition process in second language classrooms, progress has been made in assessing the product in cross-sectional research. Many studies, for example, indicate that the early French immersion programs in

Canada[11] have been among the most successful (Lambert and Tucker, 1972; Tucker and d'Anglejan, 1972; Selinker, Swain, and Dumas, 1975; Swain, 1975; Swain, Lapkin, and Barik, 1976), as has the Spanish immersion program in Culver City, California (Cathcart, 1972; Cohen, 1974; Plann, 1977). What these programs have in common is an emphasis on the content to be learned, rather than on language itself. At later levels, formal instruction was also included in varying degrees. All immersion students were at similar levels in the target language to begin with (unlike submersion programs, in which they are the minority among native speakers), and all the content-area subjects were taught in the target language until English was gradually added at later levels (see Chapter 17). These studies and many others indicate that our knowledge of the second language acquisition process *is* relevant to the classroom, and that acquisition, in fact, *does* occur there.

As early as 1975, Wagner-Gough and Hatch argued that the classroom is more than just one more environment in which acquisition occurs; rather, it can be especially conducive to acquisition. They felt that for beginners through intermediate-level learners, the classroom could potentially be more effective than the environment outside for acquiring a second language. They reminded us that it is often difficult for students to get comprehensible input from a world that is not aware of their need for it.

SUMMARY

This chapter supports two assumptions about second language acquisition: (1) Although important differences must be taken into account, a sufficient number of similarities between first and second language acquisition support a common theory, particularly when it comes to process; and (2) the classroom can be an appropriate environment for acquisition.

Learning an L1 and learning an L2 are alike in many ways and different in others. The similarities are found mainly in the process itself; the differences are found particularly in the areas of affect, cognitive functioning abilities and preferences, and certain kinds of knowledge.

Second-language acquisition appears to develop in variable stages through an interlanguage process until the learner reaches proficient L2 use. Native-speaker language no longer seems an appropriate goal for two main reasons: (1) it is unrealistic to expect second language learners to be "native"; and (2) the label no longer represents the target, especially in the case of English, considering the fact that several "Englishes" have arisen around the world.

Krashen's Monitor Model and Ellis's Variable Competence Model were developed to help clarify the second-language acquisition process in the classroom. The first emphasized the importance of comprehensible input; the sec-

---

[11] The Thunder Bay program described on pages 429–433 and the lower east side Manhattan program on pages 454–464 are examples of immersion.

ond emphasized interaction and negotiated meaning in a variety of situations. A third model worthy of consideration is Levelt's blueprint for the first language speaker which may have important implications for second language comprehension and production and has already been applied in the areas of vocabulary development and bilingual production.

Although the natural environment might be ideal for some, others might find it difficult to receive comprehensible input and to find the opportunity to participate in quality interaction about relevant issues.

READINGS, REFLECTION, AND DISCUSSION

Suggested Readings and Reference Materials

Birdsong, D., ed., (1999). *Second language acquisition and the critical period hypothesis.* Mahwah, NJ: Lawrence Erlbaum. The views of several researchers on the critical period hypothesis are included here. The hypothesis is reevaluated in light of research supporting the fact that older learners can attain the competence usually attributed to young learners of a second language. However, both sides of the argument are presented.

Cook, V. (1999). Going beyond the native speaker in language teaching. *TESOL Quarterly,* 33(2), 185–209. In this seminal article, Cook explains why the *native-speaker* goal creates unrealistic expectations and unnecessary frustration in second language learners for whom it may be unattainable.

Ellis, R. (1997). *Second language acquisition.* Oxford: Oxford University. Ellis presents a highly readable perspective of the relevant research on second language acquisition and its relationship to the theories that have been developed to explain it.

Gass, S. (1997). *Input, interaction, and the second language learner.* Mahwah, NJ: Lawrence Erlbaum. Here Gass presents her own model of the second language acquisition process, describes Universal Grammar, the role of input and output within interactionist framework, and many other issues.

Larsen-Freeman, D., and Long, M. (1991). *An introduction to second language acquisition research.* London: Longman. A comprehensive analysis of the important research in second language acquisition. Its topics include interlanguage studies, types of data analysis, theories in second language acquisition, and many others.

Levelt, W. (1989). *Speaking: From intention to articulation.* Cambridge, MA: Massachusetts Institute of Technology. In this seminal work, Levelt describes in great detail his blueprint for the first language speaker. Levelt's goal is to clarify his theoretical claims without attempting to formalize them. This work may have important implications for understanding second language learning in relation to brain functions.

Lightbown, P. and Spada, N. (1999). *How languages are learned,* 2d edition. Oxford: Oxford University. A well-developed discussion of topics such as first and second language learning, affective factors, interlanguage (learner language) development, instructed and natural environments, and common myths about language learning.

Questions and Projects for Reflection and Discussion

1. In spite of the many similarities between first and second language learning, the important differences must be considered in curriculum development. What implications might these differences have for planning the content of language programs?

2. Some people argue that a discussion of the acquisition process is not relevant to the classroom because it is difficult, if not impossible, to make it happen there. What is your stand on this issue? Base your answer on your own experience either as a language student or as a teacher.

3. Given your own experience, speculate about the role a learner's first language has in the acquisition of the second. Has its role been given too much or too little importance in the formulation of second language theory? Discuss.

4. Why do you think fossilization is unique to second language learners? Do you have any ideas about how a teacher might help second language learners overcome fossilization and move forward again in the language development process?

5. How might you define a "native-speaker"? Do you think native-speaker language should be the goal for second language learners? Why or why not? Discuss the political ramifications of your answer. What influence do you think English as a global language should have on the issues involved here? You might want to refer back to the Introduction to this book where this topic was first discussed.

6. How important do you think age is in learning another language? Relate your answer to your own experiences with language learning and to those of people you know. Use your journal to write down and organize your thoughts on this subject. Share your ideas with a small group.

7. Look again at the models presented in this chapter. What are their advantages and disadvantages? Which one appears to have the most promise for use in the future development of second language acquisition models? Do you know of other models that have been developed? What contributions might they make to future speculation about the acquisition process?

8. Levelt has developed a model for first language speakers (see page 44). How might you modify it for second language speakers? You may want to include factors mentioned by Krashen and Ellis or any others with whom you are familiar. What additional influences might you include? You may end up with more than one model. Show and explain your model(s) to a small group of peers to get their feedback. Make any changes that seem appropriate based on what you learn.

CHAPTER 3

The Role of Interaction

. . . teaching and learning involves an essentially dialogic relationship.

Gordon Wells, 1999

QUESTIONS TO THINK ABOUT

1. Is it possible to learn a second language by oneself? To what extent are teachers and peers necessary to the process? What are some of the best things teachers can do to help students learn another language? How can peers best be involved in the process?

2. Think about the times your use of language may have been corrected by a teacher. Were you ever embarrassed by the way a teacher corrected you? How should teachers handle error correction in their classrooms? Should it differ for oral and written work?

3. Consider your own experiences with formal grammar instruction either as a teacher or a student. How important was having instruction in grammar for you? Is it possible to become fluent in another language without it?

The Zone of Proximal Development (Vygotsky, 1962, 1978) is a hypothesis that may help to explain, at least indirectly, some of the cognitive requirements necessary to language acquisition. Underlying the surface complexity of this concept are fundamentals that may be extremely important to understanding how humans learn not only languages, but how they learn in general. Although this hypothesis cannot account for the actual process of first or second language acquisition, it can teach us a lot about the social nature of this process, particularly in full two-way communication.[1]

Of course, second language acquisition can take place without full two-way communication. For example, Gass and Varonis in 1985 and later Pica in 1995 found that in one-way communication there may be less need for interaction to the extent that the participants have a shared body of knowledge. However, research seems to indicate that interaction involving two-way communication is the best way to negotiated meaning and to acquisition of the target language (Gass and Varonis, 1994; Gass, Mackey, and Pica, 1998; Gass, 1997; Long, 1983a, 1983b, 1996; Pica and Doughty, 1985; Swain, 1995; and many others). Under the right conditions, such communication can lead to full participation in the language classroom (see Chapter 4).

THE ZONE OF PROXIMAL DEVELOPMENT AND SOCIAL INTERACTION

Although Vygotsky (1978), like Chomsky, did not speak directly to second language pedagogy, he did formulate ideas concerning learning and development in children that have important implications for second language teaching. Before we proceed, a comparison of Vygotsky's and Piaget's views of the *relationship of learning and development* may be beneficial. Vygotsky and Piaget were both *constructivists,* meaning that they believed that knowledge itself is structured and developed from *within* the individual through active learning.[2] This is in sharp contrast to the *behaviorists,* who thought that knowledge was structured from *without* the individual and that all the teacher had to do was imprint this knowledge on the learner's mind.

To Piaget (1979), the processes of learning and mental development are independent of each other. Learning utilizes development but does not shape its

---

[1] Burt and Dulay (1983) identified three communication phases: one-way (the learner receives input but gives no overt response); partial two-way (the learner responds orally in L1 or by simple gestures); and full two-way (the learner gives messages and responds in the target language to the messages of others).

[2] Constructivism assumes that students are able to search for their own answers; that lessons can be built around concepts and ideas, not facts and skills; that student thinking can spearhead lessons, raise important questions, and change content; that students can grapple with open-ended questions and elaborated responses, and can construct relationships, create metaphors, and build collaborative communities (see also Kaufman and Brooks, 1996).

course. Piaget believed that *maturation* precedes learning. Educators who adhere to this idea emphasize the "readiness" principle. A student must be exposed primarily to input that can be handled without difficulty. In other words, the input must be at the student's *actual* level of development.

Vygotsky differed, in that he saw the individual as having two developmental levels that interact with learning from birth forward. Vygotsky argued that *learning* precedes maturation; it creates new mental structures within the brain. Through interaction, the individual progresses from what Vygotsky called an actual developmental level to a *potential* developmental level. Between these two levels is the "Zone of Proximal Development," which he defined as "the distance between the actual developmental level as determined by independent problem solving and the level of potential development as determined through problem solving under adult guidance of and in a collaboration with more capable peers" (1978, p. 86). The potential level becomes the next actual level through learning that "presupposes a specific social nature and a process by which children grow into the intellectual life of those around them." Learning, then, should always be one step ahead of development. The idea of the Zone of Proximal Development is so powerful intuitively that it may indeed be the single most important impetus to change in the way we teach.

As Wells notes (1999):

> In the place of traditional transmissional teaching on the one hand and unstructured discovery learning on the other, his [Vygotsky's] theory places the emphasis on the co-construction of knowledge by more mature and less mature participants engaging in activity together. . . . In the place of competitive individualism, his theory proposes a collaborative community in which, with the teacher as leader, all participants learn with and from each other as they engage together in dialogic inquiry (p. xii).

Piaget stressed *biology* as the determiner in what he called the "universal" stages of development. Vygotsky did not emphasize universal stages; instead he stressed *society* as the determiner of development, although the resulting stages are similar. The stages are variable because each person's history and opportunity for interaction is different. Vygotsky emphasized a dialectical unity or an "interlacement" (a John-Steiner and Souberman term, 1978) between biological foundations and dynamic social conditions. He was convinced that higher psychological functions entail new psychological systems; they are not simply superimposed over the more elementary processes, as Piaget believed.

In addition, Vygotsky placed a great deal of stress on children's play, which he saw as being rule-governed. Children, he argued, do not typically jump around aimlessly—or at most, do so for only brief periods of time. Rather, they invent rules to make the activity fun. Even being a "mother" requires rules. Play, like school, should create a Zone of Proximal Development. Through it the "child always behaves beyond his average age, above his daily behavior; in play it is as though he were a head taller than himself" (1978, p. 102).

Although learning and development are directly related, Vygotsky suggested that they do not increase in equal amounts or in parallel ways. "Development in children never follows school learning the way a shadow follows the object that casts it" (1978, p. 91). The relationship between the two is extremely complex and uneven and cannot be reduced to a simple formula. Vygotsky was convinced that *learning itself is a dynamic social process through which the teacher in a dialogue with a student can focus on emerging skills and abilities.*

Even though Vygotsky did not make specific recommendations for teaching, many others have done so based on his theories. For example, Wells (1999) suggests that we

- engage *with* learners in challenging, personally significant activities
- observe what the students can do independently
- give them help and guidance in moving forward to solve problems, thereby forming a type of "cognitive apprenticeship"—see also Rogoff (1990)

Through a cognitive apprenticeship ". . . knowledge is co-constructed, as students and teacher together make meaning on the basis of each others' experiences, supplemented by information from other sources beyond the classroom" (see Wells, 1999, p. 160). Interestingly, Wells sees the Zone of Proximal Development as operating not only within the student, but also within a group or within the class as a whole. He calls this the "communal zone of proximal development" for which he credits Hedegaard (1990).

Freire (1970b) enlarged upon similar ideas in *Pedagogy of the Oppressed* in which he distinguished between two kinds of education: banking and libertarian (transformational). Banking education involves the act of depositing. The student is an empty depository and the teacher is the depositor. The students "receive, memorize, and repeat." There is no real communication. The role of the student is passive—a sort of "disengaged brain." On the other hand, in libertarian education the teacher and students are partners. Meaning is inherent in the communication. Through it students are involved in acts of cognition and are not simply empty heads waiting to be filled with information. The process is dialectical. Sometimes the teacher is a student and the students are teachers in a dialogue through which all individuals can benefit (see Chapter 4).

This cooperative relationship is important to second language teaching. It leads to meaningful interaction about relevant content; through such interaction, the teacher is naturally attuned to the students' emerging skills and abilities. Without this cooperative relationship, meaningful communication cannot take place. If we consider "development" to include the students' actual levels with the target language and the students' potential levels, then Vygotsky's theory makes sense for students learning a second language at any age, whether cognitive structures are already highly developed or not. Meaningful interaction seems to be the key.

The Importance of Social Interaction

One early example of the importance of social interaction to language learning came from John-Steiner (1985), who referred to the study done with Finnish immigrant children entering Swedish schools. She reported that they experienced "severe difficulties in their academic and linguistic development" because they were at first placed in very structured classrooms where there was little chance for meaningful interaction. The teacher did most of the talking and the activities were written.

John-Steiner also cited Wong-Fillmore's (1976) study of five new arrivals to the United States from Mexico. These children were paired with Anglo peers, and their communication was taped over the period of a school year. The children stretched their knowledge of the target language remarkably. Sometimes these extensions were inadequate in getting across intentions, but the peers were able to fill in the gaps.

Additional evidence of the importance of social interaction in second language teaching is found in an early study by Seliger (1977). He first became interested in social interaction as a phenomenon when he observed his own two-year-old child. She would:

> ... often push her father's newspaper aside to get his attention and then direct a stream of gibberish at him mixed with a few hardly understood words. He, in turn, could discuss the weather, the stock market, her siblings, or American foreign policy with her. It didn't seem to matter what was said as long as some interaction was taking place. As long as the child was answered, she would continue the same for quite some time.

The question Seliger posed is why a child would participate in and prolong an activity without having much understanding of what was being said to her. He concluded that this phenomenon is actually rather typical behavior and that the strategy being used may be important to the acquisition process itself.

In his study, he argued that a similar strategy is used by adults who are successfully learning a second language. Although his study was not without critics (see Day, 1984),[3] it was an important one. It attempted to measure not only a public willingness to interact in the classroom, but also a willingness to

---

[3] One of Day's findings in his study of ESOL students in Honolulu was that there appeared to be no significant relationship between a measure of public exchanges (involving both responses to general solicits by the teacher and student self-initiated turns) and scores given on an oral interview and on a cloze test.

participate in private classroom interaction. His subjects had studied English as a foreign language and were currently enrolled in an upper-intermediate level class in the English Language Institute at Queens College, C.U.N.Y. Each student fell into one of two groups: the "high input generator" group at one end of an interaction continuum, or "the low input generator" group at the other end. The members of the high input generator group interacted intensively, not only with the teacher but with each other. In addition, they initiated much of the interaction. The low input generator group, on the other hand, either avoided interaction altogether or remained fairly passive in situations in which they could have interacted. They seemed more dependent upon formal instruction.

Even though (as Day reminded us) Seliger's subjects were few in number (only three in each category), the study nevertheless had interesting implications. Scores on pretests and posttests suggested that by receiving more focused input through interaction, the high input generators were able to "test more hypotheses about the shape and use of L2 thus accounting for increased success." Low input generators, on the other hand, were particularly dependent upon the classroom environment to force interaction because they did not tend to initiate or allow themselves to become involved in it on their own.[4]

More early evidence came from the Heidelberg Project (cited in Schumann, 1978b) to support the notion that social interaction is important to second language acquisition. In this study of Italian and Spanish guest workers acquiring German in Germany, the correlations were extremely high between German proficiency and leisure social contact (.64), and between German proficiency and social contact at work (.53).

Carroll (1967) had come to a similar conclusion based on his study of university students majoring in French, German, Italian, Russian, and Spanish. Even a brief time spent abroad, where they had social interaction, had a substantial effect on proficiency.[5]

Bruner, who believes strongly in the social nature of language acquisition, chastised those who were committed philosophically to the idea that language

---

[4] At the end of the semester, Seliger gave a discrete point test of English structure (Lado-Fries) and an integrative test of aural comprehension (The Queens College English Language Institute Test of Aural Comprehension) in addition to a cloze test. It was found that the scores on the pretests were not good predictors of scores on the posttests. However, measures of social interaction were. The amount of interaction accounted for 85 percent of the variance in the posttest scores on the discrete point test and for 69 percent of the variance in the posttest scores on the Aural Comprehension test.

[5] MLA Foreign Language Proficiency Tests for Teachers and Advanced Students were administered in 1965 to 2,782 seniors majoring in foreign languages at 203 institutions. The correlations between time spent abroad and test scores were .47a, .60a, .24b, and .27b for French, German, Russian, and Spanish respectively. (Italian was probably not included because there was not a sufficient number of cases.)

Note: a. significance at the .01 level or better.
       b. significance at the .05 level or better.

learning is reducible to a linking of simple forms, which thereby become complex forms. Of course, here he was referring to methods advocated by the behaviorists and later by the cognitive-code theorists. Bruner emphasized the fact that these people "failed to take into account the inherently social nature of what is learned when one learns language and, by the same token, to consider the essentially social way in which the acquisition of knowledge of language must occur" (1978b, p. 244).

More recently, many others have supported the case for social interaction. Long (1996, and earlier), for example, discusses his still evolving *Interactional Hypothesis*. He is convinced that social interaction is indeed an important facilitator of language acquisition. Among other advantages, he points out that modifications in the input encourage the noticing of some structures. Gass (1997) agrees. Both conclude that because negotiation involves learners in comprehensible language, it pushes students beyond current levels. However, Gass reminds us that the actual results of the negotiation may not be realized until much later in the interlanguage process. Earlier, Pica (1994) had found that premodified input tailored to the level of learners made negotiation less necessary in some situations. However, she (and others) have concluded that negotiation provides the learner with more chances to notice the features of the second language due to the frequent repetitions, modifications, and feedback (Mackey, Gass, and McDonough, 2000; Mackey, 1999; Mackey and Philip, 1998; Polio and Gass, 1998; Long, Inagaki, and Ortega, 1998; Gass and Varonis, 1994. Also see de la Fuente, 2002, and Ellis, Tanaka, and Yamazaki, 1994, who looked at the effects of negotiation on vocabulary comprehension, receptive and productive acquisition and retention.) For extensive reviews of the literature on the effects on language learning of peer-peer dialogue and teacher-student interaction, in particular, see Swain, Brooks, and Tocalli-Beller, (2002) and Hall and Walsh, (2002) respectively.

THE NATURE OF THE LANGUAGE OF SOCIAL INTERACTION

Krashen, one of the early key players in the ongoing discussion about the components of interaction, concentrated on input and the role it plays in the acquisition process in his formulation of the $i + 1$. Like the Zone of Proximal Development, this concept refers to the distance between actual language development (represented by i) and potential language development (represented by $i + 1$).

This distance is perhaps realized most fully in *motherese,* that special language used by caretakers who wish to communicate with their children. Motherese involves the simplification of speech in an intense desire on the part of the caretaker to be understood by the child. According to Corder (1978), this simplification is done chiefly in terms of choosing the kinds of topics and range of speech functions, the utterance length, and the rate of speech, as well as the amount of repetition, rephrasing, and redundancy in the message. In addition, it is specifically related to situational context.

Error Treatment

Interestingly, direct corrections of ungrammatical forms in the output are seldom found in motherese. Krashen (1982) supported Roger Brown's conclusion that the caretaker seems to be more interested in the truth value of the utterance. As an example of this, he pointed to Brown, Cazden, and Bellugi (1973), who reported that "Her curl my hair" was not corrected in their study because the statement was true, whereas "Walt Disney comes on Tuesday" was corrected because in reality Walt Disney comes (on television) on Wednesday. Thus content, not form, was the emphasis.

It is interesting also that parents are usually thrilled by any effort at all that the child makes in forming utterances. For example, when the child says "Daddy home" for the first time, no one labels this a mistake or calls it substandard or even considers it an error at all. Instead it is thought to be ingenious and cute, and the child is hugged or rewarded verbally. The utterance is considered evidence that the child is indeed acquiring the language.

What if in the classroom the language teacher treated "errors" as being evidence that the language was being acquired and that generalizations (often overgeneralizations) were being formed by the student? How would that facilitate the acquisition of the language? It is probable that in such an environment, the learner would be more willing to take the risk of being wrong and would be freer and more uninhibited in developing an interlanguage. The forms would thus become acquired, as they are in L1, mainly through extensive use of modified language in meaningful situations (Wagner-Gough and Hatch, 1975; Chaudron, 1985; Ellis, 1985, 1997; Winitz, 1996).

What happens in the classroom in which the teacher is concerned both with the accuracy and fluency of the output, as most of us are? Sutherland felt that both goals "cannot realistically be achieved in the early phases of learning. Fortunately, and perhaps more importantly, they do not need to be achieved simultaneously in order to ultimately produce effective speakers" (1979, p. 25). He further argued that learners in classrooms in which accuracy is the most important factor tend to develop very little proficiency in the target language. In such classrooms, the teachers often look upon themselves as "Guardians of the Linguistic Norm" and feel that their main reason for being there is to ensure correctness. They often think that if students are allowed to make mistakes at beginning levels, they are doomed to a lifetime of linguistic errors based on the bad habits they form. However, Sutherland pointed out that "since errors persist in learners anyway—no matter what method is employed—we certainly cannot look to methods to explain this phenomenon" (1979, p. 27).

Considerable research done in the area of error correction seems to support the idea that increased direct error correction does not lead to greater accuracy in the target language (Hendrickson, 1976; Dvorak, 1977; Semke, 1984; and many more). Moreover, such emphasis on error correction can be overly directive and intimidating, and in some cases it can even lead to increased language anxiety (see Young, 1991). However, several recent studies have indicated possible advantages in providing correction in context, sometimes coupled with some sort of explanation or focus on a rule (see especially White, Spada, Lightbown, and Ranta, 1991; Carroll and Swain, 1993; Lyster, 1998; and Lyster and Ranta, 1997).

Caution must be used, however, in interpreting studies of error correction practices. Although researchers may label various teachers' corrective behaviors, they often do not provide adequate documentation or even descriptions of these behaviors, including how many times these behaviors were used, the learners' follow-up questions or practice, the pattern of behaviors, and so forth (see also Chaudron, 1991). And, more important, much of the research seems to involve short-term, experimental studies using pretest and posttest data rather than longitudinal data. It is almost impossible to learn what effect a treatment has had on the interlanguage process unless it is looked at over a long period of time. In addition, critical factors about learners seem not to be taken into account in many studies. Factors such as motivation, attitude, anxiety levels, willingness to take risks, age, cultural expectations concerning the language learning situation, and many more should not be ignored.

As discussed in Chapter 2, most errors found in the interlanguage of learners are developmental—at least after the very beginning phases, during which transfer from L1 seems to be a viable strategy. Yorio (1980) suggested that we keep careful note of the errors our students make to determine whether the errors are systematic (appear with regularity) or random (caused by memory lapse, inattention, not having acquired the rule, or overgeneralization). The systematic errors should concern us:

- Are the errors increasing? (The student is regressing.)
- Are the errors decreasing? (The student is learning.)
- Are they stationary? (The student's language is fossilizing.)

Of course, if the student appears to be regressing, something must be done before the forms have had a chance to fossilize. However, Yorio warned that teachers should not inundate students' papers with red ink, but rather should discuss errors in a meaningful way. He offered a few suggestions:

- Hold sessions at once with several students who seem to be making the same kinds of errors.
- Give students a chance to find their own errors and correct them.
- Focus on meaning, especially in oral errors, as opposed to form. (Modeling, or repeating what the learner has said but in correct form, is one way to correct indirectly.)

Yurio noted that adults often want to know the nature of the errors they are making. Students who ask for explanations are probably motivated to learn that particular rule and ready to incorporate it into their linguistic systems. However, if the student's goal is to understand and be understood in social and/or academic situations, then methods must focus on real communication in those kinds of situations.

Characteristics of Effective Input

One important question to ask is what kind of input is most conducive to forming generalizations about the language, thereby making acquisition possible? Krashen suggested that in addition to being relevant and/or interesting (see Chapter 2), the input must approximate the student's $i + 1$. It must be comprehensible in that it is near the student's actual level of development (i), but then it must stretch beyond that to include concepts and structures that the student has not yet acquired ($i + 1$). Free conversation with competent speakers does not generally produce input that can be comprehended unless the competent speakers are talking directly to the student and are aware of the student's approximate $i + 1$. Neither does TV nor radio ordinarily produce such input. The student ideally must be in a situation in which all the interlocutors desire to understand and be understood. It is often through gestures, the context itself, and linguistic modifications that the new concepts become internalized. In other words, the student needs to receive *foreigner talk.*

The term "foreigner talk" was coined by Ferguson (1975), who defined it as a simplified register or style of speech used when addressing people who are nonnative speakers.[6] Foreigner talk in the classroom is generally well formed and includes, but often to a greater degree, many of the same strategies used in regular teacher talk: exaggeration of pronunciation and facial expression; decreasing speech rate and increasing volume; frequent use of pause, gestures, graphic illustrations, questions, and dramatization; sentence expansion, rephrasing, and simplification; prompting; and completing utterances made by the student (Henzl, 1973; Gaies, 1977; Kleifgen, 1985; Wesche and Ready, 1985; Richard-Amato, 1984).

A word of caution is in order here, however. Sometimes teachers, in their efforts to make their input comprehensible, simplify it to the extent that it loses the richness and variety that it might otherwise have (see also van Lier, 1996). Teachers also may slow down and overly enunciate the simplified input to the point that students perceive it as condescending. This kind of input should always be avoided.

Teachers involved in meaningful dialogue with their students will generally automatically adjust their input in an attempt to ensure understanding, but

---

[6] An important question here is how does foreigner talk differ from regular teacher talk in the classroom? Studies have been done in an attempt to at least partially answer this question (see Kleifgen, 1985; Wesche and Ready, 1985; Richard-Amato, 1984).

they will keep the intonation natural so as not to be perceived as talking down. See the example below:

Two teachers are talking to a group of foreign students in the Intensive English Center at the University of New Mexico.

		Strategy Used
TEACHER 1:	Who's the man with the hood on his face?	question
	(points to the word "executioner" on the board)	gesture
		graphic aid
TEACHER 2:	Yeh. You've seen the pictures . . . they have	decreased rate
	black hoods (She pantomimes as she crouches	increased volume
	and ominously pulls a pretend hood over her	
	head.) . . . with the eyes. (She uses her fingers	pausing
	to encircle her eyes to appear as though she is	expansion
	looking through a mask. Teacher 1 does the	dramatization
	same, and they both scan the group as if to	simplification
	frighten them.) . . . You know . . . really creepy	expansion
	looking . . . scary . . . oh . . . what is it called?	question

(Richard-Amato and Lucero, 1980, p. 6)

Accommodation through modified input is often motivated by the students themselves. In the Western world in particular, beginners in the target language are often asked to perform beyond their levels of proficiency by the teacher. Then the teacher helps ensure success by offering the necessary accommodation during the performance (Poole, 1992; Ochs and Schiefflin, R., 1984; see especially Foster, 1998, for a detailed discussion of negotiation of meaning based on research).

The following constructed dialogue illustrates the negotiation of meaning in a typical one-to-one communication. In this kind of collaboration, the "stretching" to higher levels of development becomes more obvious.

STUDENT: I throw it—box. (He points to a box on the floor.)
TEACHER: You threw the box.
STUDENT: No, I threw *in* the box.
TEACHER: What did you throw in the box?
STUDENT: My . . . I paint . . .
TEACHER: Your painting?
STUDENT: Painting?
TEACHER: You know . . . painting. (The teacher makes painting movements on an imaginary paper.)
STUDENT: Yes, painting.
TEACHER: You threw your painting in the box.
STUDENT: Yes, I threw my painting in box.

The teacher's input is near the student's $i + 1$. It provides scaffolds upon which the student can build. The conversation is about the immediate environment, the vocabulary is simple, repetitions are frequent, and acting out is used. The focus is on meaning as opposed to form. The student is acquiring correct forms not by the process of direct correction, but through the content and the process of indirect correction or modeling. Notice that *throw* in the student's speech becomes *threw*, *in* is incorporated into the prepositional phrase, and the article *the* is picked up before *box* but then lost again. It will probably take a lot more comprehensible input containing these forms before they become firmly established in the student's mind.

Thus grammar is being acquired through the natural process of communication, without any conscious use of grammatical sequencing. Similar conclusions are borne out by many others (Long, Adams, McLean, and Castanos, 1976; d'Angeljan, 1978; Krashen, 1982; Hatch, 1983; B. Taylor, 1983; Hammond, 1988; Ioup, Boustagui, El Tigi, and Moselle, 1994).

Input in Written Texts

One modification that is especially useful to reading comprehension is *elaboration* (similar to "expansion" above). Oh (2001) investigated the effects of elaboration or expansion, as opposed to simplification, and found elaboration to be equal to or better than simplification in improving the comprehension of written texts at both high and low proficiency levels. Both elaboration and simplification improved performance on basic comprehension. However, elaboration, in particular, significantly improved the students' performance on inference items. It gave students more opportunities to understand the information provided by the text by using redundancy and clear signals concerning its structure.

INSTRUCTED GRAMMAR: WHEN CAN IT HELP?

Many applied linguists over the years have insisted that in order to acquire acceptable forms of the target language, learners must focus first on instructed grammar rules and only second on communication (see especially Higgs and Clifford, 1982).

In their frequently cited article, Higgs and Clifford claimed that students in communicative foreign language courses in which grammar is expected to be acquired inductively, through interactive processes, become victims of early fossilization from which they are unlikely to recover. However, this report lacked evidence to sufficiently support its conclusion, and in addition, the courses upon which the study was based were not described but rather only mentioned. Even more troublesome is that *fossilization* was not clearly defined.

We do know that students need to be moving through an interlanguage process, requiring interaction, before they can reach a plateau at which language may fossilize (see also page 38). Determining whether fossilization has indeed occurred requires longitudinal studies that cover several months or perhaps even years. Errors by themselves do not tell us much; it is the pattern of errors over time that is revealing.

Unfortunately, similar problems often can be found in other second language acquisition research: lack of adequate definition of one or more key concepts; basing the study on the acquisition of an artificial language rather than a natural language;[7] using cross-sectional research which measures what students can do at a specified point in time, instead of longitudinal research which reveals long-term effects and development; and a paucity of description and documentation of the instruction, communicative events, and/or the discourse upon which the studies are based. Moreover, many of the studies which compare an instructed-grammar environment with a naturalistic environment equate the first with classroom learning and the second with street learning. Of course, the classroom will usually come out best, since it is often very difficult to receive comprehensible input in the street, and the linguistic models there may not be competent speakers of the language. The common failure of street learning is often used, unfairly, to disparage naturalistic classrooms.

Rather, instructed classrooms need to be compared with natural classrooms to make a true comparison. But even this would be a bit simplistic in that no one classroom would be or could be completely one or the other. Moreover, individual learners draw from a variety of sources of which neither the teacher nor the researcher may be aware. For example, a communicative event might be consciously analyzed by the learner for its grammatical qualities; an instructed grammar event might be of value only in that it presents comprehensible input. It may be of greater benefit to refine our studies by looking at various types of grammar instruction, the timing of the instruction, learner strategies, and so forth, in relation to their effects on the interlanguage process. Studies of this type, although highly complex, would be far more valuable to informed decisions about using instructed grammar in the second and foreign language classroom.

Currently, instructed grammar is not generally considered to be the most important contributor to interlanguage development, nor is the overall order of the development affected to any great extent by instructed grammar (Van Patten, 1986; Lightbown, 1983; Pienemann, 1984; Ellis, 1997). However, there is evidence that a judicious use of instructed grammar may be helpful in at least

---

[7] When learning an artificial language which has been created for the study, subjects do not have the same motivation to learn it as they would have if the target language were a natural one. The outcome therefore is suspect.

two ways: First, students, by knowing certain rules, may be more likely to "notice the gap" between their own output and the input they receive (Schmidt, 1990, 1993); and second, students may benefit, at least for the short term, from the instruction of simple rules such as plural *s* and third-person singular *s* (Green and Hecht, 1992; Pica, 1983; Pienemann, 1984).

Rutherford and Sharwood-Smith (1988) theorized that instructed grammar can result in *consciousness raising* which they defined as ". . . a deliberate attempt to draw the learner's attention specifically to the formal properties of the target language" (p. 107; see also Rosa and O'Neill, 1999; Ellis, 1994; and Schmidt, 1994). By noticing not only the gap between what they say and what they hear, but also *how* things are said, learners can (when time allows) consciously plan their utterances. Fotis and Ellis (1991) hypothesize that these utterances can then serve as input upon which learners can internalize grammar rules. In addition, Fotis and Ellis argue that knowing about a structure may make it more salient to begin with and therefore easier to internalize. However, they suggest that the main goal of instructed grammar be to increase *explicit* knowledge rather than to increase *implicit* knowledge, where its role is not clearly understood.

Some researchers are convinced that instructed grammar increases the rate of acquisition for some structures (Doughty, 1991; Pienemann, 1984; Weslander and Stephany, 1983; Gass, 1982) and the level of attainment (Bardovi-Harlig, 1995; Ellis, 1990). Long (1988), too, concluded that there may be long-term benefits for acquisition and pointed to Pavesi (1984) who also found that instructed learners seemed to reach higher levels of attainment in their second language than did the uninstructed learners. However, this finding was weakened by Pavesi's own conclusion that the results may have been due to the fact that the instructed learners had received more elaborated and richer input than did the uninstructed learners in the study.

Concerning foreign language teaching in particular, Winitz (1996) looked at college students who had completed one semester of college Spanish. Two groups of students each received one of two treatments: *explicit* instruction in which students were exposed to a grammar-translation approach and *implicit* instruction, in which students were focused on the comprehension of sentences in Spanish through the total physical response (see Chapter 8) and pictures. Both groups had to identify Spanish sentences that were well-formed grammatically. He found that students who had had implicit instruction received significantly higher scores than those who had had explicit instruction.

Exposing students to less interaction and to more instructed grammar may have been counterproductive, considering that the time spent in the foreign language classes was very limited. However, if instruction in grammar is well-timed and based on individual needs (see Pienemann's hypothesis below), it may benefit the acquisition process.

Perhaps some of the most exciting research in the area of instructed grammar that holds great possibilities for future study comes from Pienemann, who developed the Learnability/Teachability Hypothesis. This hypothesis states that instructed grammar may help the learner progress but *only* if the learner is developmentally ready to incorporate the structure(s) taught. He does not believe that we "squirrel away" rules only to pull them out and apply them later.

Evidence Supporting the Learnability/Teachability Hypothesis

Pienemann (1984) found evidence supporting the Learnability/Teachability Hypothesis in his study of five Italian children learning German as a second language. The children were instructed in the use of inversion. The two learners who were ready to incorporate inversion into their interlanguage did, in fact, learn it; the three who had not yet reached that point did not. Then, in 1988 he replicated the study with twelve university students of German as a second language and found similar results: Those who were ready learned the structure. In addition, data gathered from the spontaneous language samples of three informants over the period of one year indicated that their interlanguage development did not coincide with the structures they were being taught in the German course they were taking (Pienemann, 1983). The conclusion was that because they were not developmentally ready for structures when they were taught, the students did not incorporate them into their repertoire of language. Ellis (1993) goes even further to say that practice with a rule that a student is not ready for can actually confuse rather than facilitate the acquisition of that rule. On the other hand, Lightbown (1998) suggests that working on some structures before the time is right may actually promote noticing and may push students toward readiness for incorporating those structures.

Generally speaking, however, if direct instruction in grammar is to achieve most of its benefits for a given structure, deciding *when* the time is right appears critical. A knowledge of the process involved in acquiring particular structures is certain to be of value to teachers making decisions about what the student may or may not be ready for. Although we already know something about the process involved with negation, question formation, relative clause formation, and past tense, we have much to learn about what happens during interlanguage development and the structures about which we can verbalize rules.

Perhaps someday we will have computer programs into which we can feed data for analysis. If properly designed, these programs may be able to help us determine which structures our students are struggling with (or perhaps avoiding) and which they may be ready for. Such programs may even be able to suggest possible courses of action in each case. Even if we can eventually use computer programs to assist us in determining when the time is right, in the final analysis, it is the student and teacher together who make this decision.

Such analysis will never be an exact science. There are too many factors involved, many of which have to do with affect: motivation, attitude, level of anxiety, and so on (see Chapter 6).

One strategy that holds promise in identifying structures for which students may be ready is teacher-generated error analysis (see pages 36–37). This focuses on information such as what structures students are trying to use in their written and oral output, and whether or not the mistakes are variable. Sometimes work with specific structures will be valuable to learners who might use them following appropriate instruction or after considerable exposure to input containing them. Of course, different students will be deemed ready for different structures. Once these structures are determined and considered teachable, small groups of students can be formed to work explicitly with a particular rule or they can be worked on by individuals.

An Individual Grammar Syllabus

What all of this means—and what will impact our teaching most dramatically in the future—is that teachers can no longer rely on a single grammatical syllabus for everyone. There may have to be as many flexible grammatical syllabi as there are students. I am proposing an *individual grammatical syllabus* for each student, which changes as the student changes. Indeed, some students may not need grammatical instruction at all; others may need and will be able to benefit from considerable work with rule application as new forms begin to emerge. In fact, adults (particularly those who are well-educated and literate) are often used to learning rules which have been explicitly taught and then working with them deductively (see Celce-Murcia, 1993). However, students should begin by spending enough of their time in interactive activities within a rich environment in order to develop an interlanguage to begin with. Without that, no matter how well the rules are taught, they will not be relevant to the language acquisition process.

We need to remember that much of language cannot be reduced to teachable rules. For example, consider the uses of what appear to be very simple concepts in English: *in* and *on*. We say *in* the car. When we say *on* the car, we mean *on top of* the car. But yet we say *on* the boat, which means *in* the boat. To get even more complex, we say *on* the ceiling. Using logic, one would think we mean *on top of* the ceiling. However, what we mean is *under* the ceiling and *attached to* it. Although there are rules governing these differences, they are for the most part subconscious. When we try to verbalize them, we generally get into trouble. The rules governing a great deal of language seem to only be internalized through a complex interactional process.

Clearly, a lot more research needs to be done before teachers can make informed decisions in the area of instructed grammar and its role in the language classroom. But perhaps we are at least beginning to ask the right questions concerning to whom, what, when, and how grammar should be taught.

Some are even experimenting with focused communication tasks that make the use of certain forms (e.g., past tense) more likely (see especially Nobuyoshi and Ellis, 1996; and Larsen-Freeman, 2002b).

Larsen-Freeman's recent work in this area is of particular interest. She proposes marrying form to both meaning and pragmatics and offers an array of communicative activities which can incorporate grammar practice. She points out that this approach differs from traditional grammar instruction in that it is the communication that generates work with given grammatical structures rather than a predetermined syllabus. The focus can be informal and part of the communication itself (see example on page 59 in this chapter) or it can involve planned activities such as highlighting the structure in a given passage, figuring out a given rule from specific data, giving students only part of a rule and letting them learn the exceptions when they make overgeneralization errors and are corrected, and so forth. She reminds us that structures inherent in total physical response-type activities (the imperative), in games such as twenty questions (*yes-no* questions), in problem-solving activities (*wh-* questions), in information-gap activities (using concepts and forms for giving directions), in role-playing (choosing pragmatically appropriate structures), and the like become salient during the interaction itself. She suggests that when the time is right, rules can be explicitly taught within a communicative framework such as in a content-based or task-based program (see Chapter 15 of this volume).

Possibly the most critical question of all is what long-term effects does grammar instruction have on the language acquisition process? Only through longitudinal research will educators ever even come close to gaining insights into this question.

OUTPUT AND THE ACQUISITION PROCESS

Just as the role of instructed grammar is controversial, so, to a lesser degree, is the role of output. Krashen (1985) minimized the role of output. He claimed that language can be acquired simply by comprehending input. He argued particularly against those who believed that output is used for hypothesis testing, a process by which the learner tries out new structures in discourse and acquires a specific rule, provided enough positive responses are received. He was convinced that second language learners test hypotheses, not through the use of output, but by subconsciously matching forms in the input to their own notions about the language. Of course, he did admit that full two-way communication, because it necessitates more negotiation of meaning, results in more comprehensible input.

Swain (1985, 1993, 1995) preferred to take a stronger stand for the importance of the role of output in her development of the Output Hypothesis. She argued that among other functions, output *is* a significant way to test out hypotheses about the target language (also see Corder, 1967; and Seliger, 1977, discussed earlier in this chapter). She concluded, on the basis of her study of English-speaking children in a French immersion program:

> Comprehensible output . . . is a necessary mechanism of acquisition independent of the role of comprehensible input. Its role is, at minimum, to provide opportunities for contextualized, meaningful use, to test out hypotheses about the target language, and to move the learner from a purely semantic analysis of language to a syntactic analysis of it (1985, p. 252).

Swain found that although immersion students comprehended what their teachers said and focused on meaning, they were still not fully acquiring the syntactic system of French. She agreed with those who have suggested that it is not only input that is important, but the input that is part of negotiated interaction. Simply knowing that one will eventually be expected to produce may serve as an impetus to notice the way things are said.

Obviously, there is less chance to give output in subject-matter classes in which the teachers do most of the talking and the students do the listening. Swain felt that the grammatical development of immersion students suffers because of their relatively limited opportunity to interact. Output has a much greater role than simply to provide more comprehensible input. She was convinced that when the second language student receives negative input in the form of confirmation checks and other repairs, he or she is given reason to seek alternative ways to get the meaning across. Just by noticing a gap between what they say and what others say helps language learners become aware of what some of their own structural and semantic problems are.

Once the meaning has been negotiated, according to Swain, students during similar future exchanges can go from semantic processing to syntactic processing. In other words, once meaning is understood, the learner is free to focus on form within the interactional situation. If Swain is right, then output is indeed more than just a means for receiving more comprehensible input. It is important to the acquisition process itself (see also Izumi and Bigelow, 2000, who came to the same conclusion based on their study of English Language Learners (ELLs).

SUMMARY

Vygotsky's Zone of Proximal Development offers insights into the essentially social nature of the language acquisition process, be it first or second. Contrary to Piaget, who proposed one level of cognitive development, Vygotsky described two levels: an actual level and a potential level. Although both were constructivists, Piaget emphasized the role of physical maturation in learning and Vygotsky stressed social interaction.

The pivotal role of social interaction in second language acquisition was supported early on by John-Steiner's conclusions based on a study involving

Finnish immigrant children in Sweden and on a study done by Lilly Wong-Fillmore of Mexican immigrant children in the United States; Seliger's research on the role of interaction in an intermediate English class at Queens College, C.U.N.Y.; Schumann's conclusions based on the Heidelberg Project; Carroll's study of foreign language students at several universities; and many recent studies.

The nature of the input is described not only by Krashen but by Brown, Cazden, and Bellugi, in addition to the many others who have looked at motherese and found that it emphasizes meaning rather than form. Applying this knowledge to second language acquisition in the classroom, Sutherland and Yorio addressed the accuracy-versus-fluency controversy and its relative significance in instruction. Sutherland argued that the two should not be dealt with simultaneously at beginning levels, at which fluency should be the chief concern. Yorio addressed accuracy and offered some suggestions for dealing with systematic (not random) errors in the student's output.

Although the role of input in the interaction is important, that of output must not be ignored. Output plays a substantial part in the acquisition process. It not only aids in receiving comprehensible input, it offers opportunities for practice and appears to be an important means for testing hypotheses and noticing the gaps.

If Pienemann's learnability/teachability hypothesis is correct, instructed grammar can aid in the process of language acquisition, but mainly if the learner is developmentally ready to incorporate what is taught. Individual, flexible grammatical syllabi and a focus on structure during appropriate communicative activities are among the many ideas advanced for effective grammar instruction.

READINGS, REFLECTION, AND DISCUSSION

Suggested Readings and Reference Materials

Larsen-Freeman, D. (1995). On the teaching and learning of grammar: Challenging the myths. In F. Eckman et al., eds., *Second language acquisition theory and pedagogy*. Mahwah, NJ: Lawrence Erlbaum. Larsen-Freeman exposes several myths about teaching grammar and offers practical ideas on how to make the teaching of it interesting and informative. She addresses such topics as the logic of certain aspects of grammar, learning styles and their connection to the teaching of grammar, grammar at the supersentential and discourse levels, and grammar as a dynamic (not static) system.

van Lier, L. (1996). *Interaction in the language curriculum: awareness, autonomy, and authenticity*. London: Longman. Here van Lier offers a comprehensive view of classroom interaction and what it is all about. He discusses the three principles upon which his ideas are based: Awareness, Autonomy, and Authenticity. Drawing from Vygotsky, Bruner, Piaget, and many others, he weaves a convincing theory for all areas of language teaching including first, second, and foreign languages.

Vygotsky, L. (1978). *Mind in society*. Cambridge, Mass.: Harvard University. Editors M. Cole, V. John-Steiner, S. Scribner, and E. Souberman spent several years compiling this volume of manuscripts and letters that might have been lost to us had it not been for their efforts. The collection highlights and clarifies Vygotsky's theories of the mind and its higher psychological functions.

Wells, G. (1999). *Dialogic inquiry: Toward a sociocultural practice and theory of education.* Cambridge: Cambridge University Press. Wells's interpretations of Vygotsky and Halliday are described at length in this illuminating book. Examples and applications abound, making it a valuable resource for teachers across the content areas.

Williams, M. and Burden, R. (1997). *Psychology for language teachers.* Cambridge: Cambridge University Press. The authors focus on a constructivist view of teaching and learning combined with a social interactionist perspective—a very welcome synthesis indeed. The book is well-written, and its ideas are very accessible to the reader.

Questions and Projects for Reflection and Discussion

1. Considering Vygotsky's ideas with regard to learning and development, what might his reaction be to each of the following:
   a. Homogeneous ability grouping for most activities
   b. A focus on audiolingual drill
   c. An individualized program approach in which an individual works alone at his or her own rate
   d. An interactive classroom in which heterogeneous grouping is the norm

2. Wells (1999) believes that teachers assisting students approximately within their Zone of Proximal Development do not necessarily need to be humans. They can also be books and other supplementary materials. They can even be works of art. To what extent can a work of art or other nonhuman entity serve as a guide or assistant to help students stretch to higher levels?

3. According to Freire, the relationship between teacher and student should be dialectical. What kind of classroom environment might foster this relationship? What sorts of activities might take place in such a classroom? Can you envision yourself teaching in such a classroom? Write about the possibilities in your journal.

4. After several visits to beginning and/or early intermediate second or foreign language classrooms, answer the following questions:
   a. In which classrooms were the lessons mainly focused on grammar?
   b. In which classrooms was meaningful interaction usually the focus?
   c. Did you notice any differences in student attitude between those involved in one type of lesson and those in another?
   d. Note the age of the students in each situation. Do you think this made any differences in student attitude?

5. In your opinion, is there a place for the explicit teaching of grammar rules in the second language classroom? If so, address the following questions, and relate your discussion to the particular language you teach. Which rules would you teach? To whom? When? Under what conditions? How? Would it make any difference if the language were being taught in a second language situation as opposed to a foreign language situation? Develop your own principles for the teaching of grammar based on your experience and on what you have learned. Share them with a small group. Ask for feedback.

6. In your opinion, how should student errors be handled in the classroom? Have your views changed in any way now that you have read this chapter? Consider the following:
   a. Level of student proficiency
   b. The age of the student
   c. Systematic versus random errors
   d. Correction of oral versus written output

Work out an error correction policy of your own, based both on your own experience and on what you have learned. Share it with a small group to get their feedback.

7. Do you see any parallel between Pienemann's Learnability/Teachability Hypothesis and Vygotsky's Zone of Proximal Development? How might it relate to Piaget's thinking? Explain.

CHAPTER 4

Participatory Language Teaching

*The dance of teachers and students as they
negotiate their respective goals, expectations,
and understandings is central . . .*

Auerbach, 2000

QUESTIONS TO THINK ABOUT

1. Think about classrooms in which you were a student. How much input did you have into making decisions about the content studied or the activities in which you participated? Did teachers consider you a person with important knowledge to share? How did their treatment of you make you feel?

2. What do you think "participatory teaching" means? What might the results of such teaching be? How might it differ from other kinds of teaching?

3. From your experience and/or observation, what strategies do good language learners appear to use to become autonomous language learners?

Although participatory language teaching involves the important aspects of communicative teaching and negotiation for meaning, it also reaches into the very core of the individual by concerning itself with that individual's place in society and with society in general. Participatory teaching finds its roots in critical pedagogy based on Paulo Freire's belief that teachers and students can establish dialectical relationships with one another from which both can benefit. The shared power that results enables students to reach academic goals and enables both students and teachers to explore together issues that affect their lives.

Shedding light on this dialogic view of learning, Diane Larsen-Freeman (1996), in her closing remarks to the World Congress of Applied Linguistics in Jyväskylä, Finland, in 1996, succinctly summarized what had been said at that conference:

> The learner is not acted upon by some (hopefully) benevolent proficient user of the target language; instead the learner's individual competence is connected to, and partially constructed by, both those with whom the learner is interacting and the larger sociohistorical forces. Following from this reasoning, teaching is not transmission, but rather is providing the scaffolding through which input is not comprehensible, but participatable. Teaching is invited, not imposed (p. 90).

Pennycook (1999) calls participatory teaching the *pedagogy of engagement*. He stresses inclusivity and discussion of relevant issues. However, he reminds us that he is not talking about the tired social issues on which many classrooms focus. The issues need to have a *transformative* dimension that goes beyond the apolitical critical thinking familiar to all of us. The issues need to be ones that make a difference in students' lives, i.e., they must be issues of *investment and desire*. Moreover, Pennycook argues that the pedagogy of engagement cannot be reduced to simply another method or approach to teaching. It involves a fundamental change in our attitude toward the teaching act itself. (See Related Reading 1.)

Participatory teaching, like other kinds of communicative teaching, considers language learning a social and cultural process, not something that happens to individuals in isolation. But it moves beyond to incorporate not only issues important to students' lives, but the way in which teachers and students relate to one another, the way in which teachers perform their roles, and the way in which the whole classroom environment contributes to transformational processes and meets students' needs. At its best, it can free students from society's negative labels, and it can empower them to assert more control over their own academic, social, political, and economic destinies.

EMPOWERMENT IN THE LANGUAGE CLASSROOM

Empowerment begins with the way teachers interact with students. Traditionally, interaction in the classroom has adhered to the Initiation/Response/Feedback (IRF) paradigm (see Bellack et al., 1966; Sinclair and Coulthard, 1975; and Mehan, 1979). The teacher asks a question (the Initiation); the student gives the answer (the Response); the teacher, more often than not, evaluates the answer (the Feedback). It may look something like this in a beginning second-language class:

TEACHER: What is this? Do you remember? [points to a picture of a penguin]
STUDENT(S): A pen-guin.
TEACHER: Yes. Very good.

As van Lier (1996) reminds us, this kind of exchange turns almost every interaction into an examination. The interaction may require little of the student (a memorized answer), or it may require a great deal of thought (the solution to a problem), or it may fall somewhere in between. Now, if it is the student who asks the question and the teacher who gives the response, we have turned this typical interactive pattern on its head. However, the example above may have its place in the classroom for certain learning situations, and it can be effective, depending upon *when, how,* and *with whom* it is used. But, this kind of interaction is definitely not what critical pedagogists had in mind, particularly if the teacher almost always is the one who initiates, the students almost always are the ones responding, and the feedback is almost always a teacher evaluation. To them, such interaction would, in most cases, be far too controlling and manipulative. Their ideal exchange would more closely resemble natural dialogue outside the classroom, except that it would be *instructional.* Below is a constructed dialogue illustrating such an exchange. It represents an attempt to meet academic goals in science:

(Students and the teacher are performing a physics experiment on pendulums.)

STUDENT 1: I wonder what would happen if we added weight to the
            pendulum bob?
STUDENT 2: It would swing slower because it's heavier.
TEACHER: Let's try it. Put on another weight and we'll time the swing.
STUDENT 1: Okay. I'm adding another half kilogram. You time the swing
            (refers to Student 2).
STUDENT 2: That's funny, the time didn't change.
TEACHER: So what did we learn?
STUDENT 1: Making it heavier didn't change it. Let's try making it lighter.
TEACHER: Yes, let's try that.

Notice that the IRF paradigm is still used, but the participants have changed roles. In the first line, it is Student 1 who initiates and Student 2 who responds. Lines 3 and 4 do not seem to follow the paradigm. Now, let's look at the last three lines. The teacher provides the initiation and feedback, as is typical. However, the feedback is not an evaluation as we know it; instead it is an agreement to complete an action just suggested by Student 1. It is an affirmation, which in a sense may be considered evaluative, but it is accomplished in a different way. The dialogue adheres to Wells's (1999) ideas about the co-construction of knowledge which, he says ". . . creates a social-intellectual climate that is both supportive and challenging" (p. 220). Learning opportunities like the one presented in this dialogue are usually anticipated and planned by the teacher. They do not just happen by chance.

The above dialogue reflects a broader definition of participatory teaching than is assumed in many discussions of the concept. In this context, participatory teaching concerns itself not only with *sociopolitical* issues and goals, but with *academic* and *personal* issues and goals as well.

Transformative Versus Transmissive Discourse

While teachers in participatory classrooms are vitally interested in what students understand and what they are learning, they work to *transform the discourse* in all aspects of instruction. They encourage students to:

- initiate topics and questions that are relevant to their own learning
- move to other topics of interest or concern
- investigate independently or with peers and/or the teacher
- reflect on what they are learning

Dialogues in which students have a personal stake and about which teacher and student have a mutual interest probably come close to what critical pedagogists intended. The knowledge that develops grows out of what the teacher and students can bring to the table. Both parties are highly motivated and enriched by the experience. One question or piece of knowledge scaffolds upon the next (see also Donato, 1994). Another example of scaffolded dialogue leading to dialectical relationships can be found in the section below on teacher/student co-authored products. While working on co-authored products, teachers and students become integral parts of the composing process and together create a written piece by scaffolding upon one another's ideas. Both form and meaning are negotiated through the interaction.

The typical IRF structure with its traditional roles may be advantageous in some circumstances, particularly for beginning students; it allows for initial teacher-lead practice and response and other teacher-fronted activities so essential to beginners. However, once students become more proficient and are able to apply strategies, especially metacognitive strategies, they are going to require more complex interactions and role alternatives. At this point, they may also have the abilities to operate independently and to participate more fully in the classroom community.

However, students cannot fully participate in the classroom in any language (be it first or second) if they have *only* been exposed to transmission education with all of its implications. In order for the students to achieve autonomy, they need to be given the chance early on to grapple with issues important to their lives and the lives of others. Of course, in the case of bilingual education, full participation can be achieved right from the beginning in the primary language.

When Paulo Freire railed against transmission (the banking model of education mentioned in Chapter 3), he expressed conviction that such education was a political ploy to keep the downtrodden in their place. In his own teaching experience with Brazilian farm workers, he developed a dialogic approach to their learning how to read. He felt that they, too, had knowledge to share and that learning could be a mutually beneficial activity. He argued that *praxis* (the combination of reflection and action) was needed in order for transformation to occur. Neither reflection nor action by themselves lead to empowerment. According to Freire and other critical pedagogists, teachers can help to make such *praxis* a reality and, at the same time, give their students greater input into what goes on in classrooms as their students begin to take full advantage of what participatory teaching offers.

The Teacher's Role

Modifying the traditional teacher's role is essential to the implementation of participatory practices. Significant changes can be made in how the teacher operates, even though the teacher/student relationship will probably always be considered unequal by society, i.e., the teacher will be expected to have greater disciplinary and worldly knowledge. Students need increasingly greater responsibility for their own learning through planning, critical exploration, decision making, and reflective thinking. This doesn't mean that the teacher has to completely turn over the reins of power to students. On the contrary, the teacher can and should be very much involved and influential concerning what happens in the classroom. What it means is that the teacher shares power and encourages student input into many areas of classroom life over which the teacher has traditionally made all the decisions—planning lessons, choosing themes and issues, deciding how knowledge will be arrived at and imparted, and so forth.

WHAT IS PARTICIPATORY LANGUAGE TEACHING?

Participatory language teaching is not a method. Nor is it an approach. It transcends both in that *it embraces the very essence of the relationship between student and teacher*. Manifestations of it are already in place in many classrooms—and have been perhaps for centuries—whenever teachers and students share power as they come together in dialogue and mutual respect. Current manifestations can be found in cooperative learning (pages 315–318), the use of peer teachers (pages 310–314), applications of the language experience approach (pages 243–246), theme cycles (a type of investigative inquiry discussed below) and in many other practices found throughout this book.

Participatory language teaching usually evolves from simple (often teacher-fronted) interaction at beginning levels to full participation in complex classroom communities at intermediate to advanced levels. Beginning communicative lessons such as learning about going to the doctor (see Chapter 9) can be scaffolds for later lessons on everything from locating the best doctors in one's area to the social implications of the inability to afford basic health insurance. Elements of participatory language teaching can appear at even the earliest levels, whenever students engage in decision-making in their second language, or it can emerge full-blown right from the beginning in bilingual programs when the primary language is the medium for discussion and instruction.

Elsa Auerbach (2000) argues "Ideal participatory classrooms probably do not actually exist; they are always in the process of becoming" (p. 149). She reminds us (as did Johnston, see pages 4–5) that teachers do have power and will always have power, no matter how much they try to give it away. The important thing, according to her, is that learning be collaborative and that students be given the chance to become informed about issues that concern them and make reasonable choices based on a critical analysis of what's at stake for themselves and the world at large. Auerbach offers the following basic principles:

1. The starting point is the experience of the participants; their needs and concerns should be central to curriculum content.
2. Everyone teaches, everyone learns.
3. Classroom processes are dialogical and collaborative.
4. Individual experience is linked to social analysis.
5. The acquisition of skills and information is contextualized.
6. The content goes back to the social context.

(Auerbach, 2000, p. 148)

Components of the Participatory Learning Experience

Following Elsa Auerbach's lead, I have developed the "Components of the Participatory Learning Experience" (see below). Note that I have added two factors that have been largely overlooked in current discussions of critical pedagogy:

- the student's *cognitive abilities*
- the student's *proficiency in the language*

Both determine the kinds of issues each student is able to identify and deal with in a meaningful way. However, students have been known to operate far beyond expectations when fully engaged in their own learning.

1. **Identification** of participants' interests, needs, problems, and concerns within the social context of the classroom and the outside world.
2. **Negotiation** of the curriculum. The curriculum grows out of the participants' prior experience, hopes for the future, and present needs (academic, personal, and sociopolitical).
3. **Dialectical relationship formation** throughout the process between students and teachers. All participants are both learners and teachers.
4. **Skills development** occurring within the context of the tasks at hand.
5. **Exploration** of the issues important to participants, leading to in-depth reading and research, composition, discussion, analysis, and reflection. Moreover, such exploration often leads to related issues of interest forming the pivot around which the next investigations are built. These explorations must be generally appropriate to students' cognitive abilities and proficiency in the language that is to be the medium of discussion and instruction.
6. **Collaborative learning** which is critical to the process.
7. **Critical analysis** during which participants deconstruct what they read and hear, accept what makes sense to them, and reject the rest.

Like the second dialogue on page 72, the above components assume a broader context for participatory teaching than most other descriptions. Again, in this context, participatory teaching concerns itself not only with sociopolitical issues and goals, but with academic and personal issues and goals as well. Although sociopolitical needs often serve as pivots around which the other goals are accomplished, academic needs must be included to make education a meaningful and transformative experience for students.

Creating a Participatory Classroom

Questionnaires can ascertain what topics interest students most, how students might rank common goals based on their aspirations, where they most need improvement, and the kinds of lessons they find most helpful and enjoyable. Students can give feedback regularly by answering questions such as these:

- What instructional activity did you participate in this week that helped you most? Why?
- Was there an activity you didn't like or didn't find helpful? Explain.
- What did the teacher do that helped you the most? The least?
- How might you change the class so it can better meet your needs?

In addition, students can rank specific activities from "most effective" to "least effective" and give brief comments explaining their decisions. Several specific participatory practices described below can further goals of critical pedagogy and serve as catalysts to help transform the student/teacher relationship.

PARTICIPATORY PRACTICES

Strategies that involve students in direct dialogue with the teacher and with each other, and that draw all into decision-making processes, can elevate students to high levels of participation. Perhaps the best known of such participatory practices is *problem-posing* as developed by Freire and elaborated upon by Nina Wallerstein and several others. Other practices described here are *dialectical writing* and *theme cycles/investigative inquiry*.

Problem-Posing

Wallerstein (1983) presented problem-posing to develop critical thinking skills in students through group dynamics. The teacher listens to students to discover issues important to them. Then the teacher finds codifications (e.g., stories, photographs, pictures, etc.) of the issues to tap into what is meaningful. For example, the students in an advanced ESL class have recently been discussing the difficulties a person faces when first arriving in another country. As a codification, the teacher has selected a picture of a lone, obviously frustrated woman waiting with her suitcases near departing taxis at an international airport in the United States. She is dressed in native garments of India. The teacher asks inductive questions about the codification to pinpoint a problem as students see it.

> What is happening here? Is there a problem?
> Have you or someone you have known experienced a similar problem?
> To what causes can you attribute this problem?
> What can we do?

The students may decide that the woman speaks no English and has been forgotten by those who were to meet her. She must survive on her own, at least for a while. A discussion ensues about the students' own experiences in similar situations and about the possible causes of such dilemmas. They decide, as a group, that they can do something to help others who find themselves in similar predicaments. They decide to create helpful pamphlets for new arrivals and make them available at their local airport. First they obtain the support and input of airport officials. Next, they outline steps for preparing the pamphlets in a variety of languages that will clearly explain important information and procedures (a map of the airport identifying restrooms, information desks, and security offices; explanations for converting money into dollars, using the telephone, finding a hotel or alternative lodging, taking a taxi or a shuttle bus, and so on). Once the pamphlets are completed and approved, the students distribute them at various locations throughout the airport.

Another possible codification for problem-posing, and one that I have used myself, is Paul Conrad's political cartoon (see Figure 4.1).

"If you don't like it here, why don't you people go back
where you came from!"

Figure 4.1. Sample Codification

While addressing problem-posing questions similar to those on the previous page, the students may talk about the irony of the situation and/or their own experiences with prejudice. During the action phase of the process, they may decide to initiate a symposium on racial tolerance within their school, investigate feelings about prejudice among peers and persons in the community, read what they can locate in the library about prejudice, and share their findings with a small group, and so forth.

The process of problem-posing has three major components: listening, dialogue, and action. The focus should be on only one problem at a time so issues don't become clouded, and teachers need to be careful to allow students to pinpoint the problem, rather than lead them to a predetermined one. Issues can involve home, school, community, nation or state, and/or world. Actions can run the gamut from developing helpful information, to speaking frankly with those who are in charge on the local level, to writing letters to members of Congress or leaders of countries. The teacher and the students need to determine effective and appropriate actions in each situation. Problem-posing often requires considerably more time than originally anticipated, but potential benefits may make the practice worthwhile. The results can include increased student interest and subsequent gains in language acquisition.

However, problem-posing is not a one-approach-fits-all formula. It will and should differ for different courses, students, and situations.

Dialectical Writing[1]

Dialectical writing has come into its own in many language classrooms as a legitimate way to ease students into the writing process. What makes dialectical writing unique is that the reader is immediately accessible. In most kinds of writing, the reader is only an abstract presence to the writer, who must anticipate reader needs, prior knowledge, and possible reactions. Dialogue journals (see page 265), in particular, can provide effective contexts for language development. Students write about what is important to them on any given day. The teacher and/or peers respond in writing.

Success with dialogue journals as effective transitions to other kinds of composition is possible with both native language speakers and language minority students at all levels. A partial explanation for their effectiveness may be that legitimate communication is taking place in the written mode. The teacher acts as a real reader as opposed to a mistake detector, the traditional role often assumed by composition teachers. Moreover, through the dialogue, the Zone of Proximal Development is being created (see pages 50–51). The student is encouraged to stretch cognitively to higher levels of meaning and expression. Because this process is a dialectical one, students can improve their writing skills and build confidence in their ability to anticipate reader needs.

Other Dialectical Writing Practices. Other dialectical writing practices include *reaction dialogues* and *teacher/student co-authored products.*

Reaction Dialogues. Reaction dialogues may have possible benefits similar to the dialogue journal. Four that I have identified include:

---

[1] Many of the ideas in this section were first presented as you see them here in a keynote to the TESOL Summer Institute at Comenius University, Bratislava, Slovakia (Richard-Amato, 1992b).

1. Teacher-presented stimulus/Student reaction
2. Student-presented stimulus/Student (peer) or Teacher reaction
3. Student product/Teacher reaction
4. Student product/Student (peer) reaction

In the first type of reaction dialogue, the stimulus can be almost anything—a story, a picture or photo, a poem, a song, an editorial, a political cartoon—and student reactions can comprise writings of various kinds—a few sentences, a paragraph, several paragraphs in essay form, and so forth. The key is that teacher and students discuss the possibilities for reaction. For example, with a story stimulus, students might agree or disagree with the characters' actions, critique the story, or describe similar experiences. With a visual stimulus, students might describe what is happening or will happen next in the picture, write a short scenario based on the picture, or simply write their opinions about the meaning the visual has for them. If students and teacher agree, the reaction does not have to be in writing at all, particularly at first; it might be a drawing. (Drawings are especially appropriate for reluctant writers and for nonliterates or preliterates.)

In the second type of reaction dialogue, it is the student who brings in the story, picture, poem, or other stimulus, and it is the other students and the teacher who react in writing. The classroom has now become more dialectical; students are now assuming a role that would traditionally belong to the teacher.

The last two types of reaction dialogues are self-explanatory. In each case, however, the process can be extended. For example, assigned expository readings can also serve as stimuli. Before class discussion of the reading, students may write a reaction relating the reading to their own life experiences and valuing systems. The teacher may respond by writing short messages and asking questions to extend and/or clarify the students' thoughts, and the student may respond to these messages with further writing. By this means, the teacher can see how students are deconstructing each reading in their own terms. Through this process, teachers and students often find themselves communicating on a much deeper and more personal level than is usually possible during whole-class discussions.

No matter who is responding, the teacher or a peer, that person is providing a written scaffold upon which the student can build, not only structurally, but contextually. Reaction dialogues, like problem-posing can lead to other lessons, compositions, projects of various kinds, and other topics of interest and concern.

Teacher/student Co-authored Products. An application of the language experience approach (see pages 243–246) that is particularly apropos to dialectical writing is the teacher/student co-authored product, in which the teacher is a facilitator and co-author rather than simply a recorder of what students say. As teacher and students compose together, the teacher records what is mutually agreed upon on the board or on a transparency for all to see. The teacher guides students, bringing out their ideas and helping them shape their language through questions and meaning clarification. Material is deleted, rearranged, modified, or expanded as the product is created. (See the extended example on pages 245–246.) As students become more proficient, one or more may exchange places with the teacher and serve as facilitators themselves. This practice can begin at very early levels of proficiency and continue through the high intermediate levels and beyond.

Theme Cycles/Investigative Inquiry

Theme cycles, a type of investigative inquiry proposed by Harste, Short, and Burke (1988), actively involve students in research and in negotiating curriculum itself. First the teacher and students individually list topics they find important and interesting. The lists are then blended by mutual agreement. The resulting list provides possibilities for the next topic of research and discussion. Teacher and students then negotiate to select one topic from the list as a starting point. Let's say the topic selected grew out of contemplating the Paul Conrad political cartoon on p. 78, and that students now want to learn more about American Indians like the ones in the cartoon. Using theme cycles, the class generates a simple list of questions, including all the things students want to learn about American Indians. Here is a sample list for possible investigation:

How did the American Indians live?

How did their cultures differ from one another?

What problems have they had to overcome in the past?

What problems do they face now?

What contributions have they made to our society?

Then students and the teacher *together* make a list of books to read, people to interview, places to visit, etc. (See an additional example of investigative inquiry on pages 324–325.) As the questions are explored, new questions arise and new discoveries are made, leading to further questions and further research. Throughout the process, students and teacher share what they learn. The teacher is a facilitator as well as a participant, ensuring that the activity is carried out successfully. All the while, skills are integrated with the content and are taught as they are needed.

MEETING STANDARDS THROUGH PARTICIPATORY TEACHING AND LEARNING

A central question often raised about participatory learning is its relationship to the current emphasis on standards: Can participatory learning prepare students to meet standards? The answer here, I believe, is a very definite yes!

Participatory learning makes it likely students will be motivated to acquire necessary skills in the first place because such skills are taught at the very time they are most needed rather than according to the mandates of a highly specified curriculum (see also Chapters 7 and 15). Moreover, within a participatory framework, standards can and should be *negotiated* whenever possible. Now this might sound like anathema to some. But not all students need or want to know the intricacies of parallel structure, for example, or how to use rhetorical questions to advantage in a composition. Much depends upon their goals and aspirations. Learning in specific content areas can be part of the negotiated instruction designed to empower students to meet agreed-upon goals.

COMMON MISUNDERSTANDINGS

Unfortunately, a few misconceptions about participatory teaching have arisen.

Myth #1: *The teacher must give up all traditional practices to establish a participatory environment.* This is simply not true. Many practices (including grammar instruction) can be effective, depending upon the proficiency levels, age levels, needs, and the cultural expectations of the students. Not only that, but basic communicative practices can serve as launching platforms for participatory practices. For example, at mid-beginning to intermediate levels, sentences to finish such as "I like to _____" can progress to "I wish I could _____," and eventually to more issue-oriented stems such as "If only _____."

     What is essential to the implementation of a participatory approach is a modification of the traditional teacher's role at all levels. As students gain maturity and proficiency and become more accustomed to sharing power in the classroom, they need to continually work toward becoming autonomous learners and effective communicators in the classroom and out.

Myth #2. *The teacher needs to turn over the reins of power to students.* On the contrary, Freire himself stressed that the teacher *can* and *should* be very much involved and influential concerning what happens in the classroom. The teacher still teaches, but so do the students. The students still learn but so does the teacher. Each participant considers the other to be an important source of knowledge and skills. Although Wells (1999) does not talk about participatory teaching as such, he argues for a strong teacher role in a "community of inquiry." And, while a dialogic relationship takes place in such a community, the dialogue is usually not between equals because of essential differences in status, education, and experience. The teacher's main role, according to Wells, is to lead and to guide students through the curriculum. He argues that the teacher is still the chief initiator and decision maker. Although the teacher maintains a leadership role, the

> ". . . leadership does not have to be exercised in a directive manner, and although the teacher is ultimately responsible for the goals to which "action" is directed, and for monitoring the outcomes in terms of students' increasing mastery of valued cultural tools and practices, it is still possible for students to have a significant part in negotiating both these processes" (p. 243).

In participatory classrooms, the learning becomes more and more collaborative as the students become informed about the issues that concern them and are able to express their opinions, explore options, and make reasonable choices based on a critical analysis of what's at stake for themselves and for the society in which they live.

LEARNING STRATEGIES AND AUTONOMY

Helping students develop appropriate learning strategies[2] is critical to participatory teaching because these strategies can allow for greater autonomy on the part of students in all areas of academia. Usually learning strategies are applied spontaneously, and they often (but not always) come to the individual naturally as the situation demands. However, frequently there are times when such strategies are applied methodically after having been learned from others (the teacher, a book, other language learners) or through deliberate trial-and-error. If used often enough, these strategies can become spontaneous.

Hedge (2000) asked a group of English language teachers from around the world to define what *self-directed learning* meant to them. From their reactions, she concluded that the teachers placed great importance on certain learning strategies, including:

- defining one's own objectives
- using language materials effectively and building on what one learns from them
- organizing the learning
- making sure enough time has been set aside for it
- depending more on oneself rather than the teacher

Hedge suggests developing a facility where students have access to computers, cassettes (for listening and recording), library materials, language games, testing materials, etc.

---

[2] In the literature on learning strategies, some researchers distinguish between strategies and tactics (see especially Seliger, 1991; and Oxford and Cohen, 1992). Strategies are the more general category under which tactics (specific behaviors or devices) fall. For the purpose of this discussion, the word *strategies* will refer to both general and specific behaviors.

The strategies our students choose to use will generally be compatible with their learning styles and preferences,[3] personalities, and cultural backgrounds. For example, students who are high-risk takers and for whom being assertive is acceptable culturally will be more willing to use overt strategies such as seeking out people (even strangers) with whom they can interact; purposely steering the discourse in ways that are beneficial; asking questions, even though some sort of disapproval might result; and so forth (Steve Wilke, personal correspondence). Although people may not be high-risk takers, they may feel comfortable making friends with native speakers of the language, seeking a language helper, debriefing after participation in interactional situations, keeping notes in a journal, and so forth.

O'Malley and Chamot (1990) have helped to organize the myriad of strategies available to language learners by identifying and describing three major categories:

1. *Metacognitive strategies.* Self-regulatory strategies that help students to plan, monitor, and self-evaluate.
2. *Cognitive strategies.* Task-appropriate strategies that help students to actively manipulate the content or skills they are learning.
3. *Social and affective strategies.* Communicative and self-control strategies that help students to interact with others to enhance learning or control their own affective states.

A metacognitive strategy might be to control one's own learning and/or to evaluate one's own progress; a cognitive strategy might be to write down key ideas during a lecture; a social or affective strategy might be to use self-talk (silently giving oneself encouragement) to lower anxiety. The authors are convinced that, through direct instruction, students can use such strategies, maintain them over time, and transfer them to new tasks when it is beneficial to do so.

Chamot (1990) argues that students need to have experience with a variety of strategies in order to choose those that work best for them. She recommends that strategy instruction start at beginning levels by providing it in students' first languages and that it be integrated within the curriculum rather than taught as a separate entity. She goes on to say that teachers should identify the strategies by name, describe them, and model them. Students who are doing less well than they might be in the language learning process should be assured that their apparent failure may well be due to a lack of appropriate strategies, and not to a deficiency in intelligence.

Oxford (1990) has developed a strategy inventory for students learning English that may be useful to help identify areas needing focus. Similar inven-

---

[3] Cognitive style relates closely to matters of culture and personality: high risk/low risk, cooperative/competitive, and so forth (see Chapter 6). It includes sensory modality preferences (auditory, visual, tactile-kinesthetic, etc.), field-dependence/independence, etc. (see Scarcella, 1990). When we tie learning styles too tightly to a specific cultural group, however, we can be in danger of stereotyping (see especially Hilliard, 1989; and Parry, 1996).

tories can be developed in any language and used in situations in which they are culturally appropriate. In Oxford's inventory, students tell how true specific statements such as the examples below are for them.

> I actively seek out opportunities to talk with native speakers of English.
>
> I ask for help from English speakers.
>
> I try to relax whenever I feel afraid of using English.
>
> I look for opportunities to read as much as possible in English.
>
> I try not to translate word-for-word.
>
> I say or write new English words several times, etc.

The simple act of completing the survey may be enough to make most students aware of many strategies that they can incorporate into their language learning practices. Other strategies may need to be expanded, modeled, and practiced before they can be incorporated.

Below is a list of strategies and helpful hints that I have shared with my own students. You may want to discuss these items, which are organized by skill area, with your students and even have some of them translated into your students' first languages so they can benefit early on.

LISTENING

- Focus attention as completely as possible on what is being said.
- Relax and let the ideas flow into your mind.
- Don't be upset if you don't understand everything.
- Try to connect what you hear to what you already know.
- Listen for key words and ideas.
- Listen for overall meaning.
- Ask the speaker to repeat or to speak more slowly, if necessary.
- Try not to be afraid to ask questions about meaning when it seems all right to do so.
- Make guesses about what is being said.
- In conversation, check out your understanding by using confirmation checks (Is this what you are saying?, etc.).
- Whenever possible, pay attention to the forms fluent speakers are using (How are they different from the forms you use?).
- Write down what you have learned—new words, meanings, concepts, structures, idioms, etc.—in a notebook.
- Find a buddy with whom you can compare lecture and discussion notes later to see if you missed any important points that were made.
- Find opportunities to listen outside of class by watching television shows and movies, going to lectures, etc.

SPEAKING

- Find fluent speakers of the language to talk with.
- Think about what you are going to say.
- Think about the grammar you are using, but do not let it interfere with what you want to say.
- Do not be afraid to make mistakes (mistakes are normal as you are learning the language).
- Use repetition, gestures, similar words, definitions, examples, or acting out to help people understand you.
- Record and write down the conversations you have with fluent speakers (ask their permission, of course); afterwards, analyze them (What was successful? Were there any breakdowns in communication? If so, what happened? Did you or your partner use any repair strategies to get back on track? Did you notice any errors?, etc.).[4] Ask your teacher or another student to help you analyze what was said.

PRONUNCIATION

- Look for opportunities to talk to fluent speakers.
- Pay attention to the rhythm, intonation, and stress of fluent speakers.
- Realize that you will not always be understood (keep trying).
- Ask people to show you how to pronounce difficult words.
- Listen to your pronunciation, and correct yourself while you speak.
- Rehearse (make up a little song or chant—have fun with the language).
- Record yourself reading passages aloud from a book.
- Try computer programs which can give you visual images of your speech (see Pennington, 1989).

Note: Not all students will desire target-like pronunciation. Some will prefer to maintain certain prosodic elements of the first language in their speech, perhaps, to retain identity with the first language culture (Morley, 1991) or for other reasons. What is important is that the student be understood.

---

[4] This idea was adapted from one that was described by Heidi Riggenbach during a presentation she gave at the Summer TESOL Institute in San Bernardino, California, 1993.

READING

- Look for opportunities to read in the new language outside of class.
- See what the reading material is about before you start to read (look the text over; think about the title/subtitles; notice the pictures—if there are any), etc. Ask questions about them.
- Read the introduction and conclusion first to guess what the material will be about.
- Notice how the reading passage is organized. (What does each paragraph do? Why do you think it is put together this way?) Ask questions about the way it is structured.
- While you read, relax and feel the words and sentences flow together.
- Ask yourself questions about the meaning as you read (What is the author trying to say here? How does it relate to what you already know? What does it have to do with what the author has just said? What might come next?).
- Do not stop reading each time you find an unfamiliar word or phrase (the meaning may come as you read further).
- If a word seems important but you still don't understand it even after you read further, check the glossary (if there is one) or look in a dictionary.
- Talk about a new idea or phrase with another student or with your teacher.
- Note any parts you do not understand and read them again later. (Are the parts you did not understand at first clearer to you now? If not, discuss them with a another student or with your teacher.)
- Map out the ideas to show how they relate to one another; tell a partner about them; summarize them in writing; discuss the issues/themes the reading presents; write about the issues or themes from your own point of view; write a critique of the reading.

VOCABULARY DEVELOPMENT

- Keep a vocabulary notebook using only the words that you think will be useful.
- At the beginning, try to learn new words as part of a story, or as part of a theme (fish, water, boat), or as part of a word group (celery, carrot). Be careful not to make your group too large.[5]
- When you are more advanced, use word maps or clustering to show relationships and to help you remember.[6]
- Try to focus on groups of words (or chunks) rather than only on individual words (see what other words are used with the vocabulary).
- Make yourself some flashcards and use them often to see if you can remember what the words on them mean. Draw pictures and/or write sentences for the words.
- Use different dictionaries including learner dictionaries as well as bilingual ones.
- Use the new words or phrases in your own writing.

WRITING

- Find out as much as you can about your topic.
- Brainstorm for ideas (discuss with other students, the teacher, family members, and others in the school or in your community).
- Make a plan; map out or cluster your ideas.
- Think about the grammar you are using, but do not let it interfere with what you want to write.
- Begin writing (do not worry about making mistakes at first); let your ideas flow.
- Rewrite, making whatever changes seem necessary.
- Think of writing as a process that develops slowly.
- Ask for advice from other students, your teacher, etc.
- Rewrite and ask for advice as many times as necessary.
- Share your writing with others.

---

[5] Some of the research on vocabulary learning has produced contradictory results. Some research supports the idea that lexical sets interfere with memory (Tinkham, 1997; and Waring, 1997); other research has concluded that lexical sets can help (Higa, 1963). See Nation (2000) for nice summary of the studies accomplished in this area.

[6] See example on pages 250–251.

Although the above lists may be useful to many students, it is important to remember that most strategies are too complex to be reduced to lists. Furthermore, we must not assume that our students are not metacognitively aware. All one has to do is listen to students' conversations about what they are doing to find they indeed are aware. Even young children have very complex ways of self-regulation that they can often verbalize. It may be wise to ask students to share with others some of the strategies they use. In addition, a debriefing session can be valuable in focusing students on the strategies they have used to complete a task and in providing them with the opportunity to learn from each other. Questions—what did you do to get started, or what helped you remember that—can be used to stimulate discussion.

Remember that practice and a focus on strategies should not be so extensive or intrusive as to interfere with learning. Sometimes too much emphasis on strategies causes students to lose the meaning of *what* they are learning as they become focused on *how* they are learning it. Furthermore, practice with strategies that may be inappropriate culturally (see especially LoCastro, 1994), or that students may not be ready for or do not need, could be a waste of precious time. On the other hand, instruction in strategies that is well timed and suited to the needs of the students can make a noticeable difference in the way they approach learning a second language.

SUMMARY

Critical pedagogy, as Pennycook and others describe it, can take us beyond meaningful communication at a basic level to communication about what most deeply affects students' lives. Such interaction goes beyond mere participation. It begins with the realization that students can learn to direct their own learning and teachers can provide an environment conducive to that end. Instruction in learning strategies is beneficial if well timed, suited to the students' needs, and compatible with students' cognitive styles and cultural expectations.

Full participation resulting in student empowerment is most likely to occur if teachers are willing to negotiate power and make classrooms less teacher-fronted. It means involving students in decision-making when it matters and it means respecting them individually and collectively.

Participatory language teaching, while not considered a method or an approach, identifies and describes the dialectical relationship that must occur between students and their teachers if both are to be active and successful members in a classroom community.

READINGS, REFLECTION, AND DISCUSSION

Suggested Readings and Reference Materials

Buehring, M. (1998). *A different angle: Co-oper Activities in communication.* Studio City, CA: Jag Publications. Intended for intermediate to advanced ESL adolescents and young adults in the U.S., this text focuses on relevant issues such as discrimination, the environment, crime and politics, illegal drugs, animal cruelty, health, defending one's beliefs, gun control, and other topics of interest. It features adapted news stories taken from newspapers and magazines and activities that require an integration of skills. Students are encouraged to look at all angles of the issues and to respect differing opinions.

Gardner, D. and Miller, L., eds. (1996). *Tasks for independent language learning.* Alexandria, VA: TESOL. This very practical anthology offers ways to help students become autonomous learners at various levels of proficiency. It includes tasks and guidelines for teachers to use in diverse situations.

Hall, J.K., and W. Eggington. (2000). *The sociopolitics of English language teaching.* Clevedon, England: Multilingual Matters. A very important anthology exploring the social, cultural, and political ramifications of teaching and learning English in today's complex world. In it can be found the selection by Elsa Auerbach referred to in this chapter, and readings by Tove Skutnabb-Kangas, Alastair Pennycook (found also in the Related Reading section of this book), Shelley Wong, and many others.

Pennycook, A. (1999). Introduction: Critical approaches to TESOL. *TESOL Quarterly,* 33(3), 329–348. This article serves as the introduction to the special issue of the *TESOL Quarterly* on the same topic. In it Pennycook discusses what it means to take a critical approach to TESOL, in what ways transformative pedagogy can change attitudes toward education, and why it is important to consider TESOL a dynamic field subject to constant critical examination.

Ridley, J. (1997). *Reflection and strategies in foreign language learning.* Frankfurt am Main: Lang. One important topic addressed by Ridley in this book is the development of learner autonomy by means of self-reflection. She concludes from her research that learners have individual learning agendas and have their own preferred ways of problem-solving and monitoring while producing language, either written or oral.

Schleppegrel, M. (1997). Problem-posing in teacher education. *TESOL Journal,* 6(3), 8–11. Here Schleppegrel clearly describes her approach to problem-posing which includes finding a "text" (the codification) and asking the students to describe the situation, raise questions which often lead to problem identification, relate the issue to personal experience, consider the larger context, and explore solutions.

Smoke, T. (1998). *Adult ESL: Politics, pedagogy, and participation in classroom and community.* Mahway, NJ: Erlbaum. Addressed in this anthology are pedagogical and personal/social issues and instructional and political strategies. It is argued that ESL courses help students become empowered in all ways, not only academic.

Walker, L. (2001). Negotiating syllabi in the adult ESL classroom. *CATESOL News,* 32(4), 5–7. This brief but pithy article offers numerous strategies for discovering what is important to students studying English. Through the use of questionnaires, Walker suggests that teachers explore the students' learning preferences and goals. She recommends that teachers ask students to rank commonly stated objectives in order of their importance. By this means, a curriculum can be developed which reflects student input. Although her ideas are intended for the teachers of adult learners, they can be applied to other levels as well.

Questions and Projects for Reflection and Discussion

1. What possibilities might participatory teaching have for your own classrooms based on what you have read and learned from others? What might be its advantages? Disadvantages?

2. What has been your own experience with self-directed learning? If you have attempted to learn another language, what strategies did you use of which you were aware? Develop your answers in a journal entry. Discuss with a small group.

3. Considering the fact that traditional teaching relies mainly upon transmission education, how wise is it for teachers to make their teaching more participatory? What might be some practical restraints? Do you feel there may be political dangers in store for teachers modifying their roles? If so, what might these dangers be and how might teachers best deal with them?

4. Design a ten- to fifteen-minute lesson using an adaptation of one or a combination of the participatory practices described in this chapter. Make sure that it would be appropriate for a group of fellow students. After presenting your lesson, ask your group in what ways it was effective and how it might be improved. Begin by sharing with them your own reactions to the lesson.

    If you are currently teaching students, use what you have learned to try out an adaptation of a participatory practice with them. Make sure the lesson is relevant and appropriate to level. If possible, have your lesson videotaped to analyze and discuss with peers. Reflect on its outcome and how you felt about doing it. Pay close attention to student response. Do you see any problems with your lesson? How might you improve it?

    Write about your experiences using participatory practices and what you learned in your journal.

5. To what extent do you feel comfortable with participatory language teaching? To what extent do you plan to incorporate it into your own teaching?

CHAPTER 5

Literacy Development and Skills Integration

. . . what people learn when they learn language is not separate parts (words, sounds, sentences) but a supersystem of social practices whose conventions and systematicity both constrain and liberate.

C. Edelsky, 1993

QUESTIONS TO THINK ABOUT

1. What do you remember about your own experiences learning to read and write in your first language? Were your experiences mainly positive or negative? Explain.

2. Now compare these experiences with those you may have had while developing literacy in another language. Were they mainly positive or negative? In what ways were they similar or different? What did you learn from them?

3. Is there is a "natural" way to teach reading and writing? If so, what might it entail? How might it be different from other ways of teaching literacy?

4. To what extent is it wise to integrate reading, writing, listening, and speaking in the language classroom? How might you go about it?

Sometimes research results on reading are used for political ends, to demonstrate that a particular method is superior to other methods. However, we need to look closely at the details upon which such studies are based. If the method requires smaller classes, more individualized work, and large amounts of time devoted to reading and being read to, then the results might be a reflection of these requirements rather than on the use of one system or another per se.

Developing literacy and other abilities in a second or foreign language should involve students in very positive, highly motivating experiences. Students often run into difficulty when learning a language is equated with the mastery of separate sets of skills and subskills. Learning to read in a first or second language is not a matter of stringing phonemes (sounds) into words, and words into phrases and sentences, and so on. Rather, it is a matter of learning to understand meaningful print in order to participate more fully in a community of readers and writers.

Yet studies are frequently cited supporting a phonemic approach to literacy in which sounds are mastered first (see especially the research of Keith Stanovich and his co-researchers). While these studies do establish a correlation between knowing how to read and phonemic awareness, they do not demonstrate that phonemic awareness causes or leads to knowing how to read (Taylor, 1998). Taylor, who refers to the phonemic awareness research reports as "spin doctoring," argues that much of this research is misleading and cited out of context. He advises teachers to look instead to the longitudinal studies of such researchers as Anne Haas Dyson, Yetta Goodman, and many others for a clearer understanding of the reading process.

A NATURAL LANGUAGE FRAMEWORK

A natural language framework is based on the notion that reading is a natural process based on an innate *motivation*. Harste, Woodward, and Burke (1984) found in their research that pre-school children growing up with print ubiquitous in their environment figured out what much of it meant without formal instruction. A natural language framework, also referred to as the "whole language approach," assumes that learning to read in a first or second language is generally a matter of wanting to make sense of text. But that doesn't mean that readers don't develop phonemic awareness. On the contrary, they do. The important questions here have to do with *how* and *when* the phonemic awareness comes about.

Written language is more abstract than speech and therefore requires more complex brain connections that very young children develop gradually as they interact with their environment. Wells (1999), referring to Halliday and Vygotsky, points out that written language is really second-order symbolism in which symbols represent spoken words, which, in turn, represent ideas. He goes further to say that the meaning of what we read and write must be determined through the written word alone, adding further complication to both processes. There are no gestures, intonation, or facial expressions to help convey meaning.

All three skills—speaking, reading, and writing—are socially motivated, active, creative processes requiring a high degree of personal involvement. For this reason, it makes sense to teach all three within a natural language framework in which motivation is high. Reading and writing, like speaking, are best learned when they are necessary for something.

Kenneth Goodman once wrote:

> If you understand and respect language, if you understand that language is rule governed, that the most remarkable thing about human beings is that they learn a finite set of rules that nobody can teach, making it possible for them to say an infinite number of things, then it is also necessary to understand that you cannot chop language up into little bits and pieces and think that you can spoon feed it as you would feed pellets to a pigeon or a rat. . . . Language doesn't work that way.
>
> . . . We have learned a lot of things. One of those things is that language is learned from whole to part. . . . It is when you take the language away from its use, when you chop it up and break it into pieces, that it becomes abstract and hard to learn (1982, p. 238).

Goodman, along with many others, was instrumental in developing a natural language perspective. He described such a perspective as "the easy way to language development." To make his point, he contrasted what makes language learning easy with what makes it difficult. One might want to look at the two columns below as ends of a continuum rather than as a dichotomy.

It's easy when:	It's hard when:
it's real and natural.	it's artificial.
it's whole.	it's broken into bits and pieces.
it's sensible.	it's nonsense.
it's interesting.	it's dull and uninteresting.
it's relevant.	it's irrelevant to the learner.
it belongs to the learner.	it belongs to somebody else.
it's part of a real event.	it's out of context.
it has social utility.	it has no social value.
it has purpose for the learner.	it has no discernible purpose.
the learner chooses to use it.	it's imposed by someone else.
it's accessible to the learner.	it's inaccessible.
the learner has power to use it.	the learner is powerless.

(Goodman, 1986, p. 8)

The right-hand column is most often associated with *bottom-up approaches*. These approaches adhere to the idea that acquiring literacy in a language begins at the most abstract level: sound and letter correspondences, syllables, words, and phrases. Students are expected to use these as building blocks to move gradually to what is more concrete and meaningful. Such approaches can be especially devastating for children who are not yet ready to think meta-linguistically. They can also be frustrating for older learners, who, although they are cognitively highly developed, have not had other means (i.e., books or other materials of interest) for accessing the written language.

The left-hand column, on the other hand, is associated with *top-down approaches*. Here students are introduced to meaningful language right from the beginning rather than to abstract bits and pieces. It may be a wordless book for which the teacher helps the student write a story, using the student's own words (see the language experience approach on pages 243–246). It may be a short message addressed directly to the student. What child or adult can resist trying to figure out a message with his or her own name on it? Through effective top-down approaches, students internalize bits and pieces as they engage personally with the reading and writing process. The abstract bits and pieces are learned as they are needed, often with the help of the teacher.

Unfortunately, natural language advocates are often accused of being against bottom-up processing—an assumption that is unfounded and misleading. More typically, it is approaches that *focus* on bottom-up processing to the exclusion of meaningful literacy events that natural language advocates are against, not the process itself. They generally recognize the interaction between top-down and bottom-up processing and the importance of that interaction. Edelsky, Altwerger, and Flores (1991) remind us that while using a natural framework, ". . . teachers *do* teach children how to spell words they are using, *do* teach appropriate punctuation for letters children are writing, *do* teach strategies for sounding out particular combinations of letters under particular circumstances" (p. 38). However, what is taught, and when it is taught, may be different for each reader depending upon the task, the situation, and individual needs. Interestingly, many good readers are not good at skills exercises, and many poor readers are (see Altwerger and Resta, 1986). What seems critical here is that developing readers be involved in reading/writing activities that are meaningful (see Chapter 13 for descriptions of such activities).

SKILLS INTEGRATION

Within a natural language framework, integrating the four skills—listening, speaking, reading, and writing—is is not difficult.[1] It should come as naturally for the teacher as it does for the students. (See Figure 5.1.) When we listen,

---

[1] The assumption is made here that the goal of any particular language program is to promote proficiency in all four skills. It should be noted, however, that not all language programs have this as a goal; some may be concerned with only one or two of the skills.

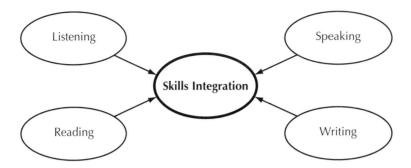

Figure 5.1 Integrating the Four Skills

opportunities for writing evolve. When we read, opportunities for speaking make themselves felt. Classrooms in which students are encouraged to flow with these opportunities will inevitably allow the skills to grow naturally.

Often, impetus for skill development comes from a need of the moment. For example, students may need to write to fulfill immediate obligations. A foreign language student in the later elementary grades may need to respond to a letter from a pen pal. A second language student at the adult or secondary level may need to fill out a job application. In these situations, students can't wait until the later levels for language to emerge. The teacher and/or peers can aid students in fulfilling these obligations. With guidance, students will frequently find themselves performing far above levels for which they are supposed to be "ready."

Integration of the four skills can take place right from the beginning without causing an undue overload on students' mental capabilities. Even during the silent period, literacy in the new language can be introduced to students who need to survive in school settings and on the street. Clear labels on various rooms throughout the school can help—especially the words designating male and female bathrooms. Words for the street are even more important: words like *stop*, *danger*, and *keep out* are crucial for survival. In the foreign language classroom, teachers can label common objects around the room after students have acquired or partially acquired their oral forms.

Beginners at any age may be highly motivated by story experience (see Chapter 11), which allows students to participate in a rich language environment even before they can utter a word in the target language. Later, students can read simple stories with accompanying pictures in both second and foreign language classes. Speech development may be accelerated simply through involvement in a character's conflict. Natural curiosity may push students into more and more complex levels of communication, incorporating all the skills of which they are capable. If teachers are there to take advantage of these teachable moments—what I call *the natural curiosity phenomenon*—they can guide students in reading and writing tasks far beyond what might have been considered possible in the traditional teacher-oriented, inflexibly structured classroom.

Students begin their transition into literacy well before they actually begin to speak through exposure to labels, signs, ads, and other pieces of written language necessary for survival. At this point, then, reading and writing skills can come not only from simple, highly motivating reading materials, but also from the students' own experiences.

Some strategies that seem to work particularly well with students of all ages are associated with the "language-experience approach" (see Chapter 13).

- Begin with a planned or spontaneous experience that the students all have in common (a story, a song, a picture, a trip to the local shopping center).
- After the experience, have students brainstorm, and write key words on the board or on a transparency. You may want to have each student contribute to a group story or paragraph that you write for everyone to see.
- Have students read what has been written aloud as a group and copy it into their notebooks.

Over time, students can begin to read and write simple, short texts somewhat independently of the teacher as they move to higher levels in the language acquisition process. Other helpful transitions are the matrices (see pages 182–183), charts (see pages 181, 195, and 250), and other activities that involve the comprehension of written messages in the target language.

Generally, the more similar the first language and culture are to those of the target group, the more likely will be the transfer of specific as well as general reading skills. For example, if the L1 is a European language using the Roman alphabet and the L2 is English, specific transfer will probably involve many similarities in sound combinations, the written symbols, punctuation, the movement of the eyes from left to right while reading, and so forth. On the meaning level, specific transfer might involve cognates, organizational patterns, shared cultural knowledge, experiences, and expectations.

On the other hand, when the language and culture are very different, the transfer is likely to be more general. For example, if the L1 is an Asian language using an ideographic writing system, the transfer would tend to be limited to more general elements such as sensory-motor skills; the symbolic nature of written language; attitudes toward reading; and general comprehension skills such as predicting, inferencing, coming to conclusions, etc. (see also Thonis, 1984). Keep in mind, however, that knowledge gained in the content areas is always transferable across languages, regardless of the languages involved.

Learning in the First Language

Learning to read in the first language is particularly important for language minority children in order that their cognitive development not be arrested while they are trying to learn a new language system (Cummins, 1981b). Nonliterates in second language classes need special attention at the beginning of the acquisition process. If possible, they should develop literacy in their primary languages first (if their languages have written traditions) and then apply this knowledge to literacy development in the second language.[2] Nonliterates for whom an L1 mastery of literacy skills is impossible for whatever reason need to be introduced to the written form of their second language in much the same way that the other students are introduced to it, except that more preliminary work is necessary.

Students need first to focus on the symbolic nature of language through such activities as role play (see Chapter 11) or game playing (see Chapter 12). In these activities, objects can be made to represent people or things. The symbols are arbitrary, just as the words on the printed page are arbitrary representations of concepts. In addition, nonliterate students may need considerable exposure to multisensory input in order to develop a rich visual and kinesthetic representational system before they can be eased into literacy. Experience with real books, story experience and charts, pictures to be labeled, maps, graphs, and actions associated eventually with the written word (such as one finds in the physical activities, in Chapter 8) all form important preliminary steps leading into literacy at any age.

READING AS AN INTERACTIVE PROCESS

Many educators and researchers use the term *interactive* to describe the reading process, but what they mean by this term can differ dramatically. Some use *interaction* to describe the relationship between top-down and bottom-up processing within the individual reader (see especially Carrell, Devine, and Eskey, 1988). Others use *interactive* as a label for questions posed by textbook writers that are designed to ensure comprehension of a particular reading, as though the meaning of that passage were somehow static.

I prefer to think of interactive reading as a process during which meaning is created by the reader (see also Zamel, 1992), not only through interaction with the text, but also through interaction with others in the class, in the school, the community, and in the home. Rosenblatt (1985) drew a rather clear distinction between the word *interaction* as used in scientific paradigms and the word *transaction* as she uses it to describe the reading process (see also Dewey and Bentley, 1949). In scientific paradigms, interaction is seen in a mechanistic way involving separate entities acting upon one another but not affecting the nature of each other. She compares the entities to ". . . two billiard balls colliding and then going their separate unchanged ways" (p. 98). Transaction, on the other hand, indicates an ongoing process in which the entities are blended and changed as a result of the interaction. My own definition and use of the word *interaction* includes a similar transactional quality. (See Figure 5.2.)

---

[2] See especially Collier and Thomas (1989) and Ramírez, Yuen, and Ramey (1991). Note that this would not necessarily be true for a student in an immersion foreign language situation (see Chapter 17).

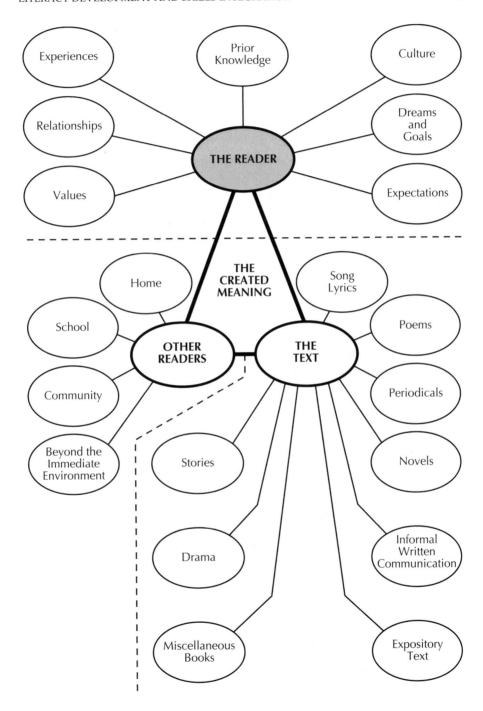

Figure 5.2. Reading as an Interactive Process

The focus of this interactive conceptualization is on the reader: the reader's values, relationships, experiences, prior knowledge, culture, dreams, goals, and expectations (or schema). The reader relates to the text, be it a story, a play, an essay, a novel, a poem, lyrics, or whatever.[3] Out of this relationship comes a preliminary interpretation, or a *created meaning*. This interpretation will be accepted or rejected by the reader either in part or as a whole, based on interaction with other readers. If there appears to be a mismatch in interpretation, the reader may return to the text to reread or to reanalyze and *recreate* the meaning. All the while, skills are being internalized, hypotheses about the meaning are being tested, expectations are being adjusted, preconceived ideas are being reevaluated, and the student is reaching increasingly higher levels of understanding.

Others, too, have emphasized the role of the reader. For example, the French philosopher, Jacques Derrida (1976, 1981), who developed the deconstructionist point of view, insisted that language has no "metaphysics of presence" of its own. In other words, it exists only when some other force gives it meaning. The reader (the "other force") reconstructs its meaning or "rewrites" it, in effect.

Although I agree with Derrida's focus on the reader as a key component in the reading process, I am dubious about the simplistic way in which he and his followers divide the world (see especially Crowley, 1989, and her references). On the one hand, they claim that the *traditional* view of reading should be avoided because it adheres to rigid forms (e.g., the expository essay, the essay of comparison and contrast, etc.), and it stresses the finality of meaning as established by expert interpretation and the authority of the author. On the other hand, they support the *deconstructionist* view because it focuses on deviating from rigid forms and static meanings and on the importance of reader interpretation as opposed to expert interpretation. I do not find the contrast itself questionable, but the dichotomy seems too simplistically drawn.

What do we gain—and lose—by dismissing the traditional view out of hand? Second and foreign language students, in particular, may *want* to know about traditional "rigid" forms used in a society that may differ in many ways from their own. They may *want* (and may indeed *need*) to be familiar with conventional models so they can incorporate what they want of them into their own writing. The deconstructionists agree that both reading and writing are communal endeavors. Why then should we as readers and writers disregard the ever-evolving conventions of a particular community for whom we want to write or whose writing we want to understand? In addition, there may be times when readers (both native and nonnative) will want "expert" interpretation. But that does not mean they have to accept it and make it their own. By looking at the two views on a continuum, we can incorporate elements from both

---

[3] Rosenblatt (1985) considers the text itself to be only a ". . . set of verbal signs" that comes into being only through transaction. Although I agree that the transaction gives it life, I believe that the text is more than ink on paper; it is a reflection of the thoughts, feelings, experience, knowledge, etc., of the author at a particular point in time and in a particular social situation.

perspectives, even though through critical engagement and analysis, we will undoubtedly lean one way more than the other.

Although the interactive conceptualization of reading presented in this chapter has elements of psycholinguistics (psychological influences within the reader's mind, particularly in respect to the READER component in Figure 5.2), it is basically a sociolinguistic representation in that the community of learners is the main influence. This is true also of the Interactive Writing Conceptualization presented later. Both representations are very rudimentary in that they do not seek to explain *how* the components work together (perhaps this is their greatest limitation). Instead, they mainly identify and show the relationships of influences involved in an interactional process as I am defining it.

FACILITATING THE READING EXPERIENCE

At almost any age level, teachers can motivate students by having them make predictions about what they are going to read and by asking questions that relate what they are reading to their own lives and to their prior knowledge and experience (see additional elements in the READER component in Figure 5.2). Teachers can provide experiences designed to familiarize students with new concepts reflected in the reading selections. In the later elementary grades and beyond, the teacher can aid understanding by helping students map out ideas as they understand them, thus giving the content a graphic dimension (see examples in Chapter 13). Teachers can ask questions that call for reflection and inference and that require higher level thinking skills and self-reflection, rather than questions requiring factual answers. Consider the list below:

1. Predicting content and outcomes
   - What do you think the story (essay, poem, etc.) will be about? (Refer students to the title, pictures, subheadings, or other clues.)
   - What sorts of problems do you think the characters might have?
   - What will happen?
2. Relating the text to prior knowledge
   - What reasons does the author give for why these things happened?
     — Can you think of other examples in which things like this happened?
     — What do you think caused them to happen?
   - What are some other things that the author (character) might have done?
3. Making inferences and supporting conclusions
   - What is the author trying to tell us here? (Refer to a specific line, paragraph, event, etc.)
   - How do you think the character (author) feels?
   - Why is the character (author) happy (angry, doubtful, relieved, etc.)?
   - Why do you think so?

4. Relating to self and one's culture
   • What would you do if you were in a similar situation (dilemma)?
   • Do these situations (dilemmas) often happen in your culture? If so, what do people usually do?
   • How does this event (fact, opinion) make you angry (glad, fearful)? Why?

Students can also be asked about organizational strategies and patterns, use of literary devices, and whatever else is appropriate to the situation—or they can be asked to generate questions of their own. Whether the questions are teacher- or student-generated, it is important to allow enough wait time so students can think first and then begin to formulate their responses.

Small-group discussions of readings allow students to share ideas within their own classroom community and to test their own hypotheses about what they are reading (see the OTHER READERS component in Figure 5.2). Because other readers come to the discussion with their own values, prior knowledge, etc., group discussions can be very potent in an interactive reading process.

Materials for Interactive Reading

Materials used in interactive learning (see the TEXT component in Figure 5.2) must be interesting and comprehensible, both semantically and syntactically, and they should include some elements slightly beyond the students' present levels. (For other considerations for materials selection, see Chapter 16). Students should be encouraged, too, to select their own materials for independent reading and for small-group participation.

WRITING AS AN INTERACTIVE PROCESS

Although separating writing from reading creates a somewhat artificial division, I do that here for ease of discussion. Like reading, writing is an interactive process, involving three basic components (see Figure 5.3).

First, the writer (like the reader) brings to the process his or her own values, relationships, experiences, prior knowledge, culture, dreams, goals, and expectations. But the writer must also consider one additional category: the audience. Writers must anticipate the possible reactions, backgrounds, etc., of those who will be reading and creating meaning out of what is being produced.

Second, the interactive process of writing includes other writers (and readers) at home, in school (mainly the teacher and peers, some of whom will probably be more advanced) and in the community and beyond. Good writers often consult or conference with other writers to ask for their reactions, comments, and suggestions.

Finally, the interactive process of writing includes other texts, written and oral—stories, drama, essays, novels, poems, formal speeches, informal written

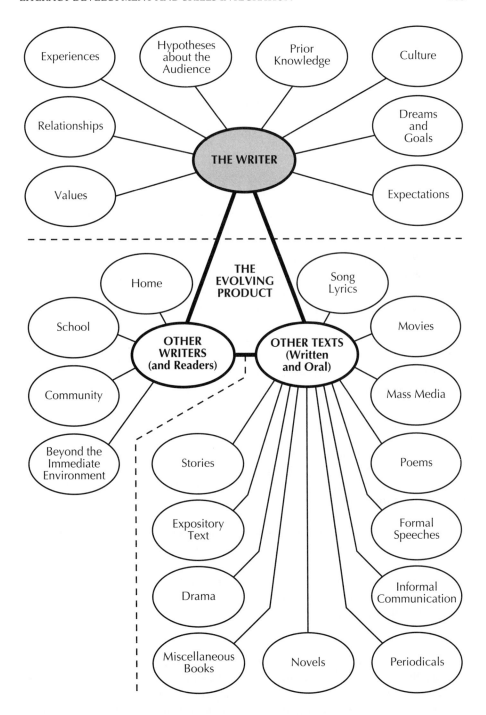

Figure 5.3. Writing as an Interactive Process

communication, song lyrics, periodicals, miscellaneous books, and so on—that can serve both as sources of information and as models.

Because the process of writing is an interactive one, the evolving product therefore does not belong solely to the person who produced it; rather it belongs in varying degrees to all influences contributing to its development and to the reader who ultimately determines its meaning on a personal level. Thus, the product truly reflects a communal effort.

FACILITATING THE WRITING EXPERIENCE

When students are writing, motivation can come from numerous sources in second and foreign language classes. Experiences with music, poetry, story-telling, role play, drama, and affective activities often provide motivation and can lead into some highly relevant, exciting topics and issues. Students need to begin the writing process with a certain amount of confidence, which can come in part from their exposure to versions of the language experience approach mentioned here and described in more detail in Chapter 13.

The writing itself can be very subjective (letters to pen pals, journal entries, simple poetry) or more objective (lists of various kinds, forms, charts, maps, compositions). The kinds of writing a student does will depend largely on that student's age, needs, concerns, and proficiency level. However, it is generally best to begin with short pieces of writing before proceeding to longer ones.

The Process and the Product

In all writing, students need to concentrate on the process and the evolving *product* simultaneously. Murray explained: ". . . You let the students write . . . . Writing must be experienced to be learned" (1982, pp. 115–116). The writing process itself involves:

- brainstorming for topics of interest and discussing them with others
- gathering information
- allowing that information to settle into some sort of overall plan (clustering and other graphic organizers might be useful in planning)
- putting the words down on paper
- consulting with others again
- revising

Revisions are particularly important to the writing process. According to Murray, they provide opportunities for the student to "stand back from the work the way any craftsman does to see what has been done. . . . The most important discoveries are made during the process of revision" (1982, pp. 121–122). Because the effective writer frequently has to pause, go back, reread, rethink, consult with other writers, rewrite, and write some more, he or she must be able to concentrate intensely on the composition without interference from the teacher or others who might want to help.

Students may need help before the actual writing begins in order to stimulate thinking, and again later, once students have had a chance to hammer out at least part of the piece alone. At that point, students may want to confer with the teacher and/or peers as needed. What points are coming across clearly? What portions are not readily understood? The listener or reader may ask questions or suggest strategies to help. Students then need time to reshape the writing to better communicate what was intended or to move in other directions. Dialoguing with other writers, especially peers, can generate a great deal of enthusiasm for the writing process and can motivate thoughts and feelings that might otherwise remain unexplored.

Approaching Errors

The most effective way to deal with errors may often be an inductive approach—simply underlining or circling the word or phrase in which a problem appears and asking the student to try to identify the error. Some errors can be tied to meaning, and teachers can guide students to identify them by asking pertinent questions. In responding to errors in verb tense, for example, the teacher might simply ask "*When* did this occur?" Often students will recognize the errors themselves, without any lengthy explanation or further probing. Reading pieces aloud in individual conference sessions often makes errors more salient.

Sometimes, however, teachers need to provide brief explanations to lead students to a better understanding of their errors. Students always need to be reminded that errors are perfectly normal during the writing process. Errors should be treated in a matter-of-fact way so that the students don't associate them with the quality of the ideas themselves. In addition, it is best not to focus on too many errors at once, but to point out patterns or to prioritize so that students understand the most important problems in their writing. Much depends on what students might be ready for at any given time. For some students, specific activities on recurring errors might help; for others, rewriting and a simple discussion of strategies may be enough to help them improve their writing.

Error correction may sometimes be handled indirectly in writing just as it is with oral production. For example, after students hand in their journals, instead of marking the errors, the teacher may simply react to the entry by repeating the words that the student has used, but in correct form in the margin. Thus, the teacher's comment serves as a model. For example, if the student writes "On Tuesday my mother sick," the teacher might respond with "I'm sorry your mother was sick." This particular type of correction often comes naturally to a teacher focused on meaning and may work well, especially with reluctant writers who are just beginning literacy development in the new language.

Teacher As Model

The teacher can sometimes serve as an effective model for the writing process. Modeling allows students to experience vicariously the frustrations and joys that go into writing and, at the same time, to be exposed to the forms and conventions of various types of composition. For example, watching the teacher execute a well-developed paragraph on the board or on a transparency can be highly motivating as well as instructive. The teacher will have to choose a topic or issue to write about (the students may want to make suggestions), brainstorm for ideas, map out a brief preliminary plan, begin a first draft, provide transitions, erase, move materials, modify, consult with the students, rewrite, and use the dictionary. If the teacher does his or her thinking out loud during the process, the students will more fully realize that even the teacher has to struggle to communicate. At more advanced levels, the teacher may even want to share previous efforts at writing; analyzing drafts written at different stages of the composition process can be very helpful to developing writers.

Portfolios

Many teachers find it helpful to have students save their work in portfolios, so that all concerned can keep abreast of the progress taking place. (See pages 139–141 for more information on portfolios.) In periodic evaluative conferences, teachers and students can talk about progress made, strengths observed, and possible future areas of work. Students often find such conferences both informative and encouraging.

CRITICAL LITERACY

Critical literacy is a way to discover how societies perpetuate and protect the values of its most powerful members. Moreover, it can examine how such power might be shared with those less fortunate who may have found themselves marginalized. Critical literacy goes beyond mere tolerance and a celebration of differences. At its best, it includes multiple literacies and points to ways in which marginalized groups in a given society may gain influence. Students need to use the acts of reading and writing to gain a better understanding of their own lives and situations and how they can work to make them better (Freire, 1970b).

Some critical pedagogues agree with Derrida and the other deconstructionists (see page 100) that rigid forms such as those found in a genre approach to teaching literacy should be avoided. Luke (1996), for example, feels that such forms tend to promote and maintain the injustices inherent in the existing power structures. However, others see a genre approach as a means to penetrate the system, discover what it is all about, and eventually effect change for the better (see Martin, 1993; and Wallace, 1992). Knowing about the various genres and how they are structured makes critical analysis possible. Wells (1999) also stresses the importance of knowing what he calls the "genres of power." He urges us to give our students "every assistance in appropriating them so that they can participate fully in the activities in which they are used" (p. 143).

Hammon and Macken-Horarik (1999) agree. Based on their research with Australian ESL primary and secondary students, they report that students should be engaged in a study of textual and cultural practices. They believe that:

> Such engagement includes an awareness of alphabetic codes, comprehension of texts, recognition of the cultural significance of specific genres, the ability to construct well-formed and cohesive texts, and the ability to undertake reflexive and critical analysis of texts. . . . They [the students] cannot be expected to run before they can walk (p. 531).

The authors caution, however, that critical literacy should not be treated as an add-on saved only for students operating at advanced levels. Students early on need to make progress toward meeting the goals of the mainstream curriculum so that they can be in a better position to deconstruct on their own terms what they are reading and learning.

Just as teachers in preparation need to have a disciplinary knowledge base in order to develop a critical perspective on the teaching process (see pages 6–9), so do their language students need such a base in order to effect change. Not only that, but they need to develop the metalinguistic strategies necessary to approach literature critically and become autonomous learners.

Pennycook (1996) perhaps sums it up best by merging the various versions of critical literacy to give us a broader view. From this perspective, critical literacy:

> . . . emphasizes the need (a) to view language education as a practice in reading the world; (b) to understand the changing face of that world, especially in terms of shifting media literacies; (c) to link language education to questions of gender, ethnicity, inequality, class, race, and so forth; (d) to consider how the needs to understand, acknowledge, and incorporate student difference and diversity can be taken seriously; and (e) to help develop abilities and awarenesses in our students that enable them to reflect critically on the word and the world (p. 170).

SUMMARY

An integrated approach to developing literacy and other academic skills in the target language can be dynamic and exciting in a natural classroom environment. Instrumental to the theoretical underpinnings of a natural language framework has been the whole language movement. This often misunderstood movement is one that has shifted our emphasis away from discrete skills and subskills to the natural elements inherent in learning to read and write for the purpose of communication.

Both reading and writing are interactional processes. The definition of *interactional* found here goes beyond the scientific use of the term and draws from a transactional perspective. From this perspective, not only does the interaction occur, but the components involved are changed, often in significant ways, by the interaction itself. The components of reading as an interactional process include the reader, other readers, and the text. Out of these the meaning is created. The components of writing as an interactional process include the writer, other writers (and readers), and other texts (both written and oral). Out of these comes the evolving product.

Acquainting students with traditional genre structure is important in order that students have the tools necessary to understand the conventions of a given community, participate in that community, and work to make it better.

Error correction for developing writers should focus on meaning and go beyond a line-by-line, word-by-word analysis whenever possible. The teacher's modeling of correct forms through the relevant communication is one way to provide indirect correction and can be particularly effective with reluctant writers. By this means, the teacher's communication serves as a scaffold upon which students can build as they move progressively to more advanced levels of proficiency.

Critical literacy can be viewed in a more narrow sense (acquiring strategies and skills needed to analyze critically) or in a broader sense (understanding change in the world and how it comes about, associating the teaching of language to issues of personal relevance and concern, increasing awareness, and so forth). Both views are important to the empowerment and the emerging independence of the second language student.

READINGS, REFLECTION, AND DISCUSSION

Suggested Readings and Reference Materials

Carson, J. G., and Leki, I., eds., (1993). *Reading in the composition classroom: Second language perspectives*, Boston: Heinle. This book presents an historical perspective of second language literacy and an analysis of the issues involved in connecting reading and writing.

Edelsky, C. (1996). *With Literacy and Justice for all: Rethinking the social in language and education*, 2d edition. London: Taylor and Francis. Edelsky offers convincing arguments for a holistic approach to literacy teaching. Included also are the political ramifications of a whole language approach. Although it focuses on L1 literacy, most of the points that it makes are applicable to L2 as well.

Freedman, S., ed. (1989). *The acquisition of written language: Response and revision.* Norwood, NJ: Ablex. This book made available several important contributions to writing pedagogy in the area of teacher and peer input into student revisions. Represented are the following authors, to name a few: Shirley Brice Heath, Courtney Cazden, Anne Gere, and Stephen Witte.

Kroll, B. (1990). *Second language writing: Research insights for the classroom.* New York: Cambridge University Press. Presented here are numerous articles describing important research of the writing process of second language learners, the variables influencing their performance, the relationship between reading and writing, and many other issues of interest to second language teachers. Included are chapters by Andrew Cohen, Ulla Connor, Joan Eisterhold, Barbara Kroll, Ann Johns, Joy Reid, and many others.

McKay, S. (1993). *Agendas for second language literacy.* New York: Cambridge University Press. The agendas for second language literacy discussed here include sociopolitical, economic, family, and educational. All are examined through a sociohistorical perspective.

Wallace, C. (1988). *Learning to read in a multicultural society: The social context of second language literacy.* New York: Prentice Hall. Here the author explores the reading event itself, sources of miscues, the integration of language skills, case studies of learner-readers, and many other topics related to learning how to read.

Zamel, V. (1992). Writing one's way into reading. *TESOL Quarterly,* 26(3), 463–485. In this article Zamel stresses the interdependence of reading and writing, and discusses both as creative processes. Her implications for instruction are particularly well-drawn.

Questions and Projects for Reflection and Discussion

1. What do you think Goodman means by "easy" and "hard" when he refers to language development (pages 94–95)? To what extent do you agree with his conclusions?

2. Would you feel comfortable learning to read and write in another language within a natural classroom environment? Why or why not? Write about it in your journal.

3. How do you think discrete points of language (e.g., spelling, sounding out consonant clusters, punctuation) should be handled within a natural classroom environment?

4. Create your own diagrams that show how you conceptualize reading and/or writing components and/or processes. Discuss them with a small group. Can you improve them in any way based on your group's feedback?

5. To what extent do you think a genre approach should be used in teaching reading in a second or foreign language? Consider, in particular, the possible effects of an emphasis on organizational forms, expert opinion, and the authority of the author.

CHAPTER 6

The Affective Domain

If we were to devise theories of second language acquisition or teaching methods which were based only on cognitive considerations, we would be omitting the most fundamental side of human behavior.

H. Douglas Brown, 1987

QUESTIONS TO THINK ABOUT

1. Think about your own experiences while studying another language. To what extent did the following help or hinder your success?

   a. anxiety

   b. motivation

   c. attitude

2. What did you and/or your teacher do to lessen your anxiety, increase your motivation, and maintain or improve your attitude? How effective were these strategies?

3. What can you do as a second or foreign language teacher to improve the overall affective environment to make your classroom a positive place in which to learn? If you have taught or are currently teaching, which of these strategies have you already tried? What happened?

4. In what ways can stereotypical notions about students from other cultures negatively affect how teachers interact with them? Has a teacher or someone else ever revealed through words or actions a stereotypical notion about you? Tell about the experience. How did it make you feel? Can stereotypical notions about others be avoided? If so, how?

The affective domain includes several variables that can either enhance second language acquisition or hinder it, depending on whether they are positive or negative, the degree to which they are present, and the combinations in which they are found.

Because these variables are difficult to isolate and are often so subtle they can scarcely be detected, studying them objectively with our current methods seems almost impossible. How does one effectively measure inhibition, for example? Or empathy? Or attitudes, for that matter? All of these intangible concepts interact to form changing patterns that usually operate out of the subconscious. We do know that factors or combinations of factors having to do with *attitudes*, *motivation*, and *level of anxiety* are central to the affective domain. These are strongly influenced by the process of *acculturation* and by certain *personality* variables.

ATTITUDES

Attitudes develop as a result of experience, both direct and vicarious. They are greatly influenced by people in the immediate environment: parents, teachers, and peers. Attitudes toward self, the target language and the people who speak it (peers in particular), the teacher, and the classroom environment all seem to have an influence on acquisition.

Attitude toward Self

Adelaide Heyde (1979) early on looked at the effects of three levels of self-esteem—global, specific (situational), and task—on the oral performance of American college students studying French as a foreign language. She found that students with high self-esteem at all levels performed better in the language they were studying. Other studies have resulted in similar conclusions (Heyde, 1977; Oller, Hudson, and Liu, 1977). In general, successful language learners appear to have higher self-esteem than those who are unsuccessful (Price, 1991).

Most people would probably agree that high self-esteem usually leads to greater self-confidence. But a student may have high global self-esteem, and at the same time experience low self-esteem in second language learning environments (Scarcella and Oxford, 1992). Moreover, the degree of self-esteem and/or self-confidence may vary from situation to situation or from task to task. Both may increase as one performs well in a variety of situations. Oller (1981) argued that the relationship between affect and learning is probably bi-directional: We may perform well because our attitude toward self is positive; we may have a positive attitude toward self because we perform well (see also Gardner, Lalonde, and Moorcroft, 1985).

Stevick emphasized the significance of *self-security*, an important facet of the attitude toward self. "Am I what I would like to be as an intellectual being and also as a social being? Do I have an adequate mind, and am I the kind of person that other people are willing to spend time with?" (1976, p. 229). If the answer to these questions is affirmative, then the individual may be better able to engage in the often humbling process of acquiring a second language.

Attitude toward the Target Language and the People Who Speak It

The attitudes that an individual has toward the target language and the target group (especially peers) seem to have a substantial effect on motivation in particular. Here stereotyping often plays a large role. Cummins (1997) is convinced that stereotypical labels frequently reflect the power relationships within society as a whole (see also Yep, 2000). Persons from other cultures are often thought of as the deficient and disadvantaged *Other* (as opposed to the more normal and enlightened *Self*).

Using different terms, Saville-Troike (1976) much earlier reported that the *in-group* (represented by the *Self*) often values characteristics that the *out-group* (represented by the *Other*) is perceived as lacking—for example, intelligence, cleanliness, human (as opposed to animal) traits, independence, self-reliance, appropriate behaviors concerning time, and the like. A major effect of stereotyping is to create or perpetuate social distance and social boundaries. Saville-Troike argued that stereotypes build social barriers that are detrimental to one's self-image as a learner.

Similarly, Harklau's (2000) ethnographic study of English Language Learner (ELL) identity found that the same students who were once considered exemplary in high school were labeled "difficult" and "underachieving" in their college ESL classes. The change in the students' attitudes due to the different treatment was dramatic. These once determined, hard-working individuals eventually became ill-behaved and combative and some dropped their ESL program altogether, even though they still felt the need for it.

When negative stereotypes are attributed to second language students in any situation, they may become *internalized* and could undermine attempts at language acquisition. Not only do negative stereotypes affect the self-esteem of second language students, but they often engender negative reactions and attitudes toward the target language and culture, which generally considers itself to be "the ideal." Students everywhere who are considered linguistically and culturally deficient or disadvantaged because they have a different first language and culture are at serious risk. Their self-esteem is in jeopardy if their teacher and peers fail to show respect for them, their first language, and their culture. If we expect language and cultural minorities to do all the accommodating and fail to reach out to them and meet them where they are, then many of our best minds will be doomed to failure in our school systems and in our society.

Attitudes toward the Teacher
and the Classroom Environment

In classrooms in which mutual respect is lacking, differing values can lead to conflicts between student and teacher, and between student and peer. A student who works together with another student to complete a project may be perceived as "cheating"; a student who does not guess on the true/false section of a test may be perceived as not caring. In reality, the first student may simply not value competition in completing a task, and the second may not feel comfortable guessing without knowing the answer. We tend to label whole societies as noncompetitive or collective, as opposed to individualistic (see Kubota, 1999 and 2001; Yep, 2000). We need to remember that people from all cultures (including our own) need to be treated as individuals with varying ways of behaving.

Scarcella (1990) addressed the issue of communication breakdowns and how to help students overcome them. She recommended the following:

- Encourage the development of friendships.
- Emphasize commonalities.
- Create a place in which the experiences, capacities, interests, and goals of every classroom member are simultaneously utilized for the benefit of all.
- Teach all students how their communication styles can be misinterpreted (p. 104).

We have all probably seen classrooms in which values clashed, student against peer. In one situation with which I am familiar, the students had been given a group task to identify problems that might be encountered on an American-style "date." Two fairly recent arrivals insisted that the couple must be chaperoned in order to prevent inappropriate behavior, but most students dismissed the idea of a chaperone as silly and argued that such a practice would never be considered in the modern world. The discussion turned into a very angry exchange among the students—one that could have been prevented had the majority of students been given a chance to voice differences early on, discuss them, and through discussion gain an appreciation of others and their differing viewpoints.

To ease tensions that might result in this kind of unpleasant situation, some teachers might feel comfortable using affective activities or *humanistic*[1] techniques (see Chapter 14). Those advocated particularly by Brown and Dubin (1975); Moskowitz (1978, 1999); and Simon, Howe, and Kirschenbaum (1992) seek to

---

[1] See footnote 1 on page 280.

create good feelings on the part of the students toward the teacher, each other, and the resulting classroom environment.

Moskowitz set out to gather evidence that the use of such techniques in language classrooms (both foreign and ESL) does indeed "enhance attitudes toward a foreign language, rapport with classmates, and the self-image of foreign language students" (1981, p. 149). She conducted two studies using the language students of eleven teachers enrolled at Temple University in courses on humanistic techniques of teaching a foreign language. The subjects were high school students studying a variety of languages: French, Spanish, German, Italian, Hebrew, and ESL. Each teacher chose one class (from beginners through advanced) in which to do the study. Often they chose classes that had been apathetic or difficult in some way. They gave three questionnaires prior to the humanistic activities and re-administered the questionnaires two months later. Had the students' attitudes changed? In both studies, significant positive increases occurred in students' attitudes toward themselves, toward the language, and toward each other.[2] The following four hypotheses were accepted (1981, pp. 145–150):

Using humanistic techniques to teach a foreign language:

- enhances the attitudes of foreign language students toward learning the target language
- enhances the self-perceptions of foreign language students
- enhances the perceptions of foreign language students toward the members of their language class and how their classmates perceive them
- increases the acceptance of foreign language students for members of the same sex and by members of the opposite sex in their class, thus increasing their cohesiveness

These studies indicated that humanistic activities increase the development of positive student attitudes overall. Moskowitz's later studies (1999), in which she replicated parts of her earlier work, support similar conclusions.

MOTIVATION

Much of the literature differentiates between *integrative* motivation and *instrumental* motivation. Gardner and Lambert (1972) defined integrative motivation roughly as a desire to integrate and identify with the target language group,

---

[2] In the *first study*, the students' identities were not revealed, and so the pre-post data were treated as though they came from two independent groups; in the *second study*, the identity of the students was retained in code so that pre-post data could be matched. Two questionnaires were administered: the Foreign Language Attitude Questionnaire and My Class and Me (see Moskowitz, 1981, p. 150). Sociometric data were collected from each student to see to what extent attitudes changed toward specific peers.

and instrumental motivation as a desire to use the language to obtain practical goals such as studying in a technical field or getting a job (see also Hedge, 2000, for similar definitions).

The studies of French classes in Canada done by Gardner and Lambert (1959) and Gardner, Smythe, Clement, and Gliksman (1976) all concluded that integrative motivation is generally stronger than instrumental motivation in predicting French proficiency. However, other evidence in this area frequently appeared contradictory. There were cases in which integration appeared *not* to be a strong motive but in which a certain urgency existed to become proficient in the target language for instrumental reasons. In such cases, instrumental motivation became the main predictor (Lukmani, 1972; Oller, Baca, and Vigil, 1977). On the other hand, the study of Chinese-speaking graduate students in the United States (Oller, Hudson, and Liu, 1977) indicated that although the students' main reason for wanting to be proficient in English was instrumental, the subjects who characterized Americans positively performed better on a cloze test. Thus the studies were very inconclusive.

What appeared to be contradictory findings may simply have been evidence indicating that the various sources of motivation studied are difficult, if not impossible, to isolate and are certainly not mutually exclusive. Many questions needed to be addressed. How do we distinguish the various sources of motivation to begin with? For example, does "integration" mean to become part of the target language group or just to socialize on a casual basis with its members?[3] If it means the latter, then might not instrumental motivation be present as well? Imagine, for example, a person who desires to socialize with the target group in order to integrate but does so in a desire to curry political favor. Or imagine that a person who is part of a marginalized cultural group wants to integrate in order to show those in power that he or she is indeed capable of learning the language and of academic success. How would one categorize such motives? Even if they could be isolated, how could they be measured? In addition, the person may not want to reveal his or her real feelings—or may not even be aware of them.

One problem here lies with the distinct possibility that motivation may have been too narrowly defined to begin with. Motivation involves not only integrative and instrumental factors, but also temporary expectancies, interests of the moment, curiosities, ego enhancement factors, personal satisfaction, and much, much more (see van Lier, 1996). These factors appear to interact in complex ways and are far more mercurial in nature than we at first thought. But one thing seems clear: motivation is an extremely important affective factor. Without it, learning any language, first or second, would be difficult, and perhaps impossible.

---

[3] Graham (1984) attempted to clarify by adding yet another category: assimilative motivation. Assimilative motivation is present when one desires to "melt" into the target group to the extent that one becomes indistinguishable from the others.

LEVEL OF ANXIETY

Two types of anxiety have been recognized in the literature on affect:

- *trait* anxiety (a predisposition toward feeling anxious)
- *state* anxiety (anxiety produced in reaction to a specific situation)

In his discussion of the two types, H. Douglas Brown (1987, 1994) notes the difference between anxiety that is debilitative and anxiety that is facilitative. Whether the anxiety is an aid or hindrance often depends upon the degree to which it is found in the individual. For example, no anxiety at all might cause the person to be lethargic, whereas a small amount might bring the individual to an optimal state of alertness.

In a study using induced anxiety, MacIntyre and Gardner (1994) found that their control group (the members of which had *not* been exposed to anxiety-arousal) performed better than the experimental groups during all phases of the learning task set before them. They also concluded that whenever anxiety-reduction strategies are employed, they must be accompanied by re-teaching strategies in order that students might have a second opportunity to learn what was missed during the time when anxiety was high. Interestingly, Gardner and MacIntyre (1993), in their report based on research, concluded that if students experience language anxiety too often, the state anxiety may turn into trait.

Others studies also support the notion that a lowered anxiety level is related to proficiency in the target language (Carroll, 1963; Chastain, 1975; Gardner, Smythe, Clement, and Gliksman, 1976; MacIntyre and Gardner, 1994). In the case of ESL, teachers and peers can promote a lowered level of anxiety by providing a sort of surrogate family to serve as a buffer until independence is reached. Sheltered classrooms in the content areas (see Chapters 17 and 18) also provide temporary refuges in which students can receive meaningful input in low-anxiety environments. Although Larsen and Smalley (1972) didn't specifically mention the classroom as serving in this capacity, they nevertheless did advocate such a haven. But students who are sheltered for too long may fossilize early as a result of isolation from target group peers. A wise teacher involves students with competent speakers (including L2 users) as early as possible and helps the students achieve independence as soon as they become ready. In the case of foreign language teaching, students can receive supplemental instruction, participate in a support group or foreign language club, or learn how to apply relaxation strategies (see especially Campbell and Ortiz, 1991).

Additional potential causes of increased anxiety in both ESL and foreign-language classes include not providing a silent period, giving direct corrections (particularly untactful ones) while students are speaking, competitiveness (see Bailey, 1995), incompatible learning styles (see Oxford, Ehrman, and Lavine, 1991) and so forth.

Below are paraphrased some of the strategies Oxford (1999) recommends to lower anxiety in the language classroom:

- Make students aware that language anxiety episodes can be temporary and do not always develop into a permanent problem.
- Provide multiple opportunities for success.
- Encourage the student to take some moderate risks.
- Help the student tolerate ambiguity in a nonthreatening environment.
- Reduce competition.
- Do not expect perfection in performance.
- Use music, laughter, and games to help students relax.
- Be fair and unambiguous in testing.
- Aid students in realistically assessing their own performance.
- Plan activities that address varied learning styles.
- Help students to recognize symptoms of anxiety.
- Encourage students to use positive self-talk and reframe negative ideas. (p. 67)

Oxford also advises teachers to "Be very clear about classroom goals and help students develop strategies to meet those goals." I would like to modify this recommendation by suggesting that students should be involved as much as possible in setting the goals in the first place. This suggestion is in keeping with the establishment of a participatory classroom (see Chapter 4).

RELATED FACTORS

Acculturation

Acculturation, too, may be an important predictor of target language acquisition (Stauble, 1980; Schumann, 1978a). Stauble argued that second language learners will succeed "to the degree that they acculturate to the target language group" if no formal instruction is attempted. Although the procedures of her research and conclusions may be open to dispute,[4] the following assumption appears reasonable:

---

[4] In Stauble's study of the process of decreolization, she made a distinction between social distance (domination versus subordination, assimilation versus preservation, enclosure, size, congruence, and attitudes) and psychological distance (resolution of language shock, culture shock, and culture stress, motivation, and ego permeability). She measured the negation development of three native Spanish speakers who had been living in the United States for over ten years. They were classified along the Schumann (1979) continuum from Basilang (minimal skills in the target language) to Mesolang (intermediate skills) to Acrolang (nativelike performance). In an attempt to account for their varying levels, she administered a questionnaire to determine their social and psychological proximity to English. She found that her subject Xavier (in the lower Mid-Mesolang phase) had the least amount of social distance (12.5%) and greatest amount of psychological distance (62.5%); her subjects Maria and Paz had the same amount of psychological distance (21%) but differed somewhat on social distance, 56% and 67%, respectively. From this she suggested that psychological distance may be more important than social distance. However, one might question this conclusion. Intuitively it would seem that the two factors would be highly correlated with one another and would be difficult to separate so distinctly. She mentions in passing that Paz demonstrated a higher degree of motivation than the other two. Perhaps this should have been pursued as a causative factor. Stauble herself admits that the validity and reliability had not yet been determined on her measurement and that the results should be considered speculative.

The assumption here is that the more social and psychological distance there is between the second language learner and the target language group, the lower the learner's degree of acculturation will be toward that group (1980, pp. 43–50).

Schumann's (1978a) research supported her conclusion. He compared the linguistic development demonstrated by six second language learners of English—two children, two adolescents, and two adults. The subject who acquired the least was Alberto, a 33-year-old Costa Rican. Of all the subjects, he was the one most socially and psychologically distant from the target language group. He interacted predominantly with Spanish-speaking friends and made no attempt to socialize with English-speaking people. He showed little desire for owning a television set and played mostly Spanish music on his stereo. Although English classes were available, he showed no interest in them. However, as Schumann pointed out, a Piagetian test of adaptive intelligence revealed no gross cognitive defects that might prevent him from learning a second language. The main reason for his low proficiency, according to Schumann, was his lack of desire to acculturate.[5]

The Acculturation Model

To explain the effect of acculturation on the second language acquisition process, Schumann developed the *Acculturation Model.* According to this model, L2 acquisition is dependent upon the amount of social and psychological distance that exists between the learner and the L2 culture. When the distances are great, the learner's language tends to fossilize during the early phases of interlanguage development. The learner may not have received the necessary input because of social isolation or may not have given the target language the attention necessary for acquisition because of psychological distance.

The Nativization Model

Andersen's (1983) *Nativization Model* also sought to explain why the language of some learners fossilizes early. He cited the effects of what he calls "nativization" (not to be confused with the "native-speaker" concept) and "denativization" upon the learner. Through nativization, the learner tends to assimilate the target language into an already determined schema of how the L2 should be and makes judgments based on knowledge of the first language and culture. Denativization, on the other hand, is an accommodation process in which the learner changes the schemata to fit the new language. Andersen

---

[5] It is interesting to note that, according to Schmidt (1984), the poorest learners in the studies referred to by Schumann and Stauble were also the oldest. Physical maturation may have been, either directly or indirectly, a contributing factor.

was convinced that the learner who tends to denativize is the most likely to become proficient.

Accommodation Theory

Giles' *Accommodation Theory* (1979) claimed that motivation is the key and that it is closely related to in-group (the L1 group) and out-group (the L2 group) identification. Giles emphasized how the individual *perceives* social distance rather than the actual social distance as described by Schumann. He argued that feelings of identity are dynamic and are dependent upon continuing negotiations between and among individuals and groups. Schumann saw these feelings as more constant and slower to change. Fossilization, according to Giles's model, occurs during "downward divergence," which takes place when the individual is not strongly motivated in the direction of the outgroup.

The Normal Acculturation Process

In his analysis of the literature, H. Douglas Brown (1987, 1994) describes the four variable stages that have been identified in the normal acculturation process.

- *First Stage.* The newcomer feels almost euphoric—excited at being in a new (sometimes exotic) place.
- *Second Stage.* As the reality of survival sets in, the newcomer moves into *culture shock*, where frustration rises, and the individual begins to feel alienated from the target culture. Self-image and security are threatened.
- *Third Stage.* The beginning of recovery—the newcomer still feels stress but is beginning to gain control over the problems that once seemed insurmountable. This state, which Brown refers to as *anomie* (see Srole, 1956), comprises initial adaptation to the target culture and loss of connection to native culture. The result can be heightened anxiety—a sense of homelessness, or hovering between two cultures. *Anomie* is a critical period in language mastery.
- *Fourth Stage.* In this stage of *full recovery*, the person becomes reconciled to his or her role in the new culture.

Under normal conditions, persons becoming acculturated pass through *all* these stages at varying rates. They do not necessarily progress smoothly from one stage to the next; regression is common, depending upon circumstances and state of mind.

Although acculturation is important to successful language acquisition in a new culture, it should not be encouraged at the expense of the student's first language and culture. Both target and native languages and cultures should be developed and maintained as much as possible during the acculturation process and beyond for a number of reasons:

- to give the student access to more than one cultural group
- to keep important aspects of the native culture alive for future generations
- to contribute to a sense of pride in one's self and in one's cultural background

This conclusion is supported by a number of studies. For example, Deyhle (1992), in her study of Navajo students, found that those students whose homes were most traditional, who maintained their own language, and who were involved in the religious and social activities of the community were the most successful in school. Phinney (1993) concluded that teenagers in general are much better adjusted if they have examined their own ethnicity in depth and value its role in their lives. Many have concluded that using students' cultural backgrounds as a transition to learning in another culture is helpful—and may even be necessary to their achieving academic success (Nieto, 1999 and Ladson-Billings, 1994—see also Related Reading 2.)

Personality

Certain personality characteristics can foster proficiency in the target language. These include:

- a willingness to take risks (Rubin, 1975; Beebe, 1983; Oxford, 1990; Brown, 1994)
- a relative lack of inhibition (Guiora, Acton, Erard, and Strickland, 1980; Guiora, Beit-Hallami, Brannon, Dull, and Scovel, 1972)
- the ability to tolerate ambiguity[6] (Oxford, 1999 and Ehrman, 1999)

Extroversion and assertiveness, although not necessarily beneficial traits (Naiman, Fröhlich, and Stern, 1978; Busch, 1982), can be helpful to the degree that they encourage more output and hence more input. In addition, empathy, under normal conditions, can lead to greater proficiency. Being able to identify with members of the target language group is important to communication. Guiora, Brannon, and Dull (1972) argued that empathy is essential in order that our ego boundaries be permeable. In other words, we need to be open to the new language and the new people. Schumann (1980) related empathy and ego permeability to a lowering of inhibitions.

> I would submit that empathic capacity or ego flexibility, particularly as operationalized under the concept of "lowering of inhibitions," is best regarded as an essential factor to the ability to acquire a second language (1980, p. 238).

These characteristics can be contradictory, however. An extremely extroverted and assertive individual may not tend toward empathy. The three char-

---

[6] A tolerance for ambiguity involves the acceptance of apparent contradictions and information that is not complete.

acteristics need to be in balance in order to have a potential positive effect on language acquisition.

Overall, research on the relationship between personality and language acquisition is inconclusive—a ripe area for further exploration.

CREATING A POSITIVE SCHOOL AND COMMUNITY ENVIRONMENT

Although the teacher may successfully establish an environment conducive to language acquisition in the classroom, what students face outside of the classroom may have an even greater impact on affect. Unfortunately, ELLs are often likely to become the victims of ridicule and sometimes outright hostility. Prejudice can come not only from native-speaking peers but from teachers, administrators, and other school staff members, as well as from the community. However subtle, the form that it takes among teachers and other school personnel can be particularly devastating. Persons of influence can affect the attitudes found in the whole school setting which often extend to the community itself.

I remember an incident that occurred when I was an ESL teacher in a large public high school. One day in the teachers' lounge a fellow teacher asked me, "How's old 'Ho Hum' [a nickname he had given the Asian student we shared] doing today?" I pretended not to know to whom he was referring, although the student's identity was obvious since we had only one Asian student in common. He continued, "You know, what's his name" and then he gave the student's real name. "Oh, he's doing just fine," I replied. As it turned out, old "Ho Hum" went on to maintain close to a 4.0 grade-point average throughout school, won the top "Junior of the Year Award," and became a star member of the soccer team. Of course, not all ELLs can achieve so much, and for those finding their languages and cultural backgrounds devalued, success in school often remains elusive.

Promoting Academic Achievement

Poor academic performance can be due to any number of factors, including, but not limited to:

- economic inequality
- ability tracking[7]
- low expectations on the part of teachers
- the pressures of standardized tests

---

[7] Ability tracking (including "gifted and talented" programs) can be very devastating to those not making the grade for the upper tracks. Eliminating such tracking, on the other hand, can have very positive effects (see especially Mehan, Datnow, Bratton, Tellez, Friedlaender, and Ngo, 1992).

- lack of respect for the individual
- social humiliation
- lack of first-language support (see also Nieto, 1999, 2000)

Some students do not succeed because negative relationships with persons of the dominant culture have caused them to resist even the appearance of assimilation. Many feel that to succeed means that they must give up too much of their own identity.

The overall school environment and the students' individual relationships with teachers are of utmost importance and will often determine whether or not academic success will be achieved. Do the school and the teacher value their languages and cultures? Are the students respected as individuals with knowledge and experience that can be built upon and shared?

Of course, we all know of language and cultural minority students who were able to overcome less than ideal conditions. Usually these students came from families that took great pride in their traditions and instilled in their children a sense of self-worth. And, in most cases, these students were encouraged by their parents to do whatever was necessary to succeed academically. An affirmation of self did much to inoculate these students against the insensitivity to which they may have been exposed in school.

Promoting Cultural Understanding

Although we cannot hope to eliminate the prejudice of all insensitive persons with whom our students come into contact, we can, perhaps through awareness training, try to make the overt expression of these prejudices unpopular. Through workshops for teachers and staff, and through the sensitizing of entire student populations and groups within the community, we can achieve a school climate that will be supportive for all of our students, not only those in second language classes.

The teacher workshop presented here seems to be particularly effective in exposing cultural biases. Similar sessions can be held for students and groups within the community. It begins with the following scenario.[8]

> A man and woman dressed in clothes that represent a very "primitive" hypothetical culture walk slowly through the audience. The woman, who is carrying a basket filled with bread, walks a few paces behind the man (her husband). Once they reach the front of the room, they turn to face the audience and kneel down, side by side. The man places his hand on the woman's head while she bows her head down, touching it to the floor three times. She then rises, walks into the audience, and begins to lead people up to the front

---

[8] Although I have not been able to locate the original source of this idea, I saw a version of it presented at the 1980 NAFSA Conference in El Paso.

of the room as though she is preparing for a ceremony. (In this case, it will be a wedding ceremony in which her husband will take a second bride.) First, she quietly leads two men (one at a time) from the audience to the front of the room. The only sounds she utters are pleasing "umms" from time to time. She motions for them to sit in the chairs she has set up previously. She repeats the same procedure, except this time she takes two women from the audience. She motions for them to kneel on the floor. Lastly, she leads the new bride to a kneeling position beside the husband. She then passes out the bread from her basket. She gives it to the men first, waits a few moments, and then gives some to the women.

The moderator asks the audience to describe this society. Usually, the audience guesses that it is a patriarchal society supported by these facts:

- the man walked ahead of the woman upon entering
- the women had to sit on the floor while the men got chairs
- the men were fed first
- the husband pushed the woman's head to the floor three times

This audience reaction is expected; they had little choice but to react from their own world view or *weltanschauung*. But in fact, the hypothetical society being portrayed is matriarchal. Consider the perspective below:

- Men walk ahead of the women to protect them from potential danger.
- Men take more than one wife because there are fewer men than women—and this disparity occurs because men's lives are more dispensable; men are expected to protect women at any cost, and men therefore die younger and in greater numbers.
- Only women can directly receive the spirits who are in the ground. Thus women bow their heads to the ground, while the men, who can only receive the spirits indirectly, must place a hand gently on a woman's head. Only during the marriage ceremony can a man receive the spirit directly.
- The bread is served to the men first to ensure the women's safety in case it has been poisoned.

This scenario is almost always followed by a lively discussion about perspectives and how they color views of reality. This kind of activity helps participants begin to look at events from the viewpoints of others and, perhaps, gain a more global perspective.

Other types of activities that promote cultural understanding are affective activities (Chapter 14), cooperative learning (Chapter 15), and many other interactive and participatory strategies mentioned throughout this volume. Nieto (2000) points out that activities that foster respect and understanding generally reduce the number of racial comments and name-calling and increase higher academic achievement overall.

The Variable Stages of Ethnicity

Another way to increase awareness of others is to take teachers, students, and community groups through the variable stages of ethnicity (Banks, 1990) by means of role-playing in hypothetical situations. Banks's typology applies to situations in which dominant and nondominant groups coexist in a variety of ways. His definitions of these stages are summarized as follows:

Stage 1: *Ethnic Psychological Captivity*
The member of a non-dominant group feels rejection and low self-esteem and may avoid contact as much as possible with the dominant group. This individual has internalized the "image" that the dominant society has ascribed to him or her and may even feel shame.

Stage 2: *Ethnic Encapsulation*
The member of a non-dominant group reacts to Stage 1 with bitterness and, in some cases, a desire for revenge. As a result, the person may turn inward to his or her ethnic group and reject all other groups, particularly the dominant one. In extreme manifestations of this stage, other groups are regarded as "the enemy" and are seen as racists with genocidal tendencies, and members of the non-dominant group who try to assimilate into the dominant group are considered traitors.

Stage 3: *Ethnic Identity Clarification*
The individual is able to clarify self in relation to the ethnic group of which he or she is a part, with a resulting self-acceptance and understanding. The person is able to see both positive and negative aspects of his or her own group, as well as the dominant group. To reach this stage, individuals must have gained a certain degree of economic and emotional security and must have had productive, positive experiences with members of other groups, particularly those in the dominant group.

Stage 4: *Biethnicity*
The individual is able to function successfully in two cultural groups, the primary group and a nonprimary group. Most individuals belonging to a non-dominant group are forced to reach this stage if they wish to become mobile socially and economically in the society in general. Interestingly, members of the dominant group do not have to do this and can (and often do) remain monocultural and monolingual all their lives.

Stage 5: *Multiethnicity and Reflective Nationalism*
The individual has learned to function successfully in several ethnic groups. The person still feels loyalty to the primary ethnic group but has developed a commitment to the nation state and to its idealized values as well.

Stage 6: *Globalism and Global Competency*
The individual has developed global identifications and has the skills necessary to relate to all groups. This person has achieved an ideal but delicate balance of primary group, nation state, and global commitments, identifications, and loyalties.

The road to biethnicity is not easy (see especially Madrid, 1991). Individuals do not necessarily move from one stage to the next in linear fashion. Rather, they tend to zigzag back and forth, and some may skip stages altogether. Fortunately, Stage 2 is often bypassed, although some feelings from it may exist temporarily as the person moves from Stage 1 to Stage 3.

Encouraging Understanding

I have found that hypothetical role-playing allows teachers, students, and community members to "experience" the first three of Banks's stages. First, I ask the participants to decide which groups they want represented (for example, Latin-American, Korean-American, Vietnamese-American, American Indian, Japanese-American, and so on.) Then they decide which group they want to join. Once in the group of their choice, they go through a set of planned activities to help them experience the different stages. In Stage 1, for example, they might bring in pieces of literature, songs, pictures, or anecdotes depicting their people experiencing oppression at the hands of the dominant group. They may want to list negative feelings about the self and the ethnic group created by this experience and discuss how each feeling came about.

A more general activity can also help participants feel the effects of this stage.

- Give each participant a paper hat (a simple headband will do).[9] On each hat write a label such as "dumb," "smart," "good-looking," "unbathed," "conscientious," "lazy," and so on.
- Place the hats on the participants in such a way that no individual will see the label he or she is wearing.
- Help the group choose a relevant topic for discussion and have them during the course of the discussion treat each other according to their labels.

Most students will be amazed at the intensity of the anger or joy they feel depending on the treatment to which they are subjected.

At Stage 2, participants may want to discuss the negative feelings they have developed. Once these feelings are fully aired, people will be better able to build positive attitudes toward their own ethnic groups, as well as the groups of others. This time, the group may want to share literature and other cultural items that cause them to feel intense pride in their own cultures.

In Stage 3, participants are encouraged to sit back a little and look at the positive attributes and achievements of other groups (share their literatures, etc.) and to achieve a realistic view of their own ethnic group in relation to others.

---

[9] This activity was adapted from one shared with me by Leah Boehne.

Still other culture awareness activities can include group discussions about issues relating to diversity, films, celebrations, and other events that bring school and community together. In participatory classrooms, students will be able to determine the issues that most concern them. They will be able to study and research these issues, discuss them, write about them, and perhaps even begin to take actions toward easing the problems (see also problem-posing on pages 77–79). The rewards of such activities can be immeasurable in terms of increased human understanding and personal empowerment.

What Makes a Difference

I want to stress again that activities and strategies by themselves are not the most important factors in establishing an accepting school and classroom environment. The most important factor by far is *the relationship that has been established between teacher and student, and student and student.* If these relationships are not as affirming and positive as they should be, then no activity or strategy, no matter how innovative, will make much difference (see also Cummins, 2000 and Nieto, 1999, 2000).

Parental Involvement

Schools should be inviting places where parents and indeed whole families feel welcome. Teachers would be wise to seek their ideas for improving the school, both academically and socially; use the home language with the help of interpreters and translators to facilitate communication with parents; encourage bilingual staff members to make home visits and in other ways serve as liaisons between school and community; ask questions of parents about their children's expectations and the ways their children seem to learn best at home; organize family meetings during which members can share experiences, problems, and so on.

Additionally, special programs can be organized to help meet families' language and cultural needs (see especially the Chinatown program described on pages 454–464). Families need to be encouraged to become partners in the education of their children by such simple acts as reading aloud with them in whatever language feels most comfortable and helping them with homework. If possible, parents should provide books for the home in both languages, and encourage their children to read them for enjoyment, to analyze and ask questions about them, and/or to use them as resources for homework.

Family members can often become important resources in bilingual classes and in second language classes (if they are reasonably competent themselves in the second language). In all classes, they can be recruited as tutors or teacher aides. Moreover, they often can be effective guest lecturers on topics/issues of relevance.

SUMMARY

Because the concepts related to the affective domain are so intangible and mercurial, they are difficult to define, describe, and measure. Yet despite their ephemeral quality, we cannot give up our attempts to understand what their role might be in second language development. Central to the affective domain are attitudes, motivation, and level of anxiety. They appear to be strongly influenced by acculturation and personality factors.

Attitudes that are largely determined by what our students have experienced and by the people with whom they identify—peers, parents, teachers—influence the way students see the world and their place in it. Motivation also is a strong force in determining how proficient the students will become. In addition, level of anxiety has its effect. If the students been given a chance to try out the language in a nonthreatening environment, they will be more likely to go through the variable stages of acculturation without it becoming a debilitating process. If the students' backgrounds and languages have been affirmed and accepted, they will be in a better position to acculturate while perserving their own identities.

Each student's emotional well-being can be enhanced by a positive school environment. In spite of the fact that prejudices cannot be eliminated completely, much can be done to make the environment a better one, not only for language learners, but for all students and their families. Cultural awareness activities can involve school personnel, students, and community members. They can sensitize people to the needs and feelings of others.

READINGS, REFLECTION, AND DISCUSSION

Suggested Readings and Reference Materials

Arnold, J. (1999). *Affect and language learning.* Cambridge: Cambridge University Press. This anthology explores affective factors and how they relate to a holistic approach to the language acquisition process. The authors represented in this book come from a variety of geographic areas, experiences and backgrounds, and perspectives. They include John Schumann, Earl Stevick, Adrian Underhill, Rebecca Oxford, Gertrude Moskowitz, JoAnn Crandall, Joy Reid, Madeline Ehrman, and many others.

Banks, J. (1993). *Multiethnic education: Theory and practice* (3d ed.). Boston: Allyn & Bacon. A sensitive exploration of the nature of ethnicity and multiethnic education in the United States. Offers guidelines for promoting a more global, open society through education. A very readable and important book for all teachers.

Horwitz, E., and Young, D. (1991). *Language anxiety: From theory and research to classroom implications.* Englewood Cliffs, NJ: Prentice Hall. A very comprehensive look at language anxiety and the effect it has on second and foreign language acquisition. Empirical research, students' perspectives, and teaching and program strategies are presented. Thomas Scovel, Harold Madsen, David Crookall, and Rebecca Oxford are among the authors included.

Igoa, C. (1995). *The inner world of the immigrant child.* Mahwah, NJ: Lawrence Erlaum. The author tells of her own journey, as a teacher, to discover the needs and feelings of immigrant children and to establish a classroom in which these needs and feelings can best be accommodated.

Richard-Amato, P. (1997). Affect and related factors in second and foreign language acquisition. In *TESOL's voices of experiences series.* Alexandria, VA: TESOL (http://www.tesol.edu). This three-hour workshop comes complete with audiotape, activities, and facilitator notes. Intended for ESL and foreign language teachers on the job and for teachers in preparation, the workshop explores the effects of factors such as anxiety, motivation, and attitudes on the language acquisition process. It also looks at acculturation and personality variables and the roles they play.

Richard-Amato, P., and Snow, M. A. (In press). *The multicultural classroom: Readings for content-area teachers.* (2d ed.) White Plains, NY: Addison-Wesley. Focusing on the needs of language minority students, this book addresses theoretical foundations for successful teaching in multicultural classrooms. It explores recommended classroom strategies and practices and later relates them to specific content areas such as math, social studies, science, and literature.

Schumann, J. (1997). *The neurobiology of affect in language.* Oxford: Blackwell. Schumann describes what his neurobiological theory is all about and how it relates to cognition. He looks at the kinds of stimuli the learner receives from the environment and how each affects the emotions and behaviors of the learner. He finds a strong connection between stimulus appraisal and motivational theory and, as before, sees affect as being critical to the language acquisition process itself.

Shulman, J. and Mesa-Bains (eds.) (1993). *Diversity in the classroom: A casebook for teachers and teacher educators.* Hillsdale, NJ: Lawrence Erlbaum. Numerous cases for reaction and response are presented here. After each case is a description of the actions actually taken by the teacher to remedy the situation and the results of those actions followed an analysis by an experienced person in the field.

Questions and Projects for Reflection and Discussion

1. In your journal, write about your own cultural heritage and how it has developed and changed. How important has it been to you over the years? Do you have any regrets concerning your cultural heritage? If you have children, what would you want to pass on to them?

2. Several language students have mentioned that learning a second language makes them feel "helpless and ineffectual." What demands are typically made on the individual in the following second language situations that might contribute to this feeling?
   a. a child going to kindergarten in a new culture
   b. a tenth-grader in beginning Spanish as a foreign language

    c. an adult going to work in a new country for the first time
    d. a university ELL attending a class oriented to native speakers

What affective factors will help or hinder the individual's ability to cope in each situation?

3. Have you ever lived in another culture? Think about the experience in relation to the normal acculturation process (see page 119). To what extent did you experience each stage? Do you remember regressing to previous stages? If so, what caused your regression in each case? Discuss with a small group of peers.

4. Savignon (1983) described an incident involving her son Daniel, a new student in a Paris school. On the first day, he met with more than a hundred students at his grade level in the school's courtyard. The school director called out the names of the students. They were to stand and tell what class they were in. When his name was called, he followed the procedure but was immediately chastised for having his hands in his pockets. When he went home that day, he vowed that he would never go back. He had had it with that school. Explain the incident in terms of what you know about attitudes, values, and the variable stages of acculturation, etc. If you had been Daniel's parent, what would you have said to him to help him put this incident in perspective?

5. What is the difference between sympathy and empathy? Think of examples of each from your own experience. Which one serves the language learner best? Explain.

6. In what ways, other than those mentioned in the chapter, can you aid your own students in developing positive attitudes, strong motivation, and reduced anxiety? Consider kinds of activities, room arrangements, and the general ambiance in the school and classroom environment.

7. Plan a culture awareness workshop for school personnel (including the secretaries, custodians, cafeteria help, etc.) in your school. Be very specific about the pre-workshop preparation, the workshop itself, and the follow-up. Share your plans with a group of peers to receive their feedback. Make any changes you want, based on what you learn.

CHAPTER **7**

Language Assessment and Standards

To the extent that a test presents authentic language and communication tasks, with both verbal (discourse level) and an extralinguistic context, it will be evoking communicative performance, and thus approach as nearly as possible the evaluation of communicative competence.

M. Wesche, 1987

QUESTIONS TO THINK ABOUT

1. Describe your own experiences as a student and/or as a practicing teacher with language assessment. Were they mainly positive or negative?

2. For what purposes do you feel second and foreign language students should be tested in the target language? In each case, what would you want to know?

3. What might a *pragmatic* test entail? How might it differ from other kinds of tests with which you are familiar?

4. Is it possible to design a language assessment program that is both instructive and evaluative? What might it look like?

5. If your classroom is largely *participatory*, what implications might this have for testing?

Misconceptions about testing abound. For example, many people believe that standardized tests are an accurate means for judging student learning, and that such tests are all that we need to make this determination. A single standardized test is often used to evaluate not only individuals (students, teachers, and administrators), but also programs, schools, and entire school districts. A low score on a standardized test has kept some students from graduating with their classmates. Curriculum has been put on hold to drill students in the name of test preparation. And in Colorado, state officials have even considered ranking teacher preparation programs in the state according to how well their graduates' students do on standardized tests!

But almost as troubling is the fact that critical decisions are often made about second and foreign language students based upon their performance on a single language test. Will the student be able to enter a program of choice? Will he or she be able to exit a basic language program and move on to more challenging course work? Important judgments like these are often based upon the very limited data provided by a language test, the scores of which mainly reflect a knowledge of grammar rules, vocabulary distinctions, and the like. Here I am reminded of the now classic story retold by Clark and Clifford (1988) about the scientific investigation of the bumblebee, carried out by an aerodynamic engineer.

> [He] carefully measured the wingspan, body weight, airflow pattern, size and placement of wing muscles, number of wing beats per second, and numerous other of the bee's physiology, and by means of elaborate diagrams, mathematical formulas, and computer-aided calculations, was able to demonstrate conclusively that the bumblebee is incapable of flight (p. 146).

Similarly, we often examine students' knowledge of language to come to conclusions about performance capabilities. Does the student of German know the rule governing the subject-AUX inversion following fronted adverbials? Does the student of English know when and how to use the subjunctive? Does the student of French recognize meaning contrasts between the *imparfait* and the *passé composé*? Based on the data obtained from tests of such knowledge, we often determine that the student is incapable (or capable, as the case may be) of successfully functioning at the level expected.

Although some of these tests have been improved in recent years by including more authentic testing components (see especially the Test of English as a Foreign Language—TOEFL), they should never be used as the *only* criteria supporting decisions that have such impact on students' lives. Evaluation of schools and individuals should be based on a *variety of assessment procedures*, with formal testing only one of them. Moreover, tests must be as free as possible of cultural, sexual, and linguistic bias (see especially Mohan, 1992).

The aim of this chapter is to explore various assessment instruments including language tests and types of formative evaluative tools such as portfolios and performance checklists. We will also look at even less formal means by which we can determine how our students are doing and whether or not they have achieved goals and standards in language development. Performance data will be discussed as they relate to decision-making and monitoring of student progress in the target language.

The same assessment instruments may or may not be applicable in the different environments where English is taught. Now that many "Englishes" exist around the world, tests need to reflect appropriate dialects or target languages.

LANGUAGE TESTS

Generally, language tests are given for one of three reasons:

- *placement*—as an instrument to place students appropriately in programs
- *diagnosis*—to diagnose students' problems in the target language with a reasonable amount of accuracy
- *achievement assessment*—to measure achievement, in other words, to what extent students have reached course or program objectives

Tests can also be categorized in other ways: *norm-referenced* versus *criterion-referenced*; *indirect* versus *direct*; and *discrete point* versus *integrative*.

Norm-Referenced Tests versus Criterion-Referenced Tests

Norm-referenced tests measure how a student does compared to how others do or have done on that same test. When administered on a large scale using accepted statistical procedures, we say that the test is "standardized." Results are given in terms of percentile rank. For example, let's say that a student scores in the 96th percentile. This means that the student did better than 96 percent of the test takers upon which the norm was based.

Criterion referencing, on the other hand, refers to how well the student has met specific objectives or a level of performance in a certain area. A driver's license test is an example of a criterion-referenced test; either you pass or you fail, based on agreed-upon standards. How you compare with others who have taken the test is not relevant.

Indirect Testing versus Direct Testing

Indirect testing is testing that does not examine the ability to perform in authentic situations. For example, a test of lexical items relating to history might be used to predict how well a student will be able to function in a history class with competent speakers of the target language. Most would agree that such a test would probably not be a very good predictor in this situation. Indirect tests do not test actual performance; rather they test enabling skills or microskills that, in theory, "add up" to what might constitute actual performance. *Direct* testing tests abilities actually used in a given context and will no doubt yield a better prediction. For example, tests that assess the ability to gather important ideas from a lecture, to write a summary or an essay expressing an opinion, or to read and understand academic written discourse will tell us more about how a student will perform in the classroom. Performance tasks, performance checklists, and observations in similar settings would also help inform our predictions of student performance.

Discrete Point Tests versus Integrative Tests

Discrete point tests grew out of a behavioristic/structural approach to language learning and teaching in which contrastive analysis was the main focus (see page 36). Discrete point tests examine the knowledge of specific elements in phonology, grammar, and vocabulary in order to determine proficiency in the isolated skill areas of listening, reading, speaking, and writing. Can the student distinguish between "pill" and "bill," for example? Can he or she recognize a past tense form or the present progressive? Does the student know the meaning of "chair" or "hippopotamus"?

    Integrative tests, on the other hand, grew out of a developmental/constructivist approach to language learning and teaching. Integrative tests examine a student's ability to use many skills simultaneously to accomplish a task. Can the student answer a question that is typical of conversation? Can he or she determine the meaning of a certain passage? Can the student tell a story that can be understood, or write an effective letter? Teachers interested in knowing what students can actually *do* in the target language ask these kinds of questions.

    These two kinds of tests are not dichotomous in nature but rather represent two ends on a continuum (see Figure 7.1).

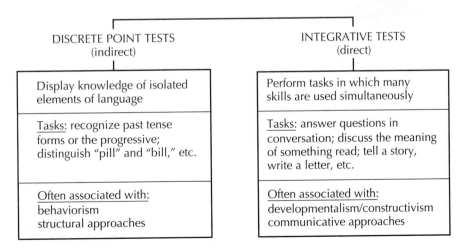

Figure 7.1 Discrete Point/Integrative Continuum

Most tests will fall much closer to one end of the continuum than the other. And to complicate matters, a test may be integrative in task but discrete point in evaluation. For example, the student may be required to write an essay (integrative in task), but the essay may be evaluated on specific errors in grammar and vocabulary (discrete point in evaluation). Generally speaking, tests that are integrative both in task and in evaluation probably tell us more about the proficiency levels of the students, whereas tests that are integrative in task and discrete point in evaluation may be best used for diagnostic purposes.

Pragmatic Tests

John Oller, Jr. (1979) described a type of integrative test called a *pragmatic* test, which he defined as an integrative test meeting two naturalness criteria:

1. The context must rely on a natural sequencing of events, and
2. a knowledge of the world and how it works must be relevant to its content (p. 70)[1]

Pragmatic tests, according to Oller, can include

- dictation (the teacher dictates sentences; the students write them down as they are being read)
- cloze procedures (passages are given in which every *n*th word is deleted; students are to supply the missing words)
- paraphrase recognition
- question answering
- oral interviews
- essay writing
- narration
- translation

Interestingly, pragmatic tests (even those of very different types) tend to correlate more highly with each other than they do with other kinds of tests. In other words, students who tend to do well on one pragmatic test will also tend to do well on others. Oller concluded that ". . . pragmatic testing seems to provide the most promise as a reliable, valid, and usable approach to the measurement of language ability" (1979, p. 71).

---

[1] An example of an integrative test that is not pragmatic might be the writing of isolated sentences to demonstrate the use of a rule in the target language. The task is highly integrative in that many skills are called for simultaneously but it is not pragmatic for two reasons: (1) the sentences lack a normal sequential context; and (2) extralinguistic data such as our perceptions of life, relationships between people, and so forth, are not important.

When choosing what kind of pragmatic test to use for general placement purposes, Oller's definition of such a test can be carried one step further. If we say that *the test tasks themselves have to approximate normal classroom communication situations*, then we would have to focus on only certain kinds of question-answering tasks, oral interviews, essay writing, paraphrasing, and narration. This is not to say that cloze activities and dictation have no value. On the contrary, they do. In fact, Oller has pointed out that both correlate very highly with other pragmatic tests of proficiency. They can be useful, particularly in providing diagnostic information—but they are not typical of normal classroom communication contexts.

DETERMINING PLACEMENT

If our goal in placing students is to divide students roughly according to proficiency levels into beginning, intermediate, and advanced classes (see definitions on pages 137–138), then a combination of the following might be all that is needed to make a reasonable determination.

- a listening comprehension task (perhaps using some simple requests requiring physical action—see Chapter 8)
- an oral interview (with pictures depicting universal experiences which may be referred to)
- some informal writing[2]
- a reading interpretation or paraphrasing section

In oral interviews, testers need to flow with the student, as in an authentic conversation, rather than ask a fixed set of questions designed to meet certain psychometric requirements. Anxiety levels are likely to be much lower in more natural, interactive situations and, although the evaluation will necessarily be highly subjective, the outcome will, in most cases, have greater applicability. Interaction between the tester and the student *can* indeed constitute real communication with varying degrees of conversational quality.[3]

A hierarchy of questions can be useful during the oral interview process. If a picture is used, the tester might begin with a general question that allows for elaboration ("What is happening in this picture?"). If there is little verbal response, the tester can move to something less general ("What do you see in this picture?"). If there is still little verbal response, the tester can move to a

---

[2] Here again, a picture depicting a universal experience might be used. In this case, the student is asked to write about the picture. What is happening in the picture? What does the student see? And so forth.

[3] Ross and Berwick (1992) present a study that indicates oral interviews can have characteristics that are typical of native-nonnative conversation. These characteristics need to be examined more carefully as they relate to authenticity. See also Van Lier, 1989, who addresses the same issue.

more specific, less difficult question ("What is this?" while pointing to an object in the picture). If necessary, the tester can go down even further on the hierarchy ("Is this a boat?" while pointing to a boat in the picture).

Much of what the tester says will depend upon what the student says. Student responses should be followed up conversationally. For example, if the tester asked, "What do you see in this picture?" and the students responds, "I see boat and water . . . I live by water," the tester might respond to the last part of this response: "Oh, you live by the water? Where?" or "It must be nice to live by the water. Do you swim there?"

The tester must be careful to match the difficulty of his or her language to that used by the student. If the tester is an experienced language teacher and is able to accommodate effectively, then we can be fairly certain that he or she knows intuitively the level at which the student is operating. Once the tester has reached the student's level of operation in each area (listening, speaking, writing, reading), the testing should be terminated and the next area of testing should be pursued.

A great deal of overlap will exist between one placement level and the next, and the levels may vary depending on the tasks. We needn't be disturbed by this. Whenever we deal with people in groups, the group will not be completely homogenous. Our goal should be to assemble groups that, while fairly diverse, will still be workable in that the "net" of input cast out will accommodate all the individuals. In particular, this will be true for interactional/participatory classrooms in which meaningful communication about relevant content is the focus.

Although some tests on the market may yield a more detailed diagnosis than most teacher-made tests, they often also lead to a focus on discrete point teaching in separate skill and subskill areas. In addition, the tests on the market are often expensive and longer than necessary. Teacher-made tests, on the other hand, may be less sophisticated and highly subjective, but they are usually short, easy to use, and flexible. Furthermore, they can include exactly those items that are appropriate to a specific situation and thus can be quite effective for the initial placement (and later reassessments) of students.

Typical Language Behaviors at Various Levels of Proficiency

The list in Table 7.1 may be useful in creating tests to place students in workable groups. Similar to the ACTFL (American Council on the Teaching of Foreign Languages) list of proficiency guidelines, it contains language behaviors typical of students at various levels of proficiency. Unlike the ACTFL list, however, it is fairly concise and easy to use, and the items within it are expressed positively. In other words, it focuses on what the students *can* do at each level rather than on what they *can't* do.

TABLE 7.1. TYPICAL LANGUAGE BEHAVIORS OF STUDENTS AT VARIOUS LEVELS OF PROFICIENCY DURING THE NATURAL PROCESS OF LANGUAGE ACQUISITION IN THE CLASSROOM

Beginning Student	Typical Behaviors
	Low
	Depends almost entirely on gestures, facial expressions, objects, pictures, a good phrase dictionary, and often a translator in an attempt to understand and to be understood Occasionally comprehends oral and written words and phrases
	Mid
	Begins to comprehend more, but only when speaker provides gestural clues; speaks slowly, uses concrete referents, and repeats Speaks very haltingly, if at all Shows increasing recognition of written segments May even be able to write short utterances
	High
	Is comprehending more and more in social conversation, but with difficulty Speaks in an attempt to meet basic needs, but remains hesitant; makes frequent errors in grammar, vocabulary, and pronunciation; often falls into silence Can read very simple text, including limited academic language Can write a little, but very restricted in structuring and vocabulary
Intermediate Student	
	Low
	(same as high-beginning above)
	Mid
	May experience a dramatic increase in social and academic vocabulary recognition, both oral and written Has difficulty with idioms generally Often knows what he or she wants to say but gropes for acceptable utterances, both oral and written Makes frequent errors in grammar, vocabulary, and pronunciation Is often asked to repeat and is frequently misunderstood, orally and in writing
	High
	Is beginning to comprehend substantial parts of normal conversation but often requires repetitions, particularly in academic discourse spoken at normal rates Is beginning to gain confidence in speaking ability; errors are common but less frequent Can read and write text that contains more complex vocabulary and structures; experiences difficulty with abstract language

Advanced Student

Low
(same as high-intermediate above)

Mid
Comprehends much conversational and academic discourse spoken at normal rates; sometimes requires repetition; idioms still present difficulty
Speaks more fluently but makes occasional errors; meaning is usually clear; at times, uses vocabulary or structures inappropriately
Reads and writes with less difficulty materials that are commensurate with his or her cognitive development; demonstrates some problems in grasping intended meaning

High
Comprehends normal conversational and academic discourse with little difficulty; most idioms are understood
Speaks fluently in most situations with fewer errors; meaning is generally clear but experiences some regression at times
Reads and writes both concrete and abstract materials; is able to manipulate the language with relative ease

Scoring Techniques

Teachers might want to set up a rating scale by which to judge students in the various proficiencies. Using four judges to rate each student yields an even more accurate placement, especially so, once the judges have had adequate experience in assessing performance (Hughes, 1989).

High rater reliability (both interrater and intrarater) is well documented in the literature (see Magnan, 1986; Shohamy, 1983; and Mullen, 1980). This means that several raters judging the same individual's performance tend to rate in very similar ways (interrater reliability) and the same rater tends to judge more than one performance by each individual in very similar ways (intrarater reliability). It is essential, however, that the raters be experienced in working interactively with second and/or foreign language students and that they be familiar with the type of scoring technique they are expected to use.

The two most commonly used scoring techniques are *holistic* and *analytic*.

Holistic Scoring

Holistic scoring requires the rater to give a single impression of the student's performance, such as "beginning," "intermediate," or "advanced" (to use the placement categories found in Table 7.1). Scorers might also rate performance by a single number—10, for example—that corresponds to a particular description of a performance level within a given category. A "10" given for a writing performance might suggest that a writer communicates effectively, organizes logically, demonstrates an effortless flow of ideas, and makes no semantic, syntactic, or mechanical errors. In contrast, a "1" might be the score for a writing performance that is very difficult to understand (no clear meaning comes through), where the ideas are listed with no logical connection between them, and where semantic, syntactic, or mechanical errors are so numerous as to interfere with what is being said.

Analytic Scoring

Analytic scoring, usually used for diagnostic rather than placement purposes, requires the rater to judge a variety of individual aspects within a general category. For example, a writing performance might include assessment of syntax, organization, vocabulary, mechanics, fluency, etc., and the writer's scores might vary—a "1" in syntax if he or she makes so many errors that they interfere with meaning, a "3" in vocabulary if the range of words is limited or words are misused but some grasp of the meaning is shown, and so forth. More specific categories within categories may be created. Mechanics, for example, might be broken down into spelling, punctuation, and capitalization, and each of these might receive a rating; organization might be broken down into overall organization, organization within paragraphs, and so on.

MAKING EVALUATION AN INTEGRAL PART OF THE CLASSROOM ENVIRONMENT

Many teachers and language programs are moving away from formal language testing as the sole criteria for placement, diagnosis, and achievement measurement. More and more, teachers are looking for assessment tools that are as authentic and direct as possible, and that involve students in tasks typical of a communicative classroom: expressing opinions, telling stories, asking and answering questions, creating meaning while reading and listening, role-playing, writing in journals, and so forth. Assessment in such situations is ongoing and instructive—in other words, formative as well as summative, process-focused rather than product-focused. Such testing provides data not only for the assessment of student progress, but also for the continual informal evaluation of teaching practices and entire programs.

Portfolios

One way to manage formative language assessment and make evaluation an integral part of the classroom environment is to use portfolios to gather student work, performance checklists, and other data. Portfolios house collections of representative student work and other performance data compiled over time. Pierce and O'Malley (1992) remind us that there is no "right" way to design and use portfolios. Rather, the design and use of portfolios should grow out of needs perceived in the specific classrooms for which they are being developed.

Portfolios may contain exemplary pieces of work as well as work in progress, with a separate section for each. Exemplary pieces can be selected by the student independently or by the student and teacher together. To select work for the portfolio, teachers might ask students, "What do you feel should go into this section of your portfolio? Why do you think this particular piece should go in? Why not that one?" In this way, even the selection of writing pieces itself becomes a learning experience, particularly if the classroom is participatory.

What else might be included in a portfolio? Any number of things, including:

- teacher observations and student self-evaluations
- performance checklists in all skill areas (see examples on pages 143–145)
- preparation notes for writing and discussion (graphic organizers, brainstorming devices, and the like)
- materials that the student has read
- summaries
- illustrations
- conferencing forms (see example relating to peer teaching in Chapter 15)
- writing samples of various kinds
- reading logs (students keep track of what they read and their reactions to what they read)
- performance logs (students note their reflections and intuitions about what they are doing while they are doing it)
- error analyses (see pages 36–37 and 64)
- oral production samples (transcribed or on cassettes)
- journal entries
- anecdotal notes based on teacher observation
- student learning journals (see page 266)
- questionnaires
- videotaped performances, and so forth.

Portfolios may be used in the classroom for the same three purposes of testing already mentioned: placement (or to be more precise in this case, *re*placement, assuming that the students have already been placed initially); diagnosis; and informally measuring achievement (often used to determine grades). In addition, the data in the portfolios can be used to provide ongoing feedback to students, their parents, and other teachers. The portfolios can even go with the students to the next teacher(s), the next grade level, or the next school.

A word of caution here: The teacher and students in the classroom should maintain control over the portfolios, their design and use. Moreover, the assessment itself, for whatever purpose, should be classroom-based in order to maintain the integrity of the portfolio. A portfolio is much more than simply a manila folder used to collect data for summative evaluation; it is an evolving thing that grows as the students grow and develop in the language learning process. It should not be reduced to rating scales and standardized pieces provided only to satisfy the requirements of large-scale testing programs.

As assessment instruments, portfolios can be instructive as well as evaluative within the classroom context. Moreover, they can allow students, teachers, administrators, and parents to see the progress that has been made over time.

Student/Teacher Conferencing

Students themselves are particularly pleased (and sometimes surprised) at the improvement they see in their work. By conferencing individually with the teacher about their portfolios, they often can come to their own conclusions about their progress, can see what their strengths are, and where they need to improve. Such conferences, if positive and nonthreatening, can be highly encouraging to students at all levels of proficiency.

The constructed dialogue below adapted from Richard-Amato and Hansen (1995—the *Teacher's Resource Book*) shows a teacher and an adolescent student conferencing about the student's progress in reading-related activities. Some of the discussion is focused on a story the students have recently read, "Atalanta," by Betty Miles, in *Worlds Together*, Richard-Amato and Hansen, 1995. The story is about a young girl who decides that she wants to determine her own future rather than have it determined for her by her father.

Sample Dialogue

TEACHER: Well, Alfredo, now that we look back over the last nine weeks, maybe together we can see what has happened here. I can see that you have done a lot of work and, of course, we have talked about much of this before. What do you think is your best work in all of this?

ALFREDO: I think the letter I wrote to Atalanta's father is the best. I put it on top there (*pointing to the portfolio*). I told her father that she had to make her own decisions about her future.

TEACHER: Why do you like that one so much?

ALFREDO: Well, I think that it is because I will have to do that in my own family. My dad wants me to be a doctor. But, you know, I think I really want to go into my own business. Like a store or something like that. I have talked to my dad about it, but he doesn't really listen.

TEACHER: I think you were wise to try to talk to your dad about this. Maybe if you keep talking, one of these times he will listen.

ALFREDO: Yeh. Maybe I shouldn't give up (*looks back at his paper*).

TEACHER: Are there any other reasons you like this piece? Maybe think about *how* you wrote it.

ALFREDO: Ummm . . . well . . . I don't know. . . .

TEACHER: I see here that you put in a lot of good words to take your reader from one idea to another. See, here you used "not only that" (*points to the paper*) to give Atalanta's father another reason for why she wants to follow her dream. Remember, we talked about using what we called "transitions" to go from one idea to another. You needed to show how ideas were connected.

ALFREDO: I remember. I really tried to do that there . . . you know, what you told me. And I think I did that on other things too. See. (*He points to another assignment.*)

TEACHER: Yes, I noticed that too. I see that you have written it down here as a strength. See here you wrote, "I am learning to use good transitions." Well, let's talk about some of the other improvements you have made, and then we'll talk about how you think you can improve in a few other areas. Maybe I can help you here . . . . First you start by telling me other places where you think you have improved . . . .

And so the discussion continues as both teacher and student talk about progress and areas for possible improvement. Together they lay out some strategies for the weeks to follow.

Performance Checklists

Performance checklists are very helpful in language assessment and, as mentioned above, can be made part of the portfolios. However, the criteria looked at should be structured as general performance objectives rather than discrete-skill items. The examples in Figures 7.2 and 7.3 (Richard-Amato and Hansen, 1995) are intended for use in the assessment of reading and writing at intermediate levels. They include instruments for self-assessment in both areas. Self-assessment is particularly helpful in participatory classrooms where students are encouraged to become autonomous learners as quickly as possible. Similar instruments, however, can be developed for teacher assessment of the student, based on observation.

Performance checklists such as those found in Figures 7.2 and 7.3 can be used to see informally what kinds of profiles emerge for each student and how they change longitudinally. Similar checklists developed by teachers can be used at other proficiency levels and for other skill areas such as listening and speaking.

Other Assessment Procedures

Anything the student accomplishes, either in or out of school can be made part of the assessment process if that process is pragmatic and ongoing.

Not only that, but the very informal discussions that take place between student and teacher can serve as checks for comprehension (in the case of

Name of Student _____ **Date** _____

Part I Check the box that best tells how often you do the things below:

When I read I . . .	usually	sometimes	not very often	comment
understand what the author is trying to say.				
understand most of the details.				
understand the vocabulary.				
read without stopping a lot.				
guess the meaning of a word by looking at the words around it.				
follow the way the author is moving through the text.				
connect what I read to my own life.				
connect what I read to what I already know.				
ask for help when I need it.				
After I read . . .				
I am able to tell someone else about what I read.				
I feel comfortable discussing the reading with others.				
I feel comfortable writing about what I have read.				

My strengths appear to be:

Areas where I can improve:

Figure 7.2. Self-Assessment Reading Checklist—Part I

Part II Put a check in front of the ones that answer the question best.

How many books did you read last month?

☐ a. none
☐ b. one
☐ c. two
☐ d. three
☐ e. more than three

What do you like to read the most? (You can check more than one.)

☐ a. books about science   ☐ g. books about the future
☐ b. books about math   ☐ h. books about the past
☐ c. books about history   ☐ i. books about the present
☐ d. books about animals   ☐ j. books about _____
☐ e. books about people   ☐ k. books about _____
☐ f. books about places

What kinds of reading do you like most? (You can check more than one.)

☐ a. short stories   ☐ f. essays that tell the opinions of others
☐ b. poetry   ☐ g. novels
☐ c. plays   ☐ h. textbooks
☐ d. autobiography   ☐ i. _____
☐ e. biography   ☐ j. _____

Where do you do most of your reading?

☐ a. in my classroom
☐ b. at home
☐ c. in the library
☐ d. _____

Which statements best tell how you feel about reading?

☐ a. Reading is one of my favorite activities.
☐ b. I am enjoying reading more and more.
☐ c. Reading is okay, but I like many other activities better.
☐ d. I dislike reading and read only when I have to.
☐ e. I would like reading more if I could read better.

Figure 7.2. Self-Assessment Reading Checklist—Part II

Name of Student _____ Date _____

Check the box that best tells how often you are able to do the things below:

When I write I . . .	usually	sometimes	not very often	comment
plan beforehand the main things I want to say.				
say what I want to say clearly.				
organize my ideas so others can follow my thinking.				
am able to develop paragraphs.				
use bridges (transitions) to go from one idea to the next.				
use enough details to make myself understood.				
feel comfortable talking about my writing with my teacher.				
feel comfortable talking about my writing with my classmates.				
rewrite to make my ideas easier to understand.				
use words that say exactly what I want to say.				
spell correctly.				
punctuate and capitalize correctly.				

My strengths appear to be:

Areas where I can improve:

Figure 7.3. Self-Assessment Writing Checklist

reading and listening) or as a means for finding out information about how the student is doing in all areas of language performance. A simple request, such as "Tell me about the book," and questions such as

- "What do you think this story (or essay) is all about?"
- "What have you learned about _____ ?"
- "Do you feel comfortable writing about _____ ?"
- "Are you having any problems with _____ ?"

will tell you a lot about how the student is doing and can be very helpful in completing the performance checklists. Moreover, knowing that the teacher is interested in what they are working on at the moment or what they have accomplished in the past can be extremely motivating to students.

Observing student behavior and providing anecdotal data are essential in an informed evaluation of student progress in the various areas of language performance. Has the student indicated that he or she has knowledge of a selected topic for writing? Is the student generally understood by other students when speaking? Do you usually understand what the student is saying orally and in writing? Do the student's questions about something read reveal logical thinking in the target language? Does the student appear to understand what you and others say? The answers to these and similar questions (although subjective in determination) will be extremely beneficial in making decisions during the evaluative process.

STANDARDS FOR ESL AND FOREIGN LANGUAGE TEACHING

Standards specify what students should know and what they should be able to do as a result of instruction in the target language. If carefully selected and judiciously implemented, they can help ensure that a program is including relevant skills in personal, sociopolitical, and academic communication, both written and oral.

Upon first blush, standards, particularly those proposed by forces outside the classroom, appear to fly in the face of participatory language teaching. It is important that standards be considered *guidelines* and that they be universal enough to fit into the agendas of most students and their teachers. Discussing the standards with students who are proficient enough to talk about them meaningfully is essential in establishing a participatory language classroom. In such a classroom, student input is crucial to decisions about selection of standards and how the standards can best be achieved. Self-assessment must also be an important part of the process in order for the students eventually to achieve learner autonomy (see also McNamara and Deane, 1995; and Smolen, Newman, Wathen, and Lee, 1995).

ESL Standards

In 1997, TESOL published *ESL Standards for Pre-K–12*[4] after receiving considerable input from people in the field (see its history in Gómez, 2000). Since that time, we have witnessed a flurry of textbooks, workshops, and demonstrations to help teachers and administrators across the nation infuse the standards as guidelines into the curriculum at all levels.

Three basic goals inform the nine standards (see Figure 7.4).

Goal 1: To Use English to Communicate in Social Settings

Standard 1: Students will use English to participate in social interaction.

Standard 2: Students will interact in, through, and with spoken and written English for personal expression and enjoyment.

Standard 3: Students will use learning strategies to extend their communicative competence.

Goal 2: To Use English to Achieve Academically in All Content Areas

Standard 1: Students will use English to interact in the classroom.

Standard 2: Students will use English to obtain, process, construct, and provide subject matter information in spoken and written form.

Standard 3: Students will use appropriate learning strategies to construct and apply academic knowledge.

Goal 3: To Use English in Socially and Culturally Appropriate Ways

Standard 1: Students will use the appropriate language variety, register, and genre according to audience, purpose, and setting.

Standard 2: Students will use nonverbal communication appropriate to audience, purpose, and setting.

Standard 3: Students will use appropriate learning strategies to extend their sociolinguistic and sociocultural competence.

Source: TESOL (1997, pp. 9-10).

Figure 7.4. ESL Standards for pre-K–12 students

(From *ESL Standards for Pre-K–12* by TESOL. Copyright © 1997 by TESOL Inc. Reproduced with permission of TESOL Inc. in the format Trade Book via Copyright Clearance Center.)

The first goal concerns English as it is used for basic social and personal functions (including interpersonal communication). The second goal focuses on English and how it is used for academic functions across the subject areas. And the third goal involves the cultural uses of English in social/personal and

---

[4] The ESL Standards and Assessment Project team from the Center for Applied Linguistics under the direction of Deborah Short has spearheaded the effort to give the standards a substantial role in curriculum development.

academic settings. (I would modify this to include sociopolitical objectives as well.) The third goal includes the ways in which English is used for more subtle functions (expressing disappointment, communicating humor, etc.), the registers and varieties of English used in different settings, and so forth.

The ESL standards themselves are accompanied by:

1. *descriptors*: categories of behaviors used to demonstrate that a specific standard has been accomplished;
2. *progress indicators* (clustered by grade-level): activities that students can participate in to show that they are indeed progressing toward the standard;
3. *vignettes*: scenarios presenting the given standard in an instructional action sequence;
4. *discussions*: explanations of the vignettes and how each works toward accomplishing the given standard.

Language assessment of various types can be tied into the standards and used to inform teachers, students and their parents, school districts, and other stakeholders about the extent to which students are meeting them. But we need to be careful. First, clustering progress indicators by grade-level is problematic in that certain kinds of learning do not necessarily parallel grade-level or age. And second, although standards used as guidelines can greatly improve the education of English Language Learners (ELLs), there may be dangers for these students when high-stakes decisions are based on tests that determine how well students meet the standards (see Irujo, 2000b). The challenge, according to Irujo, is "... to use standards-based instruction as a way to improve education for students whose first language is not English, rather than having it become another means of excluding them" (p. 7).

Two ways have been identified in which data can be obtained to test standards within the classroom (Katz, 2000):

- traditional testing
- classroom-based assessments that are part of the instructional process

Katz points out that students in today's classrooms need more complex, context-situated testing, encompassing both individual and group performance. She goes on to say that the tests should comprise multiple assessments that are authentic, dynamic, and standards-referenced, and that these tests should not be used to rank students (as traditional tests often did) but rather to chart each student's progress. She suggests that the data collected over time could include writing samples, group observations, reading inventories, oral proficiency tests, and the like, at different times during the year.

Katz also suggests several steps for aligning the standards with the assessments used to determine to what extent they have been achieved. Her steps include deciding:

1. which standards should be assessed;
2. how these standards can be approached through specific activities and in specific contexts (see also Chapter 15 in this volume);
3. whether the assessment tool will be created or selected from ones already developed;
4. what the outcome levels will be; and
5. how it will be determined that the tool used is actually measuring the standard it is supposed to measure.

If the stakes are especially high, Katz points out that great care needs to be taken in choosing the instruments used and in gathering corroborating evidence by other means.

Standards intended for mainstreamed students are often tested in large-scale assessments usually given to the majority of students at the program, school district, or state levels. However, according to Gottlieb (2000), such large-scale instruments are generally not valid in the case of ELLs[5]. Her concern is that:

> Unfortunately, many ESOL [English to Speakers of Other Languages] students are subjected to local and state assessments under inequitable conditions, and ESL and bilingual educators must conform to assessment policies that run counter to research and best practices. Still worse, when the stakes for an assessment are high, ESOL students may pay dire consequences for results that do not truly reflect their content knowledge (p. 171).

Gottlieb argues that, because these students are in the process of learning English, they should *only* be held accountable for their performance on standards that have been specifically developed for them—and, I would add, with their input whenever possible. Moreover, Gottlieb recommends that the instruments used contain textual information including maps, pictures, diagrams, graphic organizers, etc., and that the tasks and activities reflect the kinds of instruction these students have received in their classes.

Foreign Language Standards[6]

In 1996, a joint effort of the American Council on the Teaching of Foreign Languages (ACTFL), the American Association of Teachers of Spanish and Portuguese (AATSP), the American Association of Teachers of French (AATF), and The American Association of Teachers of German (AATG) resulted in the

---

[5] Cummins (1981a) concluded that district, state, and nationwide tests are generally not good instruments to use with students learning English. Even students who have been learning English in school for about three years perform about one standard deviation below grade norms in academic English skills.

[6] From the ACTFL web site (2001).

publication of *Standards for Foreign Language Learning: Preparing for the 21st Century*. The standards (finalized in 1999) were modeled on the national standards for other subjects such as math and English and focus on five goals (see Figure 7.5).

Most of the instruments used in the past to test students on their ability to function in their new language were standardized tests (norm referenced). One such test was the College Board Achievement batteries that rewarded students who had developed impressive vocabularies and had obtained a mastery over the discrete points of language. Additionally, the tests measured students' abilities to comprehend written text. Sometimes the students'

Goal 1 Communication: Communicate in languages other than English
Standard 1.1: Students engage in conversations, provide and obtain information, express feelings and emotions, and exchange opinions.
Standard 1.2: Students understand and interpret written and spoken language on a variety of topics.
Standard 1.3: Students present information, concepts, and ideas to an audience of listeners or readers on a variety of topics.

Goal 2 Cultures: Gain knowledge and understanding of other cultures
Standard 2.1: Students demonstrate an understanding of the relationship between the practices and perspectives of the culture studied.
Standard 2.2: Students demonstrate an understanding of the relationship between the products and perspectives of the culture studied.

Goal 3 Connections: Connect with other disciplines and acquire information
Standard 3.1: Students reinforce and further their knowledge of other disciplines through the foreign language.
Standard 3.2: Students acquire information and recognize the distinctive viewpoints that are available only through the foreign language and its cultures.

Goal 4 Comparisons: Develop insight into the nature of language and culture
Standard 4.1: Students demonstrate understanding of the nature of language through comparisons of the language studied and their own.
Standard 4.2: Students demonstrate understanding of the concept of culture through comparisons of the cultures studied and their own.

Goal 5 Communities: Participate in multilingual communities at home and around the world
Standard 5.1: Students use the language both within and beyond the school setting.
Standard 5.2: Students show evidence of becoming life-long learners by using the language for personal enjoyment and enrichment.

Figure 7.5. Foreign Language Standards
(Copyright © 2001. American Council on the Teaching of Foreign Languages.)

listening skills were assessed through the use of recorded speech (see also Valette, 1997).

In 1986, the American Council on the Teaching of Foreign Languages (ACTFL) developed performance standards in speaking, listening, reading, and writing. The students' abilities to communicate orally were and still are assessed using the Oral Proficiency Interview (criterion referenced) and similar tests in which a tester conducts a very structured interview to determine the student's oral proficiency by comparing the student's speech to strict guidelines. In recent years, task forces have been working on language-specific standards and hope that these standards and the Standards for Foreign Language Learning listed above will lead to greater cultural awareness and to the creative use of language in the classroom.

SUMMARY

Several types of language assessment have been presented and discussed in this chapter: norm-referenced versus criterion referenced tests; indirect versus direct tests; discrete point tests versus integrative tests. Also included in the discussion was the pragmatic test, a type of integrative test in which two naturalness criteria are relevant to the testing situation: a normal sequential context and extralinguistic data involving perceptions of life, relationships between people, and so forth.

Language assessment does not have to be a mysterious and remote activity accomplished in isolation from what is done in classrooms. The way we test does not have to be that much different from the way we teach; in fact, assessment at its best can become *an integral part of what happens in the classroom.*

Portfolios are a means by which testing can become part of the instructional process. Using portfolios, we can collect performance data to use as a basis for ongoing language assessment. Portfolios can include student work, self-evaluations, performance checklists, oral production samples (transcribed or on cassettes or video), anecdotal records, and so forth, gathered over time. Portfolios can be used to inform decisions made, not only about students and how they are doing in our classrooms, but about our own instructional practices. By making language assessment an integral part of our classroom environment, we are making evaluation a formative, authentic, direct, and pragmatic process.

Standards for second and foreign language students can be helpful in guiding curriculum development and assessment within language programs. But we must take great care in applying them to make sure that they are not used as strait jackets for curriculum planning. Moreover, we should ensure that students are involved in the selection of standards and in their implementation if they are to be compatible with participatory teaching. If used appropriately, standards can be invaluable in ensuring that programs are giving students the opportunity to develop important skills critical to their success and empowerment.

READINGS, REFLECTION, AND DISCUSSION

Suggested Readings and Reference Materials

Brown, J.D. (1998). *New ways of classroom assessment*. Alexandria, VA: TESOL. Alternative means of assessment are described in detail in this book. Included are such topics as portfolios, journals, peer and self-assessment, group assessment, making grading easier, and ways to evaluate written and oral skills.

Ekbatani, G. and Pierson, H. eds. (2000). *Learner-Directed Assessment in ESL*. Mahwah, NJ: Erlbaum. The focus of this book is on authentic second-language assessment which serves as a link to instruction. Portfolio assessment and self-assessment are among the alternative procedures explored. The validity and the reliability of various means of alternative assessment are discussed.

Genesee, F. and Upshur, J. (1996). *Classroom-based evaluation in second language education*. Cambridge: Cambridge University Press. This easy-to-read book for language teachers discusses classroom-based assessment and how it can be used to improve both learning and instruction. It includes a framework for evaluation, information collection, observations, portfolio use, questionnaires, various types of tests, objectives-referenced testing, designing test tasks, interpreting scores, and using standardized tests.

Mohan, B. (1992). What are we really testing? In P. Richard-Amato and M. A. Snow, eds. *The multicultural classroom: Readings for content-area teachers*. White Plains, NY: Longman, pp. 258–270. The author talks about the problem of content validity in relation to a variety of factors. He offers examples to illustrate how language and content tests overlap and may be confused and the ways in which language tests may be culturally biased. He points out that many such tests may be, in fact, tests of cultural knowledge.

O'Malley, J.M. and Pierce, L. V. (1996). *Authentic assessment for English language learners: Practical approaches for teachers*. Reading, MA: Addison-Wesley. This sensitively written text discusses many types of assessment that are relevant to classroom goals and instruction. As part of the assessments, students perform, create, use higher levels of thinking, integrate knowledge and skills, explore alternatives, and engage in other pragmatic tasks typically associated with good teaching.

Short, D. (1993). Assessing integrated language and content instruction. *TESOL Quarterly*, 27(4):627–656. A wealth of ideas are presented for assessing student performance in classes in which language and content are integrated. It includes a discussion (including advantages and disadvantages) of assessment matrices, skill and concept checklists, anecdotal records, inventories of various kinds, performance-based tasks, portfolios, etc., with examples in several categories.

Snow, M.A. (Ed.) (2000) *Implementing the ESL standards for pre-K–12 students through teacher education*. Arlington, VA: TESOL. An important resource for state administrators, school districts, programs, and teachers in that it contains important information about the history leading to the standards in the first place, their purpose, and how they can be used for curriculum development and assessment, both classroom-based and large-scale. Sample forms are included to aid planning and implementation.

TESOL (1997). *ESL standards for pre-K–12 Students*. Alexandria, VA: TESOL. Discusses the nine ESL standards (see Figure 7.4), behaviors to observe when evaluating, tasks for students to perform, and illustrative vignettes. See also the following titles published by TESOL:

> *Integrating the ESL Standards into Classroom Practice* (2000):
>
>> *Grades Pre-K–2*, Betty Ansin Smallwood, Editor
>>
>> *Grades 3–5*, Katharine Davies Samway, Editor
>>
>> *Grades 6–8*, Suzanne Irujo, Editor
>>
>> *Grades 9–12*, Barbara Agor, Editor
>
> *Scenarios for ESL Standards-Based Assessment* (2001)

Questions and Projects for Reflection and Discussion

1. What might you include in a test for placing students in a language program? Create a short test that would be useful to you in a specified situation. Explain how you would use it to determine levels.

2. How would you construct a test for diagnostic purposes? How might you use it? You may want to consider the discussion of error analysis in Chapter 3, pages 36–37 and 64.

3. Portfolios, as evaluative instruments, have been criticized for being "messy," much too subjective, and overly time-consuming. What would you say to educators making such judgments? Are any of these criticisms justified, in your opinion? Write about it in your journal.

4. If you wanted to use portfolios in a typical classroom in which you might find yourself, what kinds of performance data would you include? Design a plan for the use of portfolios in a hypothetical classroom. First decide who the students are and what their goals might be for learning the target language. Share your plan with a small group. Ask for their feedback.

5. How important do you think standards are for teaching language minority students? To what extent would you want them to guide your assessment procedures? How might you go about incorporating them into the way you evaluate students? Do you see any possible dangers in their use? If so, how might these dangers be avoided?

6. Now that you have reached the end of Part I, write a paper in which you describe your language teaching philosophy. Address such issues as your general approach(es); the role of grammar; language learning and teaching

strategies; integrating skills such as listening, reading, writing, and speaking; affective factors; language assessment and standards; etc. Draw your ideas from your own experience, prior knowledge, and what you have learned through current reading and discussion. Offer a well-developed rationale for each of your principles. Keep in mind that the principles you incorporate today may not be the ones you will adhere to tomorrow. Much will depend upon the knowledge you gain in the future and upon the experiences you have.

PART II

Exploring Methods and Activities: What Can We Learn?

Methods are defined generally as sets of strategies and techniques accompanied by an articulated underlying theory. Teachers' desires to know about methods often reflect their need for something concrete which through practice can inform their theories. Most do not plan to slavishly adhere to the tenets and practices of established methods, but instead to use them as interesting sources from which to draw in developing their own methodologies and local practice. For some they are a starting place. Eventually caring, informed teachers transcend the daily procedures of the classroom in the realization that dialectical relationships and power sharing are essential to student and teacher empowerment. Methods can be considered organic; their selected components can germinate, grow, and change within each individual teacher in each classroom situation.

Parts I and II of this book influence each other bidirectionally: theory informs practice; practice informs theory. Together the two create *praxis* (page 13). See especially the questions and projects suggested at the end of each chapter. The activities described within the chapters in Part II require high-quality input, negotiation for meaning, and creative language production in nonthreatening environments as the students move toward participatory learning experiences. These activities are intended for elementary, secondary, and/or university second or foreign language programs (see Chapter 17 for descriptions of program types and Part IV for "Programs in Action"). However, many activities, when given modified content, can be used in language programs for special purposes such as preparing students for various technical occupations and tasks. And although a majority of the activities are recommended for specific age and proficiency levels, most can be adapted to other levels (see pages 326–328 for sample adaptations).

The particular methods or activities chosen for specific programs will depend upon several factors: the student, the situation, and teacher/student preference. Not all the methods and activities are for everyone and every situation. They must be chosen carefully if they are to become part of a workable program (see Chapter 15). Most activities can be successfully integrated with grammar lessons when such lessons are appropriate (see Chapter 3). However, it is important that most programs keep the main focus on meaningful communication and encourage student participation whenever possible. *If students do not have input into the decision-making process once they have the ability to do so, and if their languages and cultures are not valued, then the methods and activities, no matter how creative, will fall short of their goal.*

CHAPTER 8

Physical Involvement in the Language Learning Process

If the training starts with explicit learning such as audio-lingual that emphasizes error-free production, correct form, and conscious rule learning, the risk is that most children and adults will give up before even reaching the intermediate level.[1]

J. Asher, 1972

QUESTIONS TO THINK ABOUT

1. Recall a time when you studied another language. To what extent were you involved physically in learning that language? Share the practices you considered best. Do you wish you had been involved to a greater or a lesser extent with physical activities?

2. Think of some examples of children's physical involvement while learning their first language. To what extent does learning a first language depend upon such involvement?

3. How might it be possible for older children, teenagers, and/or adults to become physically involved with learning another language? What might its effects be?

---

[1] Asher (1972) based his opinion on the early conclusions of Carroll (1960) and Lawson (1971).

THE TÒTAL PHYSICAL RESPONSE

In the 1960s, James Asher first offered the total physical response (TPR) as one alternative to the audiolingual approach which was popular at the time. His method, based on techniques advocated much earlier by Harold and Dorothy Palmer (1925), involves giving commands to which students react. For example, the teacher says, "Point to the door," and all the students point to the door. The imperatives bring the target language alive by making it comprehensible and, at the same time, fun. The students act with their bodies as well as their brains—in other words, with their total beings. Thus, the cognitive process of language acquisition is synchronized with and partially facilitated by the movements of the body.

Asher looked at the process by which children master the first language to justify his approach. Mother or caretaker directs the child to look at an object, to pick it up, or to put it in a specific place. Production is naturally delayed until the child's listening comprehension is developed and the child is ready to speak. Thus the child gradually becomes aware of language and what it means in terms of the environment and the situation.

Using total physical response strategies, second and foreign language students at all ages can remain silent until ready to speak, usually after about ten hours of instruction. At first they jump, run, sing, or do whatever is necessary to show that the request has been comprehended. Advancing gently, at their own rates, the students' aim is to achieve a productive command of the target language. Through this process, they evolve from silent comprehenders of the language to full participants in its nuances. After a few weeks of instruction, a typical class might consist of approximately 70 percent listening comprehension, 20 percent speaking, and 10 percent reading and writing (Asher, Kusudo, and de la Torre, 1974).

The commands are given to the whole class, to small groups, and to individuals. Once students have acquired basic commands, they perform double actions such as, "Walk to the window and open it." The teacher or another student demonstrates the appropriate behavior first, making the actions very clear. Then individual students in the class carry out the request. If they do not respond at first, the teacher repeats both the words and the demonstration rather than simply repeating the words. Gradually, the requests gain complexity as the students become more proficient. For example, the teacher might say, "When Lamm opens the window, Maria will run to the door and close it."

The students, when ready, move into the production phase by volunteering to give the commands while the teacher and other students carry them out. The students are allowed to make mistakes when they first begin to speak; thus anxiety is lowered. It is expected that their speech will gradually take on the shape of the teacher's as they gain confidence with their new language.

Although Asher recommended a grammatical sequencing of the materials, the lessons themselves are not focused on grammar; instead they are focused on meaning. The grammar is expected to become internalized inductively. Certain forms are more suited than others to the method and are repeated over and over during the natural course of events.

Concerning the method itself, Asher admitted that a few teachers remain skeptical of his basic approach for one reason or another. Although some have accepted TPR for the teaching of simple action verbs, they have questioned its use for teaching the nonphysical elements of language—past and future tenses, abstract words, and function words. To defuse such skepticism, Asher (1972) and Asher, Kusudo, and de la Torre (1974) offered a number of studies such as the two field tests described below.

The first field test involved adults who had taken about 32 hours of German with an instructor, using the total physical response. It was found that most of the linguistic forms of German could indeed be incorporated into the commands. Tenses were combined by using clauses in sentences such as "While John is closing the door, Annette will turn out the light." Function words were not a major problem because they were ubiquitous and were acquired naturally through repetition in a variety of situations. Abstract words such as "honor" and "justice" were manipulated as though they were objects. The words were written on cards. The instructor gave commands in German such as "Andy, pick up 'justice' and give it to Sue."

Although the experimental group had had only 32 hours of training, it did significantly better in listening comprehension than a group of college students who had received 75 to 150 hours of audiolingual/grammar-translation instruction in German. Interestingly, the experimental group, even though it had no systematic instruction in reading, did as well as the control group which had received such training. Asher (1972) surmised that if students can internalize listening comprehension of a second language, they can make the transition to oral production, reading, and writing with a fair amount of ease.

The second field test reported by Asher, Kusudo, and de la Torre (1974) involved undergraduate college students in beginning Spanish. After about ten hours of concentration in listening comprehension, the students were invited to switch roles with the teacher. As students became ready to do so, they assumed the teacher role and gave the commands for brief periods of time. Reading and writing were also accomplished at the student's individual pace. The teacher wrote on the board any phrases or words that students wished to see in writing. Skits were created and presented, and problem solving was attempted, all in the target language.

After 45 hours of instruction, the experimental group was compared with the control groups, whose hours of instruction ranged from 75 to 200. The group exposed to the total physical response exceeded all other groups in listening skills for stories. After 90 hours of instruction, the group was given a form of the Pimsleur Spanish Proficiency Test that was intended for students who had completed about 150 hours of college instruction, audiolingual style. Even with almost no direct instruction in reading and writing, the students were beyond the 75th percentile for level I and beyond the 65th percentile for level II.

According to Asher, the studies clearly indicated that TPR training produced better results than the audiolingual method. He attributed the success to the fact that TPR utilizes implicit learning, whereas the audiolingual approach relies on explicit learning. These two concepts roughly parallel Krashen's acquisition/learning distinction (see Chapter 2). However, Asher suggested that an alternative model of teaching might begin the instruction in the implicit mode and end it in the explicit mode. He felt that a student's skills at later levels may be advanced to the point at which teaching rules and correcting errors may be beneficial.

Even though Asher (1993, 1996) considered his method the main classroom activity rather than a supplement, he recommended that it be used in combination with other techniques such as skits, role play, and problem solving.

The commands themselves may be arranged around topics of interest: parts of the body, numbers, spatial relationships, colors, shapes, emotions, clothes, giving directions, and so forth. Asher recommended that only a certain number of new concepts be given at one time, depending upon the students' levels of understanding.

Below is a list of a few typical commands to use with beginners.[2] These may be modified, expanded, or combined in a variety of ways. Some possibilities for modification are suggested in parentheses.

Stand up.	Giggle.
Sit down.	Make a face.
Touch the floor (desk).	Flex your muscles.
Raise your arm (leg).	Shrug your shoulders.
Put down your arm (leg).	Wave to me (to _____).
Pat your cheek (back, arm, stomach, chest).	*(name of student)*
	Tickle your side.
Wipe your forehead (face, chin, elbow).	Clap your hands.
	Point to the ceiling (door).
Scratch your nose (knee, ankle, heel).	Cry.
	Mumble.
Massage your arm (neck).	Talk.
Turn your head to the right (left).	Whisper.
	Hum.
Drum your fingers.	Stand up.
Wet your lips.	Hop on one foot (on the other foot, on both feet).
Pucker your lips.	
Blow a kiss.	Step forward (backward, to the side).
Cough.	Lean backward (toward me, away from me).

---

[2] These commands were adapted from a mimeographed sheet (author unknown) distributed by the Jefferson County Schools, Lakewood, Colorado.

Sneeze.	Make a fist.
Shout your name ("help").	Shake your fist (head, hand, foot, hips).
Spell your name.	_____ , walk to the door (window).
Laugh.	*(name of student)*
Stretch.	_____ , turn on (off) the lights (radio).
Yawn.	*(name of student)*
Sing.	

Asher intended a lighthearted, relaxed approach to his method, one in which students are encouraged to take on some of the playfulness of childhood, a time when learning language could easily be made a game and "losing oneself" in it a natural consequence. Therefore, "barking" commands, army-sergeant style, would not be appropriate. Instead, the commands should be given in an easy, nondemanding manner.

A sample lesson for rank beginners might look like this:

The teacher has one or two volunteer students, peer teachers, or lay assistants (see Chapter 15) come to the front of the room. They are offered chairs through gesture. They sit in them. The teacher also sits in a chair. He or she gives the following commands:

1. Stand up. (The teacher demonstrates by standing.)
2. Sit down. (The teacher demonstrates by sitting.) (two repetitions of 1 and 2) .
3. Stand up. (The teacher motions to the two volunteer students or teacher assistants to stand up. They stand.)
4. Sit down. (The teacher motions to them to sit down. They sit down.) (two repetitions of 3 and 4)

The teacher turns to the class.

5. Stand up (motions to everyone to stand up and they all stand).
6. Sit down (motions to everyone to sit down and they all sit). (two repetitions of 5 and 6)

The teacher compliments with a simple "good" at various points and with a lot of smiles. Then he or she continues by giving the commands minus the gestural clues to see if the students are indeed comprehending the words. Gradually other commands such as "step forward" followed by "step backward" are added, following similar procedures. And on it goes until the students have a rather large repertoire of commands that they can comprehend. Often the order of the commands is varied to ensure that students are not simply memorizing a sequence of actions.

Some teachers like to give commands to volunteers or to the whole class (as in the example above) rather than single out individuals. They feel that anxiety is lowered if students are allowed some anonymity, especially at the very beginning levels.[3] In addition, they often prefer to use the method in small

---

[3] It is interesting to note that even those students who only observed seem to internalize the commands (see Asher, 1996).

doses, perhaps for fifteen minutes or so three or four times a week at beginning levels. Otherwise, the technique may become too tiring for the students and for the teacher. Also, if it is used extensively, there is the danger that the students will get the impression that the main function of the target language is to give commands. For these reasons, it probably makes sense to combine this approach with other kinds of activities that *reinforce* what is being taught, such as cutting and pasting, drawing, painting, chanting, story telling, singing, and other activities (see later chapters). Another reinforcement is to incorporate key concepts during a common classroom ritual such as grouping students for other activities (see also pages 233–234 and 254–255). For instance, the teacher can reinforce colors: "All students wearing the color red come to table 1; all students wearing blue go to table 2." Or, using the same method, the teacher can reinforce months of the year: "All students born in May or June come to table 1." The teacher can continue reshuffling students by giving similar commands until each group has the necessary number of students.

Below are some TPR-based activities that can readily be adapted to almost any age level (provided the students are cognitively ready).[4] Possible alternative words are given in parentheses.

Total Physical Response-Based Activities

THE POINTING GAME

With a small group of students, use a collection of pictures such as those one might find in a mail-order catalog to reinforce concepts already taught. Ask students to point to various specific body parts (a head, an arm), to colors (something green), or to items of clothing (a dress, a sweater).

IDENTIFYING EMOTIONS

After the class has acquired simple commands such as "cry" or "laugh," pictures are placed across the front of the room of people clearly demonstrating such emotional reactions. Students are asked to take the picture of a person displaying a specific reaction (someone crying, someone laughing). Later this same procedure is extended to other descriptions of emotions, perhaps more subtle ones (someone who is sad, someone who is angry).

DRESS THE PAPER DOLL

A large paper doll man, woman, or child with a set of clothes is made and mounted on a bulletin board. Velcro is used to make the paper clothes stick to the figure. Students are asked to place various items of clothing on it. Concepts such as checked, polka-dotted, and striped are taught in the same manner, along with a variety of fabrics and textures (wool, cotton, velvet, or rough, smooth, soft). For teaching the fabrics and textures, different kinds of materials are cut in the shape of the paper clothes and glued to them.

---

[4] I would like to thank Sylvia Cervantes, Carol Gorenberg, and Cyndee Gustke for the basic notions involved in "Dress the Paper Doll," "Working with Shapes," and "Following Recipes."

MANIPULATING RODS

Rods of various colors such as those used in Gattegno's Silent Way provide realia for teaching numbers, spatial relationships, colors, and the like (take the *blue* rod, take *three* red rods, put the blue rod *beside* a red rod). Rods are used also in advancing students to more complex structures (take a red rod and give it to the teacher).

BOUNCING THE BALL

Concepts such as numbers, days of the week, and months of the year are acquired or reinforced simply by having the students bounce a ball (Richard-Amato, 1983, p. 397). For instance, each one of twelve students in a circle represents a month of the year. The "March" student is directed to bounce the ball and call out "March, June." The student who is "June" has to catch the ball before it bounces a second time. Conscious attention is centered on the act of catching the ball while the language itself is being internalized at a more or less peripheral level of consciousness.

WORKING WITH SHAPES

Another idea is to cut squares, rectangles, triangles, and circles out of various colors of construction paper and distribute them to the students. Shapes (hold up the triangle), colors (hold up the green triangle), and numbers (hold up three triangles) are being taught or reinforced. Ordinal numbers are also introduced by placing several shapes in various positions along the board. A student is asked to place the green triangle in the third position or the eighth position, for example. Each student in the class is then given a small box of crayons or colored pencils and a hand-out with rows of squares, rectangles, triangles, and circles drawn on it. Commands such as "Find the first row of circles. Go to the fifth circle. Color it red." are given to reinforce not only the shape, but the ordinal number and the color.

As a follow-up, students cut out of magazines pictures of objects that have shapes similar to those mentioned above. Another follow-up is to have students cut the various shapes from colored poster board, newsprint, or wallpaper. Have them arrange the shapes into a collage.

FOLLOWING RECIPES

At later levels, making holiday rice cakes, baking valentine cookies, or preparing enchiladas provide a physical experience and also involve students in the cultures of other countries and those within the United States. First display all the ingredients for any given recipe, and introduce each item, one by one. Then present each student with a written recipe. An extra-large version to which you and the students can refer can be placed at the front of the room. While you or a student reads the recipe, other students measure, mix the ingredients, and so on. As a follow-up, students bring in favorite recipes to share. These are put together to form a class recipe book to which other recipes can be added.

INFORMATION GAPS

Information gaps (Allwright, 1979; Johnson, 1979) are created in which one student has information that another does not have but needs. One student gives a set of directions or commands to another student, who carries them out to meet some stated goal. For example,

Student A goes to the board, and Student B goes to the back of the room and faces the back wall, with a drawing in hand (simple geometric shapes usually work best at first). Student B then gives step-by-step directions to Student A so that A can reproduce the drawing. This activity is followed by a debriefing if the directions have not produced a configuration fairly close to the original. If the directions have been written down by a teacher assistant as they are given, the specific steps can be analyzed to see how they might be clarified (Richard-Amato, 1983, p. 399).

An alternative is to have Students A and B seated across from one another at a table with a divider between them, high enough so Student B cannot see what Student A is doing. Next give Student A some blocks of various sizes, shapes, and colors. Student B gets a duplicate set of blocks. Student A then is asked to build an original configuration or structure with the blocks. While Student A is accomplishing the task, he or she gives directions to Student B so that B can build a similar configuration or structure. Again, a debriefing takes place if there has been a breakdown in the communication.

Although the advantages are obvious, there appear to be a few potential drawbacks in using Asher's method. The first concerns the teaching of abstract concepts. Although words such as *honor* and *justice* might be briefly remembered through use of Asher's technique, it is difficult to see how their meanings would become clear unless they are used repeatedly in some sort of meaningful context. Asher has attempted to remedy the problem by placing translations of the words into the students' first languages on the back of cards.

Another possible difficulty is the lack of intrinsic sequencing. Although some of the applications suggested in this chapter do involve a logical sequencing, the method itself does not call for it. No matter how much fun or how fast-paced they may be, something is lost if the commands remain isolated from one another and from what we know about human experience. For example, suppose a student is asked to "turn off the light and shout 'help'" (as suggested in the list of commands earlier in this chapter). What motivation does the student have for performing these actions other than to demonstrate that he or she is comprehending? If at some point a context could be provided for such behavior, then perhaps the action would become more meaningful and thus more memorable to the progressing learner. Consider the following situation. A blind person (such as in the Audrey Hepburn classic *Wait Until Dark*) has discovered an intruder in her apartment. Cleverly, she turns off the light so that she and the intruder will be equally handicapped. In spite of this maneuver, she soon realizes she is definitely in a "no-win" situation. She might shout "help" in order to attract her neighbors. Now the commands have taken on another dimension for a student who might be asked to play the part of the blind person. Strings of seemingly unrelated sentences have now taken on meaning and become part of motivated, logical discourse (see Chapter 16).

Often physical activities can begin with a simple story, read and acted out by the teacher and one or more teacher assistants. Later the teacher acts as a director and the students perform the parts. Directions include commands such as "Sit down in the chair" or "Shake hands with Mr. Kim (a character in the story)" or "Tell Hong (another character) to take the book from the shelf." The key words and phrases eventually are written on the board or placed on cue cards. When the students are ready, they take turns being the director while the teacher and other students act out the parts. The students move from predetermined scripts or ones that they create themselves. They may even perform their own creations for other groups. (For more ideas involving role play and drama, see Chapter 11.)

THE AUDIO-MOTOR UNIT

Kalivoda, Morain, and Elkins (1971) also recognized the lack of meaningful sequencing as a weakness in the TPR method at later levels and suggested alternative ways of combining commands. Although their ideas may not be as dramatic as the one offered above, they nevertheless add a contextual dimension to the utterances. They called a particular sequence of commands an *audio-motor unit*. A ten minute tape is played on which a native speaker issues a series of commands for twenty actions, all centering on a single topic. The teacher demonstrates the appropriate responses to the commands, using whatever realia are available to make the actions comprehensible. An audio-motor unit might include such pantomimed or real sequences as "go to the cupboard," "open the cupboard door," "find the largest bowl," "take it out," "set it on the table," and so on. The students are then invited to comply with the commands. Actions may be pantomimed when it is not possible or advisable to use props. For example, climbing a real ladder can be a difficult and even dangerous task, but a pretend ladder is almost as effective using a little imagination.

Kalivoda, Morain, and Elkins liked to consider the audio-motor unit supplemental to a larger program (which, unfortunately, they do not describe). Although one unit generally lasts only about ten minutes, it can be made longer or shorter depending on student needs and on the amount of time available.

They also liked to include cultural learning in the lessons. Various customs involving eating, preparing food, telephone conversations, and introductions are taught through a series of commands given in the context of real or pretend situations.

To examine the effectiveness of the audio-motor unit, they looked at the results of a pilot program in the Southeastern Language Center at the University of Georgia (Kalivoda, Morain, and Elkins, 1971). The students were given intensive six-week courses in Spanish, French, or German. Beginning classes received one ten-minute lesson each day; advanced classes were given only one or two ten-minute lessons a week. The eight participating teachers had received only enough special instruction to make the presentations similar in execution. After the courses were over, the students filled out questionnaires so that their attitudes toward the audio-motor strategy could be studied. Of the 180 students who took part, 90 percent revealed positive attitudes. They thought that the method improved their listening comprehension and increased their vocabularies. Furthermore, they seemed to like the change of pace that it gave to the daily lessons, and they found it stimulating and entertaining. However, a few of the remaining 10 percent found it not difficult enough, boring, or silly. Some students and teachers felt that the written form of the commands should have been given and a few students thought that they should have been able to participate orally in the lesson.

Six of the eight teachers reacted positively. The benefits they reported are paraphrased below:

1. The vocabulary, structures, and syntax of the language used in their lessons were reinforced by exposure to the audio-motor strategy.
2. Students became strongly interested in the lessons through the physical acting out of cultural aspects.
3. The lessons, even though designed for the development of listening skills, had a real impact on oral production. The teachers noticed increased spontaneity and better pronunciation, although they admitted the latter was difficult to verify.
4. The nonnative teachers of the various languages felt that they improved their own skills with the languages they were teaching.

In spite of these advantages, the audio-motor unit may suffer somewhat from its dependence on a tape to give the commands. The activities could become less personalized and less flexible than those in Asher's approach, in which teachers use students' names and react to their changing needs from moment to moment. This is not to say that it is not a good idea to expose students occasionally to taped voices for which there may be no visual clues to meaning.

It must be pointed out that in both methods the teacher is the controlling force. The interaction must be almost completely teacher structured and controlled until the students gain enough proficiency to have more influence. At that time, activities such as "information gaps" mentioned earlier can be implemented, allowing students to have a more significant role in the interactional process.

SUMMARY

Asher's total physical response involves giving a series of commands to which the students respond physically. The students themselves remain silent until they are ready for oral production. At that time, they have the option of giving the commands. The students gradually develop their interlanguage, which becomes more and more like the language of their teacher. The main disadvantage, which becomes most apparent at later levels, is that the commands do not, except in some adaptations, adhere to a logical sequence based on experience. Another disadvantage is that Asher's method is likely to be of limited use in teaching nonphysical elements of language.

Kusudo, Morain, and Elkins, while following the way led by Asher, enlarged upon the basic method by adding meaningful sequence. In addition, they considered their method to be an adjunct to a much larger program rather than the focus. A disadvantage may be that a tape used to give commands takes away some of the personalization and flexibility that are integral to Asher's method.

In spite of their drawbacks, effective adaptations of either approach can pay large dividends in terms of student interest, spontaneity, and language development. Students' chances for becoming more proficient in their new language can increase when they are allowed to listen first, speak when ready, and be involved in the target language physically.

READINGS, REFLECTION, AND DISCUSSION

Suggested Readings and Reference Materials

Asher, J. (1996). *Learning another language through actions: The complete teachers' guidebook*, 5th ed. Los Gatos, CA: Sky Oaks. An important source for anyone intending to use total physical response methodology in the classroom. Covers related research and discusses in depth the techniques themselves. The lessons can be readily adapted to teaching languages other than English.

Creative Publications. Worth, IL: While catalogs are not normally found in an annotated reading list such as this, I decided to include this one because it makes available a myriad of hands-on suggestions and manipulatives for teaching concepts in math, geometry, science, social studies, languages, technology, and in many other subject areas. The manipulatives include items such as clocks, coins (play money), color tiles, blocks, cubes, cuisenaire rods, dice, dominoes, number boards, pocket wall charts, etc. Although most of the materials are intended for elementary students, many of them can be used with older students as well.

Glisan, E. (1993). Total physical response: A technique for teaching all skills in Spanish. In J. Oller, Jr., ed., *Methods that work: Ideas for literacy and language teachers*, 2d ed., Boston: Heinle, pp. 30–39. The author offers suggestions for taking the language learner far beyond the beginning proficiency levels in the target language. In addition, she presents the outline of a sample lesson in Spanish.

Gottlieb, J. (1996). *Wonders of Science*. Orlando, FL: Steck-Vaugh. This is just one of several high-interest, low-level series on the market today that include hands-on teaching and learning. The series includes six titles: *Plant Life; Land Animals; The Earth and Beyond; Water Life; Matter, Motion, and Machines*; and *The Human Body*. Although the texts are intended for grades 7–12, the reading level is for grades 2–3.

Larsen-Freeman, D. (2000). The total physical response method. In D. Larsen-Freeman, *Techniques and principles in language teaching*, 2d ed. New York: Oxford University Press, pp. 107–119. The principles and techniques of the total physical response are discussed and the reader is invited to "experience" it through a description of its implementation in a constructed classroom setting.

Questions and Projects for Reflection and Discussion

1. Why is it important that teachers not consider descriptions of methods and activities to be "prescriptions" for action? What might happen if they do? How should such descriptions be used?

2. What underlying message might students take from the fact that the teacher usually acts as the authority controlling total physical response lessons? To what extent do you feel this is necessary at beginning levels? What about at more advanced levels? Is it possible that the teacher might gradually give students greater control and still involve them physically?

3. How might the total physical response foster lowered anxiety levels (refer to Chapter 6)? Discuss.

4. Kalivoda, Morain, and Elkins (1971) stated, "Careful structuring of the audio-motor units provides for the re-entry of materials at regular intervals." Do you think this is important? Why? How might you effectively incorporate re-entries into a previous lesson from a present lesson? Create one or more examples using this technique.

5. Prepare your own version of a five-minute TPR or audio-motor activity to try out on a small group of fellow students. If the commands are simple enough, you may demonstrate in a target language with which the group is unfamiliar. In what ways was the activity successful? How can it be improved? Discuss with class members. Begin by briefly sharing your own reactions to the activity.

   If you are currently teaching students, use what you have learned to try out a similar activity with them. Make sure the lesson you prepare is relevant and appropriate to level. If possible, have your lesson videotaped to analyze and discuss with peers. Reflect on its outcome and how you felt about doing it. Pay close attention to student response. Do you see any problems with your lesson? How might it be improved?

   Write about your experiences using physical involvement to teach language and what you learned in your journal.

6. How important is it to involve the students physically in the language they are learning? Do you see any problems that might occur? How might these problems be overcome? To what extent do you plan to use physical involvement in your own teaching?

CHAPTER 9

Communicative Practices

*The essence of language is human activity—activity on
the part of one individual to make himself understood,
and activity on the part of the other to understand what
was in the mind of the first.*

O. Jespersen, 1904

QUESTIONS TO THINK ABOUT

1. What kinds of activities do you think might be typical of "communicative" practices?

2. To what extent were your own experiences with another language communicative? Share a few communicative practices that you liked the best. Do you wish that you had been exposed to more or less real communication? Why?

3. What do you think the role of instructed grammar should be in communicative language teaching?

4. What do you think a "natural" approach might be? Does it sound like something you might feel comfortable using? Why?

Communicative language teaching includes practices typically associated with physical approaches (Chapter 8) and most other practices described throughout this book. Although "the natural approach"—first proposed by Tracy Terrell and developed in collaboration with Stephen Krashen—does not embody all that is communicative in language teaching, it does describe a branch of communicative teaching found in the United States, where historically it marks a turning point in language teaching. Because the natural approach and its extensions are so highly developed and provide such an important resource for teachers, it is discussed in depth in this chapter.

THE NATURAL APPROACH: HOW IT HAS EVOLVED[1]

Krashen and Terrell were careful to make no claim for the natural approach that other interactive methods could not match if they relied on real communication as their modus operandi. Like Asher, they reminded us that students must acquire the second language in much the same way that people acquire language in natural situations (therefore the term "natural approach"). Some argue that it is not really a method at all but is, in a more general sense, an approach. However, the authors developed the natural approach as a method, and so, for the purposes of discussion, that is the way it is presented here (see Krashen and Terrell, 1983). They based their method on four principles.

- *Comprehension precedes production.* A silent period is observed during which the teacher uses the target language predominantly, focuses on communicative situations, and provides comprehensible input that is roughly tuned to the students' proficiency levels.
- *Production must be allowed to emerge in [variable] stages.* Responses generally begin with nonverbal communication, progress to single words, then to two- and three-word combinations, next to phrases and sentences, and finally to complete discourse. Students speak when ready, and speech errors are usually not corrected directly but rather are modeled during the communication and eventually become incorporated into each student's interlanguage.
- *The course syllabus focuses on communicative goals.* Grammatical sequencing as a focus is shunned in favor of a topical/situational organization. Discussion centers on items in the classroom, favorite vacation spots, and other topics and issues. Grammar is acquired mainly through relevant communication.
- *The activities are designed to lower the "affective filter"* (see description on page 40). According to Kashen and Terrell, a student engrossed in interesting ideas will be less apt to be anxious than one focused mainly on form. In

---

[1] See also Richard-Amato (1995).

addition, the atmosphere must be friendly and accepting if the student is to have the best possible chance for acquiring the target language.

The natural approach and its extensions are used with many other compatible methods and activities (total physical response and the audio-motor unit, chants, music, games, role play, storytelling, affective activities, etc.) which often produce extremely rich environments where concepts are reinforced in a variety of ways. The natural approach and all the methods and activities with which it is used should blend to form a well-integrated program if it is to work. Although recycling is not emphasized in the natural approach literature, it is important that concepts be recycled in many different ways in order for them to be mastered.

Because the focus is on real communication, many demands are made upon the time and energy of teachers. They must present a great deal of comprehensible input about concrete, relevant topics, especially at beginning levels. It is not unusual to see natural approach language teachers trudging across campus with sacks filled with fruits to talk about and eat, dishes with which to set a table for an imaginary dinner, oversized clothes to put on over other clothes, and additional paraphernalia to demonstrate the notions involved. These teachers can no longer just have students open their books to a certain page, say "Repeat after me," or assign the students to endless exercises in rule application. According to Krashen and Terrell, each teacher's chief responsibility during class hours is to communicate with the students about relevant topics and issues.

The following outline adapted from Krashen and Terrell (1983, pp. 67–70) may be useful in planning units for beginning to low-intermediate students.

Preliminary Unit: Learning to Understand

Topics

1. Names of students	5. Clothing
2. Descriptions of people	6. Colors
3. Family members	7. Objects in the classroom
4. Numbers	8. Parts of the body

Situations
1. Greetings
2. Classroom commands

I. Students in the Classroom

Topics
1. Personal identification (name, address, telephone number, age, sex, nationality, date of birth, marital status)
2. Description of school environment (identification, description and location of people and objects in the classroom, description and location of buildings)
3. Classes
4. Telling time

Situations
1. Filling out forms
2. Getting around the school

II. Recreation and Leisure Activities

Topics
1. Favorite activities
2. Sports and games
3. Climate and seasons
4. Weather
5. Seasonal activities
6. Holiday activities
7. Parties
8. Abilities
9. Cultural and artistic interests

Situations
1. Playing games, sports
2. Being a spectator
3. Chitchatting

III. Family, Friends, and Daily Activities

Topics
1. Family and relatives
2. Physical states
3. Emotional states
4. Daily activities
5. Holiday and vacation activities
6. Pets

Situations
1. Introductions, meeting people
2. Visiting relatives
3. Conversing on the phone

IV. Plans, Obligations, and Careers

Topics
1. Future plans
2. General future activities
3. Obligations
4. Hopes and desires
5. Careers and professions
6. Place of work
7. Work activities
8. Salary and money

Situations
1. Job interviewing
2. Talking on the job

V. Residence

Topics
1. Place of residence
2. Rooms of a house
3. Furniture
4. Activities at home
5. Household items
6. Amenities

Situations
1. Looking for a place to live
2. Moving
3. Shopping for the home

VI. Narrating Past Experiences

Topics
1. Immediate past events
2. Yesterday's activities
3. Weekend events
4. Holidays and parties
5. Trips and vacations
6. Other experiences

Situations
1. Friends recounting experiences
2. Making plans

VII. Health, Illnesses, and Emergencies

Topics
1. Body parts
2. Physical states
3. Mental states and moods
4. Health maintenance
5. Health professions
6. Medicine and diseases

Situations
1. Visiting the doctor
2. Hospitals
3. Health interviews
4. Buying medicine
5. Emergencies (accidents)

VIII. Eating

Topics
1. Foods
2. Beverages

Situations
1. Ordering a meal in a restaurant
2. Shopping in a supermarket
3. Preparing food from recipes

IX. Travel and Transportation

Topics
1. Geography
2. Modes of transportation
3. Vacations
4. Experiences on trips
5. Languages
6. Making reservations

Situations
1. Buying gasoline
2. Exchanging money
3. Clearing customs
4. Obtaining lodging
5. Buying tickets

X. Shopping and Buying

Topics
1. Money and prices
2. Fashions
3. Gifts
4. Products

Situations
1. Selling and buying
2. Shopping
3. Bargaining

XI. Youth

Topics
1. Childhood experiences
2. Primary school experiences
3. Teen years experiences
4. Adult expectations and activities

Situations
1. Reminiscing with friends
2. Sharing photo albums
3. Looking at school yearbooks

XII. Giving Directions and Instructions

Topics
1. Spatial concepts (north, south, east, west; up, down; right, left, center; parallel, perpendicular; etc.)
2. Time relationships (after, before, during, etc.)

Situations
1. Giving instructions
2. Following instructions
3. Reading maps
4. Finding locations
5. Following game instructions
6. Giving an invitation
7. Making appointments

XIII. Values

Topics
1. Family
2. Friendship
3. Love
4. Marriage
5. Sex roles and stereotypes
6. Goals
7. Religious beliefs

Situations
1. Making a variety of decisions based on one's values
2. Sharing and comparing values in a nonthreatening environment
3. Clarifying values

XIV. Issues and Current Events

Topics

1. Environmental problems
2. Economic issues
3. Education
4. Employment and careers
5. Ethical issues
6. Politics
7. Crime
8. Sports
9. Social events
10. Cultural events
11. Minority groups
12. Science and health

Situations

1. Discussing last night's news broadcast
2. Discussing a recent movie, etc.

The students move through three overlapping and variable stages in the natural approach:

- comprehension;
- early speech production; and
- speech emergence.

Beyond speech emergence is a fourth stage later recognized by Terrell and others as *intermediate fluency*. The time spent in any one stage differs greatly depending upon individual characteristics and preferred strategies, the amount of comprehensible input received, and the degree to which anxiety has been lowered. Some students begin speaking after just a couple hours, while others need several weeks. Children may need several months. The second stage, early speech production, may take anywhere from a few months to one year or longer. The third stage, speech emergence, can take up to three years, but usually the student is reasonably fluent in personal communication skills long before that. At this stage, the teacher does most of the talking and students do most of the listening. However, as the students become more proficient, they often assume the teacher's role in initiating input and the teacher becomes predominantly an organizer and a facilitator.

COMPREHENSION

During this first stage, the students go through a silent period. They receive comprehensible input usually from the teachers and, in some classrooms, from peer teachers and lay assistants (see Chapter 15). Often versions of the total physical response are used. Although the students' main goal is to develop listening skills at this level, many of the activities overlap into the next higher level, early speech production. Simple responses to the comprehensible input may be made by gesturing, nodding, using the L1, answering "yes," or "no," giving names of people or objects as answers to questions such as "Who has on a yellow dress?" (Kim) or "Do you want an apple or an orange?" (apple). A lot of visuals, explanations, repetitions, and so forth are used. The teacher's speech is a little slower than usual. The intonation is reasonably normal except that key words receive a bit of extra emphasis. Students are not called upon to respond individually. Instead, questions are directed to the whole group, and one or several can respond. Key terms are written on the board, perhaps on the second or third time the students are exposed to them. If students are given written forms of the words too soon, they may experience a cognitive overloading that can interfere with acquisition.

Total physical response (TPR) activities may be used to get the students into some basic vocabulary. For example, students can acquire names ("Give the book to Hong"), descriptions ("Take the pencil to a person who has short hair"), numbers ("Pick up three pieces of chalk"), colors ("Find the blue book"), and many other concepts. Notice that TPR will be involved to some degree in almost every activity suggested for this level. From my own experience with the natural approach, I have found that new concepts should be introduced gradually and that frequent checks for understanding should be made before adding other new concepts. In the sample dialogue that follows, the teacher is teaching four colors (red, blue, green, yellow) and has a strip of construction paper for each color. Notice that the language is very simple. However, the language is expected to become much richer as the teacher begins to build upon these concepts.

TEACHER: (*holding up the red strip*) This is red. This is red. (*The teacher then points to a student's red sweater.*) Is this red? (*The teacher begins to nod her head, softly uttering*) Yes.
STUDENTS: (*nodding their heads*) Yes.
TEACHER: (*pointing to a student's red skirt*) Is this red?
STUDENTS: (*nodding their heads*) Yes.
TEACHER: (*pointing to a green sweater*) Is this red? (*She begins to shake her head softly uttering*) No.
TEACHER: (*The teacher points to the red strip again.*) Is this red?
STUDENTS: Yes.
TEACHER: Yes. This is red. (*again points to the red strip*)
TEACHER: (*holding the blue strip*) This is blue. This is blue. (*The teacher points to a student's blue scarf.*) Is this blue?
STUDENTS: Yes.
TEACHER: (*pointing to a blue door*) Is this blue?
STUDENTS: Yes.
TEACHER: Good. Yes, this is blue. (*The teacher points to the red strip.*) Is this blue?
STUDENTS: No.
TEACHER: No. (*pointing to the blue strip*) This is blue and this (*pointing to the red strip*) is red.

And so the teacher continues, adding one color at a time while returning to check for understanding of colors already introduced. After working through the four colors, the teacher gives the strips to various students and asks that they be returned, color by color for reinforcement. Gradually the students begin to comprehend and use the concepts in many different meaningful contexts.

It is important not to introduce too many new concepts at once and to reinforce the ones introduced immediately. For example, the students can cut out of magazines objects of each color, paste them on sheets of paper, each labeled a different color. Or students can draw and color with crayons various objects in different colors according to the teacher's directions. A day or so later the teacher may bring in pieces of clothing of the same colors to see if their colors are remembered. At that point, the pieces of clothing themselves may be the new concepts to which the students are introduced in a similar manner.

Once the students can identify simple concepts, the teacher can reinforce these and introduce new ones by using a stream of comprehensible input: "Look at Maria's feet. She is wearing shoes. Look at Jorge's feet. He is wearing shoes, too. His shoes are brown. Look at his hair. His hair is brown. How many students have brown hair?" (nine) "What is the name of the student with red hair?" (Carolina) "Who is behind the person with the red shirt?" (Yung) "Does Yung have on a shirt or a sweater?" (sweater) "What color is the sweater?" (yellow) The teacher can carry on in this fashion about a wide variety of concrete subjects, stimulated by a picture, an object, a map, and so on.

Other sample activities, which are extensions of the natural approach, are described on the next few pages.[2]

Extensions of the Natural Approach Activities

WHERE DOES IT BELONG?

On the board, sketch and label the rooms of a house (see Figure 9.1). Then briefly talk about the house and its various rooms. (*Look at the house. It is big. It has many rooms. Here is the kitchen. Food is kept in the kitchen. People eat in the kitchen. And so forth.*) Roughly draw in each room a few typical household items including furniture to help the students correctly identify the room. Cut out pictures of other household items to be placed in the appropriate rooms. On the back of each picture place pieces of rolled up cellophane tape to make them stick to the board. (Later the tape can be removed, making the pictures reusable). Give directions such as "Put the stove in the kitchen" or "Put the dresser in the bedroom" to see if the students can correctly place the pictures. An alternative might be to use a magnetic board or a large doll house with miniature furniture.

---

[2] Many of these activities can be adapted to several age levels, provided students are cognitively able to deal with the tasks (see pages 326–328). They can also be adapted for teaching any language, second or foreign, and for most programs: English for Academic Purposes (EAP), English for Special Purposes (ESP), and others.

| Bedroom | Bathroom | Laundry |
| Garage | Kitchen | Living room |

Figure 9.1

Items typical of other places can be incorporated in similar activities. Simulated settings such as zoos, farmyards, hospitals, libraries, various work sites, cafeterias, and university campuses can be the focus.

PUT IT ON!

Bring in a variety of oversized clothes. Talk about the clothes. (*These are pants. They are blue. Here is the pocket. Point to the pocket.*) Have the students put the clothes on (over their own) according to the directions you give. The oversized clothes are taken off using a similar procedure. A camera can be used for recording the highlights of this activity. The photos can be displayed in the classroom and used at a later stage to stimulate discussion.

A follow-up provides the students with clothing catalogs, scissors, paste, and blank sheets of construction paper.[3] Take articles of clothing (which have previously been cut out) as well as a cut-out head, arms, and legs. Show the class how easy it is to create a figure by gluing these items to the construction paper. The figure will probably look very humorous, especially if you have chosen such things as enormous shoes, a little head, and a strange assortment of clothing. Have the students make their own funny figures. Through a cooperative effort, students locate the items each needs to complete a creation. In the process, the same words are repeated over and over, and a great deal of laughter can be generated, lowering anxiety.

GUESS WHAT'S IN THE BOX[4]

Fill a box with familiar objects. Describe a particular object and have the students guess which object is being described. Once the object has been correctly named, remove it

---

[3] I wish to thank Teri Sandoval for the follow-up idea.

[4] Thanks to Esther Heise for introducing this idea to me.

from the box and give it to the student temporarily. Once all the objects have been handed out, ask that the objects be returned: "Who has the rubber band?", and so forth.

GETTING AROUND

For English Language Learners (ELLs), make a large map of the campus or school using strips of butcher paper taped together (an alternative might be to block off the various locations with masking tape placed on the floor). The total area should be large enough so the students can stand on it and walk from place to place. Label rooms, buildings, or whatever is appropriate. Make sure it is clear what the various rooms in the buildings are. For example, you might place a picture of medicines in the clinic or pictures of food in the cafeteria. Using TPR, have students move around to various places. Take a tour of the campus or school itself, pointing out these same places. Once the students are familiar with the area, ask them to act as guides to new students of the same L1 backgrounds. In order to survive the first few days, new students need to know where things are before they are fluent enough to ask.

THE PEOPLE IN OUR SCHOOL

Take photos of personnel within your school. Show them to your students and talk about the job that each one does. You may want to act out the various roles: custodian, cafeteria helper, secretary, nurse, counselor, teacher, and orchestra director. Have the students point to the picture of the custodian, the principal, and so on. Now ask a volunteer student to act out the roles. See if the others can guess which roles are being acted out (see Chapter 11 for other role-play activities that would be appropriate to this level and would help reinforce concepts).

CLASSIFYING OBJECTS

Have each student make a classification booklet. Any categories can be used, depending upon the objectives you have in mind. For example, one page could be for household items, another for clothing, and a third for sports or camping equipment. Give the students several magazines or catalogs, and have them cut out pictures to be categorized. Then ask them to glue the items to the appropriate pages. You can provide comprehensible input about the pictures and do some individual TPR with each student. (*Point to the _____. Name two objects that are in a kitchen*, etc.) Previously acquired concepts can be reinforced by this means.

FOLLOWING A PROCESS

Through a series of simple commands, students learn to make things to eat (guacamole, onion and sour cream dip, sandwiches), items for play (kites, puppets, dolls, pictures), fascinating projects such as papier-mâché maps or miniature cities. You need to demonstrate first before taking the students through the step-by-step processes. Students are not expected to speak; they simply carry out the commands in TPR fashion.

MATCHING

Students match pictures of objects with words placed on heavy paper and cut into puzzle pieces (Figure 9.2). Thus, students can use kinesthetic matching as a clue if necessary. Or the student can use the word only and the matching of the puzzle pieces will simply reinforce the choice.

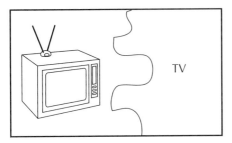 

Figure 9.2

The activities described here represent just a small sampling of the many activities that can be used with students at this stage. Of course, some are more applicable to certain ages than others. However, it has been my experience that activities sometimes considered "childish" for older learners are often enjoyed by children and adults alike. A lot depends upon how comfortable students feel, no matter their age.

The teacher needs to use lots of manipulative visuals; act out, model, or demonstrate expected responses; use body language in order to clarify meaning; use high-frequency vocabulary, short sentences, *yes/no* questions, *either/or* questions, and other questions that require only one-word answers; and rely heavily on getting the students physically involved with the target language. At the same time, activities need to be varied within any given time period for two reasons: Students' attention spans are often short, and the teacher's stamina is limited.

EARLY SPEECH PRODUCTION

Getting into Speaking

The transition into the second stage generally begins with an extension of many activities used in the comprehension stage. The teacher gradually begins to notice changes in the length of the responses. For example, to the question "Who has on a blue dress?" the teacher might get the answer "Ashwaq has dress" instead of just "Ashwaq." Once the expansions begin to appear, they come naturally and abundantly, especially if the students feel comfortable with the teacher and the ambiance of the classroom. The speech at first will contain many errors which should be dealt with *only* indirectly. To the omission of words in the student's utterance above, the teacher might respond with "Yes, Ashwaq has on the dress" instead of "No, you should say, 'Ashwaq has on the dress'" (emphasizing *on* and *the*). If allowed to develop their interlanguage naturally, the students will continue expanding their utterances to include a wide variety of structures and eventually complex language.

Some of the activities typical of this stage (or before) are described below.

Speaking-Focused Activities

CHARTS AND OTHER VISUALS

Krashen and Terrell (1983) recommend the use of charts and other visuals that will make discussion easier and will serve as transitions into reading. Write the following on the board to use as aids to conversation.

Numbers

How many students in the class are wearing
    rings? _____
    tennis shoes? _____
    belts? _____
    glasses? _____
Follow-up questions: How many students have on tennis shoes?
                       Are any students wearing glasses?
                       How many?

Clothing

Name of Student	Clothes
Carlos	jeans
Sung Hee	dress

Follow-up questions: Who is wearing jeans?
                       What is Sung Hee wearing?

Below is an example of a chart used in an ESL class to encourage interaction and to help the students to get to know one another.
First the students interview partners to fill in the chart below:[5]

	Partner 1	Partner 2	Partner 3
What's your name?			
Where are you from?			
What language do you speak?			

---

[5] This chart is adapted from one supplied by Linda Sasser of the Alhambra School District in California.

Follow-up questions: What country is _____ from?
                                    (name of student)

What languages does _____ speak?
                              (name of student)

Who speaks _____?
                    (name of language)

GROUP MURALS

Give each student a space on a huge piece of butcher paper strung across a wall. Give students pencils, rulers, wide felt-tip pens, paints, and brushes to draw pictures in their spaces and place their names at the bottom. Display the butcher paper in the classroom for a week or two, then roll it up and save it. As the students progress in the language, bring out the butcher paper again, but now for different activities. At first, ask simple questions about each picture: "Look at Juan's picture. What color is the wagon?" (green) "How many apples did Jenny paint?" (three) Later, when the students are into the stage of speech emergence and beyond, they can tell about their own pictures and those of their friends, or they can make up an oral group story incorporating each picture in some way.

OPEN-ENDED SENTENCES

Extend the streams of comprehensible input to include utterances that the student completes.
On Saturdays I _____.
My family likes to _____.
Ho likes to eat _____.

Or have the students bring in family photos to share. Using open-ended sentences, have them talk about their relatives pictured in the photos:
My sister likes _____.
My brother is _____.
My cousins are _____.

MATRICES

Open-ended sentences that are used in certain combinations for specific situations are called *matrices*. Below are a few situations in which they might be used.

First Meetings

Hi there, my name is _____.
Nice to meet you. I'm _____.
Are you a new student, too?
Yes, I came from _____.

On the Telephone

Hola.

Hola. Soy _____ . ¿Con quién hablo?

Con _____ .

At an Office

May I help you?

My name is _____ . I have an appointment with _____ .

The matrices should not be drilled in audiolingual style. Instead use role-playing situations in which a variety of responses can be given. Students simply use the matrices as aids and "starters" for as long as they need them (see Chapter 11 for similar ideas). Place the matrices on cue cards, which can serve as transitions into reading (see Chapters 5 and 13) or incorporate them into chants or lyrics (see Chapter 10).

ASKING FOR THE FACTS

Show the students simple sale advertisements (Figure 9.3) from local newspapers (in second language classes) or foreign language newspapers (in foreign language classes). An alternative might be to show the students pictures of forms that have been filled out: a hospital record, an application for welfare, or a passport (see Figure 9.4). Ask pertinent questions about each.

CAMERA $29.50
NOW ONLY $17.98

Figure 9.3

Sale Advertisement Questions:

1. What is being sold?
2. How much was it?
3. How much is it now?
4. How much will you be saving?

```
┌─────────────────────────────────────────────────────────────┐
│                    SAM'S HARDWARE STORE                       │
│                    ────────────────────                       │
│                     Job Application Form                      │
│                     ───────────────────                       │
│   Name    ____Mohamed Abdullah____    Date __5-24-03__        │
│   Address ____120 Maple Drive____   Phone _(218) 543-7841_    │
│                    (street)                                   │
│           ___Mentor___     ___Minnesota___  Sex (M or F) __M__│
│              (city)           (state)                         │
│           ___56702___                                        │
│              (zip)                                            │
│   Birth date __3-20-53__ Social Security number [4|8|0] [2|2] [3|9|6|7] │
│   Position you are seeking ____Salesclerk____                 │
└──────────────────────────────────────────────────────────────┘
```

Figure 9.4

Job Application Questions:
    1. What is the person's last name?
    2. What job does the person want?
    3. Where does the person live?
    4. What is the person's telephone number?
    5. When was the person born?

Getting into Reading and Writing

Even though speaking is their major thrust, most of the above activities can be used as transitions into reading and writing (see also Chapter 13). Key words written on the board, TPR commands that students may have listed in their notebooks, cue cards with matrices written on them, words on charts, and other visuals, all lead to reading and writing in the target language. Of course, nonliterate learners of all ages, and students whose L1 writing system is vastly different from that of the target language will need special attention (see Chapters 5 and 13). However, the teaching should always be done through meaning rather than by stringing together isolated elements such as phonemes, orthographic symbols, and the like. The natural approach, as first described by Krashen and Terrell, was concerned mainly with oral communication skills. However, they agreed for the most part that skills—listening, speaking, reading, writing—should be integrated rather than taught as separate entities.

SPEECH EMERGENCE AND BEYOND

Because speech has been emerging all along, to distinguish *speech emergence* as a separate stage seems artificial. Perhaps this is the reason Krashen and Terrell replaced it with the term *extending production* in their book *The Natural Approach*. During this third stage, the utterances become longer and more complex. Many errors are still made but, if enough comprehensible input has been internalized, they should gradually decrease as the students move toward full production. If undue attention has been paid to developmental errors, the process of acquiring correct grammatical forms in the new language could be impeded (see Chapter 3).

At this stage a large number of activities can be used that are somewhat more demanding and challenging but still within reach cognitively: music and poetry (Chapter 10), role-playing and drama (Chapter 11), affective activities (Chapter 14), and problem solving or debates at higher levels. Many of the activities already recommended in this chapter for earlier levels can be extended to provide additional opportunities for development. For example, instead of simply answering questions about an application form, the students can now fill one out; instead of just following directions, they can begin to write their own sets of simple directions to see if others can follow them. Below is a sampling of other activities that might be typical at this level and beyond.

Speech-Emergence Activities

THE PEOPLE HUNT

Give the students the following list and ask them to find a person who:
has shoelaces
wears glasses
is laughing
speaks three or more languages
is wearing black socks
hates carrots
has on a plaid blouse or shirt
lives north of Maple Street
has five letters in his or her last name
lives with a grandparent
has a six in his or her phone number
plays a guitar
They must get the signature of a person in each category.

As the students become more advanced, they can find a person who:
has parents who drive a Toyota
has been to Hong Kong within the last five years

has a family with more than six people in it
has a sister who likes to ice-skate or roller skate
has lived in more than three countries
hopes to be an actress after completing high school

CARTOONS

Take several cartoons from the newspaper, and and cut out the words in the bubbles. Place the cartoons on a blank sheet of paper, providing a place for students to write their own dialogue in the bubbles. They can exchange cartoons and end up with several versions of the action (see Chapter 11 for more storytelling activities).

DRAW THIS!

Divide the students into groups of four or five. Give one student per group a picture with simple lines and geometric shapes on it. Have these students give directions to their groups so that each group can reproduce the picture without seeing it. The student who comes closest to the original picture in each group gives directions for the next picture. You may want to brief the group on the kinds of directions that will help by giving some key words: horizontal, vertical, diagonal, perpendicular, parallel, a right angle, upper-left corner, lower right, etc. (see Figure 9.5). Pictures should become progressively more difficult as the students become more proficient.

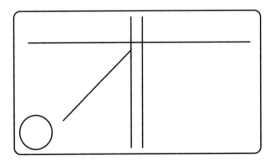

Figure 9.5

SHOPPING SPREE[6]

Set up one corner of the room as a grocery store. Stock the shelves with empty Jell-O boxes, egg cartons, milk cartons, cereal boxes, cleaning supplies, magazines, and so forth. Mark prices on the items. Have the students make out a shopping list (see Figure 9.6) and go shopping with fake money. Have students take turns being shoppers, salespersons, and cashiers. Various situations can be set up to add variety to the shopping expeditions: a shopper may have to ask where a particular item is on the shelves, may need to exchange an item, may have been given wrong change, and so forth. Similar public places can be

---

[6] Thanks to Cyndee Gustke, who introduced me to a similar idea.

Figure 9.6

simulated: a doctor's office, a bank, the post office, a drugstore, a clothing store, a garage. Various lists can be compiled, depending on each task. The situations can be an extension of matrices (see pages 182–183).

Whose Name Is It?

Write the name of a student in large letters on a piece of paper. Tape it on the back of a student volunteer. The volunteer asks *yes* or *no* questions of the class (they are in on the secret) to determine the name on the paper. "Is the person a female?" (yes) "Is she in the first desk? (no) "Does she like to sing?" (yes) "Is it _____ ?" (no). And on it goes until several volunteers get a chance. A variation of this activity is "Guess What's in the Box," described on page 178 in this chapter. The teacher gives a box with one familiar object in it. The rest of the class asks *yes* or *no* questions until the object is named (see Chapter 12 for similar activities).

Following the Written Directions

Give students sets of simple directions to follow. The directions should be on many topics of interest: how to make a model car, how to make paper flowers, how to decoupage, and so on. See if the students can read the directions and follow them. Have students work in pairs on some projects and in groups on others (see also "Following Recipes" in Chapter 8).

Map Reading

This activity is an extension of "Getting Around," described on page 179 in this chapter. Write helpful phrases on the board: turn right (left), go south (north, east, west), go around the corner (straight), on the right (left, north, south, east, west) side of the street, in the (middle, far corner) of the block, down (up) the street, until you see a mailbox (fire hydrant, bus stop), between the drugstore and the bank, across from the hardware store, and so on. Give the students maps such as the one in Figure 9.7 and have them follow your directions as they trace the route with a pencil. First do a demonstration with the class. Place the map on the overhead projector and trace a route while reading a set of directions aloud. For example, "Start at the bank, go north on Second Street until you get to Central Avenue, turn left, walk straight ahead to the gas station. It's between the grocery store and the bakery." Then divide the students into pairs and have them give each other directions while they trace the routes on their own maps.

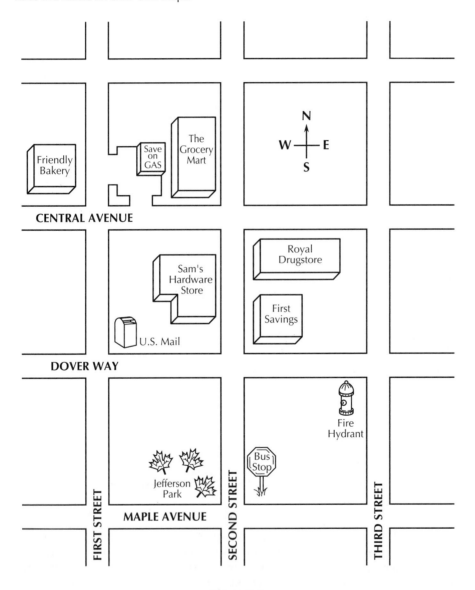

Figure 9.7

As an alternative, you might combine storytelling with the activities.[7] For example, create a story about a fugitive who moves from place to place in different ways: he walks, runs, darts, crawls, skips, and drives. The students trace the route on their individual maps as you read. Instead of drawing only straight lines, the students can draw broken lines for "walks" (– – – – – – – – –), zigzag lines for "runs" (^v^v^v^v^v^v^v^v), sideways carets for "darts" (>>>>>>), wavy lines for "crawls" (~~~~~~~~~), arches for "skips" (mmmm), and a series of plus signs for "drives" (++++++).

Follow-ups could include having the students draw maps of sections of their own communities and write sets of directions to the various places within them. Have them write ministries to go with the directions. Eventually have students participate in similar activities using real street maps of cities or highway maps of whole states or countries.

Sharing Books: The Classroom Library

Place several comfortable chairs in the corner of the classroom along with several bookcases set up at right angles to form a little library, where students have time to read individually, read to each other, and/or discuss books. Books might even be checked out through a system similar to that used in a public school or university library.[8] Students may contribute their own books to the collection.

Writing Memos

Set up situations in which students write memos. Some suggestions are given below (see Figure 9.8):

Your mother is at work. You are leaving for a baseball game. You and some of your friends want to go out after the game for pizza. Write a memo to your mother and tape it to the refrigerator door. Tell her you will be home a little late.

You are at home. Someone has called for your brother. He is still at school. Write a note asking him to return the call.

You have a job as a receptionist. A salesman has come to sell paper products to your boss. Your boss is not in. The salesman asks you to leave a message. It should say that the salesman will be back later.

You have an appointment with your professor. You must cancel it because your mother is coming to visit that day. Write a note to give to the professor's secretary. Explain the situation.

Using Local or Foreign Language Newspapers[9]

1. Ask the students to find, cut out, and paste on butcher paper a sample of each of the following. Students can work in groups or individually. This kind of activity can begin at much earlier stages if the items are simple enough.
   the price of a pound of ground meat

---

[7] I wish to thank Braden Cancilla for this idea.

[8] Cyndee Gustke suggested this idea.

[9] These activities have been adapted from the pamphlets "Newspapers in Education," *Albuquerque Journal/Tribune.*

the low temperature in a major city
a number greater than a thousand
a face with glasses
the picture or name of an animal
a sports headline
a letter to the editor
the price of a used Honda Accord
a city within 50 miles of your own
a movie that starts between 1:00 P.M. and 4:00 P.M.
an angry word
the picture of a happy person
a ten-letter word
the picture of a bride

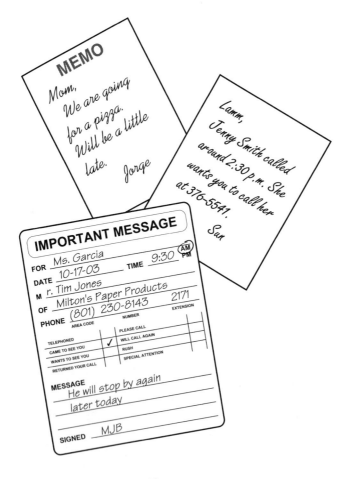

Figure 9.8

2. Have the students go through the commercial ads in a recent paper. Ask them to find three ads for products from other countries. Ask them to find three ads for products made in the state or city in which they now live.

3. Ask older students to look for suitable jobs, apartments, and other items of interest in the want ads. Have them discuss what they have found and tell why these may or may not meet their needs.

4. Ask students to look in the want ads for items to buy. Have them play the roles of potential sellers and buyers. For example, the buyers can make "telephone calls" to the sellers to gather more information about the items. (A fist held to the ear makes a good pretend phone.)

   A follow-up is to have students write want ads advertising things to sell. They might even bring these items to class. Ask them to consider these questions before writing: What do I want to sell? Who might buy it? Why might someone want to buy it? Once they have written their ads (restrict number of words and dollar value), collect them, duplicate them, and distribute them among the class. Let them buy, sell, or trade at will.

5. Finding articles about interesting people in the news can be exciting. Have students plan a "celebrity" party and make a list of those they would like to invite. Have them tell why they would like to meet those they have selected.

6. Ask students to choose a headline and write an alternative story to go with it.

PEN PALS

Mainstream English classes or organizations within or outside of the school can write personal letters to ELLs. After several exchanges of letters have taken place, the groups might get together to meet for a party or outing.

In foreign language classes students can write to each other on a regular basis in the target language, they can write to students studying the same language in another school, or they can obtain pen pals in the countries where the target language is spoken.

Establish a mailbox center in a quiet area of the classroom. Display directions for writing and information about using the center. Provide a table with three or four chairs, several types of paper, envelopes, and writing tools. To encourage letter writing, you, your assistants, and advanced students can first write letters so that each student receives one. Schedule a regular set time for students to receive, read, and respond to the letters. If students have access to computers, they might correspond through e-mail (see Chapter 16).

ORAL HISTORY

One way to show respect for the students' backgrounds is to have them develop oral histories of people from their respective countries. Students will need to first determine what questions they want to ask members of their families and people living in the neighborhood and in the community at large. The questions may need to be translated into each student's native language and the answers need to be recorded on a cassette for later transcription and translation into English. The English versions can then be shared with peers from other language groups. Photographs of the people interviewed can be put with the transcriptions. Students may place copies of the oral history transcriptions in the school library so that all students can access them (for similar ideas, see also Olmedo, 1993).

The three variable stages of the natural approach flow into one another, and it is difficult to tell where one ends and the next begins. If one were to compare these stages with the traditional levels—beginning, intermediate, and advanced—their relationship might look like this (see Figure 9.9 below).

At the comprehension stage, students develop the ability to understand spoken language and to react to simple commands. During this time students experience their "silent period" when they are not expected to speak, although they may respond with a word or two. At the early speech-production stage, students are able to produce a few words and can often recognize their written versions. At the speech-emergence stage, they begin to use simple sentences and can read and write simple text in the target language. As students become capable of fuller production (sometimes referred to by natural approach advocates as the period of "intermediate fluency"), they can express themselves in a variety of ways and can understand much of what is said. (See pages 137–138 for a more comprehensive list of typical language behaviors found at each level.)

Much overlap exists between one level and the next and one stage and the next. Students may be beginners at some tasks but advanced learners at others. In addition, an intermediate or advanced student might be thrown back temporarily into the comprehension stage typical of beginners whenever new concepts are introduced. It has been my observation that students need several "silent periods" as they move from one group of concepts to another.

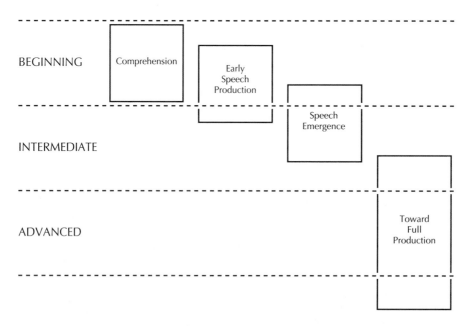

Figure 9.9. Classification of Proficiency Levels

EXPANSIONS OF THE NATURAL APPROACH

Although the natural approach has gained many advocates, particularly in the United States, it does appear to have limitations. One of these is that the method itself is oriented to oral development with beginning to low-intermediate students. While this is not a fault in and of itself, teachers need to be aware that literacy skills require more emphasis than the approach calls for and that advanced students need to be challenged through an increased emphasis on higher thinking skills.[10]

Another limitation is that it does not adequately address the formal teaching of grammar. Originally, Terrell intended that grammar develop naturally by exposing students to sufficient amounts of comprehensible input. Although he acknowledged that formal grammar should have a role, it was not made clear what that role should be.

In 1991 Terrell revealed an evolution of his thinking about the formal teaching of grammar, especially in the foreign language classroom. In an article entitled "The Role of Grammar Instruction in a Communicative Approach," he acknowledged that instruction ". . . is beneficial to learners at a particular point in their acquisition of the target language" (p. 55). He went on to say that instruction gives students structures to use as advance organizers to aid comprehension, and which help students focus on less noticeable features of language such as word endings. Moreover, such instruction serves as a basis for conscious monitoring and the creation of utterances using structures not yet acquired. However, he did *not* advocate a return to the use of a grammatical syllabus (see also the grammar discussion beginning on page 60).

A third limitation lies in the area of content and tasks. With the natural approach, the content and tasks for beginners are mainly related to everyday survival topics (foods, colors, body parts, interests, and so forth). While these may have been fine for many students, they are inadequate for those who wish to reach academic proficiency sooner in the new language. In practice, many teachers have introduced subject-matter content relating to math, science, social studies, literature, and so forth early on and have involved students in tasks that were more likely to lead to earlier success academically.

In addition, many teachers have related the new concepts taught to meaningful larger contexts to provide a cognitive hierarchical framework for them. Look again at the dialogue about colors at the beginning of this chapter. Think about how it might differ if it were related to a science unit on flowering plants, for example. Consider the dialogue below, which again is oriented to rank beginners.

---

[10] Krashen (1995) expands this notion in "What is Intermediate Natural Approach," in P. Hashemipour, R. Maldonado, M. VanNaerssen, eds. *Studies in Language Learning and Spanish Linguistics in Honor of Tracy D. Terrell*, New York: McGraw-Hill, pp. 92-105.

TEACHER: Flowers come in many colors. Here is a red flower. (*The teacher holds up a red flower or a piece of one, then holds up another red flower just like the first one.*) Is this a red flower?
STUDENTS: Yes.
TEACHER: (*holding up the same kind of flower, only this time it is yellow*) Is this a red flower?
STUDENTS: (*shaking their heads*) No.
TEACHER: (*pointing again to a red flower*) No. Good. This is a red flower.

And thus the dialogue continues in much the same way as the first one did. The language becomes more enriched (maybe within a day or two) by relating to other qualities that flowers have and by talking about *where* they grow and *how* they grow.

In the first dialogue, the focus was on colors only. In the second dialogue, although the focus is still on colors, the teaching of them is part of a larger hierarchical unit: Flowering Plants. Flowering Plants might be part of a still larger unit: Plants. The largest unit including plants and flowering plants might be labeled Living Things (see Figure 9.10).

The other activities mentioned in this chapter can also be parts of larger units and themes, depending upon their content. For example, "Guess What's in the Box" can be used for recycling math vocabulary if the box contains items such as a ruler, a compass, a pocket calculator, and the like. "Following a Process" can be part of an art lesson if it involves a process such as creating

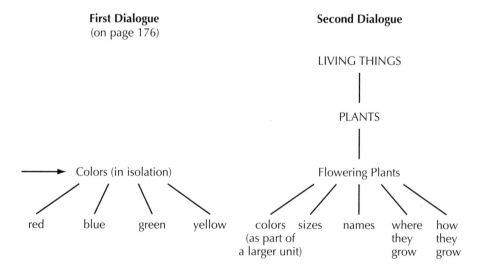

Figure 9.10

hanging mobiles. And "Charts and Other Visuals" can be used in a geography lesson comparing various countries (see Figure 9.11 from Richard-Amato and Snow, 1992).

Country	Location	Climate
Argentina	South America	Warm Summers Temperate Winters
Canada	North America	Warm Summers Cold Winters
Vietnam	East Asia	Hot Summers Temperate Winters

Figure 9.11. A Chart Used to Clarify a Geography Lesson

A hodgepodge of activities thrown together does not a curriculum make. The activities must be carefully selected and adapted, and they must logically fit into a well-planned, but flexible, hierarchy of units and themes. Within this hierarchy, key concepts will need to be reinforced sufficiently to be acquired. Unfortunately, there appears to be no mechanism inherent in the method itself for the recycling of key concepts.

Yet an additional limitation appears to be the natural approach's penchant for putting the teacher on center stage. Of course, at beginning levels the teacher's input is of utmost importance while the students are beginning to develop proficiency in the language. However, students even at beginning levels need to begin communicating more with one another and with peers (or others) who are fluent speakers of the language being learned. An emphasis on group/pair work should not be relegated only to later levels.

SUMMARY

Communicative practices such as one finds in the discussion of the natural approach can indeed lead to participatory language teaching and can serve as scaffolds upon which participatory practices are built (see Chapter 4).

According to Krashen and Terrell, the foundation of the natural approach rests on four principles: (1) comprehension precedes production; (2) production must be allowed to emerge in [variable] stages; (3) the course syllabus must be based on communicative goals; and (4) the activities and classroom environment must work together to produce a lowered "affective filter." Its evolution as a communicative approach has added to it activities having to do with literacy skills development, the inclusion of academic themes and group/pair work at beginning levels; its handling of instructed grammar; and the contextualization of learned concepts into broader, hierarchical units.

But ultimately it is the teacher in the classroom who draws from the method, combining many strategies for a particular situation. The components of this method (like those of other methods and activities described in this book) are dynamic and will evolve in different ways in different classrooms and with different teachers. Its ultimate goal is to enable students to move with relative ease from comprehension to early speech production and eventually into speech emergence and beyond.

READINGS, REFLECTION, AND DISCUSSION

Suggested Reading and Materials

Baltra, Armando (1992). On breaking with tradition: The significance of Terrell's natural approach. *The Canadian Modern Language Review*, 48(3), 265–583. The author discusses the impact of the natural approach on how we view language teaching in both second and foreign language classrooms. He makes us aware of its contribution to the movement toward interactive approaches.

Guillot, M. (1999). *Fluency and its teaching*. Clevedon, England: Multilingual Matters. This book examines the linguistic and paralinguistic factors involved in becoming fluent. Focusing on interaction, it combines theory and practice to inform the reader about how fluency can be achieved.

Krashen, S., and T. Terrell. (1983). *The natural approach: Language acquisition in the classroom*. Englewood Cliffs, NJ: Alemany/Prentice Hall. This well-known text presents essential reading for anyone planning to draw from the natural approach. The book clearly describes the method, offers theoretical justification for its use, and presents suggested activities for making it work.

Questions and Projects for Reflection and Discussion

1. In what ways did the natural approach mark a turning point in language teaching in the United States and elsewhere? Refer to the historical information provided in Chapter 1.

2. Reflect on the process by which you became proficient in a second language. How closely did your progress approximate the variable stages described in the natural approach? To what extent was your progress variable? Did your teachers appear to help or hinder your acquisition of the language? Explain.

3. Often listening, speaking, reading, and writing are treated as isolated skills by language teachers. How might you integrate them by using communicative strategies? Give some specific activities as examples.

4. Incorporate your own adaptations of natural approach practices into a ten-minute lesson to try out on fellow students. See the sample lesson format on page 322. The demonstration may be in a language unfamiliar to your group if lesson is easy enough. After your presentation, ask the group in what ways it was effective and in what ways it could be improved. Begin by sharing your own reactions to the lesson.

If you are currently teaching students, use what you have learned to try out aspects of the method with them. Make sure the lesson is relevant and appropriate to level. If possible, have your lesson videotaped to analyze and discuss with peers. Reflect on its outcome and how you felt about doing it. Pay close attention to student response. Do you see any problems with your lesson? How might your lesson be improved?

Write about your experiences using natural approach practices and what you learned in your journal.

5. How comfortable do you feel using natural approach practices? What might be some problems with this approach? Can most of these problems be overcome? Discuss.

6. How might communicative practices lead to participatory language teaching resulting in effective citizenship and self-empowerment in a classroom community? Give examples. Share them with a small group.

CHAPTER 10

Chants, Music, and Poetry

Rhythm and rhyme, assonance and pun are not artificial creations, but vestigial echoes of primitive phases in the development of language, and of the even more primitive pulsations of living matter, hence our particular receptiveness for messages which arrive in rhythmic pattern.

A. Koestler, 1964

QUESTIONS TO THINK ABOUT

1. What do chants, music, and/or poetry have in common? What role might they play in the acquisition of a first language? How important are they to the success of first language acquisition?

2. In your opinion, would older children, teenagers, and adults learning a second or foreign language benefit from them also? In what ways?

3. Think about the experiences you have had learning another language. To what extent were you exposed to chants, music, and/or poetry during the process? What effects did they have on your own success? Have you ever used them with your students? What happened?

4. Do you think chants, music, and poetry should be incorporated into a second or foreign language program? Explain.

Second language learners, like first language learners, can benefit from chants, music, and poetry. Through word/sound play, many "chunks" of useful language can be incorporated into the individual's linguistic repertoire at almost any age or level of proficiency. The use of prosodic elements, redundancy, and sometimes thoughtless repetition can produce lowered anxiety and greater ego permeability.[1] One might call such play a sort of "palatable audiolingualism." However, unlike audiolingualism, its rhythms and sound repetitions carry the student into sensually appealing activities that go far beyond mere drill. Children and adults alike can receive considerable enjoyment from indulging in such frivolity. The subject matter does not have to be meaningless but can be directly anchored in experience. The messages can be rich and multileveled and can initiate discussions that challenge even the most proficient among the group.

Meaningful word/sound play can provide students with a few tools for communication, especially valuable at beginning levels. Through these genres, students can internalize routines and patterns with or without consciously committing them to memory. Students do not even have to understand the meanings of the words within the chunks to use them for social participation (albeit in a limited fashion) and to encourage input from others. One might argue that others may at first assume that students are more fluent than they really are. However, it doesn't take long to realize the approximate levels of second language students and adjust one's speech accordingly.

Routines and patterns provide a stopgap strategy allowing entry into the new culture before considered "ready." Even though the process used to develop them is very different from that used for creative speech (Krashen, 1981b; Lamendella, 1979), routines and patterns can indeed form part of creative speech at a higher level. Myles, Mitchell, and Hooper (1999) found support for this notion in their study of early classroom learners of French as a second language. They concluded that chunks and formulas actually can form the basis for creative construction later on; they can provide "rich linguistic data" which is reexamined and used to produce creative speech (see also Towell and Hawkins, 1994).

CHANTS

The most frequently-used chants in classrooms today are jazz chants developed by Carolyn Graham, an ESL teacher and jazz musician. She provided language learners with a rhythmic means for improving speaking and listening skills. Through jazz chants, students are exposed to natural intonation patterns and idiomatic expressions in often provocative, sometimes humorous situations. Feelings are expressed in the playing out of the common rituals of everyday life.

---

[1] Guiora, Brannon, and Dull (1972) discussed the concept of language ego, which refers to the self-identity intricately involved with the risks of taking on a new language. It is responsible for boundaries that can make us extremely inhibited if too strong and impenetrable.

Because jazz chants are often in dialogue form, students learn the cultural rules of turn-taking and appropriate ways to communicate specific needs in a variety of situations. The dialogues generally include three kinds of conversational patterns: question/response, command/response, and provocative statement/response.

Graham (1978) suggested that certain steps, summarized below, be taken.

1. The teacher needs to make sure that students understand the chant's situational context. Vocabulary items and cultural ramifications inherent in the situations require clear explanations.
2. Initially, the teacher in a normal conversational voice gives each line of the chant once or twice as needed, and the students repeat in unison. Graham advises the teacher to stop at any point to correct pronunciation or intonation patterns.
3. The teacher establishes a beat by snapping the fingers (students seem to prefer this means), counting, clapping, or using rhythm sticks. Step 2 is then repeated, but this time with a firm beat.
4. The teacher divides the class into two parts (the numbers of students in each part do not matter). Using the beat already established, the teacher gives the lines. The two groups of students alternately repeat the lines as they are given.
5. The dialogue of the chant is then conducted between the teacher and the class. The teacher takes the first part, the students take the other (without the teacher to model). The teacher can use the tapes (optional) that accompany the jazz chants books (see Suggested Readings at the end of this chapter).

In my own experience with jazz chants, I have found it unnecessary to stop and correct students' pronunciation as Graham suggests. Students pick up the modeled pronunciation through the repetitions. Stopping for corrections places undue emphasis on form rather than meaning.

Chants of any kind can help students internalize matrices (see pages 182–183) and, at the same time, reinforce specific vocabulary items. In the sample chant excerpt below, sound play is embedded through the use of rhyme. The matrix includes various structures for offering and refusing food. Substitutions can include the names of the common foods one wants reinforced. Follow-ups might include total physical response activities involving food preparation (see Chapter 8) or role play taking place at the dinner table (see Chapter 11).

Would you like a fried egg?
Would you like a fried egg?
No thanks. I'm on a diet.
Please don't fry it.
Please don't fry it.

Chants can also be used to introduce a unit topic. For example, the chant below introduces a unit on sports events. Typical pictures of sports events can accompany the chant. Follow-ups can include total physical response activities (involving basic actions of the sport), sports demonstrations, local news reporting of sports events, or a trip to a sporting event as part of a "Language Experience" activity (see Chapter 13). The matrix in the following chant offers a means for talking about sports. Word substitutions can easily include a wide variety of events.

Where do you go? Where do you go?
Where do you go to see
a ball go in a basket,
a ball go in a basket?

Where do I go? Where do I go?
To a basketball game.
To a basketball game.
That's where I go to see
a ball go in a basket.

All you have to do is ask it.

Where do you go? Where do you go?
Where do you go to see
a ball kicked all around,
a ball kicked all around?

Where do I go? Where do I go?
To a soc-cer game,
To a soc-cer game.
That's where I go to see
a ball kicked all around.

You keep it on the ground.

Where do you go? Where do you go?
Where do you go to see
a girl fly through the air
a girl fly through the air?

Where do I go? Where do I go?
To a gym-nas-tics meet,
To a gym-nas-tics meet.
That's where I go to see
a girl fly through the air.

Would you do it on a dare?

There are many ways to orchestrate chants. The two parts can be used to pit males against females, those born in January through June against those born in July through December, those wearing green against the others, and so forth. To add variety, parts might be assigned to individual volunteers or to small groups of differing sizes.

Some chants are partially improvised by students. For example, the students can sit in a circle on the floor.[2] A rhythm is set by the snapping of fingers. The teacher begins the chant with something like "My name is _____. What's your name?" The teacher looks at the student on the right, who responds, "My name is _____. What's your name?" That student looks at the next student on the right, who responds, and so on around the circle. Variations can overlap into affective activities (see Chapter 14). "My name is _____ and I like _____" and "My name is _____ and I feel _____."

Although the chants above are oriented to beginning students (see page 137), intermediate and advanced students can learn idiomatic expressions through chants as well. Subtle forms of humor, decisions about the appropriateness of utterances, and symbolic content are only a few of the things to which students at higher levels can be introduced. Through the cadences, the students' pronunciation and intonation can become more natural without conscious drill.

MUSIC

Music, also, reduces anxiety and inhibition in second language students. Furthermore, it is a great motivator in that its lyrics are often very meaningful. Human emotions are frequently expressed in highly charged situations. Through music, language easily finds roots in the experience of students at any age or proficiency level. Often awareness is heightened through its prosodic elements. Kahlil Gibran once said, "The reality of music is in that vibration that remains in the ear after the singer finishes his song and the player no longer plucks the strings." Music can break down barriers among those who share its rhythms and meaning. Its unifying effect can extend across time, nations, races, and individuals.

At beginning levels, music can be used to teach basic vocabulary. Colors, body parts, simple actions, clothes, and names of people are only a few of the concepts that can be taught through music. The teacher doesn't have to be talented in music to make it a memorable experience. A gravely voice can exude as much enthusiasm as a euphonious one. Records or cassettes can provide the accompaniment in some situations. Words can be created and students' names can be inserted into stanzas coordinated with easy-to-learn melodies. For example, below are lyrics to sing to "You Are My Sunshine."

---

[2] I wish to thank Linda Cobral for sharing this idea with me.

Your name is Car-los.
Your name is Car-los.
You come from Per-u,
so far away.
And now you're with us
Until the summer.
And it is here
we want you to stay.

Your name is Sung Lee.
Your name is Sung Lee.
You're from Kor-e-a,
so far away.
And now you're with us
Maybe forever
Even after
your hair turns gray.

Your name is Ni-kom.
Your name is Ni-kom.
You come from La-os,
so far away.
And now you're with us
We are so happy.
We want to sing with you today.

Although Carlos, Sung Lee, and Nikom may not understand all the words the first few times they hear them, they will be highly motivated to find out what is being sung about them. Thus, acquisition will be highly likely.

Specific matrices can be reinforced through music. Notice the lyrics of the following song, written to the tune of "Mary Had a Little Lamb."

Danella says, "Come on, let's go.
Come on, let's go. Come on, let's go."
Danella says, "Come on, let's go.
To the zoo on Friday."

Hung an-swers, "That's fine with me.
Fine with me. Fine with me."
Hung an-swers, "That's fine with me.
Let's go to the zoo on Friday."

Friday comes and off they go.
Off they go. Off they go.
Friday comes and off they go.
To see the an-i-mals.

First they see the elephants.
El-e-phants. El-e-phants.
First they see the el-e-phants.
In the mud-dy waters.

Then they walk to the lion's den.
Lion's den. Lion's den.
Then they walk to the lion's den.
To find him pacing back and forth.

And on the song goes through as many stanzas as the teacher wants to create. Once students become more proficient, they can add their own stanzas. The words written down and duplicated along with pictures can aid the students' understanding. Total physical response can be used, with students pointing to pictures of animals while the song is sung. A trip to the zoo can stimulate additional meaningful experiences.

For those preferring "professional" songs, Hap Palmer[3] has provided a series of songbooks and records (published by Educational Activities, Inc.). Figure 10.1 presents a song he wrote on body parts and actions for beginning students.

Although these songs are beneficial mainly to beginning students, there are many songs available for intermediate to advanced students. Even the "top ten" can provide one or two. Interestingly, a serious study has been done on the appropriateness of music for teaching a second language. Murphey (1992) looked at the characteristics of fifty pop songs and found them to be repetitive, basically simple, conversation-like, and vague enough to allow for very different interpretations. He argues that "these discourse features and the song-stuck-in-my-head phenomenon make them potentially rich learning materials in and out of the classroom" (p. 771). If one uses pop songs as text, the lyrics should be duplicated so students can have their own copies to take the words home and share with families and friends.

When presenting a song in class, let the students first listen to the song played on a CD or cassette. Then hand out the words and play the song again. The third time the song is played, students will probably sing along with you and the recording. Give the students time to ask about unfamiliar words or phrases. A discussion among students relating the song to their own lives and to the lives of others can follow.

---

[3] Thanks to Raquel Mireles for making me aware of these songbooks and records.

Figure 10.1. (From Hap Palmer, 1971)

POETRY

Although poetic elements are contained in chants and music lyrics, poetry must be treated as a separate category. Poems range in length from few words to a whole book. They are generally concise, sometimes deceptively simple, and often highly charged with emotional content. They can be used at a variety of levels to reinforce ideas and introduce new ones.

The following poem by Jack Prelutsky[4] is a favorite, especially among elementary schoolchildren. It reinforces the names of concrete objects in the classroom as it presents a fantasy that we all may have had at one time or another.

The Creature in the Classroom

It appeared inside our classroom
at a quarter after ten,
it gobbled up the blackboard,
three erasers and a pen.
It gobbled teacher's apple
and it bopped her with the core.
"How dare you!" she responded.
"You must leave us . . . there's the door."

The Creature didn't listen
but described an arabesque
as it gobbled all her pencils,
seven notebooks and her desk.
Teacher stated very calmly,
"Sir! you simply cannot stay,
I'll report you to the principal
unless you go away!"

But the thing continued eating,
it ate paper, swallowed ink,
as it gobbled up our homework
I believe I saw it wink.
Teacher finally lost her temper.
"OUT!" she shouted at the creature.
The creature hopped beside her
and GLOPP . . . it swallowed teacher.

---

[4] From *The Random House Book of Poetry for Children* (1983). Thanks to Norma Ramirez, who introduced me to this poem.

Poems may not at first be understood in their entirety. In fact, students, when initially exposed to them, may understand only a few words. However, upon subsequent exposures, they begin to understand more and more.

The next poem, by Edwin Arlington Robinson, is suitable for students in university or adult programs. It can be used at high-intermediate to advanced levels to reinforce various emotions such as happiness, love, envy, loneliness, and desperation, and to teach literary devices such as symbolism and metaphor. The poem leads naturally into a discussion of Richard Cory's life and the seeming irony of his death. What was missing in his life that was essential to his happiness? The cultural ramifications and the social taboos concerning suicide are also relevant to the discussion. A good follow-up is the classic narrative song of the same title from the Simon and Garfunkel recording *The Sounds of Silence* (Eclectic Music Company). In the song, Richard Cory owns a factory and the narrator, who works for him, envies his lifestyle and is shocked at his death, just as we are. Both poem and song are very powerful and can stimulate not only discussion but compositions as well.

Richard Cory

Whenever Richard Cory went down town,
We people on the pavement looked at him:
He was a gentleman from sole to crown,
Clean favored, and imperially slim.

And he was always quietly arrayed,
And he was always human when he talked;
But still he fluttered pulses when he said,
"Good-morning," and he glittered when he walked.

And he was rich—yes, richer than a king—
And admirably schooled in every grace:
In fine, we thought that he was everything
To make us wish that we were in his place.

So on we worked, and waited for the light,
And went without the meat, and cursed the bread;
And Richard Cory, one calm summer night,
Went home and put a bullet through his head.

In addition to listening to and reading poems written by others, some students, even at beginning levels, may want to write poems of their own. Christison, in her book *English Through Poetry* (1982), recommended concrete poetry, formed from pictures and words. For example, students can draw large butterflies such as the one in Figure 10.2. Once the butterflies have been drawn, words and phrases such as "light," "flying," "beautiful," "in the air," and "a dream" can be written on the wings or the bodies. A butterfly for a student at an intermediate to advanced level might look something like the one in Figure 10.3.[5]

Also recommended for students at intermediate to advanced levels are verse forms such as word cinquain, Japanese tanka, or haiku. Below are examples, each followed by a summary of the structure that it contains.

Word Cinquain

A cat
Full of mischief
Charges, dances, pounces
Brightens my longest days
A wonder

1st line: a word or two to name the topic
2nd line: two or three words that describe the topic
3rd line: three or four words that express action
4th line: four or five words that express personal attitude
5th line: a word or two to rename the topic

Tanka

Drifting in the sky
Clouds come and go in patterns
I look to the sun
The darkness hovers around
Slowly rain begins to fall

1st line: 5 syllables
2nd line: 7 syllables
3rd line: 5 syllables
4th line: 7 syllables
5th line: 7 syllables

Haiku

Flowers wave to me
As I pass them in the field. . . .
Gentle, swirling wind

1st line: 5 syllables
2nd line: 7 syllables
3rd line: 5 syllables
(Note: There is generally a break in thought between the second and third lines.)

---

[5] This poem and illustration are by Jane Decock and come from *Harbinger*, published by the Advanced Creative Writing Classes at Jefferson High School in Edgewater, Colorado.

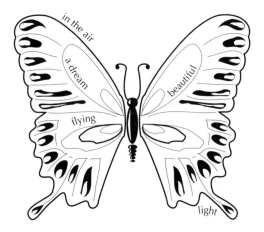

Figure 10.2. (adapted from Christison, 1982)

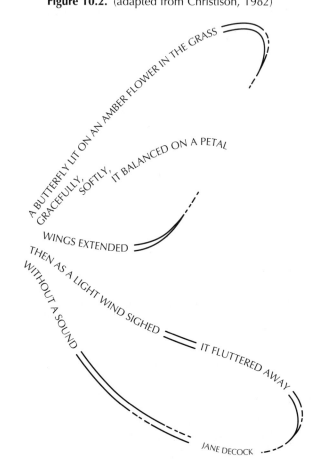

Figure 10.3

The verses can be written at first in groups with the help of the teacher or teacher assistants, using pictures to stimulate ideas. Later the students may want to try writing verses on their own.

Whether students are working in groups or individually, they should not be held to exact numbers of words or syllables for structured verse unless they can be shown how a poem might be improved by doing so.

Christison (1982) suggested that events in the students' lives provide the impetus for writing and sharing poetry. For example, students can create greeting cards to give others on special occasions. Birthdays, marriages, graduations, holidays, and other celebrations are ideal times to write and/or illustrate poetry. If the students don't want to write their own poetry, they can search in books for appropriate poems to put on their cards, giving credit to their sources.

Another idea she recommended is to have students draw or paint pictures and then find or write poems to go with them. Activities such as these can give students important reasons for reading and writing poetry, thus increasing their exposure to meaningful language.

SUMMARY

Chants, music, and poetry often produce lowered anxiety and greater ego permeability among second language learners. Beginners are often able to internalize chunks of language, allowing them to participate in social situations early on. During initial phases of language development, students often want to communicate but do not have the necessary skills. By having a communicative repertoire (however limited), students form bonds with competent speakers and thus are positioned to receive more input.

Intermediate and advanced students also gain benefits from chants, music, and poetry. Idiomatic expressions, subtle forms of humor, decisions concerning appropriateness, and symbolic content can be internalized through these media. Pronunciation and intonation patterns become more natural through use of word/sound play. Students can be exposed to situations in which highly meaningful content can be dealt with on many different levels.

READINGS, REFLECTION, AND DISCUSSION

Suggested Readings and Reference Materials

Bell, D. (1999). Rise, Sally, Rise: Communicating Through Dance. *TESOL Journal*, 8(1), 27–31. Chants and songs are combined with dance to teach language through the synchronization of voice, rhythm, and bodily movement. The goal is to improve pronunciation and fluency in the new language by placing emphasis on conversational stress patterns and rhythm.

Dunleavy, D. (1992). *The Language Beat*. Portsmouth, NH: Heinemann. Includes ways to incorporate music into classroom instruction. The book offers original songs with related activities involving choral reading, drama, creative writing, and much more.

Graham, C. (2001). *Jazz chants: Old and New*. New York: Oxford University. A popular collection of chants to use with beginning through advanced students of English as a second language. Often humorous dialogues are presented based on commonplace situations and events. Teaching notes, exercises in the various skill areas, and a cassette are included. Other titles of interest are *Small Talk, Grammar Chants, Jazz Chants for Children, Jazz Chant Fairy Tales, Mother Goose Jazz Chants, Holiday Jazz Chants*, and *Let's Chant, Let's Sing*.

Grenough, M. (1993). *Sing It! Learn English Through Song*. New York: McGraw-Hill/Contemporary. This series of all-time favorite songs consists of six textbooks covering beginning through advanced levels. The accompanying workbooks and audio programs allow students to work in skill areas such as listening, writing, grammar, and vocabulary.

Graves, D. (1992). *Explore Poetry*. Portsmouth, NH: Heinemann. Both the reading and writing of poetry for children are explored here. The author encourages teachers to integrate poetry throughout the curriculum.

Moulton, M. and Holmes, V. (1997). Pattern poems: Creative writing for language acquisition. *The Journal of the Imagination in Language Learning*, IV, 84–90. The authors present several types of pattern poems including cinquain and pattern poems about specific topics such as the five senses, heroes, and other people. Some of the patterns require specific grammatical forms within the poems; others require each line to fulfill a specific purpose such as name a person, give three words that describe that person, etc.

Questions and Projects for Reflection and Discussion

1. Compare the use of repetition and imitation in the audiolingual method (see Chapter 1) with the use of similar strategies in chants, songs, and poetry. In what ways do you think the latter might render the strategies more "palatable"?

2. What role do you think routines and patterns play in the second language acquisition process? How might the proficiency level at which students are exposed to routines and patterns make a difference in their role? Explain.

3. Choose a topic to develop a beginning lesson around. See the sample lesson format on page 322. Find a chant, some lyrics set to a popular song, or a poem to introduce or reinforce some of the key concepts. You may write your own if you wish. Present your lesson to a group of fellow students. Inform them about what other activities might be used to

reinforce the same concepts. Discuss with them the strengths of your lesson and ways in which you might improve it. Begin by sharing your own reactions to the lesson.

If you are currently teaching students, use what you have learned to try out a chant, lyrics, or a poem with them. Make sure the lesson you prepare is relevant to the content they are studying and appropriate to level. If possible, have your lesson videotaped to analyze and discuss with peers. Reflect on its outcome and how you felt about doing it. Pay close attention to student response. Do you see any problems with your lesson? How might it be improved?

Write about your experiences using chants, lyrics, or poems and what you learned in your journal.

CHAPTER 11

Storytelling, Role Play, and Drama

Drama is like the naughty child who climbs the high walls and ignores the "No Trespassing" sign. It does not allow us to define our territory so exclusively; it forces us to take as our starting-point life, not language.

A. Maley and A. Duff, 1983

QUESTIONS TO THINK ABOUT

1. How important do you think storytelling is to children acquiring a first language? What about role play and/or drama?

2. Do you think older children, teenagers, and adults learning a second or foreign language might also benefit from storytelling, role play, and/or drama? If so, in what ways? What is there about these activities that might facilitate the language learning process?

3. Recall your own experiences with one or more of these activities in learning another language. What effects do you think they may have had on your own language development?

4. Think of some ways storytelling, role play, and drama can be incorporated into a second or foreign language program.

5. How might stories and drama be used to affirm students' cultural traditions and values?

Storytelling, role play, and drama allow students to explore their inner resources, empathize with others, and use their own experiences as scaffolds upon which to build credible action. As a result, students can improve their ability to produce the target language, acquire many of its nonverbal nuances, improve the ability to work cooperatively in group situations, and effectively deal with affective issues. In the results of a questionnaire given to UCLA teachers and students, Susan Stern found support for her theory that drama has a positive effect on second language learning. It encourages the operation of certain psychological factors that facilitate oral communication: heightened self-esteem, motivation, and spontaneity; increased capacity for empathy; and lowered sensitivity to rejection (1983, p. 216).

Because they are absorbed in playing out life's experiences, second language students can overcome the self-consciousness generally associated with learning another language. In addition, by losing themselves in the struggles and conflicts of others, they can become better able to make the target language part of their memory store (see Episode Hypothesis in Chapter 16).

Before the teacher involves students in storytelling, role play, or drama, a series of warm-ups is recommended to reduce anxiety and to create a warm, active environment.

WARM-UPS

The warm-ups included here require almost no verbal language and therefore can be used with true beginners. In addition, they help establish trust and understanding among group members and lower inhibitions. The teacher can begin with a series of simple exercises involving stretching, bending, and tightening and relaxing specific muscle groups before proceeding to the activities below.

Warm-Up Activities

CIRCLE MIMICS

Students form a circle. The first student is asked to make a movement such as hopping on one foot. The second student repeats the movement and adds a new one such as shaking a fist in the air. The third student hops on one foot, shakes a fist in the air, and adds a third movement, and so on around the circle.

BASEBALL MIME

Throw a make-believe ball across the room to one of your students. After the student "catches" it, motion to the student to join you in a game of catch. Then throw the ball to other students, and motion to them to join you also. The game can remain simply a game of catch, or it can develop into a full baseball game if the students are familiar with baseball. Give one student a make-believe bat, and station the others around the room at pretend bases. Let the students take over the game.

Once students have worked out tension and lowered inhibitions, they may be ready for storytelling.

STORYTELLING

Stories have traditionally been used to teach, to entertain, and to explain the unknown. The activities offered here can be coordinated with other practices described in this book. Some of the activities are more appropriate to beginning levels; others, to more advanced levels. Most can be adapted to any age level provided they are within the students' range cognitively.

Exposing students to a story before fully understanding the words can be highly motivating for beginners at any age.[1] The same story can be used from time to time in different ways until a full understanding is achieved over a period of perhaps several months. Activities such as those presented below enable the students to participate in the language *before* actually being proficient in it, just as children do when being read to in their first language. Through these activities, curiosity in the target language can be stimulated.

Storytelling Activities

STORY EXPERIENCE[2]
Level: Beginning

Have the students form a large circle. Choose a story or a narrative poem such as the one that follows. (This particular poem is oriented to children, although adults have been found to enjoy it, too.) Pick out the concrete words that can be easily acted out. Assign to each student a word to act out. Help the students understand what the word means by demonstrating its meaning or by showing a picture to illustrate. Then read the story aloud with much feeling. Each student listens carefully for his or her word. When the word is read, the student crosses the circle, acting it out while moving across. Students on the other side make room as the actors come across.

For the following story excerpt, the teacher will need these words acted out: a fly, a spider, a bird, a cat, a dog, a cow, and a horse.

---

[1] Note that this recommendation appears to fly in the face of the arguments favoring comprehensible input. It is true that if the story were simply read aloud with little expression of feeling and if there were no physical involvement on the part of the student, then it probably would be as meaningless as most other input that is not understood.

[2] This activity has been adapted from one presented by the Barzak Institute of San Francisco at a workshop done for the Jefferson County Public Schools of Colorado in 1979.

Excerpt from *There Was an Old Lady Who Swallowed a Fly*[3]

There was an old lady who swallowed a *fly*.
I don't know why she swallowed a *fly*.
Perhaps she'll die.

There was an old lady who swallowed a *spider*,
That wriggled and wriggled and jiggled inside her.

She swallowed the *spider* to catch the *fly*.
I don't know why she swallowed a *fly*.
Perhaps she'll die.

There was an old lady who swallowed a *bird*.
How absurd, to swallow a *bird*!
She swallowed the *bird* to catch the *spider*.

There was an old lady who swallowed a *cat*.
Well, fancy that, she swallowed a *cat*!
She swallowed the *cat* to catch the *bird*.

There was an old lady who swallowed a *dog*.
What a hog, to swallow a *dog*!
She swallowed the *dog* to catch the *cat*.

There was an old lady who swallowed a *cow*.
I don't know how she swallowed a *cow*!
She swallowed the *cow* to catch the *dog*.
She swallowed the *dog* to catch the *cat*.
She swallowed the *cat* to catch the *bird*.
She swallowed the *bird* to catch the *spider*,
That wriggled and wriggled and jiggled inside her.
She swallowed the *spider* to catch the *fly*.
I don't know why she swallowed a *fly*.
Perhaps she'll die.

There was an old lady who swallowed a *horse*.
She's dead of course.

Bonne (1973)

The next story experience activity is oriented toward teenagers and adults. This time, the students in the circle hold cards of various colors: red, yellow, blue, white, and so on. Work with the students to make sure they are able to associate the words with the particular colors to which each has been assigned. The students are to listen very carefully to the words as the story is read. When the names of their colors are read, they walk across the circle, holding up the colored card.

---

[3] Those who would like the story in its entirety can refer to the version by Ruth Bonne, illustrated by Pam Adams, and published by Child's Play (International). I wish to thank Ernestine Saldivar for introducing me to this version.

More than one student may have the same color. The number of students holding each color will depend upon how many persons are involved at any given time.

A Spring Day

The door opens wide. It is Sasha. Sasha comes to my house every morning at six o'clock. We walk to work together. Today is such a beautiful, warm day. We walk on the long sidewalk. A YELLOW sun peeks through the trees. It is spring. The flowers are opening up—RED flowers, YELLOW flowers, BLUE flowers. We see a man in the street. He is riding a RED bicycle. He is wearing boots and a BLUE hat. He stops riding. He asks, "Have you seen our rabbit? He's WHITE and BLACK, mostly BLACK. He got out of the cage this morning and must have come this way." He points toward the grass behind us. We look in the direction he is pointing. Then at each other.

"No, we haven't," we say at the same time. "Sorry." The man looks very worried. He gets back on his bicycle. He begins to ride away. "Wait," I yell. "I see something here . . . behind the bush. I think . . . I see fur . . . it's WHITE and BLACK—why it is. It's a rabbit and it looks very scared. Look, it's all hunched over." The man turns around and rides back. I pick up the frightened little ball of fur and hand it to him. "Oh, thank you so very much!" exclaims the man. "My little boy will be very happy." He cuddles the rabbit in one arm as he rides away.

Once the students are familiar with the colors and feel comfortable with the activity, they pretend to be the objects as they go across the circle. One can, for example, be the sun; others can be flowers, and so forth. Even the characters and main actions of the story can be acted out once a fuller understanding is achieved.

One out of two distinct alternatives can be pursued:

- begin with a core story (the simplest form of the story) that can be gradually expanded by adding more complex syntactic structures and more and more abstract vocabulary as the students move forward in the language, or
- begin with the fully developed story and the students can "grow into it" over time.

THE NARRATIVE APPROACH[4]
Level: Beginning

The narrative approach begins with a core story that is very short (at first). The teacher draws pictures (stick figures will do) that tell a story. The teacher narrates the story using very simple language and very short sentences as he or she points to the pictures and gestures to make the meaning clear. The teacher then tells the story two or three more times, adding more details each time about the characters, the setting, etc.

Later the teacher tells different versions of the story and draws new pictures to show the changes. The new versions may use the same story but create added characters or a new ending, extend the story, or tell the story from the point of view of a different character. Then the class creates a story with blank frames for the teacher to draw in (perhaps on a transparency) as the students tell the story. The teacher then retells the story to make sure he or

---

[4] Jeff McQuillan and Lucy Tse (1998) described this approach. I want to thank Leslie Jo Adams for making me aware of their description.

she understood it correctly. Finally, the students create a story individually or in small groups while they illustrate them. If they are unable to produce the language, they can just draw the story while the teacher narrates it for the whole class.

SOUND EFFECTS
Level: Beginning

Demonstrate the sound effects that accompany the following story.[5] Beginning students only have to listen for the words that cue the appropriate effect (blanks have been inserted where the sound effects should go). Once the students understand the whole story (perhaps at an intermediate level), they can act it out. If they want, they can change the ending or rewrite it completely.

Rosita's Night to Remember

Rosita is alone in the house. Outside she hears the wind blow through the trees _____ (hooing noises). Rain begins to fall _____ (patting of fingertips on the desks). There is a scratching at the door _____ (light touch of fingernails scratching on desks). Maybe it is a lion _____ (roaring). Maybe it is a mouse _____ (squeaking). Maybe it is a monster _____ (howling). She is scared. She turns on the radio to drown out the scratching. The radio is playing a song _____ (singing—it doesn't have to be a particular tune). She turns it low _____ (the singing softens), high _____ (it becomes very loud), off _____ (it stops). At the door, the scratching continues _____ . She opens the door _____ (creaking). Her dog comes in, jumps up, and gives her a big kiss _____ (kissing sound).

As the students become more proficient, they can write their own scenarios, complete with sound effects. At advanced levels, the minidramas can even become part of full-blown radio shows complete with commercials and newsbreaks.

STORY ACT-OUT
Level: Beginning to Intermediate

Read a favorite story aloud while the students listen. Give students a chance to ask questions, then read the story again. Ask for volunteers to take the parts of the characters. Pin a sign with the character's name on each volunteer. Read the story a third time as students act it out, action by action. Then give other volunteers a chance to be the actors.

BILINGUAL STORYTELLING
Level: Beginning to Advanced

Bilingual storytelling involves telling a story in some combination of two languages. Often the teacher begins by telling the story in the students' first language and then tells the same story in the second. By offering a story that is well-known to the students in their first language, a link can be formed to the students' culture, which is one way of affirming that culture. Not only that, but familiar stories are much easier to comprehend in the new language once they've been told in the native language. In classrooms where multiple

---

[5] This story is an adaptation of one shared with me by Sylvia Pena.

languages are spoken, students can be divided into groups, depending upon which language is their native one. Advanced students of the second language can be assigned to their own native language groups and can tell the story to the others in both languages.

At intermediate levels and above, the students may read the same story in both languages. Stories can be written by the students in one language and then translated into one or more languages. *Code switching* may be used within the same story. Its parts may be told or written in alternating languages, depending on what is most appropriate for a particular story.

Folktales and legends lend themselves particularly well to bilingual storytelling.

WHAT'S THE TITLE?
Level: Intermediate

Read a story to students but leave out the title. Once the students understand the story, let them make up a title for it. Eventually the author's title can be revealed and discussed in relation to the meaning of the story.

SPINNING STORIES[6]
Level: Intermediate

Take a ball of yarn and tie knots in it at varying intervals. Some knots will be close together, others far apart. Tape a stimulating picture with people in it to the wall. After placing students in a circle, ask them what they see in the picture. Write the words on the board as they give them to you so that they will have some starters. Have students make up names and short biographical sketches for the people in the picture. Give the ball of yarn to one student in the circle. Ask him or her to begin a story about the picture while unraveling the ball of yarn. The student continues to tell the story until he or she reaches the first knot. Then the ball of yarn is passed to the next person, who continues the story until reaching the next knot. The activity continues until every student in the circle has had a chance to contribute.

GROUP STORY
Level: Intermediate

Using a language-experience type of activity (see Chapter 13), have the students create a group story. As each student makes his or her contribution, write the utterances on the board, making any necessary corrections indirectly. The stories will probably be very brief at first but will evolve into longer and more complex plots as the students gain proficiency. A series of pictures can be used to stimulate ideas.

SILLY STORIES[7]
Level: Intermediate to Advanced

You and your students can create a story together while a teacher assistant writes it on the board. Begin by offering the first half of a sentence, and have a volunteer student finish it. Other sentences can be produced in the same fashion. Pictures can be used to stimulate thought. For example:

---

[6] Adapted from an activity shared with me by Esther Heise.

[7] This idea has been adapted from Wright, Betteridge, and Buckby (1984, p. 99).

TEACHER: The elephant knocked at . . .
STUDENT 1: . . . the door to my house.
TEACHER: He asked . . .
STUDENT 2: . . . "Can I borrow a cup of straw?"

GHOST STORIES BY CANDLELIGHT
Level: Intermediate to Advanced

Ask each student to bring a scary story to tell the class in the target language. Have the students sit in a circle on the floor. Light a candle, place it in the center of the circle, and turn off the lights. Students can be told that they can volunteer by taking the candle from the center and placing it in front of them so it lights up their faces. Then they proceed to tell their stories. The candle is returned to the center as each student finishes his or her story. The teacher should demonstrate the procedure first. Background music, the volume of which can easily be adjusted to fit the situation, can be used to fill the silence between volunteers while adding to the mood. Because this activity may be a little too frightening for young children, you will probably want to limit its use to older children, teens, and adults. A flashlight may be used to substitute for a candle as a safety measure, especially for preadolescents.[8]

FINISH THE STORY
Level: Intermediate to Advanced

Present part of a story, and have students finish it orally and/or in writing. At first, most of the story can be given. Later, only a few lines such as those below may be necessary to launch students into building a climax followed by the denouement.

The boys see a dark shadow fall across the sidewalk. They look up and see . . .

The first day of her trip went well. Then she opened her suitcase. She discovered . . .

ORAL HISTORY
Level: Intermediate to Advanced

As part of a study of local history, students tell their own stories and those of their parents, grandparents, friends, and neighbors. Where did they come from? How did they get here (to this town, suburb, city, state, country)? The project can be as broad as the students want to make it. They can include stories about their experiences in the particular locale, how certain buildings came into being, how traditions developed, and so forth. Collections can be made of these stories to share with each other, with other classes, and/or with visitors to the classroom.

STORY INTERPRETATION
Level: Intermediate to Advanced

The following story is one that is sure to interest English Language Learners (ELLs) in particular because it involves the mixed feelings that accompany returning to one's homeland.

---

[8] I want to thank Cesar Montes for suggesting this precaution to me.

First motivate students to read the story with what I call "mind grabbers." Questions about their own longings to return home or about what they think it might be like to return home will serve well in preparing them for the experience in store for them. Following the story are relevant activities that can heighten its impact.

Excerpt from "Blue Winds Dancing," by Thomas S. Whitecloud

Morning. I spend the day cleaning up and buying some presents for my family with what is left of my money. Nothing much, but a gift is a gift, if a man buys it with his last quarter. I wait until evening, then start up the track toward home.

Christmas Eve comes in on a north wind. Snow clouds hang over the pines, the night comes early. Walking along the railroad bed, I feel the calm peace of snow-bound forests on either side of me. I take my time; I am back in a world where time does not mean so much now.

I am alone—alone but not nearly so lonely as I was back on the campus at school. Those are never lonely who love the snow and the pines, never lonely when the pines are wearing white shawls and snow crunches coldly underfoot. . . .

Just as a light snow begins to fall, I cross the reservation boundary. Somehow it seems as though I have stepped into another world. Deep woods in a white-and-black winter night. A faint trail leading to the village.

The railroad on which I stand comes from a city sprawled by a lake—a city with a million people who walk around without seeing one another; a city sucking the life from all the country around; a city with stores and police and intellectuals and criminals and movies and apartment houses; a city with its politics and libraries and zoos.

Laughing, I go into the woods. As I cross a frozen lake, I begin to hear the drums. Soft in the night the drums beat. It is like the pulse of the world. The white line of the lake ends at a black forest, and above the trees the blue winds are dancing.

I come to the outlying houses of the village. Simple box houses, etched black in the night. From one or two windows soft lamplight falls on the snow. Christmas is here, too, but it does not mean much—not much in the way of parties and presents. Joe Sky will get drunk. Alex Bodidash will buy his children red mittens and a new sled. . . . The village is not a sight to instill pride, yet I am not ashamed. One can never be ashamed of his own people when he knows they have dreams as beautiful as white snow on a tall pine.

Father and my brother and sister are seated around the table as I walk in. Father stares at me for a moment. Then I am in his arms, crying on his shoulder. I give them the presents I have brought, and my throat tightens as I watch my sister save carefully bits of red string from the packages. I hide my feelings by wrestling with my brother when he strikes my shoulder in token of affection. Father looks at me, and I know he has many questions, but he seems to know why I have come. He tells me to go on alone to the lodge, and he will follow.

I follow the trail to the lodge. My feet are light, my heart seems to sing to the music, and I hold my head high. Across white snow fields blue winds are dancing.

Before the lodge door I stop, afraid. I wonder if my people will remember me. I wonder—"Am I Indian, or am I white?" I stand before the door a long time. I hear the ice groan on the lake, and remember the story of the old woman who is under the ice, trying to get out, so she can punish some runaway lovers. . . .

Inside the lodge there are many Indians. Some sit on benches around the walls. Others dance in the center of the floor around a drum. Nobody seems to notice me. It seems as though I were among a people I have never seen before. . . . I look at the old men. Straight, dressed in dark trousers and beaded velvet vests, wearing soft moccasins. Dark, lined faces intent on the music. I wonder if I am at all like them. They dance on, lifting their feet to the rhythm of the drums. . . .

The dance stops. The men walk back to the walls and talk in low tones or with their hands. There is little conversation, yet everyone seems to be sharing some secret . . . they are sharing a mood. Everyone is happy . . . the night is beautiful outside, and the music is beautiful.

I try hard to forget school and white people, and be one of these—my people . . . we are all a part of something universal. I watch eyes and see now that the old people are speaking to me. They nod slightly, imperceptibly, and their eyes laugh into mine. I look around the room. All the eyes are friendly; they all laugh. No one questions my being here. The drums begin to beat again, and I catch the invitation in the eyes of the old men. My feet begin to lift to the rhythm, and I look out beyond the walls into the night and see the lights. I am happy. It is beautiful. I am home.

Follow-up Activities to "Blue Winds Dancing"

1. First, ask the students if there are any words or phrases that they do not understand. Ask them to guess at the meanings by using the context. Discuss.
2. Have volunteers retell the story to a guest who is not already familiar with it (you may want to invite someone in for this purpose).
3. Divide the students into pairs. Have one person take the part of the man who comes home and the other the part of one of the older men at the lodge. Have them make up a dialogue, write it down, and practice it. Ask volunteers to share their scenes with the class.
4. Divide the students into groups of three. Have them speculate about what it would be like to return to their homelands. Encourage them to share the problems they might have as well as the delights.

STORY WRITING
Level: Advanced

Students can be given time to write and share their own stories. They may want to make their stories autobiographical, biographical, or fictional. As a culminating activity, put copies of all the stories together in a book with illustrations and a table of contents. The books can be shared with other classes or placed in the school's library to be checked out by anyone who wants to read them.

ROLE PLAY

Role play has high appeal for students because it allows them to be creative and to put themselves in another person's place for a while. As Atticus Finch says in Harper Lee's *To Kill a Mockingbird*, "You never really understand a person until you consider things from his view—until you climb into his skin and walk around in it." Role play can be just "play" or it can have serious social implications, such as in sociodrama.

Scarcella (1983) defined sociodrama as being student-oriented rather than teacher-oriented. Students act out solutions to social problems, generally defining their own roles and determining their own courses of action. The enactment is open-ended but centers around a clearly stated conflict that is relevant to the students. Only those students who demonstrate a special interest in particular roles are chosen to play them. The steps adapted from Shaftel and Shaftel (1967), include the following:

1. introducing the topic
2. stimulating student interest
3. presenting new vocabulary
4. reading a story that clearly identifies a problem
5. stopping the story at the climax
6. discussing the dilemma
7. selecting students to play the roles
8. preparing the audience to listen and later to offer advice
9. acting out the rest of the story
10. discussing alternative ways of dealing with the problem
11. replaying the dramas using new strategies if necessary

Some sample mini-sociodramas (one might call them simply "role-play situations") are below.

Roleplay Situations

FOR ADULTS OR TEENAGERS

Sun Kim comes home from school all excited. Jeff, an Anglo-American boy, has asked her for a date. She tells her mother. Her mother is very upset.

"In Korea, you do not do any such thing," her mother reminds her.

"But, Mother, this is not Korea. This is America."

"But we are Korean," her mother insists. "You are Korean. This is not what we do. In time you will be ready. Your father and I will arrange a nice Korean man for you. We will not let you go alone with this man."

"Oh, Mother . . . but . . . I . . ."

FOR PREADOLESCENTS

"Look. I'm as big as you," Anita says to her brother John. She stretches up on her tiptoes. "Why can't I go to the movie with you?"

"Look, Squirt, you stay home this time, okay. The movie is not for you because . . . "

FOR YOUNG CHILDREN

"Mom, come here. Come here. The cat is stuck up in the tree. He won't come down. Come quick."

Mother sticks her head around the door. "Now just a minute, Sally. Don't panic. The first thing we'll do is . . ."

It's important that the students be gradually worked into the role-play situations. The teacher can get them into their roles by asking questions such as, "How old are you, Anita? What kinds of movies do your parents want you to see?" When the students seem to feel comfortable in their roles, the teacher can reread the situation and let the actors take it at the point where the story leaves off.

For the more proficient students, another activity that can be adapted to various age groups is acting out roles of characters from literature. Literature can come alive when students play the role of a character with which they are familiar. For example, if they have just read *The Pearl* by John Steinbeck (1947), one student may want to play Juana and another Kino. The characters could be interviewed as they might be on a talk show, or they might be part of a panel discussion on what money and greed can do to one's life. In addition, people from history might be brought back to life for a day or two. For example, one student might play Abraham Lincoln and another Susan B. Anthony. After students read up on their lives and times, these characters can be brought together for a TV show during which they can have discussions about relevant topics. Other characters from history could be pitted against each other in a debate about something current. It would be interesting to see how Henry VIII might feel about divorce or how Joan of Arc might react to feminist issues.

Mid-beginners also can participate in role play. Tools for communication can be taught through role-play situations. Students can be given matrices on index cards to be used as cues. Short scenes can begin with total-physical-response activities in which the teacher plays the role of the director and directs students in their parts (move to the right, sit down, walk to the table, say, "Are you ready to order?"). Matrices such as those below can be tailored to fit different situations. It is suggested that similar matrices first be incorporated into chants and lyrics (see Chapter 10).

In a restaurant:

(*Menus are given to two customers by the waiter who disappears for a few minutes and then returns.*)
Are you ready to order?
Yes, I will have the _____.
And you? (*looks at the second person*)
I will have the _____.

At the produce store:

(*A clerk is setting out baskets of strawberries. A customer approaches from behind.*)
Excuse me. Can you please tell me where the _____ is/are?
Oh, yes. It's/they're by the _____.
Thank you.

Typical greetings, simple compliments, frequently asked questions, and often-used comments can be introduced or reinforced in this manner (see also

Bardovi-Harlig, Hartford, Mahan-Taylor, Morgan, and Reynolds, 1996). Public places, in addition to those mentioned above, can be simulated to serve as settings (a post office, a doctor's office, a library, a hospital). Eventually the students can simply be given an oral description of a situation (no cue cards this time) to which they can respond through role play.

> You are in a restaurant. The waiter comes to take your order. You look at the menu and tell the waiter what you want.
> You are in a produce store. You can't find what you want to buy. You ask the clerk for help.

The most beneficial kind of role play, however, is that in which the *teacher plays a key role*. For example, if the teacher is the waiter in the restaurant or the clerk in the produce store, he or she can provide comprehensible input to extend the conversation. The teacher can prompt, expand, or offer help as needed. By this means, groups of mixed abilities can be included in the same role-play situation. Starters are offered to some, explanations provided to others, and others are given no help at all if they don't need it. Below is an illustration to show how this can work.

At a produce store (*The students have been given play money and have had prior experience counting it.*)
Pedro stands in front of the strawberries.

TEACHER: (*or teacher assistant playing the role of the clerk*) Strawberries? For you, Pedro? (*She holds up a basket of strawberries.*)
PEDRO: Aaa. . . Straw . . .
TEACHER: Strawberries? Do you want strawberries?
PEDRO: . . . Strawberries . . . (*nods his head*).
TEACHER: (*offering the basket to him*) Do you want to buy the strawberries? Yes? (*points to some play money in the box which serves as a cash register.*)
PEDRO: Yes . . . buy.
TEACHER: One dollar. Give me one dollar. (*Pedro takes some play money from his pocket but looks puzzled.*)
TEACHER: One dollar (*points to a dollar bill in his hand*).
PEDRO: One dollar (*gives the teacher the dollar bill*).
TEACHER: Thank you (*takes the money and gives him the basket*).
PEDRO: Thank you.
TEACHER: (*turning to the next customer*) Do you want some strawberries, Nor?
NOR: I want oranges.
TEACHER: Oranges, huh (*moves to the oranges*). I've got juicy ones for you.
NOR: Juicy?
TEACHER: Yes. Juicy. Lots of sweet juice (*squeezes one to show its softness*).
NOR: Oh yes. Juice.
TEACHER: They cost $1.50 a bag. Do you want a bag?
NOR: Yes. I'll take a bag (*gives the teacher the money and takes the oranges*).

Thus the teacher is able to adjust the input to fit the approximate level of each student. *No cue cards are needed*. With sufficient input, the students will begin to acquire the structures through the interaction.

DRAMA

Drama, even though an integral part of storytelling and role play, constitutes its own separate category. It includes activities involving roles, plots, and dialogues that are written in play form to be memorized and acted out on the stage or read aloud. The introductory activities recommended here are suitable as warm-ups for storytelling and role play as well.

ACT IT OUT
Level: Beginning

At lower proficiency levels, introduce students to simple dramatized emotions. First model the emotions, using exaggerated facial expressions and other movements to illustrate *joy, anger, fear, sadness,* and *doubt.* Have students model the emotions as a group (see also "Identifying Emotions" in Chapter 8). Have students refine their abilities to recognize and reproduce emotions by learning to draw them. (See Figure 11.1.)

Figure 11.1. (adapted from Evans and Moore, 1982)

For further reinforcement, have students find pictures in magazines of people expressing specific feelings. Students can cut out the pictures and paste them in a book of emotions (have them label one page "Joy," another "Fear," another "Anger," and so forth).

At a higher proficiency level, have students each write the name of an emotion on a
piece of paper to be put into a grab bag. Each student draws an emotion out of the grab
bag and acts it out while the rest of the class guesses which emotion is being portrayed. At
another time, the names of specific activities are written on the pieces of paper, the students draw them out and pantomime the activities while the class guesses what activity is
being acted out.

TV Show
Level: Beginning

Choose an interesting segment of a TV show such as a soap opera or situation comedy to
videotape. Show the video first without sound and let the students decide the emotions that
the actors are feeling. Later show the same segment, again without sound, and let students
figure out what is happening just from facial expressions and actions. Then replay the same
segment and listen to the words. How close did the students come to guessing the reality?
Discuss. It is not necessary that they understand all the words. Play it again in a few
months, and have students write and act out additional segments. Eventually, have them
write and stage their own shows.

Puppets
Level: Intermediate

Have students, particularly younger ones, each make a puppet out of heavy construction
paper and a tongue depressor (see Figure 11.2).[9] For the head, have them cut out two

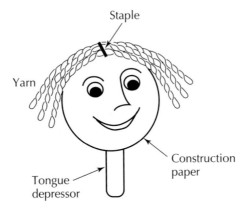

Figure 11.2

---

[9] This idea came from a handout distributed at a presentation by Susan Andrews during the Spring
COTESOL Conference 1980, Denver, Colorado.

identical shapes from construction paper and staple the edges together, leaving an opening at the neck. Placing a small wad of newspaper inside gives the puppet a three-dimensional effect. Have them place the tongue depressor where the neck should be and staple the paper to it. Yarn can be used for hair. A felt-tip pen can be used to draw eyes, a nose, and a mouth. Have them give the puppet a name and make it a character in a series of dramas or miniscenarios written and acted out by the students. An alternative is to have students make flannel-board characters to move about on a large flannel board. Glue strips of flannel to the backs of the characters so they will stick to a flannel backdrop (the flannel board).

PROP BOX
Level: Intermediate to Advanced

This activity intended for the upper elementary grades and later is an adaptation of "The Prop Box," created by Judy Winn-Bell Olsen.[10] Have each student bring to class something from home that isn't wanted anymore. It can be from any room in the house but it must be something that the teacher can keep. Place all the items in a large box (the prop box). Divide the class into groups of two, three, or four students. Ask each student to reach into the prop box without looking and draw out an item. Have the groups write short dramas or skits that incorporate all the items they have drawn out of the box as props. Students then rehearse the plays with the help of peer teachers or lay assistants (see Chapter 15) and present them to the whole class.

READERS' THEATER
Level: Intermediate to Advanced

Goodman and Tenney (1979) recommended readers' theater as a vehicle for acquiring a second language. The name "readers' theater" comes from the fact that the actors hold their scripts and read from them with expression and feeling. The actors and the narrator generally sit on tall stools arranged in a semicircle in front of the audience. The actors imagine that the wall in back of the audience is a mirror. The actors talk directly to the mirror "images" of the other characters rather than address them directly. In fact, they more or less ignore the presence of the other characters except as they appear in the "mirror." Characters who are supposed to be offstage also sit on stools, but keep their backs to the audience, facing the audience only upon their entrances. The narrator, who addresses the audience directly, plays a large role: He or she sets the scene, introduces the characters, and gives running comments about actions, feelings, and moods. In other words, the narrator provides the glue that holds the dialogue together and makes it comprehensible.

Because readers' theater involves much repetition through rehearsals for presentation, the words eventually become part of the students' repertoires without conscious memorization. The whole class, even the audience, begins to internalize the lines if they are in on the rehearsals. Reading also can be enhanced for the audience if they are able to look

---

[10] She gives credit to the Creative Environment Center, SFUSD workshop for this suggestion. Prop boxes can be used to teach other lessons, particularly in conjunction with other communicative practices (see especially Chapter 9). For example, one box could include household items, another camping equipment, etc.

at the scripts as the lines are read. Goodman and Tenney were convinced that creating a script and putting on a play can be an excellent culminating activity for units of study. Through it, concepts and structures are acquired and/or reinforced.

Goodman and Tenney suggested that the teacher first have the actors read the dialogue aloud and then ask the audience what was especially effective about the way it was read. The teacher then discusses the drama with the students to create interest in the problems of the characters. The teacher as director should model the roles to encourage the students to put aside some of their own inhibitions. Students then read the parts one more time with added expression and feeling. The audience can be called on for suggestions, including ideas, sound effects, or other elements. The teacher makes sure all the students who want to participate are part of the production in some way. See the example of a readers' theater script below:

An Unusual Birthday Celebration

NARRATOR: It is mid-afternoon. Two elderly women and a dog are on the sidewalk. They are in front of the ice-cream store on Maple Street.

MABEL: Well, Nettie, what will we get today?

NARRATOR: She smiles at Nettie. Their eyes are dancing.

NETTIE: I want something very special today . . . something new.

NARRATOR: Nettie tugs at her dog's leash.

NETTIE: Now you be a good boy and lie down.

NARRATOR: She points to the sidewalk in front of the glass door. The dog lies down obediently. The two women go into the store.

MABEL: Something new? You're going to try something new? You always want the same old thing. A cone with one scoop of chocolate. You always get that.

NETTIE: But today I want something special. Today is my birthday, you know. Seventy-six years old.

NARRATOR: She looks at all the pictures on the wall. There are ice-cream sundaes everywhere. Chocolate and caramel drip from them. They are covered with nuts, whipped cream, and cherries. Her mouth waters. Mabel says . . .

MABEL: Happy birthday!

NETTIE: Thank you.

MABEL: Yes. You must get something different to celebrate. Did you hear from your son today? Did he wish you a happy birthday?

NARRATOR: Mabel's hands flutter in the air. Nettie's smile fades.

NETTIE: No. I'm afraid he hasn't . . .

CLERK: What will you have, Ma'am?

NETTIE: I think I'll have that . . .

NARRATOR: She points to a caramel sundae.

NETTIE: I'll have . . . that caramel sundae . . . with whipped cream and nuts. No cherry, please. I'm allergic to cherries. They give me hives.

CLERK: Yes, Ma'am. Right away.

NARRATOR: She turns to look at Mabel. She catches a glimpse of the glass door and the sidewalk outside. Something is wrong. Her eyes open very wide. She screams . . .

NETTIE: My dog. Where's my dog?

NARRATOR: She runs out the door. She looks up and down the street. But she can't find him. She calls and calls . . .

NETTIE: He-re Lad-die. He-re Lad-die.
NARRATOR: . . . in a high voice. A stranger comes out from behind the building.
STRANGER: Ma'am, is this the dog you're looking for? He's right here eating ice cream.
             A little boy dropped his cone . . .
NARRATOR: Nettie runs around to the side of the building. Sure enough, there in front
             of her is the dog. He is lapping up the last bit of ice cream from the ground.
             He makes slurping sounds. Nettie is overcome with joy. She says . . .
NETTIE: Oh, my Laddie. Thank goodness he's safe.
NARRATOR: She rushes over and hugs him. The dog is now licking his chops. Mabel is
             right behind her.
NETTIE: Oh, my sweet Laddie.
MABEL: I guess he wants something special on your birthday too. Just like a dog,
             you know. They all think they're people. Come on, let's get our ice cream.
             I don't have all day, you know.
NARRATOR: The three of them head back to the door of the ice cream store.

Later, students should be encouraged to write and perform their own scripts based on pictures or musical lyrics, poetry, TV shows, and so forth. The productions eventually become whole-class projects from beginning to end.

SUMMARY

Storytelling, role play, and drama through their attention to human experience are likely to have much appeal in the language classroom. When students lose themselves in the characters, plots, and situations, they are more apt to experience lower anxiety, increased self-confidence and esteem, and heightened awareness.

Even beginning students enjoy dramatic action right from the start through prelanguage activities or warm-ups, "Story Experience," and/or producing sound effects for production. Just being a properties assistant or part of the audience has rewards.

Not only can students improve their abilities to comprehend and produce the target language, but they quickly learn to work cooperatively in group situations toward mutual goals. Being able to tell their own tales, interpret stories, deal with problems through sociodrama, write, read aloud, and produce minidramas, gives them meaningful experiences with the language that they might not otherwise have.

READINGS, REFLECTION, AND DISCUSSION

Suggested Readings and Reference Materials

Garvie, E. (1990). *Story as vehicle: Teaching English to young children*. Clevedon, England: Multilingual Matters Ltd. Here the story is presented as a way to increase intrinsic motivation in children and thereby make language acquisition more likely.

Kasser, C. and Silverman, A. (2001). *Stories we brought with us*. White Plains, NY: Pearson Education. This collection of well-known tales from many countries around the world works well with multileveled classes, grades 1-4. Two versions of each story are presented: one is written for a lower proficiency level than the other.

Phillips, S. (1999). *Drama with children*. Oxford, England: Oxford University. Many ways to get children to participate in dramatic activities are included in this book. Teachers are encouraged to photocopy selected pages for use in the classroom.

Smallwood, B. (1991). *The literature connection: A read-aloud guide for multicultural classrooms*. Reading, MA: Addison-Wesley. A helpful guide for teachers searching for read-aloud materials and guidelines (grades K-8). Of particular interest is the extensive annotated bibliography which arranges books by theme. Along with the annotations is information about grade level, proficiency level, cultural group, vocabulary, and so forth.

Stern, A. (1996). *Tales from many lands*. New York: McGraw-Hill/Contemporary. This multicultural reader, intended for secondary students and above, presents stories from several different cultures. Through the selections and their accompanying activities, students are able to link cultures and build skills at the same time at high-beginning levels. See also a similar book by Stern entitled *World Folktales* for low-intermediate levels.

Questions and Projects for Reflection and Discussion

1. How might dramatic experiences help to make the ego more "permeable" in the sense that Guiora uses the term? (See Chapter 6.)

2. What role should culture play in choosing a selection around which to build activities? What criteria might you use to guide your choice? Include important constraints that culture might present for individuals and/or groups. What might be the consequences if such constraints are ignored? Give examples.

3. Plan a lesson using storytelling, role play, or drama. Be specific about the age levels and proficiency levels of the students for whom it is intended (beginning, intermediate, or advanced). Present your lesson to a group of fellow students. Discuss with them the strengths of your presentation and ways in which you might improve it. Begin by sharing your own reactions to your presentation.

   If you are currently teaching students, use what you have learned to try out a similar lesson. Make sure the lesson is appropriate to cultural sensitivities and to level(s). If possible, have your lesson videotaped to analyze and discuss with peers. Reflect on its outcome and how you felt about doing it. Pay close attention to student response. Do you see any problems with your lesson? How might it be improved?

   Write about your experiences in your journal. What did you learn from them?

CHAPTER 12

Games

*Game playing, having apparently originated as a form
of instruction, now appears again to be coming into its
own as an instructional activity.*

T. Rodgers, 1978

QUESTIONS TO THINK ABOUT

1. Do you remember favorite childhood games that helped you to learn
   your first language? What were some of those games? In what ways
   did they help you?

2. Are teenagers and adults too old for games that might help them learn
   another language? Why or why not?

3. What advantages might games have in learning another language?

4. To what extent would you incorporate games into a second or foreign
   language course? How would you use games to teach language?

5. Can you think of a way that games might be used as a link to other
   cultures? If so, how?

Games are often associated with fun. While it is true that games are usually fun, one must not lose sight of their pedagogical value, particularly in second language teaching. Like most other activities recommended in this book, games can lower anxiety, thus making acquisition more likely. In addition, they can be highly motivating, relevant, interesting, and comprehensible.

Games can develop and reinforce concepts (e.g., colors, shapes, numbers, word definitions), add diversion to the regular classroom activities, and even break the ice, particularly in the case of true beginners. Moreover, they can introduce new ideas and provide practice with communication skills. Although some are quiet, contemplative games, others are noisy and require much verbal or physical involvement. Some are meant for small groups, others for large groups. Often classes can be divided into smaller units and several games can be played simultaneously. The teacher, peer teachers, or lay assistants (see Chapter 15) can facilitate the individual groups.

The games recommended here may involve a certain amount of group competition, but competition is generally not the focus (except perhaps in some of the nonverbal games). Games which single out and embarrass individuals in front of the class are to be avoided.

The rules of games should be very few and clearly explained. In most cases, students can begin the games and have the rules explained or repeated as the games progress. Demonstrations can also be very helpful.

Most of the games discussed below can be adapted to any age level, provided students are cognitively able to handle their content. In addition, most can be adapted to several proficiency levels (beginning, intermediate, or advanced), according to the difficulty of the tasks involved. None of the games require large outlays of money to purchase or create. Usually the materials needed can be easily collected or made by the teacher or an assistant.

Even though the categories often overlap, the games are divided into the following types, depending on their emphasis: nonverbal games, board-advancing games, word-focus games, treasure hunts, and guessing games.

NONVERBAL GAMES

Games such as relays or musical chairs help students become acquainted with each other, even before they can speak. Used sparingly, they serve as ice breakers and can be used to bring together students of mixed levels. After hearing the directions for a specific game given in the target language, the more proficient students of various language backgrounds can translate the directions into the L1 of other, less proficient students.

Nonverbal games can also be used to form groups for other games and activities. For example, at Christmas time, trees can be made of construction paper and cut into puzzle pieces to be matched (Figure 12.1).

Figure 12.1

The number of trees will depend on how many groups are necessary for the game and on the number of students in the class. For example, for classroom scrabble (described later in this chapter), fourteen students need to divide into four teams, making four trees necessary (two trees cut into three puzzle pieces and two into four puzzle pieces). The students each draw a puzzle piece out of a grab bag and find the students who have the missing pieces to make a complete tree. Thus a group is formed. The same can be done with hearts on Valentine's Day, pumpkins on Halloween, shamrocks on St. Patrick's Day, and so on. An alternative is to cut several pictures (one for each group desired) into puzzle pieces, mix them up, and have each student take one piece and find the other people with the pieces that will complete the picture. (For more ideas about forming groups, see pages 162 and 254–255.)

BOARD-ADVANCING GAMES

Using game pieces (such as buttons or little plastic cars) to represent the players, students perform certain tasks written on cards or simply roll the dice to move forward a certain number of spaces. The board itself can be as imaginative and colorful as the teacher wants to make it. The spaces must form some sort of pathway from a starting point to a finishing point which is the goal, as in Figure 12.2.

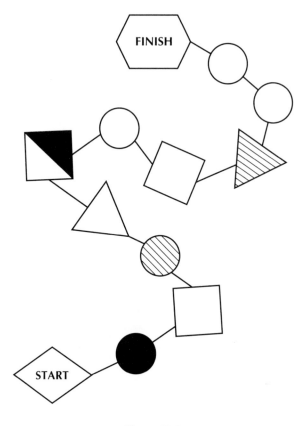

Figure 12.2

Students may take turns drawing cards with specific commands on them (jump three times, write your name on the board, sing a song from your country). Once students complete the tasks (other students can help interpret and carry out the commands), they move forward the number of spaces indicated on the cards. Additional tasks can include giving synonyms or antonyms for specific words, identifying objects on pictures, doing simple math computations, or any kind of task that will reinforce concepts or procedures. The "winner" is the one who reaches the goal first.

WORD-FOCUS GAMES

One such game requires giving students words to see how many other words they can make from them. For example the following words can be made from the word *teacher*: ear, her, teach, reach, cheer, each, hear, here, arch, tea, and eat.

By working with others in a team situation, students learn new words from the other members in the group. Seeing which group can make the most words in a certain time period may add to the excitement and probably will not raise anxiety levels since no individuals are put on the spot.

An alternative is to have teams of students see how many words they can make from a letter grid such as the one shown in Figure 12.3. Students must move along the connecting lines without skipping any letters. A single letter cannot be used twice in succession but can be returned to if there is an intervening letter. For example, in Figure 12.3, *regret* is acceptable but *greet* is not.

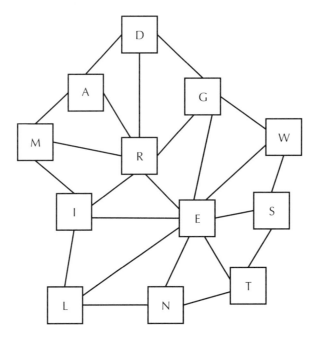

Figure 12.3

A bean bag toss suggested by Evans and Moore (1982) can be adapted to teach antonyms, synonyms, or categories of words. They suggest that the teacher make a large playing area on tagboard with a felt-tip pen. The teacher or an assistant then draws circles all over the area, and puts one word in each circle (see Figure 12.4).

Make sure that each word has its opposite (if working on antonyms), that each word has a corresponding word that means the same thing (if working on synonyms), or that each word has a corresponding category to which it belongs (if working on categories). A student stands behind a line that has been marked with masking tape and tosses a bean bag. After reading the word on which the

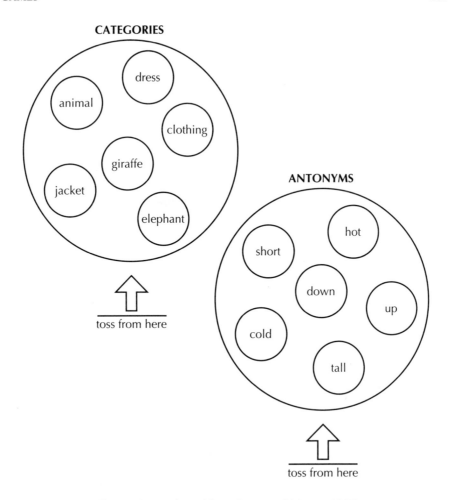

Figure 12.4. (adapted from Evans and Moore, 1982)

bag lands, the student takes a second bean bag and tries to toss it so it will land on the appropriate antonym, synonym, or a category member.

Classroom Scrabble[1] is a particularly effective word-focus game. Divide students into two to four teams with three to four students per team. Draw a Scrabble board on the board (see Figure 12.5).

Shade some of the squares; letters placed on these shaded areas receive double their normal count. Give the teams letters cut from index cards (four consonants and three vowels per team) on which you have written point values—lower point values for frequently used letters, higher point values for the rest.

---

[1] I wish to thank Deborah Floyd for this game idea.

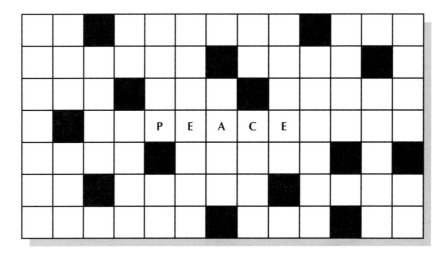

Figure 12.5

Write a message in the middle of the board, such as "Peace." The students are to build their words off the letters in the message. Roll up cellophane tape and place it behind each letter to make it stick to the board (later the tape can be removed so the same letters can be used again). The teams take turns, making as many words as they can. All words must connect to a word already on the board, either horizontally or vertically. Each team's letters are replaced after the turns, a vowel for a vowel and a consonant for a consonant. They are drawn at random by a team member from a reserve guarded by the teacher or an assistant. To keep the game moving, place a limit of about two or three minutes to complete a turn.

One commonly used word-focus game that some teachers choose to avoid is "scrambled word." The students are given words with the letters scrambled. They are supposed to unscramble them to form the intended word. For example, "cesenic" can be unscrambled to form "science." Although proficient speakers might find this fun, most second language students find such games frustrating. For them, the language may appear to be somewhat "scrambled" to begin with, so it seems senseless to cause them additional anxiety.

TREASURE HUNTS

A treasure hunt is a favorite game among second language learners. It allows them to work cooperatively in a group effort to find the items required to win and at the same time practice communicative skills. Often the items call for a group consensus: the students may have to find something they all agree is beautiful. Condon (1983) suggested that the following steps (paraphrased below) be taken in organizing a treasure hunt. The hunt can take anywhere from ten minutes to an entire day, depending on the number and kinds of items listed.

1. Divide the class into groups of from three to six members.
2. Give an identical list of treasures to each group.
3. Read the items aloud for children or less proficient students to make sure they understand the vocabulary.
4. A time limit should be given.
5. Say "Go" to indicate when the groups can begin their searches.
6. At the end of the time limit, or when the first group returns, everyone gets together to check each item, giving points (five points are suggested) for each completed item. Points are taken away for incomplete ones.

Condon mentions a few of the more interesting items that can be included:

1. List five countries the members of your group would like to visit.
2. What is the largest shoe size in your group?
3. Find something useless.
4. Make a dinner menu in English.
5. Find a photograph.
6. Collect the autographs of three people not in your group.
7. Find something that smells good.
8. Make a crazy hat for your teacher.
9. Write down six ways of making people laugh.
10. Find a picture of something good to eat.

GUESSING GAMES

Guessing games can be painless ways to develop or reinforce any number of concepts. "Guess What I Am" or "Guess Who I Am," for example, can be used to teach about animals, professions, or people in different age groups (baby, child, teenager, young adult, middle-aged adult, elderly person). Each student pantomimes a particular role, and the class guesses which role is being acted out. The student who guesses the role correctly is "it" and takes the next turn. A time limit can be set so not too much attention is devoted to any one person.

"Guess What I'm Doing" teaches or reinforces concepts associated with taking a shower, going fishing, doing homework, and so forth. "Guess What I Have" is even more focused on verbalization. The student gives verbal hints as to what object is being described, or the students ask questions about the object (as in "Twenty Questions"). The object may be hidden or in full view. It is important that the class not know the name of the object beforehand.

Alternatives include "Whose Name Is It?" or "What Am I?" In either case, one person is "it," and a sign, which the person cannot see, is placed on his or her back. On the sign has been written the name of a classmate or the name of a specific occupation. The person with the sign asks *yes* or *no* questions of the class until the correct response is arrived at. (Do I wear a hat? Do I climb ladders?) The students take turns being "it."

Games come in many different forms and can be gathered from a variety of sources: books on the subject, young people's magazines, department store game sections. However, one important source that must not be overlooked is the second language students themselves. Having students share games from their countries or cultural backgrounds can be a very exciting experience for everyone and can provide many opportunities for practice with the target language.

SUMMARY

Games can be used to develop or reinforce concepts, to add diversion to the regular classroom activities, or just to break the ice. However, their most important function is to give practice in communication.

It is recommended that competition be downplayed for most games, that the rules be few, and that they be clearly explained and demonstrated where possible.

Although the categories can overlap, the games offered here were divided into the following types depending on their emphasis: nonverbal games, board-advancing games, word-focus games, treasure hunts, and guessing games.

Various sources for game ideas are mentioned, but teachers are reminded that one of the best sources is the students themselves.

READINGS, REFLECTION, AND DISCUSSION

Suggested Readings and Reference Materials

Crookall, D., and Oxford, R., eds., (1990). *Simulation, gaming, and language learning*. New York: Newbury House. Developing learning strategies through simulation/gaming, using them as language testing devices, and using simulations on computers are only a few of the topics discussed. Included are selections by Martha Cummings and Rhonda Genzel, Robin Scarcella and Susan Stern, and many others.

Lewis, G. and Bedson, G. (1999). *Games for children*. Oxford, England: Oxford University. The games included in this book are intended for language reinforcement in the classroom. Many of the games included can be used with teenagers as well as with children.

Schultz, M., and Fisher, A. (1988). *Games for all reasons: Interacting in the language classroom*. Reading, MA: Addison-Wesley. The games described in this collection have several foci: language structure, vocabulary, pronunciation, listening, etc. They incorporate activities such as role play, physical response activities, and debate.

Shameem, N. and Tickoo, M., eds. (1999). *New ways in using communicative games in language teaching*. Alexandria, VA: TESOL. The games presented here, which come from several cultures, are designed to help students become more fluent in the language, learn strategies for socialization, be introduced to content, and develop pragmatic discourse skills. The games involve students in whole-class and small-group activity.

Questions and Projects for Reflection and Discussion

1. Form a set of criteria to use in the selection of a game for second language classroom use. Give examples of games that you might choose based on the criteria you have developed. Discuss with a small group.

2. How can a game such as a treasure hunt be used to reinforce the teaching of a story? Choose a particular story, describe the story, and tell what "treasures" you might incorporate to reinforce the concepts.

3. Recall one of the favorite games that you played as a child. How might it be adapted to a second language class?

4. Select a topic. Find and adapt, or create two or three games that you could use to reinforce the concepts associated with the topic. Try one game out with a group of fellow students. Be specific about its purpose and the age and proficiency levels of the students with whom you might use it (beginning, intermediate, or advanced). Discuss with them the strengths of your presentation and ways in which you might improve it. Begin by sharing your own reactions to the presentation.

   If you are currently teaching students, use what you have learned to try out one or more games with them. Make sure the game or games are appropriate to cultural sensitivities and to level(s). If possible, have your lesson videotaped to analyze and discuss with peers. Reflect on the outcomes and how you felt about using the game or games you selected. Pay close attention to student response. Do you see any problems with the game(s) and the strategies you used? How might they be improved?

   Write about your experiences with games in your journal. What did you learn from them?

CHAPTER **13**

Ways to Promote Literacy Development

. . . writing like a reader becomes inextricably bound up with reading like a writer.

V. Zamel, 1992

QUESTIONS TO THINK ABOUT

1. In your opinion, what kinds of activities will best promote reading and writing skills in second and foreign language learners? Relate to your own experiences with reading and writing in your first or second language. Consider experiences you already have had as a teacher or a parent.

2. Are there any kinds of activities that you would avoid? Again relate to your own experiences.

3. Do you think reading and writing should be taught simultaneously? Why or why not? To what extent do you feel they should receive separate treatment?

4. Based on your own experiences with literature, do you think language teaching could be literature-based? If so, to what extent? What are some possible advantages and disadvantages of using literature to teach language?

5. What do you know about a workshop approach to teach writing? Have you experienced it as a teacher or as a student? If so, reflect upon this experience. To what extent were the workshops successful? What problems did you encounter?

The ways to promote development of literacy skills suggested in this chapter are extensions of a natural language framework developed in Chapter 5. They are based on the premise that learning to read and write is a communal process. They assume that the student's major goal in developing these skills is to effectively create meaning either as a writer or a reader. They also assume that the learner comes to the classroom community with a rich fund of knowledge and experience to share with others within a participatory environment.

In this chapter, the following topics will be discussed:

- The Language Experience Approach
- Literature-Based Curriculum
- Writing Workshops
- Advanced Academic Literacy

THE LANGUAGE EXPERIENCE APPROACH

The language experience approach (Van Allen and Allen, 1967), was a precursor to the whole language movement (see Chapter 5). Even though it originally lacked a well-developed theoretical base, its apparent efficacy established it as a viable means for teaching reading to native speakers. Later, several versions were suggested for use with second language students (see especially Moustfa, M., 1989; and Dixon and Nessel, 1990). This approach is predicated on the notion that students can learn to write by dictating to the teacher what they already can express verbally. The teacher writes what they say and, as a result, the students' first reading materials come from their own repertoire of language.

Although applications differ for various age levels and needs, the process begins with students' experiences; e.g., going on a trip, seeing a movie, looking at a picture, reading a poem or story, etc. The students first discuss the experience with the teacher and/or fellow students and then dictate a "story" about that experience to the teacher individually. The teacher writes down exactly what the student says, including the errors. The teacher then reads aloud each sentence after it is written, giving the student a chance to make changes (some may notice their own errors and want to correct them). The teacher may wait until the story is finished before reading it back, making sure the student sees the correspondence between what is being said and what was written. The student is encouraged to read the story either silently or aloud to the teacher or to another student and then to rewrite it.

An interesting alternative, which changes the dynamics considerably, is for the whole class or small groups within the class to dictate a "group" story while the teacher writes it on the board, flip chart, or overhead transparency. What makes this alternative interesting is that the students scaffold upon each other's utterances and create Zones of Proximal Development for each other (see previous discussion on pages 50–55).

Once they are ready for display, these stories are placed in story collections or on the walls of the classroom for all to read. Students can provide illustrations to accompany their stories, adding another dimension to the printed page. As the students become more proficient reading their stories, they are gradually introduced to textbooks and other materials that are easy and are within their reach cognitively.

In perhaps a misapplication of Goodman's "whole to part" versus "part to whole" distinction (see Chapter 5), some teachers break the story into discrete elements of decreasing size. For example, teachers cut the story into sentence strips, and ask students to put the strips together again to form the whole story. Others cut the strips into sentence parts or phrases, followed by words, syllables, and finally letters and again ask the students to construct the whole, using increasingly smaller units. Other teachers have students identify letter-sound correspondences by matching them (e.g., find the *b's* in the story. Although this kind of activity might be helpful for some students, for others it is simply tedious repetition. But the greatest danger is that students might find it frustrating to see their stories turned into scrambled word/sentence/letter puzzles (I always hated those myself) or into seemingly endless phonics lessons.

Others use the story as a lesson in semantics (e.g., *Which word means "to walk slowly"? Which word is the opposite of "dangerous"?*). While this might benefit some students, most would probably be more motivated asking and answering questions related to the story's meaning. For example, if the students have just written a story about a picture of a man packing his suitcase, comprehension questions could be asked (e.g., *Where is the man going? Point to the sentence that tells that. Why is he going there? How do you know?* and so on).

Applications of the language experience approach are used at many levels and for many purposes other than composing stories. For example, charts with the information supplied by students are created, comparisons are drawn in chart or paragraph form, and idea maps or clustering devices are generated, just to name a few.

Advantages of the Language Experience Approach

Perhaps the biggest advantage is that the text is appropriate both cognitively and linguistically; it comes from the students themselves. Moreover, the student's own culture and ideas are encouraged and validated, thereby enhancing self-concepts and fostering independence. Grammar and other discrete point instruction are used as needed, and small groups are formed of students needing similar instruction. In the case of a group-created product, students learn from one another and scaffold upon each others' contributions. The teacher is a facilitator in the entire process rather than mainly an editor of what is produced.

Limitations of the Language Experience Approach

One possible limitation is that students might get the mistaken idea that writing is simply recorded speech. However, through the process of creating text, adjusting, rewriting, and so forth, students learn that the written register is not the same as recorded speech. Certain conventions and abstractions are used in written language that are not usually found in everyday speech. Moreover, students soon realize that the purposes of written language are often very different. They write things down to aid memory, to keep a record, to meet various requirements at school and in the work place, etc.

A second limitation concerns writing down student errors as part of the dictation procedure. Teachers often express reservations about this practice, thinking that they are reinforcing errors.[1] They are afraid, too, that if students see the teacher writing down their errors, they will think that all is well and that their is no mismatch between their own hypotheses about the language and what proficient users of the language know.

A third limitation involves the teacher's acting chiefly as a transcriber, when in fact the teacher could be playing a far more facilitative role. One way to make the experience more than simply a dictation and, at the same time, to make it more participatory is for the teacher and students to become integral parts of a composing process. However, care must be taken that the students have the opportunity to contribute as much as their abilities will allow and that the teacher not overshadow their efforts.

Below is an example of an alternative application. In this application, the teacher takes on a *more facilitative role* out of which a *collaborative product* is created. Notice that the teacher makes indirect corrections through modeling and uses these corrected forms in the writing. By this means, a teacher who feels uncomfortable writing errors doesn't have to.

TEACHER: (*referring to a story she has just read aloud to the students*) Let's write our thoughts about the story. Did you like the story?

ASSAD: I didn't like the story.

TEACHER: You didn't? Why? Why didn't you like it?

ASSAD: I didn't like when Maria keep the ring. It didn't belong to her.

TEACHER: Do the rest of you feel the same way? Did you not like it when Maria kept the ring? (*Five students raise their hands.*) How do some of the rest of you feel?

JORGE: It's okay.

TEACHER: What's okay?

JORGE: To keep the ring. It was her mother's ring.

---

[1] Advocates of the more "pure" versions of the language experience approach argue that this fear is unjustified and that the benefits of such a practice far outweigh the disadvantages, especially for children and for beginners of any age who are in special need of encouragement.

ASSAD: But her mother gave it to the neighbor.

TEACHER: How many of you agree with Jorge that it was all right to keep the ring? (*Three students raise their hands.*) Okay, what should we write?

JORGE: Write "Some of us want Maria keep the ring. It belonged to her mother."

TEACHER: Some of us wanted Maria to keep the ring? (*She looks at Jorge as she begins to write. Jorge nods. She writes* "Some of us wanted Maria to keep the ring. It belonged to her mother.")

And so the writing continues as the teacher guides the students, bringing out their ideas and helping them to shape the language. The teacher, in a sense, becomes a co-author, as well as a facilitator; the teacher asks questions, clarifies meaning, and makes a few contributions of his or her own. Moreover, the teacher provides language upon which the students can scaffold.

Gradually, students begin to write more independently and need less and less guidance from the teacher. Soon students are able to finish, on their own, the compositions begun as collaborations. Later, students can work with partners to create compositions. And eventually, they can write independently, with help available as needed from the teacher and peers (see Writing Workshops discussed later beginning on page 267).

LITERATURE-BASED CURRICULUM

Shirley Brice Heath (1996) once said, "Literature has no rival in its power to create natural repetition, reflection on language and how it works, and attention to audience response on the part of learners (p. 776)." Many others advocate literature as a powerful resource for the teacher to use as a focus for language teaching (Lazar, 1993; Kay and Gelshenen, 1998; Richard-Amato, 1996).

Even at beginning proficiency levels, teachers can use literature as the pivot around which curriculum revolves. For example, Story Experience (see pages 215–217) brings students into literature before they can even utter a word. Other activities using stories (found in Chapter 11) help students as they begin and continue their journey through the language learning process. All the while, writing, speaking, and listening are incorporated as they relate to the literature. Often speaking and/or reading events are turned into writing events, and so forth. In addition, the language experience approach just described can make a major contribution to the development of literacy by providing students with materials they themselves have written or have helped to write.

Why Use Literature as a Pivot?

Literature is authentic. It is not usually written solely to teach specific structures or vocabulary (unless we are talking about basal-type readers). Instead its structures and vocabulary grow naturally out of the ideas, plots, dialogues, and situations developed. That doesn't mean, however, that authentic literature does not have a particular audience in mind. Indeed, it usually does. For example, it may be written for persons of a certain age, gender, cultural background, occupation, or level of proficiency in a given language. Nor does "authentic" mean "unaltered." Literature modified for a specific age or level of proficiency can still focus on meaning (see also Bamford and Day, 1996), and its structures and vocabulary can still be a product of that meaning.

Literature can provide memorable contexts for the language. To support this argument, John Oller offered the Episode Hypothesis (see also pages 335–338), which states that "text (i.e., discourse in any form) will be easier to reproduce, understand, and recall, to the extent that it is structured episodically" (1983b, p. 12). Episodic organization requires both the motivation created by conflict and the logical sequencing that is necessary to good storytelling and consistent with experience.

Schank and Abelson (1977) earlier had gone even further and related episodic structure to the very way in which memory is organized. According to them, humans not only store information in episodic form, but that they also acquire it in that way. Literature using plot lines and characters engages students emotionally as well as cognitively. As they become involved with the characters, they often become so absorbed that they, at least momentarily, lose the barriers generally associated with learning another language.

Literature illustrates appropriate language for specific situations. Through literature, students learn what is acceptable and what is not in given situations. They learn the skills involved in turn-taking and what vocabulary and structures to use to get certain things accomplished in the new language.

Literature links students to other cultures and subcultures. By reading *The Diary of Anne Frank*, for example, students learn about the Jewish culture within Nazi-occupied Europe. From the biography *Isamu Noguchi: The Life of a Sculptor*, they learn what it was like to be a struggling Japanese-American artist during the same time period. From *The Me Nobody Knows*, they learn through poetry about the frustrations of children in the black ghettos of America. Literature can help students appreciate other peoples and their experiences.

And when the literature comes from the students' first cultures, it helps bridge a gap between the familiar and the new. Literature can also be a source of pride for students; they see their own values and traditions reflected in what they read. Not only that, but literature often presents universal themes, conflicts, and experiences that can bring people together in harmony and mutual respect.

Literature presents fodder for critical analysis, discussion, and writing. It encourages students to draw inferences, interpret, and explore personal, social, and political issues. The issues might include the racism found in *Huckleberry Finn* and other issues found in expository pieces such as editorials, essays, biographies, etc. All these genre can be very powerful to the extent that through them, students explore issues important to their lives. Literature often elicits strong emotional responses that leads to critical analysis and reflection. Moreover, literature often forms a basis for discussion, writing, or further research and provides students with ample opportunities to practice valuable skills such as summarizing and paraphrasing.

Literature encourages performance. The performance generated by literature can include reading aloud, acting out, discussion, and debate. Often, rehearsal for performance requires the natural use of repetition (not of the drill and skill variety). Choral reading, chants, readers' theater, memorization of the lines for a drama production, etc., all lend themselves to practice with the language.

Components of Literature-Based Lessons

Literature-based lessons comprise three basic elements: prereading, reading, and postreading. In this section, each element is discussed separately, along with suggested activities and strategies for each. Most of the examples come from *Worlds Together* and its accompanying *Teacher Resource Book* (Richard-Amato and Hansen, 1995) and *Exploring Themes* (Richard-Amato, 1993b), as well as other sources.

Prereading
Prereading activities have three main purposes:

- to help the student relate the text to prior knowledge and experience both in L1 and L2
- to heighten motivation for reading
- to gain cultural knowledge helpful to more fully comprehending what the writer is trying to say

Schema theory (see especially Carrell, 1984, 1985) was labeled a "theoretical metaphor" by Grabe (1991), who considers it a useful way to describe the reader's prior knowledge. However, he argued that the notion of *stable* schema structures is a myth and is not strongly supported by current research. Moreover, there is evidence that there may not be as much difference in schema across cultures as was once thought (see, in particular, Mohan and Au-Yeung Lo, 1985).

Despite skepticism concerning schema theory and the stability of schema, we know that there are expectations readers bring to a selection that either help or hinder understanding. In order for students to get the most out of what they read, teachers can help them relate text to what they already know and have experienced, and prepare them for elements of the text that may be puzzling.

To facilitate the reading process for all students, prereading activities such as the following can be developed.

Prereading Activities

1. ASKING SPECIFIC AND OPEN-ENDED DISCUSSION QUESTIONS

An example of these kinds of questions comes from *Exploring Themes,* designed for intermediate to advanced young adults. The book begins with a unit entitled "To a Distant Shore," which includes autobiographical sketches of four new arrivals. Below are the discussion questions that begin the unit.

Think about your own situation. Have you recently arrived on a "distant shore"? Are you planning to make such a move? Even if you cannot answer yes to either question, try to imagine what it might be like to leave your home and live far away. What joys are experienced by persons going from one culture to another? What problems do they face? Discuss with your class.

Instead of discussing the questions with the class, students can discuss them in smaller groups which can share their conclusions. Such questions give direction to the students' reading and thinking without being authoritative.

The next example comes from *Global Views: Reading About World Issues* (Sokolik, 1993). The questions below form part of a poll taken of the class before they read an article from the *Houston Chronicle* about manned space flights.

The following reading consists of letters to a local Houston newspaper concerning the issue of sending people into space. Before you read this passage, take a poll of your class, asking everyone these questions.

a. Do you think space exploration is a worthwhile endeavor?
b. If there is limited funding, do you think money should go to programs on earth first?
c. Do you think space exploration benefits everyone? Why or why not?

2. USING GRAPHIC ORGANIZERS (CHARTS, CLUSTERS, AND SO FORTH)

A learning chart such as the one below determines what the students already know and what they think they will learn from the reading. The following is adapted from *Worlds Together* (intended for adolescents at intermediate levels) and appears before a selection about Martin Luther King, Jr.

A Learning Chart

WHAT WE KNOW ALREADY ABOUT MARTIN LUTHER KING, JR.	WHAT WE'D LIKE TO KNOW ABOUT MARTIN LUTHER KING, JR.

After the students finish the selection, they fill in a third column, WHAT WE LEARNED ABOUT MARTIN LUTHER KING, JR.

The next example of a prereading device, in this case a cluster, comes from the same textbook. It begins the unit "What Makes a Hero?"

What do you think it means to be a hero? Perhaps a hero is someone who is unusually brave or has uncommon strength or speed. With your class, name people you think are heroes. They may be famous people (past or present). They may be people you know in your own neighborhood. They may even be make-believe people in movies you have seen or in stories or cartoons you have read. Think about what it is that makes them heroes. With your class make a cluster such as the one below in Figure 13.1. Display it in the classroom. You and your classmates may want to add heroes to your cluster after reading this unit.

THE HEROES WE KNOW ABOUT

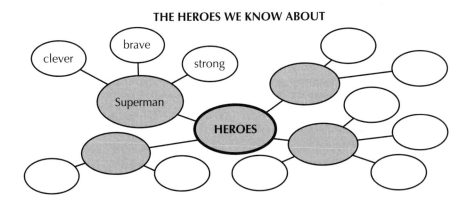

Figure 13.1

3. EXPLICITLY PRESENTING KEY WORDS

The teacher can write a few key words from the selection for all to see. The students brainstorm or say what comes to mind about these words while the teacher forms a cluster out of the ideas (see Figure 13.2).

The teacher or the students ask questions to clarify and/or extend meaning.

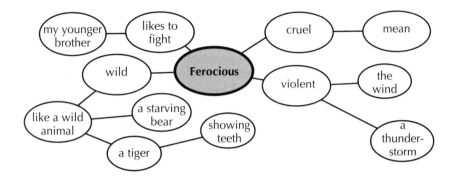

Figure 13.2

4. USING PREDICTION STRATEGIES AND ANTICIPATION GUIDES

Students can predict what is going to happen or what they think they might be introduced to in a particular selection. The title, subtitles, and illustrations are helpful in this process. Photos and other artwork, or a sample excerpt from the reading can be helpful as well. To add interest, the teacher or a student can write down the predictions as they are given and refer to them later to see which ones come closest to what actually happens or what is learned.

An anticipation guide (Readence, Bean, and Baldwin, 1981) is yet another device to help students build relevant expectations. Such a guide presents the students with statements to which they are to react. The one below precedes the essay "Romantic Deceptions and Reality" in *Exploring Themes* (Richard-Amato, 1993b).

Anticipation Guide

It is not unusual for people to have many misconceptions about love and what makes it thrive. Read the following statements. Check the ones you think are true.

a. When you feel that the romance has left your relationship, it is time to move on to a new relationship with another person.

b. It is a bad sign when one partner in a love relationship wants to make changes in the relationship itself.

c. A strong physical attraction for one's partner is necessary in order for a love relationship to blossom.

d. In a lasting relationship, partners have enough in common that they don't need outside activities with other people to lead happy, fulfilling lives.

e. Conflict should be avoided if one wants a love relationship to last.

Now read the following essay. After you read it, you will be asked to look back at your answers to this activity to see if you still feel the same way.

Students are surprised to learn from reading the essay that all of the above statements are false, at least according to the authors. When writing statements for an anticipation guide, the teacher needs to first consider what important concepts are to be learned from the reading and then write statements that will determine whether or not the students already know these concepts. Such an activity is highly motivational as students seek to check out their preconceived notions.

5. WRITING IN JOURNALS

In journals (see also pages 264–266), students write down their prereading thoughts about the issues or topics related to a specific selection or unit. They may describe their own experiences or those of others, they may express opinions, or they may write their predictions and then react to them later.

6. USING METACOGNITIVE STRATEGIES TO DEAL WITH NEW SELECTIONS

Before You Read

1. Look the book over. Think about the title. Notice the cover of the book. Is there a picture there? Are there other pictures in the book? Look at a few of them. Do they give you any ideas about what the book will be about? If the book tells a story, do the pictures give you any clues about what might happen in the story?
2. What do you think you will learn from this book?
3. Have you already learned some things from personal experience, other books, or classes that might help you understand this book?

While You Read

1. Relax and feel the words and sentences flow together.
2. Ask questions of yourself as you read. Does this seem real? Have I experienced this myself? What does this have to do with what the author has just said or what has just happened? What is coming next?
3. Do not stop reading every time you find a word you do not understand. The meaning may come to you as you read further.
4. If a word seems important and the meaning is not coming clear as you read further, then look in the glossary (if there is one) or check a dictionary. You may want to discuss the word's meaning with a classmate or your teacher.
5. If there are parts you do not understand, make a note of them so you can return later.
6. Reread for better understanding. Return to the parts you did not understand. Reread them. Are they more clear to you now? If not, discuss them with a classmate or with your teacher.

After You Read

1. What did you learn from this book? Has it changed the way you thought before?
2. Did the book turn out as you expected?
3. Talk about it with others who have read the same book. Maybe you can start a discussion group.

7. PREVIEWING THE READING

Previews that include story-specific information such as a vivid description of the characters and the situation and end with a motivator such as "Now read the story and find out how (why) the main character . . . " can be very effective. Chen and Graves (1995) found that listening to a preview of a story was the best prereading alternative offered in their study of high-scoring college freshman at Tamkang University in Taipei. Four treatments were given, one to each of the four randomly assigned groups: 1. a 200-word preview; 2. a 200-word presentation of background information; 3. a combination of the two; and 4. no pre-reading assistance at all. Although the post-tests given indicated that treatments 1 and 3 were almost equally effective, they determined that 1 (previewing alone) was the most time- and cost-effective.

One word of caution about prereading activities in general—they should not be too lengthy. Sometimes teachers attempting to cover all possible unknowns expose students to overly lengthy explanations and too many activities. Although students usually appreciate having their curiosity piqued and having a cognitive scaffold upon which to build meaning, they do not appreciate putting on hold whatever motivation they may have already gained to read the selection. Sometimes, too, teachers will impose their own interpretations upon the students beforehand, making it difficult for them to create meaning for themselves.

Reading

This is what happens *while* the students are reading. The selections themselves may contain illustrations, photographs and other artwork, subtitles, glossaries, and footnotes that offer clues to meaning and, in the case of visuals, establish the mood and/or give added life to characters and situations.

Particularly important to second and foreign language students are glossaries that are sometimes found at the bottoms of the pages. The more effective glossaries will offer not only definitions, but also common root derivations and clues to help students use the context to determine meaning. Although they may not seem a significant feature, these glossaries are extremely valuable; they provide help *while* the students are reading, when the need to understand is immediate and the motivation is strong. However, students should be encouraged to first use the context and not concern themselves with every unknown element.

Scheduling reading times during class is essential. Again, the teacher acts as a facilitator and a guide to students needing help, as long as such help is not disruptive to others. It should be remembered, however, that a wise teacher will also be seen as a reader, reading silently during these times. Thus the teacher serves as a role model for the students to emulate.

Once the students have completed the silent reading of a literary piece, they often benefit (especially at beginning to intermediate levels) from hearing the selection read aloud by the teacher or others, or by listening to it on a cassette. They need to hear the intonation, the pauses, the rhythm, and the pronunciation of the words. If the selection has been recorded, students will often want to hear it repeated several times.

Concerning reading aloud, I must give a warning. Being read aloud to can be an exhilarating experience; being *forced* to read aloud in front of a group is often the opposite. It often creates needless anxiety and sometimes even fear in those students who do not read aloud well. Moreover, it is difficult for second language readers to attend to meaning while reading aloud or while waiting to be called on. Reading aloud is a specialized skill and should be expected only of volunteers. It is important to remember that reading is generally a quiet activity accomplished in a comfortable environment either at school, in a library, or at home.

Postreading

Postreading activities should enable the student to further create meaning and extend it beyond the context of the selection itself. Here students test their hypotheses about the selection and reread when it is beneficial to do so. They share their interpretations with peers and with the teacher in an effort to express themselves and, at the same time, stretch progressively to higher levels of understanding.

Forming Discussion and Project Groups. Groups can consist of the whole class and the teacher, or of smaller numbers of students. The teacher can move from group to group, serving as a facilitator and a guide. The groups can either be formed randomly or carefully planned (see also pages 162 and 233–234).

Of the two, planned groups have at least two major advantages:

- ethnic and cultural diversity within the groups can be ensured
- students of varying abilities can be assigned to a single group

Thus, each group's work will be more likely to reflect a variety of perspectives and proficiency levels. The latter is important in that students have a greater chance of being exposed to the language and the thinking of others operating at more advanced levels (See Vygotsky discussion in Chapter 3). However, most teachers recognize that sometimes homogeneous groups are just what's needed in a given situation; e.g., when the task pertains to a particular ethnic or cultural group or when it is intended only for those having specific goals not shared by everyone.

Letting students choose their own groups often works well with adults and mature adolescents. Like the planned groups, they can produce the desired diversity of perspective and ability in some situations. However, this practice sometimes results in hurt feelings and bruised egos. Inevitably there will be some who are left out for one reason or another. To allow students more freedom of choice and, at the same time, preserve self-esteem, it may be wise for the teacher to have students write down the names of those with whom they would most enjoy working. Consideration then should be given to those choices when planning workable groups. While this alternative requires more time and effort, it does pay dividends in terms of self-esteem and motivation.

Most students will assume they have been "chosen" by someone and will be more inclined to put forth their best efforts.

Questions for Discussion. Two basic types of questions are discussed here: knowledge-based questions and reflective/inferential questions.

KNOWLEDGE-BASED QUESTIONS. Often these kinds of questions are discussed by the whole class and the teacher. Their main purpose is to ensure that the students have comprehended the main facts or points of the selection. Often they begin with what, who, when, where, and how. They allow students, under the guidance of the teacher, to know what is essential to the creation of meaning. For example, *Life, Language, and Literature* (Fellag, 1993) includes the following knowledge-based questions about Bret Harte's "The Luck of Roaring Camp."

---

1. What interesting thing happened in Roaring Camp in the beginning of the story?
2. What happened to the baby's mother?
3. What did the citizens of Roaring Camp decide to do with the baby?
4. Who was declared chief caretaker for the infant?
5. How did the baby fare in the camp?
6. How did the town change as a result of the baby?
7. What happened to the baby in the end?

It is important to remember, however, that this kind of information can be brought out (perhaps more effectively) through reflective and inferential questions.

REFLECTIVE AND INFERENTIAL QUESTIONS. Discussion questions requiring more thought and reflection can perhaps best be handled in small groups in which students have more opportunities for interaction. The teacher circulates among the groups, guiding when necessary. The examples below come from "Making Friends in a New World" in *Worlds Together*. They follow the story about a Vietnamese boy, San Ho, who comes to the United States after the Vietnamese War. Notice that, in this case, cultural expectations are directly referred to.

- How does San Ho know that he and Stephen [his new stepfather] will be good friends? What does it mean to San Ho to be a good friend? Do you agree with him? What does it mean to be a good friend in the culture you know best? List some words that you think describe a good friendship.
- San Ho was so filled with fear that he cried in the story. Is it all right to cry? Does the culture you know best encourage or discourage crying? Does age make a difference? Is it different for boys and girls? If so, why do you think it is different?

A spokesperson from each group shares the group's ideas with the class later. The teacher summarizes the ideas for all to see, as they are shared.

If the questions are personal in nature, pairs of students usually work best. For example, after the same story referred to above, one or more of the following questions are discussed with a partner.

- Why do you think San Ho felt alone in the crowd of people in the gym? Have you ever felt alone in a crowd? Why do you think this happens sometimes?
- Our friends are sometimes much older or younger than we are. For example, Stephen, an adult, was San Ho's friend. Have you ever had a friend who was much older or younger than you? Talk about your friend. Why do you think you became friends?

When they are working in small groups, it is important that students select the personal questions they want to discuss. There are some questions they might prefer to write about privately. This option should always be available.

Discussion questions promoting the expression of opinions and feelings should lead to higher-level thinking skills (application, analysis, synthesis, and so forth). In addition, students should be encouraged to form their own questions. Having the ability to pose good questions is as important as being able to answer them and is extremely beneficial to cognitive as well as language development.

Short-term Group Projects and Activities. Short-term group projects and activities (also see cooperative learning beginning on page 315) often increase student involvement and motivation. Usually such projects and activities require sharing information. An example is found after reading "Blue Winds Dancing" in *Exploring Themes.* It is the story of a Native American who returns to his reservation with great anxiety as well as anticipation (see the story on pages 221–222 of this book). Will his people accept him or has he become too "white"?

Once the story is discussed, it is suggested that students research a particular tribe of Native Americans, including the problems they have had. They may want to look at the tribe's history, culture, and contributions to society. Eventually they might share the information they find with a small group.

Other short-term group projects and activities include:

- acting out the story
- adapting the selection for readers' theater (see pages 228–230)
- forming round-table groups to discuss related problems and possible solutions
- role playing the characters

- forming collections of student writings about or related to the story
- sharing favorite literature about related themes, genre, and so forth

Although suggestions are made by the teacher or a textbook, short-term projects and activities generated by students themselves are often very effective and can involve students maximally right from the start.

Short-term group projects and activities that are teacher- or textbook-generated are best when they are tied very closely to the selection and are critical to creating its meaning. The chart below follows an excerpt from "Sarah, Plain and Tall" in *Worlds Together* (Richard-Amato and Hansen, 1995).

Finding Details to Support an Idea

We know from the story that it has been several years since Mama's death. How do we know that this family still deeply misses her? Give the details from the story that show that each of the following characters misses Mama. With your group, make a chart similar to the one below. Have one member of your group do the writing.

	Details
Caleb	
Anna	
Papa	

Not only do the students have the opportunity to work collaboratively, but they learn how to support a conclusion, a very important skill for academic success.

And the last example of a short-term project or activity comes from "To a Distant Shore" in *Exploring Themes*. Here the students use Venn diagrams to draw comparisons. They compare the situations, goals, and other characteristics of four newcomers to the United States. Notice that the things the newcomers have in common are placed in the overlapping area of the circles. Students work with a partner to complete the diagrams (see Figure 13.3).

Individual Activities and Projects. Even though the activities and projects suggested below are individually executed, they, too, are in essence communal. Often students share what they create with the teacher, a partner, or a small group and receive feedback and help when necessary. The examples given here include interviewing, taking a closer look at literature, writing in a specific genre, speech writing, journal writing, and independent reading.

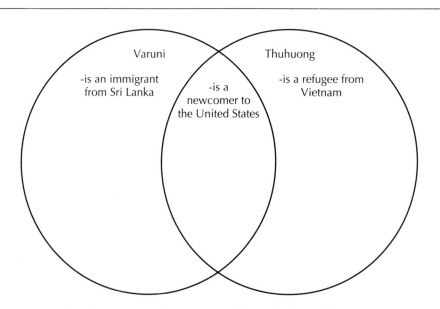

Now work with a partner and use the Venn diagram below to draw a comparison between two newcomers of your choice.

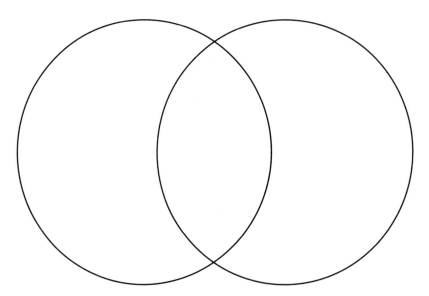

Form a group with at least two other people and share your diagrams. You may want to make changes in them based on what you learn from the others in your group.

Figure 13.3

Individual Projects and Activities

INTERVIEWING

One way for students to interact with each other and with people fluent in the target language is through interview. Students not only receive the benefits inherent in the interactional process, but they also develop skills in posing questions, asking questions, recording answers, and sharing what is learned from the experience. Here is an example from "Between Two Cultures," a unit in *Exploring Themes* (Richard-Amato, 1993b).

Are you learning English in a country where it is a commonly used language? If so, write several questions to ask fluent speakers of English. Following are a few sample questions:

–Have you ever been between two cultures? If so, what were the two cultures?
–What was it like for you to be between two cultures? What were the problems? Were there any advantages?
–Were there times when you were fearful? Explain.
–How did you overcome the problems involved in being between two cultures?

Interview several people outside your class. After each interview, write down what you can remember of the answers you received. Share a few of the more interesting answers with your class.

TAKING A CLOSER LOOK AT LITERATURE

Discovering more about literature, including characteristics of various genre types, expository formats, descriptive language, and so forth, can aid in the creation of meaning and can enhance the appreciation and enjoyment of literature in general.

The next two examples, Figures 13.4 and 13.5, both come from *Worlds Together* (Richard-Amato and Hansen, 1995). The first one, which follows the story of San Ho, explores the concept of plot or chain of events; the second one, which follows the excerpt from a biography about Martin Luther King, Jr., explores the concept of time line (or chronology).

The Plot or Chain of Events

A plot or chain of events is all the things that happen in a story. It tells which thing happens first, which one happens second, and so forth. See the sample chain below. Like all chains, it is made of links. Notice that the links are joined together. Each link contains an event that is important to creating the meaning of the story. The first four links are filled in for you already. Use as many links as you need.

Chain of Events

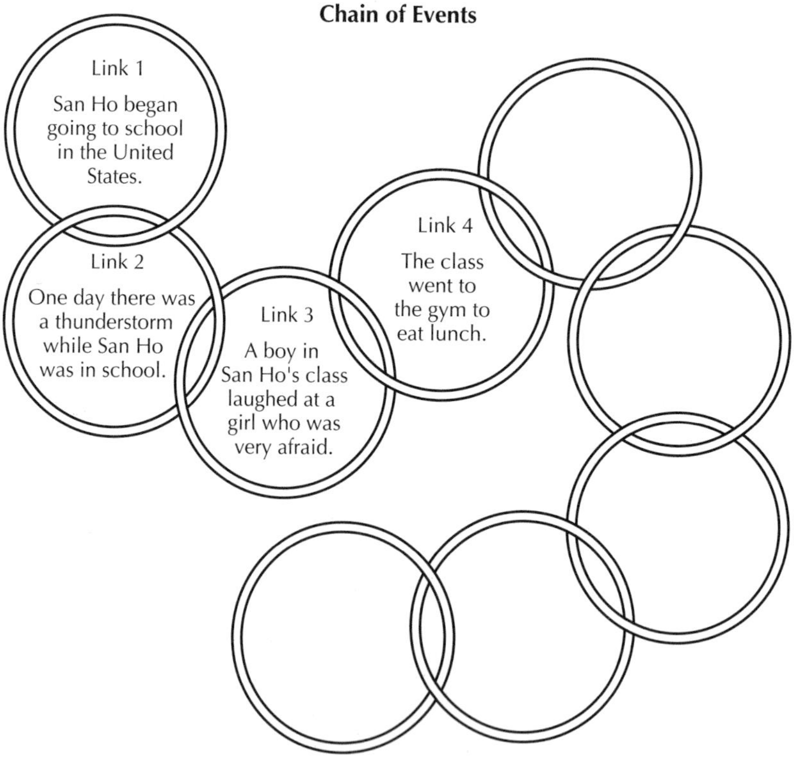

Link 1

San Ho began going to school in the United States.

Link 2

One day there was a thunderstorm while San Ho was in school.

Link 3

A boy in San Ho's class laughed at a girl who was very afraid.

Link 4

The class went to the gym to eat lunch.

Figure 13.4

A Time Line

Biographies are often written in the order of the events that happened. This order of events is called a time line. The time line may begin with the person's birth and end with the person's death.

With a partner, make a time line on your paper of Martin Luther King, Jr.'s life. See the example started for you below:

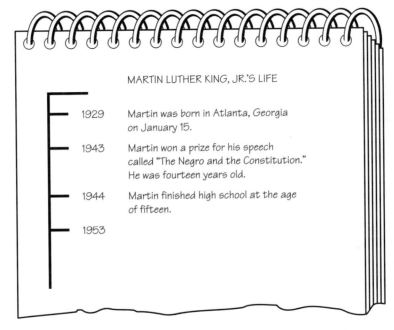

MARTIN LUTHER KING, JR.'S LIFE

1929   Martin was born in Atlanta, Georgia on January 15.

1943   Martin won a prize for his speech called "The Negro and the Constitution." He was fourteen years old.

1944   Martin finished high school at the age of fifteen.

1953

Figure 13.5

The last examples in this section come from activities developed around John Steinbeck's "The Pearl" in *Exploring Themes*. All four have to do with appreciating descriptive language.

Appreciating Descriptive Language

1. Authors often draw their readers into the excitement of a story by appeals to the senses: sight, sound, smell, touch, and taste. For example, John Steinbeck makes the night come alive by appealing to the reader's sense of sound with the words "the little tree frogs that lived near the stream twittered like birds . . .". Find several passages from the story that appeal to the senses listed below and place each in the appropriate category. There may be categories for which you can find no examples.

sight: _____
sound: _____
smell: _____
touch: _____
taste: _____

Discuss your examples with a small group. You may want to add other examples to your list based on what you learn from your classmates.

2. Descriptive language often involves a comparison between two things that are not usually thought to be similar in any way. For example, the statement "*your bicycle leaped forward like a cat*" uses such a comparison. Bicycles and cats are not usually compared to one another. Look at the following comparisons from the story in the chart below. Explain each one in the column provided. Then find one additional example of your own to place in the last space.

Comparison	Explanation
Example: ". . . Kino was a terrible machine"	Kino is compared to a machine because he seemed to be fighting without any human feelings or pity for the trackers.
". . . two of the men were sleeping, curled up like dogs"	
"And Kino crept silently as a shadow down the smooth mountain face"	

Discuss each comparison with your class and the teacher.

3. What does Steinbeck mean when he talks about the "music of the pearl," the "Song of the Family," and the "music of the enemy"? Why does he compare the movements of people's lives to music? Does this increase your enjoyment of the story? If so, how?

4. Steinbeck uses many words whose sounds suggest their meanings. The forming of such words is called *onomatopoeia* (pronounced ŏn-ä-mat-ä-pē'-ä). For example, Steinbeck uses onomatopoeia when he says that the baby "gurgled and clucked" against Juana's breast. Find several other examples of onomatopoeia in the story.

Figure 13.6 Comparison Chart

STORY GRAMMARS

A story grammar describes the structure of a story. It contains elements of storytelling such as theme, setting, characters, conflict, plot, and denouement (resolution). A story grammar is not that much different from a grammar used to talk about language. It allows the student to analyze the parts of a story and to see how they relate to one another, just as a grammar of a language allows the students to see the various parts of its structure and how the parts relate to one another. Both grammars are descriptive and both are useful tools for learning. In *Reading in the Content Areas* (Richard-Amato, 1990), a text intended for advanced adolescent and adult students of English, Ambrose Bierce's much loved story "An Occurrence at Owl Creek Bridge" is followed by an analysis of its story grammar (see Figure 13.7):

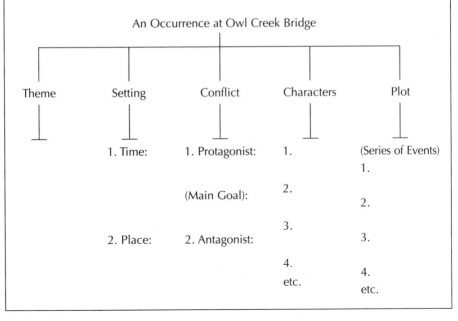

A story grammar such as the one below allows the reader to see graphically the parts of a story and how they relate to one another. Complete the story grammar, filling in the missing sections. Before you begin, consider a few definitions which may help you with the task. The theme is the main idea of the story. A protagonist is the main character or group of characters who desire something (the main goal). The antagonist, on the other hand, is usually another character or group of characters who, either directly or indirectly, prevent the protagonist from reaching the main goal. The antagonist does not necessarily have to be other characters, however. It can be nature, society, or a flaw within the protagonist. The plot is the series of events or happenings in the story.s

An Occurrence at Owl Creek Bridge

Theme	Setting	Conflict	Characters	Plot
	1. Time:	1. Protagonist:	1.	(Series of Events) 1.
		(Main Goal):	2.	2.
	2. Place:	2. Antagonist:	3.	3.
			4. etc.	4. etc.

Figure 13.7. From *Reading in Content Areas* (a Pearson Ed. publication)

WRITING IN A SPECIFIC GENRE

Students often like to try their own hand at writing in a specific genre, be it a poem, a short story, a play, and so on. It is often helpful to use what they have just read as a model. For example, following the reading of the poem "Desiderata" in *Exploring Themes* (Richard-Amato, 1993b), students are highly motivated to express their own feelings and opinions about what is important in life. One of the postreading suggestions is the following:

> Write your own "Desiderata." Include all of the things that you think are important to leading a full and rich life. Share your paper with a partner. Ask your partner to write a brief response, including areas of agreement or disagreement. You may want to react in writing to your partner's response, thus continuing the dialogue.

SPEECH WRITING

Writing a speech on a topic about which one has strong feelings can be quite exhilarating, especially if it is well-received by one's peers. Following the autobiographical piece about Martin Luther King, Jr., in *Worlds Together* (which includes an excerpt from his "I Have a Dream" speech), the students are encouraged to write a speech and share it with a small group.

> Write your own "I Have a Dream" speech. It may be about one dream or about several dreams. You may want to repeat the line "I have a dream . . ." or "I wish . . ." or similar phrases in your speech. Think about what you would like the world to be like. It could be a world without hunger, a world without war, and so forth.

With a small group, the student is asked to share his or her speech. The student can either read it to the group or record it on a cassette and play it. The members of the group are then asked to make a list of the ideas they feel to be most important in the speech. These ideas are then discussed. Do they agree with what has been expressed? Why or why not? What do they like about the speech? Do they have any questions about it? The student is then asked to rewrite the speech based on what is learned from the small group.

JOURNAL WRITING

Journals allow students to express their thoughts in writing and to relate what they read to their own lives. They may keep their entries private or share them with others. In a standard journal, students often describe their ideas and experiences, express their feelings and opinions, and/or talk about hopes and dreams. Sometimes students write about what happens on a given day in a diary; other times they choose or are given a specific topic, usually related to what they are reading or studying. But there are alternative kinds of journals. A few are described below.

The Reaction Journal

In a reaction journal, the student reacts to something very specific: a story, a poem, a picture, or a song (Richard-Amato, 1992b). These may have been selected and presented by the teacher or by fellow students. Special days are set aside as "reaction days," when students bring in and present items to which others react in their journals.

Or the reaction may be to something even more specific such as a line from a story, poem, or essay; a quote from a character in a story or play (see Figure 13.8); a description of an event; an expressed opinion; or the like. It should be something that the student finds interesting or thought-provoking. By dividing the page into two columns in a double-entry journal, the item to which the student wishes to react is written in the left column; in the right column is the reaction. The student might react by questioning, agreeing or disagreeing, analyzing, and so on.

Lines from the Reading	My Reaction
Martin Luther King, Jr. said,	I was glad that he called
"I am a citizen of the world."	himself "a citizen of the world."
(p. 197)	Too often people think only
	about themselves and their
	own country. They do not think
	of what is best for the world.
	For example, . . .

Figure 13.8 The Reaction Journal

The Dialogue Journal

Using a standard format or a double-entry format like the one described above, the students may write about a topic related to what is being read or studied. The student expresses his or her opinion or feelings in the left column; in the right column, a partner or the teacher responds. Thus the writing itself becomes a social event and takes on interesting social ramifications through its dialectical nature. Often by the means of dialogue journals, relationships are built and bonds are formed.

Peyton and Straton (1992) feel that the following are a few additional benefits that can accrue to those participating in dialogue journal writing. They say that such writing:

- makes available discourse adapted to the students' "linguistic, cognitive, and emotional levels,"
- facilitates the acquisition of advanced language functions and structures of reasoned discourse, and
- presents students with texts that are individualized and progressively more demanding.

The Learning Journal
Again the double-entry format is used. Only this time the student lists in the left column those things that he or she has learned from a given selection. In the right column, the student can write what he or she still wants to learn or how the learned information can be applied.

Journal entries, regardless of type, can form the roots from which longer, more formal writings can grow. Many a poem, story, or expository piece has sprung from a journal entry. Thus, the usefulness of the journal is extended. In this way, the journal serves as a brainstorming mechanism, a means for generating and clarifying ideas and sorting out information.

Reading Journals
Somewhat more personal in nature are reading journals. In them, students reveal their feelings about what a character says or does. They can state their reactions to the author's ideas, relate to their own experiences, and so forth. Moreover, they can talk about how they are reading. Is reading becoming any easier for them in their new language? What strategies are they using to help them comprehend? Have they discovered new means for adding to their repertoire of language, both semantically and syntactically?

Co-authored Reading Journals
An interesting alternative is for partners to select a book of the same title. During the period of time that they are reading the book, they write in a co-authored journal, also called a "buddy book journal" (Bromley, 1995; Gillespie, 1993). This is a shared journal that is passed back and forth between them. Some of the things mentioned previously may be discussed; i.e., feelings, reactions, reading strategies, and so on.

INDEPENDENT READING

Through independent reading, students can pursue subjects of interest, perhaps expanding their knowledge and vicarious experiences in areas to which they have been introduced in their lessons.

Book Reviews
Book reviews can become an integral part of the independent reading process. They can provide a means whereby students can share their impressions and make recommendations to others. Below is a sample form.

Book Review

Title of book:
Author: Type of book:
Name of reviewer: Date:

What did you feel this book was about?

What did you like about this book?

Was there anything you did not like about this book? Explain.

Do you think your classmates should read this book? Why or why not?

The reviews can be written or typed on index cards which can be filed in an accessible place in the classroom. Or the reviews can be put into a computer data base which is shared by all class members.

WRITING WORKSHOPS

Transforming the classroom into a writing workshop can be an effective way to utilize all important resources, including peers, and to reinforce the notion that writing is indeed a communal process. The teacher and peers give input when needed at whatever steps the students are ready for. The steps include:

1. coming up with an idea
2. gathering information
3. working out the idea on paper, perhaps graphically at first or in outline form
4. expanding and developing aspects of the idea
5. getting some semblance of order (moving things around, deleting, replacing)

6. providing transitional elements where appropriate
7. rendering the draft more coherent as well as cohesive
8. polishing
9. sharing with an audience

A word of caution here: Sometimes setting up a workshop results in writing as an isolated activity, removed from other events of the classroom and other language experiences. Care must be taken to ensure that writing will be an integral part of the total curriculum and that its content will be related to what the students are reading, listening to, and talking about.

Face-to-Face Conferencing with the Teacher and with Peers[2]

Although conferencing is often treated in the literature on second language acquisition separately, it can be made an integral component in a workshop approach to writing.

Conferencing with the teacher and with peers should not be disruptive to those needing a quiet place in which to think and write. Therefore, the conference itself should take place in out-of-the-way places, perhaps at stations at the periphery of the classroom (see Figure 15.2 on page 313) or in private corners. Not everyone will be ready to conference at the same time, and so those who are ready can go to a station when one is available or set up a new one if needed. It should be noted here that some students may be reluctant to join in the conferencing at first. Those not wishing to participate should not be forced to. It has been my experience that eventually almost everyone becomes caught up in the excitement generated by working with others, especially if the environment is positive. Students often receive a better sense of the reader through conferencing. Nevertheless, some students might need a little extra encouragement occasionally from the teacher and from peers.

The conferencing groups can be organized in several ways:

- The teacher selects a few students to serve as peer consultants. Those chosen can be different for each workshop until all who want to have served at least once. Each peer consultant is assigned a station. Students can be assigned to specific consultants, can select those with whom they feel most comfortable, or can go to whomever is available at the time.
- Students can be paired by the teacher to serve as consultants for each other.
- Students can form their own partnerships.

---

[2] An alternative would be conferencing through e-mail (see Chapter 16, page 347).

The way in which the conferencing groups are organized may vary from workshop to workshop, depending on the task to be accomplished and on the outcomes desired. At first the writings will probably be rather personal, short, and elementary—a listing of ideas or a cluster, a chart, a paragraph, a simple poetic form. Later the writings are more academic, longer and/or more complex—perhaps an essay, a report, a critique, a short story, a poem, a one-act play.

The purpose of the conference will be different at each phase of the writing process. When ideas are first taking shape, students will want to express these ideas orally and receive feedback. At other points in the process, students will want reactions to what they have written and may ask or be asked specific questions about what they write. At some point, they may want the teacher or a peer with whom they have established rapport to help them find and correct their errors. Usually this occurs toward the end of the writing process; however, those who are anxious about errors may request help earlier. The important thing is to give this kind of feedback when the student will most benefit from it.

It is essential that all the students go through a preparation phase before any conferencing begins. Respect for one another's ideas needs to be stressed and a focus on the positive needs to be emphasized. Some role play demonstrating effective conferencing should take place during which all students have access to the sample piece of writing being talked about. Such role play can prevent many of the problems often associated with peer conferencing; i.e., overly severe criticism, a focus on "being correct," a failure to offer positive support, and overall lack of preparation (see Leki, 1990; Hedgcock and Lefkowitz, 1992; Yoshihara, 1993).

As part of the preparation for conferencing, the following suggestions can be discussed and/or used in a role play.

What the *Writer*
Can Do During the Conference

Read the paper aloud to the teacher or peer (you may see some problem areas yourself). You may be asked to read it aloud more than once.
Ask questions such as the following:

- Which idea or ideas do you find of interest in my paper?
- Is there a main idea that holds it together?
- Are there any ideas that might be best put in a paper on another topic?
- Do you have any questions about what I am saying?
- Is there anything you would say more about if you were me?

What the *Teacher* or *Peer*
Can Do During the Conference

Listen carefully as the paper is being read. Take a few notes if you want to. If you have trouble understanding the reader, look at the paper with the reader while it is being read. Ask the writer to read it again, if necessary.
Ask questions such as the following:

- What part do you like the best about your paper?
- What idea do you think is the most important?
- Are there any ideas that might be best put in a paper on another topic?
- Why did you choose this topic?
- How do you feel about . . . ?
- Can you tell me more about . . . ?
- When did this happen?
- Should this go first or last?
- What kinds of details might you add here?
- What do you want the reader to learn from this?
- What do you plan to do now?

The following form could be filled out by the writer as a result of the conference.

Date: _____   Name of Writer: _____

Name of the conference partner: _____

What did you learn from the conference?

What changes do you plan to make on your next rewrite? _____

    The effectiveness of peer conferences has been associated with the quality of the interaction itself. Nelson and Murphy (1993) found in their study of English Language Learners (ELLs) in a writing course at a large urban university that a particular student was more likely to use a peer's suggestions in rewrites when the interaction was cooperative. When the interaction was defensive or when a negotiation for meaning was nonexistent, the student was less inclined to use the peer's suggestions. The latter was also supported by Goldstein and Conrad (1990), who looked at a similar population.

Feedback on Errors

Interestingly, the quality of the revisions may depend on the type of feedback that the student is given. Kepner (1991) found that students studying Spanish in an intermediate class at Wheaton College who had received meaning-focused written feedback rather than error-focused feedback did not "sacrifice accuracy for content." In fact, those receiving surface-error correction feedback wrote subsequent journal entries of far lower ideational quality than those receiving meaning-focused feedback. She concluded, "Correction of discrete errors should occur only at the final stages of editing, when the piece is prepared for 'publishing' or other forms of public display (p. 306)."

Zamel (1985) found in an earlier study that when the written feedback was mixed (contained both meaning-focused and error-focused feedback), the students tended to focus on the surface errors at the expense of content, the improvement of which was often ignored. It is my feeling that, as a general rule, when error-focused feedback is given, it should come near the end of the writing process, unless the student specifically requests it earlier.

More recently, Farris (1997) examined the comments that an experienced teacher had made on the papers of forty-seven students enrolled in sheltered ESL freshman composition at a California university to see which kinds of feedback appeared to be most influential. She examined the revised drafts to see how the students had utilized the comments in their modifications and whether or not the modifications seemed effective. She concluded that, overall, the comments were generally heeded and led to substantial and effective revisions (less than 5 percent were rated negative). The comments that appeared most influential were requests for information, summary comments on grammar, longer comments, and those comments that were text-specific. A strategy that she judged particularly effective was to require students to write a "revise-and-resubmit" letter reacting to the feedback received, telling how each suggestion would be handled in the revision and explaining why some would be disregarded. This practice seemed to ensure that it was the student who was in control of his or her own revisions and that if the reason(s) given for not making a specific revision were strong enough, then the student was justified in not making the recommended change. She noted, too, that teachers need to take great care in structuring any written questions they might have because students are frequently confused by the teachers' questions. She cautioned, however, against coming to too many conclusions based on her study because students operating at proficiency levels lower than those of her subjects and students not already familiar with composition classes taught in the United States might respond very differently. She also suggested that analyzing variations in comments and their effects on revisions across instructors would be helpful.

Cultural Considerations

Even though there may be cultural tendencies within different groups with respect to reading, it is important not to assume that all individuals within these groups will have the same tendencies (see also Parry, 1996). All students should be treated as individuals who are capable of bringing a variety of strategies to each situation as it presents itself. Although teachers have been made more sensitive to cultural differences and norms concerning writing and approaches to writing, there is a danger when assumptions are made about individual writers, even those from the same culture. For example, some cultures are assumed to use circular organizational patterns when thinking and writing. If the teacher assumes that *all* students from one of these cultures will have a hard time with linear organizational patterns, then the teacher might very well be coming to the wrong conclusion and, at the same time, doing these students a great disservice (see also Zamel, 1997). Students vary *within and between* cultures, depending upon circumstances and experiences and how both are interpreted by the individual. Not only that, but students are often highly skilled at "hopping borders" and achieving what might be expected in two very different cultural situations without difficulty. Teachers would be wise to explore with each student his or her background and use that background as a transition to help the student develop compositional skills in the new language (see also Nieto, 1999).

In this section on a workshop approach to writing, I have offered suggestions for teacher and peer conferencing based on what has worked in the classroom situations I have facilitated myself. It should be noted that there are many other ways in which this type of activity can be carried out, some of which may be more effective than what you see here. For further ideas on a similar subject, the reader might take a look at the section on pages 310–314 detailing peer teaching. Although the role of the peer is different in peer teaching situations, many of the ideas may be appropriate to teacher and peer conferencing and can be easily adapted.

Information about Assessment tools, including portfolios (their development and use) can be found in Chapter 7 on language assessment.

ADVANCED ACADEMIC LITERACY

Academic goals need to be pursued right from the beginning in second and foreign language classroom settings, especially if students expect to be able to function successfully in academic environments in a timely manner (see also Chapter 17).

Many of the already mentioned strategies and activities can be adapted for advanced academic applications. For example, the language experience approach can yield a group-generated analysis of an experiment on the effects of one chemical on another. Prereading, reading, and postreading strategies and activities can be applied to a seminal article on pre-World War II influences on modern political thought. A writing workshop approach can be used to develop a critical paper on Jungian philosophy, and so forth. The applications are virtually limitless.

At advanced levels within a second or foreign language program, students need to be exposed to the kinds of reading and writing (and listening/speaking) tasks that will be expected of them in later coursework: reading abstract materials, getting down the key ideas from lectures, writing critiques and summaries, and so forth. Once students are in a mainstream academic environment, they will need a place where they can go for assistance and support, perhaps in the form of an adjunct program or a learning center (see related programs described in Chapter 18).

Sustained-content language teaching is one important way to prepare students for academic work (Murphy and Stoller, 2001). The editors maintain that an extended exploration of a single content area (math, social studies, science, geography, etc.) or a topic within a content area can enhance students' abilities to learn the language skills associated with advanced literacy development, speaking, listening, academic vocabulary, grammar, etc. Not only that but a sustained approach encourages students to pursue extensive reading in the areas chosen for investigation, use multiple print and nonprint sources, look at various perspectives, and use the critical thinking necessary to successfully form comparisons and contrasts, to synthesize, and evaluate.

Within a second or foreign language academic program, students need knowledge and experience (including guided experience) in all areas that are likely to lead to academic success. These areas include but are not limited to the following:

1. *Text-structure schema and conventional text-constructing devices*

It is important for students to have a knowledge of the text-structure schema and the text-constructing devices commonly used by the academic community within a given society and within a given field of study. Being familiar with the structures associated with argumentative composition, chronological development, definition, procedural description, and analysis, to name a few examples, is useful to students studying in a variety of fields. The related text-constructing devices such as specific introductory elements, conclusions, headings, transitions, and other organizational signals, aid the students in gaining perspective on what they read, in seeing relationships, and in following lines of thought. In addition, there is evidence that students who have text-structure knowledge appear to comprehend and recall more of what they read than those who do not (see especially Carrell, 1983, 1984, 1985). Not only is such knowledge beneficial to students as readers (and listeners), but it helps students construct their own compositions, so they can be better understood by academic audiences.

2. *Cognitive and metacognitive strategies for reading and writing in the various academic content areas*

Important strategies for reading as an aid to learning include underlining, highlighting, paraphrasing in the margins, outlining, idea mapping, using the dictionary, identifying key ideas, using context to determine meaning, and many more.

Strategies for writing include brainstorming mechanisms, researching, using quickwrites[3] and graphic representations of ideas (see clustering devices used earlier in this chapter), drafting compositions, combining text-structures, and so forth.

Additional tasks such as answering questions, posing questions, anticipating questions, reacting in various ways, summarizing, using specific composition formats and combinations of formats, collecting information for specific writing tasks, test-taking and preparation, and notetaking involve a wide variety of strategies of their own. Talking about strategies in "What Works for Me" sessions can be extremely beneficial. So can practice with such strategies. However, it should be remembered that such practice should not be isolated from the content with which the students are currently involved; on the contrary, the strategies experienced should be an integral part of what the students are learning.

3. *Synthesizing information from a range of materials in a single area of study*

Krashen (1981c) called this kind of reading "narrow reading" (see also Shih, 1992). Such reading is more akin to what students will be doing in their academic coursework (see also Murphey and Stoller, mentioned above). Shorter, less complex readings can be used first, followed by those that become progressively longer and more complex. These readings can then become the basis for a variety of academic writing (and speaking) experiences. Thus the students will have the background knowledge necessary to the intelligent, logical treatments of related assignments.

4. *Other areas*

In addition to synthesizing information in a single area of study (number 3 above), Horowitz (1986) has identified six other categories. Based on an examination of actual writing assignment handouts and essay examinations given to students at Western Illinois University, he found that out of fifty-four examples, the following types of tasks emerged:

---

[3] Quickwrites allow students to write down whatever comes to mind without stopping to make corrections or worry about format. It is one way to get preliminary ideas down on paper. Peter Elbow (1993) calls the quickwrite an "evaluation-free zone" and strongly encourages its use in getting students to take risks, follow hunches, and increase their fluency in writing. Students can return later and restructure their quickwrites, making them more palatable to potential readers.

Category	Number of Examples
Summary of/reaction to a reading (in psychology, communication arts and sciences, history, home economics, special education, and learning resources)	9
Annotated bibliography (biology)	1
Report on a specified participatory experience (anthropology, psychology, educational foundations, and home economics)	9
Connection of theory and data (communication arts and sciences, psychology, economics, and home economics)	10
Case study (administrative office management, marketing, and psychology)	5
Synthesis of multiple sources (communication arts and sciences, psychology, biology, geology, sociology, accounting, zoology, management, special education, and marketing)	15
Research project (communication arts and sciences, psychology)	5

Figure 13.9

In studies such as this one, the departments from which the examples come and the number of examples will vary from term to term and from campus to campus. It is critical that the language instructor know the kinds of tasks that his or her students will be expected to carry out. Not only that, but knowing the specific nature of the tasks provides valuable information for the instructor who really cares about preparing students for what is to come. Horowitz found that out of the fifty-four tasks, thirty-four of them were highly controlled and accompanied by detailed instructions, calling for specific content organization. Related to these tasks, Horowitz emphasized the importance of the student's being able to select relevant data from sources that will be appropriate for the task, reorganize the data in response to questions, and encode data into academic forms of the language.

Rose (1983), in a study similar to Horowitz's, looked at assigned topics for composition and take-home test questions given by faculty members in seventeen departments at the University of California, Los Angeles. The topics and questions generally required a knowledge of expository and argumentative modes and the ability to synthesize information and relate to the theoretical assumptions associated with a given field of study.

Concerning writing for an academic audience, in particular, Reid (1992) stresses the importance the academic community places on traditional formats and accepted conventions of expression. In her discussion of surface errors in English, she refers to Vann, Meyer, and Lorenz's (1984) survey of academic readers, which found that respondents tended to be least accepting of those errors that were generally associated with the writing of nonnative speakers (e.g., word order and word choice, *it* deletion, tense and relative clause errors). Perhaps the academic audience needs to become more informed about the nature of errors typically made by second language writers so that they can see them in light of the normal language development process. But, in the meantime, students need to be prepared for the kinds of feedback they may receive from an audience that may or may not respond in a way that is helpful. It is beneficial, too, to give students the opportunity to write for *real* audiences from time to time (see especially Johns, 1993).

Finding out specifically what it is that students will need the ability to do seems essential to any serious academic preparation program (see also Tarone and Yule, 1989). Not only that, but while students are in preparation, instructors should be working closely with content-area teachers/professors—that is, if they are known and available. This collaboration, in all likelihood, will make the transition much easier for students. See Chapter 17 for other ideas about transitioning into academic programs.

SUMMARY

There are many ways we can promote literacy development in a second or foreign language. Using versions of the language experience approach, it is possible for us to begin where each student is. By involving the students in a literature-based curriculum, we can use the power of language to heighten awareness and fully engage the minds of our students. Moreover, the reading-writing connection may be fully realized through such involvement. Motivation and guidance can be provided through a workshop approach to writing in which students can take full advantage of the classroom community that has been established. At later levels, the students can take on progressively more advanced reading and writing tasks to prepare for an academic environment, if functioning in such an environment is the goal. All the while, skills can be integrated and allowed to grow naturally out of the content that is being learned.

READINGS, REFLECTION, AND DISCUSSION

Suggested Readings and Reference Materials

Anderson. N. (1999). *Exploring second language reading: Issues and strategies.* Boston: Heinle. ESL teachers in particular will find this book enjoyable as well as informative. In it, Anderson presents a discussion of several reading strategies involving teaching comprehension, evaluating progress, selecting materials, etc. The book includes a teachers' voices section in which we hear from four ESL teachers. In addition, readers are offered the opportunity to reflect through questions and tasks and to explore websites on various related topics.

Atwell, N. (1998). *In the middle: New Understandings About Writing, Reading, and Learning* (2d Edition). Portsmouth, NH: Heinemann. Although this book is intended for teaching reading and writing to native-speaking adolescents, many of its ideas are applicable to second and foreign language learners at all age levels. It is an honest account, told by a teacher, of her own experiences setting up writing and reading workshops. It includes many specific examples of activities and student work.

Blanton, L. (1998). *Varied voices: On language and literacy learning*. Boston: Heinle. This book is based on ethnographic research conducted at a Moroccan school with a diverse student body, both linguistically and culturally. It explores how the children developed language and literacy within their classroom communities.

Collins, P. (2001). *Community writing: Researching social issues through composition*. Mahwah, NJ: Lawrence Erlbaum. Rooted in critical pedagogy, this book contains assignments guiding students in their research of social issues affecting them and the communities in which they live. At the same time, students collaborate as they work on a variety of writing projects that grow out of their investigations. Shorter writing pieces develop into longer compositions as each student progresses in the writing process.

Dixon, C., and Nessel, D. (1990). *Language experience approach to reading (and writing)*. Englewood Cliffs, NJ: Prentice Hall. This book presents an extensive literacy program for ELLs based on the language experience approach. Combined are both theoretical and practical ideas for teachers.

Lazar, G. (1993). *Literature and language teaching: A guide for teachers and trainers*. Cambridge: Cambridge University Press. Presented here is a rationale for using literature to teach language; an overview of approaches to literature; criteria for selecting and evaluating materials; the cross-cultural nature of texts; planning lessons and designing materials around novels, short stories, poetry, and plays; reflecting on literature lessons; and using literature for self-access purposes. Most of the tasks and activities within each chapter require analysis and critical thought.

Leeds, B., ed. (1996). *Writing in a second language: Insights from first and second language teaching and research*. White Plains, NY: Longman/Addison-Wesley. Included in this anthology are the traditions of L1 and L2 composing, the processes involved in writing and reading, teacher feedback, writing assessment, and much more. Among the authors represented are Peter Elbow, Linda Flower, Ann Johns, Ann Raimes, and Vivian Zamel.

Whiteson, V., ed. (1996), *New ways of using drama and literature in language teaching*. Alexandria, VA: TESOL. This practical book could have fit as easily into the Suggested Readings for Chapters 10 and 11. It includes such activities as "The Story Game," "Poem Charades," "Experiencing the Music of Poetry . . . ," "Acting Is Becoming," as well as strategies for dialectical journal writing, using a workshop approach to writing, readers' theater, and discussing literature via think/pair/share.

Questions and Projects for Reflection and Discussion

1. What is your opinion of the more "pure" applications of the language experience approach? To what extent do you think the teacher should take on the role of a facilitator? Might there be a danger in the teacher's contributing too much? Explain.

2. Try out a version of the language experience approach with a small group of peers. Ask them to play the role of students operating at high-beginning to low-intermediate levels (see page 137 for behaviors typical of those levels). What experience will you give them about which they can write? Decide what your role will be and how you will handle errors. After your presentation, ask your group for feedback. Begin by sharing your own reactions to the presentation.

   If you are currently teaching students, use what you have learned to try out similar activities with them. Make sure the activities are relevant and appropriate to level. If possible, have your activities videotaped to analyze and discuss with peers. Reflect on the outcome of the activities and how you felt about participating in them. Pay close attention to student response. Do you see any problems with the strategies you employed? How might they be improved?

   Write about your experiences with language experience approach practices and what you learned in your journal.

3. Select a piece of literature that will engage the minds of your students, and develop several prereading and postreading activities around it. Make sure it is appropriate to age and proficiency levels. Share your plans with a small group. What is their reaction? Can they suggest any additional activities you might incorporate into your plans?

4. Devise a way to use a writing workshop that relates to and is an extension of a unit you are developing or might develop. How will you set it up? What will you do to prepare your students so that the workshop has the best possible chance for success? Discuss your ideas with a small group.

5. How might you prepare your students for a mainstream academic environment, if that is their goal? Make a list of the tasks you would include. What if their goal were something other than an academic environment? What if their goal were to have the skills necessary to succeed in a specific trade or vocation? What would your list look like in this case? Share your list with a small group and ask for their input.

CHAPTER **14**

Affective Activities

When given the opportunity to talk about themselves in personally relevant ways, students tend to become much more motivated. The result is that they want to be able to express their feelings and ideas more in the target language. They want *to communicate. When this happens, growth becomes a reciprocal process; enhancing personal growth enhances growth in the foreign language.*

G. Moskowitz, 1978

QUESTIONS TO THINK ABOUT

1. Think back about what you learned in Chapter 6, The Affective Domain. In your opinion, what were the most important factors discussed there? What do you think "affective activities" might entail? You might want to look ahead in this chapter and scan a few of the activities presented there.

2. Have you ever participated in affective activities and/or used them in the classes you have taught? If so, describe your experience with them. Under what circumstances were they used? What effect did they have on you and/or your students?

3. How do you think affective activities might be used in a second or foreign language class? Do you think they could be of benefit to language acquisition? In what ways? Do you see possible problems in their use?

HOW DID AFFECTIVE ACTIVITIES COME ABOUT?

Many of the affective activities found in this chapter have grown, either directly or indirectly, from a much earlier interest in values clarification. Raths, Merrill, and Simon (1966) asserted that valuing is made up of three categories of subprocesses:

- prizing beliefs and behaviors
- choosing beliefs and behaviors
- acting on beliefs

The approach that they recommended aimed not at inculcating a specific set of values but rather at helping students work through the process of valuing in order to clarify what it was that gave meaning to their lives. Raths, et al., argued that exploring already-formed beliefs as well as those that were emerging could be a rewarding experience for students of all ages and could greatly enhance their self-esteem and confidence.

Many teachers today feel that, for second language learners, especially those at intermediate to advanced proficiency levels, affective activities (including values clarification) can add a valuable dimension to the language learning process. If used appropriately by an impartial, accepting teacher, such activities not only can provide meaningful dialogue in the target language, but also serve as an important means of bonding among students. This can be particularly important in ESL classes in which many different values systems are brought together (see Chapter 6). An environment that fosters an appreciation of differences can encourage individual growth and decrease hostility.

In spite of their potential benefits, however, affective activities are not for everyone. They are not for the teacher who feels uncomfortable sharing feelings and opinions. They are not for the teacher who wants to treat them as therapy sessions, although, as Moskowitz (1978)[1] points out, they may be therapeutic. And they are certainly not for the teacher who wants to use them as a way to change the beliefs of others.

If affective activities are to be effective for language teaching, they must be used by a teacher who has read in depth (see this chapter's suggested readings) or who has completed a training program. Moreover, the activities chosen must be compatible with the students' age and proficiency levels, and appropriate to the cultural environment in which they are to be used. Some cultures may con-

---

[1] Moskowitz bases her ideas on humanistic education which assumes that individuals have the freedom to rise above their circumstances. Critical pedagogy, on the other hand, considers itself postmodern and is based on the premise that such freedom may or may not be there and that there are powerful forces determined to hold cultural minorities or persons with diminished influence in a state of oppression (see the introduction to this book). Some claim that humanism can become a tool to accomplish the goals of colonialism. However, the strategies presented here are not intended to perpetuate such goals.

sider it offensive to reveal oneself or to probe the thoughts of others. However, Moskowitz (1999) has found that affective strategies, if carefully applied, seem to work across cultures and with a variety of individuals in that they promote harmony and self-acceptance.

For the teacher who decides to implement affective activities, Moskowitz lays down a few ground rules:

- Students must be given the right to "pass," meaning they must not be forced to answer questions or contribute
- They must have the right to be heard
- They must have the right to see their own opinions respected (no put-downs are allowed).

She recommends further that the students have a chance to express afterwards how they felt about specific activities and what they learned from them.

In addition, Moskowitz advises that the activities accentuate the positive and that they be "low risk" so neither teacher nor student will feel threatened by them. In other words, instead of asking students what they dislike about themselves, ask them what they like; rather than asking them what they feel guilty about, ask them what makes them feel proud. Of course, negative feelings cannot be denied when they do arise. They should be treated like any other feelings, unless, of course, they are used to diminish someone else. But not all activities can be positive in all respects. For example, we may want to ask students what they would want changed in the world or how something might be made better in their lives. What Moskowitz is saying, I believe, is that the overall focus should be positive and constructive.

WHAT IS THE TEACHER'S ROLE?

Although there appears to be some disagreement in the early literature (Simon, Howe, and Kirschenbaum, 1992; Gaylean, 1982; Moskowitz, 1978) as to the role of the teacher in affective activities, all seem to agree that the chief duty is one of facilitator. As facilitators, teachers need to encourage honest responses, establish an aura of trust, listen with genuine interest to what students say, and invite sharing—but only what students want to share. Furthermore, teachers should clarify by asking "Is this what you're saying?" or by paraphrasing with statements such as "I think you're saying . . . ."

The authors all seem to agree that teachers should be free to reveal their feelings and opinions in the discussions. However, Simon, Howe, and Kirschenbaum believe that these revelations should occur only at certain times, preferably at the end of the discussion, after students have had a chance to think things through and express their own points of view. Teachers should present themselves as persons with values (and often with values confusion);

they should share their own values but not impose them. In this way, teachers present themselves as adults who prize, choose, and act according to the valuing process. Teachers have the same opportunities to share values as any other members of the class. The particular content of teachers' values holds no more weight than that of others.

On the basis of my own experience with affective activities, I agree that it is important for the students to realize that teachers,[2] like other people, are engaged in the valuing process. However, it may be naive to think that the teacher's point of view will be perceived as carrying no more weight than anyone else's, particularly when the teacher is acting as a facilitator. The problem then appears to be how teachers can make it known that they are developing and refining their own values without allowing their beliefs to unduly influence the students. Perhaps the answer lies in how we view a facilitator's role as opposed to a participant's role. It is my opinion that the teacher should not attempt to be a facilitator and a participant simultaneously. As a facilitator, the teacher should remain objective throughout the activity. It is the facilitator's job to prepare and lead the students into a particular activity, to enforce the ground rules, to listen thoughtfully and nonjudgmentally, to clarify, to accept each student as he or she wants to be accepted, and to provide transitions as well as closures at the end of each activity. The participant's role also includes listening thoughtfully and nonjudgmentally, clarifying others' ideas, and accepting others on their own ground, but it does not require that one remain impartial. A participant has the right to state his or her opinions and feelings about the subject, as long as others' rights to opinions are respected.

For a teacher to express his or her ideas without giving them undue weight, a clear shift of roles must take place. The teacher can become a participant on occasion, and volunteer students can become facilitators (somewhat akin to the dialectical relationship between student and teacher described by Freire in Chapter 3). This role switch not only provides a chance for teachers to model behaviors, but also can create a great deal of excitement and motivation for students, who realize that they too can take on the responsibility of facilitating the discussion.

There are other ways in which teachers can express opinions without being overly imposing. For example, the teacher can step down from the role of facilitator without reversing roles. However, it may be prudent to do this only when the students ask for the teacher's opinion on a certain issue of interest and only after students have had a chance to express themselves fully, as Simon, Howe, and Kirschenbaum suggest. The teacher also may want to use himself or herself as an example in a demonstration as part of the preliminary instructions, especially if the issue involved is not a controversial one.

---

[2] When I use the word *teachers* here, I also mean peer teachers and lay assistants if they are included in the program (see Chapter 15).

WHEN CAN AFFECTIVE ACTIVITIES BE USED?

Affective activities, which can be used in the classroom at almost any time, can be particularly beneficial in certain situations. On days when students are feeling especially tense or emotionally down, such activities can have comforting effects. For example, before final exams or other threatening events, the teacher might attempt an overt enhancement of self-concepts by seating the students in a circle and having each of them concentrate on one person at a time. Then each says one thing he or she especially likes about that person. During the session, someone (perhaps an advanced student) can record on separate sheets of paper what is said about each person so that the students can go home at the end of the day with the positive comments in writing (Richard-Amato, 1983).

On lighter occasions, the teacher may want to center on a theme such as "exploring career options" with teenagers and adults or "choosing a pet" with children. Or sometimes a particular activity is very compatible with what is being discussed in response to a story, song, or poem (see page 206). If a character in a story has to decide between marrying for love and marrying for money, for example, an affective activity on related choices might be in order. Such activities tie content to real life. Flexibility helps the teacher recognize these teachable moments and take advantage of them in ways that maximize the benefits of each activity. Particularly at advanced levels, the teacher may want to use several activities to stimulate thought for writing assignments. Similar activities may also serve as appropriate means for culminating library research.

GETTING READY

Most of the activities presented in this chapter are for small groups (from two to ten students). Groups can be formed in any number of ways.

- Students can be grouped sociometrically by having students write down the names of students with whom they feel most comfortable. After collecting their papers, the teacher can plan what might be some workable groups.
- In an ESL class, the teacher might want to have the various cultures represented in each group or might prefer to group students from homogeneous cultures. The act of grouping itself might be an affective activity. Groups can be set up on the basis of favorite colors, seasons, foods, and the like. For example, the teacher might say, "Today we will have four groups. The group to which you belong will be determined by your favorite season of the year. All people who like fall come to this table; spring to that table . . . ."

- Or random units might be formed by simply having the students number off. The method selected to form groups may depend on the activity chosen, the number of groups needed for the activity, the number of students in the class, and/or whether or not the groups need to be of equal numbers (see also pages 162 and 233–234).

Most of the activities suggested in this chapter are intended for intermediate to advanced levels although some, particularly those recommended in the next section, can be accomplished with beginners. Most of the activities can be modified to accommodate several different proficiency levels and can be adapted easily to various age groups simply by changing the content (see Chapter 15). Many of the questions and statements used as examples in the exercises that follow reflect the interests of teenagers and adults but can be changed to reflect those of younger children. Topics appropriate to children might include animals, toys, being the youngest or oldest in the family, discipline at home, holidays such as Halloween and Valentine's Day, TV cartoons, allowances, what you want to be when you grow up, and so forth. Activities should always be tailored to the needs, interests, and capabilities of the students and they must be activities with which the teacher feels comfortable.

PREPARING THE STUDENTS

Students should be exposed early on to some of the basic vocabulary that will be particularly useful for affective activities: emotions, feelings, favorite things to do, preferences in foods, colors, clothing, occupations, classes, and so forth. These can be taught through several of the methods presented in previous chapters. For example, introduce students to emotions by demonstrating and then asking to display them (to cry, to laugh, etc.); to foods by preparing various foods according to directions; to clothing by putting on and taking off sweaters, jackets, and other garments; to colors by manipulating objects of various colors. These concepts can be reinforced through discussion, or in warm-ups for role play. As students move into the mid-beginning proficiency level (see page 137), they can begin to express feelings and preferences through activities such as the chants in Chapter 10, where they can supply the missing words. Establish a beat by snapping fingers, and then begin and ask students to follow suit: "My name is _____ and I feel _____ (happy, sad, tired, etc.)" or "My name is _____ and I like _____ (apples, pizza, movies, dancing, to read, etc.)."

Eventually, students move into the high-beginning level, and the vocabulary becomes a little more sophisticated with words like *beautiful, stubborn, smart, safe,* and *selfish*. And as students approach intermediate levels and above (see pages 137–138), they may pick up such words and phrases as *self-confident, self-conscious, ridiculous, secure, spiteful, stimulated, enthusiastic, open-minded, to know oneself,* and *to lay it on the line.* Many of the words and structures commonly used in expressing feelings and opinions will come naturally through affective activities. There may be times, however, when the teacher wants to provide supplementary vocabulary and perhaps even some open-ended sentences (Moskowitz calls them "stems") to reinforce certain vocabulary and structures by building exercises around them:

> If I were older, I would . . .
> One thing I do well is . . .
> I want my friends to . . .
> I wonder if . . .
> I like you because . . .
> My brother (sister) makes me feel . . .
> People seem to respect me when I . . .
> People can't force me to . . .
> One thing I like about my family is that . . .
> When people tease me, I . . .
> If I could have one wish come true, I would wish for . . .

In addition, students should be encouraged to ask for help when attempting to share something that is temporarily beyond them rather than simply to pass. Students should be invited to consult with more proficient peers or with the teacher. Not only does such mentoring benefit the learner, but it can also benefit the student who acts as the "teacher." Thus, others can serve in helping roles similar to the counselors used in conjunction with Curran's counseling learning approach.[3]

If students seem reluctant to use affective activities, starting with activities involving characters in literature may be a good idea. For instance, the teacher might have the students read a story with well-developed characters, then role-play the characters to reveal what they might choose in a particular situation. An easy next step then is to ask: "And what would you have chosen in this situation?" For example, if students are reading about a couple who fight because one wants to buy an expensive home, own a flashy car, and take frequent trips to Europe, whereas the other would rather live modestly, drive a simple car that runs well, and vacation in the Sierras in a camper, they can role-play the characters in affective activities. Or students might make up a story about the people in a picture and then role-play those characters, using appropriate affective activities. Once comfortable in role-play situations, students may be more at ease doing the same activities without role-playing, but using their own opinions, feelings, and beliefs.

---

[3] Curran (1972) described an approach whereby the teacher or others proficient in the target language serve as counselors and linguistic models for students. At the beginning, the students are completely dependent on the counselors, who help them translate their utterances from L1 to L2. As they become more and more proficient in the new language, it is expected that they will work toward complete independence.

Another aid for reluctant students (all students may be a little reluctant at first) is to begin with less threatening issues. For example, the teacher might begin with, "Tell us about your favorite movie," rather than "Describe a moment when you were really embarrassed." Several of the ideas presented below may also serve as warm-ups to the other activities.

AFFECTIVE ACTIVITIES

Ideas to Consider

VALUES SURVEY[4]

Ask students questions and give them three or more choices from which to select the answer. Write the questions and possible answers on a sheet of paper, make copies, and distribute to the class. When giving the instructions, stress that there are no right or wrong answers.

Which would you rather be?
___ an astronaut
___ a business person
___ a teacher
___ a mechanic
___ a social worker
___ a mathematician
___ a carpenter

If you had $2,000, what would you do with it?
___ give most of it to some worthy cause
___ put it in the bank or invest it
___ buy a nice present for yourself

Where would you like to spend your vacation?
___ by the ocean
___ in New York City
___ at a ski resort
___ on a camping trip

Which is most important in choosing a spouse?
___ looks
___ personality
___ interests
___ values

What kind of gift do you prefer?
___ something someone made
___ money so you can buy something you want
___ a gift that somebody buys for you

---

[4] Adapted from Simon, Howe, and Kirschenbaum (1992).

How would you most like to spend an afternoon with a friend?
___ on a picnic in the mountains
___ at the movies
___ bowling

Which do you like least?
___ a person who is loud and obnoxious
___ a person who is dishonest
___ a person who gossips

What would you most like to do alone?
___ eat at a restaurant
___ attend a party
___ go to a movie
___ visit the zoo

Which car would you buy if you could?
___ a small, compact car
___ a sports car
___ a medium-sized, comfortable car
___ a pickup truck
___ a sport utility vehicle (SUV)

Which is most important to you?
___ to plan for your future
___ to show others that you care about them
___ to get all the possessions you can

Having students complete the same survey several months later to see if their values have changed can yield interesting results.

THE SEARCH[5]

Write the following on a sheet of paper, make copies, and distribute to the students (see "The People Hunt" in Chapter 8 for a similar activity):

Find someone who . . . (write the name of the person in the blank following each item).

likes to go to libraries _____
has eaten okra _____
has been to a water polo game _____
would like to have a cat as a pet _____
saw a funny movie in the last week _____
is trying to break a habit _____
would like to be an actor _____
wants to take a trip to Mars some day _____
plays a guitar _____

[5] Adapted from Moskowitz (1978, pp. 50–52).

went swimming recently _____
likes to tell jokes _____
can do the tango _____

Give the students about five minutes and then call time. Ask the whole class questions such as the following: Who likes to go to libraries? Who has eaten okra?, and so forth.

An alternative might be to have the students take similar search sheets home to use with family members, neighbors, or friends.

VALUES VOTING[6]

One sure way to get all the students involved in affective issues is to use this rapid-fire activity. Begin with the question "How many of you _____?" The blank can be filled in with items such as those below. Students raise their hands if the phrase is true of them.

    have a dog
    are afraid of storms
    think parents should be stricter with their kids
    do not like movies
    enjoy loud music
    plan to go to college
    have been in love
    wear seat belts in the car
    like to eat chocolate
    disapprove of smoking cigarettes
    want to end all wars
    think school is exciting
    work part-time
    want to get better grades in school
    like to sing
    are concerned about the environment

The teacher can write the above items on the board or on a transparency and follow each with the names of the students who raised their hands. Based on the responses, other questions can be asked: Who has a dog? What is _____ (name of student) afraid of? Who enjoys loud music? etc.

MY FAVORITE POSSESSION

Have the students decide which objects in their households are most valuable to them. Tell them to imagine that their houses are about to be destroyed by a natural disaster (earthquake, tornado, hurricane, or fire) and that they are each allowed to save only one thing (all humans and animals are already out of danger). What one thing would they save and why? Have them talk about their answers in small groups.

---

[6] Adapted from Simon, Howe, and Kirschenbaum (1992)

A COLLAGE ABOUT ME

Give students several magazines out of which they can cut pictures. Have them make collages—paste pictures together on individual poster boards of things that are particularly revealing about themselves. Items can include favorite activities, colors, foods, clothes, products, sayings, poems, jokes, and so on. After dividing the students into groups of about six, have them talk about their collages and what each item reveals. The collages can then be hung around the room for all to see.

An interesting follow-up might be to have students find the collage made by someone else that comes closest to revealing their own values.

MY OWN SPACE

If the room is large enough, give each student (especially younger ones) some bulletin board space. (Freestanding bulletin boards work well for this purpose.) Each student can use the space for things that are important to him or her but that could be replaced if lost or damaged: favorite sayings, reprints of family pictures, art work, compositions, poetry, and pictures from magazines. Students may want to rearrange their spaces from time to time and put up new things.

PRETEND PEN PALS

Ask the students to pretend they are writing to pen pals for the first time. In their letters, have them talk about such topics as their physical appearance, family, pastimes, favorite classes, and activities. Ask them to include questions they would want to ask the person with whom they are corresponding. Divide them into groups of four, and have them share their letters. The group might want to suggest additions to each letter. A follow-up could be the real "pen pal" activity suggested in Chapter 9.

An alternative might be to have the students describe themselves to a stranger with whom they will be sharing a room at college or sharing a tent at camp.

A HELPING HAND[7]

With your assistance, have students make two separate lists (Figure 14.1):

- a list of things they know how to do that they can teach others
- a list of things with which they need help

Collect these lists, choose those tasks that can be worked on in class, and give the students time to help and be helped as appropriate. The activity could be repeated at various times throughout the year and could involve many different tasks.

Students can follow up the activities by answering the following questions:

What is one new thing I learned today?
Who helped me?
What would I like to learn tomorrow?
Who can help me?
What did I help someone do today?

---

[7]Adapted from Farnette, Forte, and Loss (1977, p. 25).

You can get into the act if you wish. Learning from the students such things as how to fold paper birds Japanese style or how to count in Korean can be very challenging and exciting.

Figure 14.1

DEAR ABIWAIL[8]

Ask the students to play the role of assistant to the famous personal advisor, Abiwail. Have them write answers to the following letters (these particular sample letters are oriented toward teenagers).

> Dear Abiwail,
>
>   I can't seem to get this boy at school to talk to me. I try to get his attention by wearing clothes I think he will like and by saying things to attract him. Nothing seems to work. I did catch him staring at me one day, but when I am near him, he ignores me. What can I do? I think I am in love with him.
>
> Lovesick

---

[8] Adapted from Farnette, Forte, and Loss (1977, p. 59).

Dear Abiwail,

   Last week I did a terrible thing and I feel very guilty. In fact, I can't do my school work. I just think about what I did all the time. When I was in the hardware store near my house, I was looking at some tools. The next thing I knew, I put a small wrench in my pocket and walked out with it. No one saw me do it, but I feel just awful. My parents always taught me never to steal. How can I make myself feel better?

Guilty in Memphis

Dear Abiwail,

   I can't seem to make any friends. Everyone around me has many friends and they laugh and talk all the time. But me, I'm alone. I think maybe I'm boring. I just can't think of anything interesting to talk about when I'm with someone. I try to act cool so no one will know what I'm really feeling. I think I'll go crazy if I can't have at least one friend. Help me please.

Only the Lonely

THE MOST INFLUENTIAL PERSON

Ask students to think about which persons have most affected their lives. Ask them to write about these people and include information such as descriptions (they may have pictures to share), how long they have known these people, and what these people did that made such an impact. Divide them into groups to share their writings.

REACHING THE GOAL

Ask students to decide on a goal (either academic or social) and map their approach to it, trying to anticipate possible obstacles (see Figure 14.2). Work out one to use as an example. When the students have completed the exercise, divide them into small groups for a discussion of their goals and the steps they will take to overcome the obstacles.

A QUOTE TO LIVE BY[9]

Have students choose a favorite quotation such as "To have a friend, you must be a friend" or "If you love something, you must set it free." Provide a few books of quotations from which the students can select their sayings, or give them the option of creating their own. Divide the class into small groups to discuss the meanings of their sayings. Make available felt-tip pens with which to illustrate the sayings they have chosen. Give each student a poster board or large sheet of paper that can later be displayed in the room. At the high school or university level, the teacher might ask the students to develop effective paragraphs or essays using the quotes as topics.

---

[9] Adapted from Moskowitz (1978, pp. 232–234).

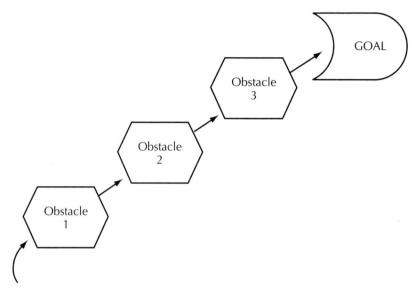

Figure 14.2

JOURNAL KEEPING

Daily journal entries are a good way to record reactions, feelings, and experiences in the target language. Encourage students to make "I" statements, such as "I was angry when I found out that . . ." or "Today I knew that . . . ." From time to time, ask students to hand in their journals for your response. Don't correct mechanical errors; instead write positive and encouraging comments.

GETTING TO KNOW YOU THROUGH INTERVIEW

Interviews are another good opportunity to practice the target language and to help students clarify values. Keep in mind that students should always have the right to pass.

1. Even though most students may already be acquainted, new students may come in from time to time and need to be introduced. At intermediate or advanced levels, one effective way to do this is to write the questions such as those below on cards (one or two per card), distribute them, and pair the students up to briefly interview each other, using the questions on the cards. Allow about six minutes per pair— three minutes for each interview. Then ask each student to introduce his or her partner and provide the partner's answers to the questions on the card, as well as any other information received. Below are some sample questions:

   What place do you like to go to when you're all alone? Describe it.
   What person do you admire most? Tell about that person's qualities.
   If you could choose any time period in which to live, which would you choose? Give your reasons.
   Where would you like to take your next vacation? Explain your choice.
   Which famous person would you like to have as a personal friend? Why?
   Which classes you are taking do you like best? Why?

2. Ask students to bring questions to class to ask each other. (You can provide them with a list of sample questions to help them get started.) On the day of the interviewing, have the students sit in a circle, and have one volunteer begin by asking a question. Let students volunteer to give answers. The student who volunteers to answer can then ask the next question.

3. Explain that you will interview two students, and ask for volunteers. Either or both can answer the questions, which should be nonthreatening in nature.[10] Here are a few possibilities:

Who is your favorite female athlete? Explain your choice.
What do you think is the best thing one person can give to another person?
What kind of person do you usually choose as a friend? What characteristics must he or she have?
What is the funniest situation you've ever found yourself in?
Out of all the people in the world, past and present, who is the one you most admire? Why?
Have you ever made a choice that surprised everyone? What was it?
Do you have any advice to give us that you think would be good for us to hear?
Which has been your best year in school? Why?
Has any news in the paper or on TV really worried you lately? If so, what was it and why did it disturb you?
How would you change this school if you could?
If you could have one question answered about life, what would your question be?
What would you change about the society in which you live?

Follow up answers with other appropriate questions before going on to the next question, or react by simply repeating what the students say in order to ensure that the intended meaning comes across. Once you complete the interview, give the class a chance to ask questions, too.

Alternatively, ask the volunteers to select topics about which they would like to be interviewed. You might post a list somewhere in the room to suggest possible categories: sports, movies, vacation, school, dating, socio/political issues, and so on.

4. Invite students, teachers, and administrators (who speak the target language) from outside the class to come in to be interviewed. Students, with your help, can prepare questions beforehand. Other questions will grow out of the interviews themselves.

5. Send the students out into the school or university campus to interview other students. (This is especially appropriate for an ESL class.) Have them form the questions beforehand and return to report the most interesting answers they received.

Alternatively, have students write up an opinion poll and ask students outside of class to respond orally while their opinions are recorded. Questions calling for a "yes,"

---

[10] It must be pointed out that what might seem nonthreatening to one student may not be to another. Sometimes even an innocent question such as "Where does your mother work?" might bring tears to one who has just lost a mother. The teacher simply has to use his or her best judgment and encourage the students to do the same in asking questions. As teachers and other facilitators become more experienced and skillful in using affective activities, they may want to take higher risks in some situations in order to maximize the results.

"no," or "maybe" answer, such as "Do you think most drugs should be legalized?" are easiest to tabulate. The results can be tallied once the students return to class.

STAND UP AND BE COUNTED![11]

Place five large signs around the room far enough apart so groups have room to form by them without crowding. Label the signs "Strongly Agree," "Agree Somewhat," "Neutral," "Disagree Somewhat," and "Strongly Disagree." Read a statement, and ask students to move to the sign that best describes their reaction. Then have a volunteer from each group tell the whole class why he or she has chosen that particular position. Each group is heard out fully before a verbal exchange among groups is allowed. Only one person should talk at a time. Below are sample statements to which students can react:

Childhood is the happiest time of life.
Men and women should share equally the chores of running a household.
Grades in school should be outlawed.
Pets should be allowed to live in homes for the elderly.
Most people are dishonest when given the chance.

In advanced classes, follow up with advanced writing activities or library research if the issues are ones about which a great deal has been written.

CONCENTRIC CIRCLES[12]

Have students sit on the floor in two concentric circles with equal numbers in each circle. The members of the inner circle should face outward, toward corresponding members of the outer circle, who face inward. Begin with a question such as "What do you find especially difficult about learning a second language?" and ask the students in the outer circle to answer the question first. As soon as a lull in the conversation becomes apparent (after a minute or so),[13] ask the students in the inner circle to answer the same question. Then the inner circle remains stationary while the outer circle rotates clockwise until each student is aligned with the next person to the left. Ask a different question, and this time have the inner circle answer first. After those in the outer circle answer, the inner circle rotates counterclockwise to the next person, and so on. Make sure to give students time to think about the question before you begin the timing.

An alternative, with somewhat different interpersonal dynamics, uses groups of three. One person in each group answers the question while the others listen. When time is called, the second member of each group answers the same question, and then the third member. Below are a few sample questions:

Describe one thing you would like to learn to do well.
Is there anyone in the world with whom you would like to change places? Explain your answer.

---

[11] Adapted from Simon, Howe, and Kirschenbaum (1992).

[12] I first heard of this activity from another teacher (whose name is unknown to me) at a workshop several years ago. Later I came across a version of it in Moskowitz (1978, pp. 78–79).

[13] During some affective activities, time is called after each response to indicate that it is now someone else's turn to react. The turn should stay with only one person until the facilitator says that time is up. If that person finishes his or her response early, the group can either use the remaining time to ask questions to clarify or its members can simply reflect silently until it is the next person's turn.

If you could run this school or university, what would you change about it?

What do you really like about the person (or people) sitting across from you?

What is the biggest problem faced by the younger generation living at home?

If you were the President of the United States, what is the first thing you would try to do?

What was the nicest thing anyone ever did for you?

What is one thing you wish you had the courage to do?

SUMMARY

One important reason for using affective activities in the classroom is to help students reach an understanding of those beliefs and behaviors that give meaning to their lives. At the same time, these activities can provide motivating dialogue in the target language and serve as a way to bring individuals and groups closer together.

Although many benefits can accrue from the use of affective activities, they are not suited to everyone. Teachers who are not comfortable sharing feelings and opinions, teachers who want to turn them into therapy and/or sensitivity training sessions, or teachers who are interested in imposing their own belief systems on others are not good candidates. Before attempting to use them, teachers should be familiar with the literature and, if possible, be specially trained in the techniques.

The activities themselves must be appropriate to the proficiency and age levels of the students as well as to the cultural environments in which they are used. They should be nonthreatening and generally positive in nature. Certain ground rules must be adhered to concerning the right to pass, the right to be heard, and the right to have one's opinion respected. If the classroom atmosphere is warm and accepting and the teacher wise and caring, affective activities can carry the students far in the language acquisition process.

READINGS, REFLECTION, AND DISCUSSION

Suggested Readings and Reference Materials

Moskowitz, G. (1999). *Enhancing personal development: Humanistic activities at work*. In Arnold, pp. 177–193. This important chapter presents the logic behind the use of humanistic activities in teaching second languages. Included is the research supporting the positive effects of such activities on the attitudes students have toward themselves, each other, and toward the language they are learning. Teachers, too, noticed improvement in their own self-esteem and in satisfaction with their teaching.

Schoenberg, I. (1997). *Talk about values: Conversation skills for intermediate students*. White Plains, NY: Pearson Education. Topics such as honesty, views toward growing old, gift-giving, and choosing a mate are used to stimulate discussion about values. There are no right or wrong answers. The book is intended for adults, both young and old. Mature teenagers may find it beneficial as well.

Simon, S., Howe, L., and Kirschenbaum, H. (1992). *Values clarification: A handbook of practical strategies for teachers and students* (2d edition). New York: Hart. Contains a series of activities and explains how to use them for furthering the process of values clarification. Includes decision making, problem solving, and many other means for confirming and developing values. Even though a few of the topics suggested in this book may be a little high risk for most teachers and students, many of the activities lend themselves readily to successful language teaching.

Questions and Projects for Reflection and Discussion

1. To what extent do you feel our values are culturally determined? Is there a set of values basic to all cultures? Explain. What role does individual experience seem to play in the process of the development of a values system?

2. Green (1983) early on stressed the characteristics of a successful values clarification teacher.

    > Use of values clarification in the classroom requires a teacher who (1) is willing to examine his or her own values; (2) can accept opinions different from his or her own; (3) encourages a classroom atmosphere of honesty and respect; and (4) is a good listener (1983, p. 180).

    What might be the consequences in the classroom for the teacher who tries to use values clarification, but who lacks even one of these characteristics?

3. What are several situations in your own teaching for which affective activities could be adapted? Plan in detail a few such activities for at least two situations. You might consider using them as part of a literature or history unit of some kind, as a follow-up to the study of the lyrics of a song, as a unit to commemorate a special holiday, or for any other situation in which such activities might be appropriate.

4. Choose one of the affective activities planned above and try it out with members of your class. State clearly the situation, the proficiency and age levels for which it is intended, and the possible follow-ups you would use. Give the class members a chance to express their feelings about it afterwards. In what ways was it successful? How can it be improved? You may want to begin by sharing your own reaction to your activity.

    If you are currently teaching students, use what you have learned to try out a similar activity with them. Make sure the activity is relevant and appropriate to level. If possible, have your lesson videotaped to analyze and discuss with peers. Reflect on its outcome and how you felt about doing it. Pay close attention to student response. Do you see any problems with your activity? How might it be improved?

    Write about your experiences using affective activities and what you learned from using them in your journal.

PART III

Putting It All Together: Some Practical Issues

No book can dictate a program or a methodology. What may be good for one group of learners in one particular setting may not be appropriate for those in other situations. The brief descriptions below of second and foreign language programs suggest some of their implications for students and for learning. See Chapter 17 for a fuller description of these program types in relation to bilingual education and other related programs.

The differences between a second language program and a foreign language program are not always clear, particularly where English is concerned. For example, Kachru (1992) distinguishes English instruction in three groups of countries: the *inner circle* (the United States, England, Canada, Ireland, Australia, and New Zealand), where English is the language of communication in most situations; the *outer circle* (the Philippines, India, Singapore, etc.) where English is used in government, education, and in other important domains; and the *expanding circle* (China, Russia, etc.) where English is used as an international language, but is not routinely used within the society itself.[1]

In dealing with these distinctions, some have divided the programs into more highly refined categories. For example, Nayar (1997) proposes dividing English as a second language programs into two subcategories: ESL, for inner circle situations in which English is the main language of communication; and EAL (English as an Associate Language), for programs in outer circle countries where there has been a substantial British or U.S. political presence and where English is used in some domains of the society for communication. He also defines EFL (English as a Foreign Language) as English programs

---

[1] See Tollefson (2000) for an enlightening discussion of the three groups identified by Kachru.

in expanding circle situations where there has been no substantial British or U.S. political presence and where English has no special status as an internal language of communication.

Because the following discussion pertains to all languages, not just English, I will use only the two basic classifications—second language and foreign language—realizing that there are many distinctions within each, and that these distinctions may have quite different implications for teaching. If we think of the two classifications as being on opposite ends of a continuum, with many programs falling somewhere in between, we get a more realistic picture of the variations.

SECOND LANGUAGE PROGRAMS

Second language programs were referred to in the Introduction (see footnote 1) as programs *in which the target language is the dominant language for communication in the area or domain where it is being taught.* Generally, students in such programs are interested in learning to survive physically, socially, and academically in their new culture. They are, in most cases, surrounded by the target language in the community, the workplace, and the school or university campus. Sometimes, however, second language students live in communities in which their first language and culture are predominant. This means that, although they have the advantages of L1 language and cultural maintenance, they may lack the target language input available to those in more integrated situations. For them, having considerable contact with proficient speakers of the target language as part of the curriculum would be especially important to their interlanguage development.

In outer circle countries (see Kachru above), English still falls into the "second language" category to the extent that the student has sustained access to the domain where it is being used, be it on the job, in dealings with government, or in other settings within the country. However, there will probably be as many varieties of English and political ramifications as there are countries and domains where it is being taught. Often, academic institutions will use English as the medium of instruction to some extent and a substantial use of code-switching between English and other languages will occur. In addition, the motivation to acquire the language may not be as strong as it is in other English second language programs. Much will depend upon the extent to which students need the language for their academic and/or social survival.

FOREIGN LANGUAGE PROGRAMS

Foreign language programs were referred to in the Introduction as programs *in which the target language is not the dominant language in the area or domain where it is being taught.* Students have a variety of reasons for being in these programs. Their goals may be:
- *Integrative.* They may want to communicate with people from another language group or survive in another culture.
- *Instrumental.* They may want to study in another country or get a job which requires that they be bilingual.
- *Personal.* They may simply feel that understanding another language is enriching.

The environment outside the classroom, however, does not give foreign language students the opportunity to be immersed in the target language. They are in special need of meaningful interaction since the classroom may be their only source. On the other hand, because they may not receive a sufficient quantity of high-quality input in the classroom to become proficient (many foreign language classes meet only one hour a day), they may find a judicious formal application of rules to be necessary in facilitating the acquisition process.

Other factors may also inhibit learning. The culture of the students may prevent some methods or activities from being as effective as they might be in other circumstances. However, students may be willing to experiment with unfamiliar strategies if their teachers discuss these strategies using the first language. In such situations, as in all others, teachers must be sensitive to individual and cultural preferences. Another factor to consider is that students in foreign language programs may be less motivated to function in the target language because it is not required for everyday survival.

Foreign language programs have their own implications for curriculum planning as well. For example, instrumental programs that are offered strictly for a single academic purpose (e.g., interpreting research findings in another language) or for other specific purposes (e.g., becoming acquainted with a new medical procedure used in another culture) may not include the development of communication skills at all. In these programs, learning to read and being familiar with a certain technical vocabulary may be all that is necessary.

CHAPTER 15

Devising a Plan

Just as there is no one set of ideal teaching materials, so there is no universal teaching method suited to the many contexts of language learning. . . . The most effective programs will be those that involve the whole learner in the experience of language as a network of relations between people, things, and events. The balance of features in a curriculum will and should vary from one program to the next, depending on the particular learning context of which it is a part.

S. Savignon, 1983

QUESTIONS TO THINK ABOUT

1. Think about the kind of program in which you are teaching or will be teaching. Is it a second or a foreign language program? What do you anticipate will be some of the implications for teaching because of the kind of program it is?

2. Can you think of ways to involve peers who are already proficient in the target language with the students in your classroom? What do you think the advantages might be? What problems might occur?

3. Have you ever experienced cooperative learning either as a teacher or as a student? If so, what was your reaction to it as a management strategy? To what extent was it effective?

4. How teacher-dominant do you think language classrooms should be? Do you think the proficiency level of the students would make any difference? If so, how?

5. What do you think a syllabus for language teaching should look like? How specific should it be?

Van Lier (1996) describes a language teaching syllabus as

> . . . a collection of maps with information and options, a guide, but one which
> leaves the students the freedom to stop where they want to, to travel alone for
> a while or in groups, to go off on some tangent if it seems interesting, but
> always coming back to the main road, and keeping the destination in mind.
> The syllabus—as Triptik—does not tell you where (and how far, how fast) you
> want to go, it gives you the advice and assistance that you ask for (p. 20).

A syllabus for language learners can indeed map out either a very rigid
and highly specified journey (it's Monday so we must be in Prague) or a journey that begins where the students are and takes them as far as possible in the
acquisition process. In a participatory classroom, students will have input into
planning the trip and into the side tours that interest them, or for which they
have a need. If they want to stop for more maps, they can. As van Lier suggests,
if students want to pursue something alone occasionally, they can. If they want
to travel in groups, they can. What matters is that they stay the course.

A single method by itself will probably not serve a language teaching program well. Neither will the concatenation of several methods and activities. What
we need is an interweaving of courses of action, each providing what is required
at the moment, all working together to form a highly integrated curriculum into
which students have had input to the greatest extent possible. A good curriculum
will reflect students' needs, their goals and aspirations, their ages and competency levels, their learning styles. And a good curriculum will also reflect your
teaching preferences—the approaches with which you are most comfortable.

INTEGRATION OF METHODS AND ACTIVITIES

There are many possibilities. A program that integrates methods and activities
might be organized, at least at beginning levels, around basic topics and situations similar to those suggested by Krashen and Terrell (see pages 171–175):
body parts, physical actions, clothing, occupations, emotions, recreation, going
shopping, etc. Early on, the program might begin to ease into subject-area concepts, themes, and sociopolitical issues including their related proficiencies.[2]
The subject areas might include art, math, business, computer processing,
physical education, social and natural sciences, and literature. Whatever the
content, it must be relevant to the students and their needs and concerns. And
it must include areas of knowledge in which the teacher has some expertise,
although most areas can be explored together if the program is a participatory
one in which dialectical relationships have been established.

---

[2] Most of the suggestions here are applicable in all second and foreign language teaching situations
in which content is the focus.

Students might first be introduced to key concepts during low-beginning levels, through physical approaches (see Chapter 8). The *same* concepts can be reinforced, while new ones are introduced, through activities typical of other communicative approaches (see Chapter 9). As students move toward mid- and high-beginning levels, chants, simple poetry, and/or music lyrics (Chapter 10) can be added either to introduce a set of concepts or to reinforce them. During this period, techniques from storytelling, role play, and drama (Chapter 11) can be highly motivating while providing the many passes through the material necessary for acquisition to occur. Games (Chapter 12) can be effective if played occasionally to develop or reinforce concepts or to teach the vocabulary and structures of game playing itself. During the high-beginning through advanced levels (see pages 137–138), if the program is to be participatory, the teacher will want to involve the students to a much greater extent in the planning process. At these levels, the teacher can introduce and reinforce concepts through affective activities (Chapter 14) and through more advanced applications of the above approaches. All the while, literacy in the target language (Chapter 13) and its related proficiencies can be taught in an integrated fashion rather than as separate sets of skills and subskills.

Various methods and activities might also be combined on a much smaller scale, either within a unit (several lessons about the same topic) or within a single lesson. In the two examples following, we have several methods, activities, and strategies merged *within a unit*, and in the third example, we have them merged *within a single lesson*.

Integrated Unit One: An Example for Intermediate-Level Children

Susan Ashby, a teacher in the Alhambra School District of California, illustrates how storytelling, music, affective activities, and poetry can be integrated with aspects of the physical approaches and communicative teaching. All can work together to produce a unified whole—in this case, a subject-area *unit on birds.* She suggests that the unit (intended for use with children at intermediate levels) begin with the Mexican folktale, "The Pájaro-cu"—the story of a bird that, at the beginning of the world, appeared before the eagle (the king) stark naked because he had no feathers. The eagle was so offended that he sent the featherless bird into exile. A dove took pity on him and began a campaign to clothe him. Each bird willingly contributed a feather. The result was a bird so colorful and beautiful that he became vain and would have nothing to do with the other birds. He decided to leave the country. The other birds were sent to look for him. In their search, the various birds began to sing out the different calls by which they are now known. Although the lost bird (called the *pájaro-cu*) has never been found, the other birds still sing their characteristic songs but no longer expect an answer.

First, discuss the meaning of the story by asking questions like the following:

1. Do people, like the Pájaro-cu, ever get sent away—into exile? If so, why?
2. Once the Pájaro-cu became more colorful and beautiful than the other birds, he would have nothing to do with them. Why do you think he would have nothing to do with them? Do people ever behave this way? Explain.

To appeal to various modes of learning, the teacher can use any number of different strategies:

- Display a series of colored pictures of birds and talk with the students about the different types and the features that most birds have in common.
- Have students pantomime to the beat of a drum the movements of different kinds of birds: big birds, delicate birds, birds that run, walk, and soar. Using movements to music (see Chapter 10), let students dance, playing the roles of different types of birds.
- Have students sketch and paint the bird, perhaps combining crayons and watercolors to give the hues a jewel-like appearance.
- Help students find sayings such as "Birds of a feather flock together" and "A bird in the hand is worth two in the bush." After discussing the meanings of the sayings, have students use them to label their pictures.
- Stimulate discussion through poetry. A poem that Ashby finds particularly effective and stimulating for discussion is "Gooloo" by Shel Silverstein.

The Gooloo bird
She has no feet
She cannot walk
Upon the street.
She cannot build
Herself a nest,
She cannot land
And take a rest.
Through rain and snow
And thunderous skies,
She weeps forever
As she flies,
And lays her eggs
High over town,
And prays that they
Fall safely down.

Integrated Unit Two: An Example for Advanced-Level Young Adults

Heather Robertson, an instructor in the American Culture and Language Program at California State University, Los Angeles, combines affective activities and role play to provide a cultural awareness unit for English Language Learners (ELLs) in a course entitled "Readings in Sociology." The course is intended for advanced students who will soon be seeking admission to the university.

Day One: Students listen to and take notes on a minilecture on how appropriateness of behavior is judged in many cultures. They then take a quiz on the lecture during which they are encouraged to use their notes. As homework, students read a section from a college-level sociology text reinforcing the same concepts.

Day Two: During the next lesson, students discuss what sorts of behaviors are considered appropriate in their cultures, but which they have found are not appropriate in the United States. They share opinions on how most Americans might react to persons deviating from the norm. For homework after the second class, students are asked to imagine situations into which they incorporate specific behaviors designed to bring about overt or subtle reactions from Americans—either those born in the United States or those who had lived in the United States a long time. The behaviors might include facing the "wrong" way in an elevator and standing "too close" to someone while speaking.

Day Three: Students present their homework and decide which situations they would like to act out around the campus. The students who feel uncomfortable with being actors can volunteer to be observers and recorders of the reactions of the subjects. After deciding on roles, the students predict the kinds of responses they expect to get. The observers and recorders are told to watch the subjects carefully and record in writing their reactions. Even a wry smile or raised eyebrow should be noted.

Day Four: The last day is reserved for reporting the results and for a discussion aimed at achieving some sort of perspective. Did the subjects react as predicted? What were the feelings of the actors? The observers? Had they been in similar situations before? How had they (the observers and recorders) reacted the first time? Through a sharing of such responses, students may be better able to deal with the feelings, whatever they might be.

Integrated Lesson One: An Example for Beginning-Level Children

Sandy Nevarez, a resource teacher in the ABC Unified School District of California, combines characteristics of several approaches *into a single lesson* that is part of a subject-area unit on insects or bugs. (See pages 320–323 for suggested lesson formats.) Navarez incorporates elements of communicative approaches (including physical activities) as well as poetry to produce a "soup fit for toads." She tells the students (primary children at beginning levels) that they are about to prepare a real delicacy—toad soup. Prior to the activity, the students are introduced to the names of various insects or other bugs and are given small pictures of them (duplicated on paper and cut out). The teacher has provided a pot in which to make the soup, along with the various ingredients needed: a raw egg, water, honey, cooked spaghetti noodles, and sand mixed with small rocks. Each ingredient should be kept out of view until it is needed, thus increasing anticipation. The dialogue can go somewhat like this:

TEACHER: What are some bugs that toads like? Put them in the pot. (The teacher looks at each picture and says its name as the students put them in the pot.) Very good. Now we have many bugs in the pot. We have spiders, bees, flies, mosquitoes, ladybugs, and many others. The soup should be very good, don't you think? (The students nod but with some doubt.) Could our soup use a raw egg? (She breaks an egg into the soup, adds water, and stirs the mixture around with her hand.) Ooooooh, it feels slimy. It feels sliiiimy. (She lets the students feel in the pot.) How does it feel? Does it feel slimy?

STUDENTS: (muttering while grimacing) Slimy. Slimy.

TEACHER: Okay. Could our soup use some noodles? Yes, it could use some noodles. (She dumps in a fistful of cooked noodles and stirs it around, again with her hand.) Squishy. It feels squishy and ishy and soooo slimy. (Again she lets the students feel.) How does it feel? Squishy and ishy?

STUDENTS: Yes.

TEACHER: Slimy?

STUDENTS: Yes.

TEACHER: Sooooo squishy and ishy and slimy. (The students make faces to indicate their disgust.)

The teacher continues in this manner, adding the other ingredients and using other rhyming words: sticky, icky (for honey), and lumpy, bumpy (for sand with rocks). Through the highly comprehensible input, the physical involvement, and the sensual quality of the words and actions, the students become completely absorbed in the activity, making acquisition highly probable.

DECIDING THE FOCUS OF THE PROGRAM

There is some disagreement about the proper focus for communicative programs. Some say teachers and their students should focus on proficiencies/competencies (Omaggio, 1993); others say they should focus on tasks (Long,

1985, and Nunan, 1989, 1991); yet others say they should focus on content (Brinton, Snow, and Wesche, 1989; Snow and Brinton, 1997).[3]

Proficiency or Competency-Based Instruction

Proficiency or competency-based programs focus on the "mastery of basic and life skills necessary for the individual to function proficiently in society" (National Center for Educational Statistics, 1982, p. 80). Often the syllabus is organized around learning outcomes that have been divided into skills and subskills:

- the ability to recognize and write common abbreviations
- the ability to auditorially distinguish certain vowel sounds
- the ability to spell a list of two-syllable words
- the ability to verbally produce and write the alphabet
- the ability to punctuate a dialogue correctly
- the ability to use negatives in obligatory positions
- the ability to distinguish between "some" and "any"
- the ability to use prepositions of location correctly, and so on

Often checklists are used to make sure students have these proficiencies or competencies before they can move on to the next task or the next level.

Task-Based Instruction

Long (1985) defined tasks as ". . . the things people will tell you they do if you ask them and they are not applied linguists" (p. 89). These might include filling out a form, typing a letter, checking a book out of the library, and so on. A task-based syllabus first requires a needs identification. Once the needs have been identified, they are classified into task types (e.g., tasks related to working in a bank or tasks related to driving a car); task difficulty is assessed within each task type; and a syllabus is prepared. Meaning is negotiated as the learners try to accomplish goals related to each task.

Nunan (1991) related task-based instruction to experiential learning. He gave an example using steps to develop a pedagogic task (p. 282):

1. Identify the target task (e.g., giving personal information in a job interview).

---

[3] In addition, there are many other alternatives, including product-based instruction, theme-based instruction, literature-based instruction, etc. Most can be directly related or subsumed by the three foci described above. For example, product-based instruction relates closely to task-based instruction in cases in which a product is a result of the task at hand. Theme-based instruction and literature-based instruction can both logically be subsumed under content-based instruction.

2. Provide a model (e.g., students listen to and extract key information from an authentic or simulated interview).
3. Identify the enabling skill (manipulation drill to practice *Wh-* questions with *do-* insertion).
4. Devise a pedagogic task (interview simulation using role cards).

Nunan claimed that this procedure provides students with the opportunity to accomplish the following:

- develop language skills meeting their needs
- be exposed to native-speaker [I would change this to "proficient-speaker"] or user language
- receive explicit instruction and guided practice
- mobilize emerging skills by rehearsing

H. Douglas Brown (1994) asserted that some tasks may be synonymous with teaching techniques (e.g., a role-play task/technique or a problem-solving task/technique). According to him, "[task-based instruction] views the learning process as a set of communicative tasks that are directly linked to the curricular goals they serve, and the purpose of which extend beyond the practice of language for its own sake" (p. 83). Brown presented important questions for teachers such as: Do the tasks specifically contribute to communicative goals? Are their elements carefully designed and not simply haphazardly or idiosyncratically thrown together?

Content-Based Instruction

Brinton, Snow, and Wesche (1989) define content-based instruction as

> . . . the integration of content learning with language teaching aims. More specifically, it refers to the concurrent study of language and subject matter, with the form and sequence of language presentation dictated by content (p. vii).

Content-based teaching is usually associated with the *academic* course content found in school subjects such as math, science, history, literature, etc. Survival topics taught at beginning levels of second language development such as getting a job, going to the doctor, and so forth, are not generally considered "content-based." Rather they are "task-based" (see Long's definition above). What Brinton, Snow, and Wesche were advocating (among other things) was that academic content be used in second language classes and that it integrate language skills around a content topic such as ocean fish, travel destinations, the effects of illegal drugs on society, and so on. Any of the topics, depending upon the students' needs and interests, could last for a short time period or be extended over a long time period (see *sustained-content language teaching* on pages 272–273). Such topics would probably be most appropriate for students operating at high-beginning to advanced levels (see pages 137–138), although preparation for them could begin much earlier. The academic content is generally selected by the teacher, and the modified input is specially tailored to their needs. A language course based on academic content in second language situations (as opposed to foreign language situations—see pages 297–299) is *transitional* in nature. Students expect to be placed eventually in sheltered, adjunct, or mainstream courses in the content areas for which they are being prepared (see Chapter 17 for a description of each type of course).

Which Focus Appears Most Promising?

This question raises at least two subquestions:

1. Will any of these approaches lead to a syllabus concentrating on isolated elements of language for study? Such a concentration should be avoided.

    In my opinion, the only focus described above that leads to a syllabus concentrating on isolated elements of language for study is proficiency/ competency-based instruction. It is not much different in this respect from the grammar-based approaches of the past. Here I am reminded of Newmark's seminal article, "How Not to Interfere with Language Learning" (1983). He said that we learn language in natural chunks, exponentially, rather than additively. The "interference" occurs when we artificially isolate parts from wholes. This is exactly what a proficiency/ competency-based curriculum appears to do. This is not to say that proficiencies and competencies are not important. On the contrary, they should be *part of* the curriculum, but not *the focus* of the curriculum.

2. Which approach would make the most sense cognitively to learners in a particular teaching situation?

    Although a focus on task-based instruction might make sense cognitively to learners, particularly its applications intended for those operating at true beginning levels and for those in special programs,[4] I would have to say that, overall, content-based instruction appears to make the most sense as a focus for situations in which successful communication and/or academic competency are the goals. In such situations, tasks generally need something to belong to in the way of content. A course that jumps from task to task may lack both cohesion and a reason for being.

For a workable hierarchy in which the three foci are integrated into a program, see Figure 15.1:

---

[4] An example would be an English for Special Purposes (ESP) program whose goals are often highly specified for a particular technical field such as medicine or computer technology. In such programs, a task-based approach might work best.

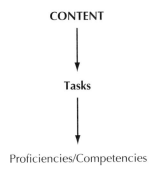

Figure 15.1

If the content were ocean fish, for example, then the tasks might involve finding out as much as possible about ocean fish and sharing that information with a small group; helping the class and the teacher set up an aquarium in the classroom to study; describing the animals in the aquarium; and so on. Proficiencies and competencies might involve being able to spell the names of various ocean fish, being able to correctly punctuate a paragraph about the habitat of various ocean fish, and so forth.

USING PEER TEACHERS AND LAY ASSISTANTS

In an ideal ESL and foreign language teaching situation, every student would receive:

- An adequate amount of meaningful, relevant input aimed roughly at the Zone of Proximal Development (see Chapter 3)
- A sufficient number of opportunities to enhance the self-image and develop positive attitudes
- Regular encouragement, motivation, and challenge
- Plenty of opportunity for input and output
- Continual feedback
- Appropriate linguistic models (competent users of the target language are usually best)
- Formal language instruction when beneficial to the language acquisition process (see pages 60–65)

The quantity or amount of each of these necessary to the acquisition of the target language depends on the individual student and on each situation. But to ensure that student needs are met, peer teachers and/or lay assistants may prove to be necessary additions to the program. Like the teacher, they can facilitate communication through negotiating for meaning, offering comprehensible input, and giving encouragement and feedback. They can provide a social link to the rest of the students in the school and to the community. In addition, they can serve as linguistic models to help prevent early fossilization and give formal language instruction when needed. Potential peer teachers who are fluent in the target language are usually available within the schools themselves. For example, foreign language classes can draw from the advanced students in the language; adult programs can draw from the community at large; ESL classes at the junior and senior high schools and at universities can draw from the student body at large; and elementary school classes can draw from the upper grades. Where tasks are not cognitively demanding, peer teachers can be much younger. However, younger peer teachers will require more supervision from the teacher than will older ones. Lay assistants who are fluent in the target language can be invaluable at all levels and are often an overlooked community resource.

In their investigation of bilingual students working with less proficient peers in content-area classes, Klingner and Vaughn (2000) found that scores on the English vocabulary tests improved significantly on the posttests, both for those needing help and for those doing the helping. The finding that both the students and their peer teachers/tutors benefited supports the conclusions of much earlier research on peer teaching/tutoring (see especially Poole, 1971; and Rust, 1970).

Peer teachers and lay assistants should meet certain qualifications: They must have the necessary skills, enjoy aiding others, have a lot of patience, be supportive, and be willing to work hard. In addition, they will need preparation workshops (especially effective at secondary and adult levels) to aid them in the following areas:

- Development of cultural sensitivity (see also Chapter 6)
- Knowledge of the instructional procedures the teacher chooses to use
- Familiarity with the materials available to them
- Pertinent background information on the students with whom they will be working—cultural information, individual background information, possible problems, and so on
- Strategies for creating friendly, supportive relationships

See the chart below for strategies that might be discussed at a preparation workshop for peer teachers.

Strategies for Helping Others

- Learn the student's name and use it frequently.
- Smile readily.
- Be friendly. Get to know the student.
- Be a good listener. Encourage the student to talk. Ask questions to find out more or to clarify what the student is saying.
- Recognize and show enthusiasm for the student's accomplishments. Praise genuinely, and make praise as specific as possible. Try to build intrinsic motivation by getting the student to reflect on what he or she has done. Phrases like "You must be very happy that you were able to _____" encourage the student to be self-motivating.

- Find out about the student's culture, learning preferences, background, goals, and aspirations.
- Be accepting of the student's right to his or her own opinions and beliefs. Avoid put-downs.
- When asking questions, give the student enough time to respond. Be patient.
- Give the student sufficient time to work at his or her own pace without feeling hurried.
- If the student does not understand a concept after several attempts, go to something that you know the student can do successfully. Later when you return to the more difficult task, it may come more easily.
- If the student is obviously troubled or upset, give him or her a chance to talk to you about it. The task at hand can wait.
- Use language that the student can understand. Repeat and/or rephrase frequently if the student is a beginner. Use pictures and/or act out concepts whenever necessary.
- Keep directions short and simple.
- Be honest. If you don't know the answer to a question, admit it. Often you and the student can find answers together.
- If the student is proficient enough in a language you have in common, ask the student to reflect upon and give you input about his or her perceived needs and feedback on what is being learned, and how it is being taught.
- Remember that the teacher is there to help you when you need it. Do not hesitate to ask for assistance.

In addition to preparation workshops, peer teachers and lay assistants need to meet with the teacher regularly to make flexible lesson plans and to talk about possible problems and various approaches. Student input is essential whenever possible. The following is an evaluation checklist to ensure frequent communication between the teacher and peer teacher or lay assistant concerning student progress. Students should be conferred with regularly to discuss progress and future directions and plans (see sample conference on page 141).

EVALUATION CHECKLIST

Name of peer teacher or lay assistant _____ Date _____

Name of student _____

1. What did the student accomplish today?

2. Were there any problems?

3. How does the student feel about what he or is learning? What can you do to better meet the student's needs?

4. What activities will you work on tomorrow?

5. Can the teacher help you in any way?

Comments:

Room Arrangements[5]

Two room plans have worked well for me in incorporating peer teachers and lay assistants (see Figures 15.2 and 15.3). See what you think of them.

In Figure 15.2, each peer teacher or lay assistant has a *private work station* where the students to whom he or she has been assigned go for assistance. These students remain at the tables in the center of the room while working on their own. This particular configuration works well when the tasks are mainly one-to-one, requiring a certain degree of privacy. Figure 15.3, on the other hand, illustrates the *flexible cluster work station* where the students assigned to

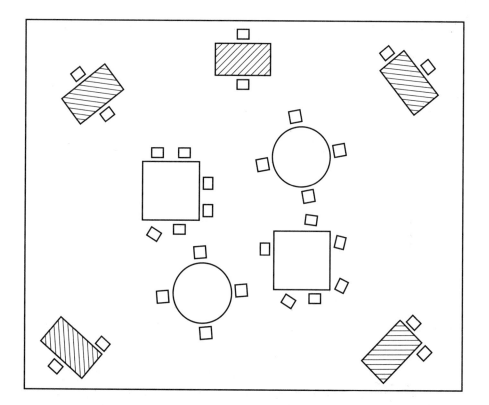

Figure 15.2. Private Work Stations

Comfortable chairs are found at each table. The tables with diagonal lines running through them are work stations for the peer teachers and lay assistants. The teacher, too, might have a work station. Note that for whole-class activities, the students can all be at the tables in the middle.

[5] From Richard-Amato (1992a, pp. 282–283).

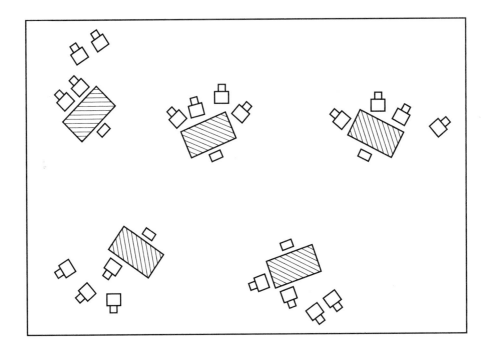

Figure 15.3. Flexible Cluster Work Stations

Movable desks cluster around the tables which serve as work stations for peer teachers and lay assistants. A similar station may be set up for the teacher. Note that for whole-class activities, the tables can be moved to the periphery of the room and the movable desks can be moved to the center to form a circle or any other configuration needed.

a particular peer teacher or lay assistant sit together with the peer teacher at the apex. This arrangement is ideal when group instruction or a group project is undertaken. However, the cluster is flexible enough so that by rearranging the desks, the peer teacher and lay assistants can still work somewhat privately with one or more members of the group.

The task of organizing a program using peer teachers and lay assistants may at first appear overwhelming. However, once these aides are familiar with procedures and once they are assigned to workable groups (perhaps three or four students of similar proficiency levels), the program seems to take on a momentum of its own. At that point, the time and talents of the teacher can be put to optimal use. The teacher is able to concentrate on students needing special help, peer teachers and lay assistants wanting additional guidance, whole-class activities, and overall structural concerns.

COOPERATIVE LEARNING AS A MANAGEMENT TECHNIQUE[6]

In cooperative learning, students help other students within groups of four to five persons in an effort to reach goals. Cooperative learning approaches can be effective at many age levels from the late elementary grades up through adult levels and can be effective in both second and foreign language teaching situations.

In cooperative learning, an *interdependence* is established among the students in each group as they strive for the achievement of group or individual objectives. This approach draws from both behaviorism and humanism. On the one hand, it frequently offers group rewards (in the form of points or grades) as its prime motivation; on the other, it urges students to develop more fully their own individual identities while respecting those of others. Students, however, need to be able to handle the cognitive challenges cooperative learning presents.

The results of early studies done on cooperative learning (Slavin, 1983) indicated great potential for some aspects of the method to produce academic success, especially in classes of mixed ethnicity. In almost all the studies (89%) in which group rewards were based on individual achievement, there were noted achievement gains. On the other hand, in studies in which only individual grades were given, or a group grade was given based on a group product, achievement was roughly the same as that found in the control classes. Moreover, several studies indicated that medium to low achievers seem to benefit most and that their accomplishments were not made to the detriment of high achievers (Martino and Johnson, 1979; Armstrong, Johnson, and Balow, 1981).

One possible drawback of cooperative learning, if it is used extensively at beginning to intermediate levels with second or foreign language students, is the possibility of early fossilization (see Chapters 3 and 6). Wong-Fillmore (1985) reported that students who are not proficient in the target language do not provide adequate models for each other. This was true also in the immersion programs (see Chapter 17). However, Crandall (1999) feels that this argument is overblown. She states:

> Possibilities of uncorrected or miscorrected student contributions are less important in the overall development of second language competence than opportunities for negotiation of meaning and interaction (p. 242).

Cooperative learning groups can provide comfortable environments in which the students can practice giving output and negotiating for meaning (see Long and Porter, 1984; Pica and Doughty, 1985; Porter, 1986). The danger, if indeed

---

[6] I wish to thank Carole Cromwell, Linda Sasser, and Leslie Jo Adams for sharing their ideas about cooperative learning with me. However, it is improbable that each will agree with every one of my conclusions.

there is one, would seem to come when not-yet-competent peers are the *major* source of input during the language acquisition process.

Versions of cooperative learning can be incorporated very successfully in most subject areas, especially in intermediate to advanced language classes and in mainstream content-area classes. It is particularly effective in the latter, where ELLs can be grouped with more competent speakers of the target language who are also more knowledgeable content-wise. Cooperative learning, too, provides for changing leadership depending on the content and skills being learned and upon who can best teach what to whom (see also "A Helping Hand" on page 289). Wells (1999) describes similar flexible collaboration this way:

> . . . most activities involve a variety of component tasks such that students who are expert in one task, and therefore able to offer assistance to their peers, may themselves need assistance on another task. But it can also happen that in tackling a difficult task as a group, although no member has expertise beyond his or her peers, the group as a whole, by working at the problem together, is able to construct a solution that one could not have achieved alone. In other words, each is "forced to rise above himself" and, by building on the contributions of its individual members, the group collectively constructs an outcome that no single member envisaged at the outset of the collaboration (pp. 323–324).

He goes on to say that there is nothing wrong with collaboratively trying to solve problems for which no one person has the answer in a sort of "pooling of ignorance." It is at these times when the greatest advances in learning are often made, he believes.

Kagan (1986) described five distinct types of cooperative learning, which I have briefly summarized below. (The examples for possible use are mine.) Types 2-5 seem to work best with groups of mixed ethnicity (in the case of ESL) and mixed ability levels. In addition, many other versions of these basic types have evolved over the past few years.

1. *Peer Tutoring*. Teammates teach each other simple concepts. This type is often used for math or language arts and would be particularly applicable in a mainstream content-area class that includes ELLs.
2. *Jigsaw*. Each member of the group is given the chief responsibility for a specific portion of the learning unit. These members work with the members of other groups who have been given the same assignment. They form "expert groups." However, eventually each member must learn the whole unit by sharing information with the others in the group. This type of cooperative learning is often used in the mastery of text material in social sciences. For example, a unit on the contributions of women in the United States might be studied by each group. One group member might be responsible for women's contributions to science, another on their contributions to literature, a third on their contributions to

politics, and so forth. Each student is graded individually on his or her understanding of the whole unit.

3. *Cooperative Projects.* The members of the group work together to complete a group project such as a presentation, a composition, or an art project. Members receive individual grades based on the evaluation of the group product.

4. *Cooperative/Individualized.* Students work alone on a particular assignment or project but their progress contributes to a group grade. They may help each other so that each can achieve the best possible results.

5. *Cooperative Interaction.* Students work as a unit to learn. However, there is no group grade received. Each member of the group is graded individually even though completion of the unit (e.g., a lab experiment, a panel discussion, a dramatic presentation) requires a cooperative effort.

Although the above suggestions are mainly for long-term projects, some very simple applications of cooperative learning can be incorporated in short-term activities at any level for which the specific content is appropriate. Following are some examples:

1. In a version of the activity commonly known as *numbered heads together,* the class is divided into several groups of four or five, and each student is given a number within the group. Each student (depending upon the number assigned) does one small portion of the group's work. For example, if a class in adult basic education is studying cultures, the teacher might give the groups several short passages, each describing an important custom in the United States. The person who is assigned the number four in each group could be responsible for reading the passage about how late one can be to a dinner party without being considered rude. The same person is then responsible for sharing this information with the others. The person assigned to number three could do the same for a passage describing who is expected to pay when one is asked to go to a movie, and so forth. Any number of topics can be handled in this manner.

2. *Think/pair/share* requires students to think about a question or issue, share their thoughts in pairs, and then share them with the class or a larger group (Kagan, 1994). For example, if the students are presented with a question about saving the environment for future generations, they might first want to jot down the aspects of the environment that need protection and what might be done in each case; get together with a partner and share these ideas for the purpose of getting feedback; and last, tell the whole class or a large group about their ideas, which by now have probably been modified more than once to reflect what they have learned in the process. At each stage, they are given the opportunity to more fully develop their ideas before presenting them to the whole class or a large group (see also Crandall, 1999).

3. The members of each group can study together for a test or work together to complete an assignment.

4. The group can complete a short-term group project such as a brief skit, a description of a scene, a collage, or a small-group discussion. Each member receives a group grade.

In his book *Cooperative Learning: Resources for Teachers*, Kagan (1985) describes a highly structured cooperative learning system consisting of team building, management techniques, and rewards based on a fairly complex system of points. However, some teachers might prefer to downplay behavioristic goals (points and other extrinsic motivational devices) and concentrate on humanistic goals (personal development and respect for others). In spite of the early claims made for cooperative learning in its unadulterated forms, my experience suggests that similar results can be had by focusing on the development of intrinsic motivation by encouraging the student to focus on what he or she has accomplished.

One research study on cooperative/collaborative group work brought mixed results for English learners. Leki (2001) found in her research at a large state university in the United States that English-speaking bilingual students often felt intimidated and found their efforts thwarted while working with native-English speakers. When they did find their work yielding positive results, it was usually because the teacher had intervened to make sure they received equal opportunities to participate.

Several researchers were among those who found evidence for one or more of the following conclusions (Leki, 2001; Tinto, 1997; Jacob, Rottenberg, Patrick, and Wheeler, 1996; Felder and Brent, 1996; D.M. Johnson, 1994; and Cowie, Smith, Boulton, and Laver, 1994). Group learning appears most successful in situations in which it:

- is well-organized
- is structured to give equal roles to language minority students when they are mixed with native speakers
- is carefully monitored and frequently assessed by a teacher who intervenes when necessary
- requires participants to have prior instruction in working in groups effectively
- presents tasks that engage the group's interest and for which the outcomes are not predetermined
- offers English learners multiple opportunities for receiving the input and output necessary for acquisition

PLANNING LESSONS

Before a lesson plan is devised, some sort of needs/interest assessment should have taken place, perhaps at the unit level with as much student input as possible. Then general objectives and expected behaviors (see especially Lesson Format 2 below) can grow out of the assessment as flexible lesson plans are developed. After the lesson is completed, lesson evaluation is important. How well has the lesson worked? Does it need to be modified in any way before trying something similar again? Did it accomplish what it was supposed to accomplish? At this point, student evaluations can be very helpful in determining answers to these questions. Also having a peer come to observe or recording the lesson for future evaluation with a peer can be beneficial. See section on teacher research and professional development on pages 328–330.

At beginning to low-intermediate levels, the same concepts need to be reinforced over and over again using different activities in different situations. Too often, inexperienced teachers present concepts once and then let them drop, never to be returned to again.

In the Lesson Example on pages 305–306, for instance, rhyming words are reinforced through a follow-up chant constructed by the teacher, which students repeat while clapping or snapping their fingers.

> How does the toad stew feel?
> Slimy and sticky?
>> Yes!
>> Slimy and sticky.
> Squishy and icky?
>> Yes!
>> Squishy and icky.
> Is that how it feels?
> Is that how it feels?
>> Yes!
>> That's how it feels.
>> That's how it feels.

In another activity, the instructor tapes pictures of insects to the walls and the students write a group paragraph, language experience style (see pages 243–246). Much later, students might create simple poetry about insects, using the rhyming words (see Chapter 10).

Teachers need to remain flexible in planning the content of their units. Some of the best lessons teachers have will be those spontaneous ones that grow out of a special need or interest that presents itself at the moment. Wells (1999) emphasizes a similar point. Teachers need not be committed to completing a predetermined lesson; instead they might move in directions prompted by student response. He states,

> . . . the teacher always has to be responsive to the students' goals, as these emerge in the course of activity, and by collaborating with them in the achievement of their individual goals, to enable them to extend their mastery and at the same time their potential for further development. From a teacher's perspective, therefore, one is always aiming at a moving target.

In my mind, flexibility is a large part of what good teaching is all about.

Concerning the structure of lessons for beginners in particular, Wong-Fillmore (1985) concluded that teacher lessons that are consistent and well-organized and have similar formats with clear beginnings and endings appear to be most effective. Familiar routines provide a scaffold for the learning of new materials.[7] Of course, students will need to have as much input into the curriculum and into lessons as their proficiency will allow them, and teachers need to flow with their changing needs and goals.

The routine outlined below in Lesson Format 1 is similar to the plan described much earlier by Madelyn Hunter and Douglas Russell (1977) for classroom lessons, but *with an important difference*. Whereas the original Hunter-Russell model appeared to be highly teacher-centered and teacher-controlled, this model allows for greater student input and participation.[8] As the students gain competence, they can gradually take on a larger role in choosing the content and even the structure of the lessons themselves.

Lesson Format 1

1. PERSPECTIVE (OPENING)

Address the following questions when appropriate:

> What have you learned to do? (previous activity)
> What concepts have you learned? (previous activity)
> How does it make you feel? Proud of yourself? More confident?

Give a preview of possibilities for the new lesson.

2. STIMULATION

The following are a few options:

> Pose a question to get students thinking about the coming activity and the major concepts involved.
> Help the students to relate the activity to their lives and to their prior knowledge.
> Begin with an attention grabber: an anecdote, a little scene acted out by peer teachers or lay assistants (see pages 310–314), a picture, or a song.
> Use it as a lead into the activity.

---

[7] Her conclusion is based on a study she did with colleagues at the University of California at Berkeley. They observed the input given in thirty kindergarten through fifth-grade classrooms over a five-year period. In addition, she observed and recorded teachers in another ten classrooms in which there were Limited English Proficient (LEP) students.

[8] The same type of plan can be used by peer teachers and lay assistants for their work with small groups and individuals.

3. Instruction/Participation Phase (teacher/student contributions)

Below are examples:

> Read and discuss the story or poem, sing the song or have it sung, do the chant, search for the issues, agree upon expectations, check for understanding, divide into groups, and so on. Encourage student involvement to the largest extent possible, depending on the student's emerging capabilities in the target language.

4. Closure

Address these questions when they are appropriate:

> What did you learn?
> How did you feel about doing the activities?

Give a preview of the possibilities for future lessons. Get student input.

5. Follow-up

> Use other activities to reinforce the same concepts and introduce new ones.
> Give students the opportunity to do independent work in class or as homework.

Note that some elements of the lessons are downplayed and others emphasized depending upon the situation and upon the proficiency levels of the students. For instance, a full development of the Perspective would probably not be appropriate for low-beginning students because not much of it would be understood unless it were given in the primary language. Nor would it be appropriate for young children. Simple statements such as, "I think you know what watercolors are. It will be fun to see what you do with them," would be sufficient. On the other hand, fully developed, highly comprehensible instructions during the Instruction/Participation Phase would be very appropriate for low-beginning students and young children. Furthermore, the teacher should keep in mind that students will probably, at first, not understand every word in the lesson, nor should they expect to. It takes time and many passes through similar structures and concepts to acquire the target language.

Van Lier (1996) suggests that lessons be balanced in that they contain both planned and improvised elements. He reminds us that ". . . most students also need points of stability in lessons, and these are achieved by recycling tasks, planning certain sequences of activities in predictable ways, ritual beginnings, endings, and transitions, and so on" (p. 200). Lesson Format 1 above provides for the ritual that students often find helpful and safe.

For teachers who prefer to use a type of lesson plan that requires detailed and focused preparation prior to the lesson but that leaves the description of the lesson completely open, the lesson format below presents an alternative. It is one I developed for my students at California State University, Los Angeles.

The particular lesson used as an example here was adapted from one given to
me by Elsa Ortega, a student.[9]

Lesson Format 2

USING THE FIVE SENSES

Name of Student: <u>Elsa Ortega</u>   *Date: <u>October 20</u>*
Age level: <u>teenagers or adults</u>   *Proficiency level: <u>high-beginning to</u>*
                                                               <u>low-intermediate</u>

Concepts introduced: Concepts introduced by the students themselves as part of the
language experience portion of the lesson later on (for some, the concepts will be new; for
others, they will be recycled—see next item below); the poetic format demonstrated in the
lesson; punctuation and capitalization as it is often (but not always) found in poems.

Concepts recycled: A rather extensive range of emotions: happiness, sadness, loneliness, excitement, pride, anger, peacefulness, jealousy, envy, hatred, etc., and the five
senses: sight, sound, taste, smell, and touch.

Behaviors expected as a result of this lesson: Students should be able to demonstrate
the understanding of the concepts introduced in the language experience portion of the
lesson. They should be able to use with relative ease the poetic format demonstrated,
including the way it is usually punctuated, with appropriate elements capitalized.

Materials needed: Several large pictures showing people in situations in which strong
emotions are likely to be felt; a board on which to write; paper (for students), unless they
are expected to use their own; thick, medium, and thin felt-tip pens in different colors,
and/or brushes, and paints for artwork.

Description of the activity:
1. Review the recycled emotions mentioned above by showing the students the pictures of people in different situations likely to bring about strong emotions (i.e., a
   teenage girl at the store who can't get the attention of the sales clerk, a child handing his sick dog to a veterinarian, an old man hugging an old woman, etc.) As students mention various emotions, write them in noun form on the board for all to see.
2. Ask the students if they remember what the five senses are. Write them on
   the board.
3. Tell students that they are to help you write a poem about an emotion using the
   following format (found in *Scholastic Action*, September, 1984, p. 23):

   Title: Name of the Emotion
   line 1: What color is the emotion?
   line 2: What does it sound like?
   line 3: What does it taste like?

---

[9] Note that the Hunter/Russell version presented earlier could be easily incorporated in the
   "Description of the Activity" by those liking its structure.

line 4: What does it smell like?
line 5: What does it look like?
line 6: How does it make you feel?

4. Choose an emotion that the students are not likely to choose. Using elements of language experience (see pages 243–246), write a poem with the students, following the above format.
5. Ask each student to choose an emotion and write a poem using the same format (write the format on the board if you have not already done so). They may work with a partner if they so choose.

Strategies used to check for understanding:
Can the students talk about the various emotions? Do they show a clear understanding of them in their poems? Do they show an understanding of the format and why they are or are not following it exactly (some may choose to vary the format)? Do they demonstrate in their own poems that they understand appropriate use of punctuation and capitalization, even though they may deviate from it for a logical reason (poetry allows for deviation more than other genres)?

Follow-up lesson(s):
1. Ask each student to complete pieces of artwork to accompany their poems. If they choose instead, they may cut pictures out of old magazines to accompany their poems.
2. Have them share their poems in small groups. Later, ask volunteers to share their poems with the whole class.

Self-evaluation of the lesson: How did the students respond? What were the strengths of the lesson? What could I improve in the lesson?

Below are a few poems written by Elsa's students as a result of this lesson.

Pride

Pride is the brightest red.
It sounds like 1,000,000 trumpets playing.
Pride tastes like turkey,
And smells like the prettiest rose.
Pride looks like a person holding his head up high.

Greg Barela

Happiness

Happiness is a colorful rainbow in the sky.
It sounds like people cheering.
It tastes like soft, sugary cotton candy,
And it smells like jasmine blooming at night.
Happiness looks like people dancing.
It makes you feel good.

Heather McBrian

THEME CYCLES/ INVESTIGATIVE INQUIRY

If a participatory classroom is the goal, one way to decide on the content and organization of lessons is to use a *theme cycles* approach (see also Chapter 4) or some
similar investigatory process. The lesson plan associated with theme cycles represents a mutual effort on the part of both the teacher and the students. Of course,
students must be proficient enough in the target language to participate fully.

Theme cycles present not just a general topic as a label around which isolated lessons in math, science, social studies, etc., and their related skills revolve;
instead, the topic is a subject for *investigative inquiry*. During the inquiry, students use math, science, social studies, and so forth, as knowledge bases from
which to draw. The process begins with an investigation that evolves into a
negotiated curricular plan. Questions lead to more questions that lead to even
more questions and further investigation. Thus the curriculum is constructed in
a joint effort between the students and the teacher.

Harste, Short, and Burke (1988) outline procedures for curriculum development using theme cycles. I summarize them below:

1. Both teachers and students make a list of topics that interest them and
   blend the two lists by mutual agreement to form the basic curriculum
   plan.
2. Through negotiation, one topic is selected as a starting point.
3. Students and the teacher create a web or chart, identifying "What We
   Know" and "What We Want to Know" about the topic. Figure 15.4
   illustrates the creation of a chart focused on the topic *Space*.
4. Students and teachers together develop a list of resources: books,
   people to interview, places to visit, etc.
5. Students choose the questions in the "What We Want to Know" column
   that are the most pressing.
6. With the help of the teacher, students become involved in whole group,
   small-group, and individual learning activities to explore the questions
   selected.

Topic: Space

What We Know	What We Want to Know
Mars, Venus, and Jupiter are planets in space. Neil Armstrong and Sally Ride are astronauts. The sun is a star. The moon revolves around the earth.	What else is there in space? What is the sun made of? How do you become an astronaut? How is it possible to revolve around another object without falling?

Figure 15.4

7. New questions are added to the chart as new discoveries are made.
8. At the end of particular segments of study, students present what they have found out to one another.
9. Other charts such as the one in Figure 15.4 are created. And so the process continues.

The authors stress the importance of building a supportive classroom environment before trying to negotiate curriculum. Throughout the process, the teacher acts as a facilitator and a participant to ensure its being carried out successfully.

INFUSING STANDARDS INTO THE CURRICULUM

Standards are crucial to any successful language program. If they are offered as guidelines, as are the ESL standards (see page 147) and the foreign language standards (see pages 149–150), then they can be used flexibly in the classroom without unduly constraining the autonomy teachers and students need in order to progress toward a participatory classroom. For example, take a look at Lesson Format 2 above. The immediate behaviors expected as a result of the lesson include the student's ability to demonstrate the understanding of the specific concepts introduced, to use with relative ease the poetic format which was demonstrated, and to punctuate and capitalize appropriately. These behaviors are closely associated with standards having to do with being able to grasp content; to express oneself in writing, including poetry; and to use the conventions involved in punctuation and capitalization for a variety of formats. Standards can also be infused into Lesson Format 1 above, into a theme cycles or investigative inquiry approach, and into virtually any lesson format employed in the classroom.

Standards specify what students should know and what they should be able to do as a result of instruction in the target language (see Chapter 7). They can help assure stakeholders (students, teachers, the school, the school district, etc.) that relevant skills necessary to reaching personal, sociopolitical, and academic objectives are being included in the language program. If selection and implementation are judiciously carried out, they can help students and teachers clarify what skills are necessary to each student's development as an autonomous learner and effective citizen in the community, both locally and globally.

One of the dangers of which teachers should be aware has been mentioned already (see Chapter 7). Sometimes teachers and/or the school districts of which they are a part, in their effort to ensure that students meet predetermined standards, will use them as strait jackets for the curriculum. Santiago (1997) also talks about this fear. She observes, "Often, teachers are put in a position where they become a hindrance to the learning process by prescribing too closely what children should learn and thereby failing to create the necessary conditions for learning" (p. 74). She goes on to say, "We fail our students by saturating them with what we think they should know at a certain age instead of finding out where they are and what they know, and continuing from there" (p. 78). Her observations support the importance of applying Vygotsky's concept of Zone of Development (see pages 50–55). In order to help students stretch to higher levels of understanding, we need to start approximately where they are and build from there. A highly specified curriculum and timetable with little input from teachers and their students leaves almost no possibility for doing that.

Van Lier (1996) goes even further to condemn such pre-established constraints on classrooms. He argues that the curriculum itself must be process-oriented in that it is

> . . . motivated by our understanding of learning rather than by a list of desired competencies, test scores, or other products. The setting of goals and objectives, and the construction and assessment of achievement, are themselves integral parts of the curriculum process, rather than pre-established constraints that are imposed on it from the outside (p. 3).

Of course, standards by themselves are not inherently evil. It is the way in which they are implemented that can make them seem that way. Many teachers, however, when faced with standards handed down as "edicts from above," have learned to deal with them as best they can. Many try to allow for as much student input and attention to students' immediate needs as possible and are able to do so, at least to some extent, within even the most rigid systems. Many of these same teachers have fought and continue to fight to have these systems changed so that they are more flexible and in tune with the ever changing needs of their students.

ADAPTING THE CONTENT

A majority of the activities recommended in this book can be adapted to almost any age level. Following is an example of how an affective activity (see Chapter 14) developed for use with adults can be modified for use with children. At both levels, the students are grouped into pairs. The responses are timed so all students have a chance to express themselves on each item.

Adapting for Age

Describe how you feel when . . .

> *For adults* (mid- to high-intermediate levels)
>   someone gives you a compliment.
>   you are late for a meeting at which you are the speaker.

your boss asks you to work four extra hours and you are very tired.
you receive an all-expenses-paid vacation to the Bahamas.

For children (mid- to high-intermediate levels)
your friend says you have a nice smile.
your teacher scolds you for coming late to class.
your favorite movie is on TV and your mother tells you to go to bed.
someone offers to treat you to a chocolate sundae.

Some activities can be easily modified for different proficiency levels. For example, in the activity below, the students are going on a treasure hunt through the local newspaper. The first group of treasures is for students at beginning levels, the second is for students at intermediate levels. See descriptions of the levels on pages 137–138.

Adapting for Proficiency Level

LOW- TO MID-BEGINNING LEVELS

Directions (should be given orally and demonstrated): *You are going on a treasure hunt. You will use the pictures in a newspaper. See how many pictures of these things you can find. Cut out the pictures.*

Find something . . .

small
soft
made of glass
square
short
narrow
heavy
sticky
longer than a pencil

MID- TO HIGH-INTERMEDIATE LEVELS

Directions (can be given orally, in written form or both): *Go on a treasure hunt in the local newspaper. Find pictures of the items and cut them out. Paste them on a piece of paper. Write the name of the category above each picture. For example, you are asked to find something that looks comfortable. You might cut out the picture of a bed. Paste it on your paper. Write the words "something that looks comfortable" above it.*

Find something . . .

that tastes good.
that has a pleasing smell.
that can be harmful or even dangerous.

that is a good buy.
that is durable.
that is accurate.
that you would like to buy.

Find something that is used . . .

to beautify something.
to control something.
to change something.

In the first version of the activity, the items are very concrete and simple; in the second version they are more abstract. Modifications can also be made in the content, depending upon various interests, background, goals, and so forth.

EXAMINING YOUR TEACHING

Teachers who want to better their practices *do* participate in teacher research, but usually on a very informal basis. In fact, these teachers may not even realize that they are doing any research at all. Bassano and Christison (1995a), both very experienced teachers and authors, asked their students in ESL classes questions about what their teachers were doing right, what had helped them most in acquiring the language, which activities they preferred, and whether or not the curriculum was meeting their needs. The authors reported, "Like many teachers involved in classroom observation and data collection at the time, we did not view our activities as research, nor did we believe that our work was particularly significant for the language teaching profession" (p. 89). Good teachers, just by progressing through a normal day, are involved in informal research. They determine from students' reactions, from test results, and from an analysis of their students' work how well they have taught and in what ways they may need to improve. Their data may also include feedback, not only from the students, but from parents, administrators, and other teachers. They often are involved in needs assessments which they then use to guide curriculum planning. And if they want to create participatory classrooms, they also find out what issues most concern and/or interest their students and use these as foci of the curriculum, particularly at intermediate to advanced levels in the case of second-language classrooms or at all levels in bilingual classrooms. To them, teaching itself becomes a rich and transformative experience.

Those teachers wishing to participate in more formal types of teacher research, the results of which they eventually plan to make public, will find some resources available to them. One such resource is Donald Freeman's book entitled *Doing Teacher Research: From Inquiry to Understanding* (1998). He argues that to investigate the classroom in a rigorous way, research must be redefined so that it becomes part of the teaching process itself. The research begins with thinking out one's assumptions about teaching and learning and uses these assumptions to develop the questions from which the inquiry will flow. It means being open to changing predetermined thinking by challenging it at every step of the way so that the results will be transformative. According to Freeman, questions for research should be open-ended and have the potential to produce understandings and principles rather than specific solutions or courses of action. Usually, such "research-able questions" (his name for them) lead to other questions for similar research. A research-able question he uses as an example is this: What is the impact of praise on group dynamics? This question requires the teacher-researcher to look at the main question and the subquestions that grow out of it from the student's point of view. The teacher-researcher's data may include among other things: an examination of journals and diaries, observations and documentation of student behaviors, a videotaped record of classroom events, a transcription of what the students say, indicating gestures, pauses, etc., and, perhaps, interviews with the students.

The following questions are among those he lists that can be made part of the framework included in any teacher research plan:

> What is the inquiry?
> What are the research-able questions/puzzles here?
> What are the supporting questions/puzzles?
> What is the background or rationale of the research?
> Where will the research be done?
> Who will be the participants in your study?
> What data are relevant to the research questions?
> How do you/the researcher plan to collect them?
> How will you/the researcher analyze them?
> What is the provisional time line or schedule?
> Why will the research matter?
> (p. 122)

Michael Wallace (1998), in his book *Action Research for Language Teachers*, takes a more personal approach to teacher research. He sees it as problem-focused with intended outcomes that are very pragmatic. The problems researched may relate to classroom management, using appropriate materials, teaching in areas such as reading and speaking, student behavior, and so forth. Data might include field notes and logs, diaries, journals, personal accounts, verbal reports (such as think-aloud) transcribed into protocols, interviews, questionnaires, case studies, and the like. An analysis of the data then becomes the basis for making decisions. Action research, according to him, can be used by teachers in conjunction with results of academic research of various kinds to inform decisions. However, unlike experimental research, it does not attempt to make general statements or make extensive use of statistical analysis. Its main goal is to encourage and facilitate reflective thinking and professional development.

Teachers collectively may use their own research to help them make decisions as part of an effort to reform their school. For example, they may want to take a look at groups of students who drop out of school to discover some of their reasons for doing so. They may want to know to what extent the academic needs of language minority students are being met. They may want to know what the attitudes of teachers are toward students who come from different cultural and language backgrounds.

The types of research teachers are able to do will depend mainly upon the questions they want to look into and the constraints within the school and classroom. Often lack of time and resources, large class sizes, and scheduling problems make more formal investigations very difficult in crowded schools. However, for teachers who are able to pursue teacher research, the dividends can be great in terms of their own professionalism and increased understanding about the learning process and the factors affecting it in their schools and classrooms. But teacher research should never become just another burdensome endeavor in which teachers feel compelled to participate. Even at its most informal levels, teacher research can produce valuable information to inform practice and improve teaching overall.

SUMMARY

Developing a methodology for both second and foreign language classrooms involves the synthesis of emergent theory and practice into a program that works. Developing such a program often means drawing from several methods and activities in order to create an integrated curriculum that will meet the needs of the students and the situation. Motivational goals, the particular concepts being taught, learning and teaching preferences, cultural factors, and age and competency levels of the students are all important considerations.

For beginners and low-intermediate students in particular, lessons need to be structured in such a way that students will receive optimal exposure to important concepts. The lessons should be well organized and contain familiar routines in order to serve adequately as vehicles for new information. Content needs to be modified to be appropriate for various age and proficiency levels. For intermediate and advanced students, theme cycles or other investigative procedures that require greater proficiency in the target language may offer the most challenges for both students and their teachers in participatory classrooms.

Focusing the program on content appears to be cognitively sound for most programs, particularly when relevant tasks and proficiencies are allowed to grow out of the content chosen. The resulting proficiencies can be tied into important standards which may have been infused into the program.

Peer teachers and other assistants can be trained to help the teacher provide sufficient amounts of comprehensible input, self-image enhancement, encouragement, motivation, and opportunity for negotiating meaning. At the same time, they can serve as linguistic models to help prevent early fossilization. In addition, the peer teachers and other assistants can help make it possible for students to move from cognitively undemanding tasks to more demanding ones and to integrate the four skill areas as they flow with the students' needs and interests.

Versions of cooperative learning also can serve as effective classroom management tools, particularly in intermediate to advanced second language classes or in mainstream content-area classes in which ELLs are included. When the conditions are favorable, students can make substantial strides in communicative and academic competence through cooperative efforts.

Examining one's practice can be ongoing and very informal at one end of the spectrum, or it can be limited to a specific time frame and quite formal with publication in mind at the other end of the spectrum. The kind of research teachers choose will depend upon their goals and the constraints under which they find themselves.

READINGS, REFLECTION, AND DISCUSSION

Suggested Readings and Reference Materials

Bassano, S. and Christison, M. A. (1995b). *Community spirit: A practical guide to collaborative language learning*. San Francisco, CA: Alta Book Center. This book highlights practical ideas and strategies for creating student-centered classrooms. Ways to increase student participation and collaboration are presented.

Crandall, J. (1999). Cooperative language learning and affective factors. In Arnold, ed., pp. 226–245. Crandall presents a very clear analysis of cooperative language learning and how it relates to affect. She describes many of its applications (along with potential problems) and gives a convincing rationale for its use.

Gebhard, J. and Oprandy, R. (1999). *Language teaching awareness: A guide to exploring beliefs and practices*. Cambridge: Cambridge University Press. This book offers assistance to teachers wanting to better their teaching through the process of discovery. It includes very practical guidelines to use while observing, keeping a journal, collecting other kinds of data, working with supervisors, and so forth.

McGroarty, M. (1992). Cooperative learning: The benefits for content-area teaching. In P. Richard-Amato and M. A. Snow, eds. *The multicultural classroom: Readings for content-area teachers*. White Plains, NY: Pearson Education/Longman, pp. 58–69. Here the author describes and supports with empirical research the linguistic, social, and curricular benefits of cooperative learning. She emphasizes the pedagogical advantages that can be realized once teachers let go of their traditional authority and become facilitators in the learning process.

Richard-Amato, P. (1992a). Peer teachers: The neglected resource. In P. Richard-Amato and M. A. Snow, eds. *The multicultural classroom: Readings for content-area teachers*. White Plains, NY: Pearson Education/Longman, pp. 271–284. Presents guidelines for the preparation and use of peer teachers, alternative models, and related research.

Snow, M.A. and Brinton, D. eds. (1997). *The content-based classroom: Perspectives on integrating language and content*. White Plains, NY; Pearson Education. This anthology discusses the theory supporting content-based instruction and its use in multiple situations with students of various age and proficiency levels.

Underhill, A. (1999). Facilitation in language teaching. In Arnold, ed., pp. 125–141. Here Adrian Underhill defines three different kinds of teacher: the Lecturer (one who has knowledge of the topic, but pays little attention to teaching techniques and methodology); the Teacher (one who has both knowledge of the topic and is skilled in a range of methods and procedures for teaching it); and the Facilitator (one who has both knowledge and skills, but also has insight into the students and seeks to enable them to be responsible for their own learning). He provides insight into each of the three roles teachers most often assume in the classroom.

Questions and Projects for Reflection and Discussion

1. Find or create a lesson that is oriented to a particular age group and adapt it to another age group. Doing the same for proficiency level, modify a lesson intended for one proficiency level (beginning, intermediate, or advanced) to make it appropriate for another. What problems needed to be considered in completing each task?

2. Think about three or four issues concerning classroom management that have bothered you recently. Which one do you feel is most pressing and/or important? Discuss the issue with peers and any students to which you might have access at this time. Then write about it in your journal. You may want to add to your entry whenever you gain additional insight through further discussion, reading, and/or experience.

   If you were to do teacher research on this issue, how might you go about it? Develop a course of action. Share it with a small group of peers to get their input.

3. Plan a workshop for a small group of peer teachers and other assistants. What important preparation will you want them to have?

4. Can you think of a few units for which you might want to incorporate some version of cooperative learning? Briefly describe how these units might be organized.

5. Teachers have described themselves as "challengers or agents of change," "nurturers," "cooperative leaders," "innovators," "providers of tools," and "artists," among other things (see de Guerrero and Villamil, 2000). How do

you see your own role(s) as a teacher? In what ways and under what circumstances do you think your role(s) might change?

6. Develop a flexible theme-based unit (a series of several lessons centered around a theme) for a second language classroom situation at a beginning or intermediate level (see page 137).[10] After considering what you think your students' goals might be and what standards they will try to reach, decide some of the major concepts you will teach and reinforce throughout and the skills you will help them develop. Describe the unit in writing. Include a brief description of the lessons and what activity or activities will be included in each. Develop fully one of the lessons, utilizing a structure similar to one of the formats or a combination of formats outlined on pages 320–323. Make sure you leave plenty of room for student input. Try the lesson out with members of your class. Make sure you state clearly the situation, the proficiency and the age level(s) for which it is intended, and how it fits into the other lessons in your unit. Ask the members of your class for feedback once you have presented your lesson. In what ways was it successful? How can it be improved? You might begin by sharing your own reactions to the lesson.

If you are currently teaching students, use what you have learned to try out a similar lesson with them. Make sure the activity is relevant and appropriate to level. If possible, have your lesson videotaped to analyze and discuss with peers. Reflect on its outcome and how you felt about doing it. Pay close attention to student response. Do you see any problems with your lesson? How might it be improved?

Write in your journal about your experiences with this and/or similar lessons and what you learned from them.

---

[10] Situations might be one of the following: An elementary, secondary, or university second or foreign language program, an adult basic education program, or a language program for special purposes such as preparing students for specific technical occupations, and so forth.

CHAPTER **16**

Tools for Teaching Languages: Textbooks, Computer Programs, Videos, and Films

. . . part of the task of selection, then, becomes the selection of segments of real world knowledge and experience . . .

R. Crymes, 1979

QUESTIONS TO THINK ABOUT

1. Think about textbooks you used when you were trying to learn another language. What did they focus on (grammar, functions, meaning, etc.)? To what extent were they effective in furthering your own language development?

2. How might computers be used in a second or foreign language classroom? What kinds of programs would you want to have available for your students? Why?

3. Do you think videos might have a place in the second or foreign language classroom? If so, what kinds of videos would you use? How would you use them?

4. Do you think Hollywood-type films have a place in the second or foreign language? Explain.

Most of the materials suggested up to this point—television programs on video, newspapers and periodicals, stories and other pieces of literature, catalogs with illustrations, games, reference books, lyrics to popular songs, maps, pictures, and others, are not specifically intended for use in second language teaching. But commercial products especially designed for second language or bilingual teaching can be just as useful if they are chosen carefully. Such materials can provide content, aid organization, give guidance when needed, complement and/or constitute lessons, and introduce and reinforce concepts. Moreover, they can serve as important resources in participatory classrooms and can allow for self-access learning.

The purpose of this chapter is not to advocate specific textbooks, computer programs, or videos or films. Rather, the purpose is to provide guidelines for evaluating and selecting these important teaching tools.

TEXTBOOKS

Some teachers and many publishers long for the days when one set of materials (complete with student texts, cassettes, workbooks, and teacher manuals) was considered the answer to language teaching needs. Today most of us realize that much more is needed to build a program. Because of the shift in emphasis to interactive/participatory approaches and to academic content, publishers feel pressure to provide materials that are communicative and logically motivated and that lead students to further inquiry. This is as true of large programs with multiple components as it is of supplemental or materials that teachers themselves have developed. Moreover, many educators are insisting that materials require teachers and students to be more active and creative and that they focus on relevant, meaningful content. Some teachers are even turning entrepreneur and publishing their own materials in an attempt to fill the gap.

Let's first address what kind of textbook content most effectively promotes language acquisition. In answer to this question, Oller (1983a) offers the Episode Hypothesis.

The Episode Hypothesis

This hypothesis states that *"text (i.e., discourse in any form) will be easier to reproduce, understand, and recall, to the extent that it is motivated and structured episodically"* (1983a, p. 12). Episodic organization requires both motivation created by conflict and the kind of logical sequencing necessary to good storytelling and consistent with experience.

As mentioned in Chapter 13, Schank and Abelson (1977) related episodic structure to memory itself. They argued that humans both acquire and store information in episodic form. Oller agreed and went one step further by applying this theory to the classroom.

Language programs that employ fully contextualized and maximally meaningful language necessarily optimize the learner's ability to use previously
acquired expectancies to help discover the pragmatic mappings of utterances
in the new language into extralinguistic contexts. Hence they would seem to
be superior to programs that expect learners to acquire the ability to use a language on the basis of disconnected lists of sentences (Oller, 1979, pp. 31–32).

Many traditional ESL and foreign language texts contain disconnected lists
of sentences or, at best, sentences that are related but are not part of any motivated or logical interaction.

Consider the following example, consisting of a group of items related
only in that each illustrates the same grammatical form.

Example 1

1. *We're having* a grammar test today.
2. Bob *is having a* party tomorrow.
3. The Smiths *are having* a good time in Paris.
4. My sister *is having* a baby in June.

(Pollock, 1982, p. 7)

Or read the next typical passage, in which the dialog is temporally structured but lacks sufficient motivation or conflict as well as logical sequencing.

Example 2

Tomás is visiting Ralph and Lucy.

RALPH: How long can you stay, Tomás?

TOMÁS: I'm going to leave tomorrow afternoon. I'm taking the bus.

LUCY: I like taking the bus, but Ralph doesn't.

RALPH: What do you want to do tomorrow, Tomás? Do you want to sleep late?

TOMÁS: No, I like to get up early. Let's go to the park. Do you like playing tennis?

RALPH: I don't like to play, but Lucy likes tennis. She plays every day.

LUCY: Ralph likes jogging. Let's go to the park early tomorrow morning. Tomás and
I can play tennis, and you can go jogging. Ralph . . .

(Sutherland, 1981, p. 11)

Compare the first two examples with the following.

Example 3

DARLENE: I think I'll call Bettina's mother. It's almost five and Chrissy isn't home yet.

MEG: I thought Bettina had the chicken pox.

DARLENE: Oh, that's right. I forgot. Chrissy didn't go to Bettina's today. Where is she?

MEG: She's probably with Gary. He has Little League practice until five.

DARLENE: I hear the front door. Maybe that's Gary and Chrissy.

GARY: Hi.

DARLENE: Where's Chrissy? Isn't she with you?

GARY: With me? Why with me? I saw her at two after school, but then I went to Little League practice. I think she left with her friend.
DARLENE: Which one?
GARY: The one next door . . . the one she walks to school with every day.
DARLENE: Oh, you mean Timmy. She's probably with him.
GARY: Yeah, she probably is.
DARLENE: I'm going next door to check.

(Brinton and Neuman, 1982, p. 33)

Which of these three examples has the best chance of being internalized? If you said Example 3, I agree with you. It captivates our interest through its episodic organization.

To reinforce the importance of episodically meaningful text, look at the following questions keyed to these three examples.

Questions for Example 1

1. Who is having a good time in Paris?
2. Who is having a party tomorrow?

Can you answer these questions without referring back to the text. Why not? Because Bob and the Smiths are not important to us, they do not connect meaningfully to our experience, nor do they connect in any meaningful way to each other.

Questions for Example 2

1. Who is visiting?
2. What does the visitor plan to do?
3. Who likes to ride on buses?
4. What does Lucy like to do?
5. Who likes jogging?

Although the sentences to which they refer are temporally related and perhaps slightly motivated, these questions are almost as difficult to answer as those for Example 1. Why? They are not logical according to our experience. Their only reason for existence seems to be to expose the student to the present progressive tense and to gerunds and to teach the comparative structure: "I like taking the bus, but Ralph doesn't," or "I don't like to play, but Lucy likes tennis." People in normal conversation do not speak like this because in natural discourse we are not concerned with exposing others to specific grammatical forms.

In addition, the conversation in Example 2 does not flow logically. When Tomás says, "I'm going to leave tomorrow afternoon. I'm taking the bus," we might expect Lucy or Ralph to respond with, "Oh, you're leaving so soon!" or something similar. Instead, Lucy says, "I like taking the bus, but Ralph doesn't." Our sense of expectancy is violated. Grice (1975) relates this sense of expectancy to the maxim of relation that is essential in normal discourse.

Questions for Example 3

1. Who has disappeared?
2. When was she last seen?
3. Where are they going to look for her?
4. How do the characters feel about her disappearance?

After rereading Example 3 quickly, can you answer these questions? Do you need to check for the answer to each question? Probably not. Why? Because the structure of the discourse is consistent with our own experience, and the dialogue is motivated and logical. As a result, we automatically become involved with the language at a subconscious as well as conscious level; we experience a heightened awareness. We are concerned about the little girl's disappearance, just as the people in the story are concerned.

In spite of what we have learned about language learning and teaching over the last twenty years or more, many of today's textbooks still contain the same kinds of content one finds in Examples 1 and 2 above. It is difficult to understand why so many publishers—and some teachers—still cling to the notion that content such as this promotes language learning in classrooms.

Although the Episode Hypothesis is universal in that it is based on the logic of experience, that experience will reflect the culture of which it is a part. The frames of experience in a particular text may be unfamiliar; certain dialogues simply may not occur in some cultures. For example, a discourse in which someone decides on a nursing home for an elderly parent may confuse or offend students from cultures in which extended families are the norm. Prereading activities can be very useful in setting a context for culturally determined schemata in the second or foreign language classroom, especially if the students intend to participate in the culture represented. (See also Chapters 5 and 13.) When English is being taught for instrumental purposes or as an international language, choosing a text that relies on the source culture (the culture where English is being taught) is important because it reinforces a culture which is both acceptable and familiar to the learner. Alternatively, you might select a text that reflects many cultures.

Selection Guidelines

When you select textbooks, you will want to ask yourself some of the questions below. Not all of these criteria will be appropriate in every situation; you need to chose those that you find most relevant and important.

Purpose and Motivation

- What underlying assumptions about language and language learning are reflected in the materials? Do you agree with these assumptions?

- Are the topics and themes covered in the materials inviting? Do you think they will interest your students?
- Do the materials encourage students to reflect on their own learning strategies and to develop new ones?
- Do the materials encourage students to inquire further about the issues covered? Do they encourage student participation in learning? Do they encourage students to become active thinkers and independent learners?
- Do the activities encourage use of creative language and negotiated meaning in a variety of situations? Do they seem to have a good chance of actually resulting in improved language use?
- Are second language characters presented positively? Are their values respected? Are they given positive roles within the material? Do the materials promote positive attitudes toward all cultures, including the target language culture? Will the activities enhance self-concepts among your students and boost confidence?

Appropriateness

- Are the materials appropriate to the language needs, goals, interests, and expectations of your students? Look not only at content but at the illustration program, range and format of activities, language level, and so on.
- Does the level of the material rise appropriately over the course of the text? Does the content become gradually more complex and academically challenging?
- If the material is part of a series, does the book dovetail nicely with those that precede and follow? Is there a clearly defined approach and "voice" that runs through all the books?
- Do activities above the beginning level call for critical thinking, or do they probe for factual information and detail?

Format

- Are the materials attractive and inviting? Is there ample white space for students to write (if they own the books)? Are the illustrations pedagogically effective or simply decorative?
- Are skill areas largely integrated, or are they approached as separate entities? (See Chapter 5.)
- Do the activities represent a wide range of varied tasks, or is the same format used repeatedly?
- Are concepts recycled several times, from unit to unit, or are they introduced and then forgotten?
- Are directions clearly written, at a level your students will understand?

- Do pre-reading activities adequately prepare and motivate students, calling on prior knowledge, without being over-long or tedious?

Authenticity

- Are students encouraged to relate the content of the material to their own lives? Are they encouraged to draw on prior knowledge?
- Do the conversations and activities seem motivated and logical according to real experience? Is the grammar natural, or is it clearly selected to illustrate a grammar point?
- Are the reading selections real, from authentic sources? If the materials have been adapted, is the adaptation effective and real? (See also pages 246–247.)

Teacher Resources

- Are the teacher resource materials clearly written and pedagogically useful? Do they contain helpful teaching suggestions? Are a range of teaching options provided?
- Do the teacher materials include ways to evaluate student progress? Are these tied coherently to the student materials? Are self-evaluation tools available for the students in the student materials?

Keep in mind also that textbook titles are sometimes misleading. Titles that imply a cast of characters, and contain the words "communicative" or "communication," do not always identify truly communicative materials. Often these books are grammar-, competency-, or function-based texts disguised to look communicative. It pays to check the content carefully before ordering them for student use.

COMPUTER PROGRAMS

Much of the software traditionally used in computer-assisted language learning (CALL) programs has been "drill and test"—the computer plays "teacher" and imparts information; the students apply the information and then are tested. Those who give wrong answers on the test are cycled back for further instruction and practice. Some programs allow teachers to use an authoring system to set up similar lessons by using the already established content, or by selecting items from a series of possible choices, or by creating new content for the program. Authoring programs are available that do not require the teacher to know advanced techniques or complex computer language.

Drill-and-test discrete point materials are still plentiful and may be appropriate at times. Hoffman (1995/1996) reminds us that such programs can be beneficial to the curriculum, especially if used outside the classroom. She argues that computers can effectively reinforce structural knowledge of a language and recommends that students be given an index of such programs, arranged from easy to difficult. Students can then choose programs in the areas in which each needs work, eliminating those in areas already mastered. Self-study activity can probably best be accomplished in a laboratory where students can work at their own pace.

Although it may be used effectively for individual study, discrete-point software can often lead to boring repetition and reduced motivation. Chun and Brandl (1992) are among the many who stress the importance of using classroom computer programs that have a highly integrative rather than a discrete-point focus. Using computers as communicative tools not only teaches computer skills, but also helps students reach language and academic objectives.

Many excellent communicative programs are available today. These include:

- Simulation programs, in which students can take fantasy trips and choose from among many options: where to go, what to eat, and so forth.
- Interfacing programs, in which students can hear prerecorded messages and interact with the computer by pressing particular keys or touching certain areas of the screen.
- Expository writing programs, in which students are asked questions to clarify their thinking about essays that are in the planning stages.
- Creative writing programs, in which students can create and illustrate stories with graphics or create poems, sometimes with line-by-line assistance for special patterns (rhymes, limericks, haiku, etc.).
- Problem-solving programs, in which students are immersed in a wide variety of problem-solving strategies, some of which even have features that allow the student to "teach the computer" to complete a task.

Computer Games

Other programs involve game-playing. Computer games, although not usually meant for second language teaching *per se*, can provide language learners with challenges in the target language. They can present simulations that call for students to make decisions, and they can require interaction with others involved in the game. Computer games are currently available in many content areas. For example, one such program introduces children to the concepts of number lines, number pairs, and graph plotting; students are asked to plot their own designs. Another program takes students on a simulated safari journey through a grid-like environment where they decipher clues in order to find the hiding place of a "mystery" animal. In the process, they get practice in making inferences, creating tactics, and collecting and organizing clues. Other computer games that can be useful in second language learning include chess, word games, memory games, teasers with missing numbers, and many more.

When choosing a software program, Bishop (2001) suggests that we focus our questions on the following areas:

- educational soundness
- ease of use by students and teachers
- age-appropriateness
- cultural sensitivity
- visual appeal
- cost-effectiveness

Perhaps teachers will find a checklist like the one in Figure 16.1 valuable in evaluating software programs.

SOFTWARE PROGRAM EVALUATION

Title of the program: _____

Publisher: _____

Name of reviewer: _____

Date reviewed: _____

Languages in which the program is available: _____

_____

1. **Use**
   How easy is the program to install? ❑ Very easy ❑ Easy ❑ Confusing or complicated ❑ Very difficult

   How easy is the program to operate? ❑ Very easy ❑ Easy ❑ Confusing or complicated ❑ Very difficult

   Comments:

2. **Age-appropriateness/level-appropriateness**
   For what audience is this program intended? ❑ ESL ❑ EFL ❑ Bilingual ❑ Sheltered ❑ Other, specify _____

   Is the program appropriate for its intended audience? ❑ Very appropriate ❑ Acceptable ❑ Inappropriate

   Comments:

For what ages or grade levels is the program designed? ❑ Primary ❑ Secondary ❑ Adult

Is the program appropriate for that age group or grade level? ❑ Very appropriate ❑ Acceptable ❑ Inappropriate

Comments:

For what proficiency level is the program designed? ❑ Low beginner ❑ False beginner ❑ Low intermediate ❑ Other, specify _____

Is the program appropriate for that proficiency level? ❑ Yes ❑ No

Comments:

What kind of use is this program most appropriate for? ❑ Classroom use ❑ Self-study at home or in a lab ❑ Other, specify _____

Comments:

3. Cultural sensitivity

If the program includes characters, was the author careful not to stereotype them by ethnicity, race, or country or origin? ❑ Yes ❑ No

Are any characters second language speakers? If so, are they given positive traits? ❑ Yes ❑ No

Is the language employed in the program sensitive to diverse ethnicities, races, and countries of origin? ❑ Yes ❑ No

Comments:

4. Visual appeal

The design of this program is: ❑ Very appealing ❑ Appealing ❑ Unattractive ❑ Very unattractive

Comments:

5. Cost-effectiveness

Price of program: _____

How often might I use this program in my classroom? ❑ Daily ❑ Weekly ❑ Once or twice during the course ❑ Other, specify _____

Comments:

6. Educational soundness

What instructional options does the program provide? ❑ Individual work ❑ Group work ❑ Pair work ❑ Other, specify _____

Description of the program:

What are the program's stated objectives?

Does the program, in your opinion, fulfill its objectives? ❑ Yes ❑ No

Comments:

7. Recommendation
Overall Evaluative comments:

What do you recommend? ❑ Purchase ❑ Don't purchase
❑ Other, specify _____

Figure 16.1 Software Program Evaluation

Canale and Barker (1986) suggested early on that computers, by incorporating integrative programs into the classroom, could serve many of the same purposes for which language itself is used. Such programs could be used as tools for thought (self-directed language), tools for social interaction (other-directed language), and tools for play and art in which the emphasis is on self-expression. They were convinced that the activities should be intrinsically motivating, provide for the autonomy of the language student, and involve problem solving in many different situations.

Today we have sophisticated multimedia programs utilizing computers, printers, interactive videodiscs, CD or DVD players, TV monitors, scanners, VCRs, digital cameras, and other electronic devices, some of which have voice-recording capabilities. Amanti (2001) suggests, among other things, that students use multimedia tools to create original programs. She offers one idea in which students of various proficiency levels collaborate to make a multimedia presentation of a field trip, including photos that can be scanned into a computer file and for which captions can be written, retelling the event. Students can then narrate a slide show presentation by reading the text on each slide, using a computer microphone. Amanti suggests that activities such as these give even shy students a chance to produce the second language in a non-threatening environment. Text and graphics (tables, charts, graphs, animation, etc.) can be used with sound to create programs of many kinds. However, Amanti emphasizes the need for setting up guidelines, evaluation criteria, and organizational plans before students embark on projects of this nature.

Involving students in special media projects may not be enough in the participatory classroom, however, Kessler and Plankans (2001) recommend that students be involved in actually creating instructional materials, particularly those involving computers. They argue that learners understand what is helpful to them in the learning process and what is not. Because the learners are the stakeholders, because they are individuals with different learning styles, because they are often computer-literate already, and because they are affected by the environment in which they will be using computers, the authors feel it is important that they be part of the program development process whenever possible.

But whether teachers and their students actually create instructional programs or not, it is important to be aware of the kinds of programs on the market that can serve as practical tools for student learning. Some of the best programs available today involve word processors and the Internet.

Word Processors

Using a word processing program can be frustrating, exhilarating, and almost always challenging to the second language student. The language used is fully contextualized and creative. Perhaps the best time for students to begin is at late beginner/early intermediate levels after they have acquired a repertoire (however limited) of language structures and vocabulary. Children, too, provided they can handle the experience cognitively, are able to work in word processing programs, especially if the programs are designed with them in mind. Some programs use extra-large characters on the screen, and the menu choices are pictorial for ease of understanding.

Students seem to learn best when they are eased into word processing gradually, with the help of the teacher, peer teachers, other assistants, or other students. One way to begin, especially for a student who has never been introduced to a computer before, is to type something about the student that he or she can comprehend with the keyboard, perhaps using the student's name. The student can then respond verbally while the teacher or aide types the words as they are said. The student can eventually proceed from the comprehending and writing of very short messages to understanding and producing fully developed text. Commands can be learned gradually, as they are needed. For example, Schneider (1997) in her class for intermediate-level English language learning adults at San Francisco City College begins by having students copy a paragraph or two into the computer, and then, change them from present to past tense or direct to indirect speech. In a computer lab, her students learn to **cut**, **copy**, and **paste** and to rewrite passages and make requested changes. Later, they learn to select and use the **find** and **replace** commands. For example, students may change the name "Sylvia" to the name "Nasim." Of course, this change necessitates other changes, which the students will probably recognize if they have already worked on agreement of forms. Being able to delete material, move whole passages to other parts of a document, select and change formats, write and send messages, and perform numerous other functions does much to facilitate the writing process.

Some programs, usually called "writing aids," are specifically designed to guide the writer through the preliminary phases of writing. For example, a few programs ask a series of questions to aid users in targeting the purpose for a specific composition. Be careful, however, of programs that give general reactions such as "How interesting!" or "Nice job!" regardless of what the student has actually written. Other programs to be wary of are those that accuse students of such offenses as being "wordy" if the sentences are too long. Parkhurst (1984) feels that such programs may focus students on mechanics at the expense of meaning, or may make students overly concerned with sentence length as opposed to clarity.

In most programs, students can store ideas and draw on these as they write, often from a "window" opened on the screen where they are creating new text.

The Internet

For most students, the World Wide Web can be an exciting resource for research and information gathering. To them, it is a helpful library filled with valuable information which may not be available on the shelves of their libraries; to others, it is a confusing maze of information so unreliable that it cannot be trusted. In reality, the Web can be both of these things, but when good research strategies are applied, the Web can be very helpful, especially when used in conjunction with other resources.

Software programs known as "browsers" provide access to "search engines" which, in turn, help identify appropriate sites on the Web. The user types a topic, key word, or phrase into a search box and the search engine hunts for related sites—often generating thousands, some of which have little to do with the subject. The more specific the key words, the more focused the results. But sometimes a broad search (like a stroll through library stacks) can produce unexpected treasures. It is best, however, to begin with a fairly broad search to see what is available and then to narrow it down to something manageable. In an effort to focus a search, some rather crude strategies have been used, bringing mixed results. For example, plus signs before a word have been used to indicate that the results must contain that word; quotation marks have been used to indicate that the words within the quotes must appear together. We are likely to see more refined strategies develop as time goes on to give the user much more control over searches.

Evaluating sources once they have been found can prove a more challenging task (Richard-Amato, 1998). Who wrote the information? How credible is the author? How current is the information? Is it fact or opinion? Is it relevant to the topic being researched? Does the information include full citations that can be verified. Are the author's sources reliable? Does the source give you the information you need to link to other relevant sites? Government sources (.gov) and education sources (.edu) can generally be trusted to provide reliable information; commercial sites (.com), may require closer scrutiny.

Using the Internet for Class Work and Personal Communication

The Internet can provide highly motivating activities, encouraging students to use language for authentic communicative purposes. Some examples include creating a classroom website and using e-mail and word-processing to provide practice and increase confidence in the ability to communicate.

Setting up a classroom website is a relatively simple task; many software programs are available to help with this process. Such a website can provide both learning resources for students and opportunities for students to get to know one another. Content might include writing guidelines and tips, sample compositions representing various genres, a dictionary designed for students in ESL, EFL, bilingual or other foreign language programs, topic ideas for compositions, and anything else the students might find useful. A classroom website might also include more personal information—biographies that students create or information in students' first languages about their home cultures.

Leslie Jo Adams uses e-mail projects with her high-intermediate English Language Learners (ELLs) to improve their writing skills. Each student acquires a free e-mail address from an Internet service provider. The students and the teacher exchange initial personal information, and then students are assigned writing topics such as "All About Me," "My School," "My Favorite Holiday," and "My Goals for the Future"—topics that will help them to feel more confident writing about themselves. Once they are ready, she connects them with students from other classes and often with ELLs from other states or countries.[1]

Soh Bee-Lay and Soon Yee-Ping (1991) describe a networking exchange between ESL and EFL students in Singapore and Quebec. Using CALL, e-mail, telephones, and fax machines, the students exchanged opinions on self-selected topics. They shared cultural stories and other pieces of literature and created an abundance of written work related to what they were reading. The two educators concluded that the exchanges were highly motivating and helped the students gain insights into a world vastly different from their own.

Nancy Sullivan (1993), too, reports positive results from electronic conversations that took place during her two-year experience working in the computer-assisted writing laboratory at the University of Texas at Austin. She concluded that students (both native and nonnative speakers of English) seemed less threatened in this situation than they would have been had they been expected to speak in front of peers and teachers. Their e-mail exchanges allowed them to initiate and/or extend their discussions about topics studied in the classroom or their assigned work. Students often collaborated while responding to and critiquing each other's papers and they negotiated meaning during problem-solving activities.

---

[1] She accesses a website that provides partner teachers from a variety of places here and abroad.

VIDEOS

Videos are another potentially valuable tool for language acquisition. Gersten and Tlustý (1998) explored whether video exchanges between peers (grades 8–12) learning English as a Foreign Language (EFL) in different countries would have a positive affect on their students' performance and participation. Their study looked at a cultural video exchange project between volunteer students from Prague and their counterparts in Regensburg, Germany. Members of the two groups communicated through letters written in English and then met to exchange the videos each had made. The students did the research, wrote the scripts, made revisions, rehearsed and acted out various scenes, interviewed people, and produced and evaluated their videos. For example, the Czech students focused their video on the city of Prague. They included information about the history of the city; its historical monuments; its famous artists, politicians, musicians, and writers; its architecture; and its food. Taping locations included a school, Saint Vitus Cathedral, the National Theatre, Prague Castle, and local restaurants. The video also featured excerpts from a well-known Czech play and interviews with a range of people including English-speaking tourists and the director of the National Theatre. Finally, the students performed historical reenactments and told stories.

Interviews with students afterwards revealed that they had all found the experience helpful in developing English proficiency and in using English to communicate in an international setting. The authors noted that the success seemed due to the students' motivation to communicate in English for authentic purposes, the pride they took in sharing aspects of their culture with a real audience, and their treatment of video as an effective tool for communication and self-evaluation.

Commercially produced videos can also be used in less wide-ranging ways as the focus of classroom lessons. Lessons can be built around all kinds of available videos, including music videos, documentaries, sports highlights, television talk shows, commercials, soap operas, and situation comedies (see in particular Stempleski and Tomlin, 1990). Simple question and answer sessions, discussions, or writing assignments based on what students have seen can comprise the follow-up.

Interactive video, which combines the benefits of both video and computer, can also serve as an excellent tool for developing communicative skills in a language. Requirements for using interactive video are more technologically complex—a videodisc player, a computer with monitor and keyboard, and an interface to connect the videodisc player to the computer. However, its benefits can be great. Chief among these is the ability to show real people in compelling scenarios which allow students to contribute input. For example, a video may show a mom and dad arguing about whether their teenaged daughter should be allowed to take a weekend trip with several friends, including her boyfriend. After we hear the parents' opinions, the characters turn to the camera and ask for help in resolving their dispute. Several pieces of advice flash on the monitor, and students are asked to read these and then press buttons representing their choices. After one character comments on the advice that has been given, the scenario continues; in some interactive videos, the continuation is based on student input. Finally, the video characters seek help from an "expert" who is part of the computer program.

Interactive video can also be used to teach the listening skills necessary for academic success. For example, while watching a videodisc lecture on some topic of interest, students are asked to press keys whenever they hear what appears to be a main idea. At the end of the lecture, all the main ideas are printed on the monitor, and students are asked to type questions on the keyboard referring to these ideas. After each question is formed, the speaker on the video answers it. An inherent problem with this kind of program, of course, is that students may ask questions for which the speaker has no answers.

Interactive video dictionaries are also available. A student types a word, the computer provides definitions and checks for spelling (it presents the student with the correct spelling if it finds an error). A speaker on the videodisc then pronounces the word and demonstrates its use in context. The word may also be printed on the screen in a sample sentence.

Many publishers produce videos to accompany their classroom materials. These range from videos produced for the publisher and keyed directly to multi-level programs to videos licensed from network television. As with software, instructors should evaluate any video materials before using them in the classroom, looking primarily at whether they serve a useful pedagogical purpose for the intended audience.

FILM

Film, like literature (see Chapter 13), can form the center of a lesson for second language learners, providing experience with authentic listening and practice in speaking and writing.

A film derived from a novel might be used in conjunction with studying that novel. For example, Hess and Jasper (1995) suggest films based on classics in American and British literature including: Pearl Buck's *The Good Earth*; Charles Dickens's *David Copperfield* and *Great Expectations*; and Daphne Du Maurier's *Rebecca*, as well as more recent novels like Harper Lee's *To Kill a Mockingbird*, Avery Corman's *Kramer vs. Kramer*, and Anne Tyler's *The Accidental Tourist*.

Hess and Jasper described their approach, using scenes from *Great Expectations* to complement reading assignments from the novel. The process included these steps:

- Students viewed the film segments with the sound off.
- In small groups, they wrote what they thought was being said.
- Students were assigned a character and asked to write down that character's words as they watched the same scenes again, this time with the sound on. The scenes were played repeatedly, so students could check for accuracy.
- Students regrouped and recreated the dialogue, using their transcriptions.
- Students approximated the dialogue without their transcriptions.
- Finally, students watched the scenes once more and then moved on to the next reading assignment.

Interspersed with reading, viewing, and recreating dialogue were discussions about cultural and personal issues, including the students' own expectations and disappointments and other relevant topics. A culminating activity was to compare the book and the film after viewing the film in its entirety.

SUMMARY

The Episode Hypothesis argues that text that is motivated and structured episodically will be more easily incorporated into our linguistic repertoire than other kinds of text. Many second language textbooks, however, are written mainly to teach specific grammar points, competencies, or structures and give little thought to what constitutes meaningful prose. This is not to say that grammar- or competency-based books should never be used. There is a place for such books, particularly as supplements. But textbooks that consider emotions as well as intellect are more likely to help students acquire language effectively.

The selection and use of textbooks, computer programs, videos, and films are not tasks that should be treated lightly. In order for these tools to be maximally useful, their substance and the activities they promote must reflect the basic philosophy of the teacher and the goals of the students. If the students' main goals are to communicate effectively and to learn subject matter in the target language, then tools should be chosen that are consistent with those objectives. This means that the materials should allow for active participation on the part of the learner and that the tasks should involve the use of natural language in meaningful contexts.

READINGS, REFLECTION, AND DISCUSSION

Suggested Readings and Reference Materials

Chapelle, C. (2001). *Computer applications in second language acquisition*. New York: Cambridge University Press. Explores the uses of computers in language teaching, assessment, and research and gives numerous examples of computer applications.

Egbert, J. and Hanson-Smith, E. (1999). *CALL Environments*. Alexandria, VA: TESOL. This very practical book for teachers of ESL discusses the critical issues surrounding the use of CALL within diverse environments and with a wide variety of language learners.

Hanson-Smith, E. (2000). *Technology-enhanced learning environments*. Alexandria, VA: TESOL. The case studies from around the world included in this volume make clear how technology has been used to teach language in multiple settings: traditional classrooms, learning centers, laboratories, and other learning environments.

Stempleski, S., and Tomalin, B. (1990). *Video in action: Recipes for using video in language teaching*. New York: Prentice Hall Regents. This book, the winner of the Duke of Edinburgh English Language Competition for 1990, presents how and when to use video effectively in language teaching.

Warschauer, M., Shetzer, H., and Meloni, C. (2000). *Internet for English Teaching*. Alexandria, VA: TESOL. Offers an overview of research, theory, and practice for incorporating computer-mediated teaching. Contains information about Internet use for online language learning, finding teacher resources, managing multimedia projects, and so forth. Teachers who are in need of an introduction to technology use in the classroom, as well as those already experienced with its use will find this book of benefit.

Windeatt, S., Hardisty, D., and Eastment, D. (2000) *The Internet*. New York: Oxford University Press. Includes classroom activities for exploring the World Wide Web, evaluating what one finds there, developing materials for language teaching, and using the Internet for communication.

Questions and Projects for Reflection and Discussion

1. Discuss how the following considerations might affect the teacher's choice of textbooks and other materials.
   a. culture in which the materials are to be used
   b. size of the class
   c. experience of the teacher in teaching a second or foreign language
   d. proficiency level of the teacher in the target language

2. How might you incorporate the types of materials listed below into the classroom? Several suggestions for the use of most of them have been mentioned throughout this book. You can probably think of many additional means for incorporation. Give specific examples.
   a. teacher-made materials
   b. student-made materials
   c. magazines and newspapers
   d. catalogs
   e. pictures and photographs
   f. television shows on video
   g. computers/a computer laboratory

3. With a small group of peers, set up important criteria for evaluating textbooks in terms of their episodic organization where applicable and other

aspects you feel are important in making your decisions. You may want to draw criteria from the sample form and suggestions presented earlier for software program evaluation.

Example:

	(check one)		
	Yes or **No**		**Comment**
Episodic Organization			
Are the characters believable?	_____	_____	
Is the dialogue logical?	_____	_____	
Is foreshadowing present?	_____	_____	
Etc.	_____	_____	
Other Important Aspects			
Are the materials appropriate to age level?	_____	_____	
Are the materials appropriate to proficiency level?	_____	_____	
Are key concepts recycled?	_____	_____	
Etc.	_____	_____	

You might want to refine the evaluation by using such categories as "usually," "sometimes," "never," and so on, and by giving numerical values to each.

Once you have your evaluation instrument completed, locate at least three to five second language or foreign language textbooks and/or supplementary materials. Analyze them using appropriate items from criteria you and your group set up. Which of these materials would you select for use in a hypothetical or real teaching situation (see footnote on page 333)? Justify your choices.

4. How might a knowledge of the Episode Hypothesis help you, other than in choosing texts and other reading materials? Consider the applicability of such knowledge to other situations used to create an acquisition-rich environment for your students. Write about the possibilities in your journal.

5. If you have access to computer software, select four programs for preview (they need not have been created specifically for language teaching). Which of the four would you select to use with your students? Justify your choices and explain how each might fit into your program, hypothetical or real.

CHAPTER 17

Teaching Language Through the Content Areas: Program Designs and Political Implications

> *. . . educators must understand the complex variables influencing the second language process and provide a sociocultural context that is supportive while academically and cognitively challenging.*
>
> *Virginia P. Collier, 1999*

QUESTIONS TO THINK ABOUT

1. What does it mean to "teach language through the content areas"? How important do you think it is to do so? Consider differences between second and foreign language teaching situations.

2. Have you ever studied another language or taught one through a content area? Was your experience a positive one? Explain.

3. To what extent might you want to incorporate subject-matter content into your own second or foreign language classes? How might you go about it?

4. What problems do you think language minority students might have in mainstream classes such as history or science? If you were their second language teacher, how would you help to prepare them for the transition to mainstream courses?

Doing well in academic or social settings in which students interact with and are accepted by educated people requires an ability to communicate effectively on a variety of topics. Students must eventually have command of the new language for both abstract thinking and problem solving. Whether the skills related to this kind of success are taught in self-contained classrooms in which a variety of subject areas are covered or in classrooms set up for the purpose of teaching specific subject matter, the lessons must be increasingly challenging academically and the environment must foster high self-esteem.

Two types of language proficiency are critical to the success of second language students in a school environment: academic and interpersonal. Academic language proficiency typically takes approximately five years or more to develop fully (see Cummins, 1981a, 1984, 1989; Collier, 1987; Ramirez, Yuen, and Ramey, 1991; Klesmer, 1994; Collier and Thomas, 1997). Interpersonal language, generally, is learned within two years (Cummins 1981a, 1984).

Teachers of ESL, bilingual education, and foreign languages can teach the target language through basic academic content, drawing from many of the methods and activities described in previous chapters. For example, physical approaches might be used to teach math skills ("Draw an octagon. Divide it in half with a vertical line.") or physical education directives ("Line up. Count off by fours."); communicative language to demonstrate how to prepare a specific food or blend colors for an art project; and chants to help students remember important information about history or math. As always, such activities must make greater and greater cognitive demands on the students.

Once students are ready for higher levels within the content areas, they can be introduced to more difficult concepts through concrete approaches and later through more abstract ones. For example, beginning students might watch a teacher demonstrate and explain a science experiment and then be asked to do the experiment themselves, following specific oral directions. Intermediate students might perform experiments using only written directions. And more advanced students might be required to conceptualize an experiment and write about the expected results under various conditions.

In this chapter, we will explore the various approaches that can be used to teach language through content-learning and vice versa, and the political implications of each. Most foreign language courses in the United States are, of course, taught independent of other content areas. English as a Second Language courses, on the other hand, are often taught in conjunction with one or more content-area programs: a submersion program; an immersion program consisting of sheltered content-area classes; and/or a bilingual program.

SUBMERSION

Students whose first language is different from that of the school and community are often "submerged" in content-area classes in which they are a minority among proficient speakers. In submersion classrooms, these students find themselves at a disadvantage: the input is often incomprehensible to them, and they are often treated as intellectual inferiors. The teachers generally do not understand their languages and know very little about their cultures. A first language may be regarded as a hindrance (subtractive)[1] to a mastery of the second. The students may or may not have the opportunity to be tutored individually. Sometimes the students who have the option of being tutored are placed in what are known as "pull-out" programs[2] that frequently put them at an even greater disadvantage, since they may miss concepts introduced in the general classroom while they are receiving pull-out instruction. Submersion programs can be dangerous, especially for young children, whose overall cognitive development may suffer as a result.

Mainstreaming

English Language Learners in sheltered classes (see page 357) are gradually transitioned into mainstream content-area classes once they become more socially and academically proficient in the target language. Before students are mainstreamed, they are generally evaluated by both the ESL teacher and the content-area teacher whose class they will enter to make sure they have been introduced to the basic concepts involved and have the necessary skills for academic work. These skills include note-taking and study skills, basic research skills including summarizing and paraphrasing, test-taking skills including writing answers in paragraph form, and so on. Students may first be placed in mainstream classes such as physical education, art, music, and math, and later in the more language-dependent natural and social sciences. The subject matter for beginners during initial transitioning is generally cognitively undemanding, the materials are context-embedded, the content-area teacher is aware of the students' need for comprehensible input, and the atmosphere is one of acceptance rather than rejection.

Sometimes a mainstream class is paired with an *adjunct* course for non-English speakers (see especially Saint Michael's College International Center described on pages 378–385). In an adjunct course, students receive assistance with language and content learning from a language teacher who works in conjunction with the mainstream course instructor. Adjunct courses have been attempted mainly at the college/university levels, probably because schedules are generally more flexible there than they are in secondary schools.

---

[1] Lambert (1974) identified two treatments of primary languages within a second language environment: subtractive and additive. A language is said to be *subtractive* when it is considered detrimental to the learning of the second language and *additive* when it is thought a beneficial adjunct.

[2] A pull-out program is one in which the students are taken out of their regular classes for certain portions of the day in order to receive special help with the target language.

IMMERSION

All immersion programs have at least one thing in common: the students are *at similar levels of proficiency* in their new language, meaning that they generally receive input specially tailored to their needs. There are two kinds of immersion programs: foreign language programs and second language programs (see also definitions on pages 279–299).

Foreign Language Immersion

In foreign language immersion programs, most (if not all) of the students are from the language majority population and are part of the dominant cultural group. They are placed in content-area classes in which a foreign language is the medium for communication and instruction. Usually the first language is added gradually later on for some of the subject-area content. The Thunder Bay French immersion program described on pages 429–433, in which all the students are from English-speaking homes, is a typical example. In foreign language immersion programs, the new language is additive and generally has the support of the parents and the community. Usually the parents have requested the program for their children and were often instrumental in setting up the program. The teacher is, in most cases, familiar with the students' first language and knows (and is often part of) their culture.

     All of these factors contribute to the high student self-esteem often found in such programs. These factors also clearly differentiate foreign language immersion programs from submersion programs, in which children are typically at a disadvantage as the content becomes more demanding cognitively and linguistically. Affective advantages, coupled with the cognitive benefit of modified input, probably account for the significant difference in the results of both programs. Children thrive in foreign language immersion programs (see studies in Chapter 2); in submersion programs they usually do not (see especially Cummins, 1981b).

     Heritage Learners are often found in foreign language immersion programs (see especially the Concordia Language Villages program description, pages 421–428). Heritage language learners in the villages are often third- or fourth-generation immigrant students who missed out on learning the language of their ancestors. They take great pride in their cultural backgrounds and are usually supported by their parents in the endeavor to revive both language and culture. In recent years, we have seen whole groups of language learners whose members are indigenous to the United States attempt to revive their language and culture by becoming Heritage Learners in immersion programs. For example, elders of the Ojibwe tribe, near Mille Lacs, Minnesota were concerned when they realized that younger members of the community were unable to participate in traditional ceremonies because they didn't know the language. A learning center was established in Rutledge, Minnesota, to revitalize the dying language and culture. Larry Smallwood, a founder of the center, lamented, "Our parents and grandparents went to boarding school, and the language was beaten out of them.

Those that didn't lose it didn't teach it to their children because they didn't want their children to face the same thing they did" (from the *Minneapolis Star Tribune*, July 19, 2000, p. B1). And so the descendants of the Ojibwe today must learn their language in the same way one might learn a "foreign" tongue—a sad commentary on the state of minority languages in our country!

Second Language Immersion

Second language immersion is found in ESL, sheltered content, and adjunct classes. In these classes, the input is still adjusted to the students' needs, but their first languages and cultures are often very different (unlike foreign language immersion). The students are considered part of the nondominant groups in the community, even though their numbers may be greater than those of the dominant group. Their teacher may or may not be familiar with their first language and culture. However, the teacher is usually prepared in current language and content teaching methodology and often has some knowledge of the various language and cultural backgrounds of the students.

BILINGUAL EDUCATION IN THE UNITED STATES

Bilingual education involves teaching students in some combination of their first and second languages. Its goals usually include being able to function effectively in the fundamental skill areas: speaking, listening, reading, writing. There are basically three types of bilingual education programs:

- In *transitional* programs, language minority students learn most of the subject matter in L1 until they are ready to be gradually transitioned to all-English classes, usually after considerable time spent in the ESL component of the program.
- In *maintenance* programs, students continue throughout much of their schooling to learn a portion of the subject matter in their L1 in order to continue improving their skills while they are developing their academic proficiency in English.
- In *enrichment programs*,[3] a portion of the subject matter is taught in L2 primarily to broaden cultural horizons or in anticipation of some future move or visit to another culture, rather than for the purpose of immediate survival. A single program may be enrichment for some and maintenance for others (see two-way bilingual education on page 359).

---

[3] Collier and Thomas (1999) use the term "enrichment program" to mean something entirely different; they use the term to refer to programs which teach cognitively challenging and complex content as opposed to remedial programs which teach watered-down content. Bilingual programs (especially maintenance ones) are enrichment programs according to their definition because they are able to teach grade-level content in the first language, keeping students from falling behind while they are learning the second language.

Bilingual programs can generally be characterized as either one-way or two-way. In both, students receive the mainstream curriculum through some combination of their first and second languages and are able to be active participants in their learning early on through their first language.

One-way Bilingual Education

In one-way programs, language minority students begin their education in the new culture by learning the core academic content in their first language. They avoid missing out on important concept formation while they are trying to master their new language, and what they have learned in their first language is easily transferred to their second (Collier, 1995). Some one-way programs are maintenance or *late exit* programs in which students continue learning at least a portion of the content in their first language, allowing them to maintain and develop their skills in the primary language. Unfortunately, most one-way bilingual programs in the United States today are transitional or *early-exit* programs. In other words, once students have acquired a sufficient amount of the target language to survive (often in social situations only), the bilingual component of their schooling is dropped. This is troublesome for two reasons:

- Students are often not ready for academic mainstreaming, since their academic skills are not yet highly developed in the target language.
- They will not be able to function with maximal effectiveness in our multicultural society, a society that *needs* people who are highly literate in more than one language.

If all of these programs were maintenance (as opposed to transitional), we as a nation would have a tremendous language resource on which to draw. Ironically, we spend much time and energy improving and expanding our enrichment foreign language programs so that our citizens will be "cultured," and yet we almost daily discourage the natural resource that many of our students already possess but need to develop—their first languages.

According to Cummins, an important goal of any second language program should be to develop proficient bilinguals (see the Threshold Hypothesis[4]). He reports:

---

[4] The Threshold Hypothesis argues that being proficient in one language facilitates being proficient in another. There are really two thresholds involved: (1) a higher threshold dividing the *proficient bilingual* (one who has obtained high levels of proficiency in both languages) from the *partial bilingual* (one who is proficient in one of the languages), and (2) the lower threshold dividing the partial bilingual from the *limited bilingual* (one who has only low-level skills in both languages).

> . . . studies were carried out with language minority children whose L1 was gradually being replaced by a more dominant and prestigious L2. Under these conditions, these children developed relatively low levels of academic proficiency in both languages. In contrast, the majority of studies that have reported cognitive advantages associated with bilingualism have involved students whose L1 proficiency has continued to develop while L2 is being acquired. Consequently, these students have been characterized by relatively high levels of proficiency in both languages (1981b, p. 38).

Cummins further states that a major success of bilingual programs in elementary schools in particular is that they encourage students to take pride in their native languages and cultures, a necessity if the students are to have positive attitudes not only toward themselves but toward the target language and the people who speak it.

One of the problems facing maintenance bilingual education associated with ESL programs is that only one or two students may speak any given language within a particular school. Most school districts require a minimum number of students in order to make the hiring of a bilingual teacher feasible. A second problem is finding qualified teachers, especially in languages for which there are fewer speakers. Often first language speakers can be hired as classroom tutors, but unfortunately these people often cannot do much more than aid in transitional bilingual situations. For some teachers the only option is to encourage students to maintain their first languages simply by not discouraging their use, and by emphasizing the advantages and opportunities for those who become proficient bilinguals.

Some one-way bilingual programs are also designed for majority language students who want to be immersed in a foreign language within their own communities (see the previous discussion of Foreign Language Immersion in this chapter).

Two-way or Dual Bilingual Programs

Two-way or dual bilingual programs are becoming popular in the United States today among students, their parents, and whole communities. Former Education Secretary Richard Riley reported in March 2000, that dual-immersion programs now number 260, and he would like to see that number grow to 1,000 or more in the future.[5] In most cases, these programs are voluntary and require parental permission. The students who enroll include both language minority students and language majority students who speak the dominant language of the mainstream culture. The language minority students learn the language of the mainstream culture, and the language majority students learn the primary

---

[5] Reported in the *TESOL Federal Update*, 2000, p. 1. Alexandria, VA.

language of the newcomers. The two groups serve as linguistic models for each other in their respective languages, and students are generally integrated for all of the school day, except when they are working on specific language instruction in their new languages. Exceptions to this integration are "developmental" programs, where basic core content is first taught in the primary language for both groups. In such programs, students do not become fully integrated for core curriculum until later. However, they are integrated for art, music, physical education, and other subjects in which the work is less cognitively demanding—see especially the Valley Center program mentioned below and described on pages 446–454.

Goals of dual bilingual programs include learning the mainstream subject matter and becoming proficient in both languages. These programs usually last at least through elementary school and sometimes follow students into the middle school and beyond. The Valley Center program, for example, is contemplating expanding its presence into the high school as it moves with its students into the upper grades.

A two-way bilingual education program comprising Spanish and English can be found in the San Diego City Schools. Students include Spanish-speaking children who begin their schooling in Spanish and who will eventually learn English, and English-speaking children who also begin their schooling in Spanish (similar to a foreign language immersion program) and who will eventually develop their English skills. Subject matter content is taught only in Spanish in grades 1–3; in grades 4–6, half of the content is taught in Spanish and the other half in English. (English reading is begun in the second grade, however.)

Spanish-speaking children are in the majority in the San Diego program, and test results so far have focused mainly on them. Herbert (1987), for example, compared students who had been in the two-way bilingual program with students who had received ESL without bilingual education. Controlling for ethnicity, gender, socioeconomic status, grade level, and the differences in pretest scores, Herbert found that students in the two-way bilingual program did significantly better at all levels tested, grades 4–6, on the CTBS math and reading tests. Moreover, they were reclassified one year earlier on the average than their ESL-only counterparts.

An important factor to consider here is not only that the Spanish-speaking children were able to begin with the language with which they were most comfortable (Spanish), but that they served as Spanish "models" for the English-speaking students, thereby helping to raise their own self-esteem. Self-esteem is a critical factor and must not be overlooked when we examine program effectiveness (see Chapter 6).

A similar advantage was found in the Spanish/English dual language in Valley Center, California, and the Cantonese/English dual language program in lower Manhattan (see their descriptions in Chapter 20). The Valley Center program is considered *developmental* in that the students are introduced to their new language (either Spanish or English) as they become ready for it; the Manhattan program, in contrast, is considered *immersion* in that *all* the children are introduced to Cantonese right from the first day, whether they are English speakers or Cantonese speakers.

Collier and Thomas (1999) also stress the development of self-esteem and other sociocultural and affective processes such as the establishment of positive relationships and anxiety reduction. According to the researchers, an affirming sociocultural environment, which is most likely to occur in two-way programs, is necessary to three important interdependent processes:

- language development
- academic development
- cognitive development

If any one of these processes is arrested for any reason, the other two will be arrested as well. For example, if cognitive development is interrupted (which is what generally happens in monolingual programs), language development and academic development will be simultaneously—and negatively—affected.

In two-way immersion bilingual education, the language majority students experience many of the same frustrations as the language minority students in the program. They are thrown into a language in which they cannot communicate, their linguistic models come from unfamiliar backgrounds, and they aren't quite sure how to deal with the resulting problems. Because of their uncertainty and their strong desire to learn, they begin to understand and accommodate to their new friends and the new language. Accommodation is no longer a one-way street, with language minority students doing all the adjusting (see also Nieto, 1999, 2000). As a result, bonds form between the two groups, and the language majority students begin to affirm and respect their language learning counterparts.

Bilingual Education: What Does the Research Tell Us?

Perhaps the most extensive research to date on bilingual education programs in the United States was done by Virginia Collier and Wayne Thomas, researchers at George Mason University (1997, 1999; Collier, 1987, 1995; Thomas and Collier, 1996, 1998). A recent analysis included over one million language minority student records collected from twenty-three school districts in fifteen states beginning in 1982. They followed these students for as long as the students remained in these school districts, looking at their academic achievement over time as measured by school district tests given at each grade level in math, science social studies, reading, and writing. Collier and Thomas

(1999) reported that when comparing various programs intended for language minority students, including ESL and bilingual education, that two-way bilingual education was most effective. The average scores of English Language Learners (ELLs) at the end of two-way programs were *above* the 50th national percentile. The next most effective programs for language minority students were one-way, late-exit programs, in which average scores for students at the end of their schooling was *at* the 50th national percentile. Students in both one-way and two-way programs took a minimum of five to six years to reach the 50th percentile, thus closing the achievement gap in their second language—in other words, they made fifteen months' worth of progress in every ten months of school.

Less effective were transitional one-way programs using current instructional approaches (average final scores for these were at the 32nd national percentile); transitional one-way programs using traditional instructional approaches (average final scores at the 24th national percentile); ESL content-based programs (average final scores at the 22nd national percentile); and finally ESL pull-out programs (average final scores at the 11th national percentile). Interestingly, a prior analysis of 42,000 student samples (Thomas and Collier, 1996) found little difference between programs in the very early grades. It wasn't until the content became more demanding in the later grades that differences among programs became significant. However, students overall did best in programs that did *not* focus on discrete points of language taught in a highly structured, sequenced curriculum in which the learner passively received knowledge. Rather, they did best in programs in which they were active learners.

In their earlier analysis (Thomas and Collier, 1996, 1998), the researchers' data and observations supported the conclusions summarized below:

Language minority students in bilingual programs appear to do best overall when

- The teaching staff is of high-quality.
- Challenging academic instruction is given in the first language for as long a time period as possible (at least six years), while the students are also receiving progressively more of the same kind of instruction in the second language. (Collier and Thomas call this kind of instruction in both languages "enriched," as opposed to remedial, meaning it builds on what the students already know and speeds up not only academic development, but cognitive and linguistic development as well.)
- Current interactive approaches are used in which students are actively involved in a discovery process and in cognitively complex learning (e.g., whole language, acquisition through the academic content areas, cooperative learning, and problem solving).

- The two languages are separated for instruction by subject area or theme, by regular time slots, and/or by teacher (that is, one teacher represents one language; a different teacher represents the other).
- The non-English language is used for at least 50 percent of the time spent on instruction and as much as 90 percent in the early grades.
- Students are integrated with English speakers in the two-way programs in a balanced ratio of 50:50 or 60:40, but not below 70:30.
- The school environment is supportive and affirming.
- Administrators within the school wholeheartedly back the program.
- The two languages are given equal status, thus creating self-confidence among *all* students.
- Close collaboration is established between parents and the school.
- The program is thought to be a gifted and talented program for *all* students.

In the United States, students who first enter at the secondary levels generally go into ESL and sheltered programs, since bilingual education is typically not an option for them. Although they would also benefit from participating in a bilingual program, lack of access to one may not be quite as harmful to them as it is to younger learners because they often have highly developed academic skills in their first languages to begin with. According to Collier and Thomas, adolescents seem to do best when English is taught through academic content, when thinking and problem-solving strategies are focused upon, when attention is paid to the students' prior knowledge, when the first language and culture are respected, and when multiple measures are used in ongoing assessment.

Collier (1995) and Collier and Thomas (1999) go further to conclude that the evidence overwhelmingly indicates that *proficient bilinguals develop cognitive advantages over, and generally outperform, monolinguals on school tests.* This may be one reason that two-way bilingualism, in particular, is sought after by many parents today for their children. For language majority students participating in two-way bilingual education, research indicates that they benefit from becoming proficient in two languages and are not at a disadvantage academically by learning content through another language (Harley, Allen, Cummins, and Swain, 1990; Genesee, 1987). Lambert and Cazabon (1994) found high levels of self-esteem and academic/personal satisfaction in both language majority and minority students in the two-way programs (in Christian, 1996).

Politics and Bilingual Education in the United States

Despite its advantages for students belonging to both the language minority and the language majority (in the case of dual language programs), bilingual education in the United States has become a political football ever since the

Bilingual Education Act was passed by Congress in 1968. But its challengers' voices reached a crescendo in the mid-1990s with a group called U.S. English who made it their mission to establish English as the "official" language of the U.S. government, arguing that the citizens' common bond as a people would be preserved. Fortunately, they did not succeed. What they failed to realize was that by attempting to make English official, they risked bringing about the opposite—increased divisiveness, rather than unity. Quebec provides an example of what can happen when the speakers of any language group try to dominate the speakers of another. Another example is Slovakia (see King, 1997), where more than 10 percent of the population is ethnic Hungarian, but the country nevertheless made Slovak its official language, requiring that it be spoken in state hospitals to patients who did not understand it and by teachers in staff meetings at Hungarian language schools. Needless to say, this action drove a further wedge between two peoples who were finally beginning to heal the wounds of the past. King points to more fortunate countries in which two or more languages co-exist in relative harmony: Finland (with its Swedish minority), Switzerland (where German, French, Italian, and Romansh are all considered "national" languages), India (which officially recognizes nineteen languages, English among them), and so forth. Most countries around the world consider other languages additive rather than subtractive; such countries more often than not encourage bilingual education and treasure its results.

In the United States, however, the status of minority languages is another story. Some worry that immigrants will be less motivated to learn English if we "coddle" them too much with education in their own languages, multilingual drivers' tests, or other measures that might aid them before they can fully understand the main language of the country. This fear seems to me unwarranted. In my own experience with immigrants over the years, I have yet to meet one immigrant who has not wanted to learn English. In Los Angeles alone, thousands of immigrants are turned away from English classes each year because there simply are not enough classes to go around. Most immigrants realize the importance of learning English and are desperately trying to do just that.

Perhaps the worst threat to bilingual education (as well as to ESL) began with the English-only movement and the Unz initiative known as California Proposition 227, approved by the voters of that state in 1998. Proposition 227 required that bilingual education be done away with altogether, and that "structured English immersion" (i.e., a crash course in ESL) be limited to one year. Such a limitation meant that students were often thrown into mainstream classes where their teachers did not have the time nor the expertise to give them appropriate English language instruction or the support they still needed. The initiative was intended to allow for few exceptions, regardless of parental preferences or students' individual needs or aspirations. Unfortunately, attempts to consider similar (but even more strident) measures have spread to other states where their advocates have achieved or are attempting to achieve more successes.

If we legally inhibit bilingual education, we are in essence infringing on the rights of parents and local communities to choose what they think is best for their children. Much of the rationale of the English-only movement has been based on an *assimilationist* viewpoint (as opposed to a *pluralistic* viewpoint). For example, in her book entitled *Forked Tongue*, Porter (1990) argues that it is not appropriate for public schools to use resources to promote bilingualism because it is an unrealistic goal. Instead, she argues that our goal should be to make all children part of the mainstream society. While it is true that children need to be able to function successfully in the mainstream society, there is no research to suggest that they need to do it at the expense of their own languages and cultures. Being proficient in two or more languages is now and always will be a tremendous advantage to successful members of our society and responsible citizens of our world. Bilingualism *is* an appropriate goal not only for our schools, but for our country as a whole. In fact, this goal becomes more and more critical as our nation becomes increasingly more diverse.

PROGRAM POSSIBILITIES FOR ENGLISH LANGUAGE LEARNERS

What comprises an effective program design for ELLs? Certainly a program to consider seriously is one that combines ESL with locally-developed versions of mainstreaming, sheltered classes, and, if possible, maintenance bilingual education. Table 17.1, adapted from Krashen (1984), presents a program that might be modified to fit any type of bilingual education. The program presented here assumes the goal of teaching *all academic subject matter in English*. In many bilingual programs, of course, the goal is to teach the *academic subject matter in two languages* throughout. These programs, based on the research findings summarized above, are the most effective of all. However, I offer the following adaptation for your critical review, mainly because for most schools, maintenance (or even transitional) bilingual education is simply not currently a reality.

TABLE 17.1. PROGRAM FOR ENGLISH LANGUAGE LEARNERS (ELLs)

Level	Mainstream	Sheltered	First Language
beginning	art, music, physical education	ESL	all core subjects
intermediate	art, music, physical education	ESL, math	social and natural sciences
advanced	art, music, physical education, math	ESL, social and natural sciences	enrichment
mainstream	all subjects	—	enrichment

(adapted from Krashen, 1984)

In this program, without modification, students at *beginning* levels are mainstreamed into subject areas in which the concepts are generally concrete and less demanding cognitively. For some students (especially those in high school), home economics and industrial arts might be added as additional mainstream electives. Students study all core subjects in their first language. During *intermediate* levels, the same students might add typing to their mainstream course selections and sheltered mathematics, but the remainder of the core subjects are still taught in the first language. At *advanced* levels, students are mainstreamed in most subjects except the social and natural sciences, which are taught in sheltered environments. The first language is used mainly for enrichment, as Krashen originally suggested.[6] The amount of time spent in ESL at each level depends on the particular needs of each student. If teaching core subjects in the first language is not possible through the intermediate levels, then these subjects are taught in the second language within sheltered classes beginning at intermediate levels. However, Krashen, who himself is a strong proponent of bilingual education, would probably agree that the program could be improved substantially if students were able to continue using the first language for at least half of their core subjects throughout.

What Can a Teacher Do?

Teachers of mainstream, sheltered, and adjunct classes in the various content areas can do much to lower the cognitive and affective burdens of the students, particularly if maintenance bilingual education is not in place or fully developed. They can modify their teaching to meet three basic objectives:

- to integrate the student (in the case of mainstream classes)
- to communicate effectively with the student
- to teach language and the subject matter in a manner conducive to acquisition

Below are some suggestions to help content-area teachers meet these goals. Although the majority of ideas can be adapted to almost any situation, a few may not be relevant for your classroom. Their relevance will usually depend on the age levels, proficiency levels, and cognitive development of the students with whom they are to be used.

For Mainstream Teachers

1. *Provide a warm environment in which help is readily available to the student.* One way to do this is to set up a "buddy" system in which proficient

---

[6] The term "enrichment" here may in reality result in a sort of token treatment of L1. The importance given to it will depend upon those operating the program. It is hoped that L1 will be used for academic as well as social communication in situations that really matter. Program directors might want to consider using L1 for a portion of the subject matter teaching provided that adequate teaching staff and materials are available.

speakers of English are paired with ELLs. Other useful management tools include peer teaching and cooperative learning (see Chapter 15). Individual instruction and group work can increase the chances that the student will receive the necessary help.

2. *If possible, use a "satisfactory/unsatisfactory" grade option until the ELL is able to compete successfully with proficient speakers.* Students may be ready sooner than expected, since many of them adapt very rapidly. It is important to remember that often the students, particularly those who are older, will already have a high level of academic understanding in the first language and may even surpass many monolingual English speakers once they have learned the new language.

3. *Record your lectures or talks on a cassette.* Students need to be able to listen to them as many times as necessary for understanding.

4. *Ask some of your proficient English-speaking students to simplify the text-book by rewriting the chapters.* The job can be made as easy as possible by giving each proficient speaker just a few pages to simplify. The simplified materials not only aid ELLs but other students who may find the regular text too difficult. The students who do the rewriting benefit also in that the task serves as a review for them.

5. *Choose proficient English-speaking students who take effective, comprehensible notes to make copies of them for ELLs.* By this means, the latter can be provided with study aids.

For Mainstream, Sheltered-Class, and Adjunct Teachers[7]

1. *Plan lessons that are related to the students' lives, utilize a lot of visuals, and provide for "hands-on" kinds of involvement.* For example, drawing, coloring, and labeling maps in geography, and pinpointing where the students came from is far more valuable than simply listening to a talk about maps.

2. *Communicate individually with the ELLs as much as time permits.* Avoid using complicated words or complex sentences. Speak slowly but keep the volume and intonation as normal as possible. Use few idioms. Incorporate a lot of body language. These strategies will be used subconsciously, for the most part, by those whose main goal is to communicate.

3. *Avoid forcing students to speak.* Allow them to speak when they are ready, in other words, when they volunteer. Students' right to a "silent period" (see Chapter 3) needs to be respected, especially when they are being introduced to new concepts.

4. *Reassure the students that their own languages are acceptable and important.* If other students from the same language group are present, do not

---

[7] Note that many of the strategies here are applicable to second language, foreign language, and bilingual education teachers as well.

insist that they use only English in class. No matter how good the intentions of the teacher, refusing to allow students to speak in their first languages is in essence saying that their languages are not good enough. Of course, students may need to be reminded that first language should not be used to exclude others from discussion.

5. *Make most corrections indirectly by repeating what the students have said in correct form.* For example, suppose an ELL says, "My book home"; the teacher can repeat, "I see. Your book is at home." It must be remembered, that simplified (ungrammatical) forms are to be regarded as normal while the student is progressing toward more complete competence in English. When the student is ready to move to another level, the indirect correction will probably be picked up and internalized after it is heard several times in a variety of situations. You might keep track of the errors students are making and work on these errors in small groups. In written production, a few suggestions can be made for improvement as long as they are balanced with positive comments. Keep suggestions simple and offer only what you think each student can handle at his or her proficiency level.

6. *Try to answer all questions that the students ask but avoid overly detailed explanation.* Simple answers that get right to the point will be understood best. If possible, point to objects and pictures, or demonstrate actions to help get the meaning across.

7. *If you are in a situation in which lectures are appropriate, try to make them as comprehensible as possible, but avoid "talking down" to the students.* Emphasize (but do not overemphasize) key words and phrases through intonation and repetition. Write them on the board or on an overhead transparency as you are talking. Give concrete examples. Use pictures and charts, map out ideas, use gestures, acting out, simplifications, expansion of ideas, or whatever is necessary to ensure understanding. Definitions, comparisons, and the like can be incorporated in the lectures to clarify new words and concepts. For example, in a history lesson you might say, "The government's funds were depleted. It was almost out of money." Thus the phrase "funds were depleted" is made more comprehensible.

8. *Check to see that what you are saying is understood.* Frequently ask questions such as, "Do you understand?" or "Do you have any questions?" and be very aware of the feedback you are getting. Students may even nod their heads but still not understand. However, blank stares or puzzled looks are sure signs that you are not being understood. Often it is better to ask more specific questions directly related to the preceding utterance. For example, after saying, "In Arizona, rainfall is minimal during most of the year," you might check for understanding by asking, "Does it rain much in Arizona?" Asking a question such as this to confirm interpretation is yet another means by which students

can be exposed to new words and concepts without losing the meaning of the message.

9. *Use confirmation checks if you are not sure you are understanding what the student is saying.* Questions such as "Is this what you're saying?" can help to confirm that you have understood correctly.

10. *Give students sufficient wait-time before expecting answers.* Students need time to formulate their ideas. Often teachers try to avoid silence and move too quickly to another student for an answer or answer the questions themselves. If, after a sufficient time, you still do not receive a response, you might want to rephrase the questions and/or answer it yourself. The question/answer process helps students to acquire the appropriate language associated with taking turns.

11. *Develop word or concept lists including technical vocabulary with which the student will need to be familiar.* Make sure that the ESL teacher receives a copy of these lists and that they are updated frequently.

12. *Encourage students to use their bilingual dictionaries when necessary or to ask questions when they don't understand important concepts.* Help them to guess at meanings first by using the context. Assure them that they do not have to understand every word to comprehend the main idea.

13. *Reinforce key concepts over and over in a variety of situations and activities.* Hearing about the concepts once or twice is not enough. Students need to be exposed to them several times through a wide range of experiences in order for internalization to take place.

14. *Whenever possible, utilize tutors who speak the native languages of the students.* Such help is especially important to students operating at beginning to intermediate levels.

15. *Request that appropriate content-area books be ordered for the library in the students' native languages.* These can be particularly useful to students in comprehending the concepts while the second language is being mastered. They also provide the students with a means for maintaining and developing skills in the native language.

16. *Become informed as much as possible on the various cultures represented by your students.* Knowing how particular students might react to classroom events and being able to interpret nonverbal symbols could help prevent misunderstanding and confusion. Be careful, however, not to stereotype the student with cultural labels. Individuals within a given culture are often very different from one another.

17. *Acknowledge and incorporate the students' cultures whenever possible.* For instance, differing number systems can be introduced in math, customs and traditions in social science, various medicines in natural science, native dances and games in physical education, songs in music, ethnic calendars in art, haiku in literature, and so on. In addition, holidays can be celebrated, languages can be demonstrated for appreciation, and literature with translations can be shared. It is important also to include

discussions of issues related to ethnicity and race so that recognition of other cultures and a respect for diversity is not limited to celebrations and the like.

18. *Prepare the students for your lessons and reading assignments.* You might ask them what they already know about the subject. Encourage them to look for main ideas by giving them at least a partial framework or outline beforehand to get them started. Ask them to predict outcomes and then to verify their predictions.

19. *Discuss some of the new vocabulary, cultural items, and structures they might find in reading selections.* If possible, provide a glossary of new vocabulary and cultural items that they can keep beside them as they read.

20. *Increase possibilities for success.* Alternating difficult activities with easier ones allows the ELLs to experience early successes. Of course, the tasks as a whole should gradually become more academically challenging as the students become more proficient.

PROGRAM POSSIBILITIES FOR FOREIGN LANGUAGE STUDENTS

One-way and two-way bilingual education are both appropriate designs for foreign language (language majority) students. Here we cannot ignore the successes of the French immersion programs in Canada and the Spanish immersion program in Culver City, California (see Chapter 2), and the immersion program in San Diego mentioned above. Either a one-way or a two-way program can ensure that students develop skills in their first language, even though it is also being fostered at home and in the community. Through both programs, students of approximately the same proficiency and age levels are given comprehensible input in the various subject areas (see especially the descriptions of the Thunder Bay early immersion program in Chapter 19 and of the two-way programs in Chapter 20). The *language village concept* (see the description of the Concordia Language Villages in Chapter 19) is also a possibility to consider. Students may want to combine traditional foreign language study in their schools with a portion of a summer spent in a village where they are immersed in the foreign language of their choice.

Unfortunately, traditional foreign language programs in the United States involve students in the target language for only a small portion of each day. Because the classroom will probably be the only source of input for the student, unless he or she also participates in a village concept program, it is vitally important that the class time be spent mainly on meaningful communication through interaction (see the high school foreign language program in Chapter 19). However, because students may not receive a sufficient amount of input, even though the focus is on interaction, they will probably need some formal instruction in order to facilitate the acquisition process—especially those students who are cognitively able to use rule application.

SUMMARY

To succeed in producing individuals who can function with maximum effectiveness in a pluralistic society, we must be concerned with the development not only of interpersonal skills but also of academic language skills in both first and second languages. Lessons must be made progressively more challenging academically regardless of the program used to teach language and content simultaneously.

ESL through locally-developed content programs, sheltered classes, mainstream courses, adjunct classes, and maintenance bilingual programs have much to offer our language minority students. Extensive research indicates that maintenance bilingual education is particularly effective in preparing students for the mainstream and for society as a whole. Language majority students, too, seem to benefit from one-way and two-way bilingual education programs wherever they are found.

It is incumbent upon teachers of language minority students to capitalize on what they already have—their first languages and cultures. Beginning where these students are and building from there is indeed the responsibility of our schools—and one we cannot minimize except to our detriment as a nation.

READINGS, REFLECTION, AND DISCUSSION

Suggested Readings and Reference Materials

Brisk, M. and Harrington, M. (2000). *Literacy and bilingualism: A handbook for all teachers*. Mahwah, NJ: Lawrence Erlbaum. Recognizing the skills that students already have and using multiple strategies to teach them are among the suggestions offered in this book. Case studies are included to help teachers reach their own conclusions about teaching reading and writing to language minority students.

Christian, D. and Genesee, F. (2001). *Bilingual Education*. Alexandria, VA: TESOL. Described here are successful bilingual education programs currently operating in our schools. All of the courses of study included, in one way or another, offer students what they need in order to function effectively in academic environments.

Díaz-Rico, L. and Weed, K. (2002). *The Crosscultural, language, and academic development handbook* (2d ed.). Boston: Allyn and Bacon. A valuable resource for ESL and Bilingual teachers and administrators across the United States. The authors have brought together current research, history, theories, important concepts, and illustrative examples, all in an effort to enlighten those working with diverse populations.

Dicker, S. (1996). *Languages in America: A pluralist view.* Clevedon, England: Multilingual Matters. The state of minority languages in the United States is the focus of this book. Common misconceptions about learning a second language, the "melting pot" mythology, the official-English movement, and the possibilities of a pluralistic, multilingual society are among the issues discussed.

Lessow-Hurley, J. (1996). *The Foundations of Dual Language Instruction* (2d ed.). White Plains, NY: Longman. Offered as an introduction to dual language classrooms and what can occur there, the author discusses issues of great interest to educators who may be contemplating how best to serve, not only language minority students, but language majority students as well. The author includes myths rooted in politics about bilingual education and presents convincing arguments for the establishment of two-way bilingual education programs in our schools.

Perez, B., and Torres-Guzman, M. (2001). *Learning in two worlds: An integrated Spanish/ English biliteracy approach* (3d ed.). Boston: Allyn and Bacon. Ways to create an appropriate learning environment for the simultaneous development of Spanish and English literacy skills are presented here.

Tse, L. (2001). *Why don't they learn English? Separating fact from fallacy in the U.S. language debate.* New York: Teachers College Press, Columbia University. This book exposes some of the myths about immigrants, including the mistaken idea that they aren't learning English. It presents such topics as the state of English language learning, why some immigrants learn faster than others, obstacles to learning English, causes of language loss, the benefits of heritage language development, the myth of "language ghettos," and many other issues of interest to language teachers.

Questions and Projects for Reflection and Discussion

1. What might be the ideal time for introducing students to a second language? Consider submersion and immersion differences and how they might affect children in the lower grades. Discuss other factors that would be relevant.

2. Find out as much as possible about the cultures that might be represented in a hypothetical or real classroom for which you might be responsible (see footnote on page 333). What strategies can you use to make the student comfortable in your classroom? How can you assure the student through actions and words that his or her primary language and culture are respected? How important is it not to use cultural stereotyping when working with your students?

3. Plan a program in which you would incorporate one-way or two-way bilingual education. Consider these questions: For what age levels or grade levels is your program intended? How would you set it up? What would be its components; e.g., instruction in the primary language, instruction in the second language, sheltered content, mainstream content, formal language instruction, assessment, etc.? How might the various components relate to one another? You might want to include a diagram to graphically

illustrate how the students would move within your program. Share your program with a small group to get their input. You may want to make changes in it based on what you learn.

4. Choose strategies from the suggestions for mainstream, sheltered-class, and adjunct teachers in this chapter and apply them to a specific lesson you prepare for language minority students in which academic content is taught. To a group of class members, demonstrate the use of one or more of your applications. Make sure you are very clear about the kind of class it is, your objectives, and the students' age and proficiency level(s). After presenting your lesson, ask your group in what ways it was effective and how it might be improved. You may want to begin by sharing with them your own reactions to the lesson.

If you are currently teaching students, use what you have learned to try out a similar lesson with them. Make sure the lesson is relevant and appropriate to level. Afterwards, reflect on its outcome and how you felt about doing it. Did you see any problems with your lesson?

Write about your experiences teaching language through academic content and what you learned from using them in your journal.

PART **IV**

Programs in Action

In order to be maximally effective, all programs for language-minority students need to be developed locally; they need to grow out of perceived local needs and desires. However, we can learn much from programs such as those presented in this section. Reading about how other teachers have implemented and developed methods, activities, and methodologies (including decisions about content, how and when to correct, how to incorporate a silent period, and so forth) can give teachers a wealth of information from which to draw. Exploring the ways in which vital questions have been answered by others can give real insights into what might work in certain situations, with specific groups of learners.

The programs described here have been divided into ESL programs (Chapter 18), foreign language programs (Chapter 19), and two-way or dual bilingual education programs (Chapter 20). Several different levels are represented—elementary through university, including adult basic education. Some are district-wide programs, others take place in a single school or college/university setting. An immersion foreign language village; a sheltered English program; a life-skills program using community resources; a college English language program; a university support program; and two dual bilingual education programs are only a few of the many presented here.

CHAPTER **18**

ESL Programs

As I stated in Chapter 17, a program possibility to consider for English Language Learners (ELLs) (K–12) might be one in which ESL is combined with locally-developed versions of mainstreaming, sheltered classes, and maintenance bilingual education. Adjunct courses might be considered, particularly at the college and university levels. Although none of the programs described in this chapter claims to be a model as such, all have features at which we may want to take a closer look. The programs include a college English language program (Saint Michael's College in Colchester, Vermont), a university support program (California State University, Los Angeles), a life-skills adult basic education program (the North Hollywood Adult Learning Center in Hollywood, California), a secondary sheltered English program (Artesia High School in Artesia, California), a high school academic program (Thomas Jefferson High School in Los Angeles), an elementary district-wide program (Alhambra School District in Alhambra, California), and a kindergarten ESL program within a Spanish bilingual school (Loma Vista Elementary in Maywood, California).

Some of the descriptions focus on the overall design of the programs, others on specific elements within them. Although the programs have been developed for specific age groups and purposes, the basic designs and activities need not be used exclusively in these situations. An imaginative teacher can probably see many ways in which most can be adapted for local educational settings (see Chapter 15).

A COLLEGE ENGLISH LANGUAGE PROGRAM[1]

The School of International Studies (SIS), established in 1954 at Saint Michael's College in Colchester, Vermont, is one of the oldest centers of its kind in the United States, and it is one of the first (if not the first) to incorporate sheltered and adjunct courses into its curriculum. Over the years, four major programs have evolved: The Intensive English Program, the Academic English Program, the Special English Program,[2] and the Master of Arts in Teaching English as a Second Language (MATESL) Program. For the purpose of this chapter, only two of these programs will be described: the Intensive English Program (IEP), and the Academic English Program (AEP).

The Intensive English Program

The IEP, which serves approximately 40–60 students each semester, is not restricted to students with academic interests only; thus it is varied in its approach and in its offerings. The program is available to students all year round with openings every four weeks. The students generally remain in the program for anywhere from 12–16 weeks, depending upon their needs and interests.

Because the program serves a wide spectrum of students, its goals are both general and academic. It offers five levels of instruction, from low beginning to advanced. Once students have completed the Institutional TOEFL, a writing sample, and an oral diagnostic test, they are placed at the appropriate level. Students operating at the lowest levels focus on oral activities in all classes; reading and writing activities are introduced to support oral language development.

Students operating at higher levels have a somewhat different schedule. In the morning, they take what is known as "The Core" which consists of integrated instruction in reading, writing, and grammar. Following The Core, students attend either a reading lab (i.e., a reading skills development class) or a grammar lab where they receive additional individualized help with grammar. In the afternoon, an oral skills class is offered along with a listening lab Monday, Wednesday, and Friday (MWF) and a special topics class Tuesday and Thursday (TTH). The lab classes may take place in the classroom or in the Language Learning Resource Center (LLRC), which offers audio, video, and computer-assisted instruction for individualized or group work. See Figure 18.1 for a sample schedule.

---

[1] I am very grateful to Sally Cummings and Carolyn Duffy at Saint Michael's College for updating the description of their evolving program first published in the second edition of this book.

[2] This is a program that is specially designed for groups from other countries who want a short-term language and cultural program tailored to their needs (e.g., a group of Colombian high school students wanting to improve their academic English skills while learning about culture in the United States).

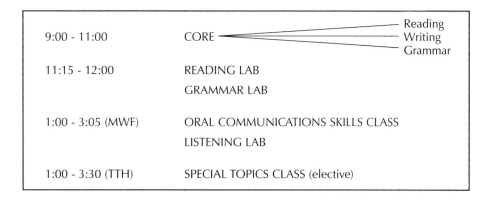

Figure 18.1. A Typical IEP Schedule

The Reading Lab

The Reading Lab provides additional work in reading skills. Typical activities include reading rate exercises; practice with previewing, skimming, and scanning texts; text organization activities; and vocabulary development exercises. Students are also introduced to extensive reading materials, and they read in specific topic areas (e.g., the history of Vermont, business issues, etc.). For novice readers, the selections are on cassettes so that students can hear them read aloud. The work is individualized and learner-centered in that students plan what they will work on with their instructor as a guide. Students also select books for independent reading (again under the guidance of the instructor) from the program's library. They respond to what they are reading either by writing in their journals or by giving oral and/or written reports.

The Core

The Core Curriculum uses an integrated skills approach. Each unit has a theme around which reading, writing, and grammar revolve. The required texts are supplemented with films, guest speakers, field trips, and authentic related readings. For example, in the reading component, a unit on education and learning styles is supplemented by an article about student test scores from *The New York Times*. A component of the Core is devoted to specific grammar instruction, with examples of the language items being studied taken from the unit's theme-based materials.

In the writing component, letters requesting information on alternative schools in the area are written. In the afternoon oral skills component, phone interviews are completed, and a field trip is taken to an alternative school. A culmination of the work accomplished up to this point is provided by viewing the classic movie *Stand and Deliver*. The in-depth discussion and writing activities that follow allow the students to synthesize what they have learned.

The Listening Lab

The Listening Lab has a dual function: (1) it supplements, extends, and enriches what students are learning in the Oral Skills class; and (2) it provides an opportunity to practice aural skills through materials that students themselves have chosen. Students can focus on activities to improve general comprehension; on specific items such as numbers, prepositions, or reduced forms; or on academic skills such as note taking.

The Oral Communication Skills Class

This class, which is usually coordinated with the Listening Lab, includes work with both academic and conversational oral and aural skills. Themes and topics introduced in the morning Core are continued in the Oral Communication Skills Class. Activities typical of this class include listening to academic lectures, conducting interviews, listening and responding to guest speakers, participating in role plays, creating videos, and having debates. A component of this class is devoted to pronunciation work and introduces students to individualized pronunciation programs such as *Pronunciation Power* for out-of-class individual practice.

The Special Topics Class

Examples of Special Topics classes from which students make choices are as follows:

1. Current Events—high-intermediate and advanced students read and discuss human interest articles from *The New York Times*.
2. Games and Puzzles—students at all levels select games consonant with their proficiency levels. Popular choices are Jeopardy and Clue. Word games of various sorts and number puzzles are among the many possibilities available.
3. English through TV—students view news items, commercials, and clips from programs such as "The People's Court." By this means, they acquire new vocabulary and improve their listening skills. In addition, the lively discussions generated by the TV shows enable students to practice communication skills.
4. Business English—high-intermediate and advanced students study aspects of business and take field trips to area businesses.

The Academic English Program

The AEP serves as a bridge to academic coursework. The AEP involves intensive English study to prepare students for the academic courses typically found at American colleges and universities. It evolved out of a need to provide a transition to the campus mainstream. Before the program was established in 1972, students often found themselves floundering for up to a year or more in courses for which they were not adequately prepared, culturally or linguistically. Drawing on Cummins's distinction between the context-rich learning environments (as represented by the ESL classes) and the context-reduced learning environments (as represented by undergraduate mainstream classes), a rationale was developed for the establishment of the AEP.

The program's courses are credit-bearing, and students who successfully complete them can transfer the credits to their undergraduate degree programs either at Saint Michael's College or at other institutions. The courses integrate both content-based and language-based teaching procedures and are taken over a two-semester time period. Students may enter the program either directly from the IEP or by applying to the program. Acceptance is based on scores from the TOEFL, and/or from the English Language proficiency tests. In addition, students take a test in academic skills prepared by the SIS. This test includes an authentic academic lecture and reading followed by a multiple-choice/essay task. Teacher recommendations and prior academic performance are part of the data used to determine appropriate placement within the program. All students entering the AEP from the IEP are first required to take a course which focuses on academic readings, lectures, and notetaking.

Within the AEP itself there are two levels: Level 1 and Level 2. Level 1, offered the first semester, is oriented to intermediate students. These students take a cooperative course, a sheltered course in college reading and writing, in addition to advanced grammar. The cooperative course has evolved over the years to include an adjunct program. It features mainstream academic content, taught by regular undergraduate faculty, and a language component, taught by a language teacher from the SIS. Level 2 is offered in the second semester and is oriented to advanced students who take sheltered courses in literature, advanced college writing and two mainstream undergraduate courses. A special undergraduate elective, Oral Presentation Skills, has been added for international students and can be taken by Level 2 students. See Figure 18.2 below.

LEVEL 1		LEVEL 2	
Cooperative Course (adjunct)	(3/4 credit)	Introduction to Literature (sheltered)	(3 credits)
Academic English for the Cooperative Course (sheltered)	(1 credit)	Advanced College Writing (sheltered)	(3 credits)
College Reading and Writing (sheltered)	(3 credits)	Oral Presentation Skills (sheltered) (elective)	(3 credits)
Advanced Grammar (sheltered)	(1 credit)	Two undergraduate courses (mainstream)	(6 credits)

Figure 18.2. AEP Courses and Credits

The Cooperative Course (Adjunct)

The first cooperative course offered at the AEP was a sheltered course in chemistry, taught by a mainstream undergraduate professor and a language instructor from the SIS. The course was sheltered in that the students taking it were all international students and the input was modified for their comprehension. Soon it became apparent that it might be better to have international students mixed with proficient English speakers to give them the skills needed to function in mainstream situations in which the input was not modified. Changes were made. The course soon lost the characteristics inherent in a sheltered program and began to resemble instead an adjunct program. The language instructor from the SIS now attends all lecture and discussion sessions, takes notes, and when appropriate records all classroom events on cassettes. The language instructor then conducts an adjunct language class in AEP for the international students in which the concepts and academic language requirements of the cooperative course are integrated. Below were the goals of the adjunct class.

The development and integration of:
    cognitive academic language proficiency
    a solid knowledge base in the content
    discussion/interaction skills
    academic grammatical competence
    library research skills
    study skills

The cooperative course became so successful that it was offered in numerous content areas: biology, human genetics, nutrition, business, economics, political science, mass communication, religious studies, and philosophy. Sally Cummings and Carolyn Duffy, both instructors in the SIS, report significant benefits of the course based on their discussions with undergraduate faculty, the international students themselves, and the proficient English speakers in the cooperative courses.

1. Benefits to members of the undergraduate faculty:
    a. The cooperative teaching approach caused many of them to reexamine their own teaching styles.
    b. They gained a better understanding of the tasks that face international students in an academic course.
    c. Their courses improved due to the new and necessary viewpoints contributed by the international students.
2. Benefits to the international students:
    a. Their opportunities for interaction with proficient English speakers increased substantially even after the course ended.
    b. They were more confident and more active class participants in all their classes once they had taken the cooperative course.

3. Benefits to proficient English speakers in the cooperative courses:
   a. They gained a new awareness of international students through the sharing of cultural values and experiences.
   b. They learned about other points of view.

College Writing (Sheltered)

The second course in Level 1 is the sheltered course in college reading and writing. This course integrates academic reading, writing, listening, and other academic skills. However, its central focus is on writing for academic purposes.

Advanced Grammar (Sheltered)

This course focuses on problem areas of grammar and allows for even more language work and additional reinforcement. When possible, coordination with the College Reading and Writing Course allows student errors that surface in writing to be addressed in greater depth.

Introduction to Literature (Sheltered)

Students in Level 2 take a sheltered course in Introduction to Literature, which includes selections from both American and international literature. They read, discuss, and write about the novels, short stories, poetry, and plays they are reading. One special feature of this course is that sometimes the plays they read are the same plays being produced by the theater department. The students are often invited to attend rehearsals.

Advanced College Writing (Sheltered)

The second course in Level 2 is a course in sheltered advanced college writing. Here students further develop their writing competence by exploring rhetorical modes of academic discourse. It is here that they become aware of their own developing styles. In addition to reading and writing essays in various rhetorical modes, they complete a library research paper. Importance is placed on peer and student/teacher conferences throughout the revision process.

Oral Presentation Skills (Sheltered)

This course was developed at the request of undergraduate faculty once they became aware that the international students needed more work in oral presentation skills. The course includes extemporaneous speaking; a focus on pronunciation problems, if needed; and a Power Point project, among other topics.

Mainstream Undergraduate Courses

In addition to the courses mentioned, Level 2 students take two mainstream courses of their choice at the undergraduate level. Before making their selections, these students are advised by the director of International Student Affairs. Once in the mainstream, they are invited to return to their teachers in the SIS, particularly to their composition teachers. They are also encouraged to use the college writing center, whose tutors are trained to assist international students. At times, they may want to seek tutorial help from MATESL practicum students.

Support Services

Student assistants organize and execute the international student orientation program and serve as hosts for international students during their first week on campus. The student assistants meet the international students at the airport, take them to a local bank, serve as English language conversation partners, and in many other ways assist them and serve as their support group.

The director of International Student Affairs conducts campus and community orientation sessions and provides ongoing support for all international students. In addition, this person serves as a liaison between the SIS and student affairs offices such as housing and health services. The Program Activities Coordinator plans evening and weekend trips off campus, and publishes a weekly bulletin highlighting upcoming events of interest, cultural information, and language-related quizzes and puzzles.

The SIS itself attempts to maximize the interaction and integration of the international students with their English-speaking peers. The Program Activities Coordinator also organizes additional activities and involves the international students in volunteer work such as serving dinner at the local soup kitchen for the homeless, planting and harvesting a garden for the food shelf, or assisting at Special Olympics events.

The SIS also sponsors weekly afternoon coffee hours during which the international students are integrated with mainstream students who are studying foreign languages. The coffee hours offer at least two benefits for all students who attend. First, the coffee hours increase the opportunities for students to interact in the languages that they are trying to learn. Second, students have a chance to increase their knowledge of the various cultures represented and to make new friends.

Yet another service provided by the SIS is the individual study components of the English Language Program, which utilize a computer-assisted instructional component for grammar, a self-study reading lab, and a writing center. The latter is staffed by students in the Master of Arts in Teaching English as a Second Language program who set up individual conferences with the international students to discuss their writing. Participation in the writing center also benefits the M.A. students themselves by giving them the opportunity to work with international students and obtain the advantages that such authentic experiences give.

Future Directions

One might wonder what the SIS would need to better provide for the needs of international students. A major strength of the SIS is its flexiblity; it can change in response to the needs of its students and in the light of current theory and research in the field of second language acquisition and second language teaching. Because of increased student interest in theme-based content as found in upper levels of the IEP, it is extending this method of organization to the lower levels as well. The SIS has found that highly motivating themes such as tourism and global issues (e.g., environment and peace education) are an excellent way to integrate language development and content. Moreover, such themes encourage analysis, synthesis, and the critical evaluation of information.

The success of its cooperative courses has spurred the AEP staff plans to develop additional courses for students at Levels 1 and 2. Experience has shown that the most successful cooperative courses are academic courses that (1) utilize the background knowledge of the international students; and (2) incorporate writing as a major learning tool. These factors will be included as criteria used for the development of new cooperative courses. In addition, the AEP will coordinate more closely between the cooperative course and the sheltered reading and writing course in order to maximize the language and content integration.

A UNIVERSITY SUPPORT PROGRAM: PROJECT LEAP[3]

Overview of the Project

Project LEAP (Learning English for Academic Purposes), a six-year project at California State University, Los Angeles, was funded by the U.S. Department of Education Fund for the Improvement of Postsecondary Education. Its main goal was to make the undergraduate general education curriculum more accessible to the university's language minority student population by enhancing the support system developed by the Educational Opportunity Program (EOP).

The students included in Project LEAP were the same students in the already existing EOP, whose program was aimed at bilingual, low income, first-generation college students, both immigrant and native English-speaking. Thirty-three percent of the students in EOP had been admitted to the university on special admission status because their SAT scores and high school grade point averages did not qualify them for regular admission.

---

[3] I want to thank Ann Snow and Janet Tricamo, co-directors of Project LEAP, for making their materials and program available to me. In addition, appreciation goes to Ann Snow who sent me an update of the program for this edition.

The EOP Study Group Program

The students in the EOP Study Group Program were advised by counselors to select certain sections among the general education courses required of all incoming freshmen. These sections were paired with one-credit study group courses[4] taught by trained peer leaders. Each study group met for three hours each week with its peer leader, who had attended the same lectures and had completed the same course readings as the students. From the peer leader, the students received assistance in comprehending course content, preparing for exams, developing individual study skills, and practicing group study techniques. Each peer leader was considered a facilitator of the many activities planned for the group.

The peer leaders (generally recommended by faculty members) were either upper division or graduate students. They had themselves received at least a "B" in the courses with which their study groups were paired. They were required to complete an initial 18-hour training program and be closely observed and evaluated weekly during their first quarter of employment as peer leaders. In addition, they attended biweekly staff training meetings.

Project LEAP

The following were the four major goals of Project LEAP:

1. to improve and expand the existing EOP study group courses
2. to provide faculty development training for the professors teaching regular general education courses
3. to effect curriculum modification to institutionalize language-sensitive instruction
4. to gain project continuity and dissemination by training future instructors and peer leaders of the study group courses

To meet these goals, Project LEAP prepared peer leaders to address more effectively the academic language (as well as content) needs of their assigned students; instructed content-area faculty teaching the general education courses in strategies for teaching academic literacy; developed a language- and content-based curriculum that could be used in all group study courses on campus, even after the project was completed; and created and/or adapted materials for the targeted general education courses.

During the project's first year, three general education courses were targeted: biology, history, and introductory psychology. Attached to each of these

---

[4] The study group courses in the already existing program and in Project LEAP were similar in concept to the adjunct courses described in Chapter 17 and to the adjunct courses associated with the Center at Saint Michael's College in Colchester, Vermont (see previous program).

courses was a LEAP study group course, led by a peer and a professional language specialist. This course aimed to integrate content instruction and related academic language skills. The time frame for the study group course was extended from three to four hours per week, and two credits were earned instead of one. During the second year of the project, political science, sociology, and speech were targeted, and during the third year, anthropology, health science, and a laboratory biology course. In the second three-year grant, faculty who taught upper division courses were trained, and courses in departments which did not previously participate such as Business and Engineering were targeted.

Academic Content/Language-Teaching Strategies

LEAP Group Study Courses

In addition to working with academic content and language, the LEAP study group courses taught students self-sufficiency and interpersonal communication skills so they might participate more actively in their assigned groups. A question-answer format was used by group leaders who initially prepared the pertinent questions (both knowledge-based and inferential) from the lectures and readings. Once students gained experience in answering questions, they brought in more and more of their own questions as they began to take on greater responsibility for the group's effectiveness. Study skills presentations were made at least three times each quarter by the peer leader or a study skills specialist from the university's Learning Resource Center. Actual course material was used in the presentations. Practice quizzes were given often by the peer leaders to emphasize the content of the readings or to help the students prepare for exams.

Below are questions from the peer leader self-evaluation form.

Discussion Leading

1. Did everyone participate in the discussion?
2. Did you give the students enough time to respond, and wait until they were through?
3. Did you give reinforcement for correct and for partially correct answers?
4. Did you make sure all the words used in the discussion were clear to the students?
5. Did you redirect the students' questions back to the group?
6. Did you test the students even though they said they understood the material?
7. Did the students do more talking than you did?
8. Was the level of difficulty of questions or materials appropriate?

Study Skills

1. Did you explain the study skill clearly?
2. Did you give the students ample opportunity to implement the skill?

3. Did you explain how they can benefit by using this skill?
4. Did you relate it to your subject area?
5. Did you explain how it can be applied to other areas?
6. Will you remember to refer to this skill again throughout the quarter?

Quizzes and Tests

1. Was it short enough for the students to complete in the allotted time period?
2. Was the level of difficulty appropriate?
3. Did you review the quiz immediately after the students completed it?
4. Did you ask the students to explain how they got their answers?
5. Do the students who missed a question know why they missed it and where to go to find the correct answer?
6. Did you make notes of the questions that were frequently missed, so that you can test the students again later?

The General Education Courses

The strategies presented below were designed by the LEAP study group leaders, language specialists, and course instructors for use in the general education courses. All the strategies were aimed to assist the students in learning the content and in improving their academic language regardless of language background. They included the following:

1. Requiring students to submit assignments in stages (especially longer papers) instead of the previous "one-shot" term paper assignment.
2. Making expectations explicit on the course syllabus.
3. Accommodating diverse learning styles in the classroom through a variety of instructional techniques (e.g., increased wait time, avoiding "spotlighting" students, group work).
4. Making explicit the critical thinking or analytical requirements of assignments by setting up guidelines.
5. Encouraging more interaction between faculty and students (e.g., making one visit to the professor during office hours a course requirement).
6. Making students more accountable for keeping up with reading assignments (e.g., pop quizzes, assigning chapter study guides).
7. Improving lectures by reviewing key concepts from the previous lecture; writing an agenda on the board for each class session; explicitly defining general academic vocabulary; referring less frequently to cultural, generational, or class-based references that might not be part of the students' background experiences.

Below are samples from some of the activities used in the general education courses. Although each sample is intended for a specific course, with some modification it could perhaps be adapted for other courses.

List-Making Exercise

RECONSTRUCTION

To answer a complicated question, you first need to compile all of the relevant information. Eventually, you will be able to answer the question: Was the Civil War and Reconstruction Era a watershed in the South? Why or why not?

1. List all of the evidence that shows change. List all of the evidence that shows continuity.

Change   Continuity

a.

b.

c.

Contributed by Carole Srole.

Sample Textbook Survey

(to accompany *Elements of Psychology,* by R. S. Feldman, 1992, McGraw-Hill)

Understanding how your textbook is organized will help familiarize you with the basic content and organization of the text. In this way, reading for academic purposes will be easier because you will understand the purpose that each of the different sections in the chapters serves.

I. *Instructions:* Working in small groups, fill in the blanks below.

Name of course: _____
Title of textbook: _____
Author(s): _____
Author(s') qualifications (e.g., university degree, professional affiliation, etc.):
_____
Copyright date: _____
Has the book been revised? _____

II. *Instructions:* Working in groups, survey your textbook and decide which of the following features it contains. Place a check in the appropriate column. Then, by analyzing each of the sections, determine the purpose that each serves. Be ready to share your ideas with the entire class.

	Yes	No
Table of contents		
Bibliography		
Name index		
Subject index		
Preface		
Glossary		
etc.		

III. *Instructions:* Using your textbook and working in small groups, answer the following questions, or locate the following information. Be prepared to explain how you found the information to the rest of the class.

1. What were the author's goals in writing the book? Where did you find the information?

   _____

   _____

2. Look at the table of contents. Is the organization of topics easy to follow?

   _____

   _____

3. On what page(s) will you find a discussion of *stereotyping*?

   _____

   _____

4. How did you find the page number?

   _____

   _____

5. How does the author explain stereotyping?

   _____

   _____

6. If you wanted to read the entire article quoted on page ___, where could you find the complete reference?

   _____

   _____

Contributed by Gloria Romero, Carolina Espinoza, and Lia Kamhi-Stein.

Grammar Exercise: Error Analysis

I. *Instructions:* The following sentences were taken from student papers. Working in pairs or small groups, analyze the structural or grammatical problems, and discuss ways to re-write the sentences.

1. The incentive was to have people buy American products instead of foreign trade.

2. Industrialization led to a transformation from an agrarian to an industrial economy, which caused much more social problems and a social class system.
3. Also government supported the business by passing vagrancy laws. These laws made business profitable. By using blacks to work in there company.
4. In 1914 congress passed the Clayton act prohibited unfair trading practices.
5. An example of this was the Sugar treaty. The sugar treaty was good for the business because they saved money in two way's and they were that they paid low wages, and did not have to pay tariff's to the Hawaiian government.
etc.

Contributed by Nick Zonen.

Identifying Cause and Effect

I. *Instructions:* Identifying the cause and effect of events and movements is a critical part of any study of history. Sometimes students don't make a clear differentiation between the cause and its results, or may even mistake one for the other. Identify the causes and effects in the following statements.

Example:
The owl and the pussycat went to sea in a beautiful pea green boat. They felt the need to get away.

Cause: They felt the need to get away.
Effect: The owl and the pussycat went to sea in a beautiful pea green boat.

1. The Emancipation Proclamation and the freeing of the slaves did not produce a society with complete equality for African Americans, and their condition remained desperate.

Cause:
Effect:

2. Because of the development of birth control, women could delay having children or avoid having them altogether; consequently, women had the opportunity to acquire an education or pursue a career.

Cause:
Effect:

etc.

Contributed by Nick Zonen.

Research

The results of program evaluation conducted at the conclusion of the first three years revealed that, overall, the performance of students in the Project LEAP study group courses approximated or exceeded that of the students in the language-enhanced general education courses. Specifically, students enrolled in the study group courses earned a higher percentage of A's and B's than those who did not participate in the study groups. Furthermore, the course grade point averages of the study group students were equal to or higher than those of comparison students in six of the nine courses. Analysis of open-ended questionnaires indicated that the Project LEAP students were very positive in their evaluation of both the study groups and enhanced general education courses. The students reported that the project had assisted them in developing their reading, writing, and note-taking skills, in particular, but many noted that they needed to improve their reading skills further.

From the faculty perspective, follow-up evaluation after six years revealed that participants were more aware of their students' language needs and had incorporated academic literacy instruction on a regular basis into their courses. They reported positive results both in content learning and in the written performance of their students. In addition, other benefits accrued. Several faculty participants published articles describing their academic literacy enhancements in such discipline-specific journals as *The History Teacher* and *Advances in Physiology Education*. Others applied Project LEAP principles to newly identified need areas such as training graduate laboratory instructors or developing strategies for teaching very large classes. Several departments changed faculty hiring practices, requiring experience and interest in teaching linguistically and culturally diverse students. Finally, more than 60 faculty members across the campus had adopted the multi-step writing assignment and library research activity developed in Project LEAP.[5]

Resources

The Project LEAP website can be found at: http://curriculum.calstatela.edu/faculty/asnow/ProjectLEAP. Several of the course enhancements can be found in the 1997 TESOL publication, *New Ways in Content-Based Instruction* and more detailed descriptions of Project LEAP can be found in the following:

Snow, M.A., and Kamhi-Stein, L.D. (in press). Teaching and learning academic literacy through Project LEAP. In J. Crandall and D. Kaufman (eds.), *Case studies in TESOL practice: Content-based instruction*. Alexandria, VA: TESOL.

Snow, M.A. (1997). Teaching academic literacy skills: Discipline faculty take responsibility. In M.A. Snow and Brinton, D.M. (eds.), *The content-based classroom: Perspectives on integrating language and content*. White Plains, NY: Longman, pp. 290–304.

---

[5] The final report to the Fund for the Improvement of Postsecondary Education (FIPSE) can be found at ERIC ED 4185989.

A LIFE-SKILLS ADULT BASIC EDUCATION PROGRAM[6]

In attempting to meet the needs of adults who are struggling not only with a new language but with providing a living for themselves and their families, the North Hollywood Adult Learning Center has made the community its classroom.

The 500 students who are enrolled in the program represent many different cultural groups from around the world: Hispanic (70 percent), Asian (12 percent), Middle Eastern (9 percent), and European (4 percent). The remaining 5 percent are native English speakers who are taking courses outside of the basic ESL program. The curriculum itself consists of six levels of ESL, running from beginning to advanced; a reading lab for students with special problems in reading; a language skills lab which emphasizes writing, spelling, and grammar; and a high school lab for those desiring a GED Certificate or a high school diploma. In the latter three, the ESL and proficient English-speaking students are mixed.

Incorporating Community Resources

Every month, the activities are built around specific life-skills topics such as the following:

Community Resources	*Mental and Physical Health*
the community and its members	medical care
autobiographical data	nutrition
cultural-social integration	personal hygiene
the world around us	dental care
police-fire-paramedic services	safety and home
the telephone	
the post office	
leisure-time activities	
athletic activities	*Government and the Law*
entertainment activities	
recreational activities	vehicles and the law
educational services	law and legal services
schools	taxes
libraries	current issues

---

[6] I would like to thank the program's coordinator Sandra Brown, who provided much information upon which this summary was based. Appreciation also goes to Harriet Fisher, Rheta Goldman, Roberto Martinez, Ethel Schwartz, Katie Treibach, and the many others I talked with during my observation.

Occupational Knowledge	*Consumer Economics*
vocational training/counseling	individual/family economy
job searches	physical concerns
the interview	financial services
on-the-job skills	consumer rights
	insurance
	consumerism
	general shopping skills
	food shopping
	meals
	clothing shopping
	housing

These topics and the information related to them serve as an important part of the content through which the structures, vocabulary, and pronunciation of English are taught. Integral to these units are trips that the students at all levels take to city government offices, occupational centers, markets, commercial businesses, factories, music/arts centers, libraries, museums, parks, hospitals, and many other places in and around the city.

On one such trip to the Farmers' Market, Rheta Goldman, a teacher of intermediate ESL, asked her students to search out the answers to the following questions:

What animals are in the window of the pet shop?
Find the post office. What shops are next to the post office?
What's the name of a store where you can get shoes repaired?
Go to the Farmers' Market newspaper stand. Can you buy a newspaper in your native language?
How much does it cost?
What kind of food can you buy at the shop next to Gill's Ice Cream Shop?
Find the glassblower. Write the names of four glass animals you can buy there.
How much does a fresh-baked pie cost from Du-Bar's Bakery?
What kinds of pies do they have today? Name three.

In addition to the trips and related activities, the students are exposed to films and real-life materials. Also, a stream of representatives from the community visit the classrooms: an immigration attorney to give advice on becoming citizens; a speaker from the Red Cross to help the students be better prepared in the event of a major earthquake; a representative from the Department of Consumer Affairs to inform them of their rights as consumers; police officers to make them aware of strategies to use in protecting themselves from crime, to name a few. In connection with the units, the students also participate in classroom activities such as role play, dialogues, conversations, discussions, and writing activities commensurate with their proficiency levels.

To aid other teachers in setting up similar programs, the coordinator and teachers at North Hollywood have compiled extensive lists of ideas in several areas: community services, consumer education, cultural awareness, employment, family life, government/citizenship/law, health, and recreation. Below is an example.

Community Services

Real-life materials/transparencies

1. *Post office* forms
2. *Bank* forms, statements, checks, travelers' checks
3. *Telephone* directory pages of Zip code maps; emergency telephone numbers; emergency number stickers for the telephone; telephone bills
4. *Driver's license* application form, test, change of address form
5. *Traffic signs*; parking/traffic citation forms; bus, train, airline schedules; bus maps from local bus company; road maps from the local Chamber of Commerce
6. *School* (elementary, secondary, adult) enrollment forms; school report card; announcement of school activity
7. *Library* card applications

Brochures
Police Department (home protection, self-defense, drugs, and so on); *fire department* (fire prevention); *automobile club* and *National Safety Council* (traffic safety); *Department of Motor Vehicles* (driver manual); *library; building and safety department* (earthquake safety); *adult school* (schedule of classes); *city councilman, state assemblyman* (booklets on local agencies and services).

Audiovisuals
Recorded tapes of telephone conversations (tell students prior to hearing the tapes that they are only simulations) with police and fire departments, telephone operators, directory assistance; Western Union; bus, train, taxi, and airline personnel; *taped conversations in the community*, at the post office, bank, with child's teacher, and so on; *taped telephone recordings* of weather, time, telephone numbers, disconnected telephones, and so on; *Teletrainers*—actual telephones with a control unit (on loan from telephone company)/free films.

Speakers
Police officer (home protection or self-defense, with film and demonstration); *fireman* (with film on fire safety and exit procedures); *paramedics* (with demonstration of life-saving equipment and techniques) *AAA* and *National*

Safety Council representatives (with films on traffic safety); *library aide; elementary, secondary* and/or *adult school principal; telephone company representative* (with film on use of telephone) *city councilman* on community services; *United Way representative.*

Trips
fire station; police department; post office; bank (before it opens); library; telephone company; local elementary school; airport.

Subjects for Discussion, Dialogue, Role Playing, and Other Activities

At the post office: sending, insuring, picking up packages; buying stamps, airletters, money orders; correctly addressing letters, and so on.

At the bank: savings/checking; deposit/withdrawal; travelers' checks, safe deposit boxes, and so on.

Emergency services: the role of police in home and self-protection; fire prevention; reporting a fire, a prowler, a break-in, an auto accident, calling the paramedics; what to do in case of a fire, earthquake, break-in, rape attempt; experiences with and attitudes toward police.

Telephone: emergency calls; long distance calls; directory assistance; wrong number; out of order; taking messages; weather report; using the telephone directory; social and business calls.

Transportation: car, taxi, bus, train, airline schedules; map reading activities; locating local services; geography of local areas; traffic safety; dangers of hitchhiking; obtaining a driver's license; at the gas station, garage; asking directions.

Education: registering child/self in school; conference with child's teacher, counselor, principal, nurse; participation in child's school activities; report cards; education in the United States compared with education in other countries; levels and types of education; special education; private schools; new approaches to education; admission requirements to colleges and universities.

Library: card application; Dewey Decimal System; overdue books; reserving books; foreign-language books; using children's books.

Philanthropic organizations: becoming involved in volunteer activities; charities; charity drives; animal protection agencies.

Community Volunteers

One of the most interesting aspects of the program is its utilization of volunteers from the community. Eighteen community workers arrive every week to assist the teachers in classrooms, to tutor students, or to help out wherever they are needed. They come primarily from the ranks of housewives and retirees. Although they receive no monetary rewards for their time, they do receive numerous rewards of a different kind. Their individual birthdays are celebrated, articles in school papers are written to honor their accomplishments, and special days are set aside to recognize the work they do. Ranging in age from 26 to 82, they form a dependable resource. Some are there only one or two hours a week; others work 15 to 20 hours. The volunteers determine, in advance, their own schedules and sign contracts confirming the agreement (see the sample contract, Figure 18.3).

Once officially accepted as staff members, the volunteers are given mail-

---

North Hollywood Adult Learning Center
Volunteer Job Description and Agreement

POSITION TITLE: Adult Basic Education Tutor

PLACE: _____ Reading Lab   _____ High School Lab

        _____ Language Skills Lab   _____ English as a Second
                                                     Language

PROGRAM OBJECTIVES: To assist students who want to learn to improve their basic skills in English as a Second Language or to earn a GED certificate or a high school diploma.

TIME COMMITMENT: Days _____ Hours _____

                         _____   _____

RESPONSIBILITIES: • To work under the guidance and supervision of the teacher to whom you have been assigned
                         • To work with either individuals or groups according to the needs of the teacher and students
                         • To follow the teacher's plans for each session
                         • To assist the teacher in any way the teacher feels will be of benefit to the students
                         • To be reliable and on time on regularly scheduled days
                         • To sign in and out on the sign-in sheet
                         • To inform the office or teacher if you must be absent (The volunteer does not: diagnose student needs, prescribe instruction, select materials, evaluate student progress, or counsel students.)

QUALIFICATIONS: • A positive attitude, interest and enthusiasm in working with adult basic education students
                       • Ability to work cooperatively with school personnel and other volunteers
                       • Adequate communication skills
                       • Dedication to fulfill all of the obligations of the position

TRAINING: BY THE TEACHER TO WHOM YOU ARE ASSIGNED

I have read and understand the above and agree to conscientiously carry out the responsibilites as described.

                                    X _____

Figure 18.3 Volunteer Job Description and Agreement

boxes and their names are added to the check-in sheets. After an orientation, they go to their assigned classrooms, where they are trained by the teacher with whom they will be working. In addition to the orientation and training, the volunteers are given suggestions in writing concerning general strategies to use when working with students (see pages 311–312 for a similar list intended for peer teacher and lay assistant training). They also receive self-evaluation checklists containing items about cooperation with others, following the teacher's directions, being friendly and encouraging, and so forth.

A SECONDARY SHELTERED ENGLISH PROGRAM[7]

We learned in Chapter 17 that a sheltered class is a kind of immersion situation in that the students are at similar levels of proficiency in the target language. We also learned that the teacher may be familiar with their first languages and usually has a knowledge of their cultures. A sheltered class can provide the comprehensible input necessary for the student to acquire the target language through content-based instruction. At the same time, it can serve as a surrogate family of sorts or a temporary buffer between the student and the mainstream.

Artesia High School in Artesia, California, is one of the schools in the ABC Unified School District that has a highly developed network of sheltered classes. The school offers 36 sections of ESL and sheltered classes to approximately 350 ELLs who represent 21 different languages. All the students in what is called the "Diverse Language Program" (ESL only) are eligible to take the special courses. Pam Branch, the school's program coordinator, reports:

> What immersion has taught us is that comprehensible subject matter teaching *is* language teaching; students can profit a great deal from subject matter classes in which the conscious focus is on the topic and not on language. Classes are taught in English, but native speakers are excluded in order to make the teacher's input more understandable for limited-English students.

Students in this program begin with two periods of ESL and three sheltered classes in specific subject matter areas (see Figure 18.4). Later, they are able to add other sheltered classes (see Figure 18.5). Gradually, they are fully mainstreamed, first in those areas that require less command of English and later in all subjects. Bilingual aides provide primary language support for the students.

---

[7] I wish to thank Pam Branch, Lilia Stapleton, Marie Takagaki, Ted Marquez, and many others with the ABC Unified School District who made it possible for me to observe their sheltered class program and include it in this chapter.

Identification and Evaluation

A home language survey and supplementary questionnaire is used first to identify ELLs in the school district. Once the student is so identified, he or she receives the Language Assessment Scale (LAS) test and, when appropriate, a battery of other tests, including subtests of the Comprehensive Test of Basic Skills (CTBS) and an informal writing sample. Each student is then rated on an oral language observation matrix that is similar to the ACTFL (American Council on the Teaching of Foreign Languages, 1982) proficiency levels 1–5. On the basis of these measures, students are placed in either Level I, II, or III.

Description of Each Level

Level I (akin to the beginning levels described on page 137) includes two periods of ESL: Skills I and Conversation I. At this level, the students can also choose from among several sheltered courses (see Figure 18.4).

Skills I focuses on survival skills such as telling time, using the telephone, filling out application forms, and so forth. *Conversation I* emphasizes various topics of interest such as those recommended by Krashen and Terrell (see Chapter 9). In both classes, physical approaches and communicative teaching are relied upon to minimize anxiety and provide sufficient comprehensible input. The sheltered classes at this level require tasks that are cognitively undemanding and heavily context embedded. For example, in *Art* students are given a wide variety of art experiences in which they can express themselves freely while studying composition and color as these are used in drawing,

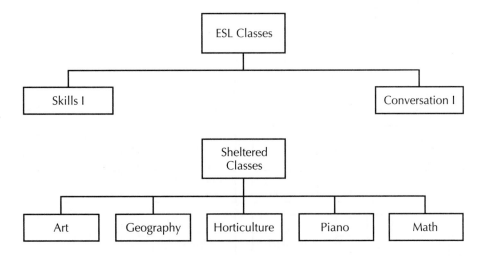

Figure 18.4. Level I

painting, and making three-dimensional objects. *Geography* also relies on concrete concepts for which pictures, maps, and globes can be used. Drawing maps or making papier-mâché ones in relief can provide a great deal of hands-on activity. *Horticulture* finds students planting and caring for a garden after diagramming and labeling the plants in a basic plan. The course not only helps students acquire the language through here and now tasks but may even open up some possible jobs for the future. *Piano* offers individualized instruction on the use of electric keyboards with headsets. If the students wish, they may elect to continue Piano into the next level. Students are placed in *Math* (in Levels I and II) according to math ability rather than level of proficiency in English. Problems are worked out on the board, and vocabulary banks are used to help students remember words already learned and to add new words for future work. Because word problems remain a continuing difficulty, the teacher helps students to break down the problems into various steps, making the tasks more manageable.

Level II (akin to the intermediate levels described on page 137) includes two periods of ESL: Skills II and Conversation II. At this level, the students have even more choices from among sheltered classes (see Figure 18.5).

Skills II and Conversation II, like their counterparts at Level I, extend survival skills through a topical organization, adding vocabulary appropriate to

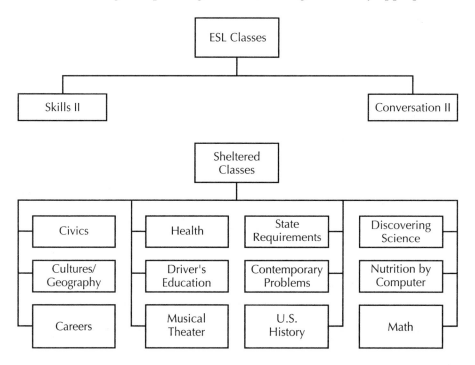

Figure 18.5. Level II

students' needs. At this level, the tasks are more cognitively demanding but are still highly context-embedded. *Careers* looks at various vocational post possibilities and helps the students to discover their own strengths and weaknesses. It makes an effort to find what kinds of jobs are best suited to each individual. The students receive practice in interview technique by role playing (see Chapter 11). *Cultures/Geography* helps students to gain an appreciation of many different cultures in relation to their geographical advantages and constraints. *Civics* takes a historical approach to the American governmental system, its organization, and the ramifications of its tenets. *Driver's Education* gives the students an opportunity to prepare for the written portion of the driver's exam and presents a reading task for which the students are already highly motivated (later they can enroll in the driver's training course, which teaches them how to actually drive a car). *Health* covers the human body and emphasizes the prevention and control of common diseases. *Musical Theater* presents American culture as depicted through Hollywood's version of Broadway musicals. *State Requirements* includes a variety of units mandated by the state of California: mental health, first aid (students receive a certificate upon completion of the unit), and fire and accident prevention. *Contemporary Problems* is a sort of catchall course highlighting issues on consumerism and interpersonal relations. Topics covered include money management, credit, insurance, self-awareness, alternative lifestyles, sexuality, and parenting. *U.S. History* is taught through frequent dramatizations of events, bringing the past alive and making it meaningful to the students. *Discovering Science* includes experiments and a lot of realia to explain physical phenomena. *Nutrition by Computer* exposes students to the benefits of a balanced diet and at the same time introduces them to computers, a rather unusual but effective combination. Students chart daily food intake, categorize foods into groups, and plan well-balanced meals.

Mainstream classes are gradually added beginning at Level II. Students are required to take mainstream physical education and can elect to take other mainstream courses such as typing or home economics.

Level III (akin to the advanced levels described on page 138) is tailored for advanced students who are into a full schedule of mainstream courses except for English. Literature is at the core of the program, and the basic skills (listening, speaking, reading, writing) are integrated into the activities evolving out of it. Students are eventually reclassified from Level III ESL once they demonstrate through a variety of means (similar to the initial battery of tests) that they are ready to move on to more challenging activities.

Staff Development

One reason for the apparent success of Artesia's program in helping students to acquire English is the emphasis the school places on staff development. All 17 of the ESL/content-area teachers have received special training in giving effective comprehensible input and in correcting through modeling and expansion. This special training is part of a series of after-school inservices provided by the district's ESL resource teachers. In addition, Krashen has consulted with the district on several occasions, offering its teachers practical applications of his theories.

Alfredo Schifini and other language arts and reading consultants in the Los Angeles area have conducted workshops in writing/reading activities. Schifini stresses that introducing the main points of a lesson increases the use of contextual clues for comprehension of the material. Recapping the major points on the board or an overhead also increases the possibility of acquisition. He feels that lectures ladened with jargon are inappropriate in a sheltered class. Instead, oral interaction should be used extensively. Students can be engaged in small-group tasks such as science experiments, mapmaking, creating murals, preparing skits, and similar activities. It is the teacher's job to demonstrate or model the task for the students to then carry out. He advises teachers, when choosing textbooks, to consider the readability, print size, paragraph length, and types of illustrations used. He recommends mapping or other kinds of graphic organization as useful techniques for helping students obtain meaning from the materials. About sheltered classes, he reminds the teachers:

> Sheltered English classrooms do not involve any magical approach to teaching. Certainly there is no "quick fix". . . . The potential exists with the sheltered model to provide truly meaningful instruction for a wide range of LEP [limited English proficient] students. It is important to restate that sheltered English should not be viewed as a substitute for bilingual education, but rather as a component in a carefully planned out developmental program designed to facilitate academic success.[8]

In addition to the inservicing provided by the ABC Unified School District, several of the staff members at Artesia graduated from the master's degree program in teaching second languages offered through a joint effort between the district and California State University, Los Angeles. All the courses in the program were taught locally to make them even more attractive to the teachers.

Staff members working in the program have come to the conclusion that a sheltered program is an effective means for teaching the target language to diverse primary-language groups for whom bilingual education is not currently considered a possibility.

---

[8] Here it should be noted that the school discontinued its bilingual program in Spanish, some think to its detriment (see Chapter 17), when it began the sheltered program.

A HIGH SCHOOL ESL ACADEMIC PROGRAM: HUMANITAS[9]

Description of the Program

Thomas Jefferson High School in the Los Angeles Unified School District was one of the first sites to become part of the Humanitas project in 1990.

The project was an interdisciplinary program designed to synthesize various disciplines such as social science, biology, history, language arts, and so forth, and break down the artificial boundaries between them. The project, funded by a grant from the Rockefeller Foundation, has now been expanded to over 30 schools in the district. The program, developed by Cleveland teacher Neil Anstead, was an attempt to integrate academic competence and language communication skills.

The ESL section of Humanitas at Thomas Jefferson High School involved students in the following coordinated classes: ESL, biology, and U.S. history. Its goals were to develop academic literacy and oral skills through a writing-based curriculum. The three classes were integrated through the same themes each semester and through coordinated assignments. In the ESL class (somewhat reminiscent of adjunct courses found at the post-secondary level), students read, wrote, and had discussions about the content being studied in biology and U.S. history.

The ELLs in Humanitas at Thomas Jefferson were all Latin American and were operating at intermediate levels of proficiency (see page 137). Every day, they met in a four-hour block (two hours of ESL, one hour of biology, and one hour of U.S. history).

The main theme for the two-semester program was human relations. The subthemes are listed below:

Fall Semester
Culture and human behavior
Identity and self-awareness
The Protestant ethic and the spirit of capitalism

Spring Semester
Immigration and racial prejudice
Individual and group power
Atomic age conflicts and resolutions

---

[9] I want to express my appreciation to Eva Wegrzecka-Monkiewicz, a teacher at Thomas Jefferson High School in Los Angeles, California, for sharing with me her numerous writings and research on Humanitas. Because of her work, I was able to summarize the program for inclusion in this edition.

Theme integration was the goal of the wide variety of assignments given. For example, during the first unit on culture and human behavior, in ESL the students presented a visual-oral self-awareness project in which they looked at their own Indian-Hispanic cultural roots; in biology they focused on biological adaptation of humans to new environments through hypothetical situations created by the students; in U.S. history they focused on the cultural heritage of Latino populations, both Indian and European, and took a historical view of cultural differences between the United States and Latin America.

Because the teachers were a team, they were able to coordinate assignments right from the beginning of the school year. Students could pursue a single assignment throughout the school day, continuing to develop it as they moved from class to class.

The products of their assignments often reflected the differences of opinion they might encounter as they discussed the content with teachers and classmates. Thus, the environment was often highly stimulating and motivating as students sought to discover information that might shed light on the issues being studied. Over time, they began to think critically, ask questions, seek answers through reading and discussion, and form their own judgments, which then became part of products they produced.

Resources

In order to make Humanitas work, certain resources were necessary. Teachers needed time to plan together, to develop teaching materials, to attend workshops, to coordinate field trips and cultural events, and to adapt materials to accommodate the students' emerging language skills. Moreover, they needed access to adequate photocopying facilities, particularly since many of the materials were created by the teachers themselves, using a large number of resources.

Research Findings

One of the results of research done by the Center for the Study of Evaluation at UCLA (Aschbacher, 1991) revealed that Humanitas students in general (not only ELLs) demonstrated significant improvement in their writing and conceptual understanding over the two semesters. A second study, reported by Wegrzecka-Monkiewicz (1992), found (among other things) that the ESL Humanitas group made greater gains in reading scores than did the control group consisting of other ELLs (see Figure 18.6). Pretest and posttest scores on the Gates-MacGinitie Reading Test were used in the comparison.

Wegrzecka-Monkiewicz attributed her results partially to the ESL Humanitas group's greater exposure to more cognitively demanding reading in their coursework. She concluded also that the integration of language and content provided an immediate and meaningful context for the language use. She recommended that ELLs be exposed to integrated academic content and

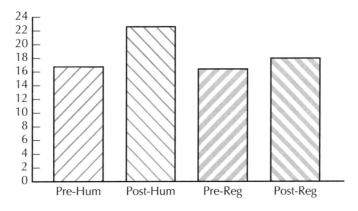

Figure 18.6. Mean Scores on the Gates-MacGinitie Reading Test

that the academic content be linked to language development early on in the language acquisition process.

AN ELEMENTARY DISTRICT-WIDE PROGRAM[10]

To meet the needs of its ELLs, grades K–3, the Alhambra School District in Alhambra, California has developed a multifaceted program and a thematic curriculum that it is now trying to extend to the higher grades. The program itself integrates features of several of the methods and activities discussed in Part II of this book: the physical approaches, communicative language teaching including chants, storytelling, drama, and many more.

Demographics

The district, which currently serves 13 elementary schools, has a total of 3,583 ELLs, representing about 30 languages. Based on the information gained from the home language surveys required of each student, the most common languages represented include Spanish, Vietnamese, Cantonese, Mandarin, and Cambodian. However, languages less common to ESL classrooms are also found in this diverse student population: Punjabi (India), Urdu (Pakistan),

[10] I wish to thank Linda Sasser at the Alhambra School District in Alhambra, California for making available the information upon which this summary is based. Appreciation goes also to the other people in the Alhambra School District who contributed, either directly or indirectly, to the development of the thematic curriculum: Lilia Sarmiento, Mary Ellen De Santos, Lourdes Brito, Marie Ibsen, Linda Naccarato, Sharon Oliver, Gina Tesner, Virginia Torres-Lopez, Cathy Tyson, and Florence Wong.

Illocano (northwestern Luzon, part of the Republic of the Philippines), and Tongan (Tonga, an island group in the South Pacific).

Although many of the language minority children arriving from other countries come from large urban population centers, there are many who come from the isolated rural regions of China and Latin America. In spite of the fact that most of the parents state that their goal for their children is a post-secondary degree, only a few of these parents have themselves obtained such a degree; however, many of them do have some formal education beyond the secondary level.

Assessment and Placement

If a language other than English is spoken in the home, the student is tested at the district's Elementary Orientation and Assessment Center. All elementary students are assessed in the primary language and in English, using a short form of the appropriate Language Assessment Scales (LAS).

The district has recently developed and is using on a trial basis Chinese and Vietnamese tests, drawing from the English and Spanish LAS format. When appropriate (for children in grades 3 and above), the district also assesses performance in mathematics, and English reading, and obtains an English writing sample.

The students who are classified by the district as ELLs generally are operating from low-beginning to intermediate proficiency levels (see page 137). Usually they are placed in one of three types of classrooms: a bilingual classroom, a language development classroom, or a language development cluster classroom. In all three types of classrooms, a bilingual paraprofessional is provided whenever possible to assist in the instruction.

A Bilingual Classroom

Bilingual classes are offered K–6 in Spanish, Cantonese, and Vietnamese, where there is a teacher available speaking the necessary language. The teacher must have been given bilingual authorization by the state of California.[11] In addition, the number of students must warrant having a bilingual class.

A Language Development Classroom

This is an intensive English environment for students operating from low-beginning to low-intermediate proficiency levels. It is taught by a state authorized Bilingual or Language Development teacher.

---

[11] Due to the passage of Proposition 227 (see footnote 3 on page 447), waivers must be obtained in order for students to enroll in these classes.

A Language Development Cluster Classroom

This is a transitional classroom that includes ELLs operating at intermediate to advanced levels, native English speakers, and language minority students who are designated as English-fluent. The ELLs are usually placed in this classroom after they have been in the Language Development Classroom for a sufficient amount of time to obtain the necessary skills. The teacher must be a certificated Bilingual or Language Development teacher.

Staff Development

In an attempt to better meet the needs of language minority students, all of the K–3 teachers in the district participated in staff development sessions. Grouped by grade level, the teachers were given information about the language acquisition process, conditions conducive to learning, and instruction in the recommended methodology. Teachers had a chance to try out various activities and strategies on each other and receive peer feedback. From time to time, they were asked to reflect upon what they had learned and upon their own growth as developing teachers. Linda Sasser, an ESL program specialist for the school district, reported that the teachers' comments on the staff development sessions were generally very positive and that she and the district were encouraged by the enthusiasm.

The Thematic Curriculum

The thematic curriculum developed for K–3 is incorporated into all three classroom designs described on pages 408–411. It is based on the premise that learning is most likely to occur when ideas and activities are integrated and interrelated in the classroom as they are in life. The thematic units link several disciplines (literature, social science, art, and so forth) around a central idea or theme. The district felt that such an organization would encourage the following:

- an emphasis on processes for constructing meaning, solving problems, and discovering relationships
- greater teacher/student involvement in planning and implementing the curriculum
- increased individual work appropriate to each student's developmental level and interests
- more effective and productive use of instructional time
- greater student involvement in dynamic, experiential learning through the myriad of resources provided

Below are graphic representations of the themes developed by the district (with teacher input) and used at level K–3 (see Figures 18.7, 18.8, 18.9, 18.10). Literature, appropriate to the proficiency and age levels of the students, was selected by the teachers to accompany each theme.

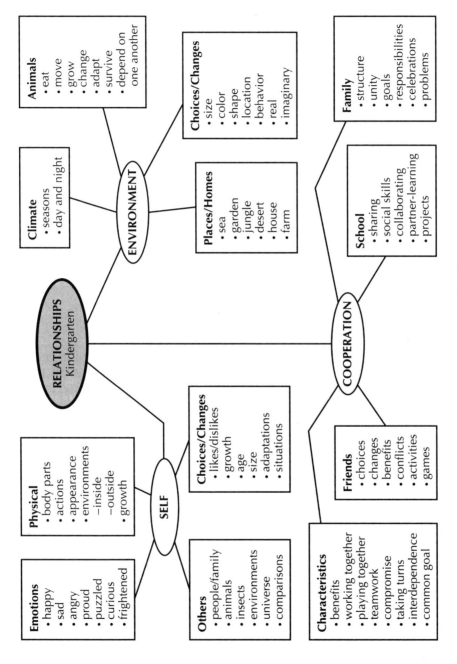

Figure 18.7. Theme: Relationships, Alhambra School District

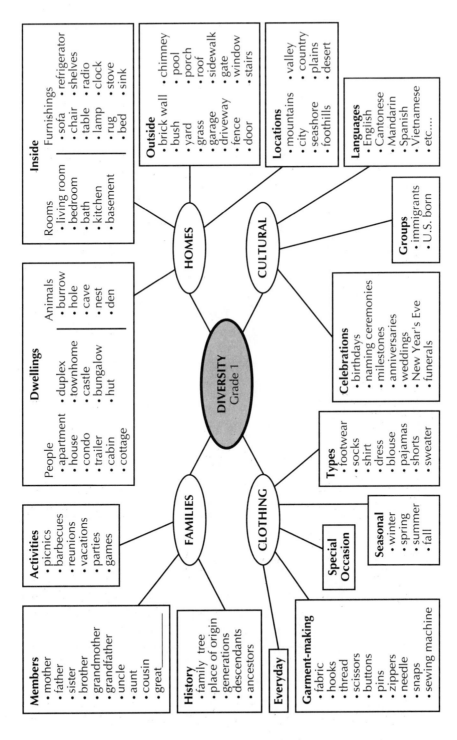

Figure 18.8. Theme: Diversity, Alhambra School District

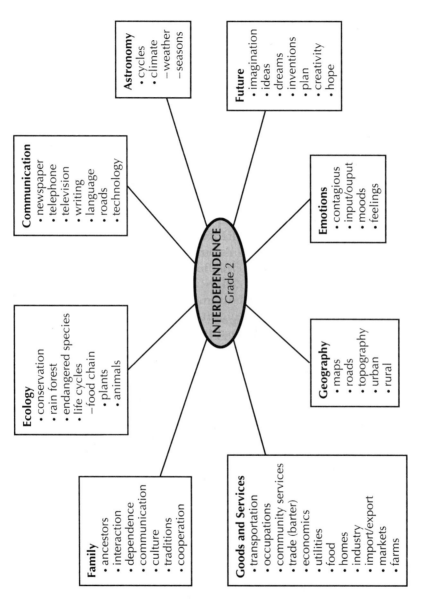

Figure 18.9. Theme: Interdependence, Alhambra School District

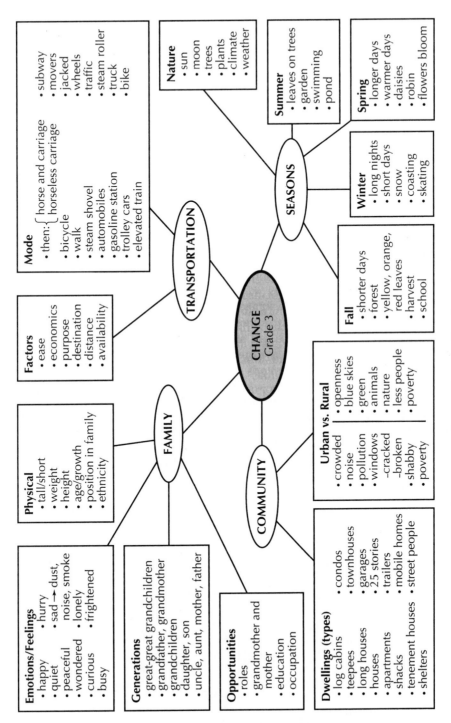

Figure 18.10. Theme: Change, Alhambra School District

Activities

The activities mentioned here are only a few of those recommended to teachers using a thematic organization. The activities, most of which are both flexible and adaptable, can be used at virtually any elementary grade level and in any thematic unit. They include clustering and other graphic devices such as Venn diagrams (see Chapter 13), concrete poetry (see Chapter 10), the language experience approach (see pages 243–246), alternative types of journals (see pages 264–266), and many more. In addition, the following are included in the recommendations:

Activity Recommendations

DRAMATIC CORNER
Level: Low- to high-intermediate

Set aside a place in the classroom where the children can go and role-play real-life situations related to the theme being studied (buying a coat, taking a pet to the veterinarian, selling shoes, etc.). The scenery is designed by the children and all of the necessary props are provided by the children or made available by the teacher. This activity enables children to experiment with language in relatively risk-free environments.

CIRCLE STORY
Level: Mid- to high-beginning

The children create a circle divided like a pie (see Figure 18.11). In each section of the pie, they make a drawing to represent an event in the story. The first event is given the number 1, the second the number 2, and so forth. The children may then cut the segments apart, eliminate the numbers, and give the pieces to a partner to reassemble. They may tell the story by looking at the pictures and/or paste their reassembled circles on construction paper and bind them together to create a class booklet for the future telling of the stories.

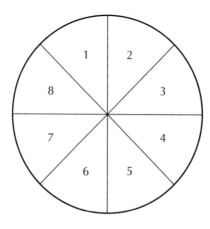

Figure 18.11. Circle Story

DRAW AND REMEMBER
Level: Low- to mid-beginning

Using strategies from the physical approaches (see Chapter 8), the children are asked to fold a sheet of paper into a predetermined number of sections and number each section. Using crayons, the children are to draw according to the teacher's directions. The pictures should be relevant to the theme's content.

> Pick up your red crayon.
> In box number 1, draw a ball.
> Put your red crayon down.
> Pick up your green crayon.
> In box number 4, draw a chair.

After the children have drawn in all of the boxes, the teacher asks questions such as these: What's in number 2? What color is the ball? What two objects are the same color? Did you draw something orange? What was it?

ECHO CHANTS
Level: Mid- to high-beginning.

In an echo chant, the children repeat a line or a portion of a line after the teacher or another student has read it aloud first. The district feels that the chant provides a "soft focus" on intonation, inflection, and pronunciation. A simple poem or a teacher-written chant can be easily converted to an echo chant by looking for the repetitive phrases or refrains. See the example[12] below:

POEM ——— conversion ————→	ECHO CHANT	
Snow on the cars.	Teacher:	Snow on the cars.
Snow on the bus.	Students:	On the cars.
Snow on the vans.	T:	Snow on the bus.
Snow on us!	Ss:	On the bus.
Snow in the puddles.	T:	Snow on the vans.
Snow in the street.	Ss:	On the vans.
Snow in the gutters.	T:	Snow on us!
Snow on my feet!	Ss:	Snow on us!
	T:	Snow in the puddles.
	Ss:	In the puddles.
	T:	Snow in the street.
	Ss:	In the street.
	T:	Snow in the gutters.
	Ss:	In the gutters.
	T:	Snow on my feet!
	Ss:	Snow on my feet!

Within the theme curriculum, teachers are encouraged to use whole-group activities (chanting, role playing, creating graphic representations discussing, etc.) and small-group instruction

---

[12] The source for this poem is unknown.

(using the Magnetic Way[13] to learn concepts related to the theme, reviewing with a partner, sharing homework). In addition, the following centers are set up where students can go during various times of the day. Examples of activities taking place in each center are in parenthesis.

Book Corner (share a big book with a friend; choose a book to read)

The Art Corner (explore color by mixing any two colors; draw pictures for a collaborative story)

Manipulative Area (sequence four pictures; cut pictures of kitchen items out of magazines)

Discovery Corner (investigate water evaporation; experiment with the effects of the sun on a planted seed)

Listening Area (follow directions on a cassette tape; listen to a story on a cassette tape)

Homework related to the theme being explored is expected of each student. They may be asked to share stories, rhymes, or chants with someone at home and come back with the responses; count the number of chairs or lamps in the house; interview adults to discover their opinions, and so forth.

Teachers are encouraged by the district to adhere to the following practices that are consonant with the philosophies supporting the physical approaches and communicative approaches (see Chapters 8 and 9): maintaining a low-stress environment, allowing for a silent period, generally focusing on content rather than form, adjusting input to accommodate the student, using an appropriate rate, checking for understanding, and giving timely feedback on student performance.

A KINDERGARTEN ESL PROGRAM WITHIN A SPANISH BILINGUAL SCHOOL

At Loma Vista Elementary School in the heart of Maywood, California, a Spanish-speaking community, every class has two components: ESL and Spanish bilingual education.[14] The kindergarten is no exception.

Beverly McNeilly, a teacher of the ESL component of the kindergarten program, takes a holistic approach to teaching English to her 31 students. In her class, English is the vehicle by which the students are exposed to stories, films, songs, games, and other items of interest. Structured ESL lessons represent only a small portion of the program; they are the first to go if any spon-

---

[13] The Magnetic Way, made available by Creative Edge, Inc. (Steck-Vaughn), consists of a large magnetic board with pieces (people representing multicultural family groups, houses, streets, buildings of various sorts, furniture, etc.) that stick to the board. Overlay pieces (clothing, interchangeable store fronts, etc.) can be placed on top.

[14] Loma Vista Elementary School is in the Los Angeles Unified School District.

taneous opportunity presents itself. For example, one day the class abandoned a lesson to watch the tree trimmers as they sawed off the limbs of an old tree outside the window.

The Subject Matter, Activities, and Classroom Management

The subject matter itself is integrated into a variety of skill areas. Target vocabulary words are generally presented in an introductory lesson and then used again and again throughout the day, whether in math, science, art, physical education, or music. The words will be reinforced naturally in the course of events. For example, as part of an art project in a unit on ocean life, the children, create starfish and coral for a mural. In math, they choose which of several drawings are "true octopi" (the ones with eight legs). Music finds the children dancing to aquatic sounds on a recording as they imagine how a shark, a crab, a whale, or a dolphin might move. The reading lesson for the day consists of a game in which the children use magnets to "catch" fish on which letters of the alphabet have been written. A science display features

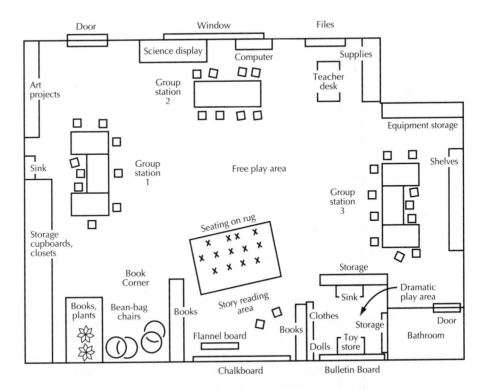

Figure 18.12. A Floor Plan of the ESL Kindergarten

shells and sand for the children to explore. The entire room environment reflects the topic in other ways with pictures, bulletin boards created by the children, and books on the theme (see Figure 18.12).

The teacher and her assistants, including one or two peer teachers from the fifth grade, manage a variety of activities for small-group participation. Group size varies from six to nine members depending on the task at hand and the number of assistants available. Instead of rigidly defined groups and timetables, fluid grouping is used. Several centers are set up each day which focus on related concepts. For example, one day during the study of mathematics, the children were divided into groups to participate in some of the activities from the still popular *Mathematics Their Way* by Lorton (1994). One group found how many designs they could make with only three Tinkertoys. Another group explored the different ways of separating six cubes into two piles. Other groups made geometric shapes with rubber bands and sequential patterns with rocks and shells. The amount of time needed to complete a task depended on each individual. Ongoing informal evaluation and the periodic pretesting and posttesting of key objectives provided evidence that children were mastering the concepts.

For the above lessons, the groups were formed based on a placement test that accompanies the Lorton book. However, usually the small-group activities are not sequentially organized and the children are allowed to select their own groups. Because they are allowed the freedom of choice, interest and curiosity remain at high levels. There are times when the group into which a student wants to go is full (all the chairs are taken). In that case, the student has two choices. He or she either can move to another activity or can participate in free or dramatic play in the areas designated for those purposes. It is in these areas that the child can reinforce concepts just learned or pursue other goals of immediate interest.

The teacher claims that she is often heartened to see the themes with which they have been working reflected in their choices of play activity. She reported:

> When we discussed transportation, block play produced trains and rocket ships. When we were concentrating on body parts, the table in the dramatic play area was an operating table, as amateur doctors came out with appropriate original language. To me, having a child produce "I'm a doctor. What's the problem? Let me see your leg"—combination of words that had never been taught her—is so much more rewarding than having little parrots.

A physical approach (Chapter 8) is combined with drama (Chapter 11) and songs and poetry (Chapter 10) to reinforce concepts. Props and pictures are used to aid understanding. For example, a skit about a firefighter's day includes the following song, which is sung to the tune of "Frère Jacques." The children act out the words as they sing the song.

Are you sleeping? Are you sleeping?
Firefighters, firefighters.
Alarm bells are ringing, alarm bells are ringing.
Ring, ring, ring . . . ring, ring, ring.

Because the lyrics are accompanied by action, even rank beginners can respond to the cues after observing their more advanced classmates. Children who are operating at the low-beginning level begin to sing along with the words. Thus, children at all levels are accommodated in this activity.

The teacher frequently reads aloud stories related to the units. Some of the children "read" the stories to each other later in the book corner, prompted only by the pictures. One of McNeilly's favorite stories to read to the children is Esphyr Slobodkina's *Caps for Sale* during a unit on clothing. She generally simplifies the story to ensure understanding. She reports that because she often repeats the same story several times in a row, she is not surprised to hear expressions from it used by the children in other situations. For instance, "Hats for sale! Does anybody want to buy a hat?" the next day became "Pencils for sale!" when one of the students was handing out the pencils.

Nursery rhymes are also used. One day she exposed the children to "Baa, baa, black sheep," and the next day she asked if they could remember it. In unison they said, "Baa, baa, black sheep, you have any wool?" This made more sense to them than the original syntax, indicating that they were focused more on meaning than on form. Other nursery rhymes such as "Pat-a-cake" and "Pease porridge hot" are introduced as they relate to the topics at hand. The rhymes are memorized by the children and seem to serve a function similar to chants (Chapter 10), appealing to the senses through their rhythmic and other poetic qualities.

McNeilly's attitude toward error correction is that "only global errors that impede communication" should be corrected. She accepts most surface form errors and primary language responses, which she considers to be perfectly healthy and normal. She feels that if the children are not overly corrected, they will be able to develop the self-confidence they need to acquire the language naturally.

To build self-esteem, the children also are given responsibilities to make the classroom function successfully. Even the rituals that begin the class each day are handled almost entirely by children, including the flag salute and attendance procedures. Children are given center stage whenever possible. On some occasions, they hold the book from which the teacher is reading aloud; on other days, they steady the flannel graph so it won't fall over while others are sticking figures to it, illustrating a story that is being read. In addition, the children's own drawings are mimeographed and made into booklets for the book corner.

The following is one of the integrated units the teacher likes to use.

Topic: Food

Whole Class Activities

Introduce vocabulary with real objects.
Use a grab bag of fruits and vegetables.
Have a fruit-tasting party.
Play the song "Alice's Restaurant." (See H. Palmer in references. Children are asked to hold pictures of food and respond to the verbal cues.)
Make vegetable soup from items brought from home.

Small Group Follow-up Activities

Make macaroni collages.
Use cookie cutters in dough made of clay.
Put illustrated cookbooks in the book corner.
Make collages, gluing pictures of food onto paper plates.
Fingerpaint in chocolate pudding.
Practice writing in thin layers of Jell-O crystals placed in trays.
String popcorn.
Bake cookies.
Set up a supermarket in the play area with food boxes, cans, and so forth; have the children "go shopping."

A Typical Day

11:00–11:45 A.M.

1. Greeting. The teacher greets the students and they greet her back.
2. Calendar coloring takes place. Today's numeral on a large calendar at the front of the room is colored in by a child volunteer. The teacher and students sing the song "What is the day to be happy?" which cues the answer to the question "What day is it today?"
3. Attendance. Children are learning to respond to visual cues. The teacher holds up flash cards and asks, "Is the person with this last name here today?"
4. Quick review of this week's concepts through the use of a picture dictionary.
5. Large-group ESL lesson. With use of posters and other realia, the Chinese New Year, which is coming soon, is discussed. Comparisons between the Chinese New Year and holidays that the children celebrate with their families are drawn.

11:45–12:25 P.M.

Small-group activities. Children choose one or more of the following:
Make paper firecrackers for the Chinese New Year.
Play a game involving guessing how many pennies are in "red packets" (made previously in preparation for the Chinese New Year).

Listen to *The Story about Ping* by Marjorie Flack as it is being read in the book corner.

Decorate paper plates with water colors; plates will later be assembled into a giant dragon for the Chinese New Year parade.

Dramatic free play.

12:25–12:45 *P.M.*

Cleanup and nursery rhymes. All the children participate in the cleanup.

Then the children retire to the rug. The "teacher of the day" (a child volunteer) leads in a chanting of some of the nursery rhymes the children have learned to date.

12:45–12:55 *P.M.*

Recess. Outdoor free play with sand toys, balance beams, and climbing apparatus for psychomotor and large muscle development. At this time the children are transitioned to the Spanish component of the program.

The Spanish bilingual teacher is also on the playground with her group of children. When recess is over, the teachers return to their respective rooms, each with a different group.

CHAPTER 19

Foreign Language Programs

Many foreign language students are finding that they can indeed acquire a second language in the classroom, particularly if interactional and participatory strategies are employed. The five programs selected for illustration here were chosen because they contain features that may be of special interest to foreign language teachers. However, none is intended as a model for replication.

The first program to be described is the Concordia Language Villages, a unique concept in foreign language teaching, utilizing immersion in creative ways to develop and maintain French, German, Russian, Chinese, Korean, Spanish, Norwegian, Finnish, Swedish, and several other languages. Next is an early immersion program in four elementary schools in Thunder Bay, Ontario, Canada, where children are acquiring French through exposure to the various subject-matter areas. Third is the Instituto Cultural Argentino Norteamericano (ICANA) in Buenos Aires, Argentina. Its approach to English as a foreign language is making it one of the fastest-growing binational centers in South America. Then comes a middle school Spanish language program at Millikan Junior High School in Los Angeles, California. Students at this school begin with an exploratory course in the seventh grade that prepares and motivates them for the two years of Spanish to follow. And last is the Spanish program at Artesia High School in Artesia, California. There students are acquiring the target language mainly through classroom interaction, but in the traditional one-period-a-day mode.

In this chapter, as in the previous one, the descriptions focus on the more salient characteristics of each program, sometimes on the overall organization and other times on specific activities and strategies. Although the programs are designed for particular age groups and specific purposes, it must again be kept in mind that most of the ideas can be readily adapted to other age levels and other kinds of programs.

A VILLAGE IMMERSION PROGRAM FOR GLOBAL UNDERSTANDING, LANGUAGE DEVELOPMENT, AND MAINTENANCE[1]

Tucked into the forests and amid the low-lying lakes of northeastern and central Minnesota is Concordia Language Villages. Its roots go back to the summer of 1961 when Concordia College[2] brought together 72 children (ages 9–12) to learn German by immersing them in the language and culture provided by the German "village" of which they became a part.

Today the villages number 12, each representing a different language and culture. Thousands of children, teenagers, and young adults now participate each year. Denise Phillippe, Associate Director for Curriculum and Staff Development, reported that in 2000 alone there were 9,084 villagers in addition to the 1,223 staff members hired that year. The staff members included deans, the counseling/teaching staff, facilitators for the various types of programs, nurses and their assistants, managers of stores and banks, maintenance people, lifeguards, and a cadre of the best cooks and bakers available. The participants and staff arrived from all 50 states and the District of Columbia, as well as from 48 countries around the world.

The Villages

The villages form miniature cultural enclaves, each having its own ethnic arts and crafts area; a dining hall where ethnic foods are served, sleeping quarters, showers, a library, an on-site clinic, large and small group meeting areas, an athletic field (most have a beach as well), a store, a bank, and even its own authentic currency. Participants can learn French, Chinese, Danish, Finnish, German, Japanese, Korean, Norwegian, Russian, Spanish, or Swedish in 11 of the villages, one for each language. The twelfth village is home to English as a

---

[1] Thanks to the many people at Concordia Language Villages for opening up their programs to me for the better part of a week. During my visitation, I had the opportunity to observe teacher/counselor/staff and participant orientations, village life (including classes), and a teacher education class. I ate many fine meals in the dining halls of various villages, witnessed several cultural presentations, and interviewed numerous students. Special thanks go to administrators and staff who supplied the details upon which this summary is based and who made my trip so enjoyable: Christine Schulze, Denise Phillippe, Sarah Happel, Donna (Daniele) Clementi, Heidi Hamilton, Laurie (Larisa) Iudin-Nelson, Jennifer (Zhenya) Ryan Tishler, Garrette (Ludo) Heysel, Tove Dahl, Karla (Yukari) Pratt, Paul (Di Baoluo) DelMain, Kerisa (Kike) Baedke, and Ruben Ayala-Brener. And to the following students for their reflective input: Annika (Gabi) Brink, Eric (Olivier) Reeves, Alex (Antone) Reeves, Mark (Marco) Sheskin, Tiffany (Iliana) Hughes, Julie (Julia) Thompsen, Katherine (Satomi) Lonsdorf, Mike (Ryu) Van Deusen, and Rachel (Reiko) Kerry. I owe a special debt of gratitude to Denise Phillippe, who served as a most gracious guide as well as a main source of information.

[2] Concordia College is a liberal arts Lutheran college in Moorhead, Minnesota. However, the purpose of the Language Villages is not to teach or promote any specific religion, and all participants are welcome, regardless of religious background.

Second Language learners and uses the nearby city of Moorhead as an extension of its English-speaking community. Of these villages, five are permanent and are located on the 830 acres owned by Concordia College on Turtle River Lake near Bemidji, Minnesota. Their names translate into "Lake of the Forest" or something very close to that.

Local and international civic groups, governments, and individuals have supported, financially and otherwise, Concordia's efforts to create permanent environments surprisingly similar to the countries they represent. For example, those entering the village of Salolampi soon discover that the dining hall, Jyringin Talo, is fashioned after a 19th-century train station in Finland, and several log cabins and a rustic sauna have been imported directly from that country. In Skogfjorden, villagers can eat at Gimle, a large dining hall whose brick walls are the back drops for Norwegian artifacts and whose ceiling is covered with intricate rosemaling. At Waldsee, participants are intrigued by the Gasthof and other buildings which are modeled after typical structures in Germany, using the traditional architectural style known as Fachwerk or half-beam. Lac du Bois and El Lago del Bosque feature buildings that are typical of those found in France and Spain respectively.

But these villages are not just for show. In the summer 2000, 47 percent of the former villagers returned, a strong indication that something very important is happening. For, in addition to helping students develop a second language and learn aspects of another culture, the villages serve as a means of extending the languages and cultures of generations of immigrants living throughout Minnesota. This use is supported by *Heritage Learners*, whose goal is to develop and maintain the language of their ancestors. These learners can be found in varying numbers among the villagers, across most language groups. It should be noted here that the German government has recently established a grant for Waldsee; one-half of this grant will be for curricular projects, and the other half will be for two-week scholarships to attend. In addition, the Sons of Norway offers about $40,000 each year in scholarships to students who want to develop and/or maintain their skills in Norwegian.

However, Christine Schulze, the Executive Director, reminds us that while preserving one's heritage is important, the primary goal of the villages is to ensure that ". . . young people are prepared to be responsible citizens in our global community." Christine was a villager herself at El Lago del Bosque in 1970 and later joined the staff, where she has worked for 26 years. She knows firsthand about Concordia Language Villages' deep commitment to global concerns. These are evident in the topics for study and discussion, as well as in the simulations presented in the villages. The topics for study and discussion are wide-ranging but relate either directly or indirectly to environmental and ecological concerns, international issues, diversity, and tolerance.

Moreover, Concordia Language Villages believes that forming relationships in the villages with people from around the world and immersing oneself in another language and culture brings a greater openness to different world views and ways of doing things. Although the village cultures are still "American" in many ways, the participants feel that they are experiencing something "culturally different." Usually, they go away with attitudes toward other peoples of the world that are positive and lasting.

Village Philosophy and the Practices of Village Teaching

Concordia Language Villages seeks to educate students for responsible global citizenship by establishing *communities of learners* in which each villager is a valued member. Through the immersion experience, villagers are encouraged to become lifelong learners as well as proficient speakers of the language of their village.

Their teachers are vital to this experience. During orientation week, new teachers are introduced to the practices common to village teaching summarized below:

1. The target language is used by the staff and villagers except when English is needed to meet safety and/or emotional needs of the participants. This practice is based on the principle that villagers need to hear and use the target language in a variety of contexts. These contexts can include completing routine tasks, meeting personal needs, actively participating in cultural activities and events, formal and informal discussions, and academic classroom experiences.

2. Early in the language acquisition process, participants are taught village-centered phrases and words—whatever is needed to participate in the daily life of the village. All signs and labels are written in the target language. The village itself is used as a classroom. Nature hikes, canoe trips, etc., provide much of the language content. It is believed that as the villagers gain the competence necessary to meet their basic needs, their speech will begin to include more abstract language in more complex contexts as interaction spreads beyond the concerns of the immediate village.

3. Error correction is handled through the modeling of correct forms and meanings rather than by the use of direct correction. However, that does not mean that forms and nuances in meaning are never the focus. On the contrary, villagers often receive direct instruction in structure and semantics within their academic work.

4. Culture is reflected throughout all the programs and is lived every day. Special cultural experiences and presentations are organized for and by the villagers, especially for the evening programs.

Types of Programs Available[3]

One-week, two-week, and four-week language programs are offered in the villages during the summer. The first two programs earn no credit and are often taken by participants seeking an introduction to a specific language and culture. The one-week sessions offer initial exposure and camp survival tips for children ages 7 to 11 and older children and teenagers ages 11 to 15. These sessions focus on very basic language instruction, arts and crafts, sports, and other hands-on experiences, depending on the interests of the age group. Sometimes a student who has already gained proficiency in one foreign language will sign up for a one-week session in another language just to see what it's like.

The two-week sessions are for participants ages 8 to 18 who have been divided into beginning, intermediate, and advanced levels. These sessions are similar in content to the one-week sessions except that they offer a more in-depth immersion experience complete with cultural simulations, cooking experiences, singing and dancing, and many other activities. Participants often take a two-week session to "brush up" on a language they have already studied in school during the academic year.

One-month programs are accredited by the North Central Association for Colleges and Schools and give villagers (grades 9–12) high school credit for language study that is equivalent to 180 hours of instruction. These sessions generally are taught by highly qualified, certified teachers and include speaking, reading, composition, vocabulary development strategies, and grammar. They are quite rigorous and require a frequent performance-based evaluation of each villager. Once final grades are given, written evaluations are sent to each participant's school and to the parents.

Other programs are available as well. One of the more popular sessions is the French Voyageurs program for young people ages 11 to 18. One-week, two-week, or four-week sessions are available. The participants not only learn French, but they learn how to survive physical challenges. The young voyageurs live in tents at a permanent campsite on Turtle River Lake. Their days are often spent canoeing on the many lakes and rivers in the area just as the French Canadian fur traders did in the 19th century. In a similar vein, the German Grüne Welle (Green Wave) for students ages 14 to 18 exposes participants to German language and culture through experiences in a wilderness setting. The focus for this course is the environment and/or important historical events.

---

[3] It should be noted that while costs to participants are not exorbitant, scholarships are available for those needing financial assistance for any of the sessions with the exception of the language abroad programs. Contributors to the scholarship funds include individuals, state agencies, foundations and corporations (both domestic and foreign), the Passport Fund program, and Concordia Language Village store sales.

Not to be overlooked are the one-month credit programs abroad. In fact, many students follow up a village experience with one of these programs. In the summer of 2000, which was typical of other summers, 86 students visited France, Germany, Japan, or Spain. They interacted daily with proficient speakers of the target language and were able to participate in many rich cultural events, as well as explore historical sites and museums. A one-week homestay with a family was also part of the agenda. While much of the time was spent experiencing the language and culture, some was set aside for a more formal study of both. To be eligible for a language abroad program, students must have at least intermediate proficiency and a minimum of two years (or its equivalent) of high school credit in the target language. Candidates are assessed through a telephone interview to ensure that they are fluent enough to fully benefit from the experience abroad.

Teachers seeking graduate credit in education or direct involvement as villagers can enroll in programs especially designed for them. A graduate course offered through Concordia College offers immersion teaching techniques. This course is taught in English by Donna Clementi, the dean of Teacher Seminars. In it, she presents the Concordia Language Villages educational philosophy of teaching, shares various methods of curriculum implementation, and helps teachers develop thematic units. During these seminars, teachers are given the opportunity to visit the villages while they are in session. In addition, teachers can become language learners themselves in week-long immersion workshops in French, Spanish, and German. Many take these courses to brush up on their own language skills or to find out what immersion is all about by experiencing it themselves.

Other programs include:

1. The village weekend programs, which run from October through May, in French, German, Spanish, Chinese, and Japanese. They are recommended to students in elementary, middle, junior, and senior high schools who are studying those languages in their schools and who want to "live" the language for a weekend. Typically, a whole class or combined classes will participate in a weekend program.
2. Adult Programs, which run September through May, in Finnish, Norwegian, Swedish, Spanish, Japanese, French, and German. For persons 18 years old and over, these range from 3-day to week-long sessions. According to Sarah Happel, Assistant Director for Public Relations, most adults enroll in these programs in order to sharpen their language skills. The courses include a workshop in rosemaling (a Norwegian art form), Norwegian Vinterfest, featuring cross-country skiing and folk dancing, a trip abroad to Norway, and immersion courses in each language.
3. College credit programs for advanced learners of French, German, and Spanish. Students must still be in high school in order to enroll in these

courses, and they must have had three years of high school language study or its equivalent. An interview determines whether a prospective student has sufficient fluency to handle the work. In 1999 and 2000, three one-month courses were offered: (a) Race, Gender, and Power in the Francophone World; (b) Germany After the Wall: Modern German Culture and Civilizations; and (c) Latin American Culture and Civilizations. Combining language learning, in-depth seminars, and workshops, these courses are offered during the summer at their respective villages. They generally are taught by international and American scholars, and educators who are both fluent in the target language and experienced in immersion techniques.

4. Elderhostel Programs which are held in April, May, and October are taught in German, Finnish, and Swedish. Again, the courses focus on language and cultural experiences in a village environment. Only persons 55 and over are eligible.

The Teaching Staff

The teaching staff is required to attend a Multivillage Orientation to gain more understanding of the mission and philosophy of the Concordia Language Villages and to become acquainted with each other. Actual preparation for village life and teaching is accomplished by the dean of each village, a variety of specialists, and returning staff members. Village counselors and teachers must be proficient speakers of the target language and must have some formal educational background in the language and culture.

The dean of each village hires staff members, makes policy and salary decisions, plans the overall curriculum, schedule, etc., and has final authority in the overall management of the village. Two facilitators—for the credit program and the non-credit program—work closely with the dean on scheduling and other matters. They also serve as resource persons for the teachers in their respective programs. Certified teachers (or their equivalents) teach the one-month credit courses, and assess the progress of each villager. Counselors usually conduct the non-credit sessions, sometimes assist credit teachers with their duties, serve as program leaders for cultural activities, including global awareness, and plan or assist in the organization of the evening programs and other cultural events. Both teachers and counselors are expected to be active participants in the daily life of the villages, take on cabin counseling responsibilities, and encourage the villagers as they move forward in the language learning process. The remaining staff, in addition to carrying out the duties relevant to their positions, also participate in village activities when appropriate. Knowledge of the target language is preferred, but not required of support staff members, including health care providers and kitchen personnel. All hired persons are expected to play a role in creating the best cultural immersion environment possible, regardless of position.

Initial Placement

Concordia Language Villages is moving toward self-placement procedures, especially in the credit courses. They have found that fewer changes are necessary if students are allowed to place themselves under the supervision of a facilitator. First the villagers complete the written portion of the self-placement procedures by developing answers to questions on paper. With the aid of a facilitator, they then group themselves into beginning, intermediate, and advanced levels by comparing their own writing to that of other villagers and/or to writing samples typical of various levels. Once with a group, the villagers move into the oral phase of the assessment process by discussing in the target language the answers to the questions they have just written about. Again with the help of a facilitator, they regroup (if necessary) based on what they learn about their own abilities to communicate orally. Then they group themselves yet again after reading posters that have been placed on the walls. In English, each poster describes language behaviors most typical of the levels. Together, the posters form a continuum, stretching around the room. For example, the first poster might feature such items as "Can I say my name in _____?" "Can I count to one hundred?" etc. A poster at a more advanced level might ask, "Do I feel comfortable talking about abstract topics such as the environment or politics?" "Can I read an abstract chapter from a textbook and understand most of it?" etc.

By this time, the students and the facilitator have a pretty realistic view of where each participant falls in relation to the rest of the group, making placement reasonably accurate.

The Curriculum

The immersion experience in the villages is rich and varied. Villagers are expected to interact daily with teachers, counselors, facilitators, and other villagers, many of whom are operating at higher levels. Thus, the villagers are likely to receive a great deal of input (some of it comprehensible and some not) and are encouraged to participate in negotiated communication, albeit limited at first. They eat meals and share cabins with seven or eight other villagers and a teacher/counselor, often in "family" groupings. Some of the villagers have even been known to experience a bit of language and cultural shock as they attempt to get their needs met in the new environment.

Although what is taught differs from village to village, teacher to teacher, and year to year, the curriculum across the villages includes similar elements: the village itself as content, global concerns, cultural traditions, music, dancing, ethnic arts and crafts, cooking, sports, history, literature, and current events. Some villages use a flexible syllabus in which the villagers have input and texts have a place, but do not determine the agenda.

For example, the French Village dean, Garrette Heysel, reports that in his program lessons are planned around a theme adopted by the whole village for a specified period of time. Themes have included the 1960s; the Ivory Coast; the color blue (ending with an evening program on artists, including Van Gogh); a day in a French student's life; and many more. Teachers are reminded that no matter what the theme, they are to incorporate listening, speaking, reading, and writing activities into units appropriate to the level they are teaching.

In other villages, the curriculum is a bit more dependent on written texts or on a predetermined syllabus. For example, the Russian village dean, Laurie Iudin-Nelson, has developed textbooks and a collection of Russian songs that form the curriculum for village teachers who wish to use them. The textbooks include basic greetings and phrases, topics of interest, grammar, and plenty of activities to ensure reinforcement and the recycling of key concepts. Laurie, who is herself a musician, has made folk, Romany, and contemporary Russian songs an integral part of the language learning process as well. A balalaika ensemble, folk dancing, a Russian choir singing folk and liturgical music, and informal campfire singing are among the musical experiences that form the basis for many language lessons.

In all the villages, the use of authentic materials to support the curriculum is considered essential. Literary pieces and songs, guest lectures, recorded television and radio programming, films, newspapers, and magazines often become the focus of units and lessons. Because there are generally 10 or fewer students per class, teachers are often able to individualize the curriculum itself to better meet the needs of each student.

Preparation for "International Days" is also part of the curriculum. The villagers and staff members come together two days during the summer to celebrate world languages and cultures with parents and members of the community. An international buffet is prepared and served, colorful presentations are given, and village experiences are shared.

Research in Progress

Currently, Concordia Language Villages is being researched by Dr. Heidi Hamilton, Associate Professor of Linguistics at Georgetown University and senior researcher with the National Capital Language Resource Center (NCLRC). Dr. Hamilton and her staff of five research assistants are attempting to identify what differences lie between the traditional approaches to foreign language teaching and the immersion found in the villages. To gather their data, the research assistants are now living in various villages. Soon the entire research team will be planning the next phases of their project. We are all looking forward to the day when this important research is completed and the results are made public.

A FRENCH IMMERSION PROGRAM
FOR ELEMENTARY STUDENTS[4]

Background

In the mid-1980s, a group of Thunder Bay, Ontario, parents (of mainly Finnish or Italian origin) first approached the Lakehead Board of Education to request a French immersion program for their children. They wanted their children to learn French so they would have more career flexibility. Why did they choose an immersion program over one of the more traditional ones? They believed, as do many parents in Canada, that foreign language immersion does, in fact, produce bilinguals. Their views were compatible with those of the Ontario Ministry of Education, which concluded that immersion is an optimal means for achieving a high level of competency in French. Immersion programs (see Chapter 17) involve a far more extensive and meaningful experience with French than can be provided by the more traditional core programs, in which students study French for one period each day, or the more recently developed extended programs in which at least one content-area class is taught in French, in addition to the core.

While their children are learning the subject matter in French, the parents feel assured that skills in the first language will not be adversely affected. Lapkin and Swain reported as early as 1984 that any fears concerning this issue have no basis in reality. This is at least partially due to the fact that the children belong to the majority culture (in the case of Thunder Bay, only 3 percent of households claim French as their home language) and that English dominates their lives outside of the school environment. Lapkin and Swain reported:

> The English achievement results for students in the early total-immersion program indicate that, although initially behind students in unilingual English programs in literacy skills, within a year of the introduction of an English Language Arts component into the curriculum, the immersion students perform equivalently on standardized tests of English achievement to students in the English-only program (1984, p. 50).

They claimed that this is true even for students who are not introduced to English until grade 3 or 4. They point out, too, that after grade 4, French immersion students sometimes outperform their English-only peers in some aspects of English language skills. Their achievement in the subject areas (math,

[4] I wish to thank the following for sharing information about their programs with me and for allowing me to observe French immersion classes in their respective schools: Ken Cressman, Nicole Gaudet, George Rendall, Lise Bagdon, Colette Aubry, John Brusset, Carol Nabarra, Glenn Coriveau, and Roy Fossum. My thanks also to Wendy Hansen for providing transportation and lodging.

science, social studies, etc.) compares favorably to that of their English-only peers (see Krashen, 1984).

In addition, parents are convinced that their children do not need particularly high IQs to be successful in French immersion programs. On this issue, Lapkin and Swain assert that IQ is not any more predictive of success in French immersion programs than it is in regular English-only programs. Students of below-average intelligence are not at a greater disadvantage in immersion programs. In fact, being bilingual may boost their confidence and have other positive results affectively.

In general, most students can expect to be competent in French intake skills (listening and reading) by the time they finish elementary school. However, in the output skills (speaking and writing), they are often less competent until they have had considerable contact with proficient French speakers. The only children found by the organization of Canadian Parents of French to be less than adequate candidates for immersion are those who exhibit a lack of ability in auditory discrimination or auditory memory. Problems in these areas are usually detected in the first year of kindergarten and affected students can be steered early on into English-only programs.

Due to the efforts of those first parent-advocates of French immersion in Thunder Bay in the 1980s and those parents, teachers, and other educators who were to follow, the program has mushroomed. It began with 36 students in one elementary school and now boasts 647 students in four elementary schools, one of which has a program extending from the second year of kindergarten (for five-year-olds) all the way through grade 8. The programs, which are allowed to grow with the students, increase by one grade level at a time as the students become older, until all the programs extend at least through grade 8. However, the school board is currently considering the incorporation of French immersion into the secondary curriculum, beginning with grade 9. Future plans also include the establishment of a French Immersion Center (where the regular English-only program would be dropped) at Redwood Public School, should the current enrollments continue. For the past two years, 16 to 17 percent of all second-year kindergarten children have been enrolled in French immersion programs throughout the district.

Enrollment and Transportation

Enrollment is on a first-come, first-served basis, and transfers from other immersion programs are accepted, provided there is room. Transportation is generally available for those accepted into the program, making it possible for a larger number of students to be involved. Students within the urban area are bused from designated neighborhood pickup points to the schools, and for those in the rural areas, transportation arrangements can be made at a reasonable cost.

Support Services

Schools with French immersion programs maintain an ever-expanding collection of books and reference materials in French. The teachers are now looking for materials oriented to the particular needs of immersion students. In addition, audiovisual resources appear to be in ample supply, and new ones are ordered yearly.

Assistance is available for enrichment or remediation from a bilingual resource teacher or a qualified special education resource teacher. Parents of children with severe problems are counseled, and recommendations are given depending upon the type of problem and upon the resources available at each school.

The home itself can be considered a "support service." Nicole Gaudet, an education officer for the district, reports, "Because the parents have made a decision about the education of their children to be in French immersion programs, they are more involved in their children's education." Parents seem more than happy to read stories in English to their children at home, work with teachers to provide experiences with proficient French speakers whenever possible, take their children to French cultural events, and volunteer to aid in classroom ventures.

Program Description

In the first two years of the program, the language for instruction is 100 percent French (except in emergency situations). In addition, all communication within the classroom is in French. In the second, third, fourth, and fifth grades, English is added but is limited to 75 minutes per day of English Language Arts. French is the language for instruction 75 percent of the time, English 25 percent of the time. During grades 6, 7, and 8, 50 percent of the instruction is in French and 50 percent in English. By the end of the eighth grade, the students will have studied history, geography, math, science, and other subjects in both languages. The subjects cover a wide range of content areas at each level (see Table 19.1).

The concepts to which the students are exposed in the French immersion program are comparable to those to which they are exposed in the regular English-only classroom.[5] In listening, the goals include helping children to listen with interest and selectivity at appropriate levels in a variety of experiences. They are taught to judge validity, make comparisons, make inferences, draw conclusions, generalize, and understand intent. During speaking, children learn to articulate their ideas and feelings confidently in a supportive

---

[5] The concepts listed here are paraphrased from the *Core Language Guide* made available by the Lakehead Board of Education. No attempt is made to list all of the goals set down by the board. A few of the more typical ones have been selected for inclusion.

TABLE 19.1. FRENCH IMMERSION CURRICULUM

Grade	K	1	2	3	4	5	6	7	8
French	X	X	X	X	X	X	X	X	X
Math	X	X	X	X	X	X	*	*X	
Environmental Studies	X	X	X	X	X	X	X		
Science								*	X
Music	X	X	X	X	X	X	*X	*X	*X
Physical Education	X	X	X	X	X	X	*X	*X	*X
Art	X	X	X	X	X	X	*X	*X	*X
History								X	*
Geography								*	X
English			*	*	*	*	*	*	*

Code: * subjects taught in English
       X subjects taught in French

Adapted from *Programme d'Immersion Précoce*, The Lakehead Board of Education, 1985.

environment, extend and synthesize various speaking skills (drama, role play-ing, conversation, discussion, oral reading, and others), and develop opinions through interaction with the teacher and peers. They learn to tell stories, inter-pret pictures, name and describe objects, explain events, evaluate, and ques-tion using verbal as well as nonverbal clues. Reading skills and processes involve exposing students to a variety of reading materials (legends, myths, folktales, poems, plays, cartoons, novels, biographies, magazine articles, recipes, directions, newspapers), enabling them to respond to print within the environment (e.g., names, labels, signs, initials), comprehend and respond to ideas, relate pictures to print, recall details, sequence events, recognize plot, understand relationships, follow directions, make judgments, distinguish fact from fantasy and fact from opinion, check for bias, predict outcomes, and so forth. Writing involves being able to label components on maps and diagrams; record personal experiences in their own words; adapt style to intended pur-pose; write from dictation; and create stories, poetry, diaries, letters, sets of directions, expositions, and reports. Even by the end of kindergarten, children have acquired a fairly extensive vocabulary in French; they are able to follow instructions and to comprehend simple stories. They can answer questions appropriately, participate effectively in drama, and sing a number of songs.

Because the immersion classes focus on subject matter rather than on the target language itself, it is important that the teachers have an adequate knowl-edge of the subject areas they teach and that they be proficient speakers of French. It is also important for the students to associate specific teachers with French and others with English. For this reason, the school district always assigns teachers to classes taught in the same language. This is especially important when there is a possibility that the same students will be present in more than one class taught by the same teacher.

Strengths and Weaknesses of the Program

Ken Cressman, the principal of Redwood Public School, feels that the French immersion program in his school has benefited the entire student body. When French cultural events are arranged, they are planned not only for the French immersion students but for everyone. It is his feeling that any cultural activity, even one in another language, can be enriching for all the students, be it singing, mime, or drama. In addition, he has observed that the French immersion students have improved the ambiance of the school in general because they tend to be more tolerant of other cultures and differences among people. When asked if one segment of the school has benefited most from the immersion program, he targeted the core French program as having perhaps received the most advantages. Although the students in this program take French for only one period a day, they profit from exposure to French immersion students with whom they can sometimes converse in a limited fashion and from whom they can often receive help with their homework.

Nicole Gaudet is also convinced that French immersion has been a real boon to the environments of all the schools of which it is a part. Because of the increased support and interest of the parents of these children, the schools' parent associations thrive, and the atmospheres of the schools are becoming more positive.

However, both Cressman and Gaudet agree that improvements can be made. Lack of materials appropriate to French immersion was one of the problems mentioned. Currently, most of the materials come from Francophone programs and are intended for native French speakers. However, teachers are busy creating their own materials and translating the ones intended for the English-only programs. Another problem mentioned was recruiting enough teachers with expertise and fluency to meet the growing needs. In addition, developing a long-range plan for inservicing was felt to be necessary means for helping the teachers to keep current once they have been hired.

Because these weaknesses are not inherent in the immersion programs themselves, both administrators believe they can be overcome with additional funds and further effort on the part of everyone involved with the programs.

A BICULTURAL INSTITUTE FOR CHILDREN, ADOLESCENTS, AND ADULTS[6]

The Instituto Cultural Argentina Norteamericano (ICANA), a private, non-profit organization, was founded in 1927 in Buenos Aires. Its primary goal was to link the education and cultural communities of Argentina and the United

[6] Appreciation goes to Blanca Arazi, the former director of ICANA, for sharing this information with me.

States. Since 1982, its enrollment has grown from 800 students to 12,000 students today, according to its former director, Blanca Arazi. She reported that the Institute's popularity in recent years is due mainly to the communicative methodologies that have emerged in its courses. She credited communicative language teaching (see Chapter 9) for serving as the main impetus for this radical departure from a past reliance on grammatical approaches as the basis for language development. She is convinced that these approaches serve as ". . . the central most important means for gaining linguistic skills."

Students

The student population at the Institute is quite heterogeneous and includes students of all ages and proficiency levels. The students represent diverse cultural and economic backgrounds. But, in spite of all their differences, they have one thing in common: their desire to communicate in English, both in oral and written forms. Their goals at each level are mainly instrumental. At the adult level, goals include preparing themselves for travel to English-speaking countries, being promoted in jobs for which fluency in English is an important asset, and bettering themselves personally as well as professionally. At the adolescent level, goals include preparing for the job market, attending school or traveling in English-speaking countries, understanding English lyrics, communicating through the use of computers, and enriching their personal lives. For children, the goals include understanding English songs, working with computers, playing American games, and understanding English-language cartoons.

Teachers

The Institute's teachers, most of whom have college degrees from local universities, number 210. Not all have college degrees. Some come from the ranks of public translators; others are about to graduate from teacher education programs. No matter their background and preparation, all are required to attend the ongoing inservice programs offered by the Institute. Stress is placed on keeping them informed about current happenings in the field and on giving them the opportunity to share ideas and discuss problems. At inservice sessions, the teachers are taught strategies on how to provide comprehensible input and how to facilitate the language acquisition process without interfering with it, without imposing their own ideas and values upon those expressing opinions, or without spoon-feeding the language to their students. In addition, teachers are asked to reflect upon their own experiences in learning a foreign language. What seemed to facilitate the process for them? What problems did they face? Each inservice program has a specific focus and stated goals. Participating also in the inservice programs are teachers, not only from all over Argentina, but from neighboring countries. Thus, the inservice program experience is very rich and stimulating.

Classes

At ICANA, classes are divided according to age level. Some classes are for children; others for adolescents; yet others for adults. All classes are appropriate for one of three proficiency levels: beginning, intermediate, and advanced (see pages 137–138). Students may select from among the four-month courses offered. Some of them meet twice a week; others meet three or four times a week. Some meet for two-hour sessions; others meet for two and one-half hours. Classes for adults at advanced levels are generally longer in duration then those for adults at lower levels, adolescents, and children. Intensive courses meet during the summer for three hours per session.

Students at all levels generally pay tuition; however, there are free conversation sessions with proficient speakers of English, interactive labs where students practice their listening skills, and video sessions during which students watch five-minute video segments and participate in prepared activities relating to the segments.

The classes revolve around topics of general interest such as the environment, healthcare and nutrition, exercise, sports, science, education, travel, and sociology. No matter the topic, it is connected to everyday life as much as possible. All activities, including oral and written activities, grow out of the main topics. Grammar and pronunciation are dealt with in a nontraditional way within the lessons themselves and only when needed.

Within the classes, students work in pairs and other small groups where they actively participate in activities designed to help them move quickly in the interlanguage development process. They frequently are involved in "mixers," activities involving interaction with the whole class and the facilitator/teacher. It is felt that by participating in such activities and correcting their own mistakes—sometimes with peer help—students will internalize new language skills. Typical activities are described below.

Small-Group Work
Working in pairs and other small groups is particularly stimulating for the students and seems to maximize their effectiveness in the new language. If the issue being discussed is somewhat controversial, then a spokesperson from each group tries to convince the other groups that his or her group is right. If the other groups are not easily convinced, then a vote settles the matter and the groups accept its results. However, that doesn't mean that minds have been changed. The students know that it is acceptable to disagree with one another. In small groups, the facilitator/teacher circulates among the groups and does not interfere, but rather encourages students to talk and become actively involved.

Mixers

From time to time, all the students are asked to interact with one another within a time limit set by the facilitator/teacher. Generally, a question or problem is posed, and students have to actively answer the question or see if they can solve the problem. The teacher and the students often alternate roles as they become facilitators and guides, resource people, managers, and so forth. Whether teacher or student, it is not easy to just sit back and let others do all the work.

Other Kinds of Activities

Affective/humanistic activities are called "field study" activities at the Institute. Through them, the teachers and students get to know each others' interests, likes, dislikes, weekend activities, favorite foods, and so on. By this means, barriers among them seem to be lowered, and a highly supportive environment results.

Games focusing on discussion, action, group competition, problem solving, or guessing provide strong motivation to learn English. At the same time, games serve as a review of structure and vocabulary from previous lessons.

Preparatory activities such as prelistening and prereading activities are used to give contextualization to the content of the courses. It is felt they increase the relevance of whatever happens during the ensuing classroom events, and they give students a chance to think about and plan a course of action.

Other activities include the use of maps, charts, graphs of comparison, radio or newspaper stories, giving and receiving directions, open dialogues, debates, discussions, role plays, and improvisations. Whatever the student activity, it must be appropriate to their age and proficiency levels, and it must appeal to their interests. The facilitator/teacher is asked to provide an example of what the students are meant to do. Students need to know what is expected of them in order that they not become too frustrated.

Language Assessment

In order to place students in the appropriate courses, they are given a battery of tests in all four skill areas. Created by the Institute, these tests include an oral interview and a written multiple-choice test. Children complete only the oral interview portion unless they already have developed some literacy in their first language and in English.

Once students are placed at the appropriate proficiency level, they are evaluated twice by means of specially designed oral and written tests. Their proficiency can also be measured by such standardized tests as the CELT and SLEP. Some opt to take the University of Michigan's Examination for the Certificate of Proficiency in English (ECPE), which is recognized worldwide.

Texts

In addition to some of the standard texts on the market in English as a Foreign Language, the programs rely heavily on what they call "real-life" materials. Such materials include articles and advertisements from newspapers and magazines, songs, television shows (including soap operas), and, of course, the work that the students themselves have done. At the levels intended for children, books about the "Sesame Street" characters, Big Bird, Cookie Monster, and so forth, are used daily. At all levels, importance is placed on involvement and the lowered anxiety and inhibitions that can result from high participation.

A MIDDLE SCHOOL SPANISH LANGUAGE PROGRAM[7]

Background

Millikan Junior High School is in the Los Angeles Unified School District, and, like many schools in that district, it serves a very large language minority population: Latin (30 percent), Asian (30 percent), Anglo (30 percent), Black (5 percent). The remaining 5 percent of the students represent various ethnic backgrounds.

The Foreign Language Department opens its courses in Spanish and French to all who want them, including students in its Special Education programs. The department's faculty is firmly committed to the idea that the foreign language experience is for all who seek a liberal education, and that through this experience, increased understanding and personal growth will result, regardless of ethnic background or other circumstances.

The students' motivation for studying a foreign language is generally instrumental—to fulfill academic requirements. However, many of the students are interested in developing basic interpersonal communication skills.

The Goals of the Foreign Language Department

The department has adopted the following goals set down by the California Foreign Language Framework to develop individuals who can:

- communicate accurately and appropriately with representatives of other languages and cultures
- understand themselves as individuals shaped by a given culture
- function appropriately in at least one other culture
- exhibit sensitivity to cultural differences in general

It is the feeling of the department that these goals can be achieved when programs stress communication over the learning of grammar rules and the mem-

---

[7] I want to thank Brandon Zaslow, the Chair of the Foreign Language Department at Millikan Junior High School, for providing me with the information upon which this summary is based.

orization of vocabulary items. The governing principle of the department's programs is, "to learn content and culture through language and to learn language through content and culture."

More specifically, the department expects that students will be able to function in informal environments, understand simple face-to-face conversation, and deal with relevant academic and survival topics. In addition, it is expected that they will be able to determine overall meaning from written discourse, create meaning through writing, and transfer learned material to new situations.

Description of the Spanish as a Foreign Language Program

The department offers two programs in Spanish: Spanish as a Foreign Language and Spanish for Spanish Speakers. For the purpose of this chapter, only the Spanish as a Foreign Language Program—Level 1 will be described in depth. Its two-year program (Levels 1 and 2) serves approximately 200 students each year, and seeks to bring eighth- and ninth-graders to intermediate levels in Spanish (see page 137) by the end of the second year. A 10-week exploratory Spanish module is offered to seventh-graders to introduce them to basic concepts and give them an overview of what to expect. Often, these students become group leaders in the Level 1 classes and sometimes serve as resources for the other students.

The following practices are a few of those developed by the department and adhered to by the teachers (one full-time and two part-time) in the Spanish as a Foreign Language Program.

  Instruction is appropriate to the learners' levels of proficiency in each of the skill areas.

  Students perform in a wide range of culturally valid situations.

  Lessons challenge students to interact with increasingly demanding academic content.

  Students perform a wide range of communicative tasks (emphasis on higher-level thinking skills).

  Teachers use paralinguistic clues (visuals, objects, etc.) and modify their speech to make input comprehensible (simplification, expansion, restatement, slower speed, use of cognates, etc.).

  Teachers frequently confirm and clarify responses and check for comprehension.

  Guided practice is both meaningful and personalized.

  Teachers provide opportunities for paired and small-group interactions and use strategies that provide for various learning styles.

Below is an overview of Level 1 and a description of sample activities.

An Overview

UNIT 1: FIRST ENCOUNTERS

Introducing oneself/saying where you are from
Understanding and spelling names and places
Greeting and leave taking/saying how you feel/being polite
Understanding prices/giving and receiving phone numbers
Asking and telling times and dates
Discussing the weather/seasons/temperature
Role playing in the target culture and U.S. contexts

UNIT 2: ACTIVE LIVES

Describing daily activities in and out of school
Asking questions about activities
Expressing what one desires/hopes/needs to do
Expressing what one likes/dislikes doing
Role playing in target culture and U.S. contexts

UNIT 3: FRIENDS AND FAMILY

Identifying others (friends and family)
Describing self and others
Talking about feelings
Talking about activities related to friends and family
Talking about sports
Talking about pets
Talking about living space at home
Talking about routine care of the home
Role playing in target culture and U.S. contexts

UNIT 4: DAILY LIFE

Talking about daily routines (discussing similarities and differences)
Focus on weekdays and weekends
Talking about clothes (colors/combinations)
Learning about healthful living/the body/medical care
Talking about food (marketing/restaurants/invitations for meals)
Talking about school/physical layout/activities in more detail
Role playing in target culture and U.S. contexts

UNIT 5: COMMUNITY LIFE

Identifying places in various communities (maps/directions)
Talking about community/cultural activities
Talking about community resources
Talking about travel
Role playing in target culture and U.S. contexts

UNIT 6: THE WORKING WORLD

Identifying abilities
Discussing career preferences
Identifying professional opportunities
Making plans for the future

Sample Activities

THE LOW-BEGINNING LEVEL

The first samples come from the unit El Cuerpo (the body) that has been developed for Spanish as a Foreign Language Program students who are operating at the low-beginning level (see page 137). Its major goal is to help students develop listening comprehension and a large receptive vocabulary. Speech will be encouraged but not expected at this point.

The unit draws from communicative and physical approaches (Chapter 8 and 9) and story experience (Chapter 11).

1. Using aspects of physical approaches, students are asked to touch specific body parts: head, chest, stomach, back, arms, hands, fingers, legs, knees, and feet. However, not all items are introduced at once. First, two items are introduced, followed by a check for understanding. Then, a third item is added, followed by a check for understanding. Then, a fourth is added, and so forth.

2. Students are divided into groups. Each group is given a life-size doll made of construction paper. Aspects of the story experience are then used to tell the story of a terrible accident involving the doll which represents a real person. The students are "doctors" and have each been given a number (they were taught numbers previously). They are instructed by the teacher to place the bandages (they have sticking putty on their backs) on the various injured body parts. Below is the story. The students will probably only understand the body parts, the word "bandage," the command "put" and some of the words are made clear through visual aids.

    The teacher says in Spanish, "Carlos has had a terrible accident (the instructor points to the picture of a person with mild injuries). He was hit by a car. Doctors, doctors, what should we do?" (The teacher holds up a card with a huge question mark on it and shrugs his or her shoulders as if puzzled.) "Put a bandage on his head, Doctor 1." (Doctor 1 in each group puts the bandage on the doll's head.) The teacher repeats the question and asks the students to put bandages on other parts, until all the targeted body parts have been recycled. Then the teacher says, "Carlos is well now" (shows a picture of the same person obviously recovered). "Take the bandage off his/her head, Doctor 2", and so forth until all the bandages have been removed.

3. For further reinforcement, students cut out pictures of the various body parts from magazines and paste them on a blank sheet of paper to form bodies of their own creation. Then they are asked to label the parts.

THE HIGH-BEGINNING LEVEL

Next are sample activities from a unit entitled Bienvenidos (Welcome). This unit has been developed for students who are operating at the high-beginning level (see page 137). The unit focuses on encouraging positive attitudes toward Mexico and on specific communicative demands such as being able to greet others, talk about time, make appointments, plan schedules, order food in a restaurant, buy necessary items for survival, etc. It centers around a story line in which the students pretend to be participating in a year-abroad program in Mexico. They arrive at their respective Spanish-speaking homes where they need to be able to get things done with language. Below are just a few activities from the unit, which is designed to last about six weeks. It should be noted that the new concepts and structures encountered will be recycled many times in a variety of circumstances.

1. Students make simulated telephone calls to their hosting peers. They give their names and spell them and they ask many questions about what to pack for their stay, etc.
2. Students write down the addresses of their hosts. Then they each write to their host, indicating their feelings about visiting the host's country.
3. Once in the host's village or city, students change their watches to reflect the time in the time zone they have entered, if it is different from their own time zone.
4. Students take the roles of hosts or guests as they introduce themselves and tell where they are from. Consideration is given to appropriate forms: first-name basis using *tú* or title plus last name basis using *usted*. Versions of this activity are repeated as needed.
5. Each student chooses favorite activities from a list provided by the host. The lists include events such as soccer games, concerts, dining out, shopping, etc. They then talk about the dates and starting times of the activities in which they will be participating.
6. Students are given calendars upon which they can write down the events in which they will participate. What is the event? Where is it? When does it start? Will someone pick them up? If so, at what time? Must they meet a person somewhere? If so, where and at what time? Students can also enter other events such as birthdays of the host family members, holidays, etc.

Strengths/Problems

One of the strengths of the program is its exploratory module for seventh-graders, giving them insight into what it might be like to learn another language. However, according to Brandon Zaslow, the Chair of the Foreign Language Department, its main strength is its focus on relevant content and culture. But this is also where its chief problem lies. The high schools into which it feeds often adhere to traditional, structure-based programs, making transitions difficult, and sometimes painful, for the students who matriculate with high expectations for continued relevant study. In spite of this problem, most of the students are able to adjust and do very well in their new settings as long as they have at least some opportunity to express themselves creatively in Spanish.

A HIGH SCHOOL SPANISH PROGRAM[8]

Although working against odds common to many high school foreign language programs, Christina Rivera uses communicative methods as much as possible in her Levels I and II (first and second year) Spanish classes at Artesia High School in Artesia, California. One of the constraints under which she works is that she must cover a certain amount of formal grammar so that the students will be ready for what is expected at subsequent levels. A second constraint is that she is able to meet with her students only one period a day, five days a week. Yet a third constraint is that, as in other California schools, the students are in foreign languages classes not always by choice. Often they are there to satisfy graduation or college entrance requirements. Thus, many of her students bring to her classes less than positive attitudes.

Nevertheless, it is her hope that by the end of the program, the students will be able to communicate effectively and appropriately in the target language. It is also her hope that students will become more sensitive to cultural differences. Activities in her classes, for the most part, center around her students' world: their objectives, their personal attempts to deal with uncertainties, and their efforts to comprehend and speak another language.

Level I

Before beginning the instruction in Spanish, Rivera takes time to educate the students in the theories upon which her methods are predicated. She feels that as a result of her doing so, the students are less apt to find her methods "strange" and are more apt to try.

Using an outline similar to what Krashen and Terrell suggest (see pages 171–175), she works on receptive skills first with Level I students. Body language, gestures, facial expressions, and tone of voice are all important in the initial phases. Through physical approaches (see Chapter 8), students learn colors by manipulating pieces of colored paper. They learn about the objects in their immediate environment, food, clothing, and many other relevant concepts by manipulation of various items. Pictures and props are used to act out scenes. Familiar stories are told as visuals are shown. And because it does not require students to respond orally, bingo is played, reinforcing concepts related to the topics covered. Simple treasure hunts (see also Chapter 12) are designed requiring students to find objects of certain colors or that have other specific characteristics.

The following activities combining communicative practices and physical approaches are typical:

1. Describe a picture from a current magazine and follow up by making statements or giving commands.

---

[8] I am grateful to Christina Rivera for making her program available to me.

Example: *This is a picture of some skirts. Notice the colors. This one* (points to a skirt) *is green. Jane* (a student in class) *is wearing a skirt. Her skirt is green. This one* (points to another skirt) *is pink. Point to the pink skirt,* etc.

Follow-up: (Thumbs up means "yes"; thumbs down means "no.") *This skirt* (points to a pink skirt) *is green* (thumbs should be pointed down). *This skirt* (points again to the pink skirt) *is pink* (thumbs should be pointed up), and so forth.

2. Ask students to draw or cut out pictures of items in a category (food, clothing, kitchen utensils, etc.). Ask them to hold up pictures of specific items. Have them take specific pictures to various places around the room.

3. Using pictures, facial expressions, and gestures, introduce the students to some of the more common emotions: happy, sad, angry, bored, fearful, etc. Hold up cue cards on which the names of the different emotions have been written. Have the students point to the picture that clearly expresses the specific emotion indicated.

4. Using numbered pictures, ask the students to say the number of the picture described by the teacher.

5. Have the students make "self" collages with items that they feel best express themselves. Later in the year they will be discussing these with class members in the target language.

As the students progress to higher beginning levels, mass media are relied upon because of their relevance and contextuality. Rivera finds commercials particularly effective. Students act out the commercials with props as the teacher gives directions. Much later, students will be writing and acting out their own commercials. Other activities she feels are appropriate to this level are described below:

1. Using a real suitcase and real clothing and other items for travel, students prepare for an imaginary trip. The teacher asks the students to place the items in the suitcase that they would take to Acapulco, Aspen, etc.

2. The students are shown a picture from a magazine. They are asked to name what they see. A list of the items mentioned is written on the board.

3. Students make a chart consisting of several of their names, the clothes they are wearing, and the color of each item (see a similar activity in Chapter 9).

4. Matrices such as the following are used as starters for scenarios:
   ¿Cuánto cuesta el _____?
   Está de venta. Le cuesta _____?
   ¡Qué bueno! (¡Qúe malo!)
   Necesito un _____.
   Por qué no vas a _____?
   ¿Cuánto cuesta?
   Cuesta _____ mas o menos.

5. Students write in a journal each day using the target language. The teacher guides them at first. They begin by writing down their favorite colors and favorite items of clothing. At later levels, the writing becomes freer as students write their feelings and thoughts.

The study of culture also is included as the students progress. Discussions are conducted entirely in the target language, aided by props, maps, and a lot of visuals. Cultural information is frequently woven into other activities such as listening to music and game playing.

Grammar is introduced at early levels. However, the concepts are those that are generally easily learned and applied. Many of the grammar activities are assigned as homework.

Level II

Level II students (those in their second year of language study) are usually somewhere in the high-beginning to low-intermediate levels. Rivera feels that many of them regress over the summer since they have had almost no exposure to the target language then. However, after spending a few weeks doing activities similar to those described above, the students will soon move into the intermediate levels, if they are not there already. Students at this level are expected to listen to Spanish language broadcasts during a part of each day for several days in sequence.[9] They may hear traffic reports, time/temperature/ weather reports, commercials, horoscope readings, song dedications, listener call-ins, interviews, sports reports, the news, or lyrics to music. They are encouraged to tape the broadcasts for repeated listening experiences. They are asked to write down what items they understand from each report. As they listen to the same reports from time to time, they are pleased to find that they understand more and more of the broadcasts. Through this process, students are exposed to proficient Spanish speakers using contemporary, idiomatic speech. They learn to take advantage of cognates, intonation, and other clues to meaning.

Affective activities (see Chapter 14) are favorites among Rivera's students at this level. It must be kept in mind that the students have spent some time preparing for humanistic activities all along. At earlier levels, emotions were identified through communicative practices and physical approaches. The journals allowed students to express their likes and dislikes and their attitudes in general. In addition, the collages contributed to their willingness to reveal themselves in low-risk situations.

Below are a few of the activities used:

1. To reinforce the terminology describing human emotions, the teacher reads a soap opera melodramatically. Cue cards with the names of various emotions can be held up by the teacher or an assistant as the story is being read. The students as a group can act out the emotion that is being displayed.

---

[9] Credit for this idea is given to Lynne La Fleur.

2. Students are asked in the target language to draw a happy baby, a mad father, and so forth. Then they are instructed to draw the following:
   a. a father who has just heard that his teenager has smashed the family car
   b. a mother seeing an "A" on her child's report card
   c. a girl seeing her boyfriend with her best friend
   d. a cheerleader after falling off the human "pyramid"
3. Students hold up small cue cards with the names of emotions written on them. Each card is held up in response to statements in the target language made by the teacher. Below are some examples.
   a. When someone is mean to me, I feel . . .
   b. At a party, I feel . . .
   c. Before a test, I feel . . .
   d. With my family, I feel . . .
   e. At the doctor's office, I feel . . .
4. Students are asked to name songs that make them feel happy, sad, like dancing, etc.
5. Students draw and label pictures about their favorite activities. They then interview each other about the activities depicted.

Eventually, the students are able to discuss problems, goals, and everyday matters in the target language. Although they may not be able to converse in perfect Spanish by the end of the second year, they seem to communicate with a minimum of anxiety.

Rivera insists that her main goal throughout the levels is to create as natural a learning environment as possible. She feels that she still has a long way to go to create an optimal classroom. However, she modestly admits that she is coming closer to her vision with each passing year.

CHAPTER 20

Two-Way Bilingual Programs

Two-way or dual bilingual programs are gaining popularity across the United States today despite the political climate of the last decade. Parents, students, and teachers have been opting for these programs, developing and supporting them in the communities where they have proven themselves to be highly beneficial. Based on on their extensive research, Collier and Thomas (1999) reported that although one-way bilingual programs produced excellent results, two-way bilingual programs appeared to be most effective overall (see Chapter 17). The first program described in this chapter is a two-way developmental Spanish/English program in the Valley Center Union School District in California. The second description is of a two-way immersion Cantonese/English program in Public School No. 1 on the lower east side of Manhattan in New York City. Both programs are highly respected in their communities—and for good reason, as the reader will see.

A DEVELOPMENTAL DUAL LANGUAGE PROGRAM: SPANISH/ENGLISH[1]

One of the more exciting dual language programs in bilingual education today is the voluntary Two-Way Developmental Bilingual Program (K–8) located at

---

[1] I want to thank Lydia Vogt, Lucy Haines, Norma Badawi, and Dr. Sarah Clayton for sharing their program with me. Appreciation also goes to the bilingual teachers whose classes I had the pleasure to observe: Natalie Weston, Mary Susan Stone, and Geri Geis. Thanks also to Debbie Mixon (math and science teacher) and Susan Benz (an aide and parent of a student in the program) for providing me with insights into their particular roles and into the program in general. But I am especially grateful to Lydia, who organized my visit and served as a most gracious and knowledgeable guide and to Kathryn Z. Weed, who made me aware of the program in the first place.

the Valley Center Union School District in California. Valley Center, a semi-rural community north of San Diego, is home to many children of migrant farm workers as well as to children from middle-class and upper middle-class families. The school district's population of 3,000 students K–8 is approximately 52 percent European-American, 26 percent Mexican-American, 11 percent Native American, and 1 percent other. Norma Badawi, Director of Special Projects, reported that in 2000, about 700 children (26 percent of the total school population) were in the two-way developmental bilingual program with the consent and encouragement of their parents. These students were served by 23 bilingual teachers and several bilingual aides throughout the school day.[2]

The program is "two-way" in that Spanish-speaking children are learning English and English-speaking children are learning Spanish. The program, which began in 1983, is still thriving and appears to be more popular than ever among the parents, teachers, and the community who have witnessed its results over and over again: students proficient in two languages before the end of elementary school! It has met the challenges of time and has developed accordingly in order to better meet the needs of its students and still be in compliance with California's Proposition 227.[3] Students and their parents are motivated by the benefits often associated with being bilingual: greater economic opportunity, increased self-esteem (particularly for minority children who become "Spanish experts" to those children learning Spanish), more career opportunities, a better understanding of other cultures, greater cognitive flexibility, and a stronger bond between the school and the community.

Just how did this program come about? It first arose out of a felt need to help students learn a second language and maintain and develop skills in their first language at the same time. Dr. Sarah Clayton, assistant superintendent and the architect of the program, began in the early 1980s by soliciting the support of the school board, the administration, the teaching staff, and the community. She presented her initial ideas to every group that would listen. When asked what recommendation she might give to others trying to begin similar programs, Dr. Clayton answered, "Persist but never insist. Don't look for satisfaction in the short term. Start small and add on every year rather than trying to do it all at once. Have long-term goals, and be patient enough to achieve them."

In her case, patience has paid off. The program has received accolades from various sources. In 1988, the California School Boards Association recognized the Valley Center Union School District for its exemplary bilingual program. In

---

[2] It is interesting to note that in grades K–3, no more than 20 students were allowed in a class (mandated by state law); in grades 4–8, 26 or 27 were the average.

[3] Proposition 227, the English Language Education for the Children in the Public Schools Initiative, was passed in 1998 in California. It requires that language minority children be taught only in English with a few exceptions. One of the few exceptions is a student with special educational needs who has obtained a parental waiver in order to be placed in an alternative program such as bilingual education. In the early grades, a parental waiver can be granted only after the child has been placed for 30 days in a structured English immersion class at the beginning of each year.

1994, The BBC (British Broadcasting Communications Corporation) presented the program live, via satellite, to their British radio audience. That same year, CABE (the California Association for Bilingual Education) awarded the district the Outstanding Elementary Program Award for substantial contributions to Bilingual Education. But, according to Dr. Clayton, her greatest satisfaction came when several students from the very first class graduated from college.

The District's Philosophy

Lydia Vogt, principal at the elementary school and a strong supporter of bilingual education, shared with me the program's basic philosophy. Below are a few excerpts that help to provide a foundation for the program's existence and for the district's work in the community.

> The Valley Center Union School District bilingual program is based upon the premise that biliteracy is desirable and attainable. Biliteracy enhances the student's potential for functional and creative thinking while providing the means for expanded communication. . . .
>
>   . . . Future benefits in higher education and in the economic segment of society are extensive for bilingually-educated students entering the work force and seeking their place in society. . . .
>
>   . . . Because the education of children is most effective when it is a cooperative effort between the home and the school, close communication is established and maintained between the two environments. . . .

Valley Center's close proximity to Mexico as well as to San Diego and Los Angeles, two ethnically diverse business centers, underscores the need for a global approach to learning and maintaining languages. Foreign trade among the Pacific Rim countries requires communication in multiple languages. California schools in general would be wise to pay attention to these realities. The increasing need for bilingual graduates, fortunately, has not gone unnoticed by the district's school board, administration, teaching staff, and the surrounding community.

Program Description

In this program, both Spanish and English learners develop and then maintain grade-level skills in two languages. The program is "developmental"[4] in that the students begin their study of the core subjects (language arts, math, science, social studies) in their *first* language while fluency in their *second* language is being developed. In the fourth grade, students formally make the transition to study core subjects in their second language. By the fifth grade, students con-

---

[4] In this context, *developmental* programs are in direct contrast to *immersion* programs in which students are taught the core subjects in their *second* language right from the beginning, while the first language remains on hold and is gradually added later (see the Thunder Bay immersion program on page 429 and the Cantonese/English dual language immersion program on page 454).

tinue to use the district's grade-level curriculum, but they are now able to do so in both English and Spanish. The ratio of first language instruction to second language instruction throughout the grades is as follows:

	First Language Instruction (percent)	Second Language Instruction (percent)
Kindergarten and first grade:	90	10
Second grade:	80	20
Third grade:	70	30
Fourth grade (beginning of year):	60	40
Fourth grade (end of year):	50	50
Fifth through eighth grade:	50	50

(See Figure 20.1 on the following pages for the specifics of this progression.)

High academic standards are maintained throughout the program in both languages. Although most children enter the program in kindergarten, exceptions can be made up to the fourth grade, but only after a careful screening to ensure that all students admitted to the program can handle the work. The school district attempts to maintain a balance between English speakers and Spanish speakers in any given classroom so each group has equal access to the other's language. In order to participate in the program, all students must have their parents' written permission or signed waivers (in the case of language minority students), and all teachers must have bilingual certification or be close to receiving it. In addition, language minority students in the lower grades can participate in the program only after being in a structured English immersion class for 30 days each school year in order to comply with the requirements of Proposition 227.

Approach to Teaching

Within the program itself, students receive instruction from a team of teachers and their assistants who are prepared to teach language through content. The teachers believe that learning basic skills in the first language under the right circumstances does not interfere with nor delay the learning of the second (see also Chapter 17).

As mentioned earlier, in the Valley Center program, Spanish-speaking children are referred to as "Spanish experts." It should be noted that English-speaking children are also known as experts; they are the "English experts." On days when Spanish is the focus for subjects such as music and art, the Spanish experts act as leaders and are responsible for helping the English learners; on days when English is the focus, the reverse is true. However, according to first-grade teacher Natalie Weston, the children are reminded early on that their goal is to eventually become "bilingual experts." Not only do they become experts in each other's languages, but they become very familiar with each other's cultures through music, games, ethnic food preparation, celebrations, and literature, as well as formal and informal discussions.

Grade Level	Student	Instruction in Spanish	Instruction in English	Alternating Languages
K	ELL	Language Arts, Math, Science, Social Studies, Health	ESL vocabulary development, Physical Ed	openings/closings, music, poetry, art, classroom management discourse
	SLL	SSL vocabulary development	Language Arts, Math, Social Studies, Science, Health, Physical Ed	
1	ELL	Language Arts, Math, Science, Social Studies, Health	ESL vocabulary development, guided reading, Physical Ed	literature (stories), math application, music, poetry, art, opening calendar, classroom management discourse
	SLL	SSL vocabulary development, guided reading	Language Arts, Math, Science, Social Studies, Health, Physical Ed	
2	ELL	Language Arts (including concept development for content areas), Math, Science, Social Studies, Health	ESL vocabulary development, guided reading, spelling, writing, Physical Ed	literature (stories), music, poetry, art, classroom management discourse
	SLL	SSL vocabulary development, guided reading, spelling, writing	Language Arts (including concept development for content areas), Math, Science, Social Studies, Health, Physical Ed	
3	ELL	Language Arts, Math, Science, Social Studies (1st 2 trimesters), classroom management discourse, opening calendar	ESL vocabulary development, guided reading, spelling, writing, Health, Physical Ed, Social Studies (3rd trimester)	handwriting, music, art
	SLL	SSL vocabulary development, guided reading, spelling, writing, Social Studies (1st 2 trimesters), classroom management discourse, opening calendar	Language Arts, Math, Science, Social Studies (3rd trimester), Health, Physical Ed	

Notes: 1) ELL means English Language Learner; SLL means Spanish Language Learner.
2) SSL means Spanish as a Second Language; ESL means English as a Second Language.
3) Both groups are together for all course work except for SSL and ESL.
4) Grades K–3 are on the trimester system; Grades 4–8 are on the semester system.

Figure 20.1. Progression to Proficiency in English and Spanish

Grade Level	Student	Instruction in Spanish	Instruction in English	Alternating Languages
4	ELL	Language Arts (1st semester), maintenance (2nd semester)	ESL vocabulary development, guided reading, spelling, writing, Physical Ed, Chorus, Geography Lab, Computers	Math, Social Studies, Science, Art, Music, Drama, Dance, Language Arts (2nd semester), classroom management discourse (languages alternate by unit)
	SLL	SSL vocabulary development, guided reading, spelling, writing	Language Arts (1st semester), maintenance (2nd semester), Physical Ed, Chorus, Geography Lab, Computers	
5	ELL		ESL (Monday through Thursday—40 min. each day) Physical Ed, Chorus, Geography Lab, Computers	Language Arts, Math, Social Studies, Science, Health, Art, Music, Drama, Dance, classroom management discourse (languages alternate by unit)
	SLL	SSL (Monday through Thursday—40 min. each day)	Physical Ed, Chorus, Geography Lab, Computers	
6	ELL	Social Studies, Science	ESL (1st semester) Language Arts, Math, Physical Ed, Band, Exploratory (2nd semester)	None
	SLL	SSL (1st semester) Social Studies, Science	Language Arts, Math, Physical Ed, Band, Exploratory (2nd semester)	
7 & 8	ELL	*Future Teachers program	*Future Teachers program	
	SLL			Social Studies, Language Arts, Science, Math

* Students tutor children in the primary grades.

Figure 20.1. Progression to Proficiency in English and Spanish (Cont'd)

During the early phases of the program's second language instructional phase (Figure 20.1), vocabulary development in the core subjects is the focus. The teachers and aides use modified input, pictures, acting out, and gestures to make the content clear in the language they are teaching. As students become increasingly more proficient, they become less dependent on the teacher and more dependent on themselves and on each other. At this point, pair work and small group work are used to give students practice in communication in the second language with peers, to learn the benefits of cooperation, and to complete group work in the content-area subjects.

Student-made books help the children develop literacy, first in their primary language and then in their second language. Family histories (replete with pictures and drawings), community reports (students go out into the community to collect data), descriptions of places and events, and fictional stories are among the more common student-made projects. Moreover, parents are encouraged to become actively involved in their children's education. Students interview parents, read their stories to them, ask for reactions and write them down to share with the class or small group, if they wish. All the while, students are being gradually introduced to the literature of both languages.

Teachers are encouraged to develop much of their own curriculum in both languages based on what is relevant and what they feel is essential to meeting the academic, psychological, and social needs of their students. Susy Stone, a teacher in the middle school, reports "What I like best about this program is the fact that we can serve such diverse needs and populations, and have the flexibility to adapt our program to students' needs as these needs change. . . ."

Language Assessment

To determine the English language proficiency level of students whose home language is not English, the Language Assessment Scales (LAS)—Forms A & B, English 1C, 2C, 1D, and 2D are used, in addition to the oral LAS. The administrator of the test determines the student's oral LAS level (1, 2, 3, 4, or 5). Students in grades 3–8 who score at level 3 or above in the oral LAS are then given the reading and writing assessment. Post-assessment forms of the LAS may be used at the end of the academic year.

Students whose home language is Spanish are given the Language Assessment Scales (LAS)—Forms Pre-LAS A, 1B, and 2B, plus the oral LAS. Again, students in grades 3–8 who score at level 3 or above in the oral LAS are given the reading and writing assessment. Students suspected of having learning disabilities in all programs are referred to the Student Assistance Services Team (SAS) for further evaluation.

The results of the assessment along with principal/teacher recommendations are sent to the parents in a language they can understand, along with a description of available programs. Parents placing their children in the two-way bilingual program know that at any time they can request a reassignment to a classroom where English is the only language of instruction. Parents are also informed that a child placed in bilingual education will be carefully monitored throughout the program. If the student is not doing as well as expected, he or she receives intervention and support programs available to all students in the primary grades. For example, if the student is having difficulty with reading in his or her first language, the student may be placed temporarily in the Reading Recovery program where one-to-one assistance is given. If a student is having problems with math, he or she may be placed in a math lab for whatever time is necessary. Other possible assistance can be found in Title I reading intervention.[5] One program employs trained literacy aides who work under the supervision of Title I teachers. In addition, there are after-school tutoring programs at all levels.

School-to-Home Program

During the summer months, bilingual personnel from the school district are invited into many of the students' homes to work on literacy training with students, their siblings, and their parents. A culmination of the summer work is helping family members prepare various projects (Continuing Learning Projects) which they later present or "showcase" at a potluck meal to which all families are invited. The projects—often elaborate—represent a wide range of study; projects in language arts, science, social studies, and math are the most common.

Funding

Funding for the two-way bilingual program comes primarily from the district's general funds and from other categorical moneys the district might receive. Supplementary funds from the Economic Impact Aid-Limited English Proficient (EIA-LEP) account help to pay for bilingual aides, staff development for teachers and/or aides for instructing those learning English as a Second Language, bilingual materials, and parental involvement projects. Title VII funds[6] have been applied for each year to help pay the coordinator's salary and to supplement the hiring of bilingual aides.

Parental Advisory Committees

The English Learner Advisory Committee meets six times a year. Parents of students learning English must constitute a majority of the committee, and at least two-thirds of the members must be migrant parents elected by their peers. Among their duties are: advising on the development of the district Master Plan for English Learners and on the goals and objectives for such learners, including migrant education goals; assistance in carrying out a district-wide needs assessment for English learners at each school; review and evaluation of

---

[5] Title I funds are intended for educational programs to help students in poverty.

[6] Title VII, an amendment to the Elementary and Secondary Education Act of 1965, provided funds earmarked for programs supporting language minority students.

programs; etc. Meetings follow a predetermined agenda and are conducted in language(s) best understood by the members.

In addition, there is an advisory group for the parents of native English-speaking children who are learning Spanish. Although the requirements and duties of this group are not so clearly defined, they operate in a fashion similar to that of the English Learner Advisory Committee. They advise the two-way developmental bilingual program and focus on the special needs of the Spanish learners in that program.

Conclusion

School districts planning to develop two-way developmental bilingual programs of their own might heed the words of Lucy Haines, principal of the elementary school and former Special Projects Director. Lucy recommends that school districts have systems in place for problem-solving as each program moves forward. "What you start may not be what you have or want tomorrow," she said, reflecting upon her own role in the process of change. She has seen her own school district's program evolve over the years into a program of which she and her colleagues are very proud.

In 2001, the school was unified with two other districts to become K–12. That means eighth-graders now have the opportunity to continue their bilingual education into grade 9. Everyone involved in the program is enthusiastic about the possibilities for the program as the school district extends it into the higher grades.

AN IMMERSION DUAL LANGUAGE PROGRAM: CANTONESE/ENGLISH[7]

In the middle of Chinatown[8] on the lower east side of Manhattan in New York City is Public School No. 1, also known as the Alfred E. Smith School.[9] From out-

[7] Appreciation goes especially to Good Jean Lau, Resource Specialist for the Dual Language Program, who made my visit possible and who so graciously made time in her very busy schedule to welcome me to the school, to set up a schedule for my observations, and to serve as a guide and resource person. I also want to thank Principal Marguerite Straus, who met with me and answered all my many questions about the school and the program itself. I am also grateful to the teachers in the dual language program who so willingly allowed me to observe in their classes and shared with me materials and ideas: Ellen Wong (Pre-Kindergarten), Lillian Joe (Kindergarten), and Susie Tsang (Grade 2). Appreciation also goes to Delores Tucker (school coordinator) and Angela Loguercio (program coordinator) for talking with me at length about their innovative program, Everybody Wins.

[8] Chinatown has over 150,000 residents making it one of the largest Chinese communities outside of Asia. But the inhabitants within this multicultural enclave have not come only from China. They also have come from Malaysia, Thailand, Korea, Burma, Vietnam, and many other countries.

[9] Alfred E. Smith was governor of New York (1919–1920) and the Democratic candidate for president in 1928.

ward appearances, the school seems not that much different from many other inner-city elementary schools: its brick and stone structure is very old; there is no grass, only sidewalk, between the school and the street; and it sits in the shadow of the taller buildings nearby. Upon entering this school, however, one realizes that there is something quite different happening here. Although the steps going up to all four floors are steep and worn, the walls and even the doors are alive with exemplary student projects, student-created pictures and collaborative murals depicting, not only symbols of the students' cultures, but the daily lives that reflect those cultures. Evidence that a *community of learners* exists here is found everywhere—from the work room reserved for parents to the nooks and crannies where power lunches take place, during which business professionals read and learn with children, one-to-one. Collaboration is also found in the school's classrooms where students are working to accomplish goals through group participation and inquiry-based learning (similar to "theme cycles" found on page 324). Moreover, students' individual endeavors are considered "works in progress" until they are finished and evaluated. The students learn by apprenticeship, but, at the same time, they are held responsible for their own learning. Moreover, they are instilled with the belief that it is each student's ability, right, and obligation to critically analyze and to question what they read and hear.

Public School No. 1, as its name suggests, was the first public school in New York City. It was organized in 1806 by a group of philanthropists who wanted the city's poor children to have a free education. At first, its 42 students met in the basement of a tenement. Since then, the school has moved several times with each population increase, finally arriving in 1897, at its present location at 8 Henry Street, where it became known to New Yorkers as the "school of immigrant children."

Based on statistics collected in 2000, the school claims 680 students (78.2 percent Asian, including Pacific Islanders, Alaskan Natives, and Native Americans; 12.5 percent Hispanic; 8 percent Black; and 1.3 percent White). Of these students, 11 percent are recent immigrants. Cantonese is the first language of the majority of its students (364), followed by English (117). The remainder speak a variety of first languages, including Mandarin, Fukinese, and Spanish. Ninety percent of the children qualify for the free school lunch program.

The School's Mission

Public School No. 1's mission includes the following goals:

1. to help children develop the skills needed to benefit from the multicultural community and the world at large
2. to expand children's awareness of their environment and help them to become life long learners within that environment
3. to help children develop critical thinking skills as well as oral and written communication skills

4. to create a rigorous learning environment within which children are
   encouraged to reach high standards[10]

In order to accomplish its mission, the school requires that all teachers make the
standards clear to the children and help them stretch to levels beyond their current capabilities. Students are expected to gain a disciplinary knowledge which
can then be used to solve problems and which serves as a basis from which they
can continue to grow and learn. Teachers are required to establish environments that make such learning possible. Within their classes, the students are
taught to self-evaluate and are given the opportunity to develop the tools necessary to achieve the state and school district standards for which they will be
held accountable.

The school's principal, Marguerite Straus, states:

> Public School 1 provides a language-rich environment in which children
> become readers, problem solvers, and responsible participants in the commu-
> nity. . . . We are committed to high rigorous standards [referring to the state
> and district standards] with the belief and expectation that all children can
> learn. Cooperative learning, peer tutoring, and inquiry-based learning chal-
> lenge children to think critically and communicate successfully. . . .

A report card which is aligned with the state and school district standards is
sent to each student's home on a regular basis. A variety of assessment tools
(including exams in English language arts and mathematics) provide input into
determining whether or not students are meeting the standards. In addition,
assessing behaviors based on performance descriptors and evaluating student
portfolios are an integral part of the process. In 2000, 56.4 percent of the students at Public School 1 had met the standards, in contrast to similar school
populations in the district where only 37 percent had met the standards.

The standards themselves are well-delineated at each grade level. Let's
look at a Reading Standard 1 intended for Grade 1 as an example.

First-Grade Reading Standard 1: Reading Habits

- Independent and Assisted Reading
  We expect first-grade students to:
    - read four or more books every day independently or with assistance
    - discuss at least one of these books with another student or a group
    - read some favorite books many times, gaining deeper comprehension

---

[10] The word *standards* throughout this section refers to the "New Standards" established by the
New York City Public Schools. They differ from the "old" standards in that they include tougher
performance objectives that are measurable by means other than multiple-choice tests. The older
standards were based on "minimum competency" tests, and as a result, some students were
judged competent, and others were not. The Board of Education felt that these tests didn't give
them enough information about how well the students were performing.

- read their own writing and sometimes the writing of their classmates
- read functional messages they encounter in the classroom (for example, labels, signs, instructions)
• Being Read To
  We expect first-grade students to:
    - hear two to four books or other texts (for example, poems, letters, instructions, newspaper or magazine articles, dramatic scripts, songs, brochures) read aloud every day
    - listen to and discuss every day at least one book or chapter that is longer and more difficult than what they can read independently or with assistance
• Discussing Books
  We expect students finishing first grade to be able to:
    - demonstrate the skills we look for in the comprehension component of Reading Standard 2: Getting the Meaning
    - compare two books by the same author
    - talk about several books on the same theme
    - refer explicitly to parts of the text when presenting or defending a claim
    - politely disagree when appropriate
    - ask others questions that seek elaboration and justification
    - attempt to explain why their interpretation of a book is valid
• Vocabulary
  We expect first-grade students to:
    - make sense of new words from how the words are used, refining their sense of the words as they encounter them again
    - notice and show interest in understanding unfamiliar words in texts that are read to them
    - talk about the meaning of some new words encountered in independent and assisted reading
    - know how to talk about what words mean in terms of functions (for example, "A shoe is a thing you wear on your foot") and features (for example, "Shoes have laces")
    - learn new words every day from talk and books read aloud.

Reading Standards 2 and 3 involve getting the meaning and learning the print-sound code respectively. The following reading materials are among those recommended to support the Grade 1 standards in reading:

Read-Aloud Books

Bourgeois, Paulette, *Franklin in the Dark*
Dorros, Arthur, *Abuela*
Lindgren, Astrid, *Pippi Long Stocking*
Martin, Bill, *Knots on a Counting Rope*
Palacco, Patricia, *The Keeping Quilt*

Sendak, Maurice, *Chicken Soup with Rice*
Viorst, Judith, *The Good-Bye Book*
Warner, Gertrude Chandler, *The Boxcar Children* (series)
Yee, Paul, *Roses Sing on New Snow: A Delicious Tale*

Level 1 Texts

D.C. Heath & Co., Little Readers. Bloksberg, *The Hole in Harry's Pocket*
Houghton Mifflin, Little Readers. deWinters, *Worms for Breakfast*
Rigby, Literacy 2000, *Jack & the Bean Stalk*
Simon & Schuster, Alladin Paperbacks, Rockwell, *Apples & Pumpkins*
William Morrow & Co., Mulberry Books, Hutchins, *Tidy Titch*
Wright Group, Sunshine Science Series, Cutting, *Ants*
Wright Group, Sunshine, Set 1, Cowley, *Quack, Quack, Quack*

The texts in the second group are considered by the school district to be richer in meaning, more challenging, and more complex in story structure than those in the first group. To learn about the remaining reading standards and the standards in other areas such as writing, mathematics, etc., and for other grade levels, go to the website for the New York City Public Schools.

Across the school district, the standards are benchmarked for grades 4, 8, and 10. At grade 4, the portfolios of the district's students are examined by district representatives who meet four times a year to look at student work and evaluate teaching practices used to reach the goals developed for the portfolio system. District-wide staff development meetings are conducted once a month for teachers, administrators, staff developers, and district representatives. Attendees read and discuss professional books and articles as they relate to district standards and talk about how the standards themselves are being implemented and assessed.

The International Academy Dual Language Program

Over 21 percent of the students (144 students) are currently enrolled in the Cantonese/English International Academy Dual Language Program (pre-K–5). Within the program, 91 Cantonese speakers are learning English, 32 English speakers are learning Cantonese, and 21 speakers of a mixture of languages are learning English and Cantonese. Both English and Cantonese are respected equally—English as the language of the broader world outside the community and Cantonese as the language of the community. The students in this program are expected to meet the same state and district standards intended for all students in the school. Of the school's 44 teachers, seven teach in the dual language program and are proficient in both languages. Unfortunately, in 2001 the school was unable to hire aides because the Title VII grant funding had run out. However, they have attempted to overcome this problem by relying on student teachers and interns from the local high schools for assistance until more funding comes their way.

The Academy, which began in 1995, has four goals: (1) to provide a complete elementary school education conducted in two languages: Cantonese and English; (2) to develop bilingual proficiency and multicultural understanding and respect; (3) to enable children to achieve high standards in all academic areas; and (4) to utilize the Academy as a comprehensive example of dual language instruction in order to reform, restructure, and upgrade education for all students in the school.

The program is designed to promote literacy in both Cantonese and English from Pre-Kindergarten through grade 5. It includes an Extended Day Program on Thursday afternoons from 3:30 to 5:30 to provide additional instruction in the Chinese culture and the Cantonese language. The Extended Day Program also offers day care centers, music/dance classes, a buddy reading program, recreational and other academic programs. During the regular school day, the ratio of Cantonese to English used varies depending upon the teacher, the content or theme, and the students in the program. Often instructions are given in both languages. The Academy is considered "immersion" because the students are exposed to their second language right from the start and in the case of Cantonese learners, it is used almost exclusively in the Extended Day Program.

Students learn to read and write in both languages through a literature-based program utilizing themes as its basic method of organization. The instruction in mathematics and science involves hands-on activities and strategy development that encourage students to think through problems and find solutions. The children serve as expert linguistic models for each other in their respective first languages, and the teachers, because they are fluent in both languages, serve as models as well. Students are often involved in self-directed research and spend considerable time choosing the best of their own work to put in the portfolios they then share with parents and other interested persons.

Typical instructional activities involve reading books in both languages,[11] learning to follow directions, exploring the neighborhood and community (libraries, stores, the police station, the hospital, etc.), using numerals, recognizing written symbols in both languages, and so forth. Other activities involve storytelling using historical literature from both cultures, field trips into the community, celebrations to commemorate Chinese and American holidays, music, art, calligraphy, games, dance, crafts, and meal preparation.

Traditional tutoring by adults, peer tutoring, and cross-grade tutoring are provided after school for those children who need and desire it. Reading

---

[11] See especially *Asia for Kids*, a catalog published by Master Communications, Inc. in Cincinnati, OH. It makes available many bilingual books in English and several Asian languages including Chinese. It also includes music and lyrics, games, and manipulatives.

Recovery, a one-to-one intervention program, is available to the children in Grade 1. Small Group Instruction (a push-in program) is available at any grade level.

An important part of the evaluation of the students in the Dual Language Program is done by the teacher, using a fairly comprehensive checklist. The areas evaluated in both Cantonese and English include the use of receptive language, the use of expressive language and articulation, cognitive development and language skills, and a knowledge of Chinese culture. (See form in Figure 20.2.)

Staff Support and Development

The team of staff members in the Dual Language Program consists of a resource specialist, a community coordinator, and one classroom teacher at each grade level. The team meets regularly to coordinate the program and plan across the grades.

Untenured teachers keep a professional portfolio for at least one year. In it, they keep the data for any teacher research in which they are involved and responses to various topics of their choice. The portfolios are given to the administrators at the end of the academic year for review and are then placed in the main office where all staff members have access to them. These teachers meet once a month to share their problems and concerns, to reflect upon their teaching, and to plan for the future.

Breakfast talks, held every Friday morning from 8:00 A.M. to 8:40 A.M., are open to all teachers and staff in the school. At these forums, teachers are able to discuss students' work and the various teaching strategies each is using. They share successes and failures, often challenge one another's ideas about best practices, and help each other become more reflective practitioners. In addition, a group of teachers meets every Tuesday morning from 8:00 to 9:30. and report back to their colleagues the highlights of their discussions. They talk about new research and analyze alternative methods of assessment to determine whether or not students are meeting state and local district standards. They are considered an in-school extension of the district-wide staff development meetings described above.

At the end of each school year, a celebration is held called "The Images of Excellence." Here, every teacher and student in the school is recognized his or her contribution to the academic environment created in the school. Student work accomplished throughout the year is displayed for all to see and admire.

Parent and Community Involvement

Public School No. 1 prides itself on its close association with parents and the community. Parents are invited to play an integral role in their children's education. To promote good teacher-parent communication, letters, announce-

Child's Name _____

Grade Level _____

Date _____

Teacher _____

Rating:
- 0 = Not Yet
- 1 = Rarely
- 2 = Sometimes/ Occasionally
- 3 = Frequently
- 4 = All the Time
- N/A = Not Applicable

1. RECEPTIVE LANGUAGE

	(CANTONESE)	(ENGLISH)
FOLLOWS SIMPLE DIRECTIONS	( )	( )

2. EXPRESSIVE LANGUAGE AND ARTICULATION

	(ENGLISH)
SPEAKS CLEARLY	( )
EXPRESSES THOUGHTS UNDERSTANDABLY	( )
USES SHORT PHRASES	( )
USES COMPLETE SENTENCES	( )
ENGAGES IN CONVERSATION WITH ADULTS AND/OR PEERS	( )
RETELLS STORY IN SEQUENCE	( )
RELATES AN EXPERIENCE, EVENT, OR STORY IN OWN WORDS	( )

SUBTOTAL: EXPRESSIVE LANGUAGE AND ARTICULATION (ENGLISH) = _____

3. COGNITIVE DEVELOPMENT & LANGUAGE SKILLS

	(ENGLISH)
ASSOCIATES LETTERS OF THE ALPHABET WITH THEIR SOUNDS	( )
RECOGNIZES INITIAL SOUNDS AND LETTERS IN WORDS	( )
RECOGNIZES FINAL SOUNDS AND LETTERS IN WORDS	( )
USES INVENTIVE SPELLING	( )
RECOGNIZES LETTERS OF THE ALPHABET (UPPER CASE)	( )
RECOGNIZES LETTERS OF THE ALPHABET (LOWER CASE)	( )
WRITES UPPER CASE LETTERS	( )
WRITES LOWER CASE LETTERS	( )
USES CONVENTIONAL SPELLING	( )
FINDS OWN TOPICS FOR WRITING	( )
WRITES SIMPLE STORIES WITH ASSISTANCE FROM ADULTS	( )
READS ON LEVEL	( )
CREATES INDEPENDENT RESEARCH PROJECTS	( )
WRITES INDEPENDENTLY	( )
APPLIES THE MECHANICS OF WRITING CORRECTLY	( )

SUBTOTAL: COGNITIVE DEVELOPMENT & LANGUAGE SKILLS (ENGLISH) = _____

4. EXPRESSIVE LANGUAGE AND ARTICULATION

	(CANTONESE)
SPEAKS CLEARLY	( )
IS ABLE TO USE BASIC DAILY COLLOQUIAL LANGUAGE	( )
IS ABLE TO RECITE SIMPLE SONGS AND POEMS	( )
ENGAGES IN CONVERSATION WITH ADULTS AND/OR PEERS	( )
RETELLS SIMPLE STORY IN SEQUENCE	( )
RELATES AN EXPERIENCE, EVENT OR STORY IN OWN WORDS	( )

SUBTOTAL: EXPRESSIVE LANGUAGE AND ARTICULATION (CANTONESE) = _____

5. COGNITIVE DEVELOPMENT & LANGUAGE SKILLS (CANTONESE)

COPIES CHARACTERS ( )
RECOGNIZES NUMERALS ( )
WRITES NUMERAL ( ) ( )
RECOGNIZES BASIC SIGHT VOCABULARY ( )
COMPREHENDS SIMPLE CHARACTERS ( )
WRITES SIMPLE CHARACTERS ( )
RECOGNIZES COMPLEX CHARACTERS ( )
WRITES COMPLEX CHARACTERS ( )
WRITES PHRASES ( )
WRITES SENTENCES ( )
WRITES SIMPLE STORIES WITH MINIMAL ASSISTANCE FROM ADULTS ( )

SUBTOTAL: COGNITIVE DEVELOPMENT & LANGUAGE SKILLS (CANTONESE) = _____

CHINESE CULTURE—Has the teacher provided the following:	**YES**	**NO**
* INTRODUCTION OF HOLIDAYS, WRITING, CALLIGRAPHY	( )	( )
* CHILDREN'S LITERATURE, POEMS AND SONGS	( )	( )
* ARTS & HUMANITIES (INCLUDES FINE ARTS, PERFORMING ARTS)	( )	( )
* OTHERS _____	( )	( )

Figure 20.2. Evaluation Form

ments, calendars, questionnaires, etc., are sent to the home in three languages: Cantonese, English, and Spanish. Translators are provided for meetings, conferences, and consultation sessions. Assistance is available for new immigrant families, and services such as the New York University Dental Program, health screenings, and annual eye and ear testing are provided. When appropriate, referrals are made to community agencies, health clinics, and family counseling services. In addition, workshops are conducted for parents throughout the academic year based on a needs assessment. These workshops include: ESL (for parents and other family members), how their children learn to read and write, computer use, standards assessment, parenting skills, family health, and social issues. Families may visit a variety of educational and cultural institutions in the community on specially organized trips. Parents actively participate in family literacy activities, open houses, parent teacher conferences, school assemblies, and cultural celebrations. Moreover, they often help out in the classroom and are involved in making important decisions. For example, parents played a large role in developing drafts of the Parent Handbook, which is available to all parents. They had input into the criteria to be included in the report cards. Perhaps most important, they were given their own workroom in the school where they hold workshops and meetings, work on crafts, disseminate information to other parents and the community, and aid in assessing the needs of newcomers to the school.

In order to assist their children with reading, parents are encouraged to read to them as often as possible and, likewise, have their children read to them; allow the children to help select the books they will read together; teach their children nursery rhymes and songs; tell and encourage the telling of stories; talk about everyday print (signs, announcements, recipes, etc.); accept without criticism their children's attempts at reading; and so forth.

Principal Marguerite Straus asks all parents/guardians to read and sign a School-Parent Compact (see Figure 20.3) if they agree with its contents and are willing to comply with its conditions.

SCHOOL-PARENT COMPACT
Public School 1

The school and parents working cooperatively to provide for the successful education of the children agree:

The School Agrees

1. To offer flexibility in scheduling parent meetings so that working parents, single parents, homeless/shelter parents have equal opportunity to meet with teachers.
2. To provide timely information regarding all programs in school and in District #2.
3. To provide translations that are accurate and clear for all parents in all necessary languages.
4. To provide an excellent education in a supportive, caring atmosphere.
5. To provide activities for parents to learn parenting strategies, as well as educational workshops and information about related services in the community.

The Parent/Guardian Agrees

1. To play an active role in supporting their child's education and to attend as many PTA meetings as possible, attend parent conferences, and parent orientations.
2. To check with their child daily for school communications review and respond when appropriate.
3. To be sure children are in school each day on time.
4. To review child's homework and provide opportunity for sharing classroom experiences.
5. To be an active participant in school-parent involvement policy.

Prinicipal: _____   Parent: _____
                                        for Title 1 & All children

---

Figure 20.3. School-Parent Compact

Community groups, local high schools, and New York University offer several programs to help Public School 1 students academically and in other ways as well. For example, America Reads provides tutors from New York University to assist with reading. Brooklyn Manhattan International High School and Cascade High School supply interns to help teachers individualize the curriculum in any area in which students need assistance. Everybody Wins, which sponsors the power lunches mentioned above, is a privately-funded, nonprofit organization founded by Arthur Tannenbaum in 1991.[12] Once a week for one and a half hours, business professionals who have formed partnerships with students come to school to share lunch, books, and conversation with their "partners." Funding for this activity is generally provided by the companies involved, and buses pick up the professionals from their places of work and return them after lunch.

Conclusion

Once the students leave the International Academy Dual Language program, they are able to choose the middle school they wish to attend. Unfortunately, none of New York City's middle schools offer dual language programs at the present time. However, such programs are under consideration for the future. Because the students live in such a rich linguistic and cultural environment, it is hoped that, in the meantime, they will not forget their Cantonese and the knowledge they have gained about Chinese culture. It is likely that their abilities to self-motivate, self-evaluate, and actively seek the information they need will remain with them as they continue through their schooling at all levels.

---

[12] This organization provides reading partners for 2,200 children in New York, New Jersey, and Connecticut and for 5,000 children across the nation.

PART V

Related Readings

This section presents edited readings from two educators whose published works have important implications for second language teaching: Alastair Pennycook, and Sonia Nieto.

The Related Readings, which are referred to in the book, are intended mainly for those desiring supplemental materials to enhance their understanding of interactional/participatory approaches and sociopolitical concerns. This section may be useful not only in the teaching of theory and methods courses at the graduate level, but to experienced teachers already in the field. The readings might be assigned in preparation for subsequent class discussions (see also the questions that end each chapter in Parts I, II, and III).

It must be noted that only two readings could be presented in this edition. The ones selected seemed to be most appropriate in that they expanded the book's current implications and provided additional areas for reflection, discussion, and/or research.

THE SOCIAL POLITICS AND THE CULTURAL POLITICS OF LANGUAGE CLASSROOMS
Alastair Pennycook

When we think of language classrooms, of language teaching and learning, it is often in terms of methods, competencies, strategies, grammar, tasks, exercises, drills, activities, and so on. Although it might already seem that such a list implies a wide diversity of ideas and approaches, I want to suggest by contrast that such a list in fact is part of a very particular view of classrooms. This perspective tends to view the classroom as something of a closed box, an educational context separated from society. Inside this box, teachers try to help their students learn a language. The language is a set of structures, pronunciations, or communicative acts that students need to master. The main concern, therefore, is how teachers can encourage the students to learn, to remember, internalize, and use the necessary pieces of language. And the main research questions have to do with how learners learn to communicate: In what order do students acquire certain structures? What kinds of communicative strategies may help learning? Does task-based learning help students more than grammar-focused learning? Is it helpful to teach generic text structures to students?

I do not want to suggest that these questions do not matter. Rather I want to argue that they form only a small part of what we need to understand in terms of what matters in language education. The problem is that so much of what we read about in TESOL and Applied Linguistics, or hear in teacher education classes, tends to view classes as closed boxes. I would like to consider an alternative view—that classrooms, both in themselves and in their relationship to the world beyond their walls, are complex social and cultural spaces. In order to do this, I shall introduce briefly two English classrooms in different parts of the world, one in Canada, another in South Asia. Although these classrooms may seem different from one's own context of work, I would suggest that there are many connections here that we need to understand.

The first classroom I discuss is Suresh Canagarajah's (1993) classroom, consisting of 22 first-year students doing a mandatory English class at the Univer-

From J. K. Hall and W. Eggington (eds.) (2000), *The Sociopolitics of English Language Teaching*, Clevedon, England: Multilingual Matters, pp. 89–103. Used by Permission.

sity of Jaffna in Sri Lanka. They are using *American Kernel Lessons: Intermediate* as a core text. The 13 female and 9 male Tamil students are mainly from rural communities and the poorest economic groups. Few of their parents have much education. English has "limited currency" in their lives outside the class and the university. The university's academic year began late because of "renewed hostilities between the Sinhala government and Tamil nationalists" (1993: 612). These tensions provide a backdrop to the classes, with government planes bombing the vicinity of the university during placement tests.

In his critical ethnography of this class, Canagarajah shows how anything from student annotations in textbooks to preferred learning styles and resistance to his own preferred teaching approaches are connected in complex ways to the social and cultural worlds both inside and outside the classroom. Despite the dramatic urgency of the real dangers outside the classroom, Canagarajah goes on to argue for an understanding of the relative autonomy of classrooms, suggesting both that they are social and cultural domains unto themselves and that they are interlinked with the world outside.

Before discussing this point further, however, I will describe briefly another classroom, an ESL class in a Chinese community center on a leafy street in Toronto, Canada (Morgan, 1997). The program has continuous intake, mixed-streaming, and no compulsory testing: "Some students have been in my class for several years, others for only a few months" (1997: 437). In the particular lesson he describes, all 15 students "claim Chinese ethnicity," 13 being from Hong Kong, with 2 from Malaysia and Taiwan; 11 were women, and 12 were over fifty. Morgan goes on to describe a "high-intermediate" lesson to practice oral and written English. The important questions for this chapter are concerned with how we relate these classrooms and the students in terms of social class (mixed in one, more homogeneous in the other), age (two rather different populations), ethnicity (in both classes a fairly homogeneous ethnic group), gender (one class fairly equally split, the other with predominantly women), and location (Toronto and Jaffna) to broader social, cultural, and political contexts.

CLASSROOMS AND THE "REAL WORLD"

As I suggested above, there is often a tendency to view classrooms as isolated spaces; classrooms are "just classrooms." I want to suggest by contrast, that classrooms are sociopolitical spaces that exist in a complex relationship to the world outside. I use the term "sociopolitical" here to address a further important dimension of how I want to approach these questions. The term political in both "sociopolitical" and "cultural political" is used not to address a formal domain of politics or policy but rather to suggest that I view questions of social and cultural relations from a critical perspective. . . . The notion of politics I am working with here is a different one. In his discussion of approaches to learner autonomy, Phil Benson (1997) has made the distinction nicely:

> We are inclined to think of the politics of language teaching in terms of language planning and educational policy while neglecting the political content of everyday language and language learning practices. In proposing a political orientation for learner autonomy, therefore, we need a considerably expanded notion of the political which would embrace issues such as the societal context in which learning takes place, roles and relationships in the classroom and outside, kinds of learning tasks, and the content of the language that is learned. (32)

It is this political understanding of the language classroom that will be the primary focus of this reading. By this I mean that I view social and cultural relations not as casual contexts of consensus but rather as sites of struggle over preferred social and cultural worlds, as domains imbued with relations of power. From this perspective, an understanding of the social politics and cultural politics of classrooms is not just about describing what is going on; it is about making critical interpretations and suggesting possible alternatives.

Initially, two main dimensions in understanding classes as sociopolitical spaces may be suggested: on the one hand, classrooms themselves are social spaces; on the other hand, the larger social context of the classroom determines social relations in the classroom. This first view suggests concerns about "democracy" in the classroom and power relations between students and teachers. Although some arguments for student autonomy or independence are based purely on a view of the psychological benefits of "independent learning," others are based on this more social understanding of classrooms and therefore are based more on a concern for social equality in learning and teaching relationships (see Benson and Voller, 1997). This approach to sociopolitical classroom relationships, however, remains rather limited if it operates simply in terms of teachers having power and students not having power, and with a belief that "democratic" classrooms involve "handing over" power to students. Such a view, I suggest, is a simplistic understanding of social relations and "power sharing," ending up with little more than an argument for group work or student input to the curriculum. This view fails to relate social relations in the classroom to the larger social context.

The second approach, which suggests that the social world outside classrooms determines what happens inside them, offers a broader scope. From this perspective it matters fundamentally what is going on outside Canagarajah's classroom. Students do not leave their social relations, their rural upbringings, or their relationships to their parents at the classroom door; instead they bring them in with them. And the screaming of the government jets over the classroom reminds us, if admittedly in an extreme way, that the outside world is never far away. Similarly, in Brian Morgan's classroom, it matters that this is a Chinese community center, that it is close to Toronto's China Town, that each segment of that Chinese community has a different socioeconomic status, and that older members of this community who attend ESL classes will not likely be part of the wealthier sections of that community. It matters that one of his students describes herself as an "astronaut's widow," referring to the Hong Kong term (*astronaut*) for those who have gained citizenship outside Hong Kong and then returned there to work.

But it is important to note also that Canagarajah argues that classrooms are "relatively autonomous" spaces. This is an important argument because it suggests that the view sketched above—that the social world outside classrooms determines what happens in them—is too deterministic. That is to say, it maps too dependent a relationship between social relations outside classrooms and social relations in classes. What we need to understand is that there is a complex interplay between classrooms and the outside world, or rather that classrooms are not so much a reflection of the outside world, but rather part of the outside world, and in fact play a role in how that outside world operates. From this perspective, the walls of classrooms become permeable, with social relations outside classrooms affecting what goes on inside, and social relations inside affecting what goes on outside. Indeed, we need to reject the common but unhelpful terminology that contrasts the "real world" with our classrooms: our classrooms are part of the real world. This last perspective has significance for understanding the implications of pedagogy.

SOCIAL RELATIONS: THE MICRO AND THE MACRO

Elsa Auerbach (1995) has explained that she sees language classrooms as socially located: "Pedagogical choices about curriculum development, content, materials, classroom processes, and language use, although appearing to be informed by apolitical professional considerations, are, in fact, inherently ideological in nature, with significant implications for learners' socioeconomic roles" (1995: 9). From this point of view, "the classroom functions as a kind of microcosm of the broader social order" (*ibid*.), that is to say the political relationships in the world outside the classroom are reproduced within the classroom. From this perspective, then, everything we do in the classroom can be understood socially and politically. And furthermore, we need to have some notion of ideology (or discourse) that suggests not only that social relations are reproduced inside classrooms but that social relations are linked to ideologies and thus to the way we think.

A key issue in a critical social view of education concerns the tension between, on the one hand, large-scale analyses of how inequitable social relations are reproduced and, on the other hand, an understanding of how people confront such social and ideological forces. If we see small-scale action, the micro-politics of the classroom, as reflecting large-scale social structure, we can start to see how social relations are reproduced in daily classroom interactions. I have also been suggesting that we need to understand ways that people can act against and resist such forces. In this section, therefore, I shall look in more detail at social reproduction in the context of education, before discussing the concepts of cultural reproduction, cultural politics, and resistance.

An optimistic liberal view of education is that it provides opportunity for all: anyone can go to school, receive equal treatment, and come out at the end as whatever they want. Yet it does not take a very sophisticated critical analysis to suggest that this is far from what actually happens. Crudely put, rich kids tend to go to private schools and get good jobs, while working-class kids tend to go to poorer state schools and work in the same social and economic positions as their parents. One might simply account for this in terms of good and bad schools: wealthy families can afford good schools, while poorer families have to send their children to schools that provide an education of lower quality. Such a solution, however, fails to look at the broader functioning of society. What we need, instead, is an understanding of how schools operate within the larger field of social relations, and a realization that schools, as a key institution within society, ultimately serve to maintain the social, economic, cultural, and political status quo rather than upset it. Indeed, Bowles and Gintis (1976) have shown that schools in the U.S. operate to reproduce the labor relations necessary for the functioning of capitalism, suggesting that social relationships outside the classroom are mirrored and reproduced in the classroom.

From this perspective, two principal dimensions explain language classrooms and their relationship to the social and political context. First, language classrooms are part of a much larger social world. As Tollefson (1991) and Auerbach (1995) argue, for example, education for Indochinese refugees, either in resettlement camps in Southeast Asia or in ESL classrooms in the U.S., needs to be understood as part of a larger social and economic policy. As Tollefson (1991) explains, "Refugees are educated for work as janitors, waiters in restaurants, assemblers in electronic plants, and other low-paying jobs offering little opportunity for advancement, regardless of whether the refugees have skills . . . suitable for higher paying jobs. Thus refugee ESL classes emphasize language competencies considered appropriate for minimum-wage work: following orders, asking questions, confirming understanding, and apologizing for mistakes" (108). Similarly, Auerbach points out that

> work-oriented content often is geared, on the one hand, toward specific job-related vocabulary and literacy tasks (reading time cards or pay stubs) and, on the other, toward 'appropriate' attitudes and behaviors and their concomitant language functions or competencies (learning how to call in sick, request clarification of job instructions, make small talk, follow safety regulations). (1995: 17)

From this perspective, then, we can see ESL in the U.S. as part of a social system that positions people of non-English speaking background into a particular socioeconomic niche.

Second, we need to understand the classroom itself as a social domain, not merely a reflection of the larger society beyond the classroom walls but also as a place where social relations are played out. As Auerbach points out, such relations between the society and the classroom can be seen at many levels, including curriculum, instructional content, materials, and language choice. For Auerbach (1995) these concerns point in two directions: on the one hand, classrooms need to "include explicit analysis of the social context" outside the classroom, and, on the other hand, "students must be involved in making pedagogical choices inside the classroom" (28). Thus we can see how classrooms need to turn outwards to the broader social worlds as well as inwards to their own social world. But we should be wary of viewing this as only a two-dimensional relationship: we also need to consider the relationships between classrooms and schools or community centers, between these and local communities, between communities and larger social institutions, and between classrooms and global relations.

What emerges most clearly from this perspective is that it is impossible to believe any longer in the myth that teaching English can be reduced to helping people gain access to social and economic power. Rather, we are part of complex social, economic, and political relations that flow back and forth through our classroom walls. Thus, the social relations inside Canagarajah's class must be seen in relation to class and ethnic relations in Jaffna and Sri Lanka. Likewise, we need to understand that the gender, age, ethnicity, and social class of Brian Morgan's "Chinese" students are inextricably linked to English and their communities and, more generally, to immigration and other policies of Canada, Hong Kong, Taiwan, and Malaysia.

CULTURAL REPRODUCTION, RESISTANCE, AND CULTURAL POLITICS

Giroux (1983) argues that theories of cultural reproduction take up where theories of social reproduction leave off: they focus much more closely on the means by which schooling reproduces social relations. One important figure whose work has become well known in this area is Pierre Bourdieu, a sociologist perhaps best known for his introduction of the now widely used term, "cultural capital." The development of the notion of cultural capital was an attempt to theorize the systems by which certain children brought certain valued attributes to school that could be exchanged for other forms of capital (e.g. social connections or school certificates), while other students' capital was not valued or exchangeable. Cultural capital, Bourdieu explains, was first developed

> as a theoretical hypothesis which made it possible to explain the unequal scholastic achievement of children originating from the different social classes by relating academic success, i.e. the specific profits which children from the different classes and class fractions can obtain in the academic market, the distribution of cultural capital between the classes and class fractions. (1986: 243)

Shirley Brice Heath's (1983) ethnography of how different communities in the Carolinas in the U.S. socialize their children into different ways of "taking from books," and how the language and literacy skills of these children were valued differently in school, fleshes out how such cultural capital is developed, valued, or devalued. In comparison to Heath's more subtle analysis of different community cultures—the Black community of Trackton and the White community of Roadville were both working-class communities—Bourdieu's more critical social analysis tends to equate forms of cultural capital with a rather over-generalized and static notion of class. Thus, although Bourdieu provides some useful tools for thinking about how schools reproduce social inequality, his view tends to be rather closed and deterministic. As Jenkins (1992) explains, Bourdieu's view of cultural reproduction does not allow for change and does not explain how people take up and resist cultural capital.

These critical understandings of social reproduction in education locate schooling in the context of social class and inequality, showing how schools are precisely part of society, both reflecting and reproducing social relations. Yet, as Giroux (1983) and Canagarajah (1993) argue, there is a danger that this view of reproduction allows no understanding of opposition and resistance, of the complex ways students and teachers act within the context of schooling. Canagarajah (1993) describes how his students resisted many aspects of the English course: "On the one hand, they oppose the alien discourses behind the language and textbook. On the other hand, they oppose a process-oriented pedagogy and desire a product-oriented one" (617). Thus, we also need to account for ways students and teachers act with a degree of autonomy within these broader social and cultural relations.

What is needed, then is a way of understanding resistance and change, a better understanding of what actually goes on in classrooms, and a sense that we, as educators, can do something. We need to escape over-deterministic, over-totalizing critical analyses to show how education may make a difference. For these reasons Giroux (1988) talks of the need to develop a language of both critique and hope in critical educational theory, and Roger Simon (1992) talks of a "pedagogy of possibility."

Nevertheless, it has been useful to look at culture as the means by which social inequality is reproduced, because this view insists that we understand culture in political terms. One of the difficulties in talking about culture in a TESOL context is the tendency for culture to be reduced to different behaviors of our students. This is a deterministic view of culture, whereby students "belong" to certain cultures (Chinese, Japanese, or Spanish) that determine the way they behave (see Kubota, 1999; Pennycook, 1998). On the one hand culture is a determining factor in one's behavior; on the other hand, culture tends to deal only with the "exotic" and superficial of cultural behavior: food, dress, and religious festivals. But if we start from the premise that cultures are not static frameworks but competing ways of framing the world, we can start to understand the cultural politics of classrooms. Thus, in both Canagarajah's and Morgan's classrooms, the

Tamil and Chinese backgrounds of their students are not reduced to learning styles or food preferences but instead are part of a complex world that students bring to the classroom, a world in which culture and ethnicity is bound up with other political domains such as social class, gender, and age.

Cultural politics, then, gives us a more open way of addressing questions of struggles over difference, such as whose versions of reality gain legitimacy and whose representations of the world gain sway over others (see Jordan & Weedon, 1995). It is clear that representations of the world that are given credence tend to be the views of powerful and influential groups. And the official sanctioning of such knowledge and culture, particularly in institutions such as schools through set curricula, reinforce the position and the worldview of those groups. From this perspective we can see the ideologies that operate in our classrooms and the social relations that they produce. This view of cultural politics allows us to see classrooms as sites where different worldviews or discourses come into dynamic contact.

THE CULTURAL POLITICS OF ELT

Once we open up this perspective of the cultural politics of classrooms, we can start to see that everything we do in the classroom is related to broader concerns. This relationship of classrooms to the outside world is a reciprocal one: the classroom is not determined by the outside world, but the classroom is part of the world, both affected by what happens outside its walls and affecting what happens there. As I suggested earlier, the very fact that we are teaching English needs to be understood in terms beyond those of national language policy. As Robert Phillipson (1992) and I (Pennycook, 1994) have argued, this global spread of English is bound up with many cultural, economic, and political forces: the dominance of U.S. media, the role of international corporations, the spread of particular forms of culture and knowledge, and the development of a very particular "world order."

As English teachers, whether we are working in a so-called English-speaking country or not, we cannot escape the implications of these global connections. As Benson (1997) observes, teachers of English "are more often than not engaged in political processes of a distinctive kind." On the one hand, the "acceptance of English as a second language very often implies the acceptance of the global economic and political order for which English serves as the 'international language.'" To understand English teaching in an international context, then, we need to be able to understand how English is connected to other global forces. On the other hand, "learning foreign languages (and again English in particular) is more often than not premised upon inequalities between learner and target communities" (Benson, 1997: 27). This is part of the social and cultural context of our teaching. It matters that Canagarajah is teaching English to his students in Sri Lanka, because of its colonial and current history in Sri Lanka and India, and because of its current role in the world. It matters that Brian Morgan is teaching English to students of Chinese background, students who live in complex relations to families in Hong Kong or Taiwan, and to the Toronto community in which they now live.

What we do in classrooms also needs to be seen in similar terms. Not only are there social relations in the classroom in terms of who speaks and who sets the agenda, but the very ways we run classes need to be seen in terms of cultural politics. Assumptions about "active" and "passive" students, about the use of group work and pair work, about self-interest as a key to motivation ("tell us about yourself"), about memorization being an outmoded learning strategy, about oral communication as the goal and means of instruction, about an informal atmosphere in the class being most conducive to language learning, about learning activities being fun, about games being an appropriate way of teaching and learning—all these, despite the claims by some researchers that they are empirically preferable, are cultural preferences. And this means that the classroom becomes a site of cultural struggle over preferred modes of learning and teaching.

As Canagarajah observes, his students started to resist his more Westernized teaching approach and opted instead for an approach to learning with which they were more familiar. Such cultural preferences cannot be mapped simply onto cultural bodies: Canagarajah is, like his students, a Tamil Lankan; but he is also a "young (in my early 30s), male, 'progressive,' Christian, culturally Westernized, middle class, native Tamil, bilingual, director of English language teaching at the university" (620). Similarly, Morgan argues that what might look a fairly homogenous label of "Chinese in Toronto" covers a vast range of diversity. We bring mixed cultural identities to teaching moments. But to say that students may have different preferences does not mean that we should just do what students want; Canagarajah feels that the students did themselves little good by pursuing this route. What it does mean, however, is that we need to understand the cultural politics of these moments.

One of Canagarajah's interests is in the ways that students react to and reinterpret the textbooks, *Kernel Lessons*, used for the class. Since these valu-able foreign texts were handed out and taken in again at the beginning and end of each class, he was able to see the annotations and comments the students made in their textbooks. These comments varied from the Tamilization of the characters, the addition of phrases (in English) such as "I love you darling," and dialogues, to the inclusion of references to the struggle for Tamil independence. Students also had difficulties interpreting some pictures, being confused, for example, by a picture of a character in prison, when he was pictured alone in his cell with a uniform and shoes (all unlikely in a Lankan context). The important point to take from this, however, is that all textbooks, all teaching materials carry cultural and ideological messages. The pictures, the lifestyles, the stories, and the dialogues are full of cultural content; all may potentially be in disaccord with the cultural worlds of the students. Everything we use in class is laden with meanings from outside and interpretations from inside.

Once we start to look at classrooms as an intersection of different ideologies and cultures, we can start to see that language learning is not an abstract cognitive, process where bits of language become lodged in the brain. Rather, it is a highly complex social and cultural process. Once we start to understand that cultural politics happen not only in the classroom and the world but also, inevitably, in the heads of our students, then we have to see classrooms as sites where identities are produced and changed. We need to understand that these identities are multiple and shifting and tied to language and language learning.

Brian Morgan illustrates this well by showing how a simple class on intonation, in fact, has a great deal to do with social and cultural relations, history, community, and identity. As we are taken through various stages of this class, Morgan shows how questions of social identity are constantly being reworked in classrooms: "Each ESL classroom is a unique, complex, and dynamic social environment . . . : Each classroom . . . becomes a resource for community development, where students re-evaluate the past (i.e. the rules of identity) in the context of the present and, through classroom reflection and interaction, forge new cultural traditions, histories, and solidarities that potentially improve their life chances for the future" (432–433). Morgan discusses how the students' exploration of different possibilities of intonation in dialogues—some more acquiescent, some more aggressive—raised questions of social and gender relations in the Chinese community. Such possibilities have major significance for the relationship between the classroom and the broader social context, as well as for our understanding of ESL methodology and research:

> ESL teachers should pay close if not equal attention to the historical and local conditions that influence identity formation when contextualizing language activities in the classroom. A far more difficult challenge for teachers, however, will be to address their own sociopolitical assumptions inscribed within TESOL's theories and technologies of language acquisition, methodology, and research. (1997: 447)

TOWARDS RESISTANCE, CHANGE, AND ENGAGEMENT

A number of teachers and researchers have met the demands of this sociopolitical and cultural political understanding of language classrooms and have developed relevant pedagogical or research strategies. I chose to discuss Morgan's and Canagarajah's classrooms not only because they show these relations but also because their articles are written as teachers/researchers. They write both as teachers teaching English and researchers trying to relate their classrooms to a broader social world. This raises further pedagogical and research-oriented questions. In order to be pedagogically more effective, we need not only better theoretical understandings of classrooms but better researched classrooms as well. As Canagarajah (1993) argues, what we are lacking at present is critical ethnographies of language classrooms, which he defines as

> an ideologically sensitive orientation to the study of culture that can penetrate the noncommittal objectivity and scientism encouraged by the positivistic empirical attitude behind descriptive ethnography and can demystify the interests served by particular cultures to unravel their relation to issues of power. (605)

That is to say, the perspective on the classroom outlined here demands a response in terms of research that keeps one eye on the workings of the classroom and another eye on the broader social and political context.

We can approach such study in a number of ways, from inclusivity, to issues, to engagement. An inclusivity focus points to the importance of making sure that people of different backgrounds are represented in our texts and our classroom possibilities. Many ESL textbooks still work with a 1970s Kellogg's® Cornflakes vision of the family: a blond, white, heterosexual family, with one daughter and one son (all of whom clearly visit the dentist regularly). An argument for greater inclusivity acknowledges that both inside and outside the classroom we live in a world different from Kellogg's®. Arguments for the inclusion, for example, of women in occupations other than at the kitchen sink, have more recently included arguments for alternative lifestyles, of gay and lesbian couples, gay and lesbian parents, single parents, people of color, people with disabilities and so on.

A different focus (though by no means incompatible) looks to include issues of identity and difference in the language teaching curriculum. This I shall call the issues focus. It is an attempt not just to have difference as a background possibility in the textbooks but also to raise more overtly such issues as a content focus in class. Thus, we may find textbooks or curricula include sections on "gay marriages" or "women in the workforce." While this does seem to put issues of difference on the agenda, there are often also problems here, since at least from within the textbook world, we tend to get a very sanitized version of difference. Much of what is presented occurs within an overarching liberal agenda that works with a bland notion of alternatives and social issues. Fundamental questions of identity get slotted into a framework of issues, so that one week we may be dealing with the environment or animal rights and another with issues of gender or sexuality. There is also a tendency to deal with a fixed set of dichotomous possibilities (e.g. nature or nurture; is homosexuality normal? etc.) (see Pennycook, 1997).

A third possibility is what I term an engagement focus. This is an approach to language education that sees such issues as gender, race, class, sexuality, postcolonialism, and so on as so fundamental to identity and language that they need to form the basis of curricular organization and pedagogy. Arleen Schenke (1996) has strongly criticized what she calls "the tired treatment of gender and 'women's lib' in many of our ESL textbooks" (156). In place of these tired liberal, issues-based approaches, she proposes what she calls a "practice in historical engagement," a focus on "the struggle over histories (and forgetting) in relation to the cultures of English and to the cultures students bring with them to the classroom already-knowing" (156). From this point of view, then, questions of difference, identity, and culture are not merely issues to be discussed but are about understanding fully how discourses structure our lives. Questions of gender or race are not themes to be discussed but make up the underlying rationale for the course. "Feminism," Schenke argues, "like antiracism, is thus not simply one more social issue in ESL but a way of thinking, a way of teaching, and, most importantly, a way of learning" (158). Such a view also informs the thinking of Canagarajah and Morgan. Understanding the social and cultural politics of classrooms ultimately has to do with a way of thinking, teaching, and learning.

Auerbach deals with the social politics and cultural politics of classrooms through what she terms "participatory action research." This research aims to do two things: (1) to give students control of the curriculum so that they start to research questions regarding language and the community that are important to them; and (2) to bring the outside community into the classroom to make it a focus of classroom work and discussion. . . . Similarly, Norton Peirce (1995), following Heath's (1983) suggestions for involving students and teachers in researching the literacy practices of their communities, argues for "classroom based social research" in order to "engage the social identities of students in ways that will improve their language learning outside the classroom and help them claim the right to speak" (1995: 26). Once we view classrooms as both social sites in themselves and as part of the larger social world, the types of materials we use and the activities we engage in become open to a range of questions of difference and identity with which it becomes impossible not to engage. Thus, it is not enough to acknowledge the social and cultural dimensions of our classrooms: we also need to engage students with the implications.

CONCLUSION: THE HEART OF THE CRUCIAL ISSUES OF OUR TIME

A typical applied linguistic view of the classroom has tended to see it as some sort of quasi-laboratory in which languages are learned and teaching methods performed (with possibly some connection between the two). This reading, by contrast, has argued for the importance of seeing the classroom as a social and cultural space. This sense of the social and cultural, furthermore, is not the liberal dream of equitable social relations and celebratory multiculturalism, but a view always concerned with questions of power. From this sociopolitical and cultural political viewpoint, the language classroom becomes a site of contestation, where different codes, different visions of the world, and different pedagogies are in competition and conflict. Auerbach suggests:

> Once we begin looking at classrooms through an ideological lens, dynamics
> of power and inequality show up in every aspect of classroom life. . . . We are
> forced to ask questions about the most natural seeming practices: Where is the
> class located? Where does the teacher stand or sit? Who asks questions? What
> kinds of questions are asked? Who chooses the learning materials? How is
> progress evaluated? Who evaluates it? (Auerbach, 1995: 12)

The classroom is a microcosm of the larger social and cultural world,
reflecting, reproducing and changing the world. This should not be seen, however, as a pessimistic view of language teaching but as a necessary understanding of the competing demands we face as teachers. Everything outside the
classroom, from language policies to cultural contexts of schooling, may have
an impact on what happens in the classroom. And everything in the classroom,
from how we teach, what we teach, and how we respond to students, to the
materials we use, and the ways we assess the students, needs to be seen as
social and cultural practices with broad implications. The challenge is to understand these relationships and to find ways of always focusing on the local while
at the same time keeping an eye on the broader horizons. The view of our classroom walls as permeable means that what we do in our classrooms is about
changing the worlds we live in. As James Gee notes:

> English teachers can cooperate in their own marginalization by seeing them-
> selves as "language teachers" with no connection to such social and political
> issues. Or they . . . accept their role as persons who socialize students into a
> world view that, given its power here and abroad, must be looked at critically,
> comparatively, and with a constant sense of the possibilities for change. Like
> it or not, English teachers stand at the very heart of the most crucial educa-
> tional, cultural, and political issues of our time. (Gee, 1994: 190)

Along with the difficulties and dangers such a view brings, it also presents
us with exciting challenges, and it can help us see that once we take the social
politics and cultural politics of our classrooms seriously, what we do as English
teachers matters, for we indeed stand at the very heart of the most crucial educational, cultural, and political issues of our time.

RELATED READING 2
THE PERSONAL AND COLLECTIVE TRANSFORMATION OF TEACHERS
Sonia Nieto

Although teaching is often approached as a technical activity—writing lesson plans, learning effective methods for teaching algebra, selecting appropriate texts, developing tests to assess student learning—anybody who has spent any time in a classroom knows that teaching and learning are primarily about relationships. What happens in classrooms is first and foremost about the personal and collective connections that exist among the individuals who inhabit those spaces. Consequently, teachers' beliefs and values, how these are communicated to students through teaching practices and behaviors, and their impact on the lives of students—these are the factors that make teaching so consequential in the lives of many people.

   We can all recall inspirational or dreadful teachers, although we may have a hard time remembering exactly what they taught or the kinds of lessons they prepared. I cannot remember her name, but the remark of one of my first teachers that it was rude to speak Spanish in the classroom still stings. It may have been nothing more than an offhand comment on her part, but those words had a powerful impact on me. In the short term, they had the effect of invalidating my use of Spanish in school. In the long term, they were to influence for many years how I would view the value of my native language. Equally rooted in my memory is the image of Mr. Slotkin, a creative and nurturing eighth-grade science teacher whose classroom was always an exciting place that made going to school worthwhile. I do not recollect any of the specific lessons he taught and, except for this one successful encounter with science, I was never particularly a science enthusiast. The relationships I had with these teachers is what made a difference, and I suspect the same is true for most people. That is why the personal transformation of teachers is a necessary process that needs to go hand in hand with structural changes in schools.

   Teaching and learning are not only about relationships, however. As Paulo Freire always insisted (1970a, 1970b, 1985), education is a *political* act. That is, it concerns decisions and actions that bear on *who* and *what* and *how* we teach, and also in *whose interest* we teach. Try as we might to separate it from the political sphere, education is always political because it focuses in a central way on questions of power, privilege, and access. As such, education is also about political commitment and social responsibility. Once teachers understand this, they no longer can point to others—the central office, the union, the principal, the prescribed basal reader—as the only or even the most important decision makers in the classroom. In spite of how teachers' actions are constricted by others, teach-

From S. Nieto (1999), *The Light in Their Eyes: Creating Multicultural Learning Communities*. New York: Teachers College Press, pp. 130–161. Used by Permission.

ers still have enormous power to create enriching and empowering relationships with students, colleagues, and members of the community in which they teach.

Environments that are both critical and empowering are not created overnight; they are developed and sustained through the relationships formed in classrooms between and among teachers, students, and families. Building these relationships implies a profound transformation of the attitudes, beliefs, and behaviors of teachers concerning the nature of learning and intelligence, the role of diversity in learning, and, in fact, the ideological stance or world view they may have in general. The process of transformation is a personal and collective journey that teachers must travel. The transformation to which I refer begins as a political commitment on the part of teachers, individually and collectively, as it is demonstrated here through the stories of several teachers with whom I have had the privilege to work over the years.

If we understand teaching as consisting primarily of social relationships and as a political commitment rather than a technical activity, then it is unquestionable that what educators need to pay most attention to are their own growth and transformation and the lives, realities, and dreams of their students. This is not to take the responsibility off the shoulders of teacher education institutions or school systems, nor is it to say that it should not be an institutional odyssey as well. I also do not intend for this focus on teachers to be read as teacher bashing. On the contrary, I believe that most teachers enter the teaching profession because of a profound commitment to young people. Although some teachers lose their enthusiasm for teaching and their hope in children, many maintain their ideals, and they actively and consistently search for ways to create learning environments that are meaningful and engaging for their students. In what follows, we will consider some ways in which teachers do this.

CONFRONTING ONE'S IDENTITY

Teachers in the United States, who are primarily White, middle-class, and monolingual, have had limited experiences with diverse populations, and they frequently perceive of diversity in a negative way. This was the conclusion reached by Kenneth Zeichner and Karen Hoeft (1996) after a thorough review of the literature concerning the role of teacher education in preparing educators for diverse classrooms. On the other hand, teachers who can call on their own experiences of marginalization, as well as those who have developed a bicultural identity and who have entered the teaching profession precisely because they see it as a way to serve their communities, find it easier to forge strong and meaningful relationships with their students. But being a member of a culturally or racially disempowered group does not guarantee that one can understand or identify with students of backgrounds different from one's own. That is, a Mexican American teacher will not necessarily be an effective teacher of Vietnamese students simply because she is Mexican

American. In fact, she may not even necessarily be a better teacher of Mexican American students if her personal experiences and background differ markedly from those of her students and she has no immediate understanding of how to bridge these differences.

For teachers of the dominant culture who have little knowledge of the cultures, experiences, or feelings of their students from bicultural backgrounds, trying to understand them poses an even greater challenge. Sometimes teachers may use their ignorance of diversity to maintain that adjusting the curriculum and instruction to their students' backgrounds makes little sense; that is, teachers may reason that if students will need to assimilate anyway, why change the curriculum? The assumption is that learning is a one-way process in which students need to learn the culture and values of the school, but that teachers need not learn the culture and values of their students. Other teachers, whether from dominant or bicultural backgrounds, recognize that they first need to understand and accept their *own* diversity and delve into their *own* identities before they can learn about and from their students.

A good example of coming to terms with one's identity and all that it entails is the following journal entry by Ann Scott during her first semester in graduate school. In it, she confronted her fear of acknowledging a White identity rooted in privilege, and she mused about what it meant to go through this process as part of her personal and professional transformation.

The Discomfort of My Identity

by Ann Scott

I'm feeling a bit anxious as a result of this class. Looking at myself in this way can be quite uncomfortable, but I know how good it is for me to have this opportunity to develop as a human being. This is an aspect of graduate school that I had not expected—and for which I'm grateful even if it's painful at times. That is, I expected to be learning about education on an intellectual level, but I did not expect to be engaged so profoundly on an emotional and spiritual level, nor to be asked to look so closely at myself and to challenge myself this way. Hard work. But the kind of hard work that I'm willing to do. . . . Placing myself in various contexts, examining my privileges and all I take for granted because of my privileges, those things I did not earn but simply inherited; recognizing how much I lose as a result of my privileges; and, perhaps most disturbing of all, recognizing just a bit how others suffer because of my privileges.

Later in the same journal entry, Ann completely immersed herself in an exercise that I often ask students to do in my graduate class. First, I assign them Peggy McIntosh's (1988) groundbreaking article on White privilege in which the author analyzes in a detailed and candid way the numerous ways in which she benefits from her Whiteness. Reading this article is often an extraordinary experience for course participants: Many Whites, some for the first time, are forced to grapple with what it means to have unearned racial privilege; Black and other people of color are often grateful that a White person has articulated a reality of which they have been painfully aware for many years. After they have read it, we engage in a far-ranging discussion—Marilyn Cochran-Smith (1977) and some of the teachers with whom she has worked call these discussions "hard talk"—about race, racism, privilege, and the negative impact they have on bicultural children. I then extend the analogy used by McIntosh by asking course participants to reflect and write in their journals about unearned privilege that they may enjoy in another area of social identity. Everybody can write something, since everybody benefits from some kind of privilege, whether it is in terms of their race, gender, social class, sexual orientation, or some other way in which their status is rewarded by society.

I have found this exercise to be particularly helpful in helping people come face to face with the silent, insidious, and unacknowledged power of institutional racism and other forms of discrimination. It provides a key learning experience for many teachers in their long journey of transformation. Ann chose to enumerate many examples of her English-language privilege (only some of which I include here), and then she though about this issue even more critically after she had finished.

The Privilege of Speaking, Reading, and Writing the English Language

by Ann Scott

Being a "native" English speaker (and reader and writer) in the United States (even though English is *not* the native language of this place) bestows all kinds of privileges on me that are so ingrained and so hidden that it takes a great deal of effort just to see the most obvious ones. I'm not sure if I've been "carefully taught not to recognize privilege" of this sort, as Peggy McIntosh thinks, or if it's simply in the nature of privilege that it is invisible to the wearer of it. Perhaps if it was visible, it would quickly become intolerable in its ugly, undeserved unjustness.

In no particular order of importance, being an English speaker in the United States means

1. I can be confident that people will understand me wherever I go in the United States, and if they don't, *they* will be seen as deficient, not me.
2. My language will be considered the essential, legal, primary, best, official, legitimate, or only way of communicating.
3. I can survive, even thrive, in my country without learning a second language.
4. I can negotiate pretty well in most places in the world with English, at least in the industrialized world, without ever learning a second language.

5. I will not be patronized because of my native language.

6. I will not be ignored or talked about as if I am not present because of my native language.

7. I will not be asked, told, or required by law or the ignorance of others to speak a language that is not native to me in the place I call home.

8. I will not suffer persecution or discrimination because my native language is other than English.

9. I will not have to worry about whether my accent will cause people to think I don't have command of English, even though I may have perfect command of English.

10. I need never become exhausted from the rigors of trying to communicate in a language that is foreign to me.

11. If I speak or write articulately in my native language. I will be considered intelligent and well educated. I will not be thought stupid or slow because of my accent or the way I speak English.

12. I will never feel ashamed of my native language.

13. I will not be pressured to forget or abandon my native language. On the contrary, I will be encouraged, even required, to study and become more fluent in it.

14. If I learn a second language, this will be seen as an asset and a source of pride, whereas for the nonnative-English speaker, being bilingual is a detriment and a source of shame.

15. I do not have to be pulled in two directions in terms of language—between my loyalties and pride in my own language and my desire to survive and belong in the dominant culture of the place I call home.

16. I do not have to feel ashamed of my parents or other family members because of the language they speak or because of their language proficiency.

17. Growing up in the United States as a native-English speaker, I have a lot of choices about educational attainment. I can be pretty lazy in school; I can do the minimum amount of work; I can even drop out of school in my early teens and still be able to speak, read, and write the dominant language adequately. (I'm not entirely sure about this one; it was true in the 1960s when I was in high school.)

About halfway through this exercise, I realized how faulty my assumptions about privilege are when I think about all the native-English speakers who are people of color, are disabled, have strong southern or rural or city accents, or are otherwise not in the dominant, Anglocentric mold. So many of the privileges I listed were also attached to my Whiteness, my WASPness. I can see gender discrimination with ease because I'm not one of the preferred people. To some extent I can recognize class privilege, but mainly I see the privileges of the classes above me. So anyway, I went back and tried to revise a lot of my list to reflect privilege specifically related to language, but many of them could be contested from the point of view of a non-Anglo native-English speaker. Perhaps, then, I should specify, when I talk about language privilege, that I mean the language spoken by Whites with specific kinds of accents or dialect, that is, a much more strictly defined language.

Wow, this stuff is really hard to do. (10.2.93)

As Ann indicated, this is hard work, but it is a process that opens up worlds of understanding that otherwise might remain closed. Courageous teachers who take this journey find, as did Ann, that it pays off in many ways both personally and professionally.

Identification with one's culture does not stop at the point of just recognizing privilege, however; if it did, then it would result only in shame and guilt. Most teachers, like most human beings in general, do not wish to remain feeling bad about themselves; they need something more positive upon which to build. This is the case with Debbie Habib, a former doctoral student who reflected deeply about her background and experiences to understand how these had affected her teaching and her life and to analyze how White privilege had influenced her differently from other White students. As a Sephardic Jew with Turkish roots, Debbie often is mistaken for Arabic, Latina, biracial, or Iranian. People who try to figure out her background often make comments such as, "You're *something*, right?" This *something*, as Debbie explains below, is seen as "a little too ethnic."

A Kid from Jersey: White Privilege and "A Little Too Ethnic"

By Deborah Leta Habib

Visiting the "Mainline" Philadelphia home of a college friend's family was an interesting cultural experience for a kid from Jersey who thought boarding schools only truly existed in Louisa May Alcott's *Little Women*. I did not lead a sheltered life, mind you. My first-generation, middle-class, lefty liberal Jewish family frequented plays and peace marches, and I was nourished on a diet of discourse and library books. In my Italian, Jewish, Black, Greek, and Catholic New Jersey community of upbringing, we just didn't do boarding schools. And so, as I was recovering from the shock of learning about a boarding school for girls where they played a game called "lacrosse" and from where my new rebellious best friend had emerged, I soon faced another challenge: I was "a little too ethnic."

Years later, I can name the emotions and experiences that shaped my sense of self with phrases like White privilege, anti-Semitism, and internalized anti-Semitism. But 15 years ago I didn't have these terms, or the reflective ability or support to make sense of it all. In middle and high school, we all hung out together, shared snacks and smokes, and visited each other's houses. But when racial violence consumed the school, I was White. I was Jewish at home, but only White at school. Everybody had to choose one, White or Black. So, a few years later, when I walked into my friend's parents' house on "The Mainline" (which had plastic coated furniture, as did my aunt's, only hers held the smells of the kitchen and the Bronx air, whereas the Mainline plastic had no smell at all), I was a little taken aback by the coldness of the greeting. I introduced myself in what I thought was a polite manner; it had always worked for my friends' parents in Jersey, who seemed to think I was nice enough. Part of me just thought these Mainline-parents had been sitting on plastic for too long, but my heart and somewhat nauseous stomach detected something else.

After a few more meetings spread over several years, I finally commented to my friend that her parents didn't seem to like me too much. "It's not that they don't like you," she said. "It's just that you're a little too ethnic for them." I thought about standing in their kitchen, me with my curly dark hair, wide nose, olive skin, and peasant build, them with their fair hair, blue eyes, and fine bones. I remembered the time that my friend and I were leaving for Europe, and her mother suggested we visit the churches and cathedrals . . . "and I'm sure there are some lovely temples too," she added, not quite knowing what to say. Considering I had rarely stepped foot in a temple before, I thought it unlikely that I would make it a focus of my trip. Was I the first Jewish person they had ever met, ever spoken with? My friend had told me that their club had an unwritten "No Jews Allowed" policy. I knew that Jews as a group were often made to feel invisible in this society and at times blatantly discriminated against or threatened. As a child, I believe I once wondered why the school calendar was organized around holidays that my family did not celebrate, and I had heard numerous stories of flight from persecution and arrival in a less than welcoming new land. But I had never been so personally aware of anti-Semitism until it seared my soul in my friend's kitchen and I experienced a form of judgment that those who did not have White privilege probably feel on a regular basis.

Fifteen years after our first meeting, I received a card from my friend's parents (she is still my close friend, so they have probably realized that I am not just a passing ethnic fad), appreciating my support in helping her coordinate her wedding and taking care of logistics so she could have time with her family. So perhaps they are beginning to accept me. Has my skin lightened, hair uncurled, ancestry changed? Or am I "one of the nice ones, not like the others"? Have they done some soul searching, examined their biases, made conscious changes in their attitudes? I would love to be sure this is it, but I am a bit skeptical.

Since that first meeting, I have learned that boarding schools not only exist, but that they serve the specific purpose of maintaining privilege in this society, and that lacrosse is a game that was first played by Native Americans. My Italian, Jewish, Black, Greek, Catholic community of upbringing now includes many Asian Americans and East Indians, one of whom owns the Dunkin' Donuts which he made kosher. My parents are active on a race relations committee which, among other things, is negotiating with the town to pave a road that would link, physically and symbolically, two neighborhoods separated by race and class. I now have the vocabulary to describe the experiences and emotions that shaped and still shape my identity. Some of these words are White privilege, anti-Semitism, and internalized anti-Semitism. They are useful as I try to unlayer and heal my ethnic identity and internalized racism with honesty and integrity. Here I sit in reflection: educator, activist, spiritual being, that kid from Jersey, the one with White privilege who is "a little too ethnic." (March 1994)

Debbie's reflections are especially useful because they help to deconstruct the White/Black dichotomy so often associated with difference. As she mentioned, in her high school you were either Black or White; there was nothing else. Given the growing presence of students from backgrounds that cannot be categorized so easily, as well as the increasingly biracial and biethnic identities of the students in U.S. classrooms, it is essential to acknowledge the complicated nature of diversity. But this recognition should not diminish the power of racial and other kinds of privilege.

A growing number of scholars are writing critically and convincingly about the need for White teachers to acknowledge and "own" their White identity if they are to become effective teachers of all students (O'Donnell & Clark, 1999; Howard, 1999). This process requires that Whites recognize their complicity in maintaining injustice if they choose to do nothing about it. Although the process of recognizing, confronting, and learning from one's unearned privileges is indispensable, it also can be tremendously painful and discouraging. To become transformative, it needs to be complemented by hopeful beliefs and actions. For many teachers, this means finding out about and becoming a White ally. Beverly Daniel Tatum (1994) speaks of this process as "the restoration of hope."

Patty Bode . . . has engaged in such a journey. Always known as a gifted art teacher, Patty had won many accolades and awards from students, parents, co-teachers, and local and national organizations for her sensitive and inclusive teaching. But she felt that "something was missing." When she started her graduate studies, she began to rethink her ideas and her classroom practices. The following is an excerpt from Patty's reflections.

On Becoming a White Ally

By Patty Bode

Before I started my graduate studies, I was proudly practicing multicultural education in my classroom, but I knew I still had an enormous amount to learn. As an art teacher, my curriculum drew from world art throughout history. I developed cross-cultural comparisons of folk artists from traditional societies throughout the globe and I researched contemporary artists who made statements about current events and social status and identity. I developed curriculum to encourage student dialogue about skin color in what I hope was a respectful way and in a safe educational environment.

I noticed an inordinate number of students of color in special education. I hoped I was doing a good job, but I knew something was missing. I was not certain what it was. I grappled with my position as a European American teacher and my place in multicultural education. I worried that somehow my practice would not be viewed as valid in a realm of study that grew out of the Civil Rights Movement with African American educators asserting the right to be accurately represented in curriculum and with concerns about the achievements of students of color.

This is why knowledge and identification of other White allies became so empowering to me. Reading the articles by Peggy McIntosh [1988] and Christine Sleeter [1994] were turning points. Their writing was not surprising or revelatory, just confirming. Their scholarship reinforced and validated my beliefs. Naming my position as a White ally underscored my role in multicultural education and provided me with a forum for dialogue among my students. When my third-grade Latino student asks me, "Ms. Bode, if you are not Latina, why do you care so much about Latino art and culture?" I am able to respond with more self-assurance and certainty. Together my students and I frame a context for Dr. Martin Luther King's words, "Injustice anywhere is a threat to justice everywhere." We talk about privilege and responsibility. We read stories about cooperation to create change. We become partners who trust each other. We promise to work together to fight racism. It all begins to make sense in the mind of a third grader. (11.12.97)

Patty Bode's is the story of a White teacher who is finding the way to honor her own identity and her role in the quest for social justice in teaching. Teachers who can identify with their students culturally, racially, in terms of social class origin, or in other ways, may find that the process is not quite as difficult because they can draw on and reflect about their own experiences with difference and consequently they are able to more readily understand the feelings and perspectives of their students. I have seen this happen time and again in my own classes. For instance, when I ask my graduate students to discuss their identity and why it is important to them or not, I have found consistently that those who identify with their culture and ethnicity are more easily able to identify with their students of diverse backgrounds. I present two examples to illustrate this. First, Tom Hidalgo, the grandson of Spanish immigrants who worked in the coal mines of West Virginia, relates how he developed his identity as a Spaniard, and how it has profoundly influenced his work as a community organizer and his interest in oral history and multicultural education as transformative processes.

Enriching Differences

By Tom Hidalgo

My ethnic background is critical to me. The first time I really remember noticing my Spanishness I was in the first grade. I remember going home and asking my parents why we had a name like Hidalgo. Nobody else in my class did. Everybody else had names like Hylton and Parsons and Jones and Green. They explained to me that their names came from England and mine came from Spain. I felt different, but also special. In fact, my sister and I were the only "ethnics" in the school of more than 800 kids! From then on I always felt special being Spanish. And lucky.

I believe that because I was different, I have always been interested in other cultures and peoples and places. I have always valued and tried to learn from differences in people. I have always noted ethnic or racial or cultural differences in people and even at a young age I remember feeling that these differences were very enriching to the environment. I'm sure this has driven much of my work and interests. (1.26.94)

In the second example, David Ruiz, a former graduate student who was a counselor for students of color in an independent school in Massachusetts, wrote simply, "I guess that being Puerto Rican is as important to me as being alive is" (9.16.94). He found it curious, but understandable, that most Whites in our class did not identify with their ethnic backgrounds. In his journal, he mused about why this might be so.

Being on the Winning Team

By David Ruiz

That the United States is characterized by Anglo-conformity seems to be apparent based on the responses given by many of the Euro-Americans in class on Wednesday. It is quite easy to be on the winning team and not ask how it is that you're winning. Most White Americans are comfortable in their dominant roles and are not really concerned about whether or not the scales of justice were tilted. Few would trade places with those other people and most would deny any wrongdoing on their part or on the part of their ancestors.

It seemed like they had conveniently forgotten their roots. Maybe it doesn't matter when you're on the barrel edge, looking into the barrel, watching all the other crabs trying to get out. . . . It is quite easy to be on the winning team and not ask how it is that you're winning. (9.21.94)

As we can see from the foregoing examples, the failure to identify with their own identity can prevent teachers from identifying more closely with their students. In conjunction with this, teachers need to develop identities as learners.

BECOMING A LEARNER OF STUDENTS

As Paulo Freire (1970b) proposed many years ago, teaching and learning need to be thought of as reciprocal processes in which students become teachers and teachers become students. If this is the case, then teachers no longer simply deposit knowledge into students' minds; rather, teachers become actively engaged in learning through their interactions with students. This is an especially timely consideration if we think about the wide gulf that currently exists in the United States between teachers, who are overwhelmingly White, middle-class, and monolingual English speakers, and their students, who are increasingly diverse in culture, ethnicity, social class, and native language. Historically in this situation, the conventional approach has been to instruct students in the ways of White, middle-class, English-speaking America and, in the process, to rid them of as many of their differences as possible.

Without denying the need to teach students the cultural capital that they need to help them negotiate society, it is also important that teachers make a commitment to become *students of their students*. This implies at least two kinds of processes. First, teachers need to learn *about* their students, a change from the one-way learning that usually takes place in classrooms. For this to happen, teachers need to become researchers. In the words of Ira Shor (Shor & Freire, 1987):

> The first researcher, then, in the classroom is the teacher who investigates his or her students. This is one basic task of the liberatory classroom, but by itself it is only preparatory because the research process must animate students to study themselves, the course texts, and their own language and reality. (pp. 9–10).

Second, as implied by Shor, teachers need to create spaces in which teachers can learn *with their students*, and in which students are encouraged to learn about themselves and one another.

The assertion that teachers can and should become learners is in no way meant to lessen their duty to teach. Nor is it to imply that there are equal power relations between teachers and students in the classroom, or that students' and teachers' knowledge have equal status in society. These are romantic notions that, taken to an extreme, relieve educators of their responsibility to teach. Years ago, for instance, I heard a teacher remark that his students were so "street smart" that they really did not need to be instructed in the academic content of the schools, something that he surely would not have said of his own children. This condescending attitude does little to help students. In fact, such comments often have more to do with teachers' feelings that their students are unable to learn or unworthy of learning academic knowledge.

Teachers have a grave responsibility to prepare students to become effective and critical participants in the world, and this is particularly true for their bicultural students, who consistently have been denied this access. Teachers need to be authoritative—that is, knowledgeable, clear, and direct—rather than authoritarian in their interactions with students. They need to teach students the kinds of skills they must have in order to make a difference in the world. This means, among other things, that students need to learn the language of power (Delpit, 1988).

Going through the paces of learning about one's students is not enough. It is not simply about learning a technical strategy, or picking up a few cultural tidbits. It is impossible, for example, to become culturally responsive simply by taking a course in which cultural responsiveness is reduced to a strategy. This does not mean that teaching is always and intuitive undertaking, although it certainly has this quality at times. But more important are the *attitudes* of teachers when they are in the position of learners. In discussing the specific case of African American students, Jacqueline Jordan Irvine (1990) has suggested that learning can be improved if the interpersonal context that exists between students and their teachers is a positive one. She developed the concept of *cultural synchronization* to describe this relationship. Cultural synchronization assumes both integrity and humility; it cannot be either deceptive or an artificial donning of cultural values. Rather, it means that teachers need to learn what can help their students learn, and then change their teaching accordingly.

Students are very perceptive, no matter how young they are, and they can spot negative attitudes or false intentions a mile away. David Corson (1995) has asserted that teachers, being human beings, are just as susceptible to the influence of negative attitudes as anybody else; however, because they have enormous power over children, their attitudes can become particularly harmful because they can be put into action in the classroom. Frances Kendall (1996) cites the appalling case of a White teacher who, in a videotape of her teaching, was found to wash her hands after every time she touched a Black child. In this case, no matter what this teacher might say, her negative beliefs were communicated unequivocally to her young students. This is not to imply that teachers who hold these beliefs cannot change, but it is to suggest that beliefs and attitudes need to change before any specific strategies can help.

In journal responses to an assignment that participants analyze the pros and cons of culturally responsive pedagogy, Lizette Román, a bilingual teacher, was critical of what she clearly saw as superficial cultural learning, but she also reflected on the necessity for teachers to learn more about their students in order to be effective with them.

Cultural Knowledge and Culturally Responsive Pedagogy

By Lizette Román

To have knowledge of another culture does not mean to be able to repeat one or two words in a student's language, nor is it to celebrate an activity or sing a song related to their culture. To acknowledge and respect is to be able to understand and apply this knowledge to everyday classroom activities. It is to be able to make changes or modifications in one's curriculum or pedagogy when the needs of the students have not been served. It is to be patient, tolerant, curious, creative, eager to learn, and, most important, nonauthoritarian with students.

In order for a teacher to promote excellence in education, there has to be a real and honest connection between the needs and cultural values of teachers and students. This is culturally responsive education. It was not until I thought more about it that I realized that both multicultural education and cultural congruency are simply *means* by which minority students will gain a better future. Students cannot learn outside of their cultural context. Factors such as achievement, dropout rates, even students' behavior and attendance are affected when schools as a whole do not take into consideration students' cultures and learning styles. All students, regardless of their ethnic group, need to feel connected with their schools, their homes, and their communities.

There are cons to culturally responsive pedagogy when teachers do not understand or acknowledge their students' culture and insist on teaching according to their own values. There are cons when a teacher stereotypes or generalizes about her students. This often has the effect of lowering expectations of the students, consequently affecting students' performance. There are cons when a teacher does not recognize a student's individuality and sees him only as part of the group. Knowledge of a particular cultural learning style is useful and serves as a guideline, but it does not necessarily represent the learning styles of all members of that culture. (11.13.96; 11.20.96)

Defining the teacher as a learner is a radical departure from the prevailing notion of the educator as repository of all knowledge, a view that is firmly entrenched in society. Ira Shor (Shor & Freire, 1987) critiqued this conventional portrait of teachers vis-à-vis their students: "The students are not a flotilla of boats trying to reach the teacher who is finished and waiting on the shore. The teacher is also one of the boats" (p. 50). Yet in spite of how terrifying it may be for teachers to act as all-knowing sages, this conception of teacher is a more familiar and, hence, less threatening one than teacher as learner. Once teachers admit that they do not know everything, they make themselves as vulnerable as their students. It is this attitude of learner on the part of teachers that is needed, first, to convey to students that nobody is above learning; and second, to let students know that they also are knowers and that what they know can be an important source of learning for others as well. It follows from this perspective that teachers need to build on what their students bring with them to the classroom.

What exactly should teachers know about their students? In the case of bicultural students specifically, teachers would do well to learn about their lives outside of school, including their families and cultures, how they see the world, what is important to them, and their values and dreams for the future. They also can learn at least one of the languages of the students whom they teach. Engaging in this kind of learning, which needs to be approached with both humility and energy, represents nothing less than a political commitment on the part of teachers. But because this learning can be done *with*, and not only *for* or *about*, students, it is neither overwhelming nor impossible. The following excerpt is a powerful example of this kind of learning.

Bill Dunn is a high school English teacher in a small urban school system. A few years ago, he decided that it was time he "came out of the closet" as a Spanish speaker, so he asked me to sponsor an independent research study in which he could document his experience. From a working-class Irish family, Bill was born, was raised, and still lives in the town in which he teaches, and he cares deeply about it. He had taught for 20 years in the same school district and he had seen a change from a mostly working-class Irish and European American school system to one that was over two-thirds Puerto Rican. He had heard a great deal of Spanish spoken over those 20 years, and when he became a doctoral student, he decided this was the perfect opportunity to explicitly learn the language. The independent research project he did allowed him to design his game plan: he would take a course in our university Spanish department and another at a local community center; he would sit in on bilingual classes at his high school; and he would keep a journal of all of these activities. Following is an extensive excerpt from the eloquent journal that was a result of Bill's immersion into the Spanish language and the lives of his students (Dunn, 1994).

Mi Semestre de Español:
A Case Study on the Cultural Dimension of
Second-Language Acquisition

By Bill Dunn

I've searched for a word to describe the cultural complexities of acquiring a second language, and eventually I settled on the word "stance." By stance I mean things: the reason why I desire to learn a second language, my attitude toward my community and the people who speak the "target" language, and many confrontations with my own cultural identity and the cultural identities of others. Stance also has a pugilistic connotation. I believe that there is an element of risk involved in living in a multicultural community. You have to be willing to take the heat. In *Pedagogy of the Oppressed* Paulo Freire [1970b] points to risk as the essence of being human. . . . To acquire a second language you must assume an attitude that reaches out to people, and to do that you must be able to see beyond your own culture.

The cultural conflicts of second-language acquisition came to me in a vivid way one day while I was involved in a totally unrelated activity. I had been aware for quite a while of the cultural turmoil of living in a language-rich environment. In fact, I don't think anyone could teach in a situation like my town without being aware of the troubled cultural waters in which we are engulfed on a daily basis. Much of the conflict is caused by language because language is in many ways culture. But the phrase which brought the cultural dimension of second-language acquisition to the surface for me occurred one day while I was working on a carpentry project. . . . I was thinking of the word for wood in Spanish, *madera*, and I wondered whether it could be used like in English to mean forest or woods. I thought to myself, "One of these days I have to come out of the closet with my Spanish." It was that particular phrase which drove home the cultural implications for second-language acquisition. Like the risks involved in revealing a homosexual orientation, there are risks involved in acquiring a second language as well. Americans are particularly poor at second-language acquisition; the dominant culture demands "English only." When you acquire a second language, you put yourself at odds with the dominant culture, and any time you go against the flow you have to be willing to take some heat for it. In a working-class town like mine you have to be willing to breach some very turbulent cultural waters. There is bound to be personal conflict on the psychic level as well because in order to acquire a second language you also have to be willing to acquire some of the habits and cultural attitudes of those who speak the language. These conflicts can be very subtle and just being aware of them can be a major first step in the right direction.

To acquire a second language, you must also acquire a second culture, and that is going to cause problems. There will be a resentment among members of your own cultural group, and occasionally suspicion among members of the target language group. (I must add, though, that my experience with native-Spanish speakers in my town has been extremely positive.) Despite these cultural barriers there are wonderful rewards and gains in letting one's cultural attitudes melt and mix with different currents. First, there is the insight into an alternate reality or perspective on the world and your environment, and second, there is a freedom in distancing yourself from the inhibiting ties of your own culture.

In my work, I often act as a bridge between different cultures. Part of my evolution as a teacher has been in self-defense: I have learned to make my life easier by making life easier for my students; but another, greater part of my experience has been a deep curiosity and yearning to understand the lives of my students. In my struggle to understand, I have learned not only a great deal about my students, but also about myself.

One thing that I have learned is that language carries a lot of cultural baggage with it. The distinctions that are made on the basis of language in my town are fascinating. We are a sort of walking, living, and breathing language lab. Obviously there exists the English–Spanish cultural distinction. There are also economic distinctions. . . . On any given day in my classroom and in the hallways of my school, I witness remarkable language interactions which often go unnoticed and are not valued, or worse, are devalued. . . . If the third floor of my school were the language wing of a prestigious boarding school, we would be answering questions for Morley Safer on *Sixty Minutes* as to why we are so successful at language acquisition when the rest of America fails so dismally. Instead we are called on by the school board to answer why our students perform so poorly on standardized tests.

I hope that you will enjoy [the following] cultural scenes. They are not the dramatic headlines that we are all too familiar with in our town. These are scenes from everyday life which in this town can be very complex.

[Dos] Escenas de cultura [Two cultural scenes]

Scene One: *A few years ago I was busy with some paper work during homeroom. Four or five students were chatting in Spanish and I found this to be very distracting. I asked them to be quiet, but they kept on talking. A little later I asked them again more forcefully. One of the students pointed out to me that there were other students speaking in English and I was not chastising them. I thought about that later in the day and I realized that this student was right. I began to wonder what it was that bothered me about the Spanish. I didn't think they were talking about me or anything like that, but I was annoyed. Shortly after that incident I began to realize that there were cultural collisions occurring beneath the surface, and I also began to understand that most people are not aware of the source of these collisions.*

Scene Two: *I'm in my classroom about a month ago. It is a senior class and there is no seating arrangement. I like to think of them as mature enough to sit where they want. There are two very attractive, well-dressed girls who always sit together. One is Black and the other is Puerto Rican. They chat a lot, and I have to constantly get their attention. On this particular day I ask them to be quiet several times. Finally the Black girl informs me that she is not going to be quiet as long as* they can talk. *With her head she motions toward the corner of the room where the bilingual kids sit. . . . I have been practicing Spanish with the bilingual kids, and in this kid's statement I sense a kind of "you like them better than us" attitude. El círculo ha cerrado (The circle has closed).*

When I decided to do this project, I was apprehensive because I was not sure how far I could get in 3 months of trying to teach myself Spanish. Puedo comunicar en español pero mi lenguage no es muy bueno [I can communicate in Spanish but my language is not very good]. Yet I feel that I have made some progress. I have also made some wonderful friends that I probably would not have met otherwise. One thing that I have noticed is that people who speak more than one language really like to talk, and I have learned a great deal just by talking to people.

In the beginning I got very excited about learning Spanish. I hadn't felt that way about learning anything in a long time. I borrowed some Spanish-language tapes and I listened to them. . . . I also worked in several different Spanish-language books. . . . Perhaps the most interesting aspect of my second-language learning was the use of television. . . . I like talk shows like *Christina* and *The Nuevo Paul Rodríguez Show* and news programs like *Noticias y Más*.

My hall duty at school is outside a Spanish One class, and I listen to what goes on in there. It seems to be a very traditional class. It also seems to me that the teacher could be using the talents of her students much more creatively. . . . Sometimes it almost seems like she is devaluing the language of her students. I have heard this from other Spanish teachers too. They put down the Spanish of the kids in this town. If I were teaching this class I would be looking for ways in which I could use the language talents of my students as a vehicle to help the monolingual students.

About a month into my study I noticed something very peculiar. I had been very excited, as I mentioned, about my project. Then everything just sort of slowed down. I found this to be very puzzling. I am guessing that things occurred on the subconscious level that caused the shutdown. My theory is that my own cultural identity was struggling to reassert itself. It was kind of like I was pushing my mind into places that it just didn't want to go. . . . As a teacher this impressed me very much. I have witnessed similar responses in my students when they come into class and just want to put their head on the desk. Again, you don't really understand this until you have experienced it for yourself. Too often we dismiss this sort of thing as laziness. It is very easy to draw the wrong conclusion. This was one of my most powerful insights into second-language acquisition. It was almost like my mind was saying, "enough with all this Spanish."

In terms of where I am now with the Spanish language, it is difficult to say. It took me a long time to get over what [Stephen] Krashen calls "the silent period." I don't know. I tend to be very inhibited to begin with so it was really difficult for me to begin to speak in Spanish. I did notice that it was very important whom I was speaking to. It is still very difficult for me to speak to a native-Spanish speaker. I'm more comfortable with someone whose second language is Spanish. I think this is a valuable insight as a teacher because many students may be very inhibited with me because I'm a native English speaker. Again, this is an insight that you don't understand until you undergo the process. . . . Another peculiarity of speaking involves who else is around. There are certain colleagues that I am very inhibited from speaking Spanish if they walk by. They tend to be teachers who are very biased in their views. This is insightful for students too. If a teacher is continually putting down a student's language and culture, that would probably be the least desirable conversationalist for the students.

When I finally came out of my "silent" period, I again got very excited about this aspect of learning a second language. Again though, it was a "roller coaster" sort of experience. One thing I can definitely point out about this aspect is that it is very hard to function in a second language when you are tired or your mind is preoccupied with other problems. Some days when I was alert the words came easily, and on other days when I was tired I just drew a blank. I think I have a greater understanding of my students because many of them come to school tired or with severe problems.

As part of my study I have been speaking with nonnative-Spanish speakers. I found them to be very sympathetic. I think they understand how difficult it is to acquire a second language when you are older. I noticed too that the [kids in the bilingual program] were more receptive toward me. I covered a class for a bilingual teacher, and the students were quite hospitable. I feel that because they are trying to accomplish a similar feat, they are more understanding. Sometimes when I speak Spanish to the mainstream [Spanish-speaking] kids they can be very critical.

I thought that it would be interesting to sit in on a bilingual class and observe. Anne, a bilingual teacher, gave me permission. . . . I knew a few of the kids and they said hello. I returned the greetings and thanked them in Spanish for allowing me to participate in their class. . . . Anne passed out a test, and I was very disappointed. I only answered a question or two, but what shocked me was I didn't understand two-thirds of the questions. I had no idea what was being asked, and I thought of all those kids in the lower tracks who are condemned to answering questions that they don't understand at the end of countless chapters that they don't comprehend. At first I felt a tremendous need to occupy myself. I reached over and took a book on the history of Puerto Rico from the bookshelf, and I started to read. . . . I knew that if I had been a student I would have been chastised for reading the book so I put it down. . . . After a while of sitting there feeling stupid and kind of neglected, I had the urge to talk to someone. I think if I had been a kid, I would have acted up or talked to someone near me even if they couldn't understand me. Then, because I wasn't really doing anything I got very, very tired. I really wanted to put my head down on the desk. I know that if I had been a student, I would have been sleeping. . . .

I came away from this class with a much deeper understanding of what it feels like to be alienated. I really felt lonely in there. I didn't feel angry, but I could certainly understand how a kid could get angry in that kind of situation. Most teachers because of their own experience of school have never dealt with these kinds of feelings, and I think they would have a hard time understanding this. I also felt that bilingual program kids tend to get isolated in most schools. They spend a good deal of the day in small groups apart from the rest of the school.

[There] are things about Puerto Rican people and culture that I admire very much. I would also have to admit that I did not always admire these things because I did not understand them at first. This is a good lesson not only for second-language learning but for any situation where different cultures come in contact. It takes time to build understanding. . . . Another aspect of my study has been a combination craft and cultural project. With my friend and colleague, Edgar Rodríguez, I have started a project to build a *cuatro* [a Puerto Rican stringed instrument]. It has been a fun undertaking, and I am looking forward to playing it. I think there has to be room in the curriculum for these kinds of things. They have to be valued as a learning experience. It is hard to describe the absolute joy that I have witnessed in many of my students' eyes when they see my project. Many of them have told me that their grandfathers play the cuatro. . . .

I now know from personal experience that second-language acquisition is a slow and difficult process, yet in most American schools we demand that nonnative-English speakers achieve fluency in a short period of time. Multiculturalism is a reality in places like my town, and I guess it comes down to whether you view it as a loss or a gain. There is a lot of conflict in my community, but there is also a lot of potential. As a nation, we cannot afford to continue to drift farther and farther apart. The trend in America over the past 2 decades has been to move away from problems. It has led to two nations, one White, affluent, and scared, and the other non-White, poor, and angry. We need to begin to reach out and understand one another. That is happening in places like my town. People are beginning to communicate. As Edgar says, "I have learned that the greatest thing in the world is to communicate." In our town, that communication is often in two languages.

As we see from his journal, Bill Dunn got more from the project than he ever imagined. Not only did he learn Spanish (he could understand most things and speak pretty well after one semester, although he is still studying it, by now having made a lifelong commitment to become bilingual), but he also learned a great deal about himself and his students in the process. Bill had always been a fine teacher because he cared about and got along with his students, and because he saw their diversity as a strength to build on. But he became an even better teacher and he developed a newfound respect for his students after he learned the energy and hard work it takes to learn academic content in a second language. His teaching practices also changed as a result of the project. For example, in his field notes he explored how many of the mistakes his students made in English were related to Spanish. Not only could he explain things to them in Spanish, but he could use examples from the Spanish language itself.

Probably the most powerful testimony to the changes he underwent as a result of learning Spanish came from his students. At the end of his journal, Bill wrote:

> At one point I asked one of my students, Julie, how she felt about an Anglo teacher trying to teach himself Spanish. Her reply was, "A lot of these teachers around here are know-it-alls. They think they know everything. When you try to learn Spanish, you are showing me that you are a learner too." I thought about Paulo Freire's theory of forming a dialogue with students and that authentic education is not A *for* B, or A *about* B, but A *with* B. My undertaking to teach myself Spanish clearly places me with my students.

IDENTIFYING WITH STUDENTS

Students are empowered as learners when they can identify with school and with their teachers, it follows that the process needs to be a mutual one. As we saw in the case of Bill Dunn, it happens when teachers make a specific commitment to identify with the everyday realities of their students. No amount of school reform or restructuring can accomplish this kind of identification. In the words of Jim Cummins (1996), implementing true educational reform that has a goal of turning around deep-seated and long-term discrimination requires *"personal redefinitions* of the ways in which *individual educators* interact with the students and communities they serve" (p. 136).

In my own research, I have found that this kind of redefinition is longed for by students (Nieto, 2000). Ron, a student who had experienced little success in school until he reached an alternative high school that was based on a model of genuine relationships with students, explained the problem eloquently:

> When a teacher becomes a teacher, she acts like a teacher instead of a person. She takes her title as now she's mechanical, somebody just running it. Teachers shouldn't deal with students like we're machines. You're a person, I'm a person. We come to school and we all [should] act like people. (p. 265)

Educational research provides compelling examples of what can happen when teachers begin to identify with their students. In a study of an ongoing collaborative research project with Yup'ik teachers in southwest Alaska, Jerry

Lipka (1991) wrote about how identifying with students can create a positive classroom climate. Lipka analyzed a lesson that was seemingly about art, but a closer look revealed that the lesson was actually about subsistence and survival and therefore based on values and skills important to this community. Lipka discovered that when Yup'ik teachers are teaching Yup'ik children and relating to them in culturally compatible ways in familiar settings, many of the factors that have been characterized as creating school failure are absent. He concluded that cultural and social *relationships* were the key to explaining the success of the teacher and students he studied.

In the case cited above, the teacher and students shared the same cultural understandings and experiences. As a consequence, the cultural congruence of the curriculum and pedagogy appeared effortless and natural. Can the same happen with teachers who do not share the same background as their students? Although it certainly takes more work, developing a strong identification with students from a different culture is possible. Research by Frederick Erickson and Gerald Mohatt (1982) reported on two classrooms of American Indian children, one taught by an Indian teacher and the other by a non-Indian. The classroom organization of these teachers differed markedly at the beginning of the school year, but by the end of the year, they were much more similar than different. How did this occur? According to the researchers, the non-Indian teacher used what they termed "teacher radar" to pick up cues from children about what strategies might be effective in teaching them. By the end of the year, the non-Indian teacher, just as his colleague, also had table groups rather than rows, and he spent more time working with small groups and tutoring rather than in whole-class instruction.

Writing more than 25 years ago, Mildred Dickeman (1973) posited that the most valuable resources available for teachers to relate classroom goals to the cultural diversity of their students were those that most often were overlooked: their students, the members of the local community, and the teachers themselves. She called on teachers to uncover their own untold stories, their ethnic heritages, and "family tragedies and achievements" (p. 24) that resulted from immigration, as a way of identifying with their culturally diverse students. Further, she suggested that teachers had available, "however forgotten, repressed, or ignored, the experiences of self and family in the context of pressure for assimilation and upward mobility" (pp. 23–24). Accordingly, Dickeman suggested that it was only when teachers learned to recognize their own alienation that they could best relate to their students.

The process that Dickeman proposed was to build on the experiences of teachers not as teachers but as people with particular histories and strengths. This process can result in a profound transformation of how teachers view their past and even their role as teachers. The purpose of identifying with one's students is not to dabble in other people's cultures, but to use the relationships that ensue to change classroom practices to be more effective with a wider range of students. It is a process that is as empowering and enriching for teachers as it is for the students with whom they work. Learning from one's students means that teachers predictably become more multicultural in their outlook and world view. As such, it implies a profound shift in attitudes and values toward students and what they have to offer. In the final analysis, it means not just talking about multicultural education as an educational program or strategy, but putting into practice a multicultural view of the world.

BECOMING MULTICULTURAL

I have argued elsewhere (Nieto, 2000), that to become a multicultural teacher, one needs to become a multicultural person first. Young people are especially keen observers of the verbal and nonverbal messages of the adults around them, and they are usually adept at spotting inconsistencies between what their teachers say and what they do. For example, teachers can talk on and on about the value of knowing a second language, but if they themselves do not attempt to learn another language, their words may sound hollow to their students. Even if their curriculum is outwardly multicultural, if teachers do not demonstrate through their actions and behaviors that they truly value diversity, students often can tell.

Becoming a multicultural person implies, as we have seen previously, that teachers need to learn more about their students and about the world in general. This means stepping out of our own world and learning to understand some of the experiences, values, and realities of others. It is sometimes an exhilarating experience, but it also can be uncomfortable and challenging because it decenters us and our world, forcing us to focus on the lives and priorities of others who are different from us. It also helps us to empathize with others whom we ordinarily might not have included within our circle of humanity. Karen Donaldson, now a well-known researcher and teacher in multicultural education, went through this very process when she began her doctoral studies with me a decade ago.

Being Black and Multicultural

By Karen McLean Donaldson

I can remember coming into the doctoral program in 1989 with one major question in mind: Would I be able to stay true to my cultural commitment of addressing the racial oppression of Black Americans? At the time, I didn't care much about looking into gender or class issues, although I was female and in a disadvantaged economic class. I believed that being Black caused more hardship for me, my family, community, and my racial ethnic group in general. Going into that first course in multicultural education, I was angry to see racism being tossed into the bowl of "isms." I thought, "Surely the injustices of racism far outweigh and are much more venomous than all of the other 'isms' put together." Before taking the course I saw racism as a Black and White issue. This is how I had been groomed all of my life: "Whites were against us and hated us." This was my total socialization experience.

As far back as I can remember, my parents taught my siblings and me about our mixed heritage, but "Negro" and later "Black American" is how we identified. It was a funny thing for me because I was the lightest one in the whole family, but there was never any doubt of who I was. My father helped with this because he taught me that being Black didn't mean what shade you were, but rather how our inner soul connected to its ancestors; being Black was a state of mind. Yet all of my life I have been asked, "What are you?" I could have passed for Jewish, Italian, Latina, Arab, and so on, but my parents instilled Black pride and knowledge in me that would never allow that.

My mother is biracial. Her father came from the Cabo Verde islands and her mother was Sicilian. When my grandmother got ill and was hospitalized, none of her Italian relatives would take the children because they were considered Black. They therefore became wards of the state and were separated into various foster homes. My mother and youngest aunt were sent to Boston and lived with Black foster parents. The other six siblings stayed in the Cape Cod area and held onto their Cape Verdean culture and language. My father, on the other hand, was born and raised in North Carolina and was Black and Indian, along with some other European mixtures; he was, that is, a product of the institution of slavery. He would often share sad stories of segregation in the South. Sometimes I would sneak out of my bed when there was company and listen to the appalling stories of racism that he had experienced as a child and adult. To know of my parents' suffering and the suffering of Black people in general made me bitter and distrustful toward Whites.

When I began the doctoral program, I asked myself why I was getting ready to take this multicultural education journey, and then I realized that all of my life I had loved learning about cultures. I had shrugged off some of the most wonderful experiences because they were so few and far between: my visits to the synagogue on the hill to learn about Jewish culture; my fifth-grade teacher from Ireland who taught me so much about Irish culture; my yearly summer visits to Cape Cod where I not only learned about my Cape Verdean heritage but about the Mashpee Indian heritage. This course brought all of that back for me. I began releasing the anger I felt, and opening up to understand that my race was not the only race that suffered in America. I opened myself to understand the intersection of race, class, and gender as well as exceptionality, ageism, language, and so on. I began to understand more of the human connection and the need to address all of these issues.

I am still dedicated to reducing racism in schools and in society, but I do this with a well-rounded view. And though I still concentrate on the continued progress of my people, I realize we all must become versed in one another's experiences and cultures if the young are to succeed in our diverse world. I think of myself now as a human rights educator and activist and I work with others in advocating for peace and justice for all human beings.

As a professor, in addition to my scholarship, I share firsthand experiences. I speak about the racial prejudice that I had toward Whites in general. In my classes, we talk about identity, conditioning, and the role power plays with regard to oppression. I teach and continue to learn about the numerous cultures in the United States and abroad. I often use the arts as a way of giving students hands-on experiences in understanding other peoples' cultures. Although I now spend much of my time doing research and writing books, teaching is still a big part of who I am. My students let me know how much they appreciate my open and nontraditional style of teaching. That first multicultural course helped in my transformation as a true humanitarian and it made me a much better teacher and individual, which in turn has enhanced my students' learning.

CHALLENGING RACISM AND OTHER BIASES

If teachers simply follow the decreed curriculum as handed down from the central office, or if they go along with standard practices such as rigid ability tracking or high-stakes testing that results in unjust outcomes, they are unlikely as ever to question the fairness of these practices. But when they engage in a personal transformation through such actions as described above—that is, when they become learners with, of, and for their students and forge a deep identification with them; when they build on students' talents and strengths; and when they welcome and include the perspectives and experiences of their students and families in the classroom—then they cannot avoid locking horns with some very unpleasant realities inherent in the schooling process, realities such as racism, sexism, heterosexism, classism, and other biases.

A compelling instance of this kind of learning happened when Youngro Yoon Song, a college teacher of Korean, took the introductory course in multicultural education with me several years ago. Many international students who have taken the course with me, especially those from Asia, initially believe that multicultural education is not an issue in their societies. That is, they do not believe that a multicultural education course will be very useful to them if they expect to teach English back in their own countries, or their native language here in the United States. Youngro began to change her mind early in the semester when she first experienced videos, discussions, and readings about racism. In a word, she began to see racism around her that she had not seen in quite the same way before. By the end of the semester, Youngro wrote about her new sense of responsibility concerning racism.

Racism

By Youngro Yoon Song

This course has given me a chance to be concerned about various kinds of prejudice (racism, sexism, ethnic stereotyping . . .). I used to consider these things as just a form of social injustice, not as my concern.

> The books, films, and articles awoke me to realize the importance of the issues that I face everyday. I began to realize that I also had prejudice and I was trained to be blind to all kinds of injustice. I began to realize that I have to do something about the issues we talked about in the class. As an educator, woman, and member of a minority people, I want to share the burden of this society. The issue is how I should do so.
>
> One thing I can do right now is to help the young generation of Koreans whom I work with at the college level to establish and be proud of their own identity as Koreans. Fortunately, I have the opportunity to teach them Korean and to share these thoughts with them. Of course, I am afraid of how much I will be able to do. But looking back on what I have learned, doing something is better than doing nothing. (12.12.90)

An almost unavoidable consequence of working closely and collaboratively with students, students' families, and other teachers is that teachers begin to discover the biased and racist ideologies behind some of the practices that they previously had overlooked. Consequently, they have no alternative but to begin to question how equitable such practices really are. This pedagogical stance, what Cherry McGee Banks and James Banks (1995) have called an *equality pedagogy*, challenges the very structure of schools, including seemingly natural and neutral practices such as tracking and disciplinary policies.

Facing and challenging racism and other biases is both an inspiring and a frightening prospect. It means upsetting business as usual, and this can be difficult even for committed and critical teachers. Kathe Jervis (1996), for example, has documented how even in a progressive middle school in New York City where teachers were solidly committed to equity and diversity, students' questions about race and racism often were greeted with silence on the part of the staff. Paradoxically, the school was consciously designed to be diverse and equitable. Yet through numerous anecdotes, Jervis demonstrated how commitment to diversity frequently remained at an abstract level, rarely making itself felt in the actual conversations that go on in classrooms or in the planned or unplanned curriculum. As often is the case, it was only through the actions of a Black teacher that racism was discussed at all. Jervis concluded, "When Whites in power don't hear the boiling lava that lies below the surface, they perpetuate silences around race. Then they are surprised when racial feelings erupt, although it is they who have paid no attention to the volcano" (p. 575).

Confronting racism and other biases means, among other things, carefully analyzing schools' policies and practices as well as the ideologies behind them, and attempting to change those that are unfair. It does not mean that teachers need to position themselves as charismatic, solitary figures, as the Don Quixotes of the schools engaged in an impossible but romantic quest. If this is the stance they take, teachers are likely to end up either completely burned out by the effort, or so alienated from their peers that they can have no appreciable impact on the general life of the school. Charismatic teachers do not last long, nor do they usually make substantive changes outside their classrooms.

Because they often consider their colleagues to be hopelessly backward or racist or ignorant, these teachers refuse to do the hard work it takes to develop alongside them. This behavior, rather than a collaborative struggle with colleagues, becomes little more than a reflection of the overly individualistic and narcissistic culture that they tend to criticize. In the end, their stance is both arrogant and self-defeating. In some ways, these teachers become just like their ineffective peers who prefer to close their doors to the outside world. And classroom hermits accomplish precious little by themselves.

When I first became a teacher educator, I often told my preservice teachers to mind their own business if they wanted to be effective with their students: I encouraged them to stay out of the faculty lunchroom (where as a neophyte teacher, I had heard many damaging and racist comments about children) and to close their classroom doors. Now my advice is just the opposite: I ask them to go to the faculty lunchroom and engage in conversations so that they can change the discourse about the students they teach, and to *open* their doors rather than close them. Opening their doors is a fitting metaphor for the kinds of collective relationships that teachers need to forge in order to make meaningful change in schools.

What I am arguing for is a stance as a *critical colleague*, that is, as teachers who can develop respectful but critical relationships with peers. In the long run, teachers who work collaboratively in a spirit of solidarity and critique will be better able to change schools to become more equitable and caring places for more students. Although we have been considering the *personal* transformation of teachers, I would submit that *even personal transformation is best accomplished as a collective journey that leads to change in more than just one classroom.*

DEVELOPING A COMMUNITY OF CRITICAL FRIENDS

Working in isolation, no teacher can singlehandedly effect the changes that are needed in an entire school, at least not in the long term. Time and again, teachers in my classes have spoken about the need to develop a cadre of peers to help them and their school go through the process of transformation. But what is needed is not simply peers who support one another—important as this may be—but also peers who debate, critique, and challenge one another to go beyond their current ideas and practices. Developing a community of critical friends is one more step in the journey of transformation.

In the excerpt below, Mary Ginley wrote about why she had returned to graduate school. Although in a doctoral program, she was not really interested in earning a doctorate. Actually, she wanted to continue to work with second graders for the rest of her career. But what she wanted from graduate school was a group of critical friends, and colleagues to help her develop as an even better teacher. Mary is a gifted and caring teacher; she is also very self-critical, a combination that makes teaching both incredibly difficult and enormously rewarding.

Why I Went Back to School

By Mary Ginley

I decided to go back to school for two reasons. One was that I needed some-one to talk to. Dora [the principal of her school, who had been a close friend and died that year] was gone and Rocío [a friend and colleague who had returned to Puerto Rico] was gone. There were so few people to talk to about what we are trying to do, what we might be doing right and where we are going wrong. I take a lot of risks in regard to curriculum and pedagogy and I needed to find people who were doing the same thing and running into the same problems—people I could trust to say, "I'm not sure this is the way to go. . . . It's not working." Without them saying, "See, I told you we need a basal reading program and a spelling book."

The other reason I returned to school was to figure out how to do it right. Why did the kids who failed to learn to read in my class, year after year, have last names like Vega, Lopez, and Rivera, while the kids who sailed along were named Moriarty, Cavanaugh, and Schwartz? Why were the kids who were constantly in trouble—on the playground, on the bus, in the class-room—always from the same part of town? I'd like to say I couldn't have done anything differently, that I did my best but it wasn't good enough, that there were too many other factors. But that would be an easy out. Dora used to say I was too hard on myself. But I'm not . . . not really. I look for excuses and find them because I hate to admit that I've failed these kids. The other reason I wanted to go back to school is to try to discover how to make school successful for all kids—not just the Moriartys, Cavanaughs, Schwartzes, and Ginleys—because so far, I haven't done it right. This course is helping: others will too. I know they will.

SUMMARY

Individual and collective stories of teachers are a useful reminder that, just as schools need to undergo an institutional transformation if they are to become places where all students learn, teachers too need to experience a similar transformation. Specifically, teachers need to learn *about* their students, *identify* with them, *build* on their strengths, and *challenge* head-on the many displays of privilege and inherent biases in the schools in which they teach. This is arduous work because it requires paying attention to many different arenas of school life, and it is inevitably accompanied by conflict. Yet as we are reminded by Paulo Freire (Schor & Freire, 1987), conflict is necessary for change to take place: "In the last analysis, conflict is the midwife of con-sciousness" (p. 176).

Conclusion

There is a solid theoretical foundation for an interactional/participatory approach to second language teaching with far-reaching implications for the classroom. Programs that involve the students in real communication about interesting, relevant subject matter and sociopolitical issues in low-anxiety environments appear to be the most effective avenues to acquisition in the classroom and learner autonomy.

This does not mean that there is little value in grammar exercises, drills of various sorts, translating, or other such activities. On the contrary, all of these may have a place, depending upon the objectives, age and proficiency levels, and cognitive development of the learner. However, it is when such relatively noncommunicative activities become the focus of the curriculum that they can be detrimental to the progression of second language students in programs in which communication and empowerment are the goals.

Developing dialectical relationships with students, involving them in the curriculum planning process, organizing interactional activities related to content, providing for a silent period, and allowing for the natural development of interlanguage require creativity, flexibility, and patience on the part of teachers. For those willing to accept the challenge, the feelings of satisfaction are great once they find their students growing and fully participating in a community of language learners.

PART VI

Case Studies[1]

Four case studies are offered in this section to stimulate reflection and discussion. Each case involves a different age group, elementary school through the college/university level.

There are many different ways to use these case studies.[2] When I used them in my own teacher education classes, I divided the participants into groups of four or five, depending upon the age levels at which they were teaching or planning to teach. Each group would receive only the case that pertained to their particular level (often I would end up with more than one group at any given level). I asked the participants to read the case study description first, and discuss the issues involved and what they might have done in that particular situation. One member of the group jotted down the group's ideas.

Then I asked them to read the second part of each case describing what the teacher actually did in each situation. Another group discussion took place as the participants reacted to what the teacher had actually done and sometimes modified their initial ideas, depending upon what they learned. Then a spokesperson from each group shared the case and the ideas of the group with the class. This procedure seemed to work. The discussions of the relevant issues were quite lively. However, most groups came to the conclusion that there were no easy answers, once the issues had been fully aired. Later, participants wrote their own case studies, based on their own experiences as learners and teachers, to share with their groups.

---

[1] The first two cases studies are from *Diversity in the Classroom: A Casebook for Teachers and Teacher Educators* (1993), edited by Judith Shulman and Amalia Mesa-Bains. They are used by permission of Lawrence Erlbaum in Mahwah, New Jersey. The third case study came from the author's own experiences, and the fourth case study was constructed by the author for this edition.

[2] See especially Colbert, Desberg, and Trimble (1996).

CASE STUDY 1: MY "GOOD YEAR" EXPLODES:
A CONFRONTATION WITH PARENTS
(FOR ELEMENTARY TEACHERS)

I thought it had been a good year. My second grade class of 32 bilingual students was a joy to teach. Like me, a third of my students were Japanese immigrants. Another third were Japanese Americans who were born in the United States, and the rest were from a mix of ethnic backgrounds. The entire class had progressed in math, according to their scores on the California Test of Basic Skills. With three weeks left of the school year, I was confident that I had covered all the math strands from the California State Framework. Moreover, because of strong parent involvement and participation, we had enjoyed a variety of enrichment activities such as art, music, dance, and other performing arts.

Early one spring morning as I prepared for class, Grace—the PTA president—walked in. Grace was a Caucasian parent and a regular volunteer in my classroom. With just five minutes to class time, she handed me a letter and said, "Don't read this now because it will make you unhappy. Wait until after school."

My puzzled look prompted her to say more. "Some parents felt you could have done a better job teaching our children. Do you think you really did a good job this year?"

I couldn't believe what I was hearing. The bell rang, but I ignored it and opened the letter. As I read, tears filled my eyes. I was too shaken to begin class. Instead, I went straight to my principal, Mr. Bryant.

Grace followed me in. Mr. Bryant seemed to be expecting me; he had been given a copy of the letter. "You may leave," he said to Grace, who was by now in tears herself. "We didn't mean to hurt you," she said to me. "We wanted you to know how we felt."

When Grace was gone, Mr. Bryant gave me a hug, offered me tea, and sent another teacher to cover my class. As I regained my composure, we discussed the letter. I learned that copies signed by parents had been sent to the principal, the district office, and the school board. Apparently, the letter had been triggered by the news that I would be teaching a combination class next year. When parents realized that I might be teaching their children again, they decided to express their concern that I had inappropriately taught the basic concepts, particularly in math.

The children had been allowed to explore and learn with manipulatives. Parents felt that they hadn't brought home enough paper and pencil homework and math worksheets. They also thought that if their children were in my class next year, they would not progress at the rate of other students. They apparently wanted their children to spend their math time on rote memorization, drill and practice, and traditional tasks.

My mind raced back to a visit I'd had with one of the mothers early in the year. She had come to me holding a stack of ditto sheets that her daughter had completed in first grade. "Look how much more she was learning last year," the mother had said.

I had explained to her my firm belief that my hands-on approach and problem-solving strategies were far more effective for all my students than traditional "drill and skill" methods. I told her that I used the mandated California State Mathematics Framework and that I had attended numerous workshops and training programs to learn how to incorporate these techniques into my teaching. The children, I pointed out, felt challenged and were highly motivated to learn math as a result. The mother had listened intently, and I thought she heard my message.

On Back-to-School night, I had carefully explained my strategies to all the parents. Throughout the school year I also kept a running communication about all curriculum, special projects, and student progress and concerns through letters, telephone calls, and weekly student checklists. Parents had numerous opportunities to contact me, but no one ever did.

What did the teacher do?

Our school has always encouraged active parent participation. My classroom was no exception. The parents who seemed unhappy with my math curriculum helped regularly in my classroom. They saw me teach hands-on, integrated math lessons and they watched their children engage in critical thinking and problem-solving activities. To reinforce skills with limited English proficient students, I often used concrete materials, visuals, sheltered English techniques, or—when I could—the child's primary language. Never did I feel that my teaching abilities were in doubt.

In the days that followed my talk with Mr. Bryant, I also conferred with other teachers, the principal, other administrators, and even professors. I wanted to know what they thought, but most of all I needed emotional support. My pride and dignity had been wounded when my professionalism and integrity were questioned. Worse, I had been accused of doing a disservice to the children. I was haunted by thoughts that I had brought this on myself, and I was full of guilt.

The network of colleagues supported me. They felt that the parents' actions reflected not a failure of mine with the children, but a lack of parent acceptance of new teaching strategies. They bolstered me with reminders that I had been selected as a mentor teacher and my work was regarded as outstanding.

But I am still puzzled. Why did parents think that their children would have different experiences in other teachers' classrooms? Each school year we address the various curriculum areas in many parent education workshops taught by mentor teachers, administrators, and specialists in the curriculum development areas. My teaching approaches are not different from those of the majority of teachers at my school. We share philosophies and use similar techniques.

Was it a personality conflict between the parents—such as Grace—and me? Was it a cultural problem, rooted in differing communication styles, learning expectations, or traditions? Why couldn't parents come directly to me when concerns first arose? Did they feel they should have had more control over what happened in the classroom? What was the true catalyst for their action?

Since this incident, our staff has had many collegial meetings to brainstorm ways of averting such problems in the future. A schoolwide grievance committee has been established, composed of the administrator, paraprofessionals, teachers, and parents. We have also established a procedure for communications. Parents must meet with the teacher first. If issues remain unresolved, all parties meet with the administrator. The final recourse is the executive parent body.

But I often still ask myself how I missed seeing warning signs. I have always put much effort into my work. It was terribly disturbing to face this quandary at the end of school. I was ready to quit the very profession I loved and to which I have dedicated years of service. Did I cause these parents to react the way they did? What did I do wrong? What should I do in the future if parents and I disagree about how best to teach their children?

CASE STUDY 2: PLEASE, NOT ANOTHER ESL STUDENT (FOR MIDDLE SCHOOL TEACHERS)

Sam Garcia, the Spanish bilingual counselor, stood outside my classroom door, grinning sheepishly as he pointed me out to the new student. I knew why they were at my door, and without really intending it, I stopped talking in mid-sentence and blurted out, "Oh, no, not another ESL Student!" Glaring at Sam I shook my head in despair and moaned, "You can't do this to my program."

He looked beyond me; his eyes refused to meet mine.

"See the boss."

"But I have!"

"You'd better go see him again. Rumor has it we're the only school that'll take in these kids the rest of the year."

"Damn," I muttered. I felt so powerless. The middle school I had chosen to teach in because of its diverse student population, its location near the heartbeat of the city, its array of special programs—Spanish bilingual, Chinese bilingual, reading demonstration, band, and home economics—was now testing my strength, my endurance, my creativity.

Sam disappeared, and the dark eyes of my new student caught mine. The class watched us closely. "Bienvenido, Fernando, bienvenido a los estados unidos, a San Francisco, a nuestra clase."

Later, during my prep period, the last of the day, I was as usual too tired to do any "prepping." I looked down the list of names and dates in my rollbook. It was May 1st, and 20 new students, including Fernando, all zero-level English, had entered my classroom since February. My "program" had been sorely affected—not enough books, paper, chairs, tables, dictionaries. Even worse, not enough teacher time for students thrust so abruptly into a new language and culture. From my experience teaching in Central America, I knew that these students were arriving in this country after completing their school year in December and then traveling during summer vacation to this new country, expecting to enter school in March or April to begin a new year. Unfamiliar with our September-June school year, they had no idea that school would soon be ending. Nevertheless, here they were, assigned to my combined 6th, 7th, and 8th grade Spanish bilingual classroom. And so far, the best I had been able to do was give each a hasty welcome, then move silently closer to hysteria over how I could make the transition work for everyone.

I knew I had to think of something quickly. The week before, 11-year-old Araceli didn't make it to the girl's bathroom in time; she hadn't been able to remember where it was and had been too shy to ask another student. The long corridors circle the building, and sometimes, on certain floors (who knows why) the bathrooms are locked. Araceli, embarrassed and frightened, went home. I, her new teacher, felt guilty, frustrated, and angry. We both needed help.

What did the teacher do?

It was too late in the year for extra help in the classroom, but I thought of my colleague Carolyn, teaching in the basement, publishing poems and stories, putting on plays, and enjoying the fruits of her year-long emphasis on writing and creative learning. She taught the sixth grade honors class during the same two-hour block my Spanish bilingual students were with me for English-as-a-Second-Language and science instruction. I wondered . . . how about pairing up each ESL student in my class with a native speaker from her class?

We met and talked and agreed! Yes! And the planning began. How should we pair the students? We went over our class lists, noting problem students. I pointed out that many of the newly arrived Spanish-speaking girls would be most comfortable with a female partner because they come from Latino school systems that traditionally separate the girls from the boys. Carolyn mentioned that she had a number of Asian girls who also were accustomed to working with each other. We made as many pairs of girls as we could. After that, our pairing was based on an attitude of "let's try these two and see if it works out; if not, we'll change it."

In planning the substance of the partnership program, I thought of my original goals in initiating the contact with Carolyn: I wanted someone besides myself to befriend my bilingual students, and I wanted my students to feel important and wanted in their new country. My aim was to provide culturally relevant material in English and Spanish that would help them learn another language and make friends too.

I put together a packet of basic information that students expect to learn when they are studying a new language. The packet contained days of the week, months of the year, numbers, simple dialogues, the alphabet (for spelling purposes), weather words, a map of San Francisco with questions about addresses and phone numbers. I had spent a number of years teaching in Central and South America and knew that certain games such as Bingo ("loteria"), Simon Says ("Simón dice"), and Twenty Questions ("veinte preguntas") crossed cultural boundaries; therefore, I included them in the packet and also introduced simple crossword puzzles based on the new vocabulary they would acquire in each language.

The packet was prepared in both English and Spanish with a blank page for writing between each section, since we knew the students would want to practice writing their new vocabulary. Even though the material was available in both languages, I pointed out to Carolyn that it was important to keep instruction in each language as separate as possible so that students did not rely on back-to-back translation as a method of learning a new language. Therefore, we agreed that our Monday session would focus on the material in English and the Friday session would be held in Spanish. Back in our own classrooms we would have our students record their experiences and feelings about the partnership program in their journals in the language of their choice.

Carolyn and I will never forget the first partnership session. The initial meeting of partner with partner was heavy with apprehension. Some paired students couldn't even bear to look at each other out of nervousness, shyness, fear. We passed out a curriculum packet to each student, had the students write their names on the packet cover, and gave initial instructions. Silence. I thought I had made a big mistake. And then, as minutes passed, there began tentative talk. Within 10 minutes, Carolyn and I were able to grin at each other. As we looked around the room, we saw body language, sign language, drawing for communication. We heard laughter, words being repeated, introductions, and yells for help too! We saw and felt an intensity of learning that had an energy of its own. Kids were interacting with kids and their attention to each other was 100 percent!

Looking back, we felt more could have been done. We found that once the students began using the simple learning packet, they had many questions that could have been answered if they each had their own bilingual dictionary. We only had two globes, yet a student's natural curiosity led him or her to want a map of the world to find out where a partner's native country was located. Even the students born in the United States had often moved from state to state or city to city, so we needed maps of the United States to allow them to show and talk about their many homes. Once the English-speaking students had mastered the pronunciation of the Spanish alphabet, they were eager to try reading in Spanish, but we had too few books.

Beyond supplies for the program, we wondered about the curriculum itself for next year. How could we challenge the students? What about science? Could students work on experiments together? What about having the students work on major interdisciplinary projects that incorporate English language arts and science?

As a trained bilingual teacher, I knew the value of native language instruction. I knew that my most successful bilingual students were those who had received the most instruction in their native language. I agreed that whatever we decided to work on in our Monday and Friday sessions would have to be presented to the students in my own classroom in prior lessons in their native language. In that way we would be building on what students already knew and understood. In addition, this approach would help the students understand the material presented to them in a new language.

We wondered about ways to pair and group the students. Given the short amount of time we initially had to put the program together, we certainly had paid too little attention to the pairings. There had been some problems. Also, absences had caused problems. These situations led us to the following questions: Do the students always have to be in pairs? Maybe they could form cooperative groups of four. Do they have to stay with the same partner all year? Wouldn't it help stretch their experiences by matching them in a variety of ways throughout the year? As teachers, we might also observe the partners and learn from their behavior. Which kids were helpful? Why? Was it behavior that we could model so that those less helpful could improve? We were excited. We were onto something. We agreed to meet at the end of the summer to lay out next year's plan.

In June, a few days after school was over, I found Alonzo Jones' journal in Carolyn's classroom and read this entry:

> This is the first time I've heard that we will meet with the ESL class about teaching them English. For our field trip together I don't know what it will be like. But I believe that it will be fun. Somehow I will do what I can to communicate and help my partner.

It's comforting for me to know that I need not be alone with my ESL students, that I have Alonzo and many others like him to help me out. I had based my Spanish bilingual program on the premise that I, as the classroom teacher, was the only one who could work with Spanish-speaking newcomers to our school. I now realize my mistake. Learning about a new language and culture can come not only from a teacher but from one's English-speaking peers.

CASE STUDY 3: CONFLICT-RESOLUTION ON CAMPUS (HIGH SCHOOL)

Teaching ESL high school students was a job I had always wanted. I had taught immigrants from Mexico several years before and had learned a lot from the experience. When I was asked to direct an ESL center in a large suburban high school, I jumped at the chance.

The next thing I knew, I was teaching 41 students from 8 different countries around the world, including several from Laos and Vietnam. I had been warned by our district coordinator to watch out for possible conflicts between the Laotians and the Vietnamese in the center due to a history of animosities between the cultures from which they had come. In order to head off any conflicts, I had decided to expose all of my students to affective and conflict-resolution activities from time to time so that they might see each other as individuals with similar concerns and needs, rather than as enemies. The activities appeared, for the most part, to be working. In fact, it was noted by the district office that, at our school, we had established an atmosphere of mutual respect. When we were asked to help quell an unpleasant situation at another school in the district by visiting and talking with the groups involved, we were confident that we might be able to do some good.

Among the students who went with me to help was one of our Laotians named Samavong, a young man of 18 whom the others knew to be a fighter from his youth in Laos. He had scars to prove it, and he wore them as badges of honor. He was studious and bright and was learning English very quickly. Not only that but he seemed to have overcome the hatred that he had at first felt for the Vietnamese in the class and had even become good friends with one of them. The two were among the emissaries who came along and, particularly because they had become friends, they seemed to make an impression on the students at the other school. Little did I know at the time that it was our *own* school we had to worry about and that the trouble that was brewing was coming from *outside* our classroom.

One day as I was passing the office belonging to one of our vice principals, he motioned me in. With a somewhat quizzical expression on his face, he asked,

"Did you hear about the big fight in the parking lot during lunch?"

My heart sank. "No," I replied. "I didn't. What happened?"

"Well it seems as though some of YOUR (emphasizing "your") Laotian students beat up some of OUR Cowboys out there." Now the Cowboys were a type of gang in the school who were known by the pick-up trucks they drove and by the baseball caps they wore. They also chewed tobacco. He continued, "The one who started the whole thing was that little one of yours with the scars on his face."

"Oh, you mean Samavong." He went on to tell me that I really ought to control my students better. I asked him if anyone had been hurt and he said that, luckily, no one had been this time, but that it could happen again and maybe with tragic results.

I left feeling very sad and disappointed. Why hadn't my students told me about it? Although I had had most of the Laotians that morning, some of the others in my afternoon class could have mentioned it. They must have known. And why hadn't they been able to handle the conflict in the first place? They had done so well with conflict resolution in the classroom. I knew, too, that the vice principal had always seemed to resent me and my students and would, no doubt, make a "federal case" out of this incident. I knew also that I had to do something to try and change the whole situation including his attitude, but I wasn't sure where to start or what to do first.

What did the teacher do?

To begin with, I rather frantically enlisted the help of the multicultural education director who had been working at our school for several months. Although he had been aware of some of the animosity between the two groups, he (like me) had not realized the tension that had begun to build. He suggested that we sit down right away with the two groups and encourage them to air their grievances. I thought it was a good idea. The Cowboys complained that the Laotians were purposely "getting in their faces" as they walked down the hallways. The Laotians said that they didn't like being called names or being made fun of. We talked about how disappointed we both were in their behavior and how it could affect the whole school if things didn't change. By the end of the session, most of the students had agreed (maybe it was just to appease us) that they were going to try and get along better in the future.

Then I decided to do an inservice for the entire staff. I had already done one inservice in the early fall which I thought had been fairly successful. I had never been trained to do inservicing and was filled with fear at the thought of it. But somehow I found it easy to talk about the students and their efforts to learn English and become part of American society. I stressed the importance of their being accepted along with their cultures and languages. I also talked about strategies content area teachers might use to make the content of their classes more accessible. I had spent a lot of time thinking about strategies beforehand and managed to come up with some ideas to start with. Then I divided them into content-area groups to come up with their own ideas and share them with the rest of us. I was glad I had done that because we all learned from each other. The only problem was that the vice principal to whom I referred earlier was not there. This time I wanted to ensure that his presence would be more likely by asking him to facilitate a group during the inservice. He almost seemed pleased at the request and accepted, much to my relief.

Sometime later, I recruited two of the Cowboys who were good students to serve as peer teachers for the ESL students. Although one of them dropped out (perhaps due to peer pressure), the other got to know several of the ESL students quite well. He even agreed to serve as a "buddy" to one of the Laotians in a course in mainstream science. Over time, we noticed a gradual softening of attitudes among students in both groups and eventually we even included some of the Cowboys in our occasional parties. But the day I knew for sure that the bitterness was beginning to evaporate was the day when two Laotian boys came to school with baseball caps on their heads. I was glad to see, however, that there was no evidence of chewing tobacco. In spite of everything, Samavong remained aloof and told me privately one day that, although he could act friendly toward the Cowboys, he would never really trust one.

CASE STUDY 4: A MULTICULTURAL COLLEGE EXPERIENCE (FOR COLLEGE/UNIVERSITY TEACHERS)

This is my first year teaching freshman English at a medium-sized community college in Los Angeles. I am not very experienced at teaching. Nor am I very experienced at working with language minority students, but I really want to help them succeed in college. I am a Caucasian woman, 33 years old, divorced with two children. I drive my car to work each day from Santa Monica where I live in a mostly white neighborhood. I attended a multiracial high school, but I graduated from a mainly white university. I have always gotten along well with people of other races and I enjoy the cultural diversity found in the Los Angeles area.

My most recent problem is a student named Miguel from Argentina. Miguel really tries, but like many of my other students, he can't seem to follow directions for assignments, and he did not do well on the mid-term exam. I thought I had given very complete, clear lectures about authors, items of historical/cultural significance to the literature we were reading, and explanations of literary terminology such as symbolism, irony, etc. But, he says he can't understand me very well. Nor can he understand the other students in the class when they participate in class discussion (which is not very often). Miguel is very quiet, so I didn't realize he was having trouble until now. Up to this point, he has only turned in one written assignment for which he received a B. The other day, I did a little checking and found out that he has never been in our college ESL program. He says that he scored very high on the TOEFL (Test of English as a Foreign Language), including the TWE (Test of Written English), so the administration put him in a regular schedule of courses. He is definitely failing my course and I suspect he is failing others as well. Now it is too late for him to drop. Another problem Miguel is having is that he does not seem to be getting along very well with the African-American students in my class. He told me that one of them (Aaron) started an argument with him and shoved him while he was in the library. I don't know what the conflict is all about, but I do know it is having a negative effect on the attitude of my whole class. I want to do well in this environment. Teaching is something I don't want to give up. What should I do? How can I best teach these students?

I should also tell you that I am now on a committee to make suggestions about curriculum, requirements, etc., for our language minority students. What can our college do to better serve students such as Miguel? What should the ESL program at our college be doing to better prepare these students for the mainstream? As far as I know, they are not doing much to help in the transition.

What did the teacher do?

First I tried to help Miguel solve the problem he was having with Aaron and the other African-American students. I asked him and Aaron to see me after class. I tried as best I could to lead them into a discussion of what had happened—not to pin the blame on anyone but to talk about how each one felt about the incident in the library. Although no one apologized, I think they came to a better understanding of each other's point of view. Later, on the advice of another instructor at the college, I did some group activities during which we talked about how we could get along better with one another. It did seem to help overall. I began to notice that the atmosphere of the classroom became a bit more positive and that the students were showing a little more tolerance toward one another.

As far as Miguel's skills go, I really didn't make much difference there. He managed to eke out a D for the semester. However, I think I might try some different strategies in my teaching in general. I just read a book about teaching second language students and I got some ideas that I think might work. I plan to do a lot more group work, ask students to share feelings and opinions more, and do a lot with peer consultation on compositions. Also I need to use more visuals including charts, maps, and other realia to make clear what I mean. I don't want to give up lecturing completely. I just want to make my lectures better for all students, not just language minority students

The committee I served on was very helpful to me. I'm not sure how much I contributed, but I certainly learned a lot! Two of the members talked about establishing an adjunct program in which mainstream courses are paired with language courses conducted by language specialists. The language specialists would help the students understand the vocabulary and key concepts taught in the mainstream course, would assist students with their compositions, would help them with the comprehension of the lectures (which would be taped) and assigned readings, and would refer them to materials on similar topics in their first languages. They also talked about setting up tutoring sessions (led by native-speakers or near native-speakers) in the library. These recommendations will be made to the administration next week.

References

Agor, B., ed. (2000). *Integrating the ESL standards into classroom practice: Grades 9–12.* Alexandria, VA: TESOL.

Alatis, J., ed. (1990). *Georgetown University Round Table on Languages and Linguistics 1990: Linguistics, language teaching and language acquisition: The importance of theory, practice and research.* Washington, DC: Georgetown University.

Alatis, J., ed. (1991). *Georgetown University Round Table on Languages and Linguistics 1991. Linguistics and language pedagogy: The state of the art.* Washington, D.C.: Georgetown University.

Allen, J., and VanBuren, P. (1971). *Chomsky: Selected readings.* London: Oxford University.

Allwright, R. (1979). Language learning through communication practice. In Brumfit and Johnson, pp. 167–182.

Altwerger, B., and Resta, V. (1986). Comparing standardized tests scores and miscues. Paper presented at the annual convention of International Reading Association, Philadelphia, PA.

Amanti, C. (2001). Technology for English language learners. *NABE News,* 25(1), 7–9.

Andersen, R. (1981). *New dimensions in second language acquisition research.* Rowley, MA: Newbury House.

Andersen, R. (1983). Introduction: A language acquisition interpretation of pidginization and creolization. In R. Andersen, ed. *Pidginization and creolization as language acquisition.* Rowley, MA: Newbury House.

Anderson. N. (1999). *Exploring second language reading: Issues and strategies.* Boston: Heinle.

Armstrong, B., Johnson, D. W., and Balow, B. (1981). Effects of cooperative versus individualistic learning experiences on interpersonal attraction between learning-disabled and normal-progress elementary school students. *Contemporary Educational Psychology,* 6, 102–109.

Arnold, J. (1999). *Affect and language learning*. Cambridge: Cambridge University Press.

Arthur, B., Weiner, R., Culver, M., Young, J., and Thomas, D. (1980). The register of impersonal discourse to foreigners: Verbal adjustments to foreign accent. In D. Larsen-Freeman, ed. *Discourse analysis in second language research*. Rowley, MA.: Newbury House, pp. 111–124.

Aschbacher, P. (1991). Humanitas: A thematic curriculum. *Educational Leadership*, 49(2), 17–19.

Asher, J. (1972). Children's first language as a model for second-language learning. *Modern Language Journal*, 56, 133–139.

Asher, J. (1993). The total physical response. Presentation at the California Education Association, San Francisco, CA, January 14.

Asher, J. (1996). *Learning another language through actions: The complete teachers' guidebook*, fifth edition. Los Gatos, CA: Sky Oaks.

Asher, J., Kusudo, J., and de la Torre, R. (1974). Learning a second language through commands: The second field test. *Modern Language Journal*, 58, 24–32.

Atwell, N. (1998). *In the middle: New understandings about writing, reading, and learning*. NH: Heinemann.

Auerbach, E. (1995). The politics of the ESL classroom: Issues of power in pedagogical choices. In J. Tollefson, ed., *Power and inequality in language education*. New York: Cambridge University Press, pp. 9–33.

Auerbach, E. (2000) Creating participatory learning communities: Paradoxes and possibilities. In J. Hall and W. Eggington, eds., pp. 143–164.

Bailey, K. (1995). Competitiveness and anxiety in adult second language learning: Looking at and through the diary studies. In H. D. Brown and S. Gonzo, eds. *Readings on second language acquisition*. Englewood Cliffs, NJ: Prentice Hall Regents, 163–205.

Bailey, N., Madden, C., and Krashen, S. (1974). Is there a "natural sequence" in adult second-language learning? *Language Learning*, 21, 235–243.

Baltra, A. (1992). On breaking with tradition: The significance of Terrell's natural approach. *The Canadian Modern Language Review*, 48(3), 564–593.

Bamford, J. and Day, R. (1996). Comments on Jeong-Won Lee and Diane Lemonnier Schallert's "The relative contribution of L2 language proficiency and L1 reading ability to L2 reading performance: A test of the threshold hypothesis in an EFL context" Two readers react. . . . *TESOL Quarterly*, 32(4), 747–751.

Banks, J. (1992). The stages of ethnicity. In Richard-Amato and Snow, pp. 93–101.

Banks, J. (1993). *Multiethnic education: Theory and practice* (third edition). Boston: Allyn & Bacon.

Banks, J. and Banks, C. M. eds. (1995). *Handbook of research on multicultural education*. New York: Macmillan, 3–24.

Bardovi-Harlig, K. (1992). The use of adverbials and natural order in the development of temporal expression. *IRAL*, 30, 199–220.

Bardovi-Harlig, K. (1995). The interaction of pedagogy and natural sequences in the acquisition of tense and aspect. In F. R. Eckman, D. Highland, P. W. Lee, J. L. Mileham, and R. R. Weber, eds. *Second language acquisition theory and pedagogy*. Mahwah, NJ: Lawrence Erlbaum, pp. 157–181.

Bardovi-Harlig, K., Hartford, B., Mahan-Taylor, R., Morgan, M. J., and Reynolds, D. W. (1996). Developing pragmatic awareness: closing the conversation. In T. Hedge and N. Whitney, pp. 324–337.

Bassano, S., and Christison, M. A. (1995a). Action research: Techniques for collecting data through surveys and interviews. *CATESOL Journal*, 8(1), 89–104.

Bassano, S., and Christison, M. A. (1995b). *Community spirit: A practical guide to collaborative language learning*. San Francisco, CA: Alta Book Center.

Beebe, L. (1983). Risk-taking and the language learner. In Seliger and Long, pp. 39–66.

Bee-Lay, S., and Yee-Ping, S. (1991). English by e-mail: Creating a global classroom via the medium of computer technology. *English Language Teaching Journal*, 45(4), 287–292

Bell, D. (1999). Rise, Sally, Rise: Communicating Through Dance. *TESOL Journal*, 8(1), 27–31.

Bellack, A., Kliebard, H., Hyman, R., and Smith, Jr., F. (1966). The language of the classroom. New York: Teachers College, Columbia University.

Bensen, P. (1997). The philosophy and politics of learner autonomy. In P. Benson and P. Voller, eds., pp. 18–34.

Bensen, P., and Voller, P., eds. (1997). *Autonomy and independence in language learning*. London: Longman.

Bialystok, E., and Fröhlich, M. (1977). Aspects of second-language learning in classroom settings. *Working Papers on Bilingualism*, 13, 2–26.

Birdsong, D., ed. (1999). *Second language acquisition and the critical period hypothesis*. Mahwah, NJ: Erlbaum.

Bishop, A. (2001). An expert's guide to products for the multilingual classroom. *NABE News*, 25(1), 12–13.

Blanton, L. (1998). *Varied voices: On language and literacy learning*. Boston: Heinle.

Bonne, R. (1973). (Pam Adams, Illus.). *There was an old lady who swallowed a fly*. Purton Wilts, England: Child's Play (International).

Bowles, S., and Ginis, H. (1976). *Schooling in capitalist America*. New York: Basic Books.

Breen, M., and Candlin, C. (1979). Essentials of a communicative curriculum. *Applied Linguistics*, 1(2), 90–112.

Brinton, D., and Neuman, R. (1982). *Getting along* (book 2). Englewood Cliffs, NJ: Prentice Hall, p. 33.

Brinton, D., Snow, M. A., and Wesche, M. (1989). *Content-based language instruction*. New York: Newbury House.

Brisk, M. and Harrington, M. (2000). *Literacy and bilingualism: A handbook for all teachers*. Mahwah, NJ: Lawrence Erlbaum.

Bromley, K. (1995). Buddy journals for ESL and native-English-speaking students. In I. A. Heath and C. Serrano, eds. *Teaching English as a second language* (second edition). Guilford, CT: Dushkin/McGraw-Hill, pp. 71–75.

Brown, H. D. (1987). *Principles of language learning and teaching*. Englewood Cliffs, NJ: Prentice Hall.

Brown, H. D. (1994). *Teaching by principles: An interactive approach to language pedagogy*. Englewood Cliffs, NJ: Prentice Hall.

Brown, H. D., Yorio, C., and Crymes, R., eds. (1977). *On TESOL '77*. Washington, D.C.: TESOL.

Brown, J. D. (1998). *New ways of classroom assessment*. Alexandria, VA: TESOL.

Brown, R. (1973). *A first language: The early stages*. Cambridge, MA.: Harvard University.

Brown, R., Cazden, C., and Bellugi, U. (1973). The child's grammar from I to III. In C. Ferguson and D. Slobin, eds. *Studies of child language development*. New York: Holt, Rinehart, and Winston, pp. 295–333.

Brown, S., and Dubin, F. (1975). Adapting human relations training techniques for ESL classes. In Burt and Dulay, pp. 204–209.

Brumfit, C. J., and Johnson, K., eds. (1979). *The communicative approach to language teaching*. Oxford: Oxford University.

Bruner, J. (1978a). From communication to language: A psychological perspective. In I. Markova ed. *The social context of language*, pp. 17–48. New York: Wiley.

Bruner, J. (1978b). The role of dialogue in language acquisition. In A. Sinclair, R. Javella, and W. Levelt, eds. *The child's conception of language*, New York: Springer-Verlag, pp. 241–256.

Brutt-Griffler, J., and Samimy, K. (1999). Revisiting the Colonial in the Postcolonial: Critical Praxis for Nonnative-English-Speaking Teachers in a TESOL Program. *TESOL Quarterly*, 33(3), 413–432.

Buehring, M. (1998). *A different angle: Co-operActivities in communication*. Studio City, CA: Jag Publications.

Burt, M., and Dulay, H., eds. (1975). *New directions in second language learning, teaching, and bilingual education*. Washington, DC: TESOL.

Burt, M., and Dulay, H. (1983). Optimal language learning environments. In Oller and Richard-Amato, pp. 38–48. Also in J. E. Alatis, H. Altman, and P. Alatis, eds. (1981), *The second language classroom*. New York: Oxford University Press, pp. 177–192.

Burt, M., Dulay, H., and Finocchiaro, M., eds. (1977). *Viewpoints on ESL*, pp. 172–184. New York: Regents.

Busch, D. (1982). Introversion-extraversion and the EFL proficiency of Japanese students. *Language Learning*, 32, 109–132.

Butterworth, G., and Hatch, E. (1978). A Spanish-speaking adolescent's acquisition of English syntax. In Hatch, ed., pp. 231–245.

Byram, M. (1998). Cultural identities in multilingual classrooms. In J. Cenoz and F. Genesee, eds. *Beyond bilingualism*. Clevedon, England: Multilingual Matters, pp. 96–116.

Campbell, C., and Ortiz, J. (1991). Helping students overcome foreign language anxiety. In E. Horwitz and D. Young, eds. *Language anxiety: From theory and research to classroom implication*. Englewood Cliffs, NJ: Prentice Hall, pp. 153–168.

Canagarajah, A. S. (1993). Critical ethnography of a Sri Lankan classroom: Ambiguities in student opposition to reproduction through ESOL. *TESOL Quarterly* 27(4), 601–626.

Canale, M., and Barker, G. (1986). How creative language teachers are using microcomputers. *TESOL Newsletter* 20(1), Supplement (3), 1–3.

Canale, M., and Swain, M. (1980). Theoretical bases of communicative approaches to second language teaching and testing. *Applied Linguistics*, 1(1), 1–47.

Carrell, P. (1983). Some issues in studying the role of schemata, or background knowledge, in second-language comprehension. *Reading in a Foreign Language*, 1(2), 81–92.

Carrell, P. (1984). Evidence of a formal schema in second-language comprehension. *Language Learning*, 34(2), 87–112.

Carrell, P. (1985). Facilitating ESL reading by teaching text structure. *TESOL Quarterly*, 19(4), 727–752.

Carrell, P., Devine, J., and Eskey, D. (1988). *Interactive approaches to second language reading*. New York: Cambridge University Press.

Carroll, J. (1960). Wanted: A research basis for educational policy on foreign language teaching. *Harvard Educational Review*, 30, 128–140.

Carroll, J. (1963). The prediction of success in intensive foreign language training. In R. Glazer, ed. *Training, research, and education*. Pittsburgh: University of Pittsburgh.

Carroll, J. (1967). Foreign language proficiency levels attained by language majors near graduation from college. *Foreign Language Annals*, 1(2), 131–151.

Carroll, S., and Swain, M. (1993). Explicit and implicit negative feedback: An empirical study of the learning of linguistic generalizations. *Studies in Second Language Acquisition*, 15(3), 357–386.

Carson, J. G., and Leki, I., eds. (1993). *Reading in the composition classroom: Second language perspectives*. Boston: Heinle.

Cathcart, R. (1972). Report on a group of Anglo children after one year of immersion in Spanish. Unpublished master's thesis, UCLA.

Cazden, C. (1972). *Child language and education*. New York: Holt, Rinehart and Winston.

Celce-Murcia, M. (1993). Grammar pedagogy in second and foreign language teaching. In S. Silberstein, ed. *State of the art TESOL essays*. Alexandria, VA: TESOL. pp. 288–309.

Chapelle, C. (2001). *Computer applications in second language acquisition*. New York: Cambridge University Press.

Chamot, A. (1990). Cognitive instruction second language classroom: The role of learning strategies. In J. Alatis, ed., pp. 497–513.

Chastain, K. (1975). Affective and ability factors in second language learning. *Language Learning*, 25, 153–161.

Chaudron, C. (1985). A method for examining the input/intake distinction. In Gass and Madden, pp. 285–302.

Chaudron, C. (1991). What counts as formal language instruction? Problems in observation and analysis of classroom teaching. In J. Alatis, ed., pp. 56–64.

Chen, H., and Graves, M. (1995). Effects of previewing and providing background knowledge on Taiwanese college students' comprehension of American short stories. *TESOL Quarterly*, 29(4), 663–686.

Chomsky, N. (1959). Review of B.F. Skinner, "Verbal Behavior." *Language*, 35, 26–58.

Chomsky, N. (1980). *Rules and representations*. New York: Columbia University.

Chomsky, N. (1995). *The minimalist program*. Cambridge, MA: MIT.

Christian, D. (1996). Two-way immersion education: Students learning through two languages. *The Modern Language Journal*, 80(1), 66–76.

Christian, D., and Genesee, F. (2001). *Bilingual education*. Alexandria, VA: TESOL.

Christison, M. A. (1982). *English through poetry*. Hayward, CA: Prentice Hall.

Chun, D., and Brandl, K. (1992). Beyond form-based drill and practice: Meaning-enhancing CALL on the Macintosh. *Foreign Language Annals*, 25(3), 255–261.

Clark, J., and Clifford, R. (1988). The FSI/ILR/ACTFL proficiency scales and testing techniques: Development, current status, and needed research. *Studies in Second Language Acquisition*, 10(2), 129–148.

Cochran-Smith, M. (1997), Knowledge, skills, and experiences for teaching culturally diverse learners: A perspective for practicing teachers. In J.J. Irvine, ed., *Critical knowledge for diverse teachers and learners*. Washington, D.C.: American Association of Colleges for Teacher Education., pp. 27–87.

Cohen, A. (1974). The Culver City Spanish immersion program: The first two years. *Modern Language Journal*, 58, 95–103.

Colbert, J., Desberg, P., and Trimble, K. (1996). *The case for education: Contemporary approaches for using case methods*. Boston: Allyn and Bacon.

Collier, V., (1987). Age and rate of acquisition of second language for academic purposes. *TESOL Quarterly*, 21, 617–641.

Collier, V., (1995). *Promoting academic success for ESL students: Understanding second language acquisition for school*. Elizabeth, NJ: TESOL—Bilingual Educators.

Collier, V., (1999). Acquiring a second language for school. In Heath and Serrano, pp. 16–21.

Collier, V., and Thomas, W. (1997). *School effectiveness for language minority students*. Washington, DC: National Clearinghouse for Bilingual Education.

Collier, V., and Thomas, W. (1989). How quickly can immigrants become proficient in school English? *Journal of Educational Issues of Language Minority Students*, 16, 187–212.

Collier, V., and Thomas, W. (1999). Making schools effective for English language learners, Parts 1–3, *TESOL Matters*, 9(4,5,6).

Collins, P. (2001). *Community writing: Researching social issues through composition*. Mahwah, NJ: Lawrence Erlbaum.

Condon, C. (1983). Treasure hunts for English practice. In Oller and Richard-Amato, pp. 309–312. Also in *English Language Teaching* (1979), 34(1), 53–55.

Cook, V. (1999). Going beyond the native speaker in language teaching. *TESOL Quarterly*, 33(2), 185–209.

Corder, S. P. (1967). The significance of learners' errors. *IRAL*, 4, 161–169.

Corder, S. P. (1978). Language-learner language. In Richards, pp. 94–116.

Corson, D. (1995). *Realities of teaching in a multiethnic school*. In O. García and C. Baker, eds. *Policy and practice in bilingual education: Extending the foundations*. Clevedon, England: Multilingual Matters, 70–84.

Cowie, H., Smith, P. K., Boulton, M., and Laver, R. (1994). *Cooperation in the multi-ethnic classroom*. London: David Fulton.

Cox, M. I. P., and Assis-Peterson, A. A. (1999). Critical pedagogy in ELT: Images of Brazilian teachers of English. *TESOL Quarterly*, 33(3), 433–452.

Crandall, J. (1999). Cooperative language learning and affective factors. In Arnold, ed., pp. 226–245.

Crawford, J. (2000). At war with diversity: U.S. language policy in an age of anxiety. Clevedon, UK: Multilingual Matters.

Crookall, D., and Oxford, R. (1990). *Simulation, gaming, and language learning*. New York: Newbury House.

Crookes, G., and Schmidt, R. (1991). Motivation: Reopening the research agenda. *Language Learning*, 41(4), 469–512.

Crowley, S. (1989). *A teacher's introduction to deconstruction*. Urbana, IL.: National Council of Teachers of English.

Crymes, R. (1979). Current trends in ESL instruction. Paper presented at the Indiana TESOL Convention, October. In J. Haskell, ed. *Selected Articles from the TESOL Newsletter* (1966–1983). Washington, DC: TESOL.

Cummins, J. (1976). The influence of bilingualism on cognitive growth: A synthesis of research findings and explanatory hypotheses. *Working Papers on Bilingualism*, 9, 1–43.

Cummins, J. (1981a). Age on arrival and immigrant second language learning in Canada: A reassessment. *Applied Linguistics*, 1, 132–149.

Cummins, J. (1981b). The role of primary language development in promoting educational success for language minority students. In *Beyond language: Schooling and language minority students: A theoretical framework*, pp. 3–49. Office of Bilingual Bicultural Education, California state Department of Education, Sacramento. Los Angeles: Evaluation, Dissemination and Assessment Center, California State University.

Cummins, J. (1984). *Bilingualism and special education: Issues in assessment and pedagogy.* San Diego, CA: College-Hill Press.

Cummins. J. (1989). *Empowering minority students.* Sacramento, CA: California Association for Bilingual Education.

Cummins, J. (1996). *Negotiating identities: Education for empowerment in a diverse society.* Ontario, CA: California Association for Bilingual Education.

Cummins, J. (1997). Minority status and schooling in Canada. *Anthropology and Education Quarterly*, 28, 411–430.

Cummins, J. (2000). Negotiating intercultural identities in the multilingual classroom. *The CATESOL Journal* 12(1), 163–178.

Curran, C. (1972). *Counseling-learning: A whole-person model for education.* New York: Grune and Stratton.

d'Anglejan, A. (1978). Language learning in and out of classrooms. In Richards, pp. 218–278.

Day, R. (1984). Student participation in the ESL classroom or some imperfections in practice. *Language Learning*, 34(3), 69–102.

Deacon, T. (1997). *The symbolic species: The co-evolution of language and the brain.* New York: Norton.

de Bot, K. (1992). A bilingual production model: Levelt's "speaking" model adapted. *Applied Linguistics*, 13, 1–24.

de Bot, K., Paribakht, T. S., and Wesche, M. (1997). Toward a lexical processing model for the study of second language vocabulary acquisition. *Studies in Second Language Acquisition*, 19(3), 309–329.

de Guerrero, M., and Villamil, O. (2000). Exploring ESL teachers' roles through metaphor analysis. *TESOL Quarterly*, 34(2), 341–351.

de la Fuente, M. J. (2002). Negotiation and oral acquisition of L2 vocabulary: The roles of input and output in the receptive and productive acquisition of words. *Studies in Second Language Acquisition*, 24(1), 81–112.

Delpit, L. D. (1988). The silenced dialogue: Power and pedagogy in educating other people's children. *Harvard Educational Review*, 58, 280–298.

Derrida, J. (1976). *Of Grammatology.* Translated by Gayatri Chakravorty Spivak. Baltimore, MD: Johns Hopkins University.

Derrida, J. (1981). *Dissemination.* Translated by Barbara Johnson. Chicago: University of Chicago.

DeVilliers, P., and DeVilliers, J. (1973). A cross-sectional study of the acquisition of grammatical morphemes in child speech. *Journal of Psycholinguistic Research*, 2, 267–278.

Dewey, J., and Bentley, A. F. (1949). *Knowing and the known.* Boston: Beacon Press.

Deyhle, D. (1992). Constructing failure and maintaining cultural identity: Navajo and Ute school leavers. *Journal of American Indian Education*, 31, 24–47.

Díaz-Rico, L., and Weed, K. (2002). *The crosscultural, language, and academic development handbook* (2d ed.) Boston: Allyn and Bacon.

Dickeman, M. (1973). Teaching cultural pluralism. In J. Banks, ed. *Teaching ethnic studies: Concepts and strategies* (43rd Yearbook). Washington, DC: National Council for Social Studies, 4–25.

Dicker, S. (1996). *Languages in America: A pluralist view.* Clevedon, England: Multilingual Matters.

Dixon, C., and Nessel, D. (1990). *Language experience approach to reading (and writing).* Englewood Cliffs, NJ: Prentice Hall.

Donato, R. (1994). Collective scaffolding in second language learning. In J. Lantolf and G. Appel, eds. *Vygotskian approaches to second language research*. Stanford, CT: Ablex.

Doughty, C. (1991). Second language instruction does make a difference: Evidence from an empirical study of second language relativization. *Studies in Second Language Acquisition*, 13(4), 431–470.

Dulay, H., and Burt, M. (1974). Natural sequences in child second-language acquisition. *Language Learning* 25(1), 37–53.

Dunleavy, D. (1992). *The language beat*. Portsmouth, NH: Heinemann.

Dunn, B. (1994). *Mi semestre de español: A case study of the cultural dimension of second language acquisition*. Unpublished independent study journal, University of Massachusetts, Amherst.

Dvorak, T. (1977). Grammatical practice, communicative practice, and the development of linguistic competence. Ph.D. dissertation, University of Texas at Austin.

Edelsky, C. (1993). Whole language in perspective. *TESOL Quarterly*, 27(3), 548–550.

Edelsky, C. (1996). *With Literacy and justice for all: Rethinking the social in language and education* (2d edition). London: Taylor and Francis.

Edelsky, C., Altwerger, B., and Flores, B. (1991). *Whole language: What's the difference?* Portsmouth, NH: Heinemann.

Egbert, J., and Hanson-Smith, E. (1999). *CALL Environments*. Alexandria, VA: TESOL

Ehrman, M. (1999). Ego boundaries and tolerance of ambiguity in second language learning. In Arnold, 68–86.

Ekbatani, G. and Pierson, H. eds. (2000). *Learner-Directed Assessment in ESL*. Mahwah, NJ: Erlbaum.

Elbow, P. (1993). Ranking, evaluating, and liking: Sorting out three forms of judgment. *College English*, 55(7), 187–206.

Ellis, N. C. , ed. (1994). *Implicit and explicit learning of language*. San Diego, CA: Academic Press.

Ellis, N. C. (2002). Frequency effects in language processing: A review with implications for theories of implicit and explicit language acquisition. *Studies in Second Language Acquisition*, 24(2), 143–189.

Ellis, R. (1984). *Classroom second language development*. Oxford: Pergamon.

Ellis, R. (1985). Teacher-pupil interaction in second-language development. In Gass and Madden, pp. 69–85.

Ellis, R. (1986). *Understanding second language acquisition*. Oxford: Oxford University.

Ellis, R. (1990). *Instructed second language acquisition*. Oxford: Basil Blackwell.

Ellis, R. (1993). Interpretation-based grammar teaching. *System* 21(1), 69–78.

Ellis, R. (1994). A theory of instructed second language acquisition. In N.C. Ellis, ed., pp. 79–114.

Ellis, R. (1997). *Second language acquisition*. Oxford: Oxford University.

Ellis, R., Tanaka, Y., and Yamazaki, A. (1994). Classroom interaction, comprehension, and the acquisition of L2 word meanings. *Language Learning*, 44, 449–491.

Elman, J., Bates, E., Johnson, M., Karmiloff-Smith, A., Parisi, D., Plunkett, K. (1996). *Rethinking innateness: A connectionist perspective on development*. Cambridge, MA: MIT.

Erickson, F., and Mohatt, G. (1982). Cultural organization of participation structures in two classrooms of Indian students. In G. Spindler, ed., *Doing the ethnography of schooling: Educational anthropology in action*. New York: Holt, Rinehart and Winston, pp. 132–174.

Ervin-Tripp, S. (1973). Some strategies for the first and second years. In A. Dil, ed. *Language acquisition and communicative choice*, pp. 204–238. Stanford, CA: Stanford University.

Ervin-Tripp, S. (1974). Is second language learning like the first? *TESOL Quarterly*, 8, 111–127.

ESL standards for pre-K–12 Students. (1997). Alexandria, VA: TESOL.

Evans, J., and Moore, J. (1982). *Art moves the basics along: Units about children*. Carmel, CA: Evan-Moor, 57.

Fanselow, J. (1992). *Contrasting conversations: Activities for exploring our beliefs and teaching practices*. White Plains, NY: Longman.

Farnette, C., Forte, I., and Loss, B. (1977). *I've got me and I'm glad*. ABC Unified School District, Cerritos, CA. Nashville, TN: Incentive Publications.

Felder, R., and Brent, R. (1996). Navigating the bumpy road to student-centered instruction. *College Teaching*, 44, 43–47.

Felix, S. (1988). UG-generated knowledge in adult second language acquisition. In S. Flynn and W. O'Neil, eds. *Linguistic theory in second language acquisition* Dordrecht, Netherlands: Kluwer Academic, pp. 277–294.

Fellag, L. R. (1993). *Life, language, and literature*. Boston: Heinle.

Ferguson, C. (1975). Toward a characterization of English foreigner talk. *Anthropological Linguistics*, 17(1), 1–14.

Ferris, D. (1997). The influence of teacher commentary on student revision. *TESOL Quarterly*, 31(2), 315–339.

Flege, J. E., and Liu, S. (2001). The effect of experience on adults' acquisition of a second language. *Studies in Second Language Acquisition*, 23, 527–552.

Flynn, S. (1987). Contrast and construction in a parameter setting model of L2 acquisition. *Language Learning*, 37(1), 19–62.

Flynn, S. (1990). Theory, practice, and research: Strange or Bliss bedfellows? In J. Alatis ed., pp. 112–122.

Foster, P. (1998). A classroom perspective on the negotiation of meaning. *Applied Linguistics*, 19, 1–23.

Fotis, S., and Ellis, R. (1991). Communication about grammar: A task-based approach. *TESOL Quarterly*, 25(4), 605–628.

Foucault, M. (1980). Power/knowledge: Selected interviews and other writings, 1972–1977. New York: Pantheon Books.

Freed, B. (1978). Foreigner talk: A study of speech adjustments made by native speakers of English in conversation with non-native speakers. Unpublished doctoral dissertation, University of Pennsylvania, Philadelphia.

Freedman, S., ed. (1989). *The acquisition of written language: Response and revision*. Norwood, NJ: Ablex.

Freeman, D., (1991). "Mistaken constructs": Reexamining the nature and assumptions of language teacher education. In J. Alatis, ed., pp. 25–39.

Freeman, D. (1992). Language teacher education emerging discourse and change in classroom practice. In J. Flowerdew, M. Brock, and S. Hsia, eds. *Perspectives in second language teacher education*. Hong Kong: City Polytechnic of Hong Kong, pp. 1–21.

Freeman, D. (1998). *Doing teacher research: From inquiry to understanding*. Boston: Heinle.

Freeman, D., and Richards, J. C. (1996). *Teacher learning in language teaching*. New York: Cambridge University Press.

Freire, P. (1970a). *Cultural action for freedom.* Cambridge, MA: Harvard Educational Review.

Freire, P. (1970b). *Pedagogy of the oppressed.* New York: Seabury.

Freire, P. (1985). *The politics of education: Culture, power, and liberation.* New York: Bergin and Garvey.

Fries, C. (1945). *Teaching and learning English as a foreign language.* Ann Arbor: University of Michigan.

Fuller, J., and Gundel, J. (1987). Topic prominence in interlanguage. *Language Learning,* 37, 1–18.

Gaies, S. (1977). The nature of linguistic input in formal second language learning: Linguistic and communicative strategies in ESL teachers' classroom language. In Brown, Yorio, and Crymes, pp. 204–212.

Gardner, D., and Miller, L., eds. (1996). *Tasks for independent language learning.* Alexandria, VA: TESOL

Gardner, R., Lalonde, R., and Moorcroft, R. (1985). The role of attitudes and motivation in second language learning: Correlational and experimental considerations. *Language Learning,* 35(2), 207–227.

Gardner, R., and Lambert, W. (1959). Motivational variables in second-language acquisition. *Canadian Journal of Psychology,* 13, 266–272.

Gardner, R., and Lambert, W. (1972). *Attitudes and motivation in second-language learning.* Rowley, MA: Newbury House.

Gardner, R., and MacIntyre, P. (1993). On the measurement of affective variables in second language learning. *Language Learning,* 43, 157–194.

Gardner, R., Smythe, P., Clement, R., and Gliksman, L. (1976). Second-language learning: A social-psychological perspective. *Canadian Modern Language Review,* 32, 198–213.

Garvie, E. (1990). *Story as vehicle: Teaching English to young children.* Clevedon, England: Multilingual Matters Ltd.

Gary, J. (1975). Delayed oral practice in initial stages of second-language learning. In Burt and Dulay, eds. pp. 89–95.

Gass, S. (1982). From theory to practice. In M. Hines and W. Rutherford, eds. *On TESOL '81.* Washington, DC: TESOL, pp. 129–139.

Gass, S. (1997). *Input, interaction, and the second language learner.* Mahwah, NJ: Lawrence Erlbaum.

Gass, S., and Mackey, A. (2002). Frequency effects and second language acquisition: A complex picture? *Studies in Second Language Acquisition,* 24(2), 249–260.

Gass, S., Mackey, A., and Pica, T. (1998). The role of input and interaction in second language acquisition: An introduction. *Modern Language Journal,* 82, 299–307.

Gass, S., and Madden, C., eds. (1985). *Input in second language acquisition.* Rowley, MA: Newbury House.

Gass, S., and Varonis, E. (1985). Task variation and nonnative/nonnative negotiation of meaning. In Gass and Madden, pp. 149–161.

Gass, S., and Veronis, E. (1994). Input, interaction, and second language production. *Studies in Second Language Acquisition,* 16, 283–302.

Gaylean, B. (1982). A confluent design for language teaching. In R. Blair, ed. *Innovative approaches to language teaching,* Rowley, MA: Newbury House, pp. 176–188.

Gebhard, J., and Oprandy, R. (1999). *Language teaching awareness: A guide to exploring beliefs and practices.* Cambridge: Cambridge University Press.

Gebhard, M. (1999). Debates in SLA studies: Redefining classroom SLA as an institutional phenomenon. *TESOL Quarterly*, 33(3), 544–554.

Gee, J. P. (1994). Orality and literacy: From the savage mind to ways with words. In J. Maybin, ed. *Language and literacy in social practice*. Clevedon, England: Multilingual Matters.

Genesee, F. (1987). *Learning through two languages: Studies of immersion and bilingual education*. Cambridge, MA: Newbury House.

Genesee, F., and Upshur, J. (1996). *Classroom-based evaluation in second language education*. Cambridge: Cambridge University Press.

Genishi, C. (1999). Poststructural approaches to L2 research. *TESOL Quarterly*, 33(2), 287–291.

Gersten, B. F., and Tlustý, N. (1998). Creating international contexts for cultural communication: Video exchange projects in the EFL/ESL classroom. *TESOL Journal*, 7(2), 11–16.

Ghim-Lian Chew, P. (1999). Linguistic imperialism, globalism, and the English language. In D. Graddol and U. H. Meinhof, eds. *English in a changing world*. Association for Internationale de Linguistique Appliquee, pp. 37–47.

Giles, H. (1979). Ethnicity markers in speech. In K. Scherer and H. Giles, eds. *Social markers in speech*. Cambridge: Cambridge University Press.

Gillespie, J. (1993). Buddy book journals: Responding to literature. *English Journal*, October, pp. 64–68.

Giroux, H. (1983). *Theory and resistance in education: A pedagogy for the opposition*. South Hadley, MA: Bergin and Garvey.

Gliedman, J. (1983). Interview (with Noam Chomsky). *Omni*, 6(2), 113–118.

Glisan, E. (1993). Total physical response: A technique for teaching all skills in Spanish. In J. Oller, Jr., pp. 30–39.

Goldstein, L., and Conrad, S. (1990). Student input and negotiation of meaning in ESL writing conferences. *TESOL Quarterly*, 24(3), 443–461.

Gómez, E. (2000). A history of the ESL standards for pre-K–12 students. In Snow, pp. 49–74.

Goodman, J., and Tenney, C. (1979). Teaching the total language with readers theater. *CATESOL Occasional Papers*, No. 5, pp. 84–89.

Goodman, K. (1982). Acquiring literacy is natural: Who skilled Cock Robin? In F. Gollasch, ed. *Language and literacy: Selected writings of Kenneth S. Goodman*, Volume II. Boston: Routledge and Kegan Paul.

Goodman, K. (1986). *What's whole in whole language*. Portsmouth, NH: Heinemann.

Gore, J. M. (1992). What we can do for you! What can "we" do for "you"? Struggling over empowerment in critical and feminist pedagogy. In C. Luke and J. M. Gore, eds. *Feminisms and critical pedagogy*. New York: Routledge, pp. 54–73.

Gottlieb, J. (1996). *Wonders of Science*. Orlando, FL: Steck-Vaugh.

Gottlieb, M. (2000). Standards-based, large-scale assessment of ESOL students. In Snow, pp. 167–186.

Grabe, W. (1991). Current developments in second language reading research. *TESOL Quarterly*, 25(3), 375–406.

Graham, C. (1978). *Jazz chants*. New York: Oxford University Press.

Graham, C. (2001). *Jazz chants: Old and New*. New York: Oxford University Press.

Graham, C. R. (1984). Beyond integrative motivation: The development and influence of assimilative motivation. Paper presented at the TESOL Convention, Houston, TX, March.

Graves, D. (1992). *Explore poetry*. Portsmouth, NH: Heinemann.

Green, K. (1983). Values clarification theory in ESL and bilingual education. In Oller and Richard-Amato, eds., pp. 179–189.

Green, P., and Hecht, K. (1992). Implicit and explicit grammar: An empirical study. *Applied Linguistics*, 13, 168–184.

Gregg, K. (1984). Krashen's monitor and Occam's razor. *Applied Linguistics*, 5(2), 79–100.

Grenough, M. (1993). *Sing It! Learn English Through Song*. New York: McGraw-Hill/Contemporary.

Grice, H. P. (1975). Logic and conversation. In P. Cole and J. L. Morgan, eds. *Syntax and semantics: Speech acts 3*. New York: Seminar Press, pp. 365–372.

Guillot, M. (1999). *Fluency and its teaching*. Clevedon, England: Multilingual Matters.

Guiora, A., Acton, W., Erard, R., and Strickland, F. (1980). The effects of benzodiazepine (Valium) on permeability of ego boundaries. *Language Learning*, 30, 351–363.

Guiora, A., Beit-Hallami, B., Brannon, R., Dull, C., and Scovel, T. (1972). The effects of experimentally induced changes in ego states on pronunciation ability in second language: An exploratory study. *Comprehensive Psychiatry*, 13, 421–428.

Guiora, A., Brannon, R., and Dull, C. (1972). Empathy and second language learning. *Language Learning*, 22, 111–130.

Hall, J. K., and Eggington, W. (2000). *The sociopolitics of English language teaching*. Clevedon, England: Multilingual Matters.

Hall, J. K., and Walsh, M. (2002). Teacher-student interaction and language learning. *Annual Review of Applied Linguistics*, 22, 186–203.

Halliday, M. A. K. (1979). Towards a sociological semantics. In Brumfit and Johnson, pp. 27–46.

Hammond, R. (1988). Accuracy versus communicative competency: The acquisition of grammar in the second-language classroom. *Hispania*, 71, 408–417.

Hammond, J., and Macken-Horarik, M. (1999). Critical literacy: Challenges and questions for ESL classrooms. *TESOL Quarterly*, 33(3), 528–544.

Hanson-Smith, E. (2000). *Technology-enhanced learning environments*. Alexandria, VA: TESOL.

Harklau, L. (2000). From the "good Kids" to the "worst": Representations of English language learners across educational settings. *TESOL Quarterly*, 34(1), 35–67.

Harley, B., Allen, P., Cummins, J., and Swain, M., eds. (1990). *The development of second language proficiency*. Cambridge: Cambridge University Press.

Harste, J., Short, K., and Burke, C. (1988). *Creating for authors*. Portsmouth, NH: Heinemann.

Harste, J., Woodward, V., and Burke, C. (1984). *Language stories and literacy lessons*. Portsmouth, NH: Heinemann.

Hatch, E., ed. (1978). *Second language acquisition: A book of readings*. Rowley, MA: Newbury House.

Hatch, E. (1983). *Psycholinguistics: A second language perspective*. Rowley, MA: Newbury House.

Hatch, E., Shapira, R., and Gough, J. (1978). "Foreigner-talk" discourse. *ITL Review of Applied Linguistics*, 39–60.

Heath, I. A., and Serrano, C. J., eds. (1999). *Teaching English as a second language*. Guilford, CT: Dushkin/McGraw-Hill.

Heath, S. B. (1983). *Ways with words: Language, life and work in communities and classrooms*. Cambridge: Cambridge University Press.

Heath, S. B. (1996). Re-creating literature in the ESL classroom. *TESOL Quarterly*, 30(4), 776–779.

Hedegaard, M. (1990). How instruction influences children's concepts of evolution. *Mind, Culture, and Activity*, 3, 11–24.

Hedgcock, J., and Lefkowitz, N. (1992). Collaborative oral/aural revision in foreign language writing instruction. *Journal of Second Language Writing*, 1(3), 255–276.

Hedge, T. (2000). *Teaching and learning in the language classroom*. Oxford: Oxford University Press.

Hedge, T., and Whitney, N. (1996). *Power, Pedagogy and Practice*. Oxford: Oxford University Press.

Hendrickson, J. (1976). The effects of error correction treatments upon adequate and accurate communication in written compositions of adult learners of English as a second language. Ph.D. dissertation, Ohio State University.

Hensl, V. (1973). Linguistic register of foreigner language instruction. *Language Learning*, 2, 203–222.

Herbert, C. (1987). *San Diego Title VII two-way bilingual program*. San Diego Unified School District, San Diego, CA.

Hess, N., and Jasper S. P. (1995). A blending of media for extensive reading. *TESOL Journal*, 4(4), 7–11.

Heyde, A. (1977). The relationship between self-esteem and the oral production of a second language. In H. D. Brown, C. Yorio, and R. Crymes, pp. 226–240.

Heyde, A. (1979). The relationship between self-esteem and the oral production of a second language. Unpublished doctoral dissertation, University of Michigan, Ann Arbor.

Higa, M. (1963). Interference effects of intralist word relationships in verbal learning. *Journal of Verbal Learning and Verbal Behavior*, 2, 170–175.

Higgs, T., and Clifford, R. (1982). The push toward communication. In T. Higgs, ed. *Curriculum, competence, and the foreign language teacher*, pp. 57–79. Skokie, IL: A National Textbook.

Hilliard, A. (1989). Teachers and cultural style in a pluralistic society. *NEA Today*, 7(6), 65–69.

Hoffman, S. (1995/1996). Computers and instructional design in foreign language/ESL instruction. *TESOL Journal*, 5(2), 24–29.

Horowitz, D. (1986). What professors actually require: Academic tasks for the ESL classroom. *TESOL Quarterly*, 20(3), 445–462.

Horwitz, E., and Young, D. (1991). *Language anxiety: From theory and research to classroom implications*. Englewood Cliffs, NJ: Prentice Hall.

Howard, G. R. (1999). *You can't teach what you don't know: White teachers, multiracial schools*. New York: Teachers College Press.

Hughes, A. (1989). *Testing for language teachers*. Cambridge: Cambridge University Press.

Hulk, A. (1991). Parameter setting and the acquisition of word order in L2 French. *Second Language Research*, 7(1), 1–34.

Hunter, M., and Russell, D. (1977). How can I plan more effective lessons? *Instructor*, 87, 74–75.

Hymes, D. (1970). On communicative competence. In J. Gumperz, and D. Hymes, eds. *Directions in sociolinguistics*, pp. 35–71. New York: Holt, Rinehart, and Winston.

Igoa, C. (1995). *The inner world of the immigrant child*. Mahwah, NJ: Lawrence Erlbaum.

Ioup, G., Boustagui, E., El Tigi, M., and Moselle, M. (1994). Reexamining the critical period hypothesis: A case study of successful adult SLA in a naturalistic environment. *Studies in Second Language Acquisition*, 16, 73–98.

Irujo, S. (2000a). ESL standards in the classroom. *TESOL Matters*, 10(3), 7.

Irujo, S., ed. (2000b). *Integrating the ESL standards into classroom practice*: Grades 6–8. Alexandria, VA: TESOL.

Irvine, J. J. (1990). *Black students and school failure: Policies, practices, and prescriptions*. Westport, CT: Greenwood Press.

Izumi, S., and Bigelow, M. (2000). Does output promote noticing and second language acquisition? *TESOL Quarterly*, 34(2), 239–278.

Jacob, E., Rottenberg, L., Patrick, S., and Wheeler, E. (1996). Cooperative learning: Context and opportunities for acquiring academic English. *TESOL Quarterly*, 30(2), 253–280.

Jain, M. (1969). Error analysis of an Indian English corpus. Unpublished manuscript, University of Edinburgh.

James, W. (1958). *Talks to teachers*. New York: Norton.

Jervis, K. (1996). "How come there are no brothers on that list?" Hearing the hard questions all children ask. *Harvard Educational Review*, 66, 546–576.

Jespersen, O. (1904). *How to teach a foreign language*. London: Allen and Unwin.

Johns, A. (1993). Written argumentation for real audiences: Suggestions for teacher research and classroom practice. *TESOL Quarterly* 27(1), 75–90.

Johnson, D. M. (1994). Grouping strategies for second language learners. In F. Genesee, ed. *Educating second language children: The whole child, the whole curriculum, the whole community*, pp. 183–211. Cambridge: Cambridge University Press.

Johnson, J. (1992). Critical period effects in second language acquisition: The effect of written versus auditory materials on the assessment of grammatical competence. *Language Learning*, 42(2), 217–248.

Johnson, K. (1979). Communicative approaches and communicative processes. In Brumfit and Johnson, pp. 192–205.

Johnston, B. (1999). Putting critical pedagogy in its place: A personal account. *TESOL Quarterly*, 33(3), 557–565.

John-Steiner, V. (1985). The road to competence in an alien land: A Vygotskian perspective on bilingualism. In J. Wertsch, ed. *Culture, communication, and cognition: Vygotsky in perspective*. Cambridge: Cambridge University Press.

John-Steiner, V., and Souberman, E. (1978). Afterword. In Vygotsky, pp. 121–140.

Jones, L., and von Baeyer, C. (1983). *Functions of American English: Communication activities for the classrooms*, p. 17. New York: Cambridge University Press.

Jordan, G., and Weedon, C. (1995). *Cultural politics: Class, gender, race and the modern world*. Oxford: Blackwell.

Kachru, B. B. (1992). *The other tongue: English across cultures* (2d edition). Urbana: University of Illinois Press.

Kachru, Y. (1994). Sources of bias in SLA research monolingual bias in SLA research. *TESOL Quarterly*, 28(4), 795–799.

Kagan, S. (1985). *Cooperative learning: Resources for teachers*. Riverside, CA: Spencer Kagan, University of California.

Kagan, S. (1986). Cooperative learning and sociocultural factors in schooling. In *Beyond language: Social and cultural factors in schooling language minority students*, pp. 231–298. Los Angeles: Evaluation, Dissemination and Assessment Center, California State University, Los Angeles.

Kagan, S. (1994). *Cooperative learning*. San Juan Capistrano, CA: Kagan Cooperative Learning.

Kalivoda, T., Morain, G., and Elkins, R. (1971). The audio-motor unit: A listening comprehension strategy that works. *Foreign Language Annals*, 4, 392–400. Also in Oller and Richard-Amato, pp. 337–347.

Kamhi-Stein, L. (2000). Adapting U.S.-based TESOL education to meet the needs of nonnative English speakers. *TESOL Journal*, 9(3), 10–14.

Kasser, C., and Silverman, A. (2001). *Stories we brought with us*. White Plains, NY: Pearson Education.

Katz, A. (2000). Changing paradigms for assessment. In Snow, pp. 137–166.

Kaufman, D., and Brooks, J. G. (1996). Interdisciplinary collaboration in teacher education: A constructivist approach. *TESOL Quarterly*, 30(2), 231–251.

Kay, J., and Gelshenen, G. (1998). *America Writes: Learning English through American short stories*. New York: Cambridge University Press.

Kendall, F. E. (1996). *Diversity in the classroom: New approaches to the education of young children* (2d revised edition). New York: Teachers College Press.

Kepner, C. (1991). An experiment in the relationship of types of written feedback to the development of second-language writing skills. *Modern Language Journal*, 75(iii), 305–313.

Kessler, G., and Plakans, L. (2001). Incorporating ESOL learners' feedback and usability testing in instructor-developed CALL materials. *TESOL Journal*, 10(1), 15–20.

King, R. (1997). Should English be the law? *Atlantic Monthly*, 279(4), 55–64.

Kleifgen, J. (1985). Skilled variation in a kindergarten teacher's use of foreigner talk. In Gass and Madden, pp. 59–68.

Klein, W. (1995). Language acquisition at different ages. In D. Magnusson, ed. The lifespan development of individuals: *Behavioral, neurobiological, and psychosocial perspectives. A synthesis*, pp. 244–264. New York: Cambridge University Press.

Kleinman, H. (1977). Avoidance behavior in adult second-language acquisition. *Language Learning*, 27, 93–105.

Klesmer, H. (1994). Assessment and teacher perceptions of ESL student achievement. *English Quarterly*, 26(3), 8–11.

Klingner, J. K., and Vaughn, S. (2000). The helping behaviors of fifth graders while using collaborative strategic reading during ESL content classes. *TESOL Quarterly*, 34(1), 69–98.

Koestler, A. (1964). *The act of creation*. New York: Macmillan.

Koffka, K. (1924). *The growth of the mind*. London: Routledge and Kegan Paul.

Köhler, W. (1925). *The mentality of apes*. New York: Harcourt Brace.

Kormos, J. (1999). Monitoring and self-repair in L2. *Language Learning*, 49(2), 303–242.

Krashen, S, (1973). Lateralization, language learning, and the critical period: Some new evidence. *Language Learning*, 23, 63–74.

Krashen, S. (1981a). The fundamental pedagogical principle in second language teaching. *Studia Linguistica*, 61.

Krashen, S. (1981b). *Second language acquisition and second language learning*. Oxford: Pergamon.

Krashen, S. (1981c). The case for narrow reading. *TESOL Newsletter*, December, p. 23.

Krashen, S. (1982). *Principles and practice in second language acquisition*. Oxford: Pergamon.

Krashen, S. (1984). Immersion: Why it works and what it has taught us. *Language and Society*, (12), 61–64.

Krashen, S. (1985). *The input hypothesis: Issues and implications*. London: Longman.

Krashen, S. (1995). What is intermediate natural approach. In P. Hashemipour, R.

Maldonado, and M. van Naerssen, eds. *Studies in language learning and Spanish linguistics in honor of Tracy D. Terrell*. New York: McGraw-Hill, pp. 92–105.

Krashen, S., and Pon, P. (1975). An error analysis of an advanced ESL learner. *Working Papers on Bilingualism*, 7, 125–129.

Krashen, S., and Terrell, T. (1983). *The natural approach: Language acquisition in the classroom*. Englewood Cliffs, NJ: Alemany/Prentice Hall.

Kroll, B. (1990). *Second language writing: Research insights for the classroom*. New York: Cambridge University Press.

Kubota, R. (1999). Japanese culture constructed by discourses: Implications for applied linguistics research and ELT. *TESOL Quarterly*, 33(1), 9–35.

Kubota, R. (2001). Discursive construction of the images of U.S. classrooms. *TESOL Quarterly*, 35(1), 9–38

Kumaravadivelu, B. (1994). The postmethod condition: (E)merging strategies for second/foreign language teaching. *TESOL Quarterly*, 28(1), 27–48.

Kumaravadivelu, B. (1999). Critical classroom discourse analysis. *TESOL Quarterly*, 33(3), 453–484.

Kumaravadivelu, B. (2001). Toward a postmethod pedagogy. *TESOL Quarterly*, 35(4), 537–560.

Lado, R. (1961). *Language testing*. New York: McGraw-Hill.

Lado, R. (1977). *Lado English series*. New York: Regents.

Ladson-Billings, G. (1994). *The dreamkeepers: Successful teachers of African American children*. San Francisco: Jossey-Bass.

Lambert, W. (1974). Culture and language as factors in learning and education. Paper presented at the Annual TESOL Convention, Denver, Colorado.

Lambert, W., and Cazabon, M. (1994). *Students' views of the Amigos program*, Research Report, No. 11. Santa Cruz, CA, and Washington, DC: National Center for Research on Cultural Diversity and Second Language Learning.

Lambert, W., and Tucker, G. (1972). *Bilingual education of children: The St. Lambert experiment*. Rowley, MA: Newbury House.

Lamendella, J. (1979). The neurofunctional basis of pattern practice. *TESOL Quarterly*, 13, 5–20.

Lapkin, S., and Swain, M. (1984). Research update. *Language and Society*, (12), 48–54.

Larsen, D., and Smalley, W. (1972). *Becoming bilingual: A guide to language learning*. New Canaan, CT: Practical Anthropology.

Larsen-Freeman, D. (1978). An explanation for the morpheme accuracy order of learners of English as a second language. In Hatch, ed. pp. 371–382.

Larsen-Freeman, D. (1991). Second language acquisition research: Staking out the territory. *TESOL Quarterly*, 25(2), 315–350.

Larsen-Freeman, D. (1995). On the teaching and learning of grammar: Challenging the myths. In F. Eckman et al., eds. *Second language acquisition theory and pedagogy*. Mahwah, NJ: Lawrence Erlbaum.

Larsen-Freeman, D. (1996). Impressions of AILA 1996. In the *AILA Review*, No. 12, 87–92.

Larsen-Freeman, D. (2000). The total physical response method. In D. Larsen-Freeman, *Techniques and principles in language teaching*, pp. 107–119. New York: Oxford University Press.

Larsen-Freeman, D. (2002a). Making sense of frequency. *Studies in Second Language Acquisition*, 24(2), 275–286.

Larsen-Freeman, D. (2002b). Teaching grammar. In M. Celce-Murcia, ed., *Teaching English as a second or foreign language* (3d edition), pp. 251–266. Boston: Heinle.

Larsen-Freeman, D., and Long M. (1991). *An introduction to second language acquisition.* London: Longman.

Lawson, J. (1971). Should foreign language be eliminated from the curriculum? *Foreign Language Annals*, 4, 427. Also in J. W. Dodge, ed. *The case of foreign language study.* New York: Northeast Conference on the Teaching of Foreign Languages.

Lazar, G. (1993). *Literature and language teaching: A guide for teachers and trainers.* Cambridge: Cambridge University Press.

Leeds, B., ed. (1996). *Writing in a second language: Insights from first and second language teaching and research.* White Plains, NY: Longman/Addison-Wesley.

Leki, I. (1990). Potential problems with peer responding in ESL writing classes. *CATESOL Journal*, 3, 5–19.

Leki, I. (2001). "A narrow thinking system": Nonnative-English-speaking students in group projects across the curriculum. *TESOL Quarterly*, 35(1), 39–67.

Lenneberg, E. (1967). *Biological foundations of language.* New York: Wiley.

Lessow-Hurley, J. (1996). *The foundations of dual language instruction*, (2d edition). White Plains, NY: Longman.

Levelt, W. (1989). *Speaking: From intention to articulation*, Cambridge, MA: MIT.

Lewis, G. and Bedson, G. (1999). *Games for children.* Oxford: Oxford University.

Lightbown, P. (1983). Exploring relationships between developmental and instructional sequences. In H. Seliger and M. Long, eds. pp. 217–243.

Lightbown, P. (1991). Getting quality input in the second/foreign language classroom. In C. Kramsch and S. McConnell-Ginet, eds. *Text and context: Cross-disciplinary perspectives on language study.* Boston: D.C. Heath/Houghton Mifflin, pp. 192–201.

Lightbown, P. (1998). The importance of timing in focus on form. In C. Doughty and J. Williams, eds. *Focus on form in classroom second language acquisition.* New York: Cambridge University Press.

Lightbown, P., and Spada, N. (1999). *How languages are learned* (2d edition). Oxford: Oxford University.

Lipka, J. (1991). Toward a culturally based pedagogy: A case study of one Yup'ik Eskimo teacher. *Anthropology and Education Quarterly*, 22(3), 203–223.

Liu, J. (1999). Nonnative-English-speaking professionals in TESOL. *TESOL Quarterly*, 33(1), 85–102.

LoCastro, V. (1994). Learning strategies and learning environments. *TESOL Quarterly* 28(2), 409–414.

Long, M. (1981). Input, interaction, and second language acquisition. In H. Winitz, ed. *Native language and foreign language acquisition: Annals of the New York Academy of Sciences*, 379, 259–278.

Long, M. (1983a). Linguistic and conversational adjustments to non-native speakers. *Studies in Second Language Acquisition*, 5(2), 177–193.

Long, M. (1983b). Native speaker/nonnative speaker conversation in the second-language classroom. In M. Clarke and J. Handscombe, eds. *On TESOL '82: Pacific perspectives on language learning and teaching.* Washington, DC: TESOL.

Long, M. (1985). A role for instruction in second language acquisition. In K. Hyltenstam and M. Pienemann, eds. *Modelling and assessing second language acquisition.* Clevedon, England: Multilingual Matters Ltd, pp. 77–99.

Long, M. (1988). Instructed interlanguage development. In L. M. Beebe, ed. *Issues in second language acquisition: Multiple perpectives.* New York: Newbury House/Harper and Row, pp. 115–141.

Long, M. (1990). Maturational constraints on language development. *Studies in second language acquisition*, 12, 273–274.

Long, M. (1996). The role of the linguistic environment in second language acquisition. In W.C. Ritchie and T.K. Bhatia, eds. *Handbook of second language acquisition*. New York: Academic Press, pp. 413–468.

Long, M., Adams, L., McLean, M., and Castanos, F. (1976). Doing things with words—verbal interaction in lockstep and small group classroom situations. In J. Fanselow and R. Crymes, eds. *On TESOL '76*, pp. 137–153. Washington, DC: TESOL.

Long, M., Inagaki, S., and Ortega, L. (1998). The role of implicit negative feedback in SLA: Models and recasts in Japanese and Spanish. *Modern Language Journal*, 82, 357–371.

Long, M., and Porter, P. (1984). Group work, interlanguage talk and classroom second language acquisition. Paper presented at TESOL 1984, Houston, TX.

Long M., and Richards, J., eds. (1987). *Methodology in TESOL: A book of readings*. Rowley, MA: Newbury House.

Lorton, M. B. (1994). *Mathematics their way*. White Plains, NY: Pearson Education.

Lozanov, G. (1978). *Suggestology and outlines of suggestopedy*. New York: Gordon and Breach.

Luke, A. (1996). Genres of power? Literacy education and the production of capital. In R. Hasan & G. Williams, eds. *Literacy in society*. New York: Longman, pp. 308–338.

Lukmani, Y. (1972). Motivation to learn and language proficiency. *Language Learning*, 22, 261–273.

Lyster, R. (1998). Recasts, repetition, and ambiguity in L2 classroom discourse. *Studies in Second Language Acquisition*, 20, 51–81.

Lyster, R., and Ranta, L. (1997). Corrective feedback and learner uptake: Negotiation of form in communictive classrooms. *Studies in Second Language Acquisition*, 19, 37–66.

MacIntyre, P. D., and Charos, C. (1996). Personality, attitudes and affect as predictors of second language communication. *Journal of Language and Social Psychology*, 15, 3–26.

MacIntyre, P. D., and Gardner, R. (1994). The effects of induced anxiety on three stages of cognitive processing in computerized vocabulary learning. *Studies in Second Language Acquisition*, 16(1), 1–17.

Mackey, A. (1999). Input, interaction, and second language development: An empirical study of question formation in ESL. *Studies in Second Language Acquisition*, 21, 557–587.

Mackey, A., Gass, S., and McDonough, K. (2000). How do learners perceive interactional feedback. *Studies in Second Language Acquisition*, 22, 471–497.

Mackey, A., and Philp, J. (1998). Conversational interaction and second language development: Recasts, responses, and red herrings? *Modern Language Journal*, 82, 338–356.

Madrid, A. (1991). Diversity and its discontents. In L. Samovar and R. Porter, eds. *Intercultural communication: A reader* (6th edition). Belmont, CA: Wadsworth, pp. 115–119.

Magnan, S. (1986). Assessing speaking proficiency in the undergraduate curriculum: Data from French. *Foreign Language Annals*, 19, 429–438.

Maley, A., and Duff, A. (1983). *Drama techniques in language learning: A resource book of communication activities for language teachers*. Cambridge: Cambridge University Press.

Marinova-Todd, S., Marshall, D. B., and Snow, C. (2000). Three misconceptions about age and L2 learning. *TESOL Quarterly*, 34(1), 9–34.

Martin, J. (1993). Genre and literacy—modelling context in educational linguistics. *Annual Review of Applied Linguistics*, 13, 141–172.

Martino, L., and Johnson, D. W. (1979). Cooperative and individualistic experiences among disabled and normal children. *Journal of Social Psychology*, 107, 177–183.

McCarthy, D. (1930). *The language development of the pre-school child*. Minneapolis: University of Minnesota.

McGroarty, M. (1992). Cooperative learning: The benefits for content-area teaching. In Richard-Amato and Snow, pp. 58–69.

McIntosh, P. (1988). *White privilege and male privilege: A personal account of coming to see correspondences through work in women's studies* (Work Paper No. 189). Wellesley, MA: Wellesley College Center for Research on Women.

McKay, S. (1993). *Agendas for second language literacy*. New York: Cambridge University Press.

McKay, S. (2000). Teaching English as an international language: Implications for cultural materials in the classroom. *TESOL Journal*, 9(4), 7–11.

McLaughlin, B. (1978). The Monitor Model: Some methodological considerations. *Language Learning*, 28, 309–332.

McLaughlin, B., Rossman, T., and McLeod, B. (1984). Second language learning: An information-processing perspective. *Language Learning*, 33(2), 135–158.

McNamara, M. J. and Deane, D. (1995). Self-assessment activities: toward autonomy in language learning. *TESOL Journal*, 5(1), 17–21.

Mehan, H. (1979). *Learning lessons*. Cambridge, MA: Harvard University.

Mehan, H., Datnow, A., Bratton, E., Tellez, C., Friedlaender, D., and Ngo, T. (1992). Untracking and college enrollment, Research Report No. 4. Santa Cruz, CA: National Center for Research on Cultural Diversity and Second Language Learning (University of California).

Mendes Figueiredo, M. (1991). Acquisition of second language pronunciation: The critical period. *CTJ Journal*, 24, 41–47.

Mohan, B. (1992). What are we really testing? In Richard-Amato and Snow, eds. pp. 258–270.

Mohan, B., and Au-Yeung Lo, W. (1985). Academic writing and Chinese students: Transfer and developmental factors. *TESOL Quarterly*, 19(3), 515–534.

Morgan, B. (1997). Identity and intonation: Linking dynamic processes in an ESL classroom. *TESOL Quarterly* 31(3), 431–450.

Morley, J. (1991). The pronunciation component in teaching English to speakers of other languages. *TESOL Quarterly*, 25(3), 481–520.

Morley, J., Robinett, B. W., Selinker, L., and Woods, D. (1984). ESL theory and the Fries legacy. *JALT Journal*, 6(2), 171–207.

Morrison, D. M., and Low, G. (1983). Monitoring and the second language learner. In J. Richards and R. Schmidt, eds. *Language and communication*. London: Longmann.

Moskowitz, G. (1978). *Caring and sharing in the foreign language class: A source book on humanistic techniques*. Rowley, MA: Newbury House.

Moskowitz, G. (1981). Effects of humanistic techniques on attitude, cohesiveness, and self-concept on foreign language students. *Modern Language Journal*, 65, 149–157.

Moskowitz, G. (1999). Enhancing personal development: Humanistic activities at work. In Arnold, pp. 177–193.

Moulton, M., and Holmes, V. (1997). Pattern poems: Creative writing for language acquisition. *The Journal of the Imagination in Language Learning*, IV, 84–90.

Moustfa, M. (1989). CI plus the LEA: A long term perspective. *The Reading Teacher*, 41(3), 276–287.

Mullen, K. (1980). Rater reliability and oral proficiency evaluations. In J. W. Oller and K. Perkins, eds. *Research in language testing*, pp. 91–101. Rowley, MA: Newbury House.

Murphy, J. M., and Stoller, F. (2001). Sustained-content language teaching: An emerging definition. *TESOL Journal*, 10(2/3), 3–5.

Murphey, T. (1992). The discourse of pop songs. *TESOL Quarterly*, 26(4), 770–774.

Murray, D. (1982). *Learning by teaching: Selected articles on writing and teaching.* Upper Montclair, NJ: Boynton Cook.

Myles, F., Mitchell, R., and Hooper, J. (1999). Interrogative chunks in French L2: A Basis for Creative Construction? *Studies in Second Language Acquisition*, 21, 49–80.

Naiman, N., Frohlich, M., and Stern, H. H. (1978). *The good language learner*. Toronto: Ontario Institute for Studies in Education.

Nation, P. (2000). Learning vocabulary in lexical sets: Dangers and guidelines. *TESOL Journal*, 9(2), 6–10.

Nayer, P. B. (1997), ESL/EFL Dichotomy today: Language politics or pragmatics? *TESOL Quarterly*, 31(1), 9–38.

Nelson, G., and Murphy, J. (1993). Peer response groups: Do L2 writers use peer comments in revising their drafts? *TESOL Quarterly*, 27(1), 135–141.

Newmark, L. (1983). How not to interfere with language learning. In Oller and Richard-Amato (1983), pp. 49–58. Also in Brumfit and Johnson, pp. 160–166.

Nieto, S. (1999). *The light in their eyes: Creating multicultural learning communities.* New York: Teachers College, Columbia University.

Nieto, S. (2000). *Affirming diversity: The sociopolitical context of multicultural education* (3d edition). White Plains, NY: Longman.

Nobuyoshi, J., and Ellis, R. (1996). Focused communication tasks and second language acquisition. In T. Hedge and N. Whitney, pp. 261–270.

Nunan, D. (1989). *Designing tasks for the communicative classroom.* Cambridge: Cambridge University Press.

Nunan, D. (1991). Communicative tasks and the language curriculum. *TESOL Quarterly*, 25(2), 279–295.

Ochs, E., and Schieffelin, B. (1984). Language acquisition and socialization: Three developmental stories and their implications. In R. Shweder and R. Levine, eds. *Culture theory: Essays on mind, self and emotion*, pp. 276–320. New York: Cambridge University Press.

O'Donnell, J., and Clark, C. (1999). *Becoming and unbecoming White: Owning and disowning a racial identity.* Westport, CT: Bergin and Garvey.

O'Grady, W. (1999). *Toward a New Nativism. Studies in Second Language Acquisition*, 21(4), 621–633.

Oh, Sun-Young (2001). Two types of input modification and EFL reading comprehension: Simplification versus elaboration. *TESOL Quarterly*, 35(1), 69–96.

Oller, J., Jr. (1979). *Language tests at school.* London: Longman.

Oller, J., Jr. (1981). Research on the measurements of affective variable: Some remaining questions. In R. Andersen, ed. pp. 14–27.

Oller, J., Jr. (1983a). Some working ideas for language teaching. In Oller and Richard-Amato, pp. 3–19.

Oller, J., Jr. (1983b). Story writing principles and ESL teaching. *TESOL Quarterly*, 17(1), 39–53.

Oller, J., Jr. (1993). *Methods that work: Ideas for literacy and language teachers.* Boston: Heinle.

Oller, J., Jr. Baca, L., and Vigil, A. (1977). Attitudes and attained proficiency in ESL: A sociolinguistic study of Mexican-Americans in the southwest. *TESOL Quarterly*, 11, 173–183.

Oller, J., Jr. Hudson, A., and Liu, P. (1977). Attitudes and attained proficiency in ESL: A sociolinguistic study of native speakers of Chinese in the United States. *Language Learning*, 27(1), 1–27.

Oller, J., Jr. and Obrecht, D. (1969). The psycholinguistic principle of informational sequence: An experiment in second-language learning. *International Review of Applied Linguistics in Language Teaching*, 7(2), 117–123.

Oller, J., Jr. and Richard-Amato, P., eds. (1983). *Methods that work.* Rowley, MA.: Newbury House.

Oller, J., Jr., and Richards, J., eds. (1973). *Focus on the learner: Pragmatic perspectives for the language teacher.* Rowley, MA: Newbury House.

Omaggio, A. (1993). *Teaching language in context: Proficiency-oriented instruction.* Boston: Heinle.

O'Malley, J., and Chamot, A. (1990). *Learning strategies in second language acquisition.* Cambridge: Cambridge University Press.

O'Malley, J. M., and Pierce, L. V. (1996). *Authentic assessment for English language learners: Practical approaches for teachers.* Reading, MA: Addison-Wesley.

Olmedo, I. (1993). Junior historians: Doing oral history with ESL and bilingual students. *TESOL Journal*, 2(4), 7–10.

Oxford, R. (1990). *Language learning strategies: What every teacher should know.* New York: Newbury House.

Oxford, R. (1999). Anxiety and the language learner: New insights. In Arnold, pp. 58–67.

Oxford, R., and Cohen, A. (1992). Language learning strategies: Crucial issues of concept and classification. *Allied Language Learning*, 3(1), 1–35.

Oxford, R., and Ehrman, M., and Lavine, R. (1991). Style wars: Teacher-student style conflicts in the language classroom. In S. Magnan, ed. *Challenges in the 1990s for college foreign language programs.* Boston: Heinle.

Palmer, H. (1971). *Songbook: Learning basic skills through music.* Freeport, NJ: Educational Activities.

Palmer, H., and Palmer, D. (1925). *English through actions* (reprinted edition 1959). London: Longman Green.

Parkhurst, C. (1984). Using CALL to teach composition. In P. Larson, E. Judd, and D. Messerschmitt, eds. *On TESOL '84: A brave new world for TESOL*, Washington, DC: TESOL, pp. 255–260.

Parry, K. (1996). Culture, literacy, and L2 reading. *TESOL Quarterly*, 30(4), 665–692.

Pavesi, M. (1984). The acquisition of relative clauses in a formal and in an informal setting: Further evidence in support of the markedness hypothesis. In D. Singleton, and D. Little, eds. *Language learning in formal and informal contexts.* Dublin: IRAAL, pp. 151–163.

Pierce, B. N. (1995). Social identity, investment, and language learning. *TESOL Quarterly* 29, 9–31.

Pierce, L. V., and O'Malley, J. M. (1992). *Performance and portfolio assessment for language minority students.* Washington, D.C.: National Clearinghouse for Bilingual Education.

Pennington, M. (1989). *Teaching languages with computers: The state of the art.* La Jolla, CA: Athelstan.

Pennycook, A. (1994). *The cultural politics of English as an international language.* London: Longman.

Pennycook, A. (1996). TESOL and critical literacies: Modern, post, or neo? *TESOL Quarterly*, 30(1), 163–171.

Pennycook, A. (1997). Vulgar pragmatism, critical pragmatism, and EAP. *ESP Journal* 16(4), 253–269.

Pennycook, A. (1998). *English and the discourses of colonialism.* London: Routledge.

Pennycook, A. (1999). Introduction: Critical approaches to TESOL. *TESOL Quarterly*, 33(3), 329–348.

Pérez, B., and Torres-Guzman, M. (1992). *Learning in two worlds: An integrated Spanish/English biliteracy approach*. White Plains, NY: Longman.

Peyton, J. K., and Staton, J. (1992). *Dialogue journal writing with non-native English speakers: An instructional packet for teachers and workshop leaders*. Alexandria, VA: TESOL.

Phillips, S. (1999). *Drama with children*. Oxford: Oxford University.

Phillipson, R. (1992). *Linguistic imperialism*. Oxford: Oxford University Press.

Phinney, J. S. (1993). A three-stage model of ethnic identity development in adolescence. In M. E. Bernal and G. P. Knight, eds. *Ethnic identity: Formation and transmission among Hispanics and other minorities*. Albany: State Univerity of New York Press, 61–79.

Piaget, J. (1955). *The language and thought of the child*. New York: Meridian Books.

Piaget, J. (1979). *The development of thought*. New York: Viking.

Pica, T. (1983). Adult acquisition of English as a second language under different conditions of exposure. *Language Learning*, 33(4), 465–497.

Pica, T. (1994). Research on negotiation: What does it reveal about second-language learning conditions, processes, and outcomes? *Language Learning*, 44, 493–527.

Pica, T., and Doughty, C. (1985). Input and interaction in the communicative language classroom: A comparison of teacher-fronted and group activities. In Gass and Madden, pp. 115–132.

Pienemann, M. (1984). Psychological constraints on the teachability of languages. *Studies in Second Language Acquisition*, 6(2), 186–214.

Pienemann, M. (1988). Determining the influence of instruction on L2 speech processing. *AILA Review* 5, 40–72.

Pierce, L., and O'Malley, J. M. (1992). *Performance and portfolio assessment for language minority students*. Washington, DC: National Clearinghouse for Bilingual Education.

Pinker, S. (1994). *The Language Instinct: How the Mind Creates Language*. New York: William Morrow.

Plann, S. (1977). Acquiring a second language in an immersion classroom. In H. D. Brown, C. Yorio, and R. Crymes, pp. 213–225.

Polio, C., and Gass, S. (1998). The role of interaction in native speaker comprehension of non-native speaker speech. *Modern Language Journal*, 82, 308–319.

Pollock, C. (1982). *Communicate what you mean* (p. 7). Englewood Cliffs, NJ: Prentice Hall.

Poole, A. (1971). *Final project report: Cross-age teaching* (No. 68-06138-0). Ontario-Montclair School District, Ontario, CA: Poole-Young Associates.

Poole, D. (1992). Language socialization in the second-language classroom. *Language Learning* 42(4), 593–616.

Porter, P. (1986). *How learners talk to each other: Input and interaction in task-centered discussions*. In R. Day, ed. Talking to learn: Conversation in second language acquisition. Rowley, MA: Newbury House, pp. 200–222.

Porter, R. (1990). *Forked tongue: The politics of bilingual education* (2d edition). Scranton, PA: Basic Books.

Postovsky, V. (1974). Effects of delay in oral practice at the beginning of second language learning. *Modern Language Journal*, 58, 5–6.

Postovsky, V. (1977). Why not start speaking later? In Burt, Dulay, and Finocchiaro, pp. 17–26.

Prabhu, N. S. (1990). There is no best method—Why? *TESOL Quarterly*, 24(2), 161–176.

The Random House book of poetry for children. (1983). New York: Random House.

Price, M. (1991). The subjective experience of foreign language anxiety interviews with high-anxious students. In E. Horwitz and D. Young, eds. *Language anxiety: From theory and research to classroom implications*. Englewood Cliffs, NJ: Prentice Hall.

Ramírez, J., Yuen, S., Ramey, D. (1991). *Longitudinal study of structured English immersion strategy, early-exit, and late-exit transitional bilingual education programs for language minority children. Executive summary: Final report*. San Mateo, CA: Aguirre International.

Raths, L., Merrill, H., and Simon, S. (1966). *Values and teaching*. Columbus, OH: Charles E. Merrill.

Ravem, R. (1978). Two Norwegian children's acquisition of English syntax. In E. Hatch, ed., pp. 148–154.

Readence, J., Bean, T., and Baldwin, R. (1981). *Content area reading: An integrated approach*. Dubuque, IA: Kendall/Hunt.

Reid, J. (1992). Helping students write for an academic audience. In Richard-Amato and Snow, pp. 210–221.

Richard-Amato, P. (1983). ESL in Colorado's Jefferson County Schools. In Oller and Richard-Amato, pp. 393–397.

Richard-Amato, P. (1984). Teacher talk in the classroom: Native and foreigner. Unpublished Ph.D. dissertation, University of New Mexico, Albuquerque.

Richard-Amato, P. (1990). *Reading in the content areas: An interactive approach for international students*. White Plains, NY: Longman.

Richard-Amato, P. (1992a). Peer teachers: The neglected resource. In Richard-Amato and Snow, eds., pp. 271–284.

Richard-Amato, P. (1992b). Using reaction dialogues to develop second-language writing skills. Keynote at the TESOL Summer Institute, Comenius University, Bratislava, Slovakia, July 15.

Richard-Amato, P. (1993a). An interactive approach to reading in a second language. Presentation at the 27th Annual Convention of TESOL, April 16, Atlanta, GA.

Richard-Amato, P. (1993b). *Exploring themes*. Reading, MA: Addison-Wesley.

Richard-Amato, P. (1995). The natural approach: How it is evolving. In P. Hashemipour, R. Maldonado, M. VanNaerssen, eds. *Studies in Language Learning and Spanish Linguistics in Honor of Tracy D. Terrell*, New York: McGraw-Hill, pp. 70–91.

Richard-Amato, P. (1996). Until I saw the sea: Creating heightened awareness in language learners. Plenary at the Puerto Rico TESOL 23rd Annual Convention and 4th Central American and Caribbean Regional TESOL Conference, Ponce, Puerto Rico, November 16.

Richard-Amato, P. (1997). Affect and related factors in second and foreign language acquisition. In *TESOL's voices of experience series*. Alexandria, VA: TESOL.

Richard-Amato, P. (1998). *World Views: Multicultural literature for critical writers, readers, and thinkers*. Boston: Heinle.

Richard-Amato, P. (2001). Sharing power: Rethinking the teacher's role. Plenary at 32d Annual Conference of CATESOL, April 20, Ontario, California.

Richard-Amato, P. (2002). Sharing power in the ESL classroom. *ESL Magazine*, January/February, 16–18.

Richard-Amato, P., and Hansen, W. A. (1995). *Worlds together: A journey into multicultural literature*, Reading, MA: Addison-Wesley.

Richard-Amato, P., and Lucero, R. (1980). Foreigner talk strategies in the ESL classroom. Course paper written for C. Cazden at the University of New Mexico, TESOL Institute.

Richard-Amato, P., and Snow, M. A. (1992). *The multicultural classroom: Readings for content-area teachers.* White Plains, NY: Longman.

Richard-Amato, P., and Snow, M. A. (In Press). *The multicultural classroom: Readings for content-area teachers* (2d edition). White Plains, NY: Longman.

Richards, J. C. (1978). *Understanding second and foreign language learning.* Rowley, MA: Newbury House.

Richards, J. C. (1989). Beyond training: Approaches to teacher education in language teaching. *Perspectives,* 1–12.

Richards, J. C. (1991). Content knowledge and instructional practice in second-language teacher education. In J. Alatis, ed., pp. 76–99.

Richards, J. C. (1998). *Beyond training.* New York: Cambridge University Press.

Richards, J. C., and Lockhart, C. (1994). *Reflective teaching in second language classrooms.* New York: Cambridge University Press.

Richards, J. C., and Nunan, D. (1990). *Second language teacher education.* New York: Cambridge University Press.

Richards, J. C., and Rodgers, T. (1986). *Approaches and methods in language teaching: A description and analysis.* New York: Cambridge University Press.

Ridley, J. (1997). *Reflection and strategies in foreign language learning.* Frankfurt am Main: Lang.

Riggenbach, H. (1993). Discourse analysis and spoken language instruction. Featured speaker at the TESOL Institute in San Bernardino, CA.

Rodgers, T. (1978). Strategies for individualized language learning and teaching. In Richards, ed., *Understanding second and foreign language learning,* pp. 251–273.

Rogoff, B. (1990). *Apprenticeship in thinking: Cognitive development in social context.* New York: Oxford University Press.

Rosa, E., and O'Neill, M. (1999). Explicitness, intake, and the issue of awareness. *Studies in Second Language Acquisition,* 21, 511–556.

Rose, M. (1983). Remedial writing courses: A critique and a proposal. *College English,* 45, 109–128.

Rosenblatt, L. (1978). *The reader, the text, the poem: The transactional theory of the literary work.* Carbondale, IL: Southern Illinois University.

Rosenblatt, L. (1985). Viewpoints: Transaction versus interaction, a terminal rescue operation. *Research in the Teaching of English,* 19(1), 96–107.

Ross, S., and Berwick, R. (1992). The discourse of accommodation in oral proficiency interviews. *Studies in Second Language Acquisition,* 14(2): 157–176.

Rubin, J. (1975). What the "good language learner" can teach us. *TESOL Quarterly,* 9, 41–51.

Rust, S. P. Jr. (1970). The effect of tutoring on the tutor's behavior, academic achievement, and social status. *Dissertation Abstracts International,* 30, 11–A, 4862.

Rutherford, W., and Sharwood-Smith, M. (1988). *Grammar and second language teaching.* New York: Newbury House.

Samway, K., ed. (2000). *Integrating the ESL standards into classroom practice:* Grades 3–5. Alexandria, VA: TESOL.

Santiago, R. (1997). Imagination in the teaching of reading: A descriptive analysis. *The Journal of the Imagination in Language Teaching,* IV, 74–78.

Savignon, S. (1983). *Communicative competence: Theory and classroom practice: Texts and contexts in second language learning.* Reading, MA: Addison-Wesley.

Saville-Troike, M. (1976). *Foundations for teaching ESL.* Englewood Cliffs, NJ: Prentice Hall.

Scarcella, R. (1983). Sociodrama for social interaction. In Oller and Richard-Amato, pp. 239–245. Also in *TESOL Quarterly*, 12(1) (1978), 41–46.

Scarcella, R. (1990). *Teaching language minority students in the multicultural classroom.* Englewood Cliffs, NJ: Prentice Hall.

Scarcella, R., and Krashen, S., eds. (1980). *Research in second language acquisition.* Rowley, MA: Newbury House.

Scarcella, R. and Oxford, R. (1992). *The tapestry of language learning: The individual in the communicative classroom.* Boston: Heinle.

Scenarios for ESL standards-based assessment. (2001). Alexandria, VA: TESOL.

Schachter, J. (1974). An error in error analysis. *Language Learning*, 24, 205–214.

Schachter, J. (1990). On the issue of completeness in second language acquisition. *Second Language Research*, 6(2), 93–124.

Schank, R., and Abelson, R. (1977). *Scripts, plans, goals, and understanding.* Mahwah, NJ: Lawrence Erlbaum.

Schenke, A. (1996). Not just a "social issue": Teaching feminism in ESL. *TESOL Quarterly* 30(1), 155–159.

Schleppegrel, M. (1997). Problem-posing in teacher education. *TESOL Journal*, 6(3), 8–11.

Schmidt, R. (1990). The role of consciousness raising in second language learning. *Applied Linguistics*, 11(2), 129–158.

Schmidt, R. (1993). Awareness and second language acquisition. *Annual Review of Applied Linguistics*, 13, 206–226.

Schmidt, R. (1994). Implicit learning and the cognitive unconscious: Of artificial grammars and SLA. In N.C. Ellis, pp. 165–210.

Schneider, L. (1997). How to turn your ESL lesson into a computer assisted language learning (CALL) lesson. *CATESOL News*, December, 12.

Schoenberg, I. (1997). *Talk about values: Conversation skills for intermediate students.* White Plains, NY: Longman.

Schultz, M., and Fisher, A. (1988). *Games for all reasons: Interacting in the language classroom.* Reading, MA: Addison-Wesley.

Schumann, J. (1978a). The acculturation model for second-language acquisition. In R. Gingras, ed. *Second language acquisition and foreign language teaching*, pp. 27–50. Arlington, VA: Center for Applied Linguistics.

Schumann, J. (1978b). *The pidginization process: A model for second language learning.* Rowley, MA: Newbury House.

Schumann, J. (1979). Lecture presented at the First TESOL Institute, University of California, Los Angeles.

Schumann, J. (1980). Affective factors and the problem of age in second language acquisition. In K. Croft, ed. *Readings in ESL*, pp. 222–247. Cambridge, MA: Winthrop.

Schumann, J. (1997). *The neurobiology of affect in language.* Oxford: Blackwell.

Scovel, T. (1988). *A time to speak. A psycholinguist inquiry into the critical period for human speech.* Rowley, MA: Newbury House.

Seliger, H. (1977). Does practice make perfect? A study of interaction patterns and L2 competence. *Language Learning*, 27(2), 263–278.

Seliger, H. (1991). Strategy and tactics in second language acquisition. In L. Malave and G. Duquette, eds. *Language, culture, and cognition: A collection of studies in first and second language acquisition.* Clevedon, England: Multilingual Matters Ltd.

Seliger, H., and Long, M. (1983). *Classroom-oriented research in second language acquisition.* Rowley, MA.: Newbury House.

Selinker, L. (1972). Interlanguage. *International Review of Applied Linguistics*, 10, 209–230.

Selinker, L., Swain, M., and Dumas, G. (1975). The interlanguage hypothesis extended to children. *Language Learning*, 25, 139–152.

Semke, H. (1984). The effects of the red pen. *Foreign Language Annals*, 17, 195–202.

Shaftel, F., and Shaftel, G. (1967). *Role-playing for social values*. Englewood Cliffs, NJ: Prentice Hall.

Shameem, N. and Tickoo, M., eds. (1999). *New ways in using communicative games in language teaching*. Alexandria, VA: TESOL.

Sharwood-Smith, M. (1981). Consciousness-raising and the second language learner. *Applied Linguistics*, 2, 159–169.

Shih, M. (1992). Beyond comprehension exercises in the ESL academic reading class. *TESOL Quarterly*, 26(2), 289–318.

Shohamy, E. (1983). The stability of the oral proficiency trait on the oral interview speaking test. *Language Learning*, 33, 527–540.

Shor, I. and Freire, P. (1987). *A pedagogy for liberation: Dialogues on transforming education*. New York: Bergin and Garvey.

Short, D. (1993). Assessing integrated language and content instruction. *TESOL Quarterly*, 27(4), 627–656.

Shulman, J. and Mesa-Bains, eds. (1993). *Diversity in the classroom: A casebook for teachers and teacher educators*. Hillsdale, NJ: Lawrence Erlbaum.

Simon, R. (1992). *Teaching against the grain: Texts for a pedagogy of possibility*. Toronto: OISE Press.

Simon, S., Howe, L., and Kirschenbaum, H. (1992). *Values clarification* (2d edition). New York: Hart.

Sinclair, J., and Coulthard, M. (1975). *Toward an analysis of discourse: The English used by teachers and pupils*. London: Oxford University Press.

Skinner, B. F. (1957). *Verbal behavior*. New York: Appleton-Century-Crofts.

Slavin, R. (1983). When does cooperative learning increase student achievement? *Psychological Bulletin*, 94(3), 429–445.

Slobin, D. (1971). *Psycholinguistics*. Glenview, IL: Scott Foresman.

Slobin, D. (1973). Cognitive prerequisites for the development of grammar. In C. Ferguson and D. Slobin, eds. *Studies of child language development*. New York: Holt, Rinehart and Winston.

Smallwood, B. (1991). *The literature connection: A read-aloud guide for multicultural classrooms*. Reading, MA: Addison-Wesley.

Smallwood, B., ed. (2000). *Integrating the ESL standards into classroom practice*: Grades Pre-K–2. Alexandria, VA: TESOL.

Smoke, T. (1998). *Adult ESL: Politics, pedagogy, and participation in classroom and community*. Mahwah, NJ: Lawrence Erlbaum.

Smolen, L., Newman, C., Wathen, T., and Lee, D. (1995). Developing student self-assessment strategies. *TESOL Journal*, 5(1), 22–27.

Snow, M. A. (1997). Teaching academic literacy skills: Discipline faculty take responsibility. In M. A. Snow and Brinton, D. M., eds. *The content-based classroom: Perspectives on integrating language and content*. White Plains, NY: Longman, pp. 290–304.

Snow, M. A., ed. (2000). *Implementing the ESL standards for pre-K–12 students through teacher education*. Alexandria, VA: TESOL.

Snow, M. A., and Brinton, D., eds. (1997). *The content-based classroom: Perspectives on integrating language and content*. White Plains, NY: Pearson Education.

Snow, M. A., and Kamhi-Stein, L. D. (2002). Teaching and learning academic literacy through Project LEAP. In J. Crandall and D. Kaufman, eds. *Case studies in TESOL practice: Content-based instruction*. Alexandria, VA: TESOL.

Sokolik, M. E. (1993). *Global views: Reading about world issues*. Boston: Heinle.

Sorenson, A. (1967). Multilingualism in the northwest Amazon. *American Anthropologist*, 69, 670–684.

Sridhar, S. N. (1994). A reality check for SLA theories. *TESOL Quarterly*, 28(4), 800–803.

Srole, L. (1956). Social integration and certain corollaries: An exploration study. *American Sociological Review*, 21, 709–716.

Stafford, C., and Covitt, G. (1978). Monitor use in adult language production. *Review of Applied Linguistics*, 39–40, 103–125.

Stauble, A. (1980). Acculturation and second language acquisition. In Scarcella and Krashen, pp. 43–50.

Steinbeck, J. (1947). *The pearl*. New York: Viking.

Stempleski, S., and Tomlin, B. (1990). *Video in action: Recipes for using video in language teaching*. Englewood Cliffs, NJ: Prentice Hall.

Stern, A. (1996). *Tales from many lands*. New York: McGraw-Hill/Contemporary.

Stern, S. (1983). Why drama works: A psycholinguistic perspective. In Oller and Richard-Amato, pp. 207–225. Also in *Language Learning* 30(1) (1980), 77–100.

Stevick, E. (1976). Teachers of English as an alien language. In J. Fanselow and R. Crymes, eds. *On TESOL '76*, pp. 225–228. Washington, DC: TESOL.

Stevick, E. (1980). *Teaching languages: A way and ways*. Rowley, MA: Newbury House.

Sullivan, N. (1993). Teaching writing on a computer network. *TESOL Journal*, 2(1), 34–35.

Sutherland, K. (1979). Accuracy vs. fluency in the second language classroom. *CATESOL occasional papers*. California Association of Teachers of English to Speakers of Other Languages, No. 5, pp. 25–29.

Sutherland, K. (1981). *English alfa* (teacher's edition). Boston: Houghton Mifflin, p. 11.

Swain, M. (1975). Writing skills of grade 3 French immersion pupils. *Working Papers on Bilingualism*, 7, 1–38.

Swain, M. (1985). Communicative competence: Some roles of comprehensible input and comprehensible output in its development. In Gass and Madden, pp. 235–253.

Swain, M. (1993). The output hypothesis: Just speaking and writing aren't enough. *The Canadian Modern Language Review*, 50, 158–164.

Swain, M. (1995). Three functions of output in second language learning. In G. Cook and B. Seidlhofer, eds. *Principles and practice in applied linguistics: Studies in honour of H. G. Widdowson*. Oxford: Oxford University Press, pp. 125–144.

Swain, M., Brooks, L., and Tocalli-Beller, A. (2002). Peer-peer dialogue as a means of second language learning. *Annual Review of Applied Linguistics*, 22, 171–185.

Swain, M., Lapkin, S., and Barik, H. (1976). The cloze test as a measure of second language proficiency for young children. *Working Papers on Bilingualism*, 11, 32–43.

Tarone, E. (2002). Frequency effects, noticing, and creativity: Factors in a variationist interlanguage framework. *Studies in Second Language Acquisition*, 24(2), 287–298.

Tarone, E., and Yule, G. (1989). *Focus on the language learner*. New York: Oxford University Press.

Tatum, B. D. (1994). Teaching white students about racism: The search for white allies and the restoration of hope. *Teachers College Record*, 95(4), 462–475.

Taylor, B. (1980). Adult language learning strategies and their pedagogical implications.

In K. Croft, ed. *Readings in English as a second language*, pp. 144–152. Cambridge, MA: Winthrop.

Taylor, B. (1983). Teaching ESL: Incorporating a communicative, student-centered component. *TESOL Quarterly*, 17(1), 69–87.

Taylor, D. (1998). *Beginning to read and the spin doctors of science: The political campaign to change America's mind about how children learn to read*. Urbana, IL: National Council of Teachers of English.

Terrell, R. (1991). The role of grammar instruction in a communicative approach. *Modern Language Journal*, 75, 52–63.

Thomas, M. (1998). Programmatic ahistoricity in second language acquisition theory. *Studies in Second Language Acquisition*, 20(3), 387–405.

Thomas, W., and Collier, V. (1996). Language-minority student achievement program effectiveness. *NABE News*, 19(6), 33–35.

Thomas, W., and Collier, V. (1998). Two languages are better than one. *Educational Leadership*, 55(4), 23–26.

Thonis, E. (1984). Reading instruction for language minority students. In *Schooling and language minority students: a theoretical framework*. Office of Bilingual Education, California State Department of Education, Sacramento, CA. Los Angeles: Evaluation, Dissemination and Assessment Center, California State University, Los Angeles, pp. 147–181.

Thorndike, E. L. (1914). *The psychology of learning*. New York: Teachers College.

Tinkham, T. (1997). The effects of semantic and thematic clustering on the learning of second language vocabulary. *Second Language Research*, 13(2), 138–163.

Tinto, V. (1997). Enhancing learning via community. *Thought and Action*, 13, 53–58.

Tollefson, J. W. (1991). *Planning language, planning inequality: Language policy in the community*. London: Longman.

Tollefson, J. W. (2000). Policy and ideology in the spread of English. In Hall and Eggington, eds., pp. 7–21.

Tomaselli, A., and Schwartz, B. (1990). Analyzing the acquisition stages of negation in L2 German: Support for UG in adult SLA. *Second Language Research*, 6(1), 1–38.

Towell, R., and Hawkins, R. (1994). *Approaches to second language acquisition*. Clevedon, England: Multilingual Matters.

Tse, L. (2001). *Why don't they learn English? Separating fact from fallacy in the U.S. language debate*. New York: Teachers College Press, Columbia University.

Tucker, G., and d'Anglejan, A. (1972). An approach to bilingual education: The St. Lambert Experiment. In M. Swain, ed. *Bilingual schooling: Some experiences in Canada and the United States*, pp. 15–21. Toronto: The Ontario Institute for Studies in Ontario.

Underhill, A. (1999). Facilitation in language teaching. In Arnold, ed., pp. 125–141.

Valette, R. (1997). National standards and the role of imagination in foreign language learning. *The Journal of the Imagination in Language Learning* (IV), 18–25.

Van Allen, R., and Allen, C. (1967). *Language experience activities*. Boston: Houghton Mifflin.

van Lier, L. (1989). Reeling, writhing, drawling, stretching, and fainting in coils: Oral proficiency interviews as conversation. *TESOL Quarterly*, 23, 489–508.

van Lier, L. (1996). *Interaction in the language curriculum: Awareness, autonomy, and authenticity*. London: Longman.

Van Patten, B. (1986). Second language acquisition research and the learning/teaching of Spanish: Some research findings and their implications. *Hispania* 69, 202–216.

Vann, R., Meyer, D., and Lorenz, F. (1984). Error gravity: A study of faculty opinions of ESL errors. *TESOL Quarterly*, 18, 427–440.

Vygotsky, L. (1962). *Thought and language*. Cambridge, MA: MIT.

Vygotsky, L. (1978). *Mind in society*. Cambridge, MA: Harvard University.

Wagner-Gough, J., and Hatch, E. (1975). The importance of input data in second-language acquisition studies. *Language Learning*, 25, 297–308.

Walker, L. (2001). Negotiation syllabi in the adult ESL Classroom. *CATESOL News*, 32(4), 5–7.

Wallace, C. (1988). *Learning to read in a multicultural society: The social context of second language literacy*. New York: Prentice Hall.

Wallace, C. (1992). Critical literacy awareness in the EFL classroom. In N. Fairclough, ed. *Critical language awareness*, pp. 59–92. London: Longman.

Wallace, M. (1998). *Action research for language teachers*. Cambridge: Cambridge University Press.

Wallerstein, N. (1983). *Language and culture in conflict: Problem posing in the ESL classroom*. Reading, MA: Addison-Wesley.

Waring, R. (1997). The negative effects of learning words in semantic sets: A replication. *System*, 25, 261–274.

Warschauer, M., Shetzer, H., and Meloni, C. (2000). *Internet for English Teaching*. Alexandria, VA: TESOL.

Wegrzecka-Monkiewicz, E. (1992). High school English as a second language: A comparative study of content based and regular programs. M.A. thesis, California State University, Los Angeles.

Wells, G. (1981). *Learning through interaction: The study of language development*. Cambridge: Cambridge University Press.

Wells, G. (1999). *Dialogic inquiry: Toward a sociocultural practice and theory of education*. Cambridge: Cambridge University Press.

Wesche, M. (1987). Communicative testing in a second language. In Long and Richards, pp. 373–394.

Wesche, M., and Ready, D. (1985). Foreigner talk in the university classroom. In Gass and Madden, pp. 89–114.

Weslander, D. and Stephany, G. (1983). Evaluation of an English as a second language program for Southeast Asian students. *TESOL Quarterly*, 17(3), 473–480.

White, L. (1989). *Universal grammar and second language acquisition*. Amsterdam/Philadelphia, PA: John Benjamins.

White, L. (1990). Second language acquisition and universal grammar. *Studies in Second Language Acquisition*, 12, 127–128.

White, L., Spada, N., Lightbown, P., and Ranta, L. (1991). Input enhancement and L2 question formation. *Applied Linguistics*, 12, 416–432.

Whitecloud, T. (1938). "Blue winds dancing." Scribner's Magazine, February. Also in *Variations: A contemporary literature program: In touch*, pp. 148–152. New York: Harcourt Brace Jovanovich, 1975.

Whiteson, V., ed. (1996). *New ways of using drama and literature in language teaching*. Alexandria, VA: TESOL.

Widdowson, H. G. (1996). Proper words in proper places. In T. Hedge and N. Whitney, pp. 62–78.

Widdowson, H. G. (1978). *Teaching language as communication*. Oxford: Oxford University.

Widdowson, H. G. (1979). *Explorations in applied linguistics*. Oxford: Oxford University.

Wilkins, D. A. (1979). Notional syllabuses and the concept of a minimum adequate grammar. In Brumfit and Johnson, pp. 91–98.

Williams, M. and Burden, R. (1997). *Psychology for language teachers*. Cambridge: Cambridge University Press.

Windeatt, S., Hardisty, D., and Eastment, D. (2000) *The Internet*. New York: Oxford University Press.

Winitz, H. (1996). Grammaticality judgment as a function of explicit and implicit instruction in Spanish. *The Modern Language Journal*, 80(1), 32–46.

Winn-Bell Olsen, J. (1977). *Communication starters and other activities for the ESL classroom*. Englewood Cliffs, NJ: Prentice Hall.

Wong-Fillmore, L. (1976). The second time around: Cognitive and social strategies in second language acquisition. Unpublished doctoral dissertation, Stanford University, Stanford, CA.

Wong-Fillmore, L. (1985). When does teacher talk work as input? In Gass and Madden, pp. 17–50.

Yep, G. (2000). Encounters with the "other": Personal notes for a reconceptualization of intercultural communication competence. *The CATESOL Journal*, 12(1), 117–144.

Yorio, C. (1980). The teacher's attitude toward the students' output in the second language classroom. *CATESOL Occasional Papers*. California Association of TESOL, No. 6, pp. 1–8.

Yoshihara, K. (1993). Keys to effective peer response. *CATESOL Journal*, 1, 17–37.

Young, D. (1991). Creating a low-anxiety classroom environment: What does language anxiety research suggest? *Modern Language Journal*, 75, 426–438.

Zamel, V. (1985). Responding to student writing. *TESOL Quarterly*, 19(1): 79–101.

Zamel, V. (1992). Writing one's way into reading. *TESOL Quarterly*, 26(3), 463–485.

Zamel, V. (1997). Toward a model of transculturation. *TESOL Quarterly*, 31(2), 341–352.

Zeichner, K. M., and Hoeft, K. (1996). Teacher socialization for cultural diversity. In J. Sikula, T. Buttery, and E. Guyton, eds., *Handbook of research on teacher education* (2d edition). New York: Macmillan, pp. 525–547.

Index